THE TROUBADOURS

An Introduction

The dazzling culture of the troubadours – the virtuosity of their songs, the subtlety of their exploration of love, and the glamorous international careers some troubadours enjoyed – fascinated contemporaries and had a lasting influence on European life and literature. Apart from the refined love songs for which the troubadours are renowned, the tradition includes political and satirical poetry, devotional lyrics and bawdy or zany poems. It is also in the troubadour song-books that the only substantial collection of medieval lyrics by women is preserved. This book offers a general introduction to the troubadours. Its sixteen newly commissioned essays, written by leading scholars from Britain, the US, France, Italy and Spain, trace the historical development and setting of troubadour song, engage with the main trends in troubadour criticism, and examine the reception of troubadour poetry. Appendices offer an invaluable guide to the troubadours, to technical vocabulary, to research tools and to surviving manuscripts.

SIMON GAUNT is Professor of French Language and Literature at King's College London.

SARAH KAY is Reader in Medieval French and Occitan at the University of Cambridge.

THE TROUBADOURS

An Introduction

EDITED BY

SIMON GAUNT

AND

SARAH KAY

CAMBRIDGE
UNIVERSITY PRESS

PUBLISHED BY THE PRESS SYNDICATE OF THE UNIVERSITY OF CAMBRIDGE
The Pitt Building, Trumpington Street, Cambridge CB2 1RP, United Kingdom

CAMBRIDGE UNIVERSITY PRESS
The Edinburgh Building, Cambridge, CB2 2RU, UK
http://www.cup.cam.ac.uk
40 West 20th Street, New York, NY 10011-4211, USA
http://www.cup.org
10 Stamford Road, Oakleigh, Melbourne 3166, Australia

First published 1999

Typeset in Baskerville 11/12.5 pt [wv]

A catalogue record for this book is available from the British Library

Library of Congress Cataloguing in Publication data
Gaunt, Simon.
The troubadours: an introduction / Simon Gaunt and Sarah Kay.
p.   cm.
Includes bibliographical references and index.
ISBN 0 521 57388 2 (hardback) – ISBN 0 521 574730 (paperback)
1. Troubadours.   2. Provençal poetry – History and criticism.
3. Civilization, Medieval, in literature.   4. Courtly love in
literature.   5. Love in literature.   6. Provençal poetry.   7. Love
poetry, Provençal.   I. Kay, Sarah.   II. Title.
PC3304.G37   1999
849'.1009–dc21   98–11652 CIP

ISBN 0 521 573882 hardback
ISBN 0 521 574730 paperback

Transferred to digital printing 2003

Contents

Contributors

WILLIAM BURGWINKLE is a Professor of French at the University of Hawai'i Manoa in Honolulu. His most recent publication on the troubadours is *Love for Sale: Materialist Readings of the Troubadour Razos*. He is currently working on constructions of masculinity and homophobic discourse in twelfth- and thirteenth-century French texts.

MIRIAM CABRÉ is a former graduate student of Cambridge University and currently holds a research fellowship at the University of Girona. She is the author of various publications on the troubadour Cerverí, including the monograph *Cerverí de Girona and his Poetic Traditions*. Her major research area is the culture of Medieval Catalonia.

SIMON GAUNT is Professor of French Language and Literature at King's College London. He has worked extensively on Medieval Occitan and French literature and is the author of *Troubadours and Irony* and *Gender and Genre in Medieval French Literature*. Together with Ruth Harvey and Linda Paterson he is one of the editors of the forthcoming critical edition of the poetry of Marcabru.

GÉRARD GOUIRAN is Professor of Romance Linguistics and Occitan at the University of Montpellier III. He works widely on medieval Occitan literature and has published editions of the poetry of the troubadours (the songs of Bertran de Born and of Falquet de Romans); *chanson de geste* (*Le Roland occitan*); romance (*Guilhem de la Barra*); and non-literary texts (*Le Livre Potentia des états de Provence*).

RUTH HARVEY is Senior Lecturer in French at Royal Holloway University of London. Her major research interests are twelfth-century court society and court literature and she is the author of numerous articles on the early troubadours and of the only

vii

monograph in English on Marcabru, *The Troubadour Marcabru and Love*. She is also one of the collaborators, together with Simon Gaunt and Linda Paterson, on the forthcoming critical edition of the poetry of Marcabru.

SYLVIA HUOT is University Lecturer in French and Fellow of Pembroke College, Cambridge. She is the author of *From Song to Book, The 'Romance of the Rose' and its Medieval Readers* and *Allegorical Play in the Old French Motet*, and co-editor with Kevin Brownlee of *Rethinking the 'Romance of the Rose'*.

SARAH KAY is Reader in French and Occitan Literature at the University of Cambridge and a Fellow of Girton College. She is the author of, among other things, *Subjectivity in Troubadour Poetry* and *The Chansons de geste in the Age of Romance*. Her current work is on the contradictions of courtly literature.

CATHERINE LÉGLU is a lecturer in French at the University of Bristol. She is the author of several articles on aspects of satirical poetry in the troubadour corpus.

MARIA LUISA MENEGHETTI is Professor of Romance Philology at the University of Siena. She works particularly on courtly romance, medieval romance lyric, and literary iconography. Her publications include *Il romanzo*, *Il pubblico dei trovatori*, and *Storia delle letterature medievali romanze*, vol. I, *Le origini*.

DON A. MONSON is Professor of French at the College of William and Mary in Williamsburg, Virginia. He works on twelfth- and thirteenth-century courtly literature in Occitan, French and Latin. He has published a book on the Occitan *ensenhamens* and various articles.

STEPHEN G. NICHOLS is the James M. Beall Professor of French and Humanities and Chair of the French Department at Johns Hopkins University. He is Director and a Senior Fellow of the School of Criticism and Theory at Cornell University and a Fellow of the Medieval Academy of America. Among the more recent books he has published are *Medievalism and the Modernist Temper* (with R. Howard Bloch), and *The Whole Book* (with Siegfried Wenzel) .

LINDA PATERSON is Reader in French at the University of Warwick. She specialises in medieval Occitan history and literature. Her major publications are *Troubadours and Eloquence* and *The World of the Troubadours: Medieval Occitan Society c. 1100 – c. 1300*.

MICHAEL ROUTLEDGE is Senior Lecturer in French and Director of European Studies at Royal Holloway University of London. His research interests include urban poets of the Middle Ages and Occitan writing on the crusades. He has published editions of the songs of the Monk of Montaudon and the works of Bertran Carbonel.

TILDE SANKOVITCH is Professor of French at Northwestern University. Her research and publications focus on French literature of the Middle Ages and the Renaissance and she is particularly interested in the work of early women writers. Her books include an edition (with W. D. Paden and P. Stäblein) of the songs of Bertran de Born and *French Women Writers and the Book: Myths of Access and Desire*.

SARAH SPENCE is Professor of Classics at the University of Georgia and editor of *Literary Imagination. The Review of the Association of Literary Scholars and Critics*. She has published widely on classical Latin and medieval literature with a particular focus on rhetoric, notably *Rhetorics of Reason and Desire: Vergil, Augustine and the Troubadours* and *Texts and the Self in the Twelfth Century*.

MARGARET SWITTEN is Class of 1926 Professor of French, Mount Holyoke College. She specialises in the music and poetry of the Middle Ages, specifically the songs of the troubadours. In addition to numerous articles, her publications include *The* Cansos *of Raimon de Miraval: A Study of Poems and Melodies* and *Music and Poetry in the Middle Ages: A Guide to Research on French and Occitan Song 1100–1400*.

Preface

This book is both a collection of self-contained essays and a text-book. The first three chapters offer an introduction to the historical context of the troubadour lyric, and then to the two main genres of the troubadour tradition, the *canso* and *sirventes*. The next five are broadly speaking literary-historical and offer an overview of the troubadours with chapters on the three main periods of troubadour production, on the women troubadours, and on Spanish and Italian troubadours, the aim being to show how the tradition evolved both in Occitania and abroad. The following five chapters give an account of the critical preoccupations of recent troubadour scholarship. The final three chapters deal, albeit selectively, with medieval reception. Each chapter gives a selective account of past scholarship, but also makes an original contribution to the field.

All references are keyed either to the bibliography or to Appendices 1 and 3. Unless otherwise stated troubadours are cited from the editions given in Appendix 1. The Appendices are intended both for reference and as tools for further research. Appendix 1 offers thumb-nail sketches of what is known of the lives and work of some fifty-six troubadours and includes references to the best available editions. Appendix 2 offers a glossary of Occitan terms. Appendix 3 is a critical introduction to research tools. Appendix 4 is a list of extant *chansonniers*.

We hope that *The Troubadours: An Introduction* can profitably be read as a book, but you may wish to consult it more selectively either by reading chapters on particular themes or issues, or by consulting the index of troubadours and their songs. Complete comprehensiveness has not, of course, been possible, but our aim has been to ensure coverage of non-canonical as well as canonical poets and to give a sense of the richness of the troubadour tradition beyond the dazzling, but nonetheless somewhat limited parameters of the twelfth-century *canso*.

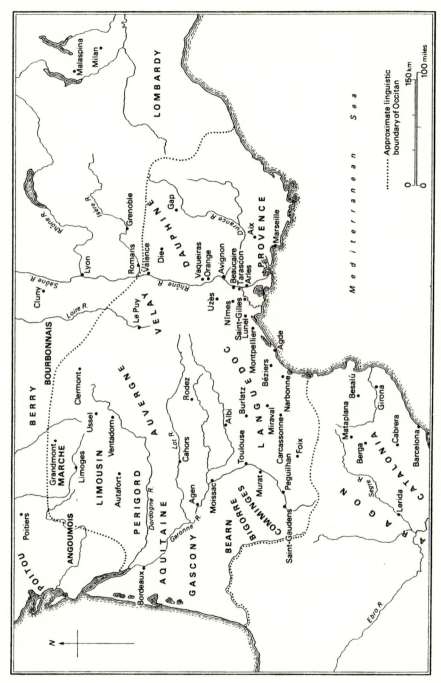

Figure 1. Map of Occitania and neighbouring Catalonia.

Introduction

Simon Gaunt and Sarah Kay

The troubadours, like other celebrities, need no introduction.
They are part of the furniture of our cultural knowledge, an unfor-
gettable heirloom in the European heritage. Who has not heard
of the courtly world they ornamented and entertained, voicing for
it the exquisite refinements of medieval love? For a glamorous
period, this tradition of poet-composer-performers (460 of whose
names we know) dazzled Southern French and neighbouring European courts with their songs (some 2,500 of which survive) in
which passion and decorum are craftily combined.[1] Although this
period was relatively short-lived (c. 1100–c. 1300), its spark was
sufficient to light the broader flame of subsequent European
poetry. The rise of courtliness, in the senses both of 'courtly love'
and 'courtly living', in which the troubadours played a determining
role, helped to shape mainstream Western culture; while their
commentaries as moralists, and as political and cultural critics,
provide vital testimony to the attitudes which underlie and helped
to form our own.

The significance of the troubadours is acknowledged in the
space assigned to them in many different academic contexts: as
part of the history of European poetry and music; as evidence for
the history of social, gender and sexual relations, and the political
and ideological world of medieval Europe; as a strand in the
linguistic diversity of the Romance languages. The range of these
contexts, however, suggests the complexity of the phenomenon.
Many of the troubadours had international careers in their life-
times, and were doubtless differently understood by different audiences; this continues to be the case. Thus in France, troubadour
scholarship is fed by regional interest but in the United States
(where the troubadours feature in comparative literature courses)
it is upheld by their potentially universal appeal; in Italy the

1

troubadours are studied as a step in the formation of Italian literature but in England as an aspect of the literature of medieval
France. The troubadours thus elicit a diversity of approaches, as
this volume shows. In particular, the last decade has seen the production of some challenging and innovative studies, and the over-
turning of some previously cherished views; the time has come,
we feel, to synthesise this work for the less specialist reader. The
purpose of this Introduction, then, is to introduce not so much the
troubadours themselves as the scholarly work addressed to them,
in order to provide readers with a context in which to situate the
chapters of this book.

The different approaches taken to the troubadours have, at a
most basic level, affected the terminology used to describe their
language. The earliest scholar to document their usage was François Raynouard, whose extraordinary *Lexique roman* was produced
between 1838 and 1844. Raynouard chose the word *roman* because
he believed that the form of Southern French used by the troubadours was a faithful reflection of the vernacular Latin spoken in
the Roman empire, more so than any other Romance language; it
alone thus deserved to be called 'Roman'. In the late nineteenth
century, however, the regional poet Frédéric Mistral headed a
revival of the language of Provence, and claimed the troubadours
as his poetic predecessors. For a long period, under his influence,
the term 'Provençal' was used to refer to the medieval literary
language. Gradually it has been overtaken by the term 'Occitan',
a backformation from the word Occitania used as early as the
thirteenth century to denote the whole of the area of Southern
France. The term Occitan accords with the broad subdivision of
medieval Romance languages according to the word for 'yes', a
subdivision recognised in the Middle Ages: in the North of France,
the word *oïl* (now *oui*) gave rise to the *langue d'oïl*, in Italy there
was the *langue de si*, and in the Midi the *langue d'oc*. The area within
which Occitan was spoken is indicated on the map on p. xiii: it
runs from just south of the Loire in the West to the Italian Alps
and down into Northern Italy in the East.

The term Provençal is especially misleading given that the earliest of the troubadours all came not from Provence, but from
Poitou and Gascony. In so far as the language of their compositions has any dialectal colouring – and it is remarkable to what

an extent it appears to have been a literary standard or *koiné* – it is Limousin (from the area of Limoges), the area which produced the first great troubadour of love, Bernart de Ventadorn. Indeed, it was not until the careers of Raimbaut d'Aurenga and Peire Rogier, past the middle of the twelfth century, that we find troubadours in Provence proper. Nor does troubadour culture halt there: it continues south and east into Italy, as well as due south into Catalonia and Spain. Throughout two centuries of movement the literary language remains much the same, a passport to intelligibility in a wide range of European courts. (To say that troubadour language is standardised does not mean that it had fixed forms. Morphology and orthography vary widely, posing problems to the novice reader. For assistance with these problems, consult Appendix 3.) Of course Occitan literature did not cease at the end of the thirteenth century, but by that date the heyday of the troubadours was past. There has been a continuous, if small-scale, Occitan literary tradition through to the nineteenth-century revival, and there is now a reasonably flourishing regional literature. But that lies outside the scope of this book.[2]

The pioneering work of Raynouard aside, troubadour scholarship was established in the late nineteenth and early twentieth centuries by a series of extraordinarily gifted German philologists, who recognised the centrality of the troubadours both to literary history and to the study of Romance philology; chief among these were Karl Bartsch, Gustav Gröber, Emil Levy and Carl Appel.[3] They opened up the field by producing large numbers of critical editions and reference works that remain unsurpassed. The contribution of German scholars to the production of basic research tools has continued unabated throughout the twentieth century. Only in Germany is work on major dictionaries and reference works still actively pursued.

Early troubadour scholarship in France had a softer edge to it. Though some early twentieth-century French scholars produced editions, they tended to be less ambitious than those produced in Germany and the most significant Francophone contributions to troubadour studies were interpretative general studies that might be regarded as at best still useful, at worst unreadable (Jeanroy, Hoeppfner). The most brilliant minds among early French medievalists (Gaston Paris, Joseph Bédier) were drawn to texts written

in the *langue d'oïl*, possibly for political reasons of which they themselves may not have been wholly conscious, and paid scant attention to the troubadours.[4]

The main themes of early twentieth-century criticism both in
and outside France were undoubtedly biography and love, and they
were picked up by a range of critics, particularly as the vexed
questions of the origin of 'courtly love' and the sincerity of courtly
poetry were debated (Lewis, Bezzola, Denomy, Nykl). Little attention was paid to the formal dexterity or literary merit of troubadour poetry by scholars of this period, which is perhaps surprising
given the attention their lyrics were receiving, precisely because
of their formal complexity, from contemporary poets such as T. S.
Eliot or Ezra Pound. Indeed, some critics from the first part of
this century did not try to conceal their dislike of the formal ingenuity of the texts to which they devoted their professional lives
(Jeanroy).

The interest in love and in the eroticism of the troubadour lyric
was maintained in Francophone criticism after the Second World
War in a number of studies that are now generally considered
idiosyncratic (Nelli, Camproux, Lazar), but outside France in the
decades after 1945 it is possible to identify distinct national
schools of troubadour scholarship and then, more recently still,
critical movements that are defined more by theoretical orientation. If, in the 1940s and 1950s, lone scholars across the globe
were making significant contributions to the field, particularly by
producing major critical editions (for example Martín de Riquer
in Spain, or Walter Pattison in the US), Germany and Italy were
undoubtedly the two main centres of troubadour scholarship.[5] The
most significant German critic of troubadour poetry in the post-
war period was undoubtedly Erich Köhler, whose publications were
to influence his contemporaries and subsequent generations of
German critics: Pollman, Mölk, Liebertz-Grün, Kasten, Leube-
Fey. Steeped in German hermeneutics and Marxist theory, Köhler
argued vigorously that the troubadour lyric mediated the tension
between the different sections of the nobility and that the erotic
'love' to which the songs were ostensibly devoted was invariably a
metaphor for other desires, other drives. Poetics were thus a cover
for politics. German scholarship after Köhler was rigorous, challenging and searching.

In Italy meanwhile, equal rigour was being applied to philology and textual criticism (Del Monte, Toja, Roncaglia, Avalle). As Romance philologists, Italian scholars of this period were primarily interested in the language and Latinate culture of the troubadour lyric. This approach is still very much in evidence among their students today and thanks to this tradition, Italy probably has more practising Occitanists than any other country in the world. The difference in approach of the two main schools of the post-war period is best illustrated in an exchange of articles between Aurelio Roncaglia and Erich Köhler on the nature of the so-called *trobar clus*, published in *Cultura Neolatina* in 1969 and 1970: the former insists upon the learned, literary and Latinate culture of the troubadours and litters his article with philological comments on the texts, the latter concentrates on the social dynamics that he believes are mediated therein and on the value of troubadour hermeneutics.

By 1969, however, the effects of new theoretical approaches to the study of literature were already being felt in medieval studies. Although the main structuralist studies of medieval vernacular lyric were in fact devoted to the lyrics of Old French poets (the *trouvères*), their influence upon troubadour scholarship is discernible in a number of major publications (Bec, Cropp, Thiolier-Méjean, and more recently Van Vleck) that take as given Zumthor's notion of *la circularité du chant*: that is, the view that medieval lyrics are self-referential formal displays dependent on the recycling, within the closed world of the genre, of a limited repertoire of formal constituents.

The influence of structuralism is perceptible as much in the resistance it engendered as in the disciples it attracted. Indeed, perhaps two of the most significant anglophone publications on the troubadours of the 1970s – Paterson's *Troubadours and Eloquence* and Topsfield's *Troubadours and Love* – were either explicitly (Paterson) or implicitly (Topsfield) responding to the structuralist premise that medieval lyric could be seen simply as a play of convention and form. Trained in the Cambridge school of practical criticism, Paterson and Topsfield breathed new life into troubadour scholarship by constructing arguments around close readings of poems. They paid attention to form and rhetoric as markers not of generic adhesion but of personal engagement, and extolled the individuality of troubadours over the homogeneity of the tradition. The purely literary appreciation of the troubadours evinced in Paterson and Topsfield's work was also typical of a number of important publications produced in the US in the 1960s and 1970s by scholars whose main interest was comparative literature: critics such as Goldin and Wilhelm influenced a generation of later North American comparatists (for example Spence, Kendrick) by devoting attention to the literary practices of the troubadours in relation to other European poetry and in the light of the prevailing New Criticism.

In the 1980s, the troubadours became the subject of increasingly sophisticated and challenging research. The publication in the early 1980s of two major studies of intertextuality (by Grüber and Meneghetti) was particularly significant. These scholars drew attention to the self-reflexive hermeticism of the troubadour lyric and to the sophisticated processes of citation, imitation and transformation that characterise the tradition. Following on from this, the late 1980s and early 1990s can perhaps best be characterised as a period of demystification: concentrating either on irony and play (Gaunt, Kendrick, Kay) or subjectivity and gender (Kay, Huchet, Cholakian, Gaunt), and armed with the findings of structuralist and poststructuralist scholarship, critics continued to turn away from taking the ostensible subject matter (i.e. love) of the courtly *canso* seriously and sought to reveal (like Köhler, only with different agendas) the underlying aesthetic, psychic and political dynamics of the tradition. If, until this point, troubadour lyric had often been held up as the most refined and moving celebration of civilised heterosexual love (Lewis, Topsfield), prevailing wisdom by the late 1980s saw it as a sophisticated game men played with each other.

Since 1945, then, concerted efforts have been made to downplay (or at the very least to reinterpret) the significance of what made troubadour poetry famous in the first place: love. As will be evident from this book, love is by no means the only subject matter for troubadour lyrics, but it is clearly the dominant theme. The demystification of the 'myth' of courtly love was undoubtedly urgent in the post-war period, but perhaps the time has come now to reassess the nature of love in troubadour poetry and to take what the troubadours said about themselves seriously again. In this respect – and in many others – troubadour studies are taking on fresh impetus. Thus, as we approach the end of the 1990s, troubadour scholars seem, like many other medievalists, to be returning to history (Paterson, Harvey) and to manuscript studies (Nichols in this volume, Burgwinkle) with renewed vigour. They are also turning to the broader corpus of troubadour lyric (Ghil, Léglu in this volume) and therefore are better able to set the love poetry in a context that helps relate it to broader social, cultural and psychic structures.

All these contemporary approaches, as well as the influence of much of the post-war criticism we have just outlined, inform this book. And as our contributors build on recent work, so they also point to potential directions for research. The troubadours are an essential part of our cultural past, and the scholarship upon them whose history we have here outlined has an exciting future.

NOTES

1 For details of the corpus, see especially Pillet-Carstens, *Bibliographie* and Frank, *Répertoire*, both in Appendix 3.

2 For the history of Occitan literature, consult Lafont and Anatole, *Nouvelle histoire*.

3 For works by these and the other scholars mentioned in this Introduction, consult the Bibliography and Appendices 1 and 3.

4 See Bloch and Nichols, *Medievalism*, on how medieval scholarship was affected by factors other than strictly academic ones.

5 There were, however, notable Belgian Occitanists in the post-war period, such as Lejeune and Pirot.

CHAPTER 1

Courtly culture in medieval Occitania

Ruth Harvey

Shortly before Christmas 1182, the Limousin troubadour Bertran de Born spent time at the court at Argentan in Normandy and this is what he says about it:

> Ja mais non er cortz complia
> on hom non gab ni non ria:
>   cortz ses dos
> non es mas parcs de baros.
> Et agra·m mort ses faillia
> l'enois e la vilania
>   d'Argentos,
> ma·l gentils cors amoros
> e la doussa cara pia
> e la bona compaignia
>   e·l respos
> de la Saisa·m defendia. (III, 49–60)

(A court where no one laughs or jokes is never complete; a court without gifts is just a paddock-full of barons. And the boredom and vulgarity of Argentan nearly killed me, but the lovable, noble person, the sweet, kind face, the good companionship and conversation of the Saxon lady protected me.)

These lines raise a number of questions, many of which have wider implications for an appreciation of medieval courtly culture. What was a court and who would have been there? What was the significance of the women often celebrated in troubadour songs? Who were the troubadours and what was their place in court society? Although we can only reconstruct the immediate conditions of troubadour performance as hypotheses, this chapter will outline some of the factors which shaped the social context of the lyric.

The presence of an Occitan poet at a court in Normandy was rather unusual: generally speaking, troubadour activity was

focused on a region further south.[1] Troubadours received a welcome in the courts of Northern Italy from the second half of the
twelfth century, while in Occitania the centres of culture and
power frequented by these poets generally looked towards the
South, across the Pyrenees. Those of Spain, especially Aragon and
Catalonia, while ever preoccupied by the reconquest of lands from
the Moors, looked north. Ever since the Provençal heiress Douce
married Count Ramon Berenguer III of Barcelona in 1112, the
Catalan house had claimed the county of Provence and it was
ruled by Aragonese-Catalan princes until the mid-thirteenth century. But these claims did not go unchallenged: Toulouse in particular repeatedly asserted its rights to Provence, both through
alliances and by military action.[2] The lesser lords of the Midi were
inevitably caught up in this protracted struggle for domination
over the lands from the Ebro to the Garonne and beyond the
Rhône.[3] Into this network of ambitions, alliances and conflicts
were also drawn the kings of England. When Eleanor of Aquitaine
was divorced from Louis VII of France in March 1152 and in May
remarried Henry Plantagenet, Count of Anjou and heir to the
Anglo-Norman realm, she took with her her vast inheritance of
Poitou and Aquitaine: Henry II ruled over lands from Hadrian's
Wall to the foothills of the Pyrenees, including the Limousin and
Périgord, where Bertran de Born's castle of Autafort was situated
and where much of the internecine strife among the Plantagenets
was fought out.[4] In consequence, the homeland of troubadour
poetry was hardly a peaceful place.

Occitan lords were prominent in the early crusading effort, both
in the Spanish *reconquista* and in Syria, and some settled there,[5] so
that many noble families of Occitania had relatives in the Christian states of the Middle East or in Spain. Probably the most
famous love-song, Jaufré Rudel's celebration of *amor de lonh*, was
inspired by a journey to the Holy Land, and other troubadour
songs exhorted knights to take the cross.[6] Peirol and Gaucelm
Faidit are thought to have gone on crusade themselves, and Raimbaut de Vaqueiras accompanied his patron, Boniface of Montferrat, on the ill-fated Fourth Crusade. Paris, on the other hand,
was relatively peripheral for many, at least until the Albigensian
Crusade brought Frenchmen into Occitania in large numbers.
This protracted and violent incursion did not, however, sound the
death-knell for the troubadours' art, as has often been claimed,

for there are at least as many poets attested in the century which followed the crusade as from the 120 years which preceded it. They produced more *sirventes* and fewer and less interesting *cansos*, and as the decades passed their creative talent diversified into new genres and avenues of expression.[7] In its heyday, the courtly culture to which the troubadours belonged was European rather than restricted to the South of France and, in their later influence, the troubadours stimulated the production of lyric poetry in courts far beyond Occitania.

Occitania itself was a large, uncentralised and diverse region. It included increasingly wealthy, urban centres such as Toulouse, Avignon, and Montpellier, which developed their own municipal government,[8] as well as small, isolated communities in inaccessible, mountainous areas such as the Carcassès, where 'the mountains were savage and the gorges terrifying', and even local men could get lost and fail to find the castle they sought.[9]

That such diverse conditions gave rise to a variety of traditions, customs and socio-political institutions is not surprising, and it is in this light that the vexed question of 'feudalism' in the Midi should be considered. Only a few, marginal areas in Occitania displayed seigneurial structures analogous to the Northern French feudal model, whereby vassals 'held land from' a lord in return for the obligations of military service and counsel and homage, involving the subordination of vassal to overlord and close vassalic ties of personal dependency. Rather, the norm among the aristocracy seems for a long time to have been *convenientiae*, egalitarian contracts between individuals in which each party promised fidelity and non-aggression, respect for the life, limb and rights of the other. The precise location of the grant or castle was specified and the vassal undertook a limited number of obligations in respect of it. To hold lands as a *fidelis*, then, meant not a general loyalty of vassal to overlord, but a specific and limited loyalty in respect of a particular castle,[10] and resulted in much looser vassalic ties with little suggestion of liege-homage, submission to and dependency on one lord alone. During the twelfth century, tighter controls and conditions began to be imposed when a lord was in a position of strength, and most dramatically after the Northern French crusaders crushed the Toulousain lords. Overall, historians have noted the diverse nature of seigneurial institutions across Occitania.[11]

To this can be added other practices regarding inheritance and *co-seigneurie* which also set Occitania apart from Northern France. Rather than passing to the first-born, Occitan patrimonies were frequently shared between all children, leading to a splintering of properties, fragmentation of resources and progressive impoverishment of families.[12] Bertran de Born, probably a *co-seigneur* himself, sang of the misery of conflict between co-owners, and Raimon de Miraval had only a fourth share in his castle.[13] Arrangements featuring male primogeniture were appearing during the twelfth century, but *co-seigneurie* still existed in areas such as the Carcassès on the eve of the Albigensian Crusade.[14]

Younger sons may not have been uniformly excluded from inheriting, but shrinking patrimonies and incomes meant that it was the court of a magnate which represented significant opportunities for advancement and enrichment. Such courts were the focus of secular power in an age of personal lordship and poor communications. Best defined rather loosely as an assembly centred on the person of the lord, a court was made up of the *familia* of his household, his companions, advisers, servants, officials, clerks, household knights and followers, including entertainers. All these *familiares* of a nobleman depended on his patronage for their promotion and remuneration. This could take various forms: food, clothing, money, riding-tackle, a mount, income from land or appointment to an office which in turn could bring rights, income and 'perks',[15] and securing such rewards required personal contact and presence at court.

This term could evoke a place or a series of places, for courts could be itinerant, especially in the case of great princes, who were obliged to travel their lands to govern and administer their subjects effectively. Staying in their own residences or those of their vassals, or in the guest-houses of monasteries, they settled disputes, heard petitions and legal cases within their jurisdiction, issued grants and mandates, and negotiated with neighbouring *seigneurs* and vassals.[16] For much of the time, his entourage went with him, so that the 'court' was wherever the lord was. In Raimon Vidal's *Abrils issia*, an early thirteenth-century verse narrative whose narrator instructs a *joglar* in courtly values and *savoir-faire*, the *joglar* relates how, having travelled from Montferrand to Provence and then Toulouse, he went to Foix, 'but at Foix I found no one, for the count had gone to Aubières'.[17] Such lordly itineraries may also explain the presence of Bertran de Born so far from home in Normandy: the troubadour was at that time engaged in a bitter dispute with his brother, Constantine, over the castle of Autafort, and it would have needed his ultimate lord, Henry II, to resolve the affair.[18]

The composition of the court would have varied according to location and occasion; it could include local vassals and clerics, tenants, visitors, and, in baronial residences, the members of the lord's family, ladies and their female companions, and other noble children (*noiritz*) whose upbringing had been entrusted to him.[19] The court was also the setting for festive assemblies on religious feasts such as Whitsun and Christmas.[20] Great festivals marked special events like noble betrothals, weddings, coronations, peace treaties, and receptions for visiting diplomats or notables. These were occasions for ostentatious displays of fine living and prodigality, and as such were a great draw for ambitious young men and for entertainers of all kinds.[21] Perhaps the most famous court festival held in Occitania was that which Geoffrey de Vigeois, with some fantasy and exaggeration, describes as staged at Beaucaire in 1174 by Henry II to mark the reconciliation of King Alfonso II of Aragon and Raymond of Toulouse, although neither king was actually present. At this court (allegedly comprising 10,000 knights), 100,000 sous were given away; the castle grounds were ploughed up and then sown with 30,000 sous' worth of coins; food was cooked with expensive wax and pitchpine torches; and Guilhem Mita was crowned King of all minstrels.[22]

Princely celebrations on this lavish scale were rare, however. More usual were smaller gatherings in seigneurial residences,[23] where what the troubadours seem to have prized were a liberal welcome, good company and stimulating conversation (*solatz*) – precisely those qualities found lacking at Argentan. Raimon Vidal's *joglar* again describes the company of lively, cultivated people he found in the great hall of Dalfi d'Avernhe's court at Montferrand:

> E la nueg si fo, co yeu vi,
> mot tenebrosa apres manjar,
> e·l solatz gran, josta·l foc clar,
> de cavayers e de joglars
> adreitz e fis e dos e cars
> e suaus ad homes cortes;

e no y ac cridat ni pus mes
de pegueza sol de primier.
Aital solatz e pus entier
aguem aqui pus que no·us dic. (*Abrils*, 158–67)

(The night was very dark after supper, and, beside the bright fire, great
was the companionship of knights and *joglars* who were skilled and
accomplished, gentle, worthy and amiable towards the courtly men; and
there was no shouting or foolishness, except at the beginning. We
enjoyed such pleasure there, more than I can say.)

This kind of intimacy represented the ideal conditions for a
troubadour performance, but the reverse of the courtly coin is
depicted by Arnaut de Tintinhac, in his condemnation of a 'vile
race' of drunken, badly behaved guests:

ricx malvatz, de pretz apostitz,
q'uns non a joi ni conortz mais
qui l'autrui afar gabeja,
la nueg que·l frons li torneja
ab lo vi en l'autrui maizo.[24]

(the wicked rich, false in worth, not one of whom has joy or pleasure
unless he jeers about other people's business when his head is spinning
from the wine, at night, in someone else's house.)

The matter of good behaviour in the households of the nobility,
cortesia, was becoming an art form. A man needed tact, charm and
discretion; he had to be elegantly dressed, cheerful, urbane, and
skilled in managing the sensibilities of other members of the
household, including his superiors. Body-language and language
itself became vitally important: the careful use of eloquence
characterised the courtier, along with an agreeable public mask.[25]
But such self-control in company could also be construed as hypocritical dissembling to cover ambition, jealousy, manipulation,
greed, and back-stabbing in what could be a very competitive
environment: advancement, material comfort and security
depended on the smile of his lordship and his recognition of one's
services.

Rewards given to one man could not, however, be given to
another and there must often have been disappointed men at
court. It is in this light that we may read Marcabru's sharp criticisms of stewards who ran the household, managed supplies and
controlled access to the lord:

Non sia lauzenia plata
cell qe la mainad' afama.[26]

(The man who starves the whole household never ceases his smooth-
tongued flattery.)

Similarly, Bernart Marti complained bitterly of richly dressed
officials apparently connected with the administration of justice:
they suspend the court-sitting, play one party off against the other
in order to increase their own *honoraria* and pervert the course of
justice, and all this through clever use of their 'forked tongues'.[27]

In the rivalries of courtiers may lie one explanation of the figures of the *lauzengiers* so execrated by the troubadours as wicked,
tale-bearing, slanderous spies.[28] In Raimbaut d'Aurenga's view,
'not one of them is pleasant to a good knight except in order to
attain his own advantage better', and some of them have ideas
above their station:

Tal cug'esser cortes entiers
qu'es vilans dels quatre ladriers,
et a·l cor dins mal ensenhat;
plus que feutres sembla sendat
ni cuers de bou escarlata
non sabon mais que n'an trobat –
e quecx quo·s pos calafata. (XXXVII, 22–4 and 43–9)

(Such a man who is common on all four sides thinks he is completely
courtly while inside his heart is churlish; no more than felt resembles
silk or ox-hide good scarlet cloth do they know any more than they have
invented, and each one fills in the gaps as best he can.)

The nature of the court changed over time and differed over the
regions making up Occitania. The ducal court of eleventh-century
Aquitaine was a far cry from the administrative bustle of Aix after
1245, where Bertran d'Alamanon complained:

I have to think about lawsuits and lawyers in order to draw up notarial
acts; then I look out along the road to see if any courier is coming, for
they arrive from all directions, dusty and saddle-sore ... And then they
tell me 'Get on your horse, you're required in court; you will be fined,
and you won't be pardoned if the hearing can't go ahead because of you.'
(VI, 28–42)

The court of Provence had become much more bureaucratic, and
more records survive to give an idea of its nature and employees.[29]
Perhaps it was more stressful and regulated by administrative

concerns, but it is equally the case that, from the outset, the troubadours always situate the heyday of elegant, civilised, courtly life in the past and their laments about contemporary decadence should be read in the light of the *topos* of a vanished Golden Age. At the turn of the twelfth century, Giraut de Bornelh asks 'Where have all the minstrels gone, and the gracious welcome you saw them receive?' There are no minstrels now praising ladies; in place of gracious conversation, he hears now at court raucous shouts, and men are more likely to want to hear trivial stories than 'a fine song about high and splendid affairs and the passing times and the passing years' (LXXIV, 31–2 and 55–60).

The number and location of courts associated with troubadour poetry was, however, very small initially. In Guilhem de Peitieu's day, only Ventadorn, Poitiers and Narbonne are explicitly mentioned. The number increases dramatically by the 1170s to include the Auvergne, Catalonia, the lower Languedoc and numerous small courts of the Limousin. From the late twelfth century, Provence becomes important and, while the *seigneurs* of Béziers-Carcassonne were destroyed by the Albigensian Crusade, Aix, Marseille, Rodez, Catalonia and the North Italian courts of Lombardy and Piedmont continued to attract the poets.[30]

Many of these centres of patronage were interconnected by marriage and through the troubadours who frequented them. Although a full picture of the associations has yet to be drawn, a few examples suffice to indicate the complexity of these networks. In his song for the Argentan court, Bertran de Born alludes to three beautiful women as 'las tres de Torena' (III, 18). These were the three daughters of Raimon II of Turenne, then all aged under twenty: Contors, who married Viscount Elias of Comborn; Helis, wife of Bernart de Casnac; and Maria, who married Eble V of Ventadorn, descendant of 'Eble the Singer'.[31] Maria, celebrated by many poets, composed a *partimen* with Gui d'Ussel (IX), whose two brothers and cousin were also troubadours and patrons.[32] Eble V is praised in a song by Elias de Barjols, who also has complimentary things to say about Raimon de Miraval, and Raimon frequented the courts of the Carcassès, whose seigneurial families were also characterised by a complex network of relationships by marriage.[33] Eble V's mother was Sybilla, daughter of Ralph de la Faye, who was the uncle of Eleanor of Aquitaine, and it is one of

Eleanor's daughters, Mathilda of Saxony, who made the Argentan court just bearable for Bertran de Born.

Who and what were the troubadours? According to our main sources of surviving information, the *vidas*, they were drawn from a wide variety of social backgrounds, ranging from great lords and kings (Guilhem de Peitieu, Alfonso II of Aragon), to the nobility (Guillem de Berguedà, Bertran de Born, Dalfi d'Alvernhe), poor knights (Raimon de Miraval, Guilhem Ademar), scions of the bourgeoisie (Peire Vidal, Elias Cairel), and a *borges* who became a bishop (Folquet de Marselha) to clerks, errant minstrels and those whose origins were so unremarkable that they were identified by the *vida*-writers only by their region of provenance and distinguished solely by the cultivation and talents they displayed. In the cases of Gaucelm Faidit, Giraut de Bornelh and Cercamon, for example, worth features more prominently than birth, yet they were welcomed by kings and counts.[34]

Cercamon is addressed as 'Maestre' (*magister*) in one song, which indicates that he had received a clerical education, studying the arts of grammar, dialectic and rhetoric.[35] Other poets, 'savis de letras' or 'ben letratz', began as clerks, canons or students, but then abandoned this calling and travelled in the secular world as poets and singers.[36] Also referred to as *maestre*, Giraut de Bornelh declares at one point that he will go back to being a scholar ('torn al mestier dels letratz') and give up singing.[37] His biography says that in the summer he travelled from court to court, accompanied by two *cantadors* to sing his songs, while he spent the winter in a school, where he 'aprendia letras' (taught rhetoric and poetic composition). It is probable that many troubadours picked up their techniques by listening to and imitating their fellows, rather than by studying Latin in a formal ecclesiastical school.[38]

That some troubadours depended for their livelihoods on what rewards they could earn for their art is likely, but the division between 'gentlemen and players', between aristocratic 'amateur' troubadours and lowly 'full-time, professional' *joglars* is not clear-cut. From the Latin *trobare*, 'to find, to invent', the term 'troubabour' had the fairly specialised sense of a man who composed lyric poetry. *Joglar*, however, covered a vast range of performers,[39] including acrobats and lewd contortionists disapproved of by the Church, animal-tamers, jugglers, musicians and performers of narratives. The Catalan lord Guerau de Cabrera produced a long

list of all the works which his ignorant *joglar*, Cabra ('Goat'), ought
to know, but the inventory is so long and includes such diverse
material (many epics and romances alongside lyrics) that it is hard
to imagine that one person could seriously have been expected to
master it all.[40] It is also noteworthy that *Cabra, juglar* includes only
four named troubadours: the lyric seems to have been considered
only as part of a much larger repertory of courtly entertainments,
even if few of the other texts Guerau mentions have survived in
Occitan.[41] Raimon Vidal's *joglar* says that he began by learning
songs by Dalfi d'Alvernhe, that is, by specialising in troubadour
courtly lyrics.[42] Others were performers entrusted by the troubadour with taking a song to a different court: often referred to by
diminutive nick-names, they are given their instructions at the
end of the song:[43]

> Huguet, mos cortes messatgers,
> chantatz ma chanso volonters
> a la reïna dels Normans. (Bernart de Ventadorn, X, 43–5)

(Little Hugh, my courtly messenger, sing my song eagerly to the Queen
of the Normans.)

According to his *vida*, Pistoleta ('Little Letter') was a *joglar* for
Arnaut de Maruelh before he became a troubadour, but other artists described as *joglars* were clearly poets in their own right and
many did not lead peripatetic lives.[44] There is some evidence to
suggest that such skilled, eloquent men would have served their
patrons in other ways too. Marcabru and Cercamon may have
exercised some administrative function in the household of William X of Aquitaine; Raimbaut de Vaqueiras became the close
companion of Boniface of Montferrat, while Bertran d'Alamanon
and Falquet de Romans were functionaries in the service of the
count of Provence and both served as diplomatic emissaries.[45] The
clear evidence for 'professional' court poets dates from the beginning of the thirteenth century and it is likely that, before then, a
fair number of poets had other roles and 'day jobs' which enabled
them to live.[46] *Joglar* then was a general term – sometimes pejorative – for all kinds of entertainer, and it may be that it was used
of individual troubadours when, for one reason or another, they
were envisaged primarily as performers.

Encouraged by the narratives in the *vidas* and *razos*, early

scholars understood the troubadours' songs rather as autobio-
graphical records reflecting 'real' experiences, including love
affairs with noble women whose identities were often discreetly
veiled by a *senhal*.[47] This relatively uncomplicated view of cultural
artefacts was definitively transcended in the early 1960s by
Köhler's sociological reading of the lyrics as stemming from the
marginal position of poor, landless knights of a particular rank,
the lesser nobility, at the courts of great magnates. Through their
spokesmen, the troubadours, this group of *iuvenes* sought to integrate themselves into court culture by constructing a system of
ethical values (*cortesia*, based on *fin'amor*, and *largueza*) which pur-
ported to be common to all the nobility.[48] Poetic courting of the
lord's wife in the *canso* would then have functioned as an elegantly
camouflaged expression of the desire of these men 'for economic
and social parity with other members of the nobility'.[49]

Kasten's 1986 study revises Köhler's arguments, but she nevertheless also sees such expressions of *fin'amor* (or, as she terms it,
Frauendienst) as informed by the sociopolitical and economic conditions of Occitania, although she accords greater importance to
the position of women. Since noblewomen like Eleanor of Aquitaine and Ermengarde of Narbonne supposedly often exercised
considerable political power, they would have had an interest in
encouraging the troubadours' panegyrics as a means of enhancing
their prestige, while the songs' amorous intrigues remained a
harmless, transparent fiction for its audience. Professional troubadours would have exploited this fashionable game as a means of
earning a living.[50]

Subsequent work has considerably modified a number of the
bases of the German scholars' readings, notably as regards vassalic
ties and feudal relations in Occitania which, as we have seen,
emerge as more diverse and difficult to pin down than had been
assumed.[51] While the troubadours' images speak of liege homage
and a vassalic dependency which prompts Bernart de Ventadorn
to kneel before his lady as before his liege-lord, such abject pos-
tures of submission do not in fact correspond to what we know of
feudal practices in the Midi.[52] Such puzzling mismatches open up
new areas of enquiry and Kay has recently suggested that one way
of reconciling the importance of the lyric's feudal metaphor, the
prominence and ambivalence of the *domna* and the aspirations of
the *fin aman* with new perspectives offered by historical research

is to see the *canso* as the forum for the negotiation of the *status* of the speaker, rather than his social rank. Informed by appeals to the feudal as 'an element in the cultural imaginary which offers scope for role-play and mystification', the troubadour lyric would be the product of a creative dialectic between the lay and clerical elements of court culture.[53]

If we can no longer simply see Bertran de Born's compliments to 'la Saisa' as evidence that he loved Mathilda of Saxony, it remains true that his amorous panegyric to one *Elena* (a *senhal* for Mathilda) in the preceding stanzas blends seamlessly with them. This mirrors a common troubadour technique which appears suggestively and flatteringly to conflate the unnamed *domna* praised by the speaker in the body of the song with the noble-woman to whom the poet dedicates the song at the end.[54]

Bertran's words also indicate the importance of women in the social life of the court, however restricted their autonomy may have been in reality.[55] Ladies and their female companions formed part of the audience for the courtly lyric: the joyful, relaxed court of Hugh de Mataplana included 'gracious ladies and the conversation was refined and pleasant', and in Arnaut de Maruelh's view, what adorns a lady above all is the wisdom and education which makes her honour each person as is fitting.[56]

Many noble patrons of poets were troubadours themselves. Guillem de Berguedà sheltered Aimeric de Peguilhan for a number of years, and Blacatz, lord of Aups in Provence, was associated with Peirol, Peire Vidal, Sordello, Falquet de Romans and others. A telling clue to the extent to which the nobility of Occitania saw lyric activity as an essential concern of the seigneurial caste is supplied by a wax seal of Bertran of Forcalquier (c. 1163): conventionally depicted as a knight on one side, the count is shown in three-quarter profile on the other dressed in a robe, seated on a decorated stool and playing a stringed instrument with a bow.[57] Great lords were known to have performed their own songs themselves: Guilhem de Peitieu 'took delight in singing of the miseries of his wretched experiences in rhythmical verse and pleasing melodies in the presence of kings, great men and Christian audiences'.[58] 'Turning everything into a joke, he made his listeners laugh uncontrollably', reports William of Malmesbury, and the disapproving monk Orderic Vitalis uses of the duke the term *histrio*, a synonym for *joglar*.[59] His contemporary, Eble II of Ventadorn, is nicknamed 'Cantator', although no songs from him have survived. In Courthézon, Raimbaut d'Aurenga took part in singing competitions: 'It is indeed fitting', he boasts, 'that one who is skilled in singing should sing in a good court ... for the blind and the deaf must know that I, of the twenty of us who will be in the lodging, shall carry off the honours ... So the day after the contest I shall wear on my head the large cloth crown', to the envy of Mita, the minstrel crowned at the Beaucaire festival.[60] He also exchanged songs with Peire Rogier.

Peire Rogier's song hints at another dimension to the role of the troubadour. He says that he has come to see the comfort and fellowship (*conort* and *solatz*) of Raimbaut's court for himself, to ascertain whether what he has heard about it is true (VIII, 11–14). The older man gives Raimbaut advice on how he should behave in order to maintain his reputation for gracious hospitality (20–1). The fame of the Lord of Orange had obviously spread, possibly as far as Narbonne, for Peire Rogier is usually associated with the Viscountess Ermengarde. But a good name is by implication a fragile thing.[61] If the troubadours were dependent on lordly courts, they also judged them; travelling between courts, they carried news and good and bad reports of one to another, both in gossip and in song. In this way, the troubadours can be seen as determining the limits and members of polite society, and binding together an exclusive community in which an appreciation of the courtly lyric and practice of the courtly virtues of hospitality, generosity and affability were seen as marks of status and cultivation.[62]

In one of the songs he composed for the *joglar* Bajona (XXXIX), Raimon de Miraval praises Peire Rogier de Cabaret, Aimeric de Montréal, the seigneur of Minerve, and Olivier and Bertran de Saissac for their generosity: Bajona's performance of this song in all the courts mentioned would enhance the reputations of this circle. Such a list is also a clear indication of whose names and reputations a contemporary audience might be expected to know. Elias de Barjols carries these assumptions one stage further when he constructs for his lady a noble lover worthy of her from the best bits of another circle of courtly lords: his *cavalher soissebut* will have the charm of Aymar de Limoges, the gracious wit of Dalfi d'Alvernhe, the generosity of Eble de Ventadorn, the gaiety of Pons de Capduelh and the poetic talents of Raimon de Miraval.[63]

This identikit paragon will also enjoy the *sen* ('wisdom') of one *En Bertran*, and it is likely that this refers to Bertran de Born, whose *dompna soissebuda* song (Poem VII) Elias is imitating here. We can infer that the first audience of this light-hearted piece would have been aware not only of the people named but also of the songs of Raimon and that by Bertran, to which this is a humorous homage.

Given the symbiotic relationship between the poets and the nobility, it is not surprising that their lyrics promoted the interests of their patrons. Over half the surviving troubadour corpus of poems are not love-songs, and the numerous *sirventes* indicate how lords were served in song in their various political, territorial and military struggles and in their conflicts either with or on behalf of the Church. While notions of 'propaganda' and 'public opinion' need careful definition in an age before mass communications and literacy,[64] *sirventes* were addressed to the same court audience as enjoyed the delicate subtleties of the *canso*.[65] The possibility that many *sirventes* were composed on the existing versification (and therefore probably melodies) of *cansos* further reinforces the connections between love and war.[66] As Gérard Gouiran has remarked, if in the tense situation of 1181 the count of Toulouse commissioned a 'chant de guerre' from Bertran de Born in order to rally his allies (Bertran, X, 1–6), it was because he thought songs to be an effective adjunct to negotiation and persuasion.[67] The political *sirventes* goad or exhort to action, praise one party and/or criticise or slander the other. They were particularly numerous in times of tension and upheaval and a great outpouring of partisan songs characterised the period of the northern French campaigns against the Midi, and the conflicts which then engulfed Provence.[68]

That courtly audiences were connoisseurs of other troubadours' songs is demonstrated by Peire d'Alvernha's famous 'galerie littéraire'. One by one, Peire reviews thirteen troubadours, devoting to each a stanza commenting on their attributes and defects and ending with himself! He has few complimentary things to say about any of them, but he bases many of his satirical remarks on their own compositions, though with an unexpected twist. Of Bernart de Ventadorn he says that

> en son paire ac bon sirven
> per trair'ab arc manal d'alborn,
> e sa maire escaldava·l forn
> et amassava l'issermen. (XII, 21–4)

(in his father he had a good servant expert at shooting with a laburnum bow, and his mother heated the oven and gathered vine-shoots [firewood].)

Here seems to be confirmation of Bernart's lowly origins, reported by the *vida* on the basis of this stanza; but Peire has taken the imagery and rhyme-words from Bernart's 'Be m'an perdut' (IX), and literalised its metaphors (which also have obscene connotations) in order to present to an informed audience a mocking image of the courtly Bernart whose father may have been Viscount Eble.[69] Similar ingenious parodies and allusions appear in Peire's treatment of his ninth target, Raimbaut d'Aurenga; Giraut de Bornelh is accused of wailing thin, miserable songs; but the fact that the whole song was composed 'At Puyvert, amidst jokes and laughter' (86) takes some of the sting from the mocking attacks. While the exact location of Puyvert is disputed, it is likely that this song was composed at a festive court at which all the troubadours mentioned would have been among the audience: the in-jokes would have more piquancy if their targets were present.[70] Such satires offer us glimpses of the performance styles, personal quirks and stage personalities of the troubadours, along with images of elderly *joglars* with dyed hair and those who shake their heads so much when singing that it looks as if they have a fever.[71]

Allusions to the works of others, their ideas or trademark metaphors create in the songs of many poets a concealed dialogue accessible, if not to all members of the audience, at least to the discerning few whose appreciation was the troubadours' main concern. While it may not have been uncommon for a performer to be asked to sing by boors who then immediately started talking amongst themselves,[72] the tone of many songs shows that they were intended for the courtly elite.[73] Those who do not understand were from the beginning stigmatised as *vilan*, the crass opposite of courtly (Guilhem de Peitieu, I, 4).

Direct addresses to them draw listeners into a song, smoothing away the distinctions between the singer and the 'I' of the lover seeking guidance from his peers:

> Era·m cosselhatz, senhor,
> vos c'avetz saber e sen. (Bernart de Ventadorn, XXV, 1–2)

(Now advise me, my lords, you who are wise and knowledgeable.)

It may have been expected that songs would be discussed and commented on by those who heard them. Raimon Vidal's *joglar* is warned not to be critical (*Abrils*, 1565–70); the troubadours' metatextual comments on their own works invite a reaction,[74] and the *tenso* between Raimbaut d'Aurenga and Giraut de Bornelh revolves around audience response to style.[75] In addition to such overt debates, the troubadours also participated in a more subtle kind of continuing, intertextual dialogue. Individual songs take up linguistic, semantic or metrical elements from the works of their predecessors or contemporaries and rework them, enabling the troubadour to refute or respond to his peers.[76] Discussion and response conducted by these means similarly point to the presence of sophisticated *cognoscenti* among the audience. Later patrons even set exegetical competitions for poets: in response to such an exercise, Guiraut Riquer composed a commentary on a song by Guiraut de Calanson for Enric II de Rodez (1280).[77] *Partimens* often present debates between poets and patrons not otherwise known for their own compositional expertise, including women such as Maria de Ventadorn and the enigmatic 'Dompna H'. Whether female participants in poetic exchanges performed their own words or had them sung by someone else is not clear: *joglaressas* existed – Gaucelm Faidit apparently married one – but seem to have had a bad reputation.[78] Once the two sides of the case had been presented, the poets purport to submit the decision to the judgement of an authoritative third party: in the debate involving Dompna H, a lady called Agnesina was to give her verdict, while Dalfi d'Alvernhe is also named as arbitrator in such 'jeux de société'.[79] It may be that from *salon* games like this was born the legend of the 'Cours d'amour' over which Eleanor of Aquitaine, Ermengarde of Narbonne and Marie de Champagne were supposed to have presided.[80]

Submitting cases to arbitration is a reminder of the judicial role of a real court. Few lyric texts concern themselves explicitly with this, but legal cases and procedures are echoed in songs and their images. Guilhem de Peitieu's 'Companho, non puosc mudar' (II) is a burlesque piece, modelled on the court case heard by a lord and his advisers: a lady brings a complaint that her *gardadors* wrongfully keep her too closely supervised; the guardians are condemned by the judge and advised to come to a compromise with the complainant![81] From the end of the twelfth century, many

troubadour songs begin with an extended allegory which equates
the speaker (lover) with a man suffering under an unjust overlord
(Love or the lady), suits which would be heard in a court, and
Ourliac notes that from the start poetry borrowed from the language of the law, evoking the experiences of the seigneurial
public.[82] Arnaut Daniel, singing of 'her who accuses him wrongly'
(VI, 6), enlists the support of lords and companions listening to
him:

> preiatz lieis don m'amors no·s tol
> qu'en aia merce cum del son;
> e diguas tug, pus ieu non l'aus nomnar:
> 'Bela, prendetz per nos n'Arnaut en cort
> e no metatz son chantar en defes.' (31–5)

(beg her from whom my love is never removed to have mercy on me as
one of her own; and everyone tell her, since I dare not speak her name,
'Beautiful Lady, for our sake, take Sir Arnaut into your court and do not
put his singing under interdiction.')

There is no documentary record of Bertran de Born's tussles
over Autafort, but if it was indeed a court hearing of that kind
which brought him to Argentan in 1182, his courtier's tact and
trobar talents enabled him to deflect his personal grievance into
humorous aspersions on the courtly culture of his day and, by
way of compensation, to celebrate the powerful charm of a single
domna.

NOTES

1 See Paterson, *World*, pp. 91–9; Paden, 'Albigensian Crusade', pp.
   173–4, also Bertran de Born, II, 17–20.
2 Higounet, 'Rivalité'; Baratier, 'Marquisat et comtés', pp. 131–66;
   Aurell, *Vielle*, pp. 19–28.
3 Duhamel-Amado, 'L'État toulousain'.
4 Gillingham, *Richard*, pp. 51–124.
5 Phillips, *Defenders*; Bull, *Knightly Piety*, pp. 70–114.
6 Riquer, *Los trovadores*, I, pp. 148–52; Hölzle, *Kreuzzüge*.
7 See Chapter 6.
8 Paterson, *World*, pp. 165–70.
9 *Chanson de la Croisade Albigeoise*, 36. 89; Barber, 'Catharism', p. 8.
10 Lewis, 'Féodalité', p. 258.

11 Martel, 'Construction', pp. 210–21; Paterson, *World*, pp. 10–19.

12 Martel, 'Construction', pp. 209–10, 215–17.

13 Bertran de Born, VI, 26; Boutière and Schutz, *Biographies* [Appendix 3, p. 301], p. 375.

14 Martel, 'Construction', pp. 218–19; Paterson, *World*, pp. 225–6; Barber, 'Catharism', p. 12.

15 Paden, 'Role'; Harvey, *'Joglars'*, p. 230.

16 Paterson, *World*, pp. 90–1.

17 *Abrils*, 631–2.

18 Gouiran, ed., *Bertran de Born* [Appendix 1, item 11], p. xiii; Gillingham, *Richard*, pp. 92–6.

19 Bloch, *Feudal Society*, I, pp. 225–6.

20 Compare Giraut de Bornelh, LIX, 57–60.

21 Paterson, *World*, pp. 90–1 and 114–19.

22 Cited in ibid., p. 114; *Raimbaut*, ed. Pattison [Appendix 1, item 50] pp. 139–40 (Mita) .

23 *Raimbaut*, ed. Pattison, p. 18; Brunel-Lobrichon and Duhamel-Amado, *Au Temps*, pp. 150, 153–6.

24 Riquer, *Los trovadores*, II, pp. 782–4, 24–8.

25 Jaeger, *Origins*; Page, *Owl*, pp. 53–9; Schmitt, *La Raison des gestes*.

26 Gaunt, Harvey and Paterson's forthcoming edition, XI, 60–1. Paterson, *World*, p. 105.

27 Poem II; Harvey, 'Allusions'; Paterson, *World*, p. 109.

28 On the *lauzengiers* in the *canso*, see Kay, 'Contradictions'.

29 Aurell, *Vielle*.

30 Paterson, *World*, pp. 91–100; Meneghetti, *Il pubblico*, pp. 60–6.

31 Gouiran, ed., *Bertran de Born* [Appendix 1, item 7], p. lxxvi.

32 Rieger, *Trobairitz*, pp. 262–74. The number of dialogue pieces involving these men suggests their role as patrons: see especially Gaucelm Faidit and Elias d'Ussel, ed. Mouzat, LVII.

33 Barber, 'Catharism', p. 12.

34 See Boutière and Schutz, *Biographies*, for all references. Compare Ghil, *L'Age de parage*, pp. 38–56 on the inclusive, 'ideological programme' of *vidas*.

35 Cercamon, VIII.

36 Brunel-Lobrichon and Duhamel-Amado, *Au Temps*, pp. 96–8; Bonnet, 'Le clerc'.

37 *Giraut de Borneil*, ed. Sharman [Appendix 1, item 27], p. 17; XXXIX, 67–70.

38 Compare Vitz, 'Chrétien'. There were fewer schools and centres of learning in Occitania than in France: see Rouche, *Histoire*.

39 See Harvey, *'Joglars'*.

40 Pirot, ed., *Recherches*, pp. 545–95.

41 Cingolani, '*Sirventes-ensenhamen*', p. 199, dates this piece 1196–8.

42 *Abrils*, 201; his repertoire includes songs by Giraut de Bornelh and Arnaut de Maruelh (*Abrils*, 44–5).

43 Paden, 'Role', pp. 91, 100–3 (nicknames).

44 On peripatetic and residential troubadours, see Paterson, *World*, p. 113.

45 Aurell, *Vielle*, pp. 125, 106.

46 Aurell, *Vielle*, pp. 126–9; Harvey, '*Joglars*', pp. 231–2.

47 The best example is Appel's edition of Bernart de Ventadorn (introduction).

48 On *iuvenes*, see Gaunt, 'Marcabru'.

49 Köhler, 'Observations'; Kay, *Subjectivity*, p. 113.

50 Kasten, *Frauendienst*, pp. 88–141.

51 Ibid., pp. 131–41; Gaunt, 'Marcabru'; Paterson, *World*, pp. 10–44; Harvey, '*Joglars*'.

52 VII, 38–40; XXXVII, 39–41; Paterson, *World*, pp. 28–36.

53 Kay, *Subjectivity*, p. 114 and 'Contradictions'.

54 Kay, *Subjectivity*, pp. 153–61.

55 Brunel-Lobrichon and Duhamel-Amado, *Au temps*, pp. 50–2; Paterson, *World*, pp. 220–41; Martindale, 'Eleanor'.

56 *En aquel temps*, 1083–84; *Razos es*, 257–60.

57 Brunel-Lobrichon and Duhamel-Amado, *Au Temps*, pp. 60–1.

58 Orderic Vitalis, cited in Riquer, *Los trovadores*, I, p. 108.

59 Riquer, *Los trovadores*, I, p. 108.

60 XXI, 1–11. On the question of the literary contests at the court of Le Puy, see Routledge, 'Troubadours'.

61 Compare Marcabru's reproaches to Alfonso VII of Castile (XXIII), in Gaunt, *Troubadours*, pp. 48–51.

62 Eulogies in the *planhs* suggest the qualities for which lords would have liked to be known: see Bertran de Born, XIII, 29–42.

63 Riquer, *Los trovadores*, III, pp. 1196–8 for notes on these men.

64 Gouiran, 'L'opinion', p. 20.

65 See Chapter 3.

66 Chambers, 'Imitation', p. 106; Meneghetti, *Il pubblico*, pp. 114–16.

67 Gouiran, 'L'opinion', pp. 20–1.

68 See Chapter 6; Aurell, *Vielle*; Asperti, 'Sul sirventese'.

69 Rossi, 'Per l'interpretazione', pp. 79–82; Paden, 'Bernart de Ventadour', pp. 408–9.

70 Riquer, *Los trovadores*, I, pp. 322–3.

71 Monje de Montaudon, XVIII; Kay, 'Rhetoric'.

72 *Abrils*, 1435–44.

73 Guiraut Riquier, Epître XIII, 1–4.

74 See for example Guilhem de Peitieu, VI, 1–7; Jaufré Rudel, I, 31–2.

75 *Giraut de Borneil*, ed. Sharman [Appendix 1, item 27], LIX; Kay, 'Rhetoric'. See Chapter 10.

76 Gruber, *Dialektik*, and see Chapter 11.
77 Epître XIII; Guida, *Jocs*, pp. 29–35. See Chapter 6.
78 Rieger, 'Beruf', pp. 232–3.
79 Riquer, *Los trovadores*, III, pp. 1247–50; Chambers, *Proper Names*, pp. 105–6.
80 Andreas Capellanus, pp. 251–71.
81 See Pasero's commentary; compare Monje de Montaudon, XVI and XV.
82 Ourliac, 'Troubadours', p. 162; Routledge, 'Monk'.

CHAPTER 2

Fin'amor *and the development of the courtly* canso

Linda Paterson

At the height of the courtly *canso* tradition Arnaut Daniel declares, 'obre e lim / motz de valor / ab art d'Amor' ('I work and file words of worth with Love's art', II, 12–14). The claim that artfully fashioned words of love are a source of value goes back to the beginnings of Occitan poetry. Guilhem de Peitieu formulates the earliest troubadour poetic of love, in a song whose social context is typical of the ensuing tradition: a song sent publicly to a male friend from whom he seeks recognition for its worth.[1]

I   Pos vezem de novel florir
         pratz, e vergiers reverdezir,
         rius e fontanas esclarzir,
            auras e vens,
         ben deu chascus lo joi jauzir   5
            don es jauzens.

II   D'amor no dei dire mas be.
         Quar no·n ai ni petit ni re?
         Quar ben leu plus no m'en cove!
            Pero leumens   10
         dona gran joi qui be·n mante
            los aizimens.

III   A totz jorns m'es pres enaisi
         c'anc d'aquo c'amiei no·m jauzi,
         ni o farai, ni anc non o fi;   15
            c'az essiens
         fauc maintas res que·l cor me ditz:
            'Tot es niens'.

IV   Per tal n'ai meins de bon saber
         quar vueill so que non puesc aver.   20
         E si·l reprovers me ditz ver:
            'Certanamens

a bon coratge bon poder,
   qui·s ben sufrens'.

V   Ja no sera nuils hom ben fis   25
              contr' amor, si non l'es aclis,
              et als estranhs et als vezis
                  non es consens,
              et a totz sels d'aicels aizis
                  obediens.   30

VI   Obediensa deu portar
              a maintas gens, qui vol amar;
              e cove li que sapcha far
                  faitz avinens
              e que·s gart en cort de parlar   35
                  vilanamens.

VII   Del vers vos dic que mais ne vau
              qui be l'enten, e n'a plus lau:
              que·l mot son fait tug per egau
                  comunalmens,   40
              e·l sonetz, ieu meteus m'en lau,
                  bo·s e valens.

VIII   A Narbona, mas ieu no·i vau,
                  sia·l prezens
              mos vers, e vueill que d'aquest lau   45
                 ·m sia guirens.

IX   Mon Esteve, mas ieu no·i vau,
                  sia·l prezens
              mos vers, e vueill que d'aquest lau
                  sia guirens.[2]   50

I   Since we see meadows newly blossoming, and orchards growing green once more, streams and springs turning clear, breezes and winds, each man ought to delight in the joy that gives him pleasure.

II   Of love I must say nothing but good. Why do I have little or nothing from it? Perhaps because I do not deserve any more! Yet it readily gives great joy to one who holds love's rights of easement.[3]

III It has always been my lot never to have joy of what I loved, nor will I do so, nor have I ever done so; for I knowingly do many things of which my heart tells me: 'It's all pointless'.[4]

IV   I have less pleasure from it for the reason that I want what I cannot have. And yet the proverb speaks the truth to me: 'A good wish certainly has a good outcome if you are patient.'

V   A man will never be truly faithful to love unless he is submissive to it, and accommodating to strangers and neighbours, and willing to serve all those in such circles.[5]

VI   Anyone who desires to love must obey the wishes of many people; and it is incumbent on him to know how to perform pleasing deeds and to take care not to speak uncouthly in court.

VII   Of the *vers*[6] I tell you that it is worth more to one who understands it well, and it is praised more as a result: for the words are all fashioned evenly to complement each other, and the melody – and I give myself the credit for this – is a good one of fine quality.

VIII Let my *vers* be presented in Narbonne, since I am not going there in person, and I wish it [*either* Narbonne *or* the *vers*] to vouch for this judgement on my behalf.[7]

IX   Let my *vers* be presented to my Stephen, since I am not going to him in person, and I wish him [*or* it] to vouch for this judgement.

The song moves from the general ('each man ought to delight in the joy that gives him pleasure') to the apparently personal ('why do I not receive more from love?') to the authoritatively general ('the proverb speaks the truth'). It concludes with a declaration of the poetic worth of the words and music in the ear of a discerning listener. Topsfield saw it as evidence of discontent with a contemporary code of love, and of a personal confession of a sense of the futility of life.[8] The use of the first person is unlikely, however, to mark a personal confession, but rather serves rhetorically as an exemplary illustration of what brings about failure in love. Far from distancing himself from the general truths about love presented in the poem, Guilhem can be seen as authorising them. The poem's structure subordinates individual experience to the universal: stanzas V–VI represent its thematic climax.[9]

The elements of Guilhem's formulation are patience, submission to love's demands, an accommodating manner to a great many others, willingness to perform services for them, pleasing actions, and polite speech at court. Unless one takes a credulous view of some of the contemporary character assassinations of Guilhem, there is no reason to suppose he would have found these irksome,[10] nor are they incompatible with his jocularity elsewhere.[11] In addition, this code of courtesy is bound up with the artistic excellence of the song and to conoisseurship on the part of its audience ('qui be l'enten', 38).[12] As an accomplished poet and courtly lover a man merits praise (*lau*, 38), acknowledgement of the worth of his creation (the song is *valens*, 42), and access to metaphorical property rights (*aizimens*, 12). Through its simultaneous claim to poetic excellence and authority in matters of love the poem encodes the regulation of social exchange, the exclusivity of the court, and the worth and privilege of the troubadour.

This is but one, early, articulation of a possible 'code' of love. There is no single set of rules for what the troubadours come to call *fin'amor*, any more than there is a single code of chivalry.[13] Not only did their poetry span over two hundred years, including the tumultuous events of the Albigensian Crusade, but inventive individuals were constantly interacting with each other in an ongoing debate or dialectic, assimilating but also challenging, subverting and outdoing each other's ideas and style.[14] Emphasising the social prerequisites for love (courteous manners), Guilhem's formulation will be overtaken by others which develop love's ethical dimensions.

According to Denomy, 'Courtly Love is a type of sensual love and what distinguishes it from other forms of sexual love, from mere passion, from so-called Platonic love, from married love is its purpose or motive, its formal object, namely, the lover's progress and growth in natural goodness, merit and worth.'[15] From this perspective *fin'amor* in the first troubadour is merely embryonic. Love, for Guilhem, effects metamorphosis, but not necessarily improvement:

> Per son joi pot malaus sanar,
> e per sa ira sas morir,
> e savis hom enfolezir,
> e belhs hom sa beutat mudar,
> e·l plus cortes vilaneiar,
> e·l totz vilas encortezir. (IX, 25–30)

(For joy of her a sick man can be cured, and from her anger a healthy man can die, and a wise man go mad, and a handsome man lose his good looks, and the most courtly one become a boor, and the totally boorish one turn courtly.)

It is Marcabru who, in the next generation, introduces a marked ethical dimension into troubadour concepts of love. A satirist and moralist, not an author of love lyrics, Marcabru attacks the immorality of those responsible for corrupting the aristocratic blood line, and the foolishness of the dizzy sexual excitement peddled by troubadours such as Jaufré Rudel.[16] Marcabru also seeks on occasion, no doubt in response to audience resistance to his negative fulminations, to distinguish *fals'amor* or *amar* (a pun on 'loving' and 'bitter') from *fin'amor*, and to formulate some definition of the latter: a love based on joy, patience, self-control, mutuality of desire, trust, purity, honesty and freedom from greed (XXXVII, 24–40); courtesy, controlled speech, personal worth and liberality (XXXII, 55–67); and monogamy (XV, 27–30). Marcabru's positive formulations are abstract and vague, but in so far as his *fin'amor* involves the love between a man and a woman, it seems close to ideas being elaborated by twelfth-century churchmen on the place of affection in marriage.[17]

Though not an author of love-lyrics himself, Marcabru was to have a profound impact on the development of the *canso* after him, in that troubadours generally make serious claims for the moral virtues of love. Peire d'Alvernha, a champion of Marcabru's ethical approach (XIII, 38–42), stresses the fruitfulness, security, 'grans sabers ni purs' ('great and pure wisdom'), and poetic integrity that spring from *bon'amor* (see especially poems V and VI). His contemporary Bernart de Ventadorn, often and rightly regarded as the troubadour who crystallises the key elements of troubadour love poetry, responds to the challenge posed by Marcabru in a number of moves. One consists in forcefully asserting the value of heartfelt love. Sincerity, he claims, is the hallmark of excellence in both love and poetry (II, 1–4). Another involves turning Marcabru's formulations back on him. Bernart attacks those (such as Marcabru) who blame love, by making a distinction, as Marcabru did, between 'true' and 'false' love,[18] and repeating Marcabru's attacks on venal women:

> Amor blasmen per no-saber
> fola gens, mas leis no·n es dans,
> c'amors no·n pot ges dechazer
> si non es amors comunaus.
> Aisso non es amors; aitaus
> No·n a mas lo nom e·l parven
> que re non ama si no pren.

S'eu en volgues dire lo ver,
eu sai be de cui mou l'enjans,
d'aquelas c'amon per aver
e son merchandandas venaus. (II, 15–25)

(Foolish people blame love out of ignorance, but this is no threat to it, for love cannot fall into disgrace if it is not vulgar love. Love is not like this; such a thing has only its name and appearance, for it loves nothing if it takes nothing.

To tell the truth of the matter, I know well where the deceit comes from – from those women who love for money and are mercenary traffickers.)

In the same song he deftly rewrites Marcabru (XXXVII, 28) by 'defining' love in terms of equal mutual desire (II, 29–32). He attributes a vague spirituality to his lady's eyes (II, 47), a strategy developed elsewhere in the invocation of God as creator of female beauty (XLIV, 50–3) and sympathetic aid to lovers (X, 15–18), and finally he echoes Marcabru's stress on *trobar naturau* (XXXIII, 7) in the claim that his own *vers* is 'fis et naturaus' (II, 50). With a few exceptions troubadours henceforth defend *fin'amor* as a source of moral goodness and worth, some emphasising the virtuous qualities of the individual, others the social benefits of the joy of the court.[19]

Once this point of the tradition has been reached, and despite the fact that there continue to be debates and shifts in emphasis, it makes sense to speak of a 'code' of love in its wider sense of a language of initiates. The courtly *canso* as a whole deploys a range of characteristic *topoi* or commonplace ideas, phrases, motifs and stylistic devices which form part of such a code. These *topoi* include, for example, the spring opening ('it is spring and I am in love'; 'it is spring, the birds are singing so I should sing'; 'it is winter but nevertheless it is spring in my heart'); the reason for singing ('I love, therefore I sing', 'someone has asked me to sing', 'since the birds sing so do I'); professions of love, constancy, timidity, sincerity and discretion by the lover; apostrophes to Love, the *domna*, the *lauzengiers*, *gardadors*; comparisons of the lover with famous lovers such as Tristan; affective expressions often swinging between joy and pain, elation and depression; and discussions of the nature of love and courtly virtues. Also constituting *topoi* of the *canso* are a range of key concepts relating to moral qualities, on the part of the lover, the *domna*, or of society. They are not stable and always need to be interpreted in the light of their context.[20]

One of these is *joi*. As in the case of Guilhem de Peitieu ('ben deu chascus lo joy jauzir/don es jauzens', VII, 5–6, see above), this is extensively used in alliterative and etymological play, and often supported by synonyms such as *gaug*. An essential property of the courtly love poet, *joi* may be the elation aroused by nature or love, or by extension the receipt of some favour from the *domna*, or sexual fulfilment. Sometimes it stands for the *domna* herself; sometimes it refers to a social atmosphere. It is also a social and moral quality belonging to *cortesia*: the *fis amans* and the *domna* are expected to be joyful and to disseminate joy.

Joven, literally 'youth', refers on the one hand to a courtly quality, and on the other to an association or brotherhood of those endowed with it. As a moral or social quality it involves generosity, especially in making gifts, and more broadly represents the font of virtue: 'As long as good *Joven* was father of the world and *fin'Amor* mother, *Proeza* (probity, virtue, prowess) was upheld in secret and in public' (Marcabru, V, 37–40). In the second half of the twelfth century, troubadours such as Rigaut de Berbezilh seem to attach the term to the *domna*, indicating her youthful vitality and commitment to courtly ideals, and at times bring the sense closer to biological youth (the lady being praised for her youth and beauty). Outside the *canso joven* can also mean the liveliness and carefree energy of men keen to fight for a just cause, in Marcabru's crusading songs for example (XXII and XXXV), or in the case of Bertran de Born, to risk life and limb in adventurous exploits rather than stagnate in the accumulation of worldly goods (XXVI, 29–35; XXVIII, 25–32). Although it is right to regard *joven* as a key troubadour concept, some troubadours such as Jaufré Rudel and Bernart de Ventadorn never mention it at all. There has been some suggestion that this might be linked to its possible Arabic origins and the contacts or otherwise of troubadours such as Guilhem de Peitieu and Marcabru with Spain.[21] Alternatively, it might relate to differences between courts, particularly to the comparative role and presence there of groups of young men.

Cortesia or 'courtliness' means having the civilised qualities and refined manners appropriate to life at court, as opposed to the roughness or baseness attributed to the peasant or *vilan*: courtesy, eloquence, the avoidance of offensive speech or behaviour, willingness to be of service to others. In the *canso* it is usually said to arise from love and to be impossible without it.

Largueza is the key quality required of those in positions of power by the not disinterested troubadours: a willingness to spend liberally (but not on the undeserving), and to uphold the courtly way of life, ideally by dispensing luxury goods, feasting, entertainment and the encouragement of troubadours and *joglars*.

Pretz and *valor* refer either to personal merit or to courtly worth in the abstract. *Valor*, a vague term for value (either innate or acquired with effort), is rarer than *pretz*. In reading troubadour poetry it is worth bearing in mind that translators are often unaware that *valor* can sometimes mean 'estate' or 'property'.[22] *Onor* has a similar blend of abstract and concrete value, meaning primarily 'land' or 'office' and by extension the honour that goes with it. In the context of the *canso*, it means a favour or reward granted by the *domna* to the lover, which increases his worth or reputation.

Mezura is self-discipline, the ability to moderate one's passions with rational control, to avoid extremes or anything that contravenes courtly behaviour. A key element of the troubadours' courtly ethos as a whole, and very different from the Tristan myth with its notion of overwhelming fatality, it is nevertheless the subject of troubadour polemic, since some, such as Bernart de Ventadorn, claim that it is impossible to retain *mezura* in love.[23]

Intellectual qualities such as *ensenhamen* (education, good manners – generally more in the social than the learned sense), *conoissensa* (discrimination), *sen* (intelligence, good sense), *saber* (knowledge, wisdom), and *sciensa* (knowledge) may also form a requisite part of the character of the courtly man or woman.

Denomy pointed out in 1933 the heretical implications of setting up a form of profane love, which as Christians the troubadours knew to be sinful and immoral, as a source of good. His explanation was to see the troubadours as operating a form of 'double truth', which had analogies in Christian attitudes to the new waves of Aristotelean science being assimilated in the West (a proposition could be held to be true according to philosophy yet false according to revelation), and which compartmentalised different aspects of intellectual and spiritual life.[24]

The troubadours' claims for the high moral ground in their unfolding concepts of *fin'amor* are indeed audacious in the context

of the Christian ethos and secular marriage practices. One of its
key ingredients was long thought to be adultery. In recent years
there has been some debate about the marital status (as well as
social rank) of the *domna*,[25] but in fact the opposition between
married and unmarried woman is rather a false one: unless the
lyric speaker addresses his wife (a joke)[26] or seeks a woman in
marriage (never?), by requesting the love of the *domna* he contravenes the 'rights' of some other man (husband, father, other male
relative) over her sexuality.[27] Some troubadours certainly do
defend the right of a woman to have one lover as well as her
husband without incurring stigma; however, it is not always clear
how seriously this is intended, and what the nature of the 'lover'
is.[28] The courtly *suitor* of a married woman was no doubt a social
reality. Uc de Mataplana, a Catalan nobleman and poet, reproached Raimon de Miraval for throwing his wife Gaudairenca out
of the family castle because she composed songs and encouraged
such suitors. A husband, Uc maintained, should accept his wife's
admirers, just as she accepts his attentions to *domnas*.[29]

But perhaps *fin'amor* was a primarily spiritual affair? Its language permits considerable moral ambiguity, so that at extreme
ends of the scholarly spectrum, *fin'amor* has been perceived on the
one hand as a cover for the sexual licence of the upper classes, and
on the other as a spiritual phenomenon, in which erotic language
conveys mystical emotion or even encrypts heretical dogma.[30]
Jaufré Rudel's *amor de lonh*, for example, has given rise to mystical
or religious interpretations,[31] God being heavily implicated in his
desire: God, he claims, formed this *amor de lonh* (IV, 36–7) and will
give him a true sight of it ('Ben tenc lo Senhor per verai/per qu'ieu
veirai l'amor de lonh', IV, 29–30); he imagines himself as a pilgrim in the *domna*'s presence (IV, 33–5), her love is like manna
(III, 19), the pains of love like the ascetic's mortification of the
flesh (I, 13–15) or reminiscent of the Crown of Thorns (III, 26).

Yet it would be perverse to deny the sensuality of troubadour
eroticism. This may be expressed in the frank enthusiasm of
Guilhem de Peitieu: 'Enquer me lais Dieus viure tan/qu'aia mas
mans soz son mantel!' ('God let me live long enough to get my
hands under her cloak!' X, 23–4), in the apparently more deferen-
tial desire for permission to kneel humbly beside her bed and take
off her well-fitting shoes, 'if it pleases her to hold out her feet
towards me' (Bernart de Ventadorn, XXVI, 29-35), or Arnaut

Daniel's suggestive wish to undress his *domna* in the lamplight ('qe·l seu bel cors baisan rizen descobra / e qe·l remir contra·l lum de la lampa', XII, 31–2). But the *canso* rarely celebrates the fulfilment of sexual desire, springing rather from the tension between desire and fulfilment: a longing intensified by obstacles such as the *gilos* (jealous ones), *lauzengiers* (slanderers or spies), *gardadors* (guards), by distance (*amor de lonh*), and by the need for secrecy (*celar*) and recourse to pseudonyms (*senhals*). If some troubadours celebrate, in anticipation, personal happiness or *joi* through mutual pleasure of the senses, others delight in the pain of impossible love, in a simultaneous 'aspiration and renunciation "have and have not"'.[32] At the time of the Albigensian Crusade, troubadours anxious to defend their world against the Inquisition stress the social and spiritual benefits of *fin'amor*, to the point where Guilhem de Montanhagol declares that love is a source of chastity since a lover would never seek anything to dishonour his lady (XII, 18).

It may seem surprising that the Church did not more openly or specifically oppose troubadour *fin'amor*. This was perhaps partly because troubadours of the satirical tradition (see Chapter 3) such as Marcabru or Peire Cardenal performed this function, perhaps also because until the Albigensian Crusade, when it began to crack down on the courtly way of life,[33] the Church did not take troubadour activities seriously. Furthermore, troubadour articulations of love were often vague and ambiguous, encouraged by the permeability of erotic and mystical language in the Middle Ages. Just as mystics such as St Bernard expressed in sensual terms the longing of the soul for union with God,[34] so Jaufré Rudel largely if not exclusively incorporated religious language into a secular longing roundly condemned by Marcabru. Guiraut Riquier addresses a courtly *domna* in the same language as he does the Virgin Mary. The term *fin'amor* itself was highly slippery (one has only to compare its use by Marcabru and Bernart de Ventadorn), and meaning was further destabilised by the ubiquitous potential for irony in troubadour lyrics.[35] And ambiguity has the great advantage that moral contradictions and social tensions are not brought out into the open: as Sarah Kay has said, 'Being evasive about satisfaction was, paradoxically, a way of satisfying everyone.'[36] Some troubadours, such as Peire d'Alvernha, seem to have been troubled by competing claims of *fin'amor* and religion. Attacked publicly by

Bernart Marti (poem V) for boastfulness and lack of integrity in breaking his religious vows as a canon, at a certain point in his poetic career Peire bade a fond farewell to 'cortez' amors de bon aire' (X, 58) – the only occurrence of the phrase 'courtly love' in the whole of the troubadour corpus – in favour of the love of the Holy Spirit, and in a crusading song defended Marcabru's rejection of 'carnal amar' (XIII, 22–42). Folquet de Marselha abandoned it as a shameful excess when he became a Cistercian monk.[37] But if these troubadours found themselves constrained to choose between carnal and spiritual love, others were happy to fuse them: in the case of Arnaut Daniel, at the pinnacle of troubadour art, daringly and knowingly.

Arnaut Daniel's *canso* 'Si·m fos Amors' (XVII), from the 'classical period' of the late twelfth century, distils many of the quintessential themes of the genre while on one level audaciously challenging the listener to explore the mystificatory processes of its language. Drawing on the lover's traditional submission to love and his worship of a lofty and shadowy *domna*-figure, it offers a perfect example of the *canso*'s tension between desire and fulfilment, which refines erotic desire into the ethical and spiritual. At the same time it develops the notion of worth or value in a startlingly explicit, though also subtly ambivalent, series of economic or monetary metaphors, which highlight possibly discordant meanings of worth inherent in the tradition:[38]

I   Si·m fos Amors de ioi donar tant larga
        cum ieu vas lieis d'aver fin cor e franc,
        ia per gran ben no·m calgra far embarc,
        q'er am tant aut qe·l pes mi poi' e·m tomba,
        mas qant m'albir cum es de pretz al som   5
        mout m'en am mais car anc l'ausiei voler,
        c'aras sai ieu que mos cors e mos sens
        mi farant far, lor grat, rica conquesta.

II   Pero s'ieu fatz lonc esper, no m'embarga,
        q'en tant ric luoc me sui mes e m'estanc   10
        c'ab sos bels digz mi tengra de ioi larc
        e segrai tant q'om mi port a la tomba,
        q'ieu non sui ies cel que lais aur per plom;
        e pois en lieis no·s taing c'om ren esmer,
        tant li serai fis e obediens   15
        tro de s'amor, si·l platz, baisan m'envesta.

III   Us bons respieitz mi reven e·m descarga
d'un doutz desir don mi dolon li flanc,
car en patz prenc l'afan e·l sofr' e·l parc
pois de beutat son las autras en comba,   20
que la gensser par c'aia pres un tom
plus bas de liei, qui la ve, et es ver;
que tuig bon aip, pretz e sabers e sens
reingnon ab liei, c'us non es meins ni·n resta.

IV   E pois tan val, no·us cuietz que s'esparga   25
mos ferms volers ni qe·is forc ni qe·is branc,
car no serai sieus ni mieus si m'en parc,
per cel Seignor qe·is mostret en colomba,
q'el mon non ha home de negun nom
tant desires gran benanans' aver   30
cum ieu fatz lieis, e tenc a noncalens
los enoios cui dans d'Amor es festa.

V   Na Mieills-de-ben, ia no·m siatz avarga,
q'en vostr'amor me trobaretz tot blanc,
q'ieu non ai cor ni poder qe·m descarc   35
del ferm voler que non es de retomba;
que qant m'esveill ni clau los huoills de som
a vos m'autrei, qan leu ni vau iazer;
e no·us cuietz qe·is merme mos talens,
non fara ies, q'ara·l sent en la testa.   40

VI   Fals lauzengier, fuocs las lengas vos arga,
e que perdatz ams los huoills de mal cranc,
que per vos son estraich cavail e marc:
amor toletz, c'ab pauc del tot non tomba;
confonda·us Dieus que ia non sapchatz com,   45
qe·us fatz als drutz maldire e viltener;
malastres es qe·us ten, desconoissens,
que peior etz, qui plus vos amonesta.

VII   Arnautz a faitz e fara loncs atens,
q'atenden fai pros hom rica conquesta.   50

I   If Love were as open-handed in giving joy as am I to her in having a pure, free/noble heart, it would never vex me to become indebted[39] for the sake of great wealth; for I now love so high that the scales[40] lift me up and drop me down; but when I consider how [imagine that?] she's at the summit of value, I love myself the more for ever daring to desire her, for I now know that my heart/body and senses/mind will make me make, thanks to them, a rich/noble conquest.

II   Yet even if I wait a long time, this does not impede me, for I have placed myself in such a rich place and remain fixed/staunch myself there,[41] for with her fair words she will keep me generous with joy, and I shall persevere until I am carried to the tomb, for I am definitely not one to abandon gold for lead; and since there is nothing in her that needs refining in any way, I shall be true and obedient to her until, if it pleases her, kissing she invests me with her love.

III A certain noble hope/wait[42] refreshes[/sells me back?] and discharges me of a sweet desire which makes my flanks ache, for patiently/as a tax/as the kiss of peace at the offertory[43] I accept the travail and endure it and husband it parsimoniously/suffer it, since the other ladies are down in the valley in terms of beauty, for to anyone who sees her the loveliest of them seems to have tumbled below her level, and it is true; for all good qualities, worth and intelligence and good sense abide with her, so that not one is diminished or lacking.

IV   And since she is worth so much, do not imagine that my firm desire will scatter[44] or fork or branch, for I shall not be hers or mine if I abstain from it,[45] by that Lord who revealed Himself in the form of a dove, for in the whole world there is no man of any name/reputation who might so desire to possess great prosperity as I do her, and I pay no heed to the vexatious ones for whom damage to love is festival.

V   Lady Best-of-Good/Wealth, do not be niggardly with me, for in your love you will find me pure white,[46] for I have no heart or power to discharge myself of the firm desire which does not come from a phial; for when I wake or close my eyes in sleep, I yield myself to you, when I get up or go to bed; and do not imagine that my yearning will ever diminish; it will never do so, for I now feel it in my head.

VI   False slanderers, fire burn your tongues, and may you lose both your eyes from foul canker, for because of you are withheld horses and marks: you hinder love, so that it almost entirely collapses; God confound you without you ever knowing how, for you cause lovers to be slandered and denigrated; it is an ill star that keeps you in ignorance, for the more you are admonished, the worse you are.

VII Arnaut has made and will make a long attentive wait, for by waiting attentively a worthy man will make a rich conquest.

There are many ambivalent expressions in this dense and complex poem. The translation here highlights its economic tropes, involv-

ing wealth and value, largess and parsimony, property and fief-
dom, money, debt, investment and exchange, interwoven as they
are with images of retention and release, rising and falling, freedom and attachment, submission and domination, erotic desire
and worship.

The *canso* begins with the clash of two different economic systems: one of 'free' exchange between lord and subject, where a
lord grants largess in exchange for a subject's fidelity, and one of
mercantile investment ('I wouldn't mind getting into debt with
the prospect of rich returns later'). The speaker's 'worth' lurches
unstably on the scales of trade or coin exchange, while also connoting the religious weighing of souls, famously sculpted on the tym-
panum of Autun cathedral; at the same time the subject of the
verb *es* in line 5, which slides from *Amors* to the unspecified *domna*,
occupies the apex of value or price, and the very act of daring
to aspire to such heights becomes a process of self-valuation and
self-enhancement. The stanza's concluding economic metaphor
reverts to a pre-mercantile 'pillage and gift' model: as a follower
of *Amor*, and thanks to his qualities of heart and mind, the speaker
will gain by conquest the *domna*'s love, and its attendant wealth
and status (implied by *ric*). This image, echoed in the *tornada*,
marks a deftly imagined move from a position of weakness and
subordination to power, wealth and dominance.

In stanza II the lover claims that if he embarks on a long, hopeful, wait, this is not placing any impediment (possibly 'debt', in
the light of line 3) upon himself, because he has 'settled in a
rich place'. The expression *m'estanc* (10) suggests on one level the
staunching of desire, on another the lover's firm commitment to
Love ('I attach myself'). Is this an allusion to the medieval treatment of debtors? In Montpellier these were customarily fastened
half-naked to a bolt on the door of the main church, near to the
money-changing tables, where they could be beaten by their credi-
tors.[47] Furthermore *paguar estanquidamen* means to pay the money
required to acquit one's debts:[48] perhaps the idea is one of paying
off the debt owed to Love by the open-handed dispensation of joy
(line 11), a further shift whereby the speaker takes on the position
of a lord with gifts to distribute. The *domna*'s worth is pure gold
(13) with nothing left to refine (14), and he looks forward to being
invested with her love, in other words both 'clothed' and put in
full possession of it as if of a property.[49] This metaphor draws on

the common medieval practice of granting a favoured subordinate a wife and the property that goes with her, and places the *domna* in the position of a passive gift of Love.

In stanza III, the notion of debt returns with *descarga* (and *reven?*) in 17, and possibly with *mi dolon li flanc* if one thinks of the beating of debtors. The phrase *en patz* means simultaneously 'patiently', 'as a tax' ('I accept the pain as a tax imposed by Love'), and, in an act of religious devotion, 'as the kiss of peace placed on the Psalter or the paten at the moment of the Offertory'. An economic interpretation of *parc* (19) suggests that the lover husbands the pains of love thriftily, in opposition to the notion of free spending elsewhere, binding together the contradictions of largess and mercantilism. The up-and-down of value continues with the *domna*'s pre-eminence over other ladies who are 'tumbling down into the valley' in comparison with her.

Stanza IV deepens the theme of self-control, abstinence resonating with the ubiquitous theme of waiting. Here the 'abstinence' is complex, not to say convoluted, since the speaker professes his intention *not* to abstain from his *ferm voler* which is nevertheless a form of abstinence in itself: abstinence from other love affairs. The invocation of the Holy Spirit develops a powerfully spiritual dimension to the love celebrated as feast or festival, whether secular or religious. It is a particularly audacious example of what Denomy referred to as the 'heresy' of Courtly Love.

In moves typical of the *canso*, the speaker addresses in turn the *domna* (stanza V) and the *lauzengiers* (stanza VI). The desired *domna* is both the 'best of goodness' and the 'best of goods'.[50] The phrase *non es de retomba*[51] is probably an elliptical allusion to Tristan's famous love-potion: Arnaut's love is not a drug-induced madness but a sublimated emotion that has acquired a rational force ('q'ara·l sent en la testa'). Finally in his invective against the *lauzengiers*, through which he appropriates the moral high ground at the conclusion of the poem, Arnaut binds together the traditional notion of courtly largess ('horses and marks') with love's freedom to be generous.

This *canso* distils many of the key traditional themes, *topoi* and strategies of *fin'amor*. Its bold privileging of competing notions of value through its economic imagery, at a historical time when the rise in the circulation of coin is displacing old economic certainties, startlingly highlights a disquieting clash of lofty spirituality and materialistic negotiation, while simultaneously fusing their contradictions. This clash is made all the more disturbing in that, while images of economic exchange were present in the love language of the first troubadours – in lovers' property rights or *aizimens* mentioned by Guilhem de Peitieu, for instance[52] – mercantile discourse would seem more aggressively to challenge an ethos founded on nobility of spirit.[53] Arnaut's poem represents a dazzling linguistic performance, a heady erotic and emotional brew, and a self-conscious reflection upon the traditional mechanisms of *fin'amor*.[54]

Fin'amor was the driving force that generated the artistic brilliance of the troubadour *canso*, the reputation of the *canso*'s individual authors, and a code of social and moral values fostering the cohesion and self-valuation of the medieval Occitan court. This flexible code proved not only powerfully innovative but also remarkably durable in the subsequent history of European literature and manners. As Arnaut's poem shows, troubadours could be well aware of its contradictions and questionable premises. They might accept them, as Arnaut seems wholeheartedly yet knowingly to do, or treat them ironically, or subject them to open discussion by means of other genres such as the *tenso* or *sirventes*; or indeed to bring elements of these other lyric genres into the *canso* itself (see Chapters 3, 11 and 12).

NOTES

1 As Riquer (*Los trovadores*, I, p. 123) says, *mon Esteve* might be a *senhal* for a woman – though it would be unusual to use a man's *name*. For poetic exchanges between men, see Gaunt, 'Poetry of exclusion', pp. 311–13.

2 Text based on Pasero VII. In stanza VII I have regularised the inflections, the MS testimony being divided, and have followed *a¹ sonetz* in 41 (*CE sonet*). In 46 and 50 I have followed Jeanroy's edition, to avoid hypermetric lines.

3 'Rights of easement' (French 'droits d'usage') are the rights to the produce and profits of a piece of land. Love is envisaged as a lord who allows such rights to favoured subjects. See Niermeyer [Appendix 3, p. 297], s.v. *aisamentum* and *manutenere* 4, and compare *PSW* [Appendix 3, p. 295] V, 116 *mantenensa*. For other interpretations see the note to this line in Pasero's edition. He translates *aizimens* as 'le regole' (the rules); compare Topsfield, *Troubadours*, p. 29, 'its precepts', and Dragonetti ('*Aizi*', pp. 133–40), 'les limites propres aux différ-

ents ordres fixés par lui': the latter is over-dependent on a particular thirteenth-century case of *aisamenta* in Du Cange [Appendix 3, p. 297], s.v.

4 For *que = de que, don*, see Jensen, *Syntax* [Appendix 3, p. 299], § 455. Pasero 'c'az essiens/fauc, maintas vez que·l cor me ditz' (for it is certain that I do so many times when my heart (however) tells me). He suggests *fauc* here might be translated as 'gioisco' ('I rejoice').

5 Dragonetti's explanation of *aizis* as the different dwellings of love's subjects according to their metaphorical distance or proximity to love ('*Aizi*', p. 140) seems over-elaborate.

6 *Vers* is the generic name for a troubadour song at this early date. The term *canso* appears c. 1160.

7 Pasero translates *lau* as 'praise' ('lode'), but see Lejeune, 'Formules féodales', p.108, who points out that it is a legal term. For the pleonastic pronoun in 44 and 48, see Jensen, *Syntax* [Appendix 3, p. 299], § 359.

8 Topsfield, *Troubadours*, p. 29.

9 See also Pasero's analysis on pp. 189–94 of his edition.

10 Martindale, '*Cavalaria*', pp. 87–116.

11 Contrast Roncaglia, 'Guillaume IX'. He sees no 'idéologie courtoise' in or before Guilhem's poetry (p. 1113).

12 See Pasero's commentary, pp. 189–94.

13 Compare C. S. Lewis's influential belief that love had a 'systematic coherence throughout the love poetry of the troubadours as a whole' (*Allegory*, p. 3).

14 See Gruber, *Dialektik*; Gaunt, *Troubadours*; and Chapter 11.

15 Denomy, 'Courtly love', p. 44.

16 See Paterson, 'Marcabru's rhetoric'.

17 Brundage, *Law*, pp. 197–8 and 'Marital Affection' in his General Index.

18 XXI, stanza II; XXII, stanzas II–III; XXXI, 33–36.

19 On the latter, see Topsfield, *Troubadours*, Chapter 8.

20 Cropp, *Vocabulaire courtois*; also Payen, 'A propos'. For analogous Old French lyric *topoi* see Dragonetti, *Technique*.

21 Cropp, *Vocabulaire courtois*, pp. 413–21 (especially pp. 414–15); see also Denomy, 'Arabic influences', p. 153.

22 Bernart Marti, II, 53.

23 Bernart de Ventadorn, VIII, 24; XIII, 22–27; see also Wettstein, '*Mezura*'.

24 Denomy, 'Arabic influences', p. 156.

25 Lazar, *Amour courtois*, p. 60; Utley, 'Must we abandon', p. 318; Press, 'The adulterous nature'; Paden, 'The troubadour's lady'; Monson, 'The troubadour's lady'.

26 Raimbaut d'Aurenga, poem VIII.

27 Gaunt, 'Marcabru', p. 56; Paterson, *World*, pp. 232–5, 240.

28 Paterson, *World*, p. 235; Paden, 'The troubadour's lady', p. 40.

29 See Topsfield, *Troubadours*, p. 221.

30 Briffault, *Troubadours*; De Rougemont, *L'Amour*; for a survey of critical opinion, see Boase, *Origins*.

31 See the introduction to Chiarini's edition, and Topsfield, *Troubadours*, Chapter 2.

32 Kay, 'Contradictions', Appendix i, p. 240.

33 See for example Montanhagol, poem I, and Raimon Vidal, *Abrils*, 906–39.

34 *S. Bernardi Opera*, I–II.

35 See Chapter 12, and Gaunt, *Irony*.

36 Kay, 'Contradictions', p. 231.

37 See Stronski's edition [Appendix 1, item 23], p. 89*.

38 Apart from Toja's edition see also that of Wilhelm, *Arnaut Daniel*, poem 17.

39 MS *H* glosses *debita*.

40 *pes* can also mean 'thought', as editors have traditionally taken it.

41 The primary sense of *estancar* is 'staunch' (see *FEW* [Appendix 3, p. 296], XII, 231, *STANTICARE). For *estanquidamen* see *PSW* [Appendix 3, p. 295], III, 305.

42 Wilhelm, stressing the Latin etymology (*respectus*, a looking back): 'a fond reflection'; Toja 'pensiero'; but see Cropp, *Vocabulaire courtois*, pp. 198–9; *LR* [Appendix 3, p. 295], V, 88; *PSW*, VII, 265; *FEW*, X, 306(8) .

43 See *PD* [Appendix 3, p. 296] *patz*, a sort of tax, and *dar, donar p., la p.*, 'to give the kiss of peace on the Psalter or the paten at the moment of the offertory', *ofrir en p.* 'to suffer patiently'.

44 *FEW*, XII, 133, SPARGERE 'zerstreuen'; apr. esparger. 'répandre; divulguer'. Some examples cited involve liquid: compare perhaps *m'estanc*, in 10.

45 Previous editors see *parc* in line 27 as a rare form of *part*, from *partir* ('if I part from her'). *PD* gives 'écarter' as one sense of *parcer, parcir*, which would produce a similar sense. But for the reflexive *se parcer de* see *PD*, 'se retenir, s'abstenir', and compare Bertran de Born, XXVIII, 11, 'Mas per aisso m'en soffrisc e m'en parc' ('but for this reason I renounce and abstain from this').

46 Compare, perhaps, TL [Appendix 3, p. 297], I, 984, 'argent blanc', for an idea of pure currency.

47 Baumel, *Seigneurie*, I, pp. 67–8.

48 *FEW*, XII, 231, *STANTICARE; *PSW*, III, 305, *estanquidamen*. The 'extinction' or 'quashing' logically implies an object 'debt' rather than 'debtor', but if Arnaut 'owes himself', the distinction disappears.

49 See Niermeyer [Appendix 3, p. 297], s.v. *investire*.

50 Other editors treat *Mieills* in the *senhal* as a comparative. It could

only be a comparative adverb, which is syntactically implausible here; I take it as a noun, analogous to the *mieills* sought by Guilhem de Peitieu (IX, 4–5) and Jaufré Rudel (VI, 30) .

51 The *es* of the majority reading could mean 'is', but can also be a form of *eis* and mean 'goes out', explicit in MSS *AB*'s *(hi)eis*, followed by Bond (Guilhem IX, *Poetry*, ed. Bond; see his note on p. 114). *Retomba* is a glass drinking-cup, bulbous-shaped flask or bottle (see *PSW*, VI, 292; TL, VIII, 1136; Alcover and Moll, *Diccionari*, IX, 443). It can connote drunkenness (compare Arnaut's poem IV, 18), and also fragility (see the examples in *PSW*).

52 VII, 12, quoted above.

53 As it does in Arnaut's equally bold imagery of the *domna* as usurer in X, 27–8.

54 Arnaut's combination of linguistic play and economic relativism is interesting in the light of the 'realism' and 'nominalism' debates highlighted by Bloch (*Etymologies*, pp. 164–9).

CHAPTER 3

Moral and satirical poetry

Catherine Léglu

If love is central to the troubadour lyric, it is not the sole motivation for song. The *chansonniers* preserve an important corpus of lyrics which range from didactic and moralising songs to songs containing political comment and personal invective, making this corpus difficult to define. Some texts attack the emerging conventions of *fin'amor*, while others address issues of social and religious behaviour. Much satirical work of the period is religiously motivated, and therefore moralising, although not all moralising or didactic texts are satirical. Moreover it is important – but occasionally tricky – to differentiate between destructive invective and meliorative attack. What is the appropriate reading approach to adopt towards these songs: socio-historical, aesthetic or rhetorical?[1] These expressions of dissatisfaction or rebellion, voiced from a number of positions within medieval society, provide a refreshing antidote to the bland good manners espoused by the poets of *fin'amor*; they also, however, raise a set of questions in their own right.

Most importantly, these texts are not marginal to the troubadour lyric, but a constituent part of it. The bibliography of troubadours by Alfred Pillet names 460 troubadours, of whom 58 are associated solely with the *canso*, leaving 360 names attributed a variety of genres. Of these, 69 are represented only by satirical or moralising songs, and there are a further 38 of whom over half the songs are satirical, political, didactic or moralising. Many of these troubadours head tiny bodies of work, between one and three songs only, but the ratio of 58 *canso* troubadours to 107 satirical or moralising specialists confirms the initial impression that, while the *canso* may constitute the core genre of the lyric, there is also a varied field of other genres.

This chapter sketches a general introduction to the various

schools of troubadour satirical and moralising poetry (although it excludes *tensos* and *coblas esparsas*). There have been a number of studies of the corpus presented here; Thiolier-Méjean's work on the *sirventes* adopts a non-political, 'formal' (aesthetic and rhetorical) approach, while Klein, Aurell and Ghil place political poems in their historical contexts.[2] Both approaches are valid, and may work together constructively, as I hope to show.

Since my purpose is introductory, I focus on songs attributed to Marcabru, Bertran de Born and Peire Cardenal, three key figures in the elaboration of distinctive styles of satirical and moralising song which are known by different generic names. Up to c. 1160 – c. 1170, all songs composed in the troubadour lyric were called *vers*, a word related to the Latin para-liturgical genre known as the *versus*.[3] It is noticeable that whereas a considerable number of troubadours after 1160 begin to use the term *sirventes* to refer to their songs,[4] a group of poets, all of whom refer either directly or allusively to Marcabru, keep the term *vers* into the 1190s. This leads to an association of the term with a style of didactic invective which may be at the root of a redefinition of the *vers* as a purely didactic composition in the later thirteenth century, used by Peire Cardenal and Guiraut Riquier. The *canso* emerged from the general term *vers* at roughly the same time, and appears to have remained more stable in its definition. (Scattered examples of minor satirical and moralising genres also survive, such as the violently satirical *estribot*, the comic *arlotes*, the *enueg* and the *plazer*.[5])

THE VERS: DIDACTIC-SATIRICAL CRITICISM[6]

The earliest datable satirical songs are attributed to Alegret, Cercamon and Marcabru. Textual references to Alegret indicate he was a contemporary of Marcabru's (see Marcabru XI), while the *vida*'s claim that Cercamon was Marcabru's master is in line with the textual echoes between the two poets, who were both under the patronage of Duke Guilhem X of Aquitaine (d. 1137). The first reference in Occitan to a *sirventes* is by Marcoat, a minor figure who refers to the death of Marcabru. These points strongly suggest that a style of satirical poetry was elaborated between c. 1130 and c. 1150, when the *canso* was also emerging but satirical poetry appears to predominate, producing a new generic name by the

end of this period. Out of this school of troubadours, Marcabru
emerges as the leading figure, with the greatest number of extant
songs, and a style which later poets emulated; it is possible to refer
to this as the 'Marcabrunian' school, including Peire d'Alvernha,
Gavaudan, Bernart Marti, Bernart de Venzac and pastiches by
other poets, such as two – probably early – songs by Raimbaut
d'Aurenga (I and II).

Marcabru establishes a distinctive way of expressing disaffec-
tion from noble society, largely through a combination of invective
and allusion to Scripture. There is a recurrent scenario of adulterous couples producing degenerate (non-noble) offspring who usurp
noble rank, and an obsession with *luxuria* which often carries
echoes of Biblical invective. The Marcabrunian satirist is heavily
marked by this theme, and by the invective and declamatory styles
found in the Latin texts of ascetic moralists such as Jerome, Peter
Damien and Alain de Lille. There are close analogies with these
writers' violent rhetoric and pessimism in the Roman satirist
Juvenal (diffused in Christianised interpretations in the Middle
Ages) as well as the Old Testament books of Jeremiah, Isaiah and
Proverbs. These songs rehearse the commonplaces of contempt
for the world, a disenchanted view of human affairs, a morbid fear
of women and of sexuality, and a general suspicion that penance
or solitary withdrawal are the only appropriate reactions.

Whether or not this places Marcabru on the side of ecclesiastical interests in the period, it certainly marks his voice as that of
a school-educated man informed by ascetic, perhaps penitential,
writings, who nevertheless chooses to express these ideas in a
secular frame.[7] However, the difference between Marcabru's world-
bound misanthropy and his follower Peire d'Alvernha's exhortations
to spiritual withdrawal is striking. Peire d'Alvernha is a much more
'clerical' speaker, as his biographical status as a former canon would
suggest. Marcabru is not so easy to classify. His 'Dirai vos en mon
lati' (XVII) will serve as an example since it rehearses ideas and
devices common to his forty-two surviving songs:

> Dirai vos en mon lati
> de so qu'ieu vei e que vi;
> non cuich que·l segles dur gaire
> segon qu'escriptura di,
> qu'eras faill lo fills al paire
> e·l pair' al fill atressi. (1–6)

(I'll tell you in my 'Latin' about that which I have seen and see now; I don't think this world will last long, according to what Scripture says, for now the son betrays the father – and the father betrays the son as well.)

The song opens uncompromisingly with the speaker sharing his experience of sin with the audience, couched in his own language, but bolstered by Scripture. The pessimistic comment that the end is nigh may herald an exhortation to penitence, but instead, the speaker prefers to paint a bleak picture of a degenerating noble class without offering prescriptions for improvement. Elements of sermon discourse also occur in the song's use of proverbial phrases, which it places in the mouths of three specified lower-class characters, a labourer, a miller and a ploughman:

> Soven de pan e de vi
> noiris ric hom mal vezi,
> e si·l tengues de mal aire
> segurs es de mal maiti,
> si no·i ment lo gazaignaire
> don lo reproviers issi.
>
> Lo mouniers jutg'al moli:
> qui ben lia ben desli;
> e·l vilans ditz tras l'araire:
> bon fruitz eis de bon jardi,
> et avols fills d'avol maire
> e d'avol caval rossi. (13–24)

(Often, a rich man feeds a bad neighbour on bread and wine; and if he got him from a bad lineage, he's certain of a bad awakening – if the peasant isn't lying from whom the proverb came.

The miller passes judgement at the mill: 'He who binds well unbinds well', and the villein says, behind the plough: 'Good fruit comes from a good garden, and a worthless son from a worthless mother, and from a worthless stallion comes a nag.')

Rather than the generic *vilain* (rustic) cited in the collections of proverbs from which these maxims come, the song presents the audience with three identified commentators on the nobility, a device pushed to the extreme in Marcabru's two extant *pastorelas* (XXIX, XXX), in which shepherdesses criticise their 'noble' inter-locutors. The decadence of noble heirs is further illustrated by the disastrous tranformations undergone by the courtly virtues of Joi, Joven and Donars (Joy, Youth and Giving); these respectively lose their path, become tricksters, scuttle away ashamedly or change

from promising young foals into braying asses (10–12, 25–30).
Marcabru envisages the courtly virtues as an ideal family, comprised of the masculine virtues Joi, Joven and Donars and their
sister, mother or mistress Proeza (Prowess). This unit is destroyed
by attacks from outside, or the corruption and betrayal of one
virtue by another (see Marcabru V, XI and XXXVI).

Song XVII then proceeds to attack one social group directly, the
married men who allow themselves to commit adultery, heedless
of the fact that this leaves their wives inadequately guarded and
tempted to retaliate in kind:

> Moillerat ab sen cabri
> atal paratz lo coissi
> don lo cons esdeven laire;
> que tals ditz: 'Mos fills me ri'
> que anc ren no·i ac a faire:
> gardatz sen ben bedoï. (31–6)

(Married men with goatish minds, you set out the cushion in a way which
makes the cunt turn thief; for such a one says: 'My son is smiling at me'
who never had a thing to do with it: you protect a stupid mind indeed.)

Surprisingly, given the apparent confidence of his attack, the song
ends with the speaker throwing up his hands in exasperation: his
words are not having any effect on his audience. It is noticeable
that the signature of this satirical moralist (his name) is treated
as a separate entity from the voice of the speaker, as if the song
and this style of ranting were merely an act:

> Re no·m val s'ieu los chasti,
> c'ades retornan aqui,
> e puois un non vei estraire
> Marcabrus d'aquel trahi,
> an lo tondres contra·l raire,
> moillerat, del joc coni. (37–42)

(It's useless for me to reprimand them, for they keep returning to it;
and since I don't see Marcabru drag a single one from this habit, then
let the cutter fight the shaver, married men, in the game of cunts!)

One of the striking features of Marcabrunian satire, aside from
its violence, is its negativity: there is no explicit positive ideal in
the songs, and those good principles that appear are almost
invariably corrupted, dismembered or killed. The obsession with
shape-shifting or corruptible virtues stretches into the realm of

language to such an extent that such concepts as *amor* are treated as pristine signs which should not be touched by interpreting (potentially distorting) words. In short, the speaker assumes a shared conservatism with his audience: their common value system is assumed to be based on social stasis, existing definitions of language and a set pattern of sexual behaviour.

A second important feature is a vision of the world that may justifiably be described as pan-sexual. Every aspect of social and moral corruption is referred ultimately to questions of uncontrolled sexuality and procreation, focusing on the married noble couple as the nexus of virtue and vice. Humanity is envisaged as subdivided into species defined in terms of social class, which should not be mixed. The weak point of the social matrix is the *con* (cunt) of the noble wife, which may be fertilised by the wrong 'species' of man, should her husband fail in his duty towards her:

> Dompna non sap d'amor fina
> c'ama girbaut de maiso,
> sa voluntatz la mastina
> cum fai lebrieir' ab gosso;
>   Ai!
> d'aqui naisso·ill ric savai
> que no fant conduit ni pai;
>   Hoc,
> si cum Marcabrus declina. (XXXI, 46–54)

(A lady knows nothing of refined love who loves a household churl; her will makes a bitch of her, like a greyhound with a mongrel cur – Ay! – From this are born the vile noblemen who like neither sport nor peace – Yes! – Just as Marcabru says.)

This obsession is reflected in the *vidas* composed about Marcabru, which describe him respectively as a foundling and as the son of a woman called Marcabruna, thereby implying illegitimate birth (Boutière and Schutz, *Biographies*, III).

Marcabru's condemnation of adultery is best explained not biographically, but poetically as an attack on the *amor*, which Marcabru distortingly represents as *amar* (bitterness or lust), celebrated by a school of poets referred to as the *troba N'Eblo* (the *trobar* of Sir Eble, XXXI, 73–81). Since Bernart de Ventadorn claims to have been of the *escola N'Eblo*,[8] it is commonly supposed that this is an allusion to the love lyric, the poetic celebration of the *amor fina* mentioned in XXXI, 46. The crude sexual encounters in steaming kitchens depicted in XXXVIII, the obscene *senhals* such as *Cropa-Fort* (Sturdy-Rump, XXXIV, 41) and the focus on peasant lovers may therefore be a violent parody of the courtly relationship between the humble poet-lover and his superior *domna*. The satire is aimed at a rival school of poets and at the ideology they profess, claiming to read their songs as overt exhortations to noble ladies to fornicate with their servants, rather than metaphorical depictions of unsatisfied desire.[9]

The Marcabrunian school of troubadours adapt this motif to ideas more frequently found in preaching, such as the notion of the temptress playing with men's emotions, but some are closer to the concerns of the *canso* than others:

> Dona es vas drut trefana
> de s'amor pos tres n'apana:
> > estra lei
> > n'i son trei,
> mas ab son marit l'autrei
> un amic cortes prezant.
> E si plus n'i vai sercant
> > es desleialada
> > e puta provada. (Bernart Marti, III, 10–18)

(A lady is perfidious towards her lover when she gives her love to three: three are outlawed, but apart from her husband I'll allow her a single pleading lover, and if she seeks out more, she's disgraced, and a proven whore.)

These images provide an uncomfortable counterpoint to the *domna* in the *canso*, but underpin the notion that praise is due to the woman possessed of self-control or discretion. As literary polemic which throws light directly on the sexual mores of the ruling class, and questions their inherited right to rule by alleging bastardy, this body of songs also functions as powerful social satire. It threatens lords who do not observe the rules of *Donars* (Giving) or virtue with accusations of bastardy, while reinforcing the common consensus that social stability depends on the control of female sexuality.

While the songs attributed to Marcabru do not advocate withdrawal from the secular world into a spiritual sphere, other troubadours of his school, especially Peire d'Alvernha and Gavaudan, adopt a position much more identifiable as that of the clergy, producing devotional lyrics (for example Peire d'Alvernha, VIII) or sermon-like songs (for example Gavaudan, IV, promoting the *Pax Dei* movement; compare Marcabru XXXV). Crusade songs are usually included in the field of satirical and moralising lyric, although they occupy a mid-way position between political propaganda and didactic sermonising. This is another demonstration of the complexity of the corpus of moral and satirical poetry; such songs as these are undoubtedly full of invective, and urge the audience to improve themselves by embarking on warfare presented as penitential pilgrimage, but are they satirical? Their approach is closer to that of a sermon or a political rallying call. Gavaudan's song V, promoting crusade in Spain and the Holy Land, moves towards an explicitly general and political, rather than personally penitential, motivation for conflict, stating that Jerusalem has fallen in punishment for Christian sins (1–2); Gavaudan reinterprets the Marcabrunian voice, making it a channel for overt ecclesiastical propaganda, as well as violent invective aimed this time at the enemy, not at those in the audience who refuse to fight:

> Profeta sera·n Gavaudas
> Que·l digz er faitz. E mortz als cas!
> e Dieus er honratz e servitz
> on Bafometz era grazitz. (V, 64–6)

(Gavaudan will be a prophet in this: the words will become deeds. And death to the dogs! And God will be honoured and served where *Bafomet* was thanked.[10])

Gavaudan's work is striking for its lack of subtlety in its appropriation – and simplification – of Marcabrunian ideas. However, there is also room for complexity, and an approach closer to the modern definition of personal satire, within this school. For example, Bernart Marti attacks Peire d'Alvernha, who composed devotional and crusade songs, for his smugness in claiming spiritual superiority to his. After a long criticism of all those who claim to compose *entiers* (whole) verse within a fallen, 'broken', context – that of human achievement and vernacular poetry – he concentrates his attack on a single target:

> E quan canorgues si mes
> Pey d'Alvernh'en canongia,
> a Dieu per que·s prometia
> entiers que peuys si fraysses?
> Quar si feys, fols joglars es
> per que l'entiers pretz cambia. (V, 31–6)

(And when Peire d'Alvernha became a canon in a canonry, why did he promise himself wholly to God, if he was to break later on? Since he did so, he's a foolish *joglar* because he changed his whole reputation.)

The attack on this poet's claims to a preaching or exemplary position is made explicit: who is he to claim superiority over human frailty?[11] Unlike these poets, Bernart Marti's songs present a man vacillating between his emotions and his stringent moral code in a way reminiscent of songs of Marcabru's such as 'Contra l'ivern' and 'Cortesamen' (XIV and XV),[12] but far removed from the quasi-sermons quoted above. As Simon Gaunt comments, 'the difference between Marcabru and Bernart does not lie in their moral standpoints: the two are in fact very close in this respect. It lies rather in Bernart's introspection and in his questioning of the feasibility of the moral standards he has set himself.'[13] Any examination of the Marcabrunian corpus should address the ambiguity underlying many of these troubadours' most stringent precepts, and the fragility of their claims to authority.

THE SIRVENTES

From its inception in the 1160s–1170s, the *sirventes* is indissociable from the name of Bertran de Born. A minor political figure in his lifetime, much of Bertran's fame is due to the enormous success of his songs and the *razos* composed around them in thirteenth-century Italian-speaking regions. A number of troubadours copied his style and the poet became a literary figure, with a biography which gave him a major role in the infamous family feuds of the Plantagenets (Boutière and Schutz, XI, pp. 65–139).[14] Though Bertran probably did not invent the term, the treatises written in the fourteenth century define the *sirventes* in terms of the style developed by him: a song built on the existing melody and form of a *canso*, addressing political events and powerful figures directly, as if composed by a *sirven*, a paid soldier, and invariably partisan.[15] These are commonly celebrations of, and incitements to, warfare, more frequently local disputes than crusades.

One of the most famous *sirventes* attributed (albeit uncertainly) to Bertran de Born is 'Be·m platz lo gais temps de Pascor' (XXXVII), a powerful example of his celebration of warfare, as well as the embryonic model for a genre developed by the Monk of Montaudon into the *plazer*, with its counterpart in the *enueg*, also initiated by Bertran.[16] It opens with a conventional spring opening, promising a *canso*, in celebration of the *joi d'amor* pursued in May-time, which veers abruptly into a celebration of another early summer sport, feudal warfare:

> Be·m platz lo gais temps de pascor,
> que fai foillas e flors venir;
> e plaz mi, qand auch la baudor
> dels auzels, que fant retentir
> lor chan per lo boscatge;
> e plaz me, qand vei per los pratz
> tendas e pavaillons fermatz,
>   et ai gran alegratge,
> qand vei per campaignas rengatz
> cavalliers e cavals armatz. (1–10)

(I really like the gay weather of Eastertide, which makes leaves and flowers bloom, and I like it when I hear the happiness of the birds, whose songs ring through the woods, and I like it when I see tents and pavilions pitched across the meadows, and I have great joy when I see armoured knights and horses lined up across the countryside.)

Unusually, this particular song has a narrative progression, recounting the battle from this initial encampment scene to the final rout:

> Et auch cridar: 'aidatz! aidatz!'
> E vei cazer per los fossatz
> paucs e grans per l'erbatge
> e vei los mortz que pels costatz
> ant los troncons ab los cendatz. (46–50)

(And I hear men shouting: 'Help! Help!', and around the moats, I see the low-ranking and the great fall down across the pastureland, and I see the dead, who have splinters of lance tipped with their silk pennons sticking out of their ribs.)

The song ends with a *tornada*, urging the addressees to wage war soon (61–3); the *sirventes* celebrates war, and promotes it as a festi-val as natural to springtime as flowers or *amor*. Bertran's love of warfare is imbued with erotic connotations; the spring opening altered to praise killing rather than courtship is only one example of this.

The *vida* composed about Bertran's relations with his overlords suggests that his songs shaped political events (Boutière and Schutz, XI A, 6). Dante's placing of a beheaded Bertran in Hell, punished for his incitement of war between father and sons (*Inferno*, Canto 28), granted him still further influence. Both probably exaggerate his power; however, the later twelfth and thirteenth centuries show a growth in the use of *sirventes* as rallying calls, morale-boosting songs or propaganda. Martin Aurell has studied the political function of a number of such songs in Provence, and shown some of them to constitute veritable campaigns, aimed at recruiting allies to a given cause or power.[17] Another strand of the *sirventes*, less powerful than Bertran's, but no less widespread, was the intense personal invective aimed at identified individuals particularly associated with Guillem de Berguedà. A Catalan nobleman who may have met Bertran in the 1170s during a period of exile after murdering a neighbouring lord, Guillem's style of vicious personal attack consists of grotesque caricatures, twisted versions of the addressees' names and scurrilous accusations of all sorts of crimes.[18] Troubadours in early thirteenth-century Italy emulate this variety of song too, and it is possible that Guillem's songs were transmitted in close parallel to Bertran's.

Guillem's rhetoric is typical of forms of invective extant in Latin poetry from Ovid's *Contra Ibem* onwards; vituperation, insinuation and pejorative description of rivals or addressees were weapons in every rhetorician's armoury, to be used to powerful, if unsubtle, effect.[19] However, Guillem's *sirventes* are possibly meant literally rather than as ludic play-insults. There is reason to suppose that such songs fuelled real hostilities as frequently as they provided displays of comic vituperation. Earlier examples, such as Marcabru's exchange with N'Audric (XX and XXb), or Peire d'Alvernha's poets' gallery (XII) are more overtly entertainment. There is a fine line between comic effect and explicit hostility, trodden by the catalogues of abuse aimed at *joglars* to be found in a subgenre often called the *sirventes joglaresc*, or such cycles as the songs exchanged between Garin d'Apchier and Torcafol.[20]

One addressee of Guillem de Berguedà's invective is the Marquis of Mataplana, a near-neighbour and rival lord whom he attacks in four surviving songs, but for whom he also composed a remorseful *planh*. This song uses its refrain to taunt the marquis directly:

Cansoneta leu e plana
leugereta, ses ufana,
farai, e de Mon Marques,
del trachor de Mataplana,
q'es d'engan farsitz e ples.
A, Marques, Marques, Marques,
d'engan etz farsitz e ples. (X, 1–7)

(An easy, smooth song, very light, without pride I'll compose, and about My Marquis, about the traitor from Mataplana, who is stuffed and filled with trickery. *Oh, Marquis, Marquis, Marquis, you are stuffed and filled with trickery.*)

In this cycle of songs (X, XI, XII, XIII), the marquis is accused of clumsiness, deformities born of repeated falls, ugliness and homosexuality (this may be contrasted with the cycle of songs against the Bishop of Urgel – songs VI, VII, VIII, IX – whom Guillem calls a eunuch, lecher, rapist, sodomite and threatens with castration); the abuse is caricatural and illogical, a display of playful rhetorical excess rather than an attempt at veracity:

Marques, ben aion las peiras
a Melgur depres Someiras,
on perdetz de las denz tres;
no·i ten dan que las primeiras
i son e non paron ges.
A, Marques . . . etc.

Del bratz no·us pretz una figa,
que cabreilla par de biga,
e portatz lo mal estes;
ops i auria ortiga
qe·l nervi vos estendes.
A, Marques . . . etc. (X, 8–21)

(Marquis, well done to the the stones of Melgur, on which you lost three of your teeth. No harm's done – they're the first set, and you can't see them yet.

I wouldn't give a fig for your arm, because it looks like a goat's leg, and you hold it badly. You need some nettles to stretch the nerve.)

Invective is a well-established rhetorical device, the mirror opposite of praise; the two are often paired as *laus et vituperatio* (praise and blame) in oratory, 'lauzar los pros e blasmar los malvatz' in Occitan poetry (Boutière and Schutz, LXXIII.2,

LXXXI.3, XCIII.6, L.5). The refrain in Guillem's song repeatedly invokes the victim's name, while the text focuses on inflicting damage on Mataplana's face and body. He emphasises the mouth and sword-arm, using the latter to hint at impotence. The marquis is made symbolically powerless to respond with either words or acts; it is significant that no responding songs from him are either extant or recorded. The process of invective here is one-sided, and the speaker holds the power of words against his silent addressee.

The troubadours cited in this section display a sense of class-identity different from that adopted by Marcabru. Rather than a liminal position on the margins of secular and ecclesiastical society, these poets speak as feudal noblemen addressing their peers and overlords.[21] Guillem's attitude towards bishops and priests is hostile, as is both poets' vision of kings. They are partisan with respect to a specific social group, and present a vision of a world kept alive by constant warrior activity and aggressive rivalries.[22]

This ethos of institutionalised aggression runs counter to the Church's attempts to ensure peace through the *Pax Dei* movement, and to transfer energies into holy wars in Iberian and Middle Eastern crusades. Guillem depicts the marquis as a nobleman who fails in his duty, since he cannot hold a sword, stay on horseback or father children; for Bertran, a baron who does not love war is disloyal to his class. The ideology of these troubadours is very much that of a warrior, and neither addresses issues of social stability except in terms of ensuring the nobility may continue to do what they do best: fighting each other.

These are no more 'real' concerns than the Marcabrunian depiction of a nobility devoted to trysts with rough trade in steamy kitchens, but they clearly articulate a different, emphatically secular, ideology. Rather than moralising, these songs are concerned with physical interaction and power. The voices of the secular moralist-preacher in Marcabru's *vers* and the belligerent knight in Bertran de Born's *sirventes* may seem irreconcilable; in fact, they are close neighbours, since prelates and lords were frequently brothers, and noblemen often repented in later life, entering religious orders and espousing ecclesiastical interests. The two voices are drawn together by the thirteenth-century troubadours, in particular Peire Cardenal, a learned man who composed *sirventes* and *vers* in all styles.

THIRTEENTH-CENTURY DEVELOPMENTS: PEIRE CARDENAL

According to Lavaud's edition, and to the *vida* by Miquel de la Tor (Boutière and Schutz, L), Peire Cardenal lived to the age of nearly one hundred, and composed prolifically in response to the massive political and social changes in Occitan-speaking regions between 1205 and 1275, focusing on the years c. 1210 to c. 1250. Lavaud accepted every attribution, however tenuous, to Peire, and produced a vast corpus of ninety-six songs which probably include pieces composed by other troubadours; it may be better to regard it as a representative sample of song-production in these years.

The Albigensian Crusade (1209–29) brought conflicts and dis-possessions which resulted in the imposition of Northern French noblemen over Occitan regions, the dispersal and mutual betrayal of many Languedoc noble families, and the development of a repressive ecclesiastical regime, comprising preaching orders, the beginnings of the Inquisition and a new university at Toulouse from the late 1220s onwards.[23] As a result of these changes, Peire's songs – and those of others, such as Guilhem Figueira and Guilhem de Montanhagol – articulate ideas that may appear para-doxical to the modern reader, in that they separate clerks, who are perceived as deceitful preachers, traitors or invaders, from *clerzia*, spiritual good. The songs are not clear-cut in their political positions, reflecting the multiple shifts in allegiance that charac-terised the years between 1209 and 1249, when it would be mis-leading to speak purely of a northern assault on a unified southern region, aided by cynical priests. It is interesting to note that this complex set of events created a tension between the different registers of satirical and moralising discourse in the Occitan lyric.

A versified sermon attributed to Peire Cardenal (LXV) lists an orthodox set of spiritual and social duties for noblemen, but urges them not to go on crusade. Good preaching needs to be dis-tinguished from bad in political rather than ethical terms, and polemic is directed increasingly towards questions of right and wrong, rather than good and evil. A powerful example is 'Clergue

si fan pastor' (XXIX). An Inquisition document of the early fourteenth century shows that this song circulated among lesser noblemen in the Pyrenees during the last quarter of the thirteenth
century, and was interpreted as anti-clerical propaganda.[24] It
appears to make a distinction between spiritual good and the
social group of clergy:

> Clergue si fan pastor
> e son aucizedor;
> e par de gran sanctor
> qui los vei revestir,
> e·m pren a sovenir
> que n'Ezengris un dia,
> volc ad un parc venir:
> mas pels cans que temia
> pel de mouton vestic
> ab que los escarnic,
> puois manget e traïc
> tot so que li-abelic.
>
> Rei e emperador,
> duc, comte e comtor
> e cavalier ab lor
> solon lo mon regir;
> ara vei possezir
> a clers la seinhoria
> ab tolre e ab traïr
> e ab ypocrezia,
> ab forsa e ab prezic;
> e tenon s'a fastic
> qui tot non lor o gic
> e sera, quan que tric. (1–24)

(Clerks make themselves pastors, but they are killers, and they look very
holy when you see them dressed up, and I find myself remembering that
Ysengrin,[25] one day, wanted to get into a sheepfold: but because of the
dogs he feared, he put on a sheepskin, with which he mocked them, and
he stole and ate everything he liked the look of.

Kings and emperors, dukes, counts and *comtors*, and knights as well, want
to rule the world; now I see clerks hold the power, by theft and betrayal,
and by hypocrisy, force and preaching; and they think it a burden if
everything isn't given them, and that's how it will be, for as long as it
lasts.)

The spiritual results of this position become more explicit in a
song such as 'Un sirventes novel' (XXXVI). This song is not a

heretical tract, despite its irreverent approach to the doctrine of the Last Judgement:

> Un sirventes novel vueill comensar,
> que retrairai al jor del jujamen
> a sel que·m fes e·m formet de nien.
> S'el me cuja de ren arazonar
> e s'el me vol metre en la diablia
> ieu li dirai: 'Senher, merce, non sia!
> qu'el mal segle tormentiei totz mos ans.
> e guardas mi, si·us plas, dels tormentans'. (1–8)

(I want to begin a new *sirventes*, which I will recite on Judgement Day to the One who made me and formed me from nothing. If He wishes to arraign me on any charge, or wants to put me in the devils' place, I'll say to him: 'Lord, have mercy, don't let this be! For the evil world tormented me all my years, and protect me, please, from the tormentors.')

This vision of a corrupt world is close to medieval ascetic writings and penitential preaching, and still within the bounds of orthodoxy. However, the *sirventes* is undeniably provocative, and reminiscent of Old French *fabliaux* which place an irreverent peasant or *joglar* in Hell or at Heaven's gates.

Heaven is accused of a miscarriage of justice against fallen humanity. The speaker argues that there is nothing just about his being sent to Hell at the Last Judgement, since the corruption of the world forces him to sin, whether he wishes to or not. Effectively, he opposes the notion of salvation (crucial to preaching campaigns against heresy) to the equally necessary threat of hellfire, and denounces the outcome as unfair, indeed illogical. The speaker envisages a debate with God, but does not associate this with any clerical status.

The radical shift in this voice is more obvious when set against the Marcabrunian preacher-penitent speaking in another song attributed to Cardenal:

> Ieu trazi pietz que si portava chiera
> quan vei far mal a la gen ni grevansa.
> E non aus dir que tortz es e sobrieira
> tan tem l'erguelh del mon e la bobansa,
> mas d'una ren mi conort a sazos:
> que Dieu es tan cortes e poderos
> que dels tortz faitz cug que penra venjansa. (LIV, 1–7)

(I bear something worse than if I wore a hair-shirt when I see people harmed or mistreated. And I do not dare say it is wrong or outrageous, so fearful am I of the pride and the pomp of the world. But I do take comfort in one thing sometimes: that God is so courtly and powerful, that I think He'll take revenge for the wrongs that have been done.)

'Un sirventes novel' clearly contains a satirical charge, as a secular sinner dares to challenge the orthodox picture of good and evil. He denounces as absurd the eschatological commonplace whereby original sin condemns humanity to do wrong compulsively until the final reckoning: he would never have sinned had he never been born, so why should he be held to account for his misdeeds?

> E farai vos una bella partia:
> que·m tornetz lai don moc lo premier dia
> o que·m siatz de mos tortz perdonans.
> qu'ieu no·ls fora si non fos natz enans. (XXXVI, 37–40)

(And I'll strike a good deal with you: you can return me to the place from which I came on the first day, or you can forgive me my wrongdoings. For I wouldn't have committed them had I not been born.)

The mocking invective of a belligerent knight is conflated with a secular preacher empowered to speak on a level with God; the effect is provocative and parodic in equal measure.

The delicate political and religious situation of this period is perceptible in songs by other troubadours. Guilhem de Montanhagol, for example, launches a fierce attack on the unjust behaviour of preachers and clerks, only to back-pedal half-way through the *sirventes*: he may resent the persecutions he witnesses, but has to rush to assert his endorsement of them too:

> Ar se son fait enqueredor
> e jutjon aissi com lur plai.
> Pero l'enquerre no·m desplai,
> anz me plai que casson error
> e qu'ab bels digz plazentiers ses yror,
> torno·ls erratz desviatz en la fe. (I, 19–24)

(Now they've made themselves Inquisitors, and pass judgement as they please. But I've nothing against the Inquisition – in fact, I like their hunting out of errors, and [I like] them, with attractive, pleasing words, without anger, to return those who have strayed, and turned away, to the faith.)

In this corpus, the strands of the Marcabrunian *vers* and the *sirventes* are joined, with a new twist owed to changing political and

social circumstances. Peire Cardenal also composed some songs
he labelled *vers*, but he now reinterprets the term using a false
etymology to *verus*, true, in order to stress the moral value of his
work (XLIII). Guiraut Riquier and Cerverí de Girona also composed *vers* in this style; these songs are soberly didactic, offering a
return to the Marcabrunian voice in its spiritual form, as represented by Peire d'Alvernha a century earlier.

To conclude, Peire Cardenal offers an apt summary of the various
strands traceable in the corpus of satirical and moralising poetry.
The songs attributed to him include personal invectives, political
propaganda, sermons, didactic poems and general satirical pieces.
Out of this vast collection, only a couple of pieces address *fin'amor*
at all. Bertran de Born, Peire d'Alvernha, Guilhem de Montanhagol and others mentioned in this chapter also composed important numbers of love songs; it is important not to isolate the satirical and moralising lyric from its *canso* counterpart, either by
over-emphasising or by isolating it. The dialectic between the
canso, the *sirventes* and the *vers* is constant and very rich, producing
such modern generic terms as the *canso-sirventes*. To marginalise
this body of satirical and moralising poetry is therefore to create
a false picture of the troubadour lyric as a whole; the edition by
Mölk of Guiraut Riquier's *cansos* in the 1960s established this poet
as 'the last troubadour' strictly in terms of his treatment of
fin'amor, but it obscured the equally sizeable body of *vers*, still only
accessible in their obsolete edition of 1853.[26] However, the *vers* of
Guiraut Riquier are neither more nor less important than the
cansos; they simply manifest the two sides of the rhetorical pairing
of *laus et vituperatio*, praise and blame, in the guise of love and
criticism.

NOTES

1 See Kay on these questions with reference to the love lyric in 'Rhetoric', and *Subjectivity*, pp. 1–16.
2 Thiolier-Méjean, in *Poésies satiriques* and *Poétique*; Klein, *Partisan Voice*,
   Aurell, *Vielle*, and Ghil, *L'Age de parage*.
3 Chailley, 'Premiers troubadours'.
4 Marshall, '*Vers* au XIIe siècle'; Bec, 'Problème des genres'; Rieger,
   Gattungen.
5 On the *estribot*, see Ricketts, 'L'*estribot*', Vatteroni, 'Peire Cardenal';

for examples of the *arlotes*, see the comic monologue by Raimon d'Av-
inho and a scurrilous song attributed to Turc or Truc Malec, Pirot,
ed., *Recherches*, Lazzerini, '*Cornar lo corn*'; for the *enueg* and *plazer*, see
Thiolier-Méjean, *Poétique*, pp. 127–205.

6 This section draws on the following: Roncaglia's re-editions and studies of Marcabru; Paterson, *Troubadours*; Gaunt, *Troubadours*; Harvey,
Marcabru; Goddard, 'Early troubadours'.

7 Kendrick, 'Jongleur'.

8 See Kendrick, *Game*, pp. 16–17; Harvey, *Marcabru*, pp. 29–30.

9 Harvey, *Marcabru*, pp. 140–53, 149, and XXXIV, 40–2.

10 Bafomet is a pejorative term for Muhammad also found in *chansons
de geste*.

11 The song is an attack on Peire d'Alvernha XI; see Gaunt, *Troubadours*,
p. 99.

12 See ibid., pp. 80–96.

13 Ibid., p. 96.

14 *Bertran de Born*, ed. Paden, Sankovitch and Stäblein, pp. 1–33. Klein,
Partisan Voice, examines Bertran's political poetry.

15 *Doctrina de compondre dictatz*, 104–8 in '*Razos de Trobar*', ed. Marshall
[Appendix 3, p. 298], pp. 95–8.

16 *Bertran de Born*, ed. Paden, Sankovitch and Stäblein, pp. 65–8.

17 Aurell, *Vielle*.

18 *Guillem de Berguedà*, ed. Riquer [Appendix 1, item 33] I, gives a full
historical study.

19 Quintilian, III, 7.10–22; *ad Herennium*, III.6.10–11, 7.13–14, 8.14.
Raby, *History*, I, pp. 348, 355, 319.

20 *Garin d'Apchier*, ed. Latella; Pirot, ed., *Recherches*; Witthoeft, *Sirventes
Joglaresc*; Méjean, 'Contribution'.

21 Gaunt, 'Marcabru'.

22 Klein, *Partisan Voice*.

23 Roquebert, *L'Epopée cathare*, Wakefield, *Heresy*, give a historical
account; Ghil, *L'Age de parage* and Aurell, *Vielle*, set the poetry in its
historical context.

24 Dufournet, *Registre d'Inquisition*, III, pp. 318–20, 328–9.

25 Ysengrin is the name of the wolf in the satirical Latin epic *Ysengrimus*
and in the Old French *Roman de Renart*.

26 *Werke Guiraut Riquiers*, ed. Pfaff.

CHAPTER 4

The early troubadours: Guilhem IX to Bernart de Ventadorn

Stephen G. Nichols

The early troubadours exercise a certain fascination for moderns. Beginnings tend to be shrouded in mystery, especially the origins of cultural movements we would like to know more about. It is the reverse situation that makes the early troubadours so fascinating. They seem to spring up, brilliant from the first *vers* or songs of Guilhem de Peitieu, and continuing through two more generations until about 1170, when the movement, initially concentrated in just a few courts, grows wider and the poets more numerous.[1]

At least three reasons may explain why these poets hold the sway they do in modern times. First, the coherence of their corpus, and its homogeneity: it is useful to be able to quote troubadours who evidently knew each other's work, who quote each other, and for whom the evolution of their poetry seems so closely entwined. A second reason for the prominence of the early troubadours is their genius in creating what has come to be called, since Roger Dragonetti and Paul Zumthor, the *grand chant courtois*.[2] Christopher Page illustrates the seductiveness of this concept in his book *Voices and Instruments of the Middle Ages* where he asserts that the poetic force of the *grand chant* or 'high style song', as he calls it, lies in the coherence of the formal elements internal to the lyric. The genius of the genre, by this account, stems from its ability to reveal only gradually the complex architectonics of its art. Performance, the lyric component of the song, orchestrates our apprehension of the work.[3]

The early troubadours, then, created the first 'modern' European examples of the individual artist, a genius set apart from the common folk, whence the connotations of value and 'high seriousness' associated with the high style. The cult of the individual artist points to the third reason for the hold the early troubadours have exercised on the modern imagination: the myth of their colourful lives. The early troubadours are among the most memorable poets of their age, an age where many artists laboured anonymously. If they did not invent vernacular poetic identity, they certainly incorporated it as part of their poetic project.

Take, for example, the larger-than-life, often obscene initiator of the genre, Guilhem de Peitieu, Count of Poitou and Duke of Aquitaine. One of the greatest lords of his time, Guilhem chose to construct a poetic identity only obliquely linked to his political persona. Guilhem's late thirteenth-century *vida* plays on all these themes:

Lo coms de Peitieus si fo uns dels majors cortes del mon e dels majors trichadors de dompnas, e bons cavallier d'armas e larcs de domnejar; e saup ben trobar e cantar. Et anet lonc temps per lo mon per enganar las domnas. (Boutière and Schutz, p. 1)

(The Count of Poitou was one of the greatest noblemen in the world as well as one of the greatest deceivers of noblewomen, a good knight in arms and a generous wooer; and he knew very well how to compose and to sing poetry. He went through the land for many years seducing noblewomen.)

Following him comes Marcabru, a baseborn cleric who stands out in bold relief for his muscular moralising. Stirred to wrath – and poetic satire – by the moral failings of his time, exemplified as he saw it by the licentiousness of Guilhem's poetry, Marcabru contradicts and recasts what he deplores by appropriating his adversaries' poetic patterns. It is Marcabru who invents the *pastorela*, with 'L'autrier jost'una sebissa' (**XXX**), thereby bequeathing us one of its liveliest specimens, a witty sitcom in which the country maid proves a sharper dialectician than her aristocratic would-be seducer.

Then there is Jaufré Rudel, whose 'Lanquan li jorn' (**IV**) evokes hauntingly his passion for a princess he has never seen, or seen but once, thereby prefiguring Dante's love for Beatrice and the Italian tradition. Jaufré's *amor de lonh* or far-away love typified, for moderns like the Pre-Raphaelites, the essence of 'courtly love'. Cercamon, described by his thirteenth-century *vida* as writing 'vers et pastoretas a la usanza antiga' ('songs and pastorelas in the old style'), perfected the integration of the lyrical description of nature and love. All of which did not prevent him from writing a satire on the decline of his civilisation worthy of Martial, 'Puois nostre temps' (**VIII**).

Bernart de Ventadorn and Peire d'Alvernha, coming as they do towards the end of the early period, refine the troubadour poetics thematically and by their numerous formal innovations: rhythmic, prosodic and melodic. Bernart's 'Can vei' (XXXI) defines lyric subjectivity for the troubadour canon, while both Bernart and Peire d'Alvernha stamp the song-as-poetics and the *tenso* or debate lyric with the dialectical vigour that inspired their successors to emulation.

These legends and others one could cite testify to the role accorded to the early troubadours as creators not only of the cultural phenomenon known as courtly love, but also of a whole mode of life implied in the term. One would not want to impugn their status as poets of genius, which they clearly were. Nevertheless, this picture, though authentic in the sense that the early troubadours were all these things and more, reflects an historicising reconstruction, a need to tell a story about the tradition and its poets in keeping with a modernist master narrative. But the facts as we find them in historical documents do not necessarily corroborate this story. Or, rather, they might be said to tell a more complex one, and one not necessarily less interesting. We should be clear on the fact that whereas the master narrative confidently describes twelfth-century events, nothing of that period remains of their work. Everything that has come down to us may be found in MS *chansonniers* of the mid to late thirteenth century onwards.

What we do know of the period, and here Page is apposite, is the importance of oral performance and transmission for representing and preserving the songs. But to define the high style song by the criterion of oral performance risks conflating the important difference between *being* something and *representing* it. It fails to differentiate between what the thing is *per se* and how it may be represented to a public. By this account, the high style song would be defined by its lyrical performance, by the fact that it was sung. But as we shall see, there were many ways to represent these songs besides singing them, many performative modes and frameworks.

Overemphasis on the oral performative mode also risks encouraging a homogeneous picture of the genre. Undoubtedly, the twelfth century did witness the rise of a brilliant court culture in the Midi, particularly in Poitou and the Southwest. The culture was an intimate one where lords and poets not only knew one another, but also exchanged roles: Guilhem de Peitieu was not the only lord who was also a poet. Poets sang their own songs or had their *joglars* sing them; either way, poetic performance passed directly through the body, through the singing voice. Poetic performance relied on the presence of the singer, poet or *joglar*, and on an audience physically present in the great hall or dining room of a castle.

However, the world of the twelfth-century performance disappeared with the political and social conditions that had given rise to it. What remained was, on the one hand, an indigenous Occitan tradition that became increasingly dominated by satire and didactic lyric (see Chapters 3 and 6), and on the other one that moved north to the literary centres of *langue d'oïl* (see Chapter 16), south to Catalonia (see Chapter 8) and east to the Veneto (see Chapters 8 and 15). These centres developed flourishing poetry of their own in the thirteenth century, but Italy and Catalonia continued to cultivate Occitan song, the archetypal 'mother tongue', as Dante would see it. In the thirteenth century, troubadour song was an international property and troubadours singing in *langue d'oc* enjoyed enormous prestige.

It is easy to imagine that the dynamic memory of the lost twelfth-century troubadour culture also fuelled the creation of the colourful myths of their lives. The *vidas*, or lives, of the poets created in the thirteenth and on into the fourteenth century function as biography generally does, that is to provide an image of culturally important people who have disappeared, but whom we want to be able to picture (see further Chapter 15). The literary image thus fills a void, a hole in history marked by the corpus we possess that recalls the creator long gone but no less real in our imagination: the body of the work cannot quite stand for the body of the poet.

No one can doubt the efficacy of the belated picture of the early troubadours. These poets composed and sang in the twelfth century under conditions – social, political and artistic – that were very different from what came later. Yet this elementary and glaring fact has been all but effaced by their modern presentation. Anthologies and editions represent the troubadour tradition as a seamless canvas running from Guilhem de Peitieu's life to the end of the thirteenth century. They portray an ordered distribution across the historical spectrum, beginning around 1100 and running to just beyond 1300. In short, a classic evolutionary schema of literary origin, vigour and decadence. Such a scenario dependent on the model of literary evolution cannot fail to assign a privileged position to origins, hence to the early troubadours who created the *vers* or troubadour song in its various permutations.

From our perspective, there might seem only a slight difference between the twelfth and thirteenth centuries. But from a poetic standpoint there was, culturally speaking, a major shift from a tradition of 'performative presence' to one of 'performative absence', as it were, where writing and reading were empowered by recourse to technologies that had hitherto been used primarily to produce and disseminate Latin texts. 'Books' and the readers that they created signalled a new concept of consumption and performance, one that placed both a temporal and a physical space between poet and audience. That new performative space is, as far as troubadour lyric is concerned, predicated on the absence of the performer and therefore, one might say, on nostalgia. The poet or *joglar* no longer embodies the song immediately in an interpretative voice that both delights and guides the listener's interpretation. Some *chansonniers* implicitly recognised this absence by seeking to supplement it with poet 'surrogates', such as the *vidas*, 'portraits' of given troubadours accompanying their songs, and by insistent attribution of every lyric. Still, viewed dispassionately, manuscript technology did open important new vistas. If the poet were absent and the song silent, the visual presence of the song was much enhanced and with it, other elements appealing to the visual and tactile senses.

If the *chansonnier* could not preserve the atmosphere and the immediacy of the oral performance where song was represented in and by the body, it could and did represent a new and different kind of lyric performance. We must not forget that *chansonniers*, too, involved the body, the body writing and the body viewed – many had 'portraits' of poets in historiated letters, while some also had marginal paintings.[4] The MS songbook could also do what no previous oral performance could achieve and that is to represent the broad sweep of the troubadour tradition. In short, each *chansonnier* could view the troubadour canon from a considered viewpoint.

In placing a premium on the oral origins of the troubadour lyric, the master narrative institutes a hierarchy between lyric performance and textual transmission. Oral performance assumes the generative role: it is in that setting that the song lives, where it is 'produced'. In this scenario, transmission takes second place as a mere amanuensis to performance. When the vehicle of transmission shifts from person to thing, from *joglar* to *chansonnier*, the gap between production and transmission becomes even wider. The *joglar* at least performed and, in so doing, interpreted. The *chansonnier*, however, would be little more than a repository, nothing like a space of textual production still less of performance.

How true is this picture? Not particularly, if one looks closely at the troubadour *chansonniers* of the thirteenth century. Indeed, what were troubadour manuscripts if not a successor to earlier forms of performance and transmission? Should it really be so surprising to find that *chansonniers* play the dual role of performance and transmission, often with incredible ingenuity? What they do not do, however, is to support the evolutionary master narrative of troubadour lyric. We find little attempt in the 'performance' of troubadour song in *chansonniers* to create or sustain a historically ordered grouping at all. Indeed, one would often be at a loss to discern in many *chansonniers* any principle of period organisation. These MSS have specific ordering principles: they treat the songs not chronologically, but in terms of form, arranging by genre or theme, and by other more elusive criteria. There is little evidence in the *chansonniers* that the early troubadours were singled out as such, and not infrequently certain of them may be found side by side with chronologically much later poets. MS *R*,[5] a *chansonnier* produced in Languedoc at the beginning of the fourteenth century, quite unusually incorporates early troubadours at the beginning of the manuscript, but not in chronological order. Marcabru, Peire d'Alvernha, Peire Rogier, Bernart de Ventadorn all have songs on folios 1–21, but their lyrics also appear much further on in the manuscript, e.g., on folios 48–50, 61, 80–5, 224–6, 249, 394, 401, 472–3. But we find no evidence that the early troubadours were characterised or even thought of as 'early', in the originary sense that modernists use this term.

So the manuscript as a performative space clearly had a profound impact on the way in which this lyric tradition was conceived. Moreover, it was the early troubadours whose work was most profoundly affected by the change, for, unlike later generations, who were transitional between a culture of voiced transmission and a mixed voice/writing one, they could not have foreseen the sea-change that beset the medium in the thirteenth century.

This is not to say that no differentiation exists between the early troubadours and songs of subsequent generations. We can discover a good deal about how early troubadours were perceived by studying the *chansonniers*. For one thing, we find that differentiation occurs on what we must assume to be aesthetic principles or degrees of popularity. *Chansonniers* follow generic classifications, with *tensos*, for example, segregated from other kinds of lyric and consigned to a later part of the MS. Since these songs involve a debate between two poets, each named in the song, they do not fit the category of 'single-authored' lyric which makes up the major opening sections of a *chansonnier*. Such sections contain the songs of a particular poet whose name and, often, 'portrait' appear at the beginning of the section. The ordering of poets varies with the logic idiosyncratic to a given *chansonnier*, the commonest being to place the poets in descending order of significance.[6]

It is difficult to discern a correlation between songs included in a manuscript and the actual extent of a poet's corpus. Bernart de Ventadorn and Marcabru have an extant corpus of over forty songs each, for example, yet their representation in *chansonniers* varies widely. Bernart de Ventadorn has thirty songs in *A*, thirty-seven in *C*, nine in *E*, thirty-three in *I*, twenty-six in *N*, twenty in *Q*, thirty-one in *R*, eighteen in *S*. His treatment in all these *chansonniers* suggests that he enjoyed canonical status, to judge by his advantageous position in the manuscripts and the relative care with which his songs are recorded. The large number of his songs in circulation makes it unlikely that the scribe of a manuscript with fewer songs, *E* for example, did not have access to more *cansos*. More likely, the selected songs represent a nuclear corpus of 'hits', a hypothesis reinforced by the presence in *E* of what we must conclude to be his 'signature' song, 'Can vei' (XXXI), widely disseminated in very many MSS (twenty-eight including fragments and citations).

The principle of selection at work in these manuscripts indicates some difference between what was considered a core of essential songs by an early troubadour in the thirteenth century, and what has become the 'core' canon in our own time. Bernart de Ventadorn's 'Lo tems vai' (XLIV) or 'Chantars no pot' (II) figure as mainstays of his lyrics in modern anthologies. Yet the first, a powerful evocation of the searing effect of time on love, occurs in only nine *chansonniers*, as does the second, a staple of Bernart's poetics for modern readers. On the other hand, 'Amors, e que·us es veyaire' (XXVII) has less visibility in Bernart's nuclear canon today, and yet it appears in roughly half of the major *chansonniers*. This is not to say that there are not points of convergence between thirteenth-century tastes and our own. 'Non es meravelha' (I) appears in twenty manuscripts, while another of Bernart's modern favourites, 'Ab joi mou lo vers e·l comens' (III) figures in twenty-three.

We may infer, then, that where a given poet appears in a manuscript, and the relative percentage of his corpus included, can tell us much about how that poet was esteemed by the compiler(s) of the *chansonnier* – and perhaps by the patron(s) for whom it was made. The number of songs included cannot be taken as an absolute criterion, of course, for we do not know how much of a poet's corpus might have been available to a given scribe. Still, the criterion offers some measure of the popularity of a given poet at a specific moment and place, for the more songs available for inclusion, the more esteemed that poet would have been. This is especially true of the early troubadours a century after they wrote. Recognition is another sign of status. If a song which we believe to be by one troubadour appears attributed to another, or else anonymously, we may assume that the troubadour in question was not well known at the time, or no longer known. On the other hand, if a poet is listed as the author of a song that is, in fact, by another troubadour, then one may infer that the first poet is sufficiently valued to have the work of others ascribed to him (see below for some examples).

When we look at *chansonniers* produced in the late thirteenth and early fourteenth centuries with the above criteria in mind, we discover that, unlike the modernist approach, which assigns a special but 'segregated' role to them, the early troubadours were dynamically integrated in the canon. To perceive these dynamics, we have to conceive the *chansonniers* as not simply transmitting lyrics, but as editing and performing them. In short, we need to understand how the manuscripts themselves 'read' and interpreted the corpus.

We cannot doubt that they did so. For, about the same time

that secular poetry began to be recorded in manuscripts in the early thirteenth century, Geoffroy de Vinsauf wrote his *Poetria nova* (*The New Poetry*, c. 1210) which became one of the most popular and influential poetic treatises of the high Middle Ages. Geoffroy's treatise departs radically from classical *artes poeticae*, which had been concerned primarily with oratory, that is the *oral* delivery of poetry and argument. His *Poetria nova* reveals the new concerns with ordering narrative for *written* presentation. Reading him, we can seize his excitement in the face of a new aesthetics, and his awareness of the need to create a new poetics for dealing with the innovation. He makes us sense that writing was not simply a tool for remembering, but a technique for thinking.

Whereas classical rhetoric was concerned primarily with the immediate rhetorical effects of oral delivery – argument, deliberation and panegyric – Geoffroy's *Poetria nova* stressed techniques for organising and presenting the *narrative of writing*.[7] Consequently, for Geoffroy, the order of the book as arrangement or *dispositio* becomes paramount. The poet has two choices: to follow the natural sequence of events, the historic order, or to invent a synthetic order based on aesthetic or other principles. Geoffroy writes that the latter 'strives on the footpath of art' ('tum limite nititur artis'), while the former 'follows the highway of Nature' ('tum sequitur stratum naturae').[8] Natural order renders an unimaginative sequence flatly. The same brief space may be made at least pleasing and perhaps even interesting by a synthetic style: 'skillful art so inverts the material that it does not pervert it; art transposes, in order that it may make the arrangement of the material better. More sophisticated than natural order is artistic order, and far preferable, however much permuted the arrangement be.'[9]

Geoffroy speaks about arranging or transposing existing materials. The artist or poet 'finds' (in the medieval sense of *trobar*, *trouver*) his material already in the world and makes his poetry as a construction, a reconstruction and a reordering. As Guilhem de Peitieu had already put it so brilliantly, the flowers of rhetoric are the product of artistic construction in the poetic workshop or *obrador*. The song 'Ben vueill' (VI) thematises Guilhem's poetics, and was, not surprisingly (given the poetic self-consciousness of the early troubadours), one of two of his most frequently reproduced *vers* in *chansonniers*:[10]

Ben vueill que sapchon li pluzor
d'un vers, si es de bona color,
qu'ieu ai trat de bon obrador;
qu'ieu port d'aicel mester la flor,
    ez es vertatz,
e puesc ne trair lo vers auctor
    quant er lasatz. (VI, 1-7)

(I want all to hear if a song that I've produced in my workshop is of good quality [*color* = sign of quality in refining or smelting]. For I possess the flower of my métier, and that's the truth. The song itself will testify to this, once it's finished [lit: 'laced up', meaning that the versification has been worked out satisfactorily].)

When Guilhem de Peitieu and later Geoffrey of Vinsauf place the art of *trobar* at the heart of the poetic process, they are also describing exactly what the manuscript matrix invited the scribe to do with the material he sought to include in his *chansonnier*. From this viewpoint, the work of the scribe is not so very much different from that of the poet, since the art of the manuscript is the art of *dispositio*: artistic arrangement and construction. This permits us to think of the manuscript matrix not as a haphazard affair, but as a space that could be planned as carefully as a poetic composition. The *dispositio* or order of the manuscript resides exactly in the logic of its poetic intent. We can speak of a centre of intelligence for manuscripts just as we speak of the centre of gravity of objects, playing its role as the *metteur en scène* for a whole collection of disparate poems which the *chansonnier* gathers and to which it gives a purpose, just as the poet elaborates a meaning for a poem. The difference is that the *chansonnier* gives a meaning – or a sense of a whole – to a large body of pre-existing works, and in that sense of the whole lies the 'intelligence' of the *chansonnier*. The *poet* creates a sense or an identity – a poetic logic – for a single poem; the *scribe* for an entire corpus. In that sense, the *chansonniers* may be said to have created the troubadour corpus in the thirteenth century.

We can actually witness how the *chansonniers* interpret and represent the troubadours. We find that the early troubadours have been treated with an extraordinary heterogeneity from one MS to another, belying the modernist myth of homogeneity. One may discern six basic principles by which *chansonniers* manipulate troubadour lyric for performative or interpretative purposes.

These principles go from the most arbitrary, where it would be difficult to argue intentionality, to clear manipulation of the basic form of a lyric that necessarily changes meaning, and on to the staging of dramatic confrontations between poets that suggests a whole new performative dimension for the earliest poets:

> *Reattribution of songs*. This involves the attribution of a song by one poet to another who seems more 'probable' as its author. For example, because of the popularity of his 'Lanquan li jorn' (IV), Jaufré Rudel became known for songs beginning with 'Lanquan'. Several MSS assign 'lanquan' songs by Guilhem Ademar and Grimoart Gausmar to Jaufré. But songs may be misattributed simply because they seem 'more like' the repertoire of one early poet than another. MS a^1, fol. 499, attributes Guilhem de Peitieu's 'Ab la dolchor' to 'en iaufre rudel', for example. However, thirty-six folios earlier, on fol. 463, a^1 'correctly' attributes this song to 'lo coms de peiteus'.

> *Variation in the ordering of stanzas*: a well-known tendency of early medieval lyric to manifest unstable ordering in the stanzas of a given song from one manuscript to another, or to lose stanzas in transmission. Traditionally considered a phenomenon of scribal or MS corruption, stanzaic variation may, in fact, represent different interpretations, a deliberate rearrangement of meaning for specific effects.[11]

> *Recomposition of stanzaic elements*: a phenomenon whereby one or more lines of one stanza may be switched with one or more lines of another. While recombining stanzaic elements is less intrusive than rewriting stanzas (see the next principle), it does alter both the meaning of a stanza and the sense or mood of the song as a whole, sometimes dramatically. Again, such dramatic recomposition may be analogous to a conductor's 'arrangement' of a musical score to achieve a new performance.

> *Apocryphal stanzas* created for a particular version of a song and either not found in other *chansonniers* or found in only one or two related ones. This is a clear case where the manuscript offers a version of the song different from others. Such stanzas take the impulse of recomposition one step further

towards an entirely new composition by substituting wholly different, rather than recombined components.[12]

Variable intensity of lyric elements. Taken together, the recomposition of stanzaic elements and the substitution of entirely new stanzas permit us to postulate something like a principle of 'strong' and 'weak' constituent parts. Lines within stanzas, or certain stanzas themselves, may have had a lesser lyric intensity within the high medieval aesthetic, permitting them to be more readily displaced, transposed or recomposed. One may then speak of 'weak' lyric elements, as opposed to 'strong-voiced' lyric in the case of those not susceptible of later manipulation. Recomposition and substitution should have much to tell us about the context and intentionality of a MS, since it is unlikely that so deliberate an intervention in a song would be unmotivated.[13]

Dramatic juxtapositions within the MS of poets or groups of poets historically or thematically disparate from one another in order to stage a dramatic confrontation or a debate. Such juxtapositions correspond to Geoffrey of Vinsauf's concept of artistic ordering, on the one hand, while conforming to the troubadour penchant for the *tenso* or debate, on the other. Dramatic juxtaposition, coupled with the three preceding principles, illustrates the concept of a manuscript 'centre of intelligence'.

By way of concluding, let us look briefly at examples of some of these principles in manuscript versions of poems by Bernart de Ventadorn and Guilhem de Peitieu. We shall find that far from a homogeneous, fixed corpus, the poetry of the 'early troubadours' continued to be 'composed' or certainly recomposed, and thus revitalised in the written 'performances' of the manuscripts. Loss of 'voice' did not seem to freeze this lyric into lifeless immobility like some museum specimen.

The section in *N* devoted to Bernart de Ventadorn begins on folio 137 with 'Estat ai' (XXX), a song which appears in as many as fourteen *chansonniers*, but which can be found today only in editions of Bernart's work.[14] The song has *coblas doblas* (paired stanzas) rhymed $a^8 b^7 a^8 b^7 b^7 a^8 a^8 b^7$ (where letters indicate rhyme sounds and numbers the syllable-count of each line; see Chapter

9). It thereby incorporates a principle of inversion or switching in its metrical scheme along with pairing of lines and stanzas. The version in *N*, when compared with the 'authentic' version given in modern editions, inverts elements within the pairing of stanzas, and indeed whole pairs of stanzas to produce a different sense of progression in the poem. The third lines of the two opening stanzas have been switched around, so that 'E sui m'en tart aperseubuç' ('I only realised belatedly') appears in stanza I in place of 'Mas er m'en sui reconoguç' ('But now I'm fully conscious'), now in stanza II.[15] This apparently minimal switch underlines the poet's growing disenchantment with his lady, an anti-courtly but very natural emotion. Unquestionably, the song joins those illustrating the self-knowledge and self-examination which love fosters in its initiates, chief among whom are its poets. In this vein, the poem can be seen either to dramatise a momentary revolt against the vicissitudes of Love's service, and the lady's indifference (a pique repented as soon as it has been voiced), or else to play out the end of love triggered by self-examination. The former, of course, corresponds to the classic scenario of courtly love; it is the preferred version of modern editions. The latter gives us a different meaning and mood for the song, certainly no less aesthetic, but arguably more dramatic.

In addition to transposing these lines, *N* also brings forward the final pair of stanzas as they occur in the modern editions, where the lover contemplates reconciliation, to the middle of the poem where they become stanzas III and IV instead of V and VI. By reordering the stanza pairs, and inverting the second half of two stanzas, *N* produces a darker mood that makes rupture inevitable. What for the editions is the middle pair – the two stanzas where the lover momentarily imagines separating from the *domna* – here becomes the final act, the act of rupture. *N* reinforces this gesture by recombining elements of these two strophes. The last four lines of stanza V read as the *cauda* for stanza VI, while the *cauda* of VI ends stanza V.[16] What was simply a meditation on revolt in the edited version, reads here as rupture and transference of affections:

> Mas bel m'es c'ab lei contenda,
> c'autra n'am, plus bell'e meillor,
> que·m val e m'aiud' e·m socor,
> e·m fai de s'amor esmenda. (stanza IV, *N*, fol. 137c)

(It pleases me to fight with her, for I love another, more beautiful and better, who suits me and helps and aids me, and who rewards me with her love.)

If the lover enjoys contending with his lady, the MS space seems to encourage a similar contention over the meanings of these songs. *Fin'amor*, the psychology and aesthetic of love, a more authentic term than 'courtly love', has a broader, more nuanced and, finally, more realistic range of expressions when we see how diversely the same song can render the same situation according to how one 'arranges' it. Medieval scribes and their audiences clearly enjoyed implementing the full range of lyric permutations.

Such permutation need not involve manipulating the form of an individual song. The effect and meaning of lyric can be transformed in startling ways by dramatic juxtapositions of troubadours from different historical periods who would not normally be read together. A singular example of dramatic juxtaposition occurs in the latter part of *N*. Over a space of eight or nine folios, the scribe responsible for this *chansonnier* juxtaposes five songs of the first troubadour, Guilhem de Peitieu, with six songs by *trobairitz*, female troubadours who lived long after Guilhem's death in 1127.[17]

Dramatic juxtaposition of this sort reminds us of the generic virtuosity of the troubadours, certainly, but also of the phatic thrust of this lyric: from the beginning, it reached out to engage an interlocutor. Apostrophe governs the troubadour lyric mode. Examples abound in the early troubadours: so, for example, Guilhem's 'Companho fairai un vers tot covinen' (I) to Peire Rogier's 'Dous' amiga, no·n puesc mais' (IX), or Marcabru's 'Estornel, cueill ta volada' (XXV) to Peire d'Alvernha's 'Rossinhol, el seu repaire' (I).

Several unusual circumstances signal the intention of the scribe to set off Guilhem's and the *trobairitz*' songs as debates, as contrasting worldviews; so contrasting, indeed, as to point to a serious fault line in the principles of *fin'amor*. The juxtaposition of Guilhem with the *trobairitz* cannot be accidental. Only here do *trobairitz* songs figure, and it is also the only place in the manuscript where a corpus of songs is repeated integrally: the same five songs of Guilhem's which precede the *trobairitz* corpus are repeated immediately afterwards in approximately reverse order. The same hand has copied all of the songs so we cannot suppose that two scribes working independently accidentally copied the same songs. Nor can the order have resulted from an accident of binding: the poems make a continuous sequence, i.e. the first and last *trobairitz* poems begin and end on 'Guilhem' folios.

Moreover, the first song in the initial Guilhem section (fol. 228a–c), and the last song in the repeated section (235b–236a) are the *fabliau*-like 'Un uers farai poi me semeil' (V). Sometimes referred to as the 'red-cat' song, this bawdy lyric purports to recount how the poet, disguised as an anonymous deaf-mute, endures a week of amorous exploits at an inn with two wives of fellow aristocrats. Since this is one of the most explicitly sexual troubadour songs, the scribe is unlikely to have forgotten that he had copied it only eight folios earlier. Furthermore, the order of the repeated songs in folios 228a–230b and 233c–236a has been planned so that the whole sequence of lyrics begins and ends with the same ribald song.[18] The manuscript has deliberately 'sandwiched' the women troubadours between copies of the same five Guilhem songs, beginning and ending with the most ribald. The intent can only have been satirical.

Guilhem's poems, surrounding the selection of four poems by Na Castelloza, one by the Comtessa de Dia, and one by Na Azalais de Porgairagues, might be seen as a cynical provocation, a means of responding to the women by subjecting them to a male corpus. But such a proposition would presuppose passivity on the part of the women's texts, which are, on the contrary, among the strongest lyrics in the corpus.[19]

In fact, the *trobairitz*' poems make a vigorous counter to Guilhem's, enabling one to envisage the section as a specular exchange where the women debate this famous seducer and traducer of women. Having read the responses of the women to the archetypal male poet, the manuscript then invites a re-reading of Guilhem's songs, 'turned inside out' as it were by the altered order in the repeated series which makes the original middle lyric the beginning and the original beginning song, the finale.

The debate genre was a flourishing one in Occitan poetry and, as a matter of fact, this manuscript closes with thirty-four *jocs partitz* or *tensos* on folios 275–92. So the repetition of Guilhem's five songs would constitute a review of the nature and substance of his poetry in light of the women's love poetry. The whole section thus begins to look like a deliberate debate whose topic is the age-old question of the male and female response to love. It also makes a striking comparison between contrasting modes of lyric, a progress report on how far the tradition had come since its early days. We saw from the *vida* of Guilhem quoted on p. 67 above that he had an anti-courtly reputation, yet was recognised as a first-rate poet. If Guilhem, particularly in his most negative and brutal song V that begins and ends this sequence, represents the heroic forces that initiate love and poetry, then the *trobairitz'* poems offer a philosophical meditation on that initiating move.

Their poetry, fully evoking desire, their own sexuality and its consequences, seeks to understand the order of love as part of a higher system, and then to meditate on how to accept the inevitable for themselves, while behaving with understanding and integrity towards their lover. Their poems, contrasted so clearly with those of their archetypal male rival, demonstrate how poetry can offer a programme, valid for male and female alike, for ruling oneself and one's fate.

This confrontation between an early and later troubadours dramatically conveys the lesson that in the world of the *chansonniers* that bequeathed the troubadours to history, the category of earlier and later troubadours yields to a more subtle dialectic, one that interrogates fundamental premises of the love lyric.

NOTES

1 See Chapter 1 and Meneghetti, *Pubblico*, pp. 60–6.
2 Dragonetti, *La Technique poétique*; Zumthor, *Langue et techniques poétiques*.
3 Page, *Voices*, p. 14.
4 A 'historiated letter' is a large, painted initial used to designate the beginning of a new section of a MS. Troubadour lyrics were recorded in sections devoted to a particular troubadour with his or her 'portrait' represented within the enlarged capital letter of the first word of the first song of a section in some *chansonniers*.
5 On the alphabetical sigla designating *chansonniers*, see Appendix 4.
6 See Zufferey, *Recherches*, pp. 33–5.
7 Murphy, *Three Medieval Rhetorical Arts*, p. 35, n. 11.
8 *Poetria Nova*, lines 87–8, Faral edn in *Les Arts*, p. 200.
9 Murphy, *Three Medieval Rhetorical Arts*, p. 36 (= lines 97–100, Faral edn in *Les Arts*, p. 200).
10 'Ben vuell' (VI) appears in four MSS (*C*, *D^a*, *E*, *N*), compared with seven for 'Pos de chantar m'es pres talenz' (XI) (*C*, *D^a*, *I*, *K*, *N*, *R*, *a'*). This compares to 1 MS each for three songs, 2 MSS for five, and 3 MSS for one.

11 On strophic ordering, see also Chapter 14.

12 For an example from Jaufré Rudel, see Kay, 'Continuation'.

13 Here too a good example is provided by Jaufré Rudel's corpus, which illustrates richly the principles of stanza reordering, recombination, 'strong' and 'weak' lyric elements, and apocryphal *coblas*. Jaufré's signature song 'Lanquan li jorn' appears in all sixteen MSS containing Jaufré songs. Only MS *C* has the stanza ordering found in Jeanroy's edition. At least two and sometimes three stanzas have been recomposed, usually with elements from a stanza that has been 'dropped' in a given MS. See *Jaufré*, ed. Pickens, pp. 150–215, for versions of this song.

14 Even Riquer's three-volume anthology, which has nineteen of Bernart's songs, does not include 'Estat ai': a clear example of aesthetic criteria differing between the thirteenth century and today.

15 *N*'s inversion of these lines may also be found in *aIK*.

16 *IK* make the same transpositions, but not *a*, which is interesting since *a* does transpose lines 3 and 11 as *N* does. While *a* does not follow *IKN* in the more radical transformation, it does invert lines 19–20 to lines 27–8, and transposes stanzas 5–6 into a 6–5 order.

17 On the juxtaposition of the Guilhem and *trobairitz* poems in *N*, see also Nichols, 'Why material philology?'; Bossy and Jones, 'Gender and compilation'.

18 The songs in question by Guilhem are, in the sequence of the first section (fols. 228a–230b), '[U]n uers farai poi me semeil', '[A]b la dolchor del temps nouel', '[B]en uoill que sapcho li pluisor', '[C]ompagno non pus mudar qu'eo nom effrei', '[P]os de chantar m'es pris talenz'. The order of this sequence (1–5) becomes 3,4,5,2,1 in the repetition (fols. 233c–236a).

19 The songs are: Na Castelloza, '[A]mics s'ie·us trobes auinen' (fols. 230c–231a), '[I]a de chantar non degr'auer talan' (fols. 231a–c), '[M]out aurez fag lonc estage' (fols. 231c–232a), '[P]er ioi d'amor m'auegna' (fols. 232a–c); La Comtessa de Dia, '[A] chantar m'er de cho qu'eu non uolria' (fols. 232c–233a); Azalais de Porgairagues, '[A]r e·m al freit tems uengut' (fols. 233a–c).

CHAPTER 5

The classical period: from Raimbaut d'Aurenga to Arnaut Daniel

Gérard Gouiran

Classicism is a strange notion to use to define any period of troubadour composition. Is there any troubadour more 'classical' than Bernart de Ventadorn, considered here amongst the 'early troubadours'? Are not all of the troubadours in fact united by their commitment to toiling on the margins, in a way which preserves them permanently from classicism? If Raimbaut d'Aurenga and Arnaut Daniel are classical troubadours, then one might as well say that Rimbaud too is a classical poet.

Yet despite the troubadours' determination to be extraordinary, in the etymological sense of the word, which might be expected to lead to their thorough-going individualism, one can still sense that there is a bond, a sense of common ground between those of them who followed in the footsteps of the great Limousin poet. Whence does this feeling stem? This is not the place to put in question the very notion of classicism; but let me nevertheless propose that this period, roughly the second half of the twelfth century, is classical because there existed a consensus on major ideas and attitudes whose validity the poets by and large acknowledged. Despite the growth of genres which were previously minor, the privileged medium of the lyric is the *canso*, whose sole subject is *fin'amor* and whose undisputed means of expression is the commonplace, the *topos*. Once these prerequisites have been observed, the rest is entirely at the poet's discretion and, as with all classicism, it is noteworthy that the strictness of the rules in no way shackles the freedom of genius: the higher the hurdle, the more prodigious the leap. This imagery of competitive exertion is all the more apt in that, once these rules have been assimilated by all, the songs of the troubadours become one song where voices answer each other in such a way as constantly to further amorous reflection and poetic creation. And this within a form which is always striving to surpass the compositions of predecessors who must consequently be outdone in terms of theme as well as expression, in an aesthetic where matter and form are never in opposition to one another.[1]

One can see this practice in the use of one of the most traditional *topoi* of the Occitan lyric, the nature opening. We know that a good number of songs begin with a description of nature, usually in spring but also, as this interest in exploiting the margins comes into play, in the winter months. This nature opening, a *locus* full of plants and birds, which some have seen as an element of ancient folklore, allows the troubadour to set forth his state of mind as in harmony with, or in opposition to, the world he describes, or to show how love acts as a filter by coming between the poet and the reality it governs. This play existed well before the classical age of *trobar*, and, to look no further than Bernart de Ventadorn, how could we forget these opening lines?

> Ara no vei luzir solelh,
> tan ne son escurzit li rai;
> e ges per aisso no·m esmai
> c'una clardatz me solelha
> d'amor qu'ins el cor me raya.   (V, 1–5)

(Now I do not see the sun shining any more, so obscured are its rays; and for all that I am not dismayed, for I am lit by a beam of love which shines inside my heart.)

The way these set-piece expressions about the world transfigured by love are inserted into the intimidating framework of *rims derivatius* without the least obscurity is dazzling. Clearly Raimbaut d'Aurenga, contemporary and friend of Bernart, did not forget them:

> Er resplan la flors enversa
> pels trencantz rancx e pels tertres.
> Quals flors? Neus, gels e conglapis,
> que cotz e destrenh e trenca,
> don vei mortz quils, critz, brais, siscles
> pels fuelhs, pels rams e pels giscles;
> mas mi ten vert e jauzen jois,
> er quan vei secx los dolens crois.
>
> Quar enaissi o enverse
> que·lh bel plan mi semblon tertre,
> e tenc per flor lo conglapi,
> e·l cautz m'es vis que·l freit trenque,

e·lh tron mi son chant e siscle,
e paro·m folhat li giscle;
aissi·m sui ferms laçatz en joi
que ren no vei que·m sia croi.[2]

(Now the inverted flower blossoms on the sharp rocks and on the hill-sides. Which flower? Snow, frost and hail, which bite, torment and cut, and kill warbling, cries, shrieks, and trills throughout the leaves and boughs and branches; but joy keeps me verdant and happy, now that I see sad and base people dried up.

Indeed, I invert this world and the beautiful plains seem to be hills to me, I take hail to be a flower, and the cold, I believe, is the heat which cuts it, the claps of thunder are songs and trills to me and the leaves seem to me to cover the branches again; I have attached myself to joy so firmly that I see nothing which seems base to me.)

The two poems share the 'world upside-down' motif and the use of derived rhyme, though whereas Bernart exploits this technique within the structure of the stanza, Raimbaut uses it to link consecutive stanzas.

Even when the poetry seems exclusively concerned with its own formal virtuosity, troubadours still contrive, as though it were a point of pride, to introduce the traditional *topos* where it is least expected, as for example in the famous *sestina* by Arnaut Daniel:

Lo ferm voler qu'el cor m'intra
no·m pot ges becs escoissendre ni ongla
de lauzengier qui pert per mal dir s'arma;
e pus no l'aus batr'ab ram ni ab verga,
sivals a frau, lai on non aurai oncle,
jauzirai joi, en vergier o dinz cambra.[3]

(The firm desire which enters into my heart cannot be taken away from me by either the beak or the nail of the slanderer who loses his soul through his scandalmongering; and as I do not dare to hit him with a branch or with a rod, at least in secret, there where I have no uncle, will I enjoy joy, in a garden or inside a chamber.)

Indeed for the initiated, those *entendenz* to whom the troubadours address their songs, the words *ram*, *verga*, or *vergier* inevitably recall the traditional return of spring, and *bec* the birds associated with it.

This play on the *topos*, which thus appears to be anything but a strait-jacket, infiltrates other genres, such as the *descort*; Raimbaut de Vaqueiras begins his famous multilingual composition with:

> Eras quan vei verdejar
> pratz e vergiers e boscatges,
> vuelh un descort començar
> d'amor per qu'ieu vauc aratges ... (XVI, 1–4)

(Now that I see meadows, gardens and woods growing green again, I want to begin a *descort* on the love which makes me delirious ...)

This introduction is well suited to a work which goes on to accumulate the commonplaces characteristic of the lyric in the different languages deployed.

The finest example of this play is surely provided by a *sirventes* by Bertran de Born, who employs with consummate art the technique of the displaced parallel so characteristic of troubadour lyric:

> Cant vei pels vergiers desplegar
> los cendatz grocs, indis e blaus,
> m'adousa la vos dels cavaus
> e·l sonet que fan li juglar
>   que viulen de trap en tenda,
> trombas e corn e graile clar.
> Adoncs voill un sirventes far
>   tal que·l coms Richartz l'entenda. (XXIV, 1–8)

(When I see in gardens banners of yellow, indigo and blue silk being unfurled, I am filled with sweet delight by the neighing of the horses and the melodies of the *joglars* who go from tent to pavilion playing the viol, trumpets, horns and high-pitched clarions. That is why I want to compose a *sirventes* such that King Richard may hear it.)

Once the first line has led listeners to believe that the traditional white flowers of spring and the love songs of the birds are about to burst forth in the garden, the second surprises them with an alternative reality: the colours are those of banners, the sound is that of steeds. The concert of birds is replaced by that of men, which is infinitely more varied, as were the colours of the flags. The traditional nature opening has been countered by a 'culture opening' since, for Bertran, the imagination of men unquestionably stems from their unchanging second nature. Note also the sense of causality: just as the description of nature automatically led to the *canso*, that of culture leads to the *sirventes* and so here war becomes the most refined manifestation of aristocratic existence.

The offhand manner in which Peire Vidal acquits himself of his seasonal dues is similarly adroit in its rehandling of conventional material:

> Be·m pac d'ivern e d'estiu
> e de fregz e de calors,
> e am neus aitan cum flors
> e pro mort mais qu'avol viu,
> qu'enaissi·m ten esforsiu
> e gai Jovens et Valors.
> E quar am domna novella,
> sobravinen e plus bella,
> paro·m rozas entre gel
> e clar temps ab trebol cel. (XXXVI, 1–10)

(I am as pleased with winter as with spring, with the cold as much as with warmth, and I love snow as much as flowers and a worthy dead man more than a live coward, for Youth and Worth keep me strong and joyful. As I love a young lady, full of grace and of beauty, I see roses in the middle of the frost and fair weather in a stormy sky.)

In other cases, the song's opening comparison – as already happened with the early troubadours – can place love in relation to something other than nature, and this type of comparison, which was to flourish with Rigaut de Berbezilh before enjoying its later well-known success with the poets of Italy and the French Pléïade, is illustrated by Gaucelm Faidit:

> Al semblan del rei thyes
> qan l'ac vencut l'emperaire,
> e·il fetz tirar, qan l'ac pres,
> sa carret'e son arnes,
> don el chantav'al maltraire,
> vezen la roda virar,
> e·l ser, plorav'al manjar,
> chant on plus ai malananssa,
> qan cossir q'en alegranssa
> mi pot mon maltraich tornar,
> e plor qan vei joi ni be
> als autres, e mi sove
> q'ieu n'aic pro, ar non ai re. (XXXVIII, 1–13)

(Just like the Teutonic king whom the emperor, once he had defeated him, took prisoner and forced to drag his chariot and equipment, as a result of which he would sing of his sufferings, seeing the wheel of fortune turn, and shed tears when he ate at night, in just such a way do I sing in the depth of my misfortune, imagining that it can change my suffering into happiness, and I weep before the joy and the good fortune of others, at the thought that I had much of it and that I have none any more.)

This strophe reiterates fairly exactly the motif of Bernart de Ventadorn's lark (XXXI), but for once the *topos* lies in the idea expressed rather than in the image which is its vehicle.

The comparison established by Peire Raimon de Tolosa between the song which grows from the sorrow of love and the candle which feeds a light that destroys it is so magnificent that it is hard to think of it as a commonplace:

> Atressi cum la candela
> que si meteissa destrui
> per far clartat ad autrui,
> chant, on plus trac greu martire,
> per plazer de l'autra gen.
> E, car a dreit escien
> sai qu'eu fai folatge,
> c'ad autrui don alegratge
> et a mi pen'e tormen,
> nuilla res, si mal m'en pren,
> no·m deu plaigner del dampnatge.[4]

(Like the candle which destroys itself in order to give light to others, I sing, at the worst of my torture, for the pleasure of others. And, as my conscience is very aware that I am committing a folly in bringing joy to others and pain and torment to myself and, if I suffer for it, no one should feel sorry for my hurt.)

Another introductory *topos* is the link between love and song, whether this is seen as straightforwardly causal, as in Bernart de Ventadorn (II, 1–4), or as taking any number of other extremely diverse forms. This is one of Miraval's favourite opening themes:

> A penas sai don m'apreing
> so q'en chantan m'auzetz dir;
> cum pieitz trac e plus m'azir,
> mieills e mon chan esdeveing:
> gardatz, qand er qi·m n'enseing,
>   si sabrai esdevenir
> ni ma bona dompna·m deing;
> que jes de saber no·m feing,
> ni nuills hom no·i pot faillir
> que de lieis aia soveing. (VI, 1–10)

(I know not where I will go to search for that of which you hear me speak in my songs; the more I suffer, the more I am sad, and the better is my song: imagine how great my success will be when there is someone to instruct me and if my beautiful lady accepts me; for I do not find knowledge distasteful and there is no one who could lack it if he has my lady in his thoughts.)

The contradictory effects of singing also inspire a famous song by Folquet de Marselha:

> En chantan m'aven a membrar
> so qu'ieu cug chantan oblidar,
> mas per so chant qu'oblides la dolor
>   e·l mal d'amor,
>   et on plus chan, plus m'en sove,
> que la boca en al re non ave
>   mas en 'merce!'
>   perqu'es vertatz e sembla be
> qu'ins el cor port, dona, vostra faisso
> que·m chastia qu'ieu no vir ma razo. (V, 1–10)

(When I sing, I remember that which I try to forget by singing; but I sing in order to forget the sorrow and the distress of love, and the more I sing, the more I remember, for my mouth never manages to say anything but 'have pity!' The truth, and it is clear, is that I am carrying in my heart your image, my lady, which advises me not to change my topic.)

Everything in this passage down to the image of the lady's face engraved on the heart of the troubadour (a motif which was to enjoy enormous success in Sicilian poetry) strikes us as a tribute to Bernart de Ventadorn (VI, 39–40).

Let us now move on to the great poets of this period, and first of all to the so-called master of the troubadours, Giraut de Bornelh. This is no empty title, since numerous *chansonniers* pay him the honour of opening with his works – works which are, moreover, quite exceptionally abundant and diverse. Even if this preference demonstrates the difference in taste which separates us from the past, Giraut clearly knew how to give a new lease of life to the major themes imposed by tradition:

I
> Non pues sufrir c'a la dolor
> de la den la lengua non vir
> e·l cor a la novela flor,
> lanquan vei los ramels florir
> e·il chant son pel boscatge   5
> dels auzeletz enamoratz.
> E si tot m'estau apensatz
> ni pres per mal auratge,

can vei camps e vergiers e pratz
ieu renovel e m'asolatz.   10

II   Qu'ieu no m'esfors d'autre labor
         mas de chantar e d'esjauzir;
         c'una nueit sonjav'en pascor
         tal somge que·m fetz esbaudir,
         d'un esparvier ramatge   15
         que m'era sus el ponh pausatz
         et si·m semblav'adomesgatz,
         anc non vi tan salvatge,
         mas pueis fo maniers e privatz
         e de bons jetz apreiszonatz[...]   20

VI   Qu'ieu ai vist acomensar tor
         d'una sola peir'al bastir
         e cada pauc pugar aussor
         tro c'om la podia garnir.
         Per qu'ieu pren vassalatge   55
         d'aitan, si m'o aconseyllatz,
         que·l vers, pueys er ben asonatz,
         trametray el viatge,
         si trob qui lai lo·m port viatz,
         ab que·s deport e·s don solatz.   60
                                              (XXXVII)

(I cannot refrain from bringing my tongue back to the aching tooth, any more than I can hold back my heart from turning to the new flower when I see the branches flowering and when the songs of amorous birds resound around the woods. And although surrounded by worries and concerns, upon seeing fields, gardens and meadows, I am rejuvenated and happy.

I exert myself in no other task than singing and bringing joy; thus, one spring night, I had a dream which filled me with happiness: a sparrowhawk from the woods had landed on my fist and he seemed tame to me; I had never seen such a wild one, but afterwards he was tame and friendly and bound with fine straps ...

I saw a tower starting to be built, beginning from a single stone and constantly rising until it could have been garrisoned. Thus, if you advise me to, I will show enough audacity to set my song on the journey – once it has been well set to music, and provided that I find someone to swiftly transport it there – so that she can enjoy and take pleasure from it.)

I confess my admiration for the image, so nearly in bad taste, of the tongue playing with an aching tooth, and the way the song

then suddenly bursts into the splendour of spring before giving
way to striking dream images: the verticality of the tower of love
and war, and the bird sprung up from the depths of the unconscious . . .

Even if they are more traditional in conception, Arnaut de
Maruelh's songs have an undeniably majestic grandeur:

> La grans beutatz e·l fis ensenhamens
> e·l verais pretz e las bonas lauzors
> e·l cortes ditz e la fresca colors
> que son en vos, bona domna valenz,
> me donon gienh de chantar e sciensa,
> mas grans paors m'o tolh e grans temensa,
> qu'ieu non aus dir, domna, qu'ieu chant de vos,
> e re no sai si m'er o dans o pros.
>
> Qu'ieu vos am tan, domna, celadamens
> que res no·l sap mas quant ieu et Amors
> ni vos eyssa, tan grans sobretemors
> m'o tol ades que no·us aus far parvens;
> tal paor ai qu'ira e malsabensa
> m'aiatz, domna, quar vos port benvolensa,
> e pus no·us aus ren dire a rescos,
> dirai vos o sevals e mas chansos. (I, 1–16)

(The great beauty, the perfect education, the true merit, the praise-
worthiness, the courtly speech and the fresh complexion which you possess, beautiful lady of great worth, give me the understanding and the
knowledge to sing, but I am held back by great fear and great nervousness, for I do not dare say, my lady, that it is of you that I sing, and I do
not know if that is to my profit or to my disadvantage.

For I love you, my lady, so secretly than none but Love and I know it, not
even you, so extreme is the terror which prevents me from manifesting it
to you; I am so afraid that you would be angry and dissatisfied with me,
my lady, because of my affection, and, as I dare to say nothing to you in
secret, at least I will tell you it in my songs.)

Of course, one could claim that there is merely a succession of
topoi here, and indeed that they have reached the point of diminishing returns: the spell-binding *carmen* is on the verge of being
replaced by formulae which no longer have the power to create
poetic magic. This illustration of the theme of *celar* (secrecy), that
absolute discretion which is one of the pillars of *fin'amor*, and of
the total submission which places the fate of the troubadour in
love in the hands of a superhuman lady who simultaneously

kindles the song in his heart and dampens it on his lips, is nonetheless superbly successful.

In addition to exploiting this strictly amorous vein, the period
is also characterised by reflection on composition. Of course,
fin'amor is a source of inspiration, but no one holds this necessary
pretext for *trobar* to be sufficient, and there are many exordia
which assimilate the roles of craftsman and poet, as in this work
by Arnaut Daniel:

> Ab gai son coindet e leri
> fatz motz e caputz e doli,
> que seran verai e cert
> quan n'aurai passat la lima;
> qu'Amors marves plan'e daura
> mon chantar, que de lieis mou
> cui Pretz manten e governa.[5]

(To a gay, gracious and happy tune, I compose by planing and smoothing
words which will be exact and precise once I have filed them; Love is
eager to polish and to gild my song, which is inspired by her who sustains
and governs merit.)

Language itself becomes the subject matter of poetry, and an
erudite succession of well-combed and ill-kempt sounds (to use
Dante's terminology) foregrounds the sonority of songs in which
the poets of the *trobar car* successfully combine, to good effect,
traditional *topoi* with an audacious use of metrical form and sound,
as in these lines, by Raimbaut d'Aurenga, which seem to have
been woven out of thin air:

> Ara non siscla ni chanta
> 　　rossigniols
> 　ni crida l'auriols
> en vergier ni dinz forest,
> ni par flors groja ni blava,
> 　　e si·m nais
> 　　jois e chans
> 　e creis en veillians;
> car no·m ven com sol
> 　　somnejans. (XIV, 1–10)[6]

(Now one cannot hear the nightingale warbling nor singing, nor the
oriole calling in the garden or in the forest; we see neither yellow nor
blue flowers, and yet a joy and a song are born in me whilst I am awake,
for it is not happening, as is usual, when I am asleep.)

Arnaut Daniel's extraordinary texture of sonorities is no whit inferior to Raimbaut's; even if its extreme elaboration leaves the modern reader perplexed, it must have been just as puzzling to contemporary audiences:

L'aur'amara	fa·ls bruels brancutz		
clarzir	que·l dous'espeys'ab fuelhs,		
e·ls letz	becx	dels auzels ramencx	
te balbs e mutz,	pars	e non-pars.	
Per qu'ieu m'esfortz	de far e dir	plazers	
a manhs? Per ley	qui m'a virat bas d'aut,		
don tem morir,	si·ls afans no m'asoma.		

Tan fo clara	ma prima lutz		
d'eslir	lieys, don cre·l cors los huelhs,		
non pretz	necs	mans dos angevencs	
d'autra. S'eslutz	rars	mos preyars,	
pero deports	m'es e d'auzir	volers	
bos motz ses grey	de lieys, don tan m'azaut		
qu'al sieu servir	suy del pe tro qu'al coma. (IX, 1–14)[7]		

(The harsh wind clears the branched bushes, which the zephyr thickens with leaves, and keeps the beaks of birds on the branch, those alone as well as those in couples, stammering and silent. Why is it that I strive to do and to say things which are pleasing to many? Because of her who has brought me low from on high, and I am afraid of dying as a result of this if she does not put an end to my torments.

So bright was my first look in making out her who causes one's heart to trust one's eyes that I don't reckon at the value of two Angevin coins the secret messages of any other lady. It is rare for my prayer to be brought forth, but it is a pleasure for me to hear the wishes and the good words, with no wickedness in them, of her with whom I am so taken that I am entirely in her service, from my feet to my hair.)

It was not just the *canso* which gloried in such astonishing displays of skill, and Bertran de Born did not hesitate, in his *sirventes*, to imitate Raimbaut d'Aurenga, adapting the song 'Ara non siscla' to Angevin politics in order to address these reproaches to Richard Lionheart:

> Entre Dordoinha e Charanta
> es trop mols,
> so·m dis N'Auriols,
> q'enqier no·i a ren conqest.
> Et er l'anta si·s suava,
> ni qe lais

> benananz
> e gortz e tiranz
> cels q'amar non sol
> e poissanz. (XXXI, 41–50)

(Between the Dordogne and the Charente, he shows himself to be too
weak, from what Lord Auriol tells me, for he has made no conquests
there yet. And he will be covered in shame if he appeases those whom
he likes not, and leaves them prosperous, fat, rebellious and powerful.)

He even, in a *sirventes* which sets out to compete with Arnaut's
'Si·m fos Amors' (XVII), concludes by admitting his inability to
write another strophe, because he has run out of rhyme words:

> Di·m a·N Rotgier et a totz mos parens
> que no·i trob plus omba ni om ni esta. (XXVIII, 43–44)

(Tell Roger and all my relatives that I can find no more rhymes in *-omba*,
-om, nor *-esta*.)

Indeed, although the *canso* continues to be the most valued genre
in the classical period, this period also saw the rise of the *sirventes*,
to which Bertran certainly contributed.

The debate genre also flourished, and alongside discussions on
literary subjects, like that which opposes Raimbaut d'Aurenga and
Giraut de Bornelh, there are a number of debates on love casuistry
(often purely for entertainment), such as this battle of words proposed by Savaric de Mauleon to Gaucelm Faidit and Uc de la
Bacalaria:

> Gaucelm, tres jocs enamoratz
> partisc a vos et a N'Hugon
> e chascus prendetz lo plus bon,
> e laissatz me cal qe·us voillatz:
> una dompn'a tres prejadors
> e destreing la tant lor amors
> qe, qan tuich trei li son denan,
> a chascun fai d'amor semblan:
> l'un esgard'amorosamen,
> l'autr'estreing la man dousamen,
> al tertz caucia·l pe rizen –
> Digatz a cal, pois aissi es,
> fai major amor de totz tres. (Gaucelm Faidit, LI, 1–13)

(Gaucelm, I challenge Uc and yourself to a *tenso* on three choices to do
with love, so each of you take the better part and leave me whichever
you like: three men are courting a lady and she responds to their love so

well that when all three are before her she makes a sign of love to each. She looks at the first affectionately, sweetly proffers her hand to the second, and brushes the third with her foot whilst smiling. State to which of the three she shows the most love in this situation.)

Here is another which a certain Ademar proposes to the doubtless ageing Raimon de Miraval:

> Miraval, tenzon grazida
> voil que fassam, si·us sap bon,
> e digatz mi ses faillida
> s'om deu laissar per razon
> sidonz, pos es veillezida,
> ses negun'autr'uchaizon.
> Respondetz d'oc o de non!
>
> N'Aesmar, tost hai chauzida
> la part del preç e del pron:
> drutz q'a domna conqezida
> no·n deu moure partizon,
> q'ades val mais la gauzida
> qan dura longa sazon;
> perqu'aqi non veig tenzon. (XLIV, 1–14)

(Miraval, I would like us to make a pleasant *tenso*, if it please you; tell me truly whether it is fair to abandon one's lady for no other reason than that she has grown old. Answer yes or no!

Lord Ademar, I have quickly chosen the side of merit and advantage: when a lover has conquered a lady, he must not provoke a separation between them, for pleasure is worth more the longer it lasts; I don't think there is anything to be discussed in this matter.)

It emerges that Ademar's intention was to poke fun at the older troubadour who no doubt imagined that his gentlemanly reply was in strict accordance with the courtly code:

> Miraval, molt m'es estragna
> dompna, pos ha·l pel ferran;
> perq'eu lau q'ab vos remagna,
> q'ambdui seretz d'un semblan:
> veils e veilla s'acompagna,
> e joves ab joves van;
> perq'eu veill domnei desman. (XLIV, 15–21)

(Miraval, I find a lady repugnant once she has grey hair; therefore I suggest that she should stay with you, because you two will be of one appearance: the old man and the old woman go together, whereas young people suit other young people; I refuse to court old women.)

Luckily, this parlour game – which, while it demands a fair amount of skill, does not preclude the participation of patrons, who were probably delighted to make their voices heard in such collaborations, and more inclined to be generous as a result – often gave way to compositions in which the troubadour supplied both voices (although we can never be absolutely certain of this), such as 'Si·us quer conselh' by Giraut de Bornelh (LVII), or 'Amics, en gran' by Raimbaut d'Aurenga (XXV). It is to this class of fictive *tenso* that belongs a curious and beautiful song by Guilhem de Saint Leidier (IX), often considered to be the only allegorical poem in the medieval Occitan lyric:

> En Guillem de Saint Deslier, vostra semblanza
> mi digatz d'un soin leugier que·m fo salvatge:
> qu'ieu somjava, can l'autr'ier en esperanza
> m'adurmi ab lo salut d'un ver messatge,
>> en un vergier plen de flors
>> frescas, de bellas colors,
>> on feri uns venz isnels
>> que frais las flors e·ls brondels.
>
> Don, d'est sompni vos dirai, segon m'esmanza,
> q'eu en conoisc ni m'es vis en mon coratge:
> lo vergiers, segon q'en penz, signifianza
> es d'amor, las flors de domnas d'aut paratge,
>> e·l venz dels lauzenjadors,
>> e·l bruiz dels fals fenhedors,
>> e la frascha dels ramels
>> nos·s cambi'en jois novels.   (IX, 1–16)

(Lord Guilhem of Saint-Didier, tell me your opinion about a fleeting dream of which I can make no sense: the other evening I fell asleep full of optimism, having been greeted by a true messenger, and I dreamt of a garden full of fresh flowers with beautiful colours, and in which a strong wind was blowing, breaking off flowers and buds.

My lord, I will tell you how I interpret and understand this dream in my heart of hearts: the garden, to my mind, signifies love, the flowers ladies of great nobility, the wind slanderers, and the uproar of false, feigning lovers, and the broken branches transport us to new joys.)

One of the usual effects of classicism is to suppress all but the major genres; Bernart de Ventadorn would fit this model very well, having composed practically nothing but *cansos*, whereas we have just seen that the troubadours of the subsequent generation favoured a wider variety of genres. Even forms of lesser standing, like the *alba*, tempted Giraut de Bornelh; it is less surprising to find a little gem of an *alba* attributed to Raimbaut de Vaqueiras (XXV), since he delights in cultivating minor genres such as the *estampida* and the *descort*. The formal complexity of his *alba* affords him the pleasure, which is far from being a classical one, of innovation.

In addition to political *sirventes*, poets of this period composed crusading and religious poetry, such as Gaucelm Faidit's 'Del gran golfe' (LVI) and Folquet de Marselha's 'Hueimais no·y conosc' (XIX). These are not the only occasions when troubadours may have fulfilled a quasi-official role as spokesmen, and the death of nobles gives them the perfect pretext to compose some of their most stately pieces, the *planhz*. This highly codified genre, descendant of the Latin *planctus*, shows once again that constraints are far from hindering poetic expression, as is demonstrated by Gaucelm Faidit in a famous lament for King Richard I (L), and by Bertran de Born mourning Henry the Young King, eldest son of Eleanor of Aquitaine (XIV). The disappearance of his protector was such a cruel loss for Bertran that there is no need to invoke 'poetic sincerity', as is so often done with the troubadours, to account for this *planh*: plain ordinary sincerity will have been sufficent inspiration.

One could go on enumerating examples of this rich and fertile contradiction between *topos* and originality; it would, indeed, provide the basis for an original account of classicism. However, if one understands by classicism a tendency to establish some kind of order over a previous, bountiful disorder, a carefully cultivated French park as opposed to an English garden, then nothing is more alien to the spirit of the troubadours. Granted, the garden of the 'classical' troubadours is a place where certain flowers, certain groves, certain statues and certain architectural features are indispensable, but both the intrinsic conception and the arrangement of these elements remain totally free.

In fact, the period we have just surveyed is classical only if we take classicism to mean quintessence. In the last quarter of the twelfth century there is no longer any contest between the *vers* and the *canso*, the *canso* constituting, by common consent, the genre to end all genres. Similarly, despite some dissenting voices – and these always in humorous vein – the courtly code, the *cursus amorum* (that is, the course love affairs must follow), is never really questioned. *Fin'amor* is the foundation of song: it is its spirit while the *topoi* are the material forms from which any song is constructed, and which can be elaborated poetically in an extraordinary variety of ways. Other genres also come to maturity, but one could say that they know their place, not experiencing the sort of infinite division into sub-genres which typifies the post-classical period.

The final defining feature of classicism, and the most difficult to detect and to explain, is the power of inspiration. It is this which distinguishes our period from that in which, even if we find the same principles of composition and ideology being applied, the poetic text becomes nothing but a recapitulation, and in which the great voice of the troubadours falters. It is not that the poets are bad: far from it, for they handle *topoi* with skill and construct their songs confidently: but they lack the assurance which comes with legitimacy and without which classicism could not exist.

Translated by Matthew Bardell

NOTES

1 See Gruber, *Dialektik*, and also Chapter 12, below.
2 Cited from Gouiran, *Lo Ferm Voler*, pp. 64–5 (= Pattison XXXIX, 1–16).
3 *Lo Ferm Voler*, pp. 74–5 (= Toja XVIII, 1–6).
4 Cited from *Le poesie de Peire Raimon de Tolosa*, ed. Cavaliere, IV.
5 Gouiran, *Lo Ferm Voler*, pp. 70–1 (= Toja, X, 1–7).
6 Pattison prints this song differently, in seven-line stanzas with internal rhymes.
7 I adopt the layout of Riquer, *Los trovadores*, II, 624–5.

CHAPTER 6

The later troubadours

... noels digz de nova maestria ... ?

Michael Routledge

Around the middle of the thirteenth century, Guilhem de Montan-hagol used the familiar convention of the 'lost golden age' to assert the value of his own and his contemporaries' compositions:

> Non an tan dig li primier trobador
> ni fag d'amor,
> lai el temps qu'era guays,
> qu'enquera nos no fassam apres lor
> chans de valor,
> nous, plazens e verais. (VIII, 1–6)

(The first troubadours did not say or do so much with regard to love, back in the good old days, that we are unable to compose after them songs which are new, pleasing and true.)

Thematic originality is paramount and still possible, but must be accompanied by renewal in style:

> Quar dir pot hom so qu'estat dig no sia
> qu'estiers non es trobaires bos ni fis
> tro fai sos chans guays, nous e gent assis
> ab noels digz de nova maestria.
>
> Mas en chantan dizo·l comensador
> tant en amor
> que·l nous dirs torn' a fays. (VIII, 7–13)

(For one *can* say that which has never been said; without this no trouba-dour is good or true unless he composes a song which is gay, new and well-measured, with new ideas in a new style. But those who went before say so much in their love songs that it becomes wearisome drudgery to find anything new to say.)

Guilhem was expressing, with evident exasperation, an 'anxiety of influence' which, given the century and a quarter of troubadour song which separates him from Guilhem IX, is hardly surprising.

Indeed, it is hard to find in thirteenth-century *cansos* any thematic innovation. There may be greater variety in metrical form in the works of any one troubadour, but the forms themselves are generally those developed and elaborated in the previous century. There is little stylistic or lexical experimentation, none to rival Marcabru, Raimbaut d'Aurenga or Arnaut Daniel. There are signs of a broadening of the range of imagery, notably with reference to the language of commerce, not unconnected perhaps with an increased measure of bourgeois patronage, especially in the wealthier towns of Provence and Languedoc. Bertran Carbonel of Marseille frequently and unapologetically uses commercial similes in his *cansos* and *coblas*:

> Aisi com sel que·s met en perilh gran
> ab son aver per talan d'enrequir,
> e·ls mals que n'a li·n aven a sofrir
> per lo guazanh que en vai esperan,
> o ai ieu fach, dona, c'ai dat a vos
> lo cor e·l cors com a la plus plazen
> e que val mays . . .   (IV, 1–7)

(Like a man who takes a great risk with his money, out of a desire to make a fortune, and manages to put up with the misfortunes he has to suffer because of the profit he hopes for, I have done likewise, lady, since I have given to you my heart and body as to the most pleasing lady and the one who is of greatest worth . . .)

The lady is equated with a profitable financial investment. Debate about the finer points of *fin'amor*, about how to write songs and what subjects are appropriate, seems to be especially popular and is carried on through *tensos* and *partimens* or through exchanges of *coblas*. There is often a crepuscular tone to these exchanges, a sense that almost everything has indeed been said. Isnart d'Entrevenas, one of the numerous troubadours who enjoyed the patronage of Blacatz, responds to an innocuous but hackneyed song by his protector by expressing mock admiration and offering advice: 'I am so envious of Blacatz's *sonet* that I'm composing *descortz*, *retroenguas* and *chansos*; and, since he seems to like it, I would compose a *sirventes* if only I knew how. But since I don't, I'll compose a *danza* which will be pretty and suitable, such as true lovers can sing, on the subject of what is pleasing. If it please Sir Blacatz, since he's written a new tune, his *canso* would be better if he put into it some hills and meadows, some gardens and leafy orchards, Spain and Almeria, France and Lombardy, Berthe and her oxen, the long days of May, the sweet month of the year, St John's wort and flowery Eastertide'.[1] Isnart is drawing attention to the few favourite subjects and much-imitated images (including, of course, those from Jaufré Rudel's most famous song!) that his patron's song does *not* contain.

Received wisdom has it that the troubadour lyric as a whole went into rapid decline after the Albigensian Crusade of 1209–29, suggesting that Montanhagol was wasting his time striving to keep alive a way of writing that was already dying on its feet. It is argued that dispossessed southern barons could no longer support troubadours, that poets feared to write because of the Inquisition and that consequently many troubadours left Occitania for the more favourable cultural climate of Spain or Italy. Recent work by William Paden has shown that the known facts concerning the social and political effects of the crusade, the number of troubadours who flourished in the thirteenth century, and their sojourns in Spain and Italy simply do not support such a view.

Simon de Montfort, leader of the crusading army in the early years of the Albigensian Crusade, had adopted a policy of dispossessing the local nobility, but this did not survive his death in 1218, and many of the *faidits* (dispossessed lords) 'were restored to their possessions, either under the treaty of 1229 or by royal grant afterwards'.[2] Even the most convinced supporters of the 'Albigensian eclipse' theory admit that there is little if any evidence of troubadour poetry being infected with catharism, and the Cathar writings which survive make no mention of troubadour poetry or song. The picture of the Inquisition in Occitania in the thirteenth century as an all-pervasive thought police is anachronistic, and the alleged watering-down effect which religious repression is supposed to have had on troubadour writing seems to owe much to Jeanroy's overinterpretation of Guilhem de Montanhagol's 'Ar ab lo coinde pascor', a song in which the poet claims that love is not sinful but leads to virtuous deeds:

> e d'amor mou castitatz,
> qar qi·n amor ben s'enten
> non pot far qe pueis mal renh. (XII, 18–20)

(From love proceeds chastity, for anyone who properly devotes himself to love cannot then behave badly.)

Whilst the statement 'd'amor mou castitatz' is striking in this
context, it seems excessive to construct on this basis a theory
which claims, as Jeanroy appeared to do, that the presence of the
Inquisition brought an end to troubadour poetry (or banished it
to Spain and Italy) and, at the same time, that thirteenth-century
troubadours were singing of 'un amour épuré dont la chaste
expression ne pouvait donner l'éveil à la censure la plus soupçon-
neuse' (a pure love whose chaste expression would not give rise
to the slightest suspicious censure).[3] If troubadours really lived in
fear of arousing the censure of the inquisitors, Guilhem would
have been more circumspect about the Dominicans, the spearhead
of the Inquisition:

> ... E meron mal clerc e prezicador,
> quar devedon so qu'az els no·s cove,
> que hom per pretz non do ni fassa be ...
>
> ... Enquer dizon mais de folor
> qu'aurfres a dompnas non s'eschai.
> Pero si dompna piegz no fai,
> ni·n leva erguelh ni ricor,
> per gent tener no pert Dieu ni s'amor.
> Ni ja nulhs hom, s'elh estiers be·s capte,
> per gen tener ab Dieu no·s dezave;
> ni ja per draps negres ni per floc blan
> no conquerran ilh Deu, s'alre no y fan. (I, 5–7 and 28–36)

(The clerks and the [Order of] Preachers have deserved ill because they
forbid that which does not suit them, namely that people should, out of
a sense of honour, bestow gifts or offer help.

They say things which are even more foolish, maintaining that it is not
fitting that ladies should wear cloth of gold. But if a lady does nothing
worse and does not make it a matter of pride or vanity, she will not risk
losing God or his love because of her elegant dress. Indeed, no-one is
estranged from God because they dress well, provided that they behave
well in other respects; and no-one ever won God's love just by wearing
black clothes or a white habit and doing nothing else.)

Such songs by Guilhem and his contemporaries reflect an
awareness of the inquisitors and of the more repressive attitude
to courtly society which they sought to impose, but such awareness
does not suggest tame submission, much less acceptance of defeat.
In the same song, dating from 1233 or 1234, soon after Gregory

IX had entrusted the Inquisition to the Dominicans, Guilhem is explicitly, perhaps even prudently, orthodox in his views:

> Quar Dieus vol pretz e vol lauzor,
> e Dieus fo vers hom, qu'ieu o sai ... (I, 10–11)

(For God demands worth and praise, and God was truly man, I know this ...)

He makes clear that he does not share the Cathar doubts about the Incarnation. But, in a song which begins by deploring the loss of *valor* in the world, such orthodoxy does not stop him criticising the inquisitors and perhaps implying that an element of personal vindictiveness or lust for power might enter into their judgements:[4]

> Ar se son fait enqueredor
> e jutjon aissi com lur plai. (I, 19–20)

(Now they have turned themselves into inquisitors and they judge just as it suits them.)

Montanhagol was writing from about the end of the Albigensian Crusade to about 1268. He spent time at the court of Raimon VII in Toulouse, and whilst he also went to the court of Jaime I of Aragon and perhaps to that of Alfonso X of Castille, this was by no means a question of exile. He was successful in finding patronage both in France and beyond the Pyrenees. His songs demonstrate a lively and partisan interest in political events: in one he cheers on the uprising against the French of 1240–2, in another laments the marriage of Beatrix of Provence with Charles d'Anjou, the event which signalled the final establishment of French hegemony in the Midi. The case of Guilhem demonstrates that a view of troubadours as muzzled or cowed by the crusade or the inquisitors cannot be sustained.

Direct reference to the Albigensian Crusade in surviving songs is not abundant, but there is a noticeable increase in the number of political *sirventes*, and in what Eliza Miruna Ghil has called 'ce *trobar* dans le combat', alongside the epic account of the crusade, known as *La Canso de la Crotzada*.[5]

One of the earliest reflections of the expedition of 1209 is the *planh* by Guilhem Augier Novella for Raimon Rogier Trencavel, Viscount of Béziers and Carcassonne. The crusade, declared by Innocent III and led by the papal legate, Arnaud Amaury, had already taken Béziers and, soon after the crusaders under Simon de Montfort had successfully laid siege to Carcassonne, Trencavel died in prison. Guilhem de Tudela, author of the first part of the *Canso de la Crotzada*, appears anxious, even before reaching the point in his narrative where he recounts this death, to counter rumours which claimed that Trencavel had been poisoned on de Montfort's orders:[6]

But the viscount was later to die of dysentery. The wicked scoundrels and other wretches, who know nothing about what happened and what did not, claim that he was treacherously murdered at night: by Jesus Christ on his throne, the count would not for anything in the world consent to anyone killing him.

To make doubly sure, Tudela later gives a more circumstantial account of Trencavel's death and of the solemn funeral which de Montfort gave him. But rumours there certainly had been, as the *planh* makes clear:[7]

> Mort l'an, et anc tan gran otratge
> no vi hom ni tan gran error
> fach mai ni tan gran estranhatge
> de Dieu et a Nostre Senhor,
> cum an fag li can renegat
> del fals linhatge de Pilat
> que l'an mort; e pus Dieus mort pres
> per nos a salvar, semblans es
> de lui qu'es passatz al sieu pon
> per los sieus estorser, l'aon. (III, 11–20)

(They have killed him; and never was seen such an outrage, nor such a sin, nor such a departure from [the will of] God or Our Lord as that committed by the renegade dogs, those men of Pilate's lineage, who killed him; and since God accepted death to save us, may He be merciful to him who likewise has passed away to save his people.)

What is most striking about this stanza is the explicit identification of Trencavel with Christ as redeemer. The consequence of such an identification is that, if the Saracens in the Holy Land are seen as usurping God's territory and if Trencavel is to be identified with Christ, then the northern barons are the usurping infidels. This is further signalled in the epithets 'can renegat' and 'del fals linhatge de Pilat', traditional terms of abuse for the Saracens.[8] At the same time, in stanzas strongly reminiscent of Bertran de Born's *planh* for Henry the Young King, Guilhem presents a secular litany, an image of Trencavel as representative of courtly virtues:

> Ric cavalier, ric de linhatge
> ric per erguelh, ric per valor,
> ric de sen, ric per vassallatge,
> ric per dar e bon servidor,
> ric d'orguelh, ric d'umilitat,
> ric de sen e ric de foudat,
> belhs e bos, complitz de totz bes,
> anc no fo nulhs hom que·us valgues.
> Perdut avem en vos la fon
> don tug veniam jauzion. (41–50)

(Most noble of knights, most noble in lineage, most noble in pride, most noble in worth, most noble in understanding, most noble in bravery, most noble in giving, and a good servant, most noble in pride, most noble in humility, most noble in sense and most noble in folly, handsome and virtuous, filled with all goodness, never was there a man who was your equal. In you we have lost the fountain from which we all came away rejoicing.)

The notion of courtly virtues perishing with the death of an individual is not new, but the metaphor of the fountain, the image of Trencavel as a redeemer and the identification between the viscount and his people combine to make this one of the first and most striking expressions of a culture under threat, an assertion of the values of the troubadour tradition as *parage*, a distinctive feature of southern life, maintained by the nobility.

The *sirventes* 'A tornar m'er' is attributed to two troubadours from Tarascon, Tomier and Palaizi, apparently working in collaboration, and deals with the siege of Beaucaire in 1216. The garrison of northerners were trapped in the citadel by southern barons led by Raimon VII, Count of Toulouse, but de Montfort's reinforcements had been besieging the town since June. On the night of 15 August, de Montfort's troops attempted to take the town but were repulsed. After negotiations the garrison was given safe passage out of Beaucaire, and the Northerners withdrew. The *sirventes* was written very soon afterwards and with close knowledge of events – the poets specify that de Montfort escaped by boat, a point not mentioned by the *Canso*:[9]

S'il vol venir per querre son trabus
no·ill lau qu'el torn a Belcaire jazer
on escampet la veilla de son bus,
si qu'anc puois jorn no fetz mas dechazer:
ar es l'enjanz de lui e dels clerjatz. (I, 9–13)

(If he wants to come in search of his tribute, I wouldn't advise him to come back to spend the night in Beaucaire, from which he escaped yesterday in his boat. So every day since then he has done nothing but suffer failures: now the disappointment is for him and for the clerics.)

Tomier and Palaizi urge the Provençal barons to behave with courage and to reject illusory offers of a truce. As Martin Aurell has pointed out, they do so with a passion which leads one to guess that some of the nobility were suffering from a lack of enthusiasm which the troubadours saw as their duty to combat.[10] Two more *sirventes*, one relating to Avignon's attempt to relieve the siege of Toulouse in 1217 and the other to Louis VIII's attack on Avignon in 1226, show a similar closeness to events and express themes widely encountered in songs of this period. In 'Si co·l flacs', Tomier and Palaizi re-use a *topos* first encountered in Marcabru's '*Pax in nomine Domini*', setting one crusade against another:

Pauc a en Deu d'esperansa
qui·l Sepulcre desenansa,
car clergue e sel de Franssa
preson pauc la desonransa
de Dieu, qu'en penra venjansa.
        C'ab lur raubaria
an tout los camins e·ls portz d'Acre e de Suria. (II, 43–9)

(Anyone who fails to support [the cause of] the Sepulchre can have little hope in God; for the clerics and the French care little about the dishonour inflicted on God, for which He will have his revenge. For in their marauding greed they have seized the roads and the passes which lead to Acre and to Syria.)

They return to this point in the third *sirventes*, accusing the cardinal, Romain de Saint-Ange, of neglecting the *real* crusade and of preferring the easy pickings available in Provence. The legitimacy of the expedition against the southern heretics is questioned in many songs of the period. Nowhere is it more forcefully expressed than in the celebrated *sirventes* against Rome by the Toulousain troubadour Guilhem Figueira.

This lengthy song (160 lines) pulls no punches in its indictment of the clergy's meddling in politics, which Guilhem sees as a threat to civilisation:[11]

> No·m meravilh ges, Roma, si la gens erra,
> que·l segle avetz mes en trebaill et en guerra,
> e pretz e merces mor per vos e sosterra. (12–17)

(It is no wonder to me, Rome, if people fall into error, for you have plunged the whole world into trouble and war, and because of you glory and mercy die and are buried.)

Not only is Rome's support for the Albigensian Crusade responsible for losses in the eastern crusade ('Rome, I would have you know that your vile dealings and your folly caused Damietta to be lost', 29–30), but the expedition cannot be a crusade since it is waged against Christians, and thus no indulgence can be gained by participants:

> Roma, veramen sai eu senes doptansa
> c'ab galiamen de falsa perdonanssa
> liuretz a turmen lo barnatge de Franssa
>   lonh de paradis;
>   e·l bon rei Lois
> Roma, avetz aucis, c'ab falsa predicanssa
>   ·l traissetz de Paris. (36–42)

(Rome, truly I know without a doubt that by means of the lure of a false indulgence you delivered up to torment, far from Paradise, the barons of France: and, Rome, you killed good King Louis because, with your false preaching [of a crusade] you lured him away from Paris.)

The reference to the king is explained by the fact that Louis VIII died at Montpensier in 1226 from a disease contracted in Languedoc, a disease that, it is implied, he would never have contracted had he not responded to Rome's call to take part in this false crusade. Where traditional crusade songs identify the road to heaven with the road to Jerusalem, Guilhem maintains that the road to Avignon or Toulouse leads to hell:

> ... qu'a salvacion, Roma, serratz la porta.
>   Per qu'a mal govern
>   d'estiu e d'invern
> qui sec vostr'estern, car diables l'en porta
>   inz el fuoc d'enfern. (52–6)

(... for, Rome, you close the door to salvation. And so, be it summer or winter, a man follows a bad guide if he follows in your tracks since the devil carries him off into the fire of hell.)

In aiming his *sirventes* at Rome, Guilhem attacks papal support for the expedition, but he also uses the proper noun as a symbol for the clergy in general. Animosity between nobility and clergy had been a feature of twelfth-century courtly literature, already detectable in Guilhem IX's 'Farai un vers, pos mi sonelh' (V), but in the thirteenth century it almost becomes a genre in its own right. The crusade gives a focus to this latent anticlericalism which seems to be an integral part of the thirteenth-century version of *cortesia*, despite the fact that some of the greatest exponents of this theme were themselves clerics.[12]

Indeed, Peire Cardenal, the troubadour who, chronologically and quantitatively, dominates the century, was himself a canon of Le Puy, but also the author of savage attacks on the clergy.[13] In 'Tartarassa ni voutor', a *sirventes* based on the rhyme and metre of Bernart de Ventadorn's 'Era·m cosselhatz', Peire depicts the clerics, with their unfailing nose for a rich patron, as kites or vultures, including 'franses e clerc' with usurers and traitors in a list of those who have overturned the whole world. Lest anyone should think that he is preaching against Christianity itself, Peire concludes this song with a prayer for the redemption of sinners:

> Dieus verais, plens de doussor,
> Senher, sias nos guiren!
> Gardas d'enfernal dolor
> peccadors e de turmen,
> e solves los del peccat
> en que son pres e liat,
> e faitz lur veray perdo,
> ab vera confessio! (LXXIV, 33–40)

(True God, full of sweetness, Lord, be our protector! Keep sinners from the pains and torments of hell, and free them from the sin that imprisons and binds them; grant them true pardon through true confession!)

But such an implicit profession of faith is more than a means of allaying suspicion. Peire is also the author of devotional lyrics. The potential for a fusion of the troubadours' *domna* and the Virgin had always been implicit in the imagery of the *canso*. In the late thirteenth century, however, this is made explicit. Peire combines the pleading stance of the poetic persona with a litany and with a rhetoric of praise that has come full circle back to Biblical models:

> Vera vergena, Maria,
> vera vida, vera fes,
> vera vertatz, vera via,
> vera vertutz, vera res,
> vera maire, ver' amia,
> ver' amors, vera merces:
> per ta vera merce sia
> qu'eret en me tos heres.
> *De patz, si·t plai, dona, traita,*
> *qu'ab to Filh me sia faita.* (XXXVIII, 1–10)

(True Virgin Mary, true life, true faith, true truth, true way, true virtue, true creature, true mother, true friend, true love, true mercy: grant through your true mercy that your heir may give me my inheritance. If it please you, lady, come to an agreement with peace so that peace may be made between me and your Son.)

Ironically, even Guilhem Figuera's *Roma* is metrically modelled on an anonymous song of devotion to the Virgin, 'Flors de paradis'.

Guiraut Riquier is an outstanding exponent of such Marian poetry. In Guiraut's *cansos* we can see clearly the transformation from the address to the *domna*, referred to by means of the *senhal* 'Bel Deport', to the address to the Virgin. There is no difficulty in following this shift chronologically since Guiraut's songs appear in the manuscript with their dates of composition. An early *canso*, written in 1254 in his home town under the patronage of Amalric of Narbonne, differs little in style and content from the norms of the mid to late twelfth century. The poet's stance, the texture and imagery are all familiar:

> Tant m'es plazens le mals d'amor,
> que, si tot say que·m vol aucir,
> no·m vuelh ni m'aus ni·m puesc partir
> de midons ni virar alhor;
> quar tals es, qu'ieu penray honor,
> si fis lieys aman pusc murir,
> o si·m rete, cen tans maior;
> doncx no·m dey tarzar al servir. (I, 1–8)

(I find the pain of love so pleasing that, though I know it intends to kill me, I neither wish nor dare to leave *midons* nor to turn elsewhere; for she is such that I will derive honour simply from dying as her faithful lover or, if she should keep me, a hundred times greater honour; therefore I must not be slow to serve her.)

In a *vers* written in 1273 at the court of Alfonso X of Castille,[14] Guiraut continues to use the conventional vocabulary of the *canso*, but with meanings which are at once new and familiar:[15]

> Humils, forfaitz, repres e penedens
> entristezitz, marritz de revenir
> so qu'ay perdut de mon temps per falhir.
> Vos clam merce, Dona, verges plazens,
> maires de Crist, filh del tot poderos,
> que no gardetz cum suy forfaitz vas vos;
> si·us plai, gardatz l'ops de m'arma marrida. . . .
>
> . . . Mas esper ai que·m siatz vos guirens
> del greu perilh mortal que·m fa marrir,
> de que no puesc per ren ses vos issir:
> tans e tan greus trobi mos fallimens!
> E donc pregatz vostre Filh glorios
> que·m fassa far sos plazers e mos pros,
> qu'aissi·m podetz tornar de mort a vida. (1–6 and 15–21)

(Humble, guilty, standing accused and repentant, disconsolate, saddened as I return am I, because I have wasted my time in sinning. I call to you for mercy, Lady, gracious Virgin, mother of Christ, Son of the Almighty, that you should not consider how I have offended against you but, if it please you, look upon the need of my sorrowing soul. . . .

. . . But I maintain hope that you may be to me a protectress against the grievous deadly peril which causes my distress and from which I cannot escape at all without your aid: so grievous do I find my sins! and so beseech your glorious Son that he should cause me to do what pleases him and what benefits me, for thus can you turn me away from death towards life.)

Words such as *forfaitz*, *falhir*, *marritz*, *merce* are the everyday currency of the troubadour lyric for conveying the notion of some imagined failing committed by the poet–lover, the suffering which the consequent distance from the *domna* imposes and the hope of her indulgence which might save him from death, from the absence of love. Here the context shifts the denotation of these words and images back into the religious and moral range, without totally removing their courtly connotations.

In what was probably his final poem, Guiraut refers to himself as being among the last of the troubadours ('Be·m degra', 16). He is not actually the last poet writing in Occitan in the thirteenth century – the creation in 1323 of the *Consistòri del Gai Saber*, a poetry society resembling the *puys* maintained by northern French towns, demonstrates that poetic activity survived Guiraut – but certainly his work signals a change, so much so that it has been suggested that the term 'troubadour', in the sense of composer-performer, is no longer appropriate.[16] Guiraut's works, collected together in one manuscript, are all preceded by their date of composition. They include lengthy letters addressed to patrons. One of these consists of Guiraut's critical analysis – his *Exposicio* – of a song by Guiraut de Calanso. In what appears to have been a literary game, Guiraut and three other troubadours were supplied by their patron, Henry II of Rodez with the written text of the song 'A lieys qu'eu am'. After five years, Henry set his seal to a *Testimoni* in verse, stating that he despaired of anyone else but Riquier submitting an analysis, and so was awarding him the prize. There is no mention of performance, though it cannot be excluded, but it is evident that, in this period, which also saw the compilation of many of the troubadour *chansonniers*, the written record becomes privileged over performance.

This is further illustrated in the fashion for syntheses and compendia. The monumental *Breviari d'amor* of Matfre Ermengaud de Béziers, written in 1288, includes the 'Perilhos tractat', a synthesis of the ideology of *fin'amor* illustrated with quotations from over sixty troubadours. The *Razos de trobar* and the fourteenth-century *Leys d'amors* propound the rules governing form, genre and content with examples from the works of numerous troubadours. Performance is transformed in another sense through the composition of *vidas*, *razos* and romances which change the lyric 'I', the performing 'I', into a narrative character.

As we have seen, the thirteenth century was not particularly innovative in terms of the traditional subjects of the *canso*, the rhetoric of praise, although the devotional poems of Peire Cardenal, Guiraut Riquier and others changed its focus. In terms of the poetry of blame, however, the *sirventes* acquired an immediacy of impact, a sharpness of focus and a breadth of appeal which far surpassed twelfth-century examples of the genre. In their response to the Albigensian Crusade *sirventes* gave added reality to such traditional poetic topics as nostalgia for a lost golden age or the rivalry between the noble and the clerk, but above all they upheld, with force and passion, Occitania's claim to an independent, humane culture.

NOTES

1 Translated from 'Die Werke des Trobadors Blacatz', ed. Soltau, p. 243.
2 Paden, 'Troubadours', p. 170.
3 Jeanroy, *Poésie lyrique*, II, p. 166.
4 See Chapter 3, where this poem is further discussed.
5 The political voice of the troubadours is extensively discussed in Aurell, *Vielle*, and Ghil, *L'Age de parage*.
6 *Laisse* 37, 15–23, translated from *Chanson de la Croisade*, ed. Gougaud.
7 Quotations are from 'Die Gedichte des Guillem Augier Novella', ed. Müller.
8 Compare Gavaudan (1195) in 'Senhors, per los nostres peccatz' (V, 34–6): 'ab Luy venseretz totz los cas/Cuy Bafometz a escarnitz/e·ls renegatz outrasalhitz' (with his help you will defeat all the dogs whom Mahomet has led astray and the impudent renegades).
9 Quotations from 'Tomier et Palaizi', ed. Frank (see Palaizi, p. 307 below).
10 Aurell, *Vielle*, p. 47.
11 Quotations from Riquer, *Los trovadores*, III, pp. 1272–9.
12 The invading army is routinely referred to as 'clerc e Frances'.
13 See Chapter 3.
14 Himself the author of the *Cantigas de santa Maria*.
15 Quotations from Oroz, *Lirica religiosa*, p. 230.
16 Zufferey, *Bibliographie*, pp. xiii–xiv.

CHAPTER 7

The trobairitz

Tilde Sankovitch

While few medieval cultural phenomena have been discussed
more assiduously and persistently than that of *fin'amor*, which
made its appearance in the poetry of the troubadours, the contributions of the women troubadours, or *trobairitz*, were long neglected. Although the poetry of the *trobairitz* has been available in
print, at least in part, since the late nineteenth century, there
were few critical studies until a renewed interest was spurred by
a growing concern with all aspects of female culture in the Middle
Ages. In 1976 Meg Bogin published her edition of *trobairitz* poems,
and since then there have been several new editions, as well as
a substantial number of critical appraisals and analyses of what
constitutes a small but provocative body of poems.[1]

In troubadour poetry woman, as *domna*, is omni-present, but the
function she fulfils is a passive and silent one, since she figures
mainly as the necessary object of the poet–lover's desire. *Fin'amor*,
to use Julia Kristeva's words, 'holds only nothingness in store for
the other, particularly the other sex . . . The one who constitutes
himself through it creates himself in and for himself.'[2] The *domna*
is relegated to being the poet's 'mirror', and in fact is called
exactly that in a number of poems. The 'nothingness', the empty
space, the 'mirror' of woman, of the mute 'other' sex, is filled by
the troubadour with the discourse, the definition and description,
of himself. In this poetic situation and expression enters the
woman aspiring to language, the *trobairitz*, and the question to ask
is: how does she manage to effect that entrance? How does she
obtain access to expression and fashion her own discourse? In
order to answer this question – how do the *trobairitz* compose
poetry? – we must first ask exactly what they composed.

The outlines of the *trobairitz* corpus remain indeterminate. A
substantial number of texts are anonymous, yet bear linguistic

indications that women may have composed them; and, to add to
the divergence of opinions concerning the constitution of the
corpus, certain critics believe all anonymous as well as certain
named *trobairitz* may be fictitious.[3] Different editions offer various
numbers of texts, ranging from a scant twenty-three (Schultz-
Gora) or a hardly more generous twenty-five (Bec), through thirty-
six (Bruckner *et al.*), to forty-six (Rieger). I tend to agree with
Geneviève Brunel-Lobrichon, who proposes to 'grant that the
cansos and *tensos* attributed to the *trobairitz* were written by women',
and with François Zufferey who emphasises 'the arbitrariness of
discrimination founded on anonymity'.[4]

For those *trobairitz* whose names we have, there is little biographical information. *Vidas* exist for only five women, while
others are mentioned in *vidas* or *razos* pertaining to troubadours.
In any case, the information contained in these metatexts is only
occasionally reliable. What we do know is that the *trobairitz* write
mainly in two genres: the *canso* and the debate poem. In the first
genre, we encounter two *trobairitz* – the Comtessa de Dia and Castelloza – who have left us four *cansos* each, and we also have single
cansos by Azalais de Porcairagues, Bieiris de Romans, Clara d'An-
duza, and Tibors de Sarenom: a total of twelve poems. For the
debate poem we have twenty-four texts. Of these, two are dialogues between named women (Alaisina Yselda and Carenza;
Almuc de Castelnou and Iseut de Capion), and one is a conversation between two anonymous women, indicated only as *domna*
and *donzela*. There are also eight dialogues between named male
troubadours and named women (Alamanda, the Comtessa de Pro-
ensa, Guillelma de Rosers, Lombarda, Maria de Ventadorn, Ysab-
ela, Felipa and Dompna H); and thirteen dialogues between
named troubadours and anonymous women. In other genres practised by the *trobairitz* we have three *sirventes* (two anonymous, one
by Gormonda de Monpeslier), a *salut* (letter) by Azalais d'Altier,
and an anonymous *planh*. Although there are probably a substantial number of anonymous or misattributed poems that are, in
fact, the work of women, it is evident that the preserved *trobairitz*
poems constitute a small body of work, compared to the troubadour corpus of c. 2,500 poems.

How to explain this disparity? On the one hand it is likely that
not all the texts composed by women survived, and that, in fact,
many of them may never have been recorded at all,[5] but it is also

true that it was difficult for women – as it has been through the ages – to gain access to the self-articulation that was unproblematic for men. Their entrance into the world of Occitanian culture as active practitioners constitutes a remarkable instance of literary activity on the part not of one exceptional woman, but of a group of women who, from c. 1170 to c. 1260 engaged in the dynamic exercise of poetic imagination and expression. The *trobairitz* were among the first women in Western Europe to embrace the world of vernacular literary discourse, of language not limited to the ephemeral, precarious enunciations that constitute the exchanges of daily life, but of a language meant to be heard and preserved beyond the circumscribed sphere of the domestic.

What made it possible for them to do so was the milieu of the twelfth- and thirteenth-century Occitan courts, where, during a 'golden interval' women of the nobility (the class to which the *trobairitz* seem to have belonged) enjoyed certain political, economic and social privileges, and played central roles as organisers, animators and audiences of cultural manifestations.[6] These are still essentially voiceless roles, however, and to make the transition from *taciturnitas* (admirable silence, the most desirable quality of women who tend, according to their detractors, to excessive garrulity) to overt speaking is nothing less than subversive.

What happens when woman, traditionally relegated to the function of confirming man's identity, of being his mirror, his creation, the object that reflects and grounds him, starts to claim her own presence? What happens, to borrow Luce Irigaray's words, when the object starts to speak (*Speculum*, p. 167)? Or in Susan Gubar's terms, 'what if woman decided to create rather than be created?' ('The Blank Page', p. 81)? When the *domna* turns *trobairitz* this is exactly what occurs: woman changes from object to subject of enunciation. Do we then witness a volte-face, an exact reversal of the roles and procedures found in troubadour poetry? Scholars examining the *trobairitz* – an exhilarating enterprise – agree that more than a simple reversal takes place, that 'differences' exist between the male and the female poets, but they are not always capable of pinpointing these divergences precisely. What these multiplying studies suggest, however, is interesting and rewarding. To give a few examples: Marianne Shapiro, analysing significant instances of what she calls 'unconventionality' in the works of the *trobairitz*, remarks that 'in none of the women's poems . . . does the masculine beloved appear to incarnate or substitute, as she [i.e. the *domna*] had, for a total scheme of ideals' ('Provençal Trobairitz', p. 564); Joan Ferrante suggests that there may be a specifically female rhetoric in the poetry of the *trobairitz* ('Notes'); Pierre Bec sees the women authors as favouring what he calls 'psycho-poetic' values (fidelity, trust, emotivity) over 'socio-poetic' ones (moderation, generosity, reputation) (*Chants*, p. 34), and finds the *assag* or love test,[7] rarely mentioned in the works of the troubadours, a frequent *topos* in *trobairitz* poetry.

These indications of difference are valuable, and they point the way to further investigations, but we should of course avoid generalisations, and we may prefer to talk about particularities, about female inscriptions, rather than about 'differences', for that term is still deviant, secondary, other. Each *trobairitz* finds her own voice, or rather, her multiple voices, her own ways of dealing with the sphere of courtly literature, a sphere revolving around man-made notions and rhetorical codes, and she is also situated clearly in a female rather than in a male poetic orbit, tracing a female rather than a male trajectory into and through the unfamiliar, and potentially dangerous, domain of poetic composition. If the *trobairitz* wants to explore that domain, and come out, not only alive but with the trophy of artistic self-expression, she must chart her path carefully.

In *This Sex Which Is Not One*, Luce Irigaray proposes specifically female itineraries for entering into and traversing male territories, male discourses, itineraries that we could call 'desire-lines', unofficial pathways through established spaces.[8] The itineraries, or strategies, that interest me here are mimicry, and the recovery/preservation of a female 'elsewhere'. For Irigaray mimicry is the assumption of a prescribed feminine role in order to undermine and transform that role or function, and affirm that women 'are not simply reabsorbed in this function. *They also remain elsewhere*' (p. 76). As far as the woman poet is concerned, mimicry may, in a first movement, allow her entrance into the textual sphere, and, if handled deftly, allow her not to be drowned in it, but, in a second movement, it may enable her to escape into her own 'elsewhere', her own feminine poetic pleasure, thanks to what Irigaray calls a 'crossing back' through the imitative mirror/discourse, emerging on the other side as, literally, her own poet: the poet of herself.

That is not to say that the *trobairitz* does not make abundant

use of troubadouresque formal procedures and rhetoric, but rather
that she adapts and thus transforms these courtly conventions
according to her own needs and desires. Elaine Showalter writes
that 'women writing are not *inside* and *outside* of the male tradition;
they are inside two traditions simultaneously' ('Feminist criticism', p. 264), and Irigaray uses the same topographical terms in
a scenario in which the female 'outside' may appear in the dominant, male, 'inside' of the already firmly established traditional
space, thus anamorphosing that space,[9] and creating her own 'elsewhere'. The *trobairitz* does so in subtle and fluid ways that vary
from one author and poem to the next. There is no systematicity
here, as may seem to be the case in male discourse, but rather a
ludic inventiveness that it is not easy to categorise or limit.

Fin'amor is often, rightly, considered a game, as play (see also
Chapter 12). The anthropologist Clifford Geertz talks about 'deep
play' in which 'much more is at stake than material gain: namely
esteem, honor, dignity, respect – in a word: status' (*Interpretation*,
p. 433). The courtly game is certainly that for the troubadour,
and the *trobairitz* plays too, but for her the game may not have the
same goals, although it is 'deep' play as well. For her the ludic is
an escape from the self-satisfied 'seriousness of meaning' (with its
implications of univocal truth) that, according to Irigaray, characterises the masculine imaginary (*This Sex*, p. 163). By exceeding
the limits of that culturally constructed and imposed imaginary,
she seeks to accomplish her ludic goal of discovering a possible
place for the female imaginary, a space where she can undertake
her own language work (see Chapter 13 on the concept of the
imaginary).

To do this is not a simple matter for women authors in a culture
in which woman, especially in her corporeality, is often presented
as evil. For male poets, sexuality is a poetic attribute, and in their
erotic poetry love is a function of sexual and social experience
combined. While there is a persistent male sexual discourse that
runs through the centuries, for women, burdened with sexual
taboos, shame and guilt, the relationship with their sexuality has
almost always, of necessity, been repressed and silenced. It is
therefore remarkable that, as Stephen Nichols notes, '[w]ith as
much candor as originality women explicitly confronted the
hidden dimensions of desire' ('Medieval women writers', p. 78).
Using the vocabulary and the scenarios of the troubadours the

trobairitz penetrates into courtly expression, bringing into it her awareness both of the need to masquerade as feminine (that is, to adopt the role imposed upon her by culture), and of her desire to re-cover her own creative pleasure. She engages, as it were, in an undercover exercise that may allow her to establish 'the erotic connection between who I am and how I speak' (Mairs, 'Carnal acts', p. 10).

Irigaray finds that '[t]here are more and more texts written by women in which another writing is beginning to assert itself even if it is still repressed by the dominant discourse' (*This Sex*, p. 134); in the work of the *trobairitz* signs, traces, of this 'other writing' are already present, and we recognise a sly, pervasive intention of difference, a persistent tone of covert disruptive experimentation. Indeed, an intention and a tone is what we notice when we read the poems of the *trobairitz*, rather than repeated details of similarity or coincidence, and rather than repeated linguistic or thematic traits that would merely imitate the fixity of established discourse.

The only *canso* we have of Azalais de Porcairagues, 'Ar em' (XXVII), has posed a puzzle for editors and readers because of an obvious lack of thematic unity that results in an impression of fragmentation and incoherence. The poem combines, in an apparently haphazard way, a conventional nature opening (in the first stanza: one of only two nature openings in *trobairitz* poetry) with elements of *planh* and of *canso*. I suggest that we see here a female aesthetics at work, an aesthetics not of well-constructed forms, of linear development, and of logical unity, but of fluidity, of multiplicity, of simultaneity; an aesthetics of disruption and impropriety.

The nature opening, while miming the traditional aspects of the 'nature-in-winter' motif, serves here not as a declaration of erotic/poetic aphasia (as the motif often does in troubadour poetry) but as a statement of female aphasia overcome. Winter is a time of sterility and silence, when snow and ice cover the world,

> e·l auçellet estan mut
> c'us de chantar non s'afraingna;
> e son sec li ram pels plais
> que flors ni foilla no·i nais
> ni rossignols non i crida. (2–7)

(and the little birds are mute, for not a single one tries to sing; and the branches are dry in the hedges, for neither flower nor leaf sprouts there, and neither does the nightingale sing there ...)

Paradoxically, the seasonal dormancy in nature of the sort of activity often metaphorised by the troubadours as signifying their poetic creativity – birds singing, plants burgeoning – seems to make it possible for Azalais to compose. Whether the suspension of procreation, or the temporary halt in the courtly mating games (where the troubadours/lovers, twittering like birds, need silent female participation) facilitate her poetic work, she proceeds from her agile mimicry of the nature opening into a similarly adept mimicry of *planh* and *canso* in which two stanzas of the former genre frame three stanzas of the latter. Azalais usurps both genres in a catachrestic way:[10] through the unusual structure of embedded juxtaposition both *planh* and *canso* function improperly in the 'whole' of the poem, and, in fact abolish all notions of wholeness, logical sequence and coherence. By thus destroying poetic propriety she becomes the new, improper, proprietor of language, and, at the same time, she undermines the authoritarian conventions of courtly behaviour and the rules of *fin'amor* by situating them in an overall syntax of incongruity. The grieving lexicon of the *planh* (in stanzas two and six) simultaneously allows her to insert her radical 'otherness' into the text: 'Tant ai lo cor deseubut/per qu'eu soi a toz estraingna' (9–10; 'My heart is so troubled that I am from everyone estranged').

The topic of the *assag*[11] appears twice in this poem. In the fifth (*canso*) stanza it is part of a 'typical' courtly situation (37–40). But in the sixth (*planh*) stanza, the *assag* is mentioned alongside a series of famous architectural monuments in the city of Orange (evoked, probably, because of Raimbaut d'Aurenga, possible object of the *planh*):

> A Dieu coman Belesgar
> e plus la ciutat d'Aurenga
> e Gloriet'e·l caslar
> [...]
> e l'arc on son fag l'assai. (41–3; 46)

(I commend to God [the castle of] Belesgar and also the city of Orange, and the Glorieta and the fortress ... and the arch where the tests are made.)

The last line, rendered here literally, has been considered problematic by translators who interpret it as designating the Roman arch in Orange, either as the monument on which representations of great deeds, resulting presumably from strenuous tests of courage, are carved in commemoration (Bruckner, Bec), or as the official site where testing itself takes place (Rieger). In either case, this seems to refer, not to a private activity, but rather to public deeds of arms. While, in principle, the *assag* is a sexual test imposed by the *domna* on the lover, and, according to Bec, offers a symbolic guarantee of female supremacy and power, and of an authentic femininity (*Chants*, pp. 41–3), Azalais hints, through her repetition of the *assag* theme, that, in fact, the *assag*, erotic or martial, is about male accomplishments rather than female authority, and that, like other courtly inventions, it exploits a hackneyed cultural representation of woman for purposes of male exaltation and power.

It is interesting that Azalais addresses this poem of mimicry and subversion, of 'inside' and 'outside', to a woman ('a la fenida', line 55, maybe Ermengarde of Narbonne). Irigaray remarks that '[t]here may be a speaking-among-women ... that may also be the place where a speaking (as) woman may dare to express itself' (*This Sex*, p.135) and Azalais de Porcairagues may have found it the perfect site for her mimetic play that denounces the law-giving pretensions of male-authored troubadour poetry.

A *canso* by the Comtessa de Dia shows how the *trobairitz* may traverse the mirror of prevailing discourse and come back with articulations of her own pleasure. In 'Estat ai' (XXXVI), she questions essential elements of the courtly code: to the norm of *mezura* (moderation) she opposes a desire for excess; to the norm of secrecy a desire for revelation:

> Estat ai en greu cossirier
> per un cavallier q'ai agut,
> e vuoill sia totz temps saubut
> cum eu l'ai amat a sobrier. (1–4)

(I have been in grave distress because of a knight whom I used to have, and I want it known for all times how I have loved him to excess.)

She opposes sexual frankness to veiled allusions – 'Ben volria mon cavallier/tener un ser en mos bratz nut' (9–10; 'I should like to hold my knight naked in my arms one evening') – and to a standard representation of woman as the holder of moral power she opposes her impatient yearning for sexual power:

Cora·us tenrai en mon poder
e que iagues ab vos un ser,
e qe·us des un bais amoros? (18–20)

(When will I have you in my power, and lie with you one evening, and give you an amorous kiss?)

The husband figure, usually discreetly kept in the shadows among the indistinct mass of *lauzengiers* (false flatterers) and *gelos* (jealous ones), here is clearly named and, in the scenario of her desire, displaced from the marriage bed and replaced by the lover: 'Sapchatz, gran talan n'auria / qe·us tengues en loc del marit' (21–2; 'Know that I would very much wish to have you in the husband's place').

Disregarding societal and discursive strictures, the Comtessa imagines the exterior territory of her desires. She eroticises her own body and formulates her own pleasure in terms of holding and touching rather than through the dominant visual economy, and, rather than portraying the lover as an absent foil, gives him a place next to her in her bed, once the place of her erasure, now the ludic place of pleasure: he would be delighted 'sol q'a lui fezes coseillier' (12; 'if only I would be his pillow').

Turning to another *trobairitz*, Castelloza, we see that she concentrates her intensity on the one overriding shape she wishes love to take: that of suffering. That she indeed intends to express her penchant for the linkage between love and pain, between pleasure and submission, is made clear in each of her *cansos* as she infers that 'she gains satisfaction because of her suffering, and not in spite of it' (Paden *et al.*, 'Poems', p. 166). She repeatedly expresses her wish to follow her own path towards pleasure (see XXX, 55–6 and XXXII, 31–2). She defends herself against those who reproach her for what seems like a perversion of love, for as she says of her erotic leanings, 'tant gen mi conve,/e cel q'o ditz non sap cum s'es de me' (XXIX, 25–6; 'it suits me so well, and the one who says that [i.e. reproaches her] does not know anything about me'). Castelloza's single-mindedness in knowing what 'suits' her is a remarkable instance of feminine self-recovery and deviation from convention. She mimes the suffering and forbearance that are accepted parts of the courtly scenario, and, exaggerating them into abject submission, exceeds the limits of their acceptability. Her excess stains that discourse with the marks of her sexual/discursive difference.

The singularity of the only surviving *canso* by Bieiris de Romans – 'Na Maria' (XXVIII) – lies in the fact that this love poem is addressed to a woman, the Lady Maria of the title, leading to speculations as to whether the *canso* is a lesbian poem. Whether this poem is or is not an articulation of lesbian desire is less important than the ludic strategy that takes place here: a woman poet uses all the terms a troubadour might address to a *domna*, but instead of addressing them to a man, she speaks them to a woman. It is precisely the unsettling derailing of the reversal, the surprising twist imposed on the expected scheme, that brings out the ludic and subversive aspect of the poem. Bieiris is playing, perfectly, at being a man, using all the right words, but knowing very well that her femininity, even if hidden behind her linguistic cross-dressing, erases the 'manliness' of the discourse. Bieiris seems to look into a concave mirror, which, according to Irigaray, 'allows for the relation of woman to "herself" and to her like . . . [and] disturb[s] the staging of representation according to too-exclusively masculine parameters' (*This Sex*, p. 155). From this particular *canso* the masculine is absent.

The poems so far discussed are *cansos*. What about the *tensos* or dialogue genre?[12] If we admit the *tensos* between named troubadours and anonymous *domnas* into the corpus, we have twenty-four texts as opposed to twelve *cansos*; even without these poems, we have eleven texts, or almost the same number as that of the *cansos*. Given that among the c. 2,500 troubadour poems there are only 194 examples of the dialogue genre (Frank, *Répertoire*, p. xvi), the genre is clearly privileged by the *trobairitz*. Why does dialogue seem to offer the woman writer a particularly ready access to the realm of song?

One reason is the situational aspect of the dialogue poem, its structure as courtly conversation. Social interaction, including conversation, is an aspect of the patroness/hostess role in which women were accepted, and they may thus slip unobtrusively from 'ordinary' to 'literary' conversation. In fact, the number of cases of anonymous *trobairitz* conversing poetically with known male authors may be due, at least in part, to that very unobtrusiveness that rendered the women quasi-invisible.

The *tenso* between Alaisina Yselda and Carenza Alais (I) explores the links between sexuality and procreation, and the possibility of breaking the links by situating desire and creativity elsewhere than in married sexuality and in biological reproduction. In this poem, two young sisters, one named, the other anonymous, endowed with all possible talents and gifts (9–11), question the obviously older and wiser lady Carenza about the desirability of marriage with the attendant physical burdens of childbearing and of physical deterioration:

> Na Carenza, penre marit m'agença
> mas far infanz cuit qu'es gran penitença
> que las tetinas pendon aval jos
> e lo ventrilh es rüat e'nojos. (17–20)

(Lady Carenza, taking a husband pleases me, but I think that making babies is heavy penance, for one's breasts start to droop and one's belly stretches and becomes ugly.)

These perceptions are not surprising in young women who may have observed the effects of multiple pregnancies on their mother's body. The enigmatic part of the poem is the advice Carenza gives the two sisters. After having recognised their many outstanding qualities she tells them:

> per qu'ie·us conselh per far bona semença
> penre marit coronat de scïença,
> en cui faretz fruit de filh glorïos.
> Retenguda's pulcel'a cui l'espos. (13–16)

(therefore I advise you, in order to make good seed, to take a husband who is crowned with learning, in whom you will make fruit of glorious progeny. Kept back is a girl by whoever marries her.)

The repeated use of the verb *far* (to make) in these lines emphasises the degree of activity and of responsibility for their own destiny Carenza advises her young questioners to assume. As for the identity of the bridegroom, only indicated as *coronat de scïença*, according to various interpretations he might be Christ, or simply an intelligent, cultured man.[13] If we opt for the identification of the bridegroom with Christ – that is for the interpretation that has Carenza advising her interlocutors to enter into the religous life – we have a confirmation that the most common experience for a high-born woman, namely to bear heirs for her husband, does not allow for artistic or intellectual endeavour and that creativity may better be pursued in a non-married state. If we read the concluding line of the quoted advice quite literally (as I have done in the translation), it reinforces the subversive criticism of the traditional wife-mother role.

This *tenso* is unique in its *mise-en-scène*, which is closer to the counter-culture of women than to the prevailing courtly culture.[14] It does not retain the structure of courtly conversation contained within the boundaries of *fin'amor*. In most dialogue poems with feminine voices these parameters are respected. What we see in this extraordinary *tenso* is a conglomeration of three women resolutely on the margins rather than in the centre of the courtly situation, discussing concerns that pertain to their outsider status and sexuality, and that, in their unconventional (that is 'un-pretty') physical specificity, expose and explode the artificiality of courtliness.

In Lombarda's *tenso* with Bernart Arnaut, 'Lombards volgr'eu eser' (VIII) Bernart, who speaks first, tries to woo Lombarda by using three rather trite ploys: he pretends to submit to her by giving up his name in favour of one – Lombard – supposedly derived from hers, in order to signify that she possesses him, while in fact he simultaneously invades her name and affirms his possession of it by evoking Lombardy among the properties over which he rules; next, he compares her favourably with two other ladies: 'Alamanda no·m plaz tan ni Giscarda' (2; 'Alamanda does not please me as much, nor Giscarda'), thus revealing himself as a judicious comparison shopper rather than as a passionate lover; and he calls her 'Mirail-de-Prez' (17; 'Mirror of Merit'), since 'ab sos oiltz plaisenz tan jen me garda' (3; 'with her pretty eyes she looks at me so pleasingly'), so that he feels justified in calling her his mirror, the mirror in which his merit and his self-satisfaction are reflected. But in Lombarda's *coblas*, the mirror speaks, as Irigaray had suggested it might (*Speculum*, pp. 167–8), and Lombarda wittily subverts each of Bernart's amorous strategies by taking them literally. She thus demonstrates their ridiculous artificiality, and indulges fully in ludic language: as Irigaray puts is, 'to escape from a pure and simple reversal of the masculine position means in any case not to forget to laugh' (*This Sex*, p. 163). If he adopts her name she will do the same, but one name will not do: 'Nom volgr'aver per Bernat Na Bernada/e per N'Arnaut N'Arnauda apellada' (21–2; 'I should like to have for Bernart the name Lady Bernarda and for Sir Arnaut the name Lady Arnauda'). She thus becomes two women, upsetting the courtly design of exclusive love. Then, literalising his mention of Alamanda and Giscarda, she confronts him, not with one mirror, but with four – the two ladies and her two selves – and summons him to disclose what is truly ''l mirail on miraz' (28; 'the mirror in which you look'). She thus transports him into a house of mirrors, the antithesis, in its glimmering confusion, of the one faithful, unchanging, mirror. Next she turns the mirror – in which Bernart is not reflected – into an instrument of self-examination, allowing her access to her 'self-affection' reflected in and recorded by her proper name: Lombarda.[15] Bernart is reduced to a dwindling, mute, ghost-like figure:

> mas del cor pes
> on l'aves mes
> qe sa maiso ni borda
> no vei qe lui taises. (33–6)

(but I wonder about your heart, where you have put it, for its house or hut I do not see since you keep it silent.)

In this exchange we do not see a simple reversal of roles between male and female poets: rather we see Lombarda traversing the mirror playfully, mimetically, making fun of hoary courtly *topoi*, and, retraversing it, emerging into an 'elsewhere' of her own design. Her strategies in this poem are therefore typical of those used elsewhere by *trobairitz* to enter into poetry by miming the prevailing discourse, often in a questioning and disruptive mode that disturbs it profoundly. These remarkable women give visibility to the subtle but forceful signs of their 'outside' as it emerges in the 'inside' of the courtly system.

NOTES

1 All citations are from *Trobairitz*, ed. Rieger [Appendix 1, item 7]; for other editions (Bec, Bogin, Bruckner *et al.*) see the entry 'Trobairitz' in the bibliography. Important recent studies of the *trobairitz* include the essays in Paden, ed., *Voice*, Bruckner, 'Fictions' and Gravdal, 'Metaphor'.

2 Kristeva, *Tales*, p. 113.

3 See, for example, Chambers, '*Las trobairitz soiseubudas*', p. 48.

4 Brunel-Lobrichon, 'Images', p. 219; Zufferey, 'Toward a delimitation', p. 35.

5 Rieger (*Trobairitz*) names and discusses a substantial number of *trobairitz* who are mentioned in a variety of documents, but of whom no texts have survived (pp. 93–153) .

6 Paden, ed., *Voice*, p. 11.

7 The *assag* or *assais*, mentioned by several *trobairitz*, was a test imposed by the *domna* on her lover. It has been speculated that it was a sexual test, in which the lover had to remain chaste in a situation of physical intimacy. See Nelli, *Erotique*, pp. 199–209 and Bec, *Chants* [*see under Trobairitz*, p. 308 below], pp. 40–3.

8 The expression 'desire lines' is used in architectural contexts to denote the unplanned pathways marked by walkers who ignore the established, 'official' paths. See Muschamp, 'Student center', p. B4.

9 The term 'anamorphosis' designates a distorted image which is unrecognisable unless viewed from the proper angle. For literary applications, see Lacan, *Ethics*, pp. 139–54 and Žižek, *Looking Awry*, pp. 90–1; see also Chapter 13. I use the term here to indicate that the 'outside' of the female author may be recognised within the 'inside' of a given, seemingly conventional, textual space, when that text is read from the correct 'angle', thus undoing the original cultural distortion.

10 The site of catachresis (the improper use of a word or figure, here extended to the improper use of genre conventions) seems to be, according to Irigaray, the place *par excellence* where the feminine may appear. See also Butler, *Bodies*, pp. 37–8.

11 See note 7.

12 I refer to all poems that are structured as dialogues as *tensos*.

13 See Bogin, *Women Troubadours* [*see under Trobairitz*, p. 308 below], p. 145; Dronke, *Women Writers*, p. 102; Nelli, *Ecrivains*, p. 255; compare Bec, *Burlesque*, p. 202.

14 By the counter-culture of women I mean a culture directed and conducted by women, and centred primarily around the preoccupations, interests, activities and interactions of women.

15 According to Irigaray, women are 'so irremediably cut off from their "self-affection" that from the outset ... they are exiled from themselves, and lacking any possible continuity/contiguity with their first desires/pleasures, they are imported into another economy, where they are completely unable to find themselves' (*This Sex*, p. 133).

CHAPTER 8

Italian and Catalan troubadours

Miriam Cabré

When court poets in Northern Italy and the Crown of Aragon began to compose in the vernacular, they adopted Occitan as their poetic language and the influence of this seemingly foreign culture would continue even when works start to be composed in Italian and Catalan. In Italy, the troubadour tradition has an obvious impact, from the mid-thirteenth century, in the *scuola siciliana* and later in the *stilnovisti*. In Catalan literature, the troubadours have a direct influence well into the fifteenth century.[1] This complete absorption of troubadour poetry makes Northern Italy and the Crown of Aragon unique among the areas that underwent the influence of Occitan culture. Originally, their geographical proximity to Occitania had made them a convenient extension to the troubadour circuit, ready to welcome such prestigious influence, but in the thirteenth century they became the main focus of late troubadour culture. Both areas had political links with the county of Provence, and were deeply involved in the power struggle that was taking place in Europe. This chapter will examine the factors involved in the adoption of the troubadour tradition in Northern Italy and the Crown of Aragon, and the orientation taken by this tradition in the hands of local troubadours.

The prestige of Occitan poetry is attested to by its role in the shaping of other vernacular traditions, such as the works of French *trouvères*, and German *minnesänger*. Its influence was aided by the mobility of troubadours as well as the wide diffusion of their poetry. Even from an early period troubadours travelled outside the original domains of their poetic tradition. Often the first evidence of contacts with foreign lands is mentions of their rulers as either potential patrons or sympathisers of the same political cause. We have several such early references to the areas that concern this chapter. Marcabru and Peire d'Alvernha both refer to the rulers in Castile and the Crown of Aragon, and seemingly visited Spain. The first ruler of the Crown of Aragon to appear in troubadour poetry was Ramon Berenguer IV (1131–62). During the Third Crusade, in 1190, Peirol mentioned the Marquis Corrado de Monferrato, whose court would be the first Italian centre to receive Occitan troubadours. Within the Italian and Iberian peninsulas, the presence of visiting troubadours is also documented in other kingdoms, where Occitan was not the sole literary language. King Alfonso X of Castile (1252–84) fostered a wide range of cultural initiatives in several languages.[2] As an important political figure, he aroused the interest of many troubadours, and as a patron of the arts, he protected, among others, Guiraut Riquier. However, the king chose Galician-Portuguese, the prevailing poetic language in his court, to compose his *Cantigas de Santa María*. Even the Italian Bonifacio Calvo added two *cantigas* and a multilingual poem to his Occitan corpus during his stay in Alfonso's court. However, despite the predominant role of Galician-Portuguese poetry in the Castilian court, some of its elements can be traced back to the Occitan tradition.[3] In the kingdom of Sicily, meanwhile, Emperor Frederick II promoted poetic activity. This *scuola siciliana*, although strongly marked by Occitan influence, adopted Italian as its poetic language. While no overtly political poetry was composed in Frederick's entourage, the choice of language was in itself a political statement. At the peak of his confrontation with the pope, the emperor was seeking to manipulate his image through the poetic output of his entourage. It was the prestige of troubadour literature, above other vernacular traditions, which made it an obvious model, with the additional advantage of its proven value as a tool of propaganda.[4]

The impact of the Occitan tradition in Northern Italy and the Crown of Aragon went beyond formal or thematic borrowing. Visits from Occitan troubadours were followed by local production. The identity of the first native troubadour in Italy is disputed. The Guelph harangue 'D'un serventes faire', by Peire de la Caravana, has been dated 1194 or 1195, but his Italian birth is uncertain.[5] Thus Rambertino Buvalelli, who held the position of *podestà* in several Italian cities, as well as diplomatic posts on behalf of the city of Bologna, is usually hailed as the first Italian troubadour.[6] It has been suggested that he came into contact with troubadour poetry during his years as a law student at the University of Bologna.[7] Beyond this alleged first contact, Rambertino was closely linked to the Marquis of Este, one of the first Italian magnates to sponsor troubadour poetry. All of Rambertino's poems are love songs dedicated to Beatrice d'Este, the marquis's daughter. However, since the Marquis of Este was the Guelph leader and Rambertino a leading politician, the very act of dedicating his poetry to Beatrice could be read as a political gesture. As the foundation of the *scuola siciliana* exemplifies, politics and poetry were often bedfellows. Troubadour poetry had been ideologically charged since its origins and probably more so after the gradual French domination of the Midi.[8] After the Albigensian Crusade, the male line of the dynasties of Toulouse and Provence died out, and were replaced by two French princes in 1246 and 1249, respectively. The rising of French power irreversibly changed the nature of the courts in the area, and caused a large number of exiles (*faidit*), some of them troubadours, to travel to peripheral areas, such as Italy and Spain. The cultural background of these exiles reinforced the exportation of the troubadour tradition by previous Occitan visitors.

In the thirteenth century, Italy was the focus of international conflicts. Northern Italian cities rallied for or against the emperor's sovereignty over them. Originally the anti-imperial focus was the alliance of cities called the Lombard league, but the pope soon lent them support, and the rivalry polarised between the papacy and the emperors. Thus the Guelph and Ghibelline parties were formed, embodying respectively opposition to the Empire or the Church. At the core of this confrontation, which was particularly intense during the thirteenth century, feudal and urban powers intersected. Feudal lords often became the *podestà* of warring cities, as well as being acknowledged as faction leaders. There were endless factions and shifting alliances.[9] The involvement of poetry with these tensions is exemplified by the earliest poem with an Italian topic, Peire de la Caravana's 'D'un serventes faire', encouraging the Italian cities to fight together against the emperor.[10] The power of poetry to convey these messages effectively and to exacerbate the conflicts is explicitly revealed in a 1252 edict by the *podestà* of San Gimignano: 'quod nulla persona castri et curtis St. Gem. canere debeat aliquas cantiones inter Guelfis et Ghibellinis' (Safiotti, *Giullari*, p. 102; nobody in the castle or court of San Gimignano shall sing any song about

Guelphs and Ghibellines). The tensions in Italian politics were not isolated from the interests of other countries, as France, the pope's traditional ally, exemplifies. At the climax of the tensions between the papacy and Manfred of Sicily (who had succeeded Frederick II), Charles d'Anjou, the new Count of Provence and younger brother of King Louis IX, rose as the pope's champion. As a result, in 1266 Charles took possession of the kingdom of Sicily, offered to him by the pope, after defeating Manfred in battle. As a prominent Guelph figure and an increasingly powerful ruler, Charles polarised the opinions of Guelph and Ghibelline partisans. His exploits, in both Provence and Italy, were the object of commentaries by a large number of troubadours.[11] Some of them were based in the Crown of Aragon, which, as we will see, was also deeply involved in these events. This is especially true of one of its kings, Pere *el Gran* (1275–85), who had dynastic claims to Provence and was married to Manfred's daughter and heiress.[12]

In addition to being a political weapon, poetry lent prestige to patrons and poets alike. This has been put forward as one of the reasons why troubadours were so well received in the most influential courts of Northern Italy: Monferrato, Savoia, Este, Malaspina, and Da Romano (Bologna, 'Letteratura', pp. 102–4). Raimbaut de Vaqueiras and Peire Vidal are among the first troubadours known to have visited Italy, where they enjoyed the hospitality of Bonifacio de Monferrato and dedicated love poems to Bonifacio's daughter Beatrice. In a panegyric to her (XVIII), Raimbaut chose as a structuring metaphor the *carrocio* (*carros* in Occitan), the ox-cart which symbolised the Lombard league. The use of a war metaphor as a device for a collective panegyric of noble ladies was taken up by Aimeric de Peguilhan. His poem, now lost, represented a battle between the daughters of Corrado Malaspina, to which Guilhem de la Tor wrote a sequel: the truce (*treva*) agreed through the mediation of Italian ladies.[13] While echoing the politicised environment, these pieces also reflect the pleasurable side of court poetry. The same could be said of the seemingly insult-hurling debates which, despite their apparent crudeness, often are unlikely to be more than a court game. Aimeric de Peguilhan is the most significant troubadour in the court of Azzo VI d'Este, where he enjoyed a prolonged stay. He wrote there his famous complaints against the *joglaret novell* ('upstart little *joglars*', 'Li fol e·il put' (XXXII), among whom he sarcastically mentioned

Sordello. Both poets had an exchange of *coblas* in a similar tone, 'Anc al temps' (XXX). Aimeric accused Sordello of leading a dissolute life and of cowardice, for he never saw a man receiving such a beautiful blow ('tant bel cop') in the head, which almost killed him. He mockingly praises Sordello's sweet character and his reaction to such attacks:

> mas el a·l cor tan umil e tan franc
> q'el prend en patz totz colps, pois no·i a sanc. (XXX, 7–8)

(he is so meek and generous at heart that he takes peacefully all blows, as long as there is no blood.)

Sordello's retaliation turns Aimeric's self-portrait as a venerable figure of authority into that of boastful wimp:

> Anc persona tan avara
> no crei que homs vis
> cum el veils arlots meschis
> n'Aimeric ab trista cara.
> Sel qe·l ve a pez de mort;
> e se tot a son cors tort
> e magr'e sec e vel e clop e ranc,
> mil aitans dis . . . qe·l no fes anc. (XXX, 9–16)

(Nobody has ever seen such a stingy person as that mean old beggar, the sad-faced Aimeric: seeing him is worse than death. Even though he has a crooked body, scrawny, puny, old, limping and wobbly, he boasts a thousand times of what he has never done.)

This type of slander was a frequent feature of Sordello's early years in Italy, and it continued during his long stay in Provence. There is documentary confirmation of his presence in the retinue of Count Raimon Berenguer IV of Provence and he stayed in the entourage of his successor Charles d'Anjou.[14] However, the Mantuan poet owes a great deal of his fame, as reflected in his colourful *vida* and magnified by Dante's *Commedia*, to his early connection with the Da Romano brothers, Alberico and Ezzelino. At their request, he is said to have abducted their sister Cunizza from her husband Riccardo di San Bonifazio. The event obviously caused a stir at the time, and Sordello was teased about it in a *tenso* with Joanet d'Albusson, 'Digatz me' (XIII). Around 1220 Uc de Sant Circ arrived at the Da Romano court where he would remain for forty years. His account of the Cunizza affair in Sordello's *vida* has been interpreted as his patron's official version of the events

(Meneghetti, 'Uc de Saint Circ', pp. 120–3). It is a specific example of Uc de Sant Circ's role as Alberico's spokesman (Peron, 'Trovatori e politica', pp. 23–30). After Sordello left Italy there are some years unaccounted for, during which he seems to have visited several courts. Peire Bremon Ricas Novas mocks his wandering by referring to his acquaintance with 'every baron from Treviso over to Gap' (*Poetry of Sordello*, ed. Wilhelm, p. xvi). Before he settled into the retinue of the counts of Provence, it seems that Sordello stayed in the court of Barral de Baus and was also protected by Blacatz. When the latter died, Sordello dedicated to him one of his better-known pieces, a *planh* (XXVI) where he substitutes the expected pattern of lament with a satire against contemporary rulers, structured around the folk motif of the eaten heart. Sordello proposes, as the only solution to the irreversible moral decline among the ruling classes after Blacatz's death, that his heart be taken out and distributed among them. A list of magnates who would benefit from Blacatz's *cor* follows. Sordello thus inaugurates a genre highly codified both in structure and content, a hybrid of the *planh* and the *sirventes*, which Peire Bremon Ricas Novas and Bertran de Lamanon swiftly imitated.[15] This poem probably prompted Dante's image of Sordello as a concerned patriot in Purgatorio (VI–IX) and he is generally considered the most interesting figure among Italian-born troubadours. However, because of the geographical distribution of his career, other non-Italian troubadours better typify troubadour activity in Italy. This would be the case of Aimeric de Peguilhan, whose occasional pieces and poetic exchanges at the court of Este mirror the environment and fashion in Italian courts. Equally, during his stay at the court of the Da Romano Uc de Sant Circ became a major representative of the non-lyric, more academic, activity that characterises late troubadour culture, thanks to his corpus of *vidas* and *razos* (see also Chapter 15).[16]

The adoption of this originally courtly poetry by urban poets has been judged as an Italian contribution to the development of troubadour poetry: the introduction of 'new social and cultural groups ... in particular, lawyers and administrators' (Bologna, 'Letteratura', p. 131), a tendency that would recur in the *scuola siciliana* and among the *stilnovisti*. The acceptance of this 'courtly civilisation' by the 'urban civilisation' (Roncaglia, 'Corti', 107–8) occurred within the intricate web of alliances and rivalries which entangled cities and courts. Urban poets, as was indeed the case with Rambertino Buvalelli, could have contacts and common (or antagonistic) interests with the courts from which troubadour poetry emanated. The main urban circle of troubadour activity was Genoa, whose patriciate produced numerous poets, among whom the judge Lanfranc Cigala stands out. From his known political career, it is significant that he was the Genoese ambassador to Provence in 1241. Despite his influential position and political interests, his corpus contains only a few Guelph topical pieces. Like Rambertino Buvalelli, Lanfranc wrote mainly love songs, which have earned him probably the highest artistic valuation of all the Italian troubadours among modern scholars. The intellectualising tendency of his love poetry has been suggested as a forerunner for the approach later taken up by the *stilnovisti* (Ugolini, *Poesia provenzale*, xxxix–xlvi).

The development of troubadour poetry in the Crown of Aragon confirms the importance of both social prestige and politics as factors in the adoption of this poetic tradition.[17] It was certainly present in aristocratic courts, but from the beginning the main nucleus of production was the royal entourage. The factors outlined to account for Italian troubadour activity are applicable here: its use as court entertainment, vehicle of propaganda and ideology, and a prestigious social exercise. However, the weight of the royal patron marks an important difference in the Catalan troubadour milieu. It was by royal initiative that Occitan poetry was first imported into Catalan lands during the reign of King Alfons (1162–96).[18] Among his domains, Provence was at the centre of a dispute with the counts of Toulouse and the French Crown. He decided actively to sponsor troubadour poetry, as befitted his title as a great Occitan lord, and to import it into his lands south of the Pyrenees (M. de Riquer, 'Littérature'). At one stroke, he managed to please his Provençal subjects and also to create a cultural link across his lands. King Alfons further encouraged troubadour production by composing poetry in Occitan himself, thus initiating a tradition of poetic creation and promotion among members of his royal family (Cluzel, 'Princes'). His extant works are a *canso* and a *tenso* with Giraut de Bornelh, 'Be·m plairia' (LVIII, ed. Sharman) about the worth of a rich man's love. The 'maestre dels trobadors' had a relevant role in the development of Catalan troubadour poetry, as attested by the works of the most influential Catalan troubadour, Cerverí de Girona. Giraut's works (together with those of Cerverí) account for a substantial part of the anthology collected in MS *Sg*, which was intended as a model corpus and attests to a Catalan line of transmission.[19]

King Alfons was among the targets of one of the best-known Catalan troubadours, Guillem de Berguedà (d. 1196).[20] Although the troubadour appears sometimes in the king's entourage, more often he was a keen participant in the fights among the nobility. In this pursuit, he used troubadour poetry and its established channels of diffusion as a political weapon (see also Chapter 3). The relatively mild 'Cantarey' (V) shows his advantageous combination of character assassination (the Viscount of Cardona and the Bishop of Urgell are portrayed as treacherous and beggar-like), with a light popularising tone and a well-known tune. This contrast accentuates Guillem's sarcasm and facilitates the circulation of the song. Since all of the events mentioned in his poetry (except what is obviously plain abuse) are documented, it seems licit in this particular case to interpret his satire biographically, as a very sharp tool, the use of which went beyond mere courtly entertainment. Like his friend Bertran de Born, who referred to him as 'Fraire', Guillem's most famous facet is this vitriolic attack on his many enemies, but he also has a considerable corpus of love lyrics. Among them, 'Qan vei' (XXVI) was widely disseminated (fourteen MSS) and imitated. The poetic fame of another notable Catalan troubadour, Guillem de Cabestany, also owes much to a single particularly well-transmitted *canso*, 'Lo doutz cossire', which is extant in more than twenty MSS (Cots, 'Poesías', pp. 278–90). However the notoriety emanating from Guillem de Cabestany's *vida*, which links him with the legend of the eaten heart, far exceeds his literary fame (Riquer, *Los trovadores*, II, 1065–6; see also Chapter 16).

The success of King Alfons's manoeuvre is patent in the view held by later troubadours of Catalonia and Occitania as a single entity (Aurell, *Vielle*, pp. 55–8). His immediate successors kept the tradition of troubadour patronage alive, but it was his great-grandson, Pere *el Gran*, who fully exploited the latent possibilities of troubadour poetry. King Pere used literary activity to project a public image of himself as the ideal prince, and to justify some controversial policies. Troubadour poetry was also an offensive weapon against his rival in his two main international targets, Sicily and Provence, namely Charles d'Anjou. Even before Pere *el Gran* became king, his court was a leading centre of anti-Angevin propaganda and he had already began to stand out as a Ghibelline supporter.[21] He systematically sheltered *faidits* from Provence, among them the troubadour Paulet de Marselha. Clear examples of anti-Angevin poetry written in Prince Pere's entourage are Cerverí's 'Sirventes' (XXXVI) and Paulet de Marselha's 'Ab marrimen et ab mala sabensa' (VIII: I. de Riquer, 'Poesías', pp. 187–92). The king himself composed an extant *cobla* against the French in the wake of their papally sanctioned invasion of King Pere's lands (M. de Riquer, 'Trovador valenciano'). However, his interest in troubadour literature was not only political. According to his protégé, Cerverí, he also composed some lighter pieces and was a fine judge of poetry. Cerverí had a clear function as the main pawn of his patron's propaganda policy, but his role goes far beyond that of a partisan poet.[22] It amounts to a new position in the Catalan royal court, characterised by the unusual length and closeness of the relationship between troubadour and patron. The most remarkable effect of the self-awareness resulting from Cerverí's position is his creation of a literary character identified with the first person. Through this character, Cerverí embodies his opinions about the function of poet and poetry in the context of the court. His style is characterised by wit and craft, which manifest themselves in word-play, elaborate and unusual structures, and sophisticated metrical schemes, together with a taste for experimenting with genres and adding new materials to the framework of the troubadour tradition. In addition to political pieces, Cerverí's vast corpus contains formally elaborate love songs, moralising *vers*, popularising dance songs, narrative poems and sophisticated panegyrics. His works came to be greatly influential in later Catalan literature, acting as a bridge between the troubadour tradition and later local developments.

The common traits between Italian and Catalan troubadour culture largely derive from the fact that these regions are the main centres of late troubadour activity. Broad trends such as the spread of lay literacy, the rise of written production in the vernacular, and the growth of courts and their administrative staff resulted, in both Catalan and Italian courts, in a series of

paraliterary troubadour activities. In parallel to the contemporary
academic developments, the late troubadour world witnessed the
compilation of song-books and *florilegia*, the production of Occitan
treatises, and the creation of *vidas* and *razos*.

The works of Sordello and Cerverí exemplify this poetic production. The situation in the courts where they lived, as reflected
in their works, has points of contact.[23] Both were in the entourage
of a powerful lord, in the midst of the professional intellectual
class that supplied the court with its administrative staff, which
was rapidly growing and diversifying. There is documentary evidence of the progress of Cerverí and Sordello in this milieu, to
judge by their increasing financial rewards.[24] Analysis of chancery
documents, together with these troubadours' works, gives us a picture of the development of contemporary courts, where new
elements, new functions and new tensions were arising. One of
the fields where friction between court professionals is manifest
is in the confusion between troubadours and ill-reputed *joglars*.[25]
Despite the evidence of his progress in the royal entourage, chancery documents refer to Cerverí as *ioculator* up to the end of his
career. Sordello was still being teased by fellow troubadours, at a
stage when court documents refer to him as *miles* (knight) or *do-
minus* (lord). Sordello's *tensos* and *partimens*, his most distinctive
pieces, respond to the thirteenth-century taste for *jocs* and love
casuistry. Within this context of poetic competition, playful or in
earnest, he is accused of being a *joglar*. For instance in the *tenso*
'Digatz me' (XIII), Joanet d'Albusson and Sordello refer to each
other in demeaning terms and allude to their *joglaria*. In the dialectic used to deny the charges, Sordello and his rival knowingly
confirm them. However, in his *sirventes* against Peire Bremon Ricas
Novas, 'Lo reproviers', Sordello refutes energetically his condition
of *joglar*:

> Ben a gran tort car m'apella joglar,
> c'ab autre vau et autre ven ab me,
> e don ses penre, et el pren ses donar,
> q'en son cors met tot qant pren per merce.
> Mas eu non pren ren don anta m'eschaia,
> anz met ma renda e non vuoill guizerdon
> mas sol d'amor; per qe·m par q'el dechaia
> et eu poje, qui nos jutga a razon. (XXIV, 17–24)

(He is very wrong to call me a *joglar*, because he follows others while others follow me, and I give without taking while he takes without giving, for he wears what he is mercifully given; instead, I do not take anything that would shame me, but, on the contrary, I spend my income and do not expect other reward than love; for all this, it seems to me that he lowers himself, and I am elevated, when rightly judged.)

Cerverí also alludes to unworthy envious people who accuse him of being a *joglar*, for instance in his 'Maldit bendit' (CXV), and he relentlessly protests that his status is that of a troubadour: 'ne suy juglars ne·n fau captenimen' (I am not a *joglar* nor do I behave like one), he affirms in 'Lo vers del saig' (LXXXIII, 32). However, unlike Sordello, Cerverí does not deny that he derives economic benefits from his poetry, but reacts by sublimating his condition as a dependant into the figure of the wise adviser of his patron:

> Eu soy sirvens e serviray breumens
> d'un sirventes al bo rey d'Arago. (XXXV, 9–10)

(I am a servant and will presently serve the good king of Aragon with a *sirventes*.)

He complements this validation of his role with theoretical arguments about the high value of poetry, as means of moral advice and social improvement.

Both Sordello and Cerverí recycle the subject-matter of moral literature and apply it to the immediate context of the court. Sordello's two moral *sirventes* deal with topics such as *mezura*, the relative value of poverty and wealth, and the responsibility of rulers to set a model of behaviour. In the vernacular, these are new, fashionable themes, which respond to the demands of a new audience (Segre, 'Forme'). Sordello himself wrote a treatise, in verse, the *Ensenhamens d'onor*, which gives instruction on correct behaviour, containing both general moral advice and love etiquette. In Cerverí's works, moral literature topics are pervasive and in using them he reinforces his image as a self-styled adviser to his patron. With a similar effect, Cerverí re-uses new-fashioned and learned materials, in tune with contemporary scholastic practices. He adapted the three basic school texts, proverbs, fables and psalms, as well as allegorical romance. His poems often borrowed structuring or didactic devices from sermons and scholastic treatises. From administrative and judicial practice, he took epistles, declarations of war and libels as poetic models. In fact he transmuted almost anything in his environment into poetic matter or devices. His use of scholarly methods and subjects fits with the image of *savi*, which underpins Cerverí's defence of his position as a poet. This is the characterisation that Cerverí evokes when portraying himself in an *exemplum* of the wrong values prevalent in the court, where only wealth and not wisdom are heeded:

> [D]itz de paubre no poria
>   gran mal far,
> car hom no·l cre per gran vertat que dia,
> que s'eu totz sen de Salamo dezia,
> e·l reys c'a vist un cabirol volar,
> tuit dirion – per que·ls ditz deu temer? –
> qu'eu mentria e·l reys diria ver. (LXXX, 15–21)

(A poor man's words cannot be very harmful, since nobody believes him, however great the truth he tells; since, if I told the whole of Solomon's wisdom, while the king said that he had seen a roe deer flying, everybody would say – why should he be afraid of (my) words? – that I had lied and the king had told the truth.)

Cerverí's vast corpus (119 items) acts as a window onto the cultural trends of the thirteenth century. Both he and Sordello illustrate the involvement of late troubadour poetry with new elements from their evolving cultural environment. This resulted in a renewed troubadour tradition, and coloured its eventual transformation into new schools. Cerverí's perception of his image and of his corpus as a whole is also in tune with the new self-awareness of late medieval poets. Cerverí did for himself what Dante did for Sordello: he created a literary character based on his own lyrics which enhanced his literary reception.

NOTES

1 For instance, on Italy see Sapegno (*Compendio*, pp. 31–2). A much fuller treatment is given in Bologna's contribution to the multivolume *Letteratura Italiana*. For the history of Catalan literature, see M. de Riquer, 'Trobadors catalans', pp. 12–14. I am grateful to Stefano Asperti for his indications and bibliographical information. I would also like to thank Ann Giletti for her help.

2 For the patronage in Alfonso X's court, see Burns, ed., *Emperor of Culture*, and Ballesteros Beretta, *Alfonso X*.

3 See D'Heur, *Troubadours d'oc*.

4 Antonelli ('Politica', pp. 58–92) discusses fully Frederick II's active promotion of the *scuola siciliana*.

5 For troubadour activity in Italy, see Ugolini, *Poesia provenzale*; Bertoni,

'Poesia provenzale'; De Bartholomaeis, *Poesie provenzali*; Bologna, 'Letteratura'; Roncaglia, 'Corti', pp. 105–22; Folena, 'Tradizione' (see pp. 23–8 for 'D'un serventes faire').

6 The *podestà* was a magistrate who was appointed by the citizens for a set period of time to rule the city, as an alien power above the quarrelling factions.

7 Rambertino Buvalelli has also been linked with the onset of troubadour poetry in Genoa, where he was the *podestà* for three years. See Viscardi, 'Trovatori italiani', pp. 986–7. For a modern edition of his poems, see Rambertino Buvalelli, *Poesie*, ed. Melli.

8 For Guilhem IX and his choice of language, interpreted as a stand against clerical Latin, see Antonelli, 'Politica', pp. 12–27.

9 For an English summary, see Salvatorelli, *Concise History*. For a more detailed discussion, see Tabacco, 'Storia politica e sociale'.

10 Peron, 'Trovatori e politica'. For Peire de la Caravana's pieces, see Folena, 'Tradizione', pp. 24–8.

11 For a full study of the influence of Charles d'Anjou in troubadour poetry and transmission, see Asperti, *Carlo*.

12 The international projection of Italian politics is lengthily laid out in Runciman, *Sicilian Vespers*.

13 'Pos N'Aimerics a fait mesclança e batalla' (*Le poesie di Guilhem de la Tor*, ed. Blasi, p. 29). For a commentary, see Folena, 'Tradizione', pp. 39–40 and 78–83.

14 Sordello signed as a witness in some transactions and also appears as the beneficiary of donations. Documentary references can be found in the introduction to *Sordello: le Poesie*, ed. Boni, and in *Poetry of Sordello*, ed. Wilhelm [Appendix 1, item 55], pp. xix–xxii.

15 For Sordello's influence, see *Poetry of Sordello*, ed. Wilhelm, pp. xxv–xxix.

16 See Guida, *Primi approcci* and Meneghetti, *Pubblico*, pp. 237–76.

17 See Milà, *De los trovadores*, Alvar, *Poesía trovadoresca*, and especially M. de Riquer, 'Trobadors catalans'.

18 Bisson, *Medieval Crown* offers a general view of the history of the period. For a more detailed account, see Soldevila, *Pere el Gran*.

19 The influence of Giraut de Bornelh on Cerverí is outlined in I. de Riquer, 'Giraut de Bornelh chez les grammariens'. For a more detailed discussion of the Catalan MSS which transmit Giraut's works, see I. de Riquer, 'Giraut de Bornelh en las obras de Ramon Vidal'. For a study of MS *Sg*, see Asperti, *'Flamenca'* .

20 M. de Riquer has studied in detail the historical background in *Guillem de Berguedà*, ed. Riquer, I.

21 Wieruszowski, 'Corte', discusses King Pere's Ghibelline career. For the anti-Angevin propaganda created in the court of Pere *el Gran*, see Aurell, *Vielle*, pp. 168–75, and Cabré, *Cerverí de Girona*.

22 For a study of Cerverí's works, see Cabré, *Cerverí de Girona*.

23 For a general view of troubadour courts, see Paterson, *World*, pp. 90–119 and for the Da Romano court, Meneghetti, *Pubblico*, pp. 245–50.

24 The relevant documents are mentioned in M. de Riquer, '*Verses proverbials*', *Poetry of Sordello*, ed. Wilhelm and *Sordello: le Poesie*, ed. Boni.

25 See Harvey, '*Joglars*', and Cabré, '"Ne suy joglars"', for a more detailed discussion of this complex issue.

CHAPTER 9

Music and versification
Fetz Marcabrus los motz e·l so

Margaret Switten

The new song of the early twelfth century brought a new way of crafting verses and a new music. It flourished in the cloister as in the court, in Latin as in the vernacular.[1] Its salient features were the control of verse length by number of syllables and the linking of verses by end-line rhyme, to which the music corresponded by a tendency towards balanced phrase structures and regular cadence patterns. New systems of sonorous coordinations thus emerged. The most significant vernacular repertory of 'new songs' to be preserved was created by the troubadours. How did the troubadours exploit these new sound systems, verbal and musical? This chapter will propose some responses to that question.

At the outset, I admit that the question is, in many ways, unanswerable. The reason is not complicated: no medieval sounds have come down to us. What we have are written records, and the written records for troubadour song, like many medieval records, are difficult of interpretation. I shall first point out some of the difficulties, then describe textual and musical elements of the song; examine approaches to coordinated analysis and performance; and conclude with a few illustrative examples. Examples are grouped at the end of the chapter (pp. 156–62 below).

MANUSCRIPTS

Only one manuscript from the time of the early troubadours contains songs in Old Occitan: BNF, fonds latin, 1139, from Saint Martial of Limoges, part of which can be dated c. 1100. In the oldest section of this manuscript, among Latin songs called *versus*, are three religious songs in Occitan, or Occitan and Latin, all with music. In contrast, the first *chansonniers* containing troubadour songs date from the mid thirteenth century – from a time when troubadour song in its classic formulations was drawing to a close. This poses a paradox, frequently noted: the gap between the creation of troubadour songs and their preservation in writing. We do not know how the songs crossed this gap.

As compared to *trouvère* manuscripts, troubadour *chansonniers* preserve relatively few melodies. While most *trouvère* manuscripts contain melodies, only two troubadour manuscripts (*G* and *R*) have music, and then not systematically throughout. Fortunately, two *trouvère* codices (*W* and *X*) have troubadour sections, thus giving us four main sources for troubadour music. About 10 per cent of troubadour poems survive with melodies, roughly about 250 melodies for some 2,500 texts. As may be seen from Appendix 1, some melodies for many important troubadours have been preserved, but for others we have no melodies at all.

These features intensify the usual problems of manuscript variability and attribution (see Chapter 14). Medieval manuscripts do not give us a single, authoritative 'song'. What we call one song was probably many songs as 'it' moved from performance to performance, eventually to be embedded in manuscripts. Manuscripts surely reflect the activity, at different stages, of composers, performers and scribes. Different manuscript versions raise the issue of how to determine the composition of a given song. They also raise the issue of how to determine the 'creator' of the song. Examination of words and music together seems to assume that one person composed both. We readily make this assumption: the (often problematic) author attributions in manuscripts are routinely applied to both text and melody. The numerous passages where an 'author' lays claim to composition of both text and melody justify this assumption as a working principle – provided we remember, however, that it is not proved or even provable that text attributions always apply to the tunes. Such uncertainties problematise concepts such as 'author's intention' or 'author's original work' as applied to the study of text–music relationships and shift our attention to the concept of performance as the moment when two different sonorous systems are combined into a single artistic expression.

Apart from their instability, written records bring uncertainties of interpretation probably more acute for melodies than for texts. In the sources (except *X*), melodies are normally preserved in the square notation used for Chant: a single note per syllable is indicated by a square-shaped symbol with or without a stem; symbols are linked together for a group of notes per syllable (see Examples 3a and 4a). This notation (called 'non-mensural') conveys pitch with adequate precision, but not rhythm. A 'semi-mensural' notation (where some symbols could have durational meaning) used for a few songs in *R* (such as Example 1) gives partial but contradictory information about rhythm. This situation has led to considerable debate among scholars. Further, the music sources do not indicate whether or how instruments might have been used. I will return to these matters under 'Performance' (pp. 149–50 below).[2]

VERSIFICATION

The troubadours were virtuosic versifiers. The chief elements of versification are metre (defined for this repertory as number of syllables per line) and rhyme. Although these elements may seem conventional to us, possibilities of combination and re-combination served as a powerful stimulus to troubadour invention of new patterns of verbal sound. Moreover, it is useful to historicise versification, to realise that practices we tend to con-sider stable developed over time: this allows integration of experi-mentation and irregularity into our critical thinking.

Important recent book-length studies of versification include those of Frank Chambers and Dominique Billy; the indispensable reference tool is István Frank.[3] Chambers adopts a chronological approach, following the practices of individual troubadours; his explanations are clear and accessible. However, while recognising irregularities, Chambers proceeds from the notion that numerical counting of syllables was intended to be exact; thus he normalises. The inadvisability of normalising all texts was cogently argued by John Marshall and incorporated into the theoretical, rigorously structural, work of Billy.[4] Regular syllable count may remain the basis of analysis of troubadour song, but recognising that irregu-larity is not always mere scribal error permits an understanding of historical developments during a period when the adoption of exact syllable counting was more a process than a sudden event.

Syllable count for all troubadour songs is furnished by Frank's *Répertoire*. It is instructive to remember that designations of verse types do not necessarily correspond to actual number of syllables.

According to a system of counting dating at least from the fourteenth-century treatise the *Leys d'amors*, the basis for identifying
types of metre is the place of the final accent in the line of verse.
Counting includes only the last accented syllable, and the verse
length is defined by that syllable. Thus in an eight-syllable line
with final accented syllable, all syllables are counted:

1	2	3	4	5	6	7	8
Ab/	ioi/	mou/	lo/	vers/	e·l/	co/	mens

      (With joi I begin the *vers* and start it)

whereas in a line accented on the next to last syllable, the final
unaccented syllable is not counted:

1	2	3	4	5	6	7	8	'
Mas/	tant/	m'au/	ci/	ab/	bel/	mar/	ti/	re

      (But slays me with such fine martyrdom)

In modern parlance, when there is an accent on the final syllable,
the end-word is called 'masculine'; an end-word with an accent on
the next to last syllable is called 'feminine'. Medieval treatises do
not use the terms 'masculine' and 'feminine' either to describe
lines or to describe rhymes, but speak of *accen agut* (acute accent)
or *accen greu* (grave accent).[5] All lines are named by number of
syllables: thus, eight-syllable, or octosyllabic, ten-syllable, or decasyllabic, to give as examples frequently used metres. When the
same metre is used throughout the stanza, one speaks of 'isometric' stanzas; changes in metre within the stanza determine
'heterometric' structures. Numerous poetic effects are created by
the choice of isometric or heterometric stanzas and by the distribution within the stanza of lines having final accented
('masculine') endings and next-to-final accented ('feminine') endings.

Further considerations of accent in troubadour verse include
the caesura and accents determined by stress patterns of the language. The caesura itself may be considered a pause, but the syllable preceding the pause is normally accentuated. Caesurae are
typically found in the troubadour repertory in decasyllabic lines
(after the fourth syllable, less often after the fifth or sixth).
Shorter lines do not have fixed caesurae, but one may presume
variable accents corresponding to sense groups, much as in
modern French poetry. The line of verse, anchored by the number

of syllables and the accent at its close, diversified by the varying accents that play across these defining features, is manipulated with great sophistication by the troubadours.[6]

The second element of versification, rhyme, also offers a dizzying array of possibilities. Rhyme is simultaneously sound, sense and signpost: this multiplicity of functions makes it a privileged poetic space. In the early twelfth century, it had all the attractiveness of a new technology. Rhyme is generally defined as the identity of sounds from the final accented vowel to the end of the word, and it can be further described by the number of syllables included in the identical sounds (degree or richness of rhyme) and by the quality and nature of the sounds themselves. Rhymes mark line ends, and serve to establish inter- and intra-stanzaic linkings. Within the stanza, rhyme schemes (such as *ababccdd* or *abbacdcd*) define stanza types, and techniques such as *coblas unissonans* or *coblas capcaudadas* link stanzas together. Technical discussion of these matters may be found in Frank, *Répertoire*, in Chambers and with great detail in Billy.[7] But the rhyme is not merely a technical device; it is a source of sonorous beauty and, by the relationships it creates, of substantive argument. Troubadours revelled in sound contrasts and gradations; some sought unusual words, harsh or smooth. Raimbaut d'Aurenga's 'Ar resplan' (XXXIX), for example, weaves its themes from rare and derivative rhymes (see Chapter 5 on this poem). Choice of a single rhyme-word crystallises meaning, as in Jaufré Rudel's 'Lanquan li jorn' (IV), where the rhyme-word *lonh*, expanded into the phrase 'amor de lonh' (with always the same musical cadence), governs the poem and, indeed, some modern interpretations of *fin'amor*. A prestigious example of meaning produced by selection and manipulation of rhyme words is Arnaut Daniel's 'Lo ferm voler' (XVIII), probably the earliest *sestina*.[8]

MUSIC

Durable scholarly problems in the study of music include manuscripts and transmission (briefly described above), rhythm (about which more in a moment), and style and structure. In her recent book, Elizabeth Aubrey treats form and style in considerable detail.[9]

A good way to approach troubadour music is to devise strategies one can deploy to appreciate how the melodies work, starting from the basic concepts that (a) notes and note groups are joined to syllables; (b) that a melodic phrase corresponds to a poetic line of verse; (c) that the phrase may be closed by a cadence; and (d) that most troubadour songs are strophic, so the melody is contained entirely within the stanza and repeated for each succeeding stanza.

In the narrow sense, melodic style (or texture) is defined by number of notes per syllable: syllabic style has one note to a syllable; melismatic style (a melisma is a group of notes) has several notes to a syllable. Normally, troubadour melodies combine these contrasting styles, and the style of a particular song is characterised by the relative weight accorded to each. But song textures are fluid. In the manuscripts, associations between notes and syllables often vary from one version of a song to the next. Melismas are ornamental. And since singers were under no constraint to adhere to a written 'score', adorning and varying melodies must have been important performance techniques, doubtless used to demonstrate skill in interpreting the text. Thus exact distribution of notes per syllable surely changed with different performances, even where the basic texture remained the same.

On a more complex level, melodic style can be defined by how a melody moves. Does it follow step-wise progressions or are there large skips? Is the initial motion of the melody maintained throughout a phrase, or are there sharp reversals of direction? Is the range of the melody (its highest and lowest note) wide or limited? Often a troubadour melody reaches swiftly upwards to a peak during the last portion of the stanza, and the listener learns to appreciate this moment. Motion between phrases is significant: starting a new phrase on the same note as the preceding one expresses continuity while a large leap proposes new material. One feature of melodic unfolding that differentiates it from verbal progression is the use of repetition. Melodic repetition frequently engages entire phrases, and this repetition is a major formal criterion. Texts cannot support such repetition except in the special case of refrains. An equally important musical technique is the repetition of small melodic ideas or motives (see Example 4b) which structure the melodic flow and provide coherence.[10] Finally, individual pitches stand out through repetition; these repeated tones often suggest an undergirding structure, or even, in conjunction with the final note or cadence, a tonal centre.

A cadence is the note or series of notes that closes a musical utterance, and one can think of it as analogous to rhyme, yet the two are very different. The pitch a melody reaches both at the ends of phrases and at the end of the piece is important. But troubadour melodies do not always move towards clearly defined pitch goals. A melodic cadence is less predictable than a rhyme. As modern listeners, we are often disconcerted when, in different versions of a melody, concluding pitches are not the same at the ends of phrases, or even at the end of the piece. However, as the examples to be discussed will show, it is instructive to consider the final note of a piece and relate it to the final notes of individual phrases to see if some structural pattern emerges.

MUSIC AND TEXT

Since troubadour song brings music and poetry together, this relationship is a key focus of any discussion. As I have argued elsewhere, two basic approaches to the study of text–music relationships in troubadour song may be identified: structural and rhetorical.[11] The former emphasises parallel patterns or shapes (metrical rather than semantic); the latter emphasises the production and communication of meaning. The two are tendencies rather than mutually exclusive procedures.

The structural approach rests on the comparison of metrical and melodic formal characteristics, chiefly repeated elements, to determine how stanzas are put together and how structures are created. Such analyses have often drawn upon the unfinished treatise by Dante Alighieri, *De vulgari eloquentia*, composed in Latin between 1303 and 1305. Since Dante used troubadour and *trouvère* songs as models, his treatise has influenced modern critics' perception of text–music relationships. Focusing on the stanza (*stantia*) as the 'receptacle,' the 'room' (*mansio*) where the art of song is forged, Dante emphasised the proportioned arrangement and distribution of parts. He defined several patterns, giving them names still widely used. A pattern without division or repetition of phrases was called *oda continua*. Various possibilities with a mid-stanza division and phrasal repetitions before or after it were described, of which the most widely used have been: *pedes* (pre-division repetition) with *cauda* (no post-division repetition); and *pedes* with *versus* (post-division repetition).[12] These three patterns correspond to melodic schemes ABCDEFG, ABAB CDEF, ABAB CDCD or rhyme schemes abcdef, abab cdef, abab cdcd. As Dante's views have usually been interpreted, they would posit full 'agreement' between melodic and rhyme schemes as an ideal compositional model. However, Dante's terms, and the structural concepts that have been drawn from them, only partially correspond to the varieties of troubadour creativity. Appreciation of these requires the finer-grained approaches to defining structures that include small irregular units and unusual as well as regular coordinations of music and text.

Structural analysis provides important insights, but it gives little sense of how a song plays out in time. Abstract schemes omit essential information and impose a deceptive normalisation. Emphasis on the stanza alone fails to take into account the repetition of stanzas that creates an irreversible temporal pattern. The unfolding *in time* of textual and musical elements is an issue that needs to be addressed.

The second type of basic approach, the rhetorical approach, allows us to confront this issue. Rhetorical purpose is different from the idea of 'text painting' or 'madrigalism'. Rarely can troubadour melodies be said to 'imitate' word meanings. But they can reflect, through sound and syntax, expressive values of texts. The aim of rhetorical analysis is to discover the combinations and coordinations of *all* the resources of language and music brought into play as the song unfolds.

Those who seek rhetorical interpretations, considering the composer, performer or scribe as a 'reader' or 'interpreter' of the poem, sometimes emphasise the first stanza of the song. It is usually the only stanza with music in the manuscripts (the same melody being then repeated for following stanzas), giving the impression that the inventor of the melody might have had it specifically in mind. A main question then becomes: how can the music relate to succeeding stanzas? The first stanza does set the subject and the tone. But as the melody is repeated for succeeding stanzas, it is cast in a new light by association with different texts. And although melodic and metrical patterns are set by the first stanza, many intricate rhyme schemes and refrain patterns can only be deployed over the entire song. Therefore, at its best, the rhetorical approach includes an examination of *how* the first stanza conditions the rest.

Rhetorical analysis must also account for the widespread use of *contrafacta* or borrowing and exchange of tunes and texts. Sometimes a tune from, say, a *canso* (love song) has been borrowed for a *sirventes* (political song). If text and melody are related *only* on the level of form or shape, then texts and melodies can easily be interchanged. If, however, specific melodies are seen as responses to specific texts, the practice of *contrafacta* problematises the rhetorical approach. In this context, it is useful to think of contrafaction as a type of 'intertextuality,' opening a new range of interpretative models (see Chapter 11). Further, the fluidity of melodies in the manuscripts raises difficult issues of interpretation, especially when, in multiple versions of a song, melody versions are so different as to constitute essentially different tunes. With rhetorical analyses, special care must be taken not to base interpretations on the concept of a fixed association between words and melodies, or on the notion of author's intention, narrowly defined. For each song – and indeed for its several variations where there are variations – the range of possible musico-poetic juxtapositions must contribute to an understanding of rhetorical effectiveness.

PERFORMANCE

The song lives in the physical act of singing. The knottiest issue in performance is rhythm. Owing to the ambiguity of the medieval musical notation, no modern theory enjoys complete adherence.[13] Should we give equal time to each syllable? Should we impose a system of longs and shorts on the song? The last solution is now largely discredited; the first, sometimes called the isosyllabic hypothesis,[14] if strictly applied, is too rigid; but combined with linguistic accents and poetic diction, it offers valuable practical solutions. Another controversial issue is the use of instruments. Lack of precise manuscript indication combines with iconographical and other evidence that suggests their use to create an ambiguity that does not allow definitive solutions. Previously, instruments were enthusiastically omnipresent in performances; recent work has brought a clearer assessment of historical probabilities: for troubadour song, use of instruments was probably discreet.[15]

Consideration of performance must also include the complex relationships between performers (who may or may not have been the composer), audience and performance space.[16] The main performing space was surely the court; the main critical task is to examine possible interactions between performers and a court public. The audience was presumably mixed. The performers were likely a range of figures – poets, *joglars* – and also women. Ongoing research, especially in social history, is bringing fresh assessment of the role of women.[17] Theories of male political dominance by marginalising women tend to exclude them.[18] But Occitan women likely held considerable power, participating in political life as castellans, though less frequently than men. Positing the active presence of women in performance situations subtly enriches the interchanges we imagine as the songs' initial reception.

Audience reception of musical performance has not benefited from the kind of scrutiny accorded to reception of texts. How was the song heard? What musical contexts guided understanding? Surely one main context was the Chant, another monastic songs such as *versus*, and still another 'popular' songs now lost to us. A sophisticated audience surely appreciated inter-musical relations, as it appreciated subtleties of versification, melodic composition and textual rhetoric as they came together in performance.

MUSIC AND VERSIFICATION: A BRIEF SAMPLING

The examples at the end of the chapter, arranged in roughly chronological order, represent several periods of troubadour song.[19] Discussion of them will illustrate and summarise main points treated above.

Example 1: Bernart de Ventadorn, 'Ab joi mou lo vers' (III), preserved in *G*, *R* and *W*. Comparison of *G* and *R* reflects the variability of troubadour melodic composition and transmission. Regarding melodic characteristics, both versions combine syllabic and melismatic styles. The position and length of melismas are sometimes the same in both versions; more usually, different distributions of notes and note groups pertain. Nonetheless, the repeated pitch *f* at the end of most phrases and at the close of the piece establishes *f* as the tonal centre; the prominence of *c* gives it secondary tonal importance; and the cadence on *g* in line 7 forms a contrast to the other cadences before the final close. The melody in *R* corresponds to Dante's *pedes* and *cauda*, ABAB CDEF. The *G* version does not (nor does the version in *W*), especially in the first portion of the song; differences can be plotted by comparing successive lines in *G* to *R*. The structure may have been regularised by the scribe of *R*; and to adopt his regularisation, excluding other versions (following Gennrich),[20] is to engage in an abusive normalisation that obscures what we must imagine as the medieval reality. The heterometric *coblas unissonans* combine eight- (masculine), seven- (feminine) and ten-syllable lines with a rhyme scheme ababc′c′dd. The turn of the stanza (lines 4–5) illustrates transition by variation of rhythm and rhyme through which rhyme relations are highlighted. The rhythmic shift by end-line accent, 'masculine' to 'feminine': *-éns/-ánsa*, plays on both similarity and difference of rhyme sounds. The effect is striking in the first stanza, when *coméns* (line 1) expands to *comensaméns* (line 4) then shifts to *comensánsa* to conclude development of this key notion.

Example 2: The Comtessa de Dia, 'A chantar' (Rieger XXXV), our only *trobairitz* melody. The regularly balanced opening phrases, ABAB CDB, the stately ten-syllable lines, the expressive rise through a triad *f–a–c* in line 6, the emotional centre of every stanza, and the return to the B phrase to close, all create a captivating musical expression. The song has only one stanza in MS *W*. The language of the MS illustrates problems brought about by 'Frenchifying' Old Occitan (in *trouvère* manuscripts and in lyric insertion romances). As Occitan songs travelled north, the texts were adapted to a French-speaking environment.[21] The example shows both Old Occitan and Old French, and the problematic relationship of 'Frenchification' to the melody. The versification of this song demonstrates a frequently used device to link what are technically *coblas singulars*. The rhyme scheme is a′a′a′a′ba′b. The rhyme sound a changes with every stanza providing a variety of colours. Stanzas are linked by the rhyme sound b, *-ens*, which stays the same and anchors the song, its sound and its meaning, since rhyme words in *-ens* carry particular force.[22]

Example 3: Raimon de Miraval, 'Bel m'es' (XXXVII). In this song, one may examine structuring by short repeated motives and the recurrence of entire phrases but not in a set pattern. The *oda continua* label sometimes applied to it is, at best, misleading.

Division in two parts is proposed by the cadence on *d* in lines 4 and 9, and by the upward leap of a fifth in line 5 contrasting with the downward leap of a fourth in line 1. The rising motif 'a' unites lines (1), 2 and 4, and returns in line 8 to link the last part of the song to the first. Lines 6 and 7 are exactly repeated – though in the second part of the melody and not the first where one expects such repetition. But 6 and 7 also recall line 3 in their concluding portion (motif 'b'). While absolute identity is avoided by the shifting text accent (in line 3, 'b' occurs to a masculine rhyme, in lines 6–7 to a feminine rhyme), echoing of motives relates the middle section of the tune also to the first part. Such motivic interrelationships provide strong melodic coherence. Verse form combines seven-syllable masculine and feminine lines with a rhyme scheme abbacd'd'cc. The rhyme-sounds play on studied distinctions: diphthongs *ei/ai*, with identical final elements *i* and slightly differentiated accented vowels *e/a*, contrast with the single high vowel of *-ut*. Musical motif 'b' both connects and varies melodically the diphthong in *plais/vaire, traire*: in line 3 *ai* has a two-note group, in lines 6–7 a six-note group, expanding the diphthong in the feminine rhyme before the final *-ut*. Expansion is framed by the linking in lines 5–8 of *rimes embrassées*: cd'd'c to what one could call *cadences embrassées*: fccf. Music and versification are joined in an effective sonorous development. The tense rhyme *-ut* will conclude the song in the key word *perdut*, twice repeated in the *tornadas*, summing up the major theme: painful loss of joy and of one's castle in the crucial year 1213.[23]

Example 5: Guiraut Riquier, 'Fis e verays' (Mölk XVII), an example from the later flowering of troubadour art. Frequent repetitions on the level of the phrase, exploiting the settled paradigm ABABx (specifically ABABCAB here), and melismatic style are typical of Riquier. Riquier also represents the case, unique to the troubadour repertory, of a group of songs signed and dated as by the composer's own hand: rubrics like the one given here situate Riquier's songs in both *R* and *C*. The complexity of the versification provides a glimpse of troubadour virtuosity: *coblas alternadas capcaudadas retrogradas* with seven ten-syllable lines, all masculine, rhyme scheme abbcdde, thus three *rims estramps* (*uelh*, *-es*, *-ans*) – to which is added a refrain word that conveys the central theme:

I	II	III	IV	V	*tornadas*	
uelh	ans	uelh	ans	uelh		
ort	or	ort	or	ort		
ort	or	ort	or	ort		
ames	*ames*	*ames*	*ames*	*ames*	*ames*	*ames*
or	ort	or	ort	or	or	or
or	ort	or	ort	or	or	or
ans	uelh	ans	uelh	ans	ans	ans

Because the rhyme scheme changes and the melody is repeated, as the song unfolds there occur different associations between rhyme sounds and melodic cadences. For example, the sounds -*uelh* and -*ans* will be heard alternately to the cadences of lines 1 and 7, and since the cadences of lines 4 and 7 are the same, the refrain word will be linked alternately to these sounds and the meanings they carry, as they appear in line 7. Thus stanza I links *ames/enans*; stanza II *ames/vuelh*. Rhyme schemes beginning abbc can create an effect of surprise: an audience by this late date expects rhyme a to come back. The surprise here creates tension: rhyme a does not come back to end the first section, but the melodic cadence brings closure. Syntactically, no strong pause is marked at the end of line 4; *ames* is an imperfect subjunctive, which seems to propel the song forward. Thus there is tension between musical pause and textual movement: in this tension lies the frustration of love.

Now let us take up Example 4, Peire Vidal, 'Be·m pac' (XXXVI), to glimpse an entire song through selected stanzas given in the example. This *canso* with political and crusading overtones is representative of Peire Vidal in the sometimes whimsical unfolding of its text. The song was possibly twice reworked to add the first *tornada* and then the sixth stanza. But if stanza VI was a later addition, the transition to it is prepared by what precedes. The ten-line *coblas unissonans* combine seven-syllable metres with masculine and feminine rhymes in a sequence abbaabc′c′dd. This sequence incorporates a two-line prolongation of the rhymes of the first part into a basic scheme abba [ab] ccdd. Lines 5 and 6 are thus transitional, relating both to the first and to the second parts of the stanza. Rhyme sounds a and b contrast: -*iu*/-*ors*; c and d share a vowel and a consonant: -*ella*/-*el*, differentiated only by the unaccented syllable of the feminine rhyme. The metrical shape thus created is unique. Of the sounds chosen for the rhymes, -*ors* is the most thematically charged since it brings a constellation of terms associated with *amors* in its wake. Two terms stand out: *combatedors* and *secors*. *Combatedors*, an unusual designation, is paired with *fenhedors* in stanza II, and the negative set carries over to *vilas domneiadors* in stanza III, until *fis conoissedors* ushers in *mellors* and then a positive series *valors, lauzors, doussors* in stanzas IV and V (not reproduced in the example). The lady's merit vanquishes all enemies. *Secors* plays a double role in stanza VI: it is the pivot on which turns the shift from secular to sacred, from the possibility of the lady's *secors* to the call to help the Lord. The final rhyme sound *-el* is part of a series of Biblical references – Gabriel, Abel, Israhel (IV), Rachel (V), Daniel – until the Byzantine Emperor Manuel in stanza VII. These infuse the song with a religious aura before we arrive at stanza VI. The rhyme *-ella* carries one whimsical image, again typical of Vidal: the heart drawn from beneath the armpit in stanza III.

The melody, among the loveliest in the troubadour repertory, exhibits an extraordinary range, an affinity for motion by chains of thirds, graceful adornment. It is in three manuscripts: *G, R* and *X*, with practically identical versions in *G* and *X* (*R* is similar structurally but more compact in range). The melody is through-composed, thus Dante's *oda continua*. But that fact gives us no concept of its structure. Cadence notes for each phrase provide initial clues: c–g–c–c–a–g–c(octave above)–e–g–c. The note c stands out; hierarchically the lower c carries greater weight and suggests (without clearly affirming it) an initial division of the melody into two parts: four lines closing on c followed by six lines again closing on c. The relative highness or lowness of the melody, exploiting the upper and lower portions of the range, brings contrast. Lines 1–4 move in the lower portion; lines 5–8 sweep through the entire range, from low g to high f, almost a double octave and surely a place for the singer to display his talent; lines 9–10 fall back into the original portion of the range. The structure is refined: an initial four lines, followed by four lines contrasting in range, with two lines bringing closure by a return to the beginning. To flesh out these structural points, one could take note of repeated inital melismas in lines 1 and 10; of melodic 'rhyme' in 1, 3 and 10; of the spectacular rising thirds f–a–c at the beginning of line 7 leading to the climax of the melody on f. One further consideration clinches the initial impression of a division after line 4: the motion to the next line drops a fourth from g to c, contrasting with the rising motion proceding from lines 1–2 and 3–4. Moreover, lines

5 and 6 have the only stepwise rising link in the piece – one could almost call the movement from 5 to 6 a continuation of musical sense from one line to the next, a kind of equivalent of poetic enjambment. If the melody is through-composed, having no repetition of entire phrases, it is not without structural divisions that give it shape, and with its abundance of four-, five-, six- and even eight-note melismas, it is a bravura piece of remarkable energy.

Considering now text and melody together, the first stanza sets the stage for a *canso*: love unites all contraries ('dead noble' vs. 'living coward' strikes a humorous note), sustained by youth and merit. Lest the short seven-syllable line seem frivolous, the richly adorned melody gives it weight and substance. The melodic division after the fourth line sets off the contraries, pausing enough for a smile on *avol viu*. Lines 5 and 6 then move forward, syntactically and musically joined, as these central lines will be in every stanza of the poem. The apex of the melody (high f) is touched in lines 7–8, the two lines with feminine rhyme; in this portion of the melody, syllabic style increases dynamic tension and forward motion, to which the lengthening of the rhyme is counterpoised. The complete expansive melodic gesture rising to and falling away from the climax covers lines 5–8 (from low g to high f and back to e) and corresponds to the rhetorical statement of reasons for singing. The last two lines then return to the first contrasts as the melody settles back into its initial range. At the close of the first stanza, the main rhetorical elements are in place, and a tone both serious and mocking has been established.

In the succeeding stanzas, new textual configurations will be heard to the same melody. The first four-line melodic statement will propose though not impose matching syntactic and semantic statements. Lines 5–8, given prominence by the melodic range, often contain explanations or justifications. The whimsical image in stanza III, mentioned above, is the more amusing because it comes when the melody peaks: the unexpected juxtaposition of the feminine rhymes *sembella* and *aissella* deflates the musical rhetoric. Perhaps most striking throughout the song is the correlation of the final rhymes in *-el* with the melody's return to its original space. This emphasises a list of names and a series of comparisons that are unusual for a *canso*, but they fit with this song's generic ambiguity and create thematic unity. Moreover, the *-el* rhyme also includes *cel*, *fel* and *mel*, which return in the *tornadas*, so that the first stanza and the last tornada close on the same word, *cel*.

Example 1 Bernart de Ventadorn, 'Ab joi mou lo vers e·l comens'; comparison of versions in *R* and *G*

(1) The text in *R*, line 3, is: 'Et ab que bona sia la fis', thus an extra syllable and an extra note. Adding or deleting notes, splitting or combining note groups are common adjustments of melodies in the manuscripts to number of syllables. *R* has semi-mensural notation. See van der Werf, *Extant*, p. 30*.

(From joy I begin the *vers* and with joy will it continue and end; and only if the end is good, will I consider good the beginning. Through the good beginning come to me joy and happiness; so I must welcome the good ending for I see all good actions praised upon conclusion.)

Example 2 The Comtessa de Dia, 'A chantar m'er de so qu'ieu non volria'

(1) In line 2, the scribe (possibly confused about the gender of the speaker) wrote 'amigs' but left the last note of the melody in place; a possible emendation to 'amige' in the manuscript seems to address that problem. In line 7, the 'Frenchified' rhyme 'ence' corresponds to the melody as written. The melodic cadence of line 2 fits the Old Occitan text; to sing line 7 in Old Occitan, one must consolidate the final three-note melisma plus one note in a single group.

(I am obliged to sing of that which I would not, so bitter am I over the one whose love I am, for I love him more than anything; with him, mercy and courtliness are of no avail, not my beauty, nor my merit, nor my good sense, for I am deceived and betrayed just as I should be if I were ungracious.)

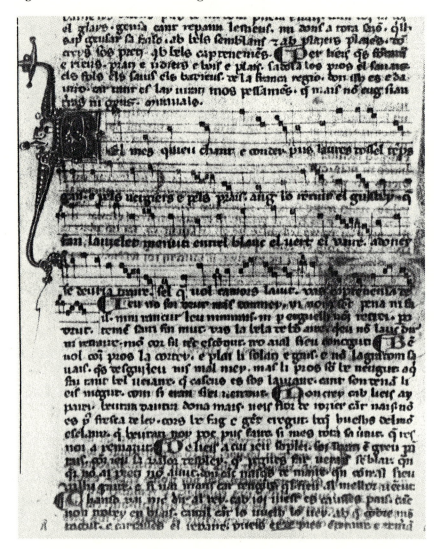

Example 3a Raimon de Miraval, 'Bel m'es q'ieu chant e coindei', MS *R*

Folio 83v, upper left detail. Square notation on a four-line staff with an F clef of the form ⁊⁊,
except that for the last melisma, there is a three-line staff to fit the space.
Cliché Bibliothèque Nationale de France, Paris.

Example 3b Raimon de Miraval, 'Bel m'es q'ieu chant e coindei'

(1) This note could be *f*.

(It pleases me to sing and be agreeable since the air is warm, the weather delightful, and in the orchards and hedges I hear the chirping and warbling of the little birds among the green and the white and the multicoloured (foliage and flowers). Then he who wants love to help him should strive to behave like a lover.)

Example 4a Peire Vidal, 'Be·m pac d'ivern e d'estiu', MS *G*

Folio 40v. Square notation; staves of 5–7 lines to accommodate the range; C and F clefs, the latter of the form ⨎. Unlike *R*, only underlaid text is run-on. Other stanzas have one verse to a line. Verse 7 has one missing syllable. The note group over the second syllable of 'novella' has an unusual stem in the middle as though two groups had been placed together. In the transcription, this group has been separated to cover the 8 actual syllables. Line 1, first melisma could end on *f*.

Example 4b Peire Vidal, 'Be·m pac d'ivern e d'estiu'

II Ma don'a pretz soloriu
  Denant mil combatedors,
  E contra·ls fals fenhedors
  Ten establit Montesquiu:
  Per qu'el seu ric senhoriu   15
  Lauzengiers non pot far cors,
  Que sens e pretz la capdella;
  E quan respon ni apella
  Siei dig an sabor de mel,
  Don sembla Sant Gabriel.   20

III E fai·s temer plus de griu
  Als vilas domneiadors,
  Et als fis conoissedors
  A solatz tan agradiu,

  Qu'al partir quecs jur'e pliu   25
  Que domn'es de las mellors:
  Per que·m train'e·m sembella
  E·m tra·l cor de sotz l'aissella,
  Don m'a leyal e fizel
  E just pus que Dieus Abel. [. . .]   30

VI En Fransa et en Beriu
  Et a Peitieus et a Tors
  Quer nostre Senher secors
  Pel Turcs que·l tenon faidiu,
  Que tolt l'an e·l vas e·l riu   55
  On mondava·ls pechadors;
  E qui ara no·s revella
  Contr'aquesta gen fradella
  Ben mal sembla Daniel
  Que·l dragon destruis e Bel.   60

I Winter and summer please me as do cold and heat; I like snow as much as flowers and prefer a dead noble to a living coward, for thus do Youth and Merit keep me joyous. Since I love a new lady most gracious and beautiful, roses appear amidst ice and clear weather in a troubled sky.

II My lady has superior merit before a thousand enemies, and against false hypocrites holds Montesquiu firmly so no *lauzengier* can attack her authority, for wisdom and merit guide her; and when she answers or calls, her words are honey so she resembles St Gabriel.

III More than a griffon she makes herself feared by vulgar suitors, and perfect connoisseurs are so warmly greeted that, on leaving, each swears and pledges that she is one of the best ladies; therefore she attracts and lures me and draws my heart from beneath my armpit, so I am loyal and faithful to her and more just than God towards Abel . . .

VI In France and in the Berry, in Poitiers and in Tours, Our Lord seeks help against the Turks who hold him in exile, for they have taken the sepulchre and the stream where he purified the sinners; and who now does not rise up against this cursed people resembles not at all Daniel who destroyed the dragon and Bel.

MS *R*

1. Fis e ve- rays e pus ferms que no suelh,
2. Suy vas a- mor en- dreg mon Belh De- port,
3. Non que m'a- ja fag sem- blan de co- nort,
4. Mas que.m so- ven qui fuy ans que a- mes,
5. E que.m cos- sir qui fo- ra ses a- mor,
6. Et aug per qui.m te- no.l co- noys- se- dor,
7. Per qu'ieu am fis quar d'a- mar ay l'e- nans.

Example 5 Guiraut Riquier, 'Fis et verays e pus ferms que no suelh'

La XVIIa canson d'en Guiraut   The XVIIth *canso* by Guiraut
Riquier l'an M CC LXXV   Riquier in the year 1275

II   L'enans que n'ay m'es mout plazens e grans,
        Qu'ieu non saupi penre ni far honor,
        Ni negus faitz d'azaut no m'ac sabor,
        Tro·m fes plazer amors qu'ieu lieys ames,
        Qu'ab mi no fon en lunh fag d'un acort,
        Sal quar son pretz creysser dezira fort,
        Que s'ylh o vol, ieu atretant o vuelh.

I   For my Fair Delight, I am noble, true, and more constant than usual towards love. Not that she's shown me comfort, but because I recall who I was ere I loved and consider who I would be without love, and hear whom the connoisseurs take me to be. For I love nobly because by love I am enhanced.

II   The enhancement I have is most pleasing to me, for I knew not how to win or do honour, and no gracious deed appealed to me, until love made it pleasing that I should love her who was in no agreement with me, except that she greatly desires to increase her merit, and if she wants that, I want it just as much.

(1) The scribe did not place flat signs consistently. See Van der Werf, *Extant*, p. 53.

NOTES

1 Arlt, 'Zur Interpretation' and *'Nova Cantica'*; Grier, 'New voice'.
2 For MSS, transmission, notation and editing problems, see van der Werf, *Chansons*, pp. 26–45 (definitions of mensural and semi-mensural notation are given on p. 157), *Extant*, pp. 3–28, 'Music', pp. 121–39; Switten, *Music and Poetry*, pp. 3–20, 75–9; Aubrey, *Music*, pp. 26–65.
3 Frank, *Répertoire* (see Appendix 3, p. 301); Chambers, *Versification*; Billy, *L'Architecture*.
4 Chambers, *Versification*, pp. 8–9; Marshall, 'Isostrophic', 'Textual transmission', 'Versification lyrique'; see also Switten, *Music and Poetry*, pp. 86–7.
5 *Leys*, I, 100. Chambers, *Versification*, pp. 11–12 cites two ambiguous examples from later troubadours of 'masculine/feminine' possibly referring to rhymes. The terminology was regularly applied to nouns in grammatical treatises. See also Kay, 'Derivation', pp. 162–5.
6 Switten, *Music and Poetry*, pp. 85–93.
7 See also Roubaud, *Fleur*, pp. 185–240.
8 See Switten, 'De la sextine', for interaction of rhymes and music.
9 Aubrey, *Music*, pp. 132–236; see also Switten, *Music and Poetry*, pp. 104–19.
10 Switten, *Miraval*, pp. 22–40; Aubrey, *Music*, pp. 184–94.
11 Switten, 'Music and words', pp. 14–16. For representative types of analysis, see Stevens, *Words and Music*; Treitler, 'Medieval lyric'.
12 *De vulgari*, II, ix–xi.
13 Van der Werf, *Chansons*, pp. 35–45, 'Music', pp. 121–3; Aubrey, *Music*, pp. 240–54; Switten, *Music and Poetry*, pp. 82–6; 96–7.
14 Stevens, *Words and Music*, 413–16, 500–4. Van der Werf, '"Not-so-precisely measured"', proposes *pitches* of equal length.
15 Page, *Voices and Instruments*; Aubrey, *Music*, pp. 254–62.
16 Kay, *Subjectivity*, pp. 132–70, treats some of these issues.
17 Until forthcoming publications, such as Cheyette, 'Women', elaborate these approaches, see Bruckner, *Songs of Women* [see under *Trobairitz*, p. 308 below], pp. xxxvi–xxxviii; Switten, 'Comtessa', in Rosenberg, *Songs*, p. 95.
18 Such as the Duby model of male power. For Duby's work, including deficiencies in depiction of women, see Evergates, 'Georges Duby'.
19 Example texts come from editions in Appendix 1, except 4 from Switten, *Miraval*, p. 160. For melodic transcriptions, I use rhythmically neutral black dots (a smaller dot for the *plica*) and a modern G clef.
20 Gennrich, *Nachlass*, II, *Kommentar*, p. 27.
21 Pollina, 'Troubadours dans le Nord'.
22 Bruckner, 'Fictions', p. 882; Switten, 'A chantar' in Rosenberg, *Songs*, p. 96.
23 Miraval had lost his castle before composing this song in 1213 to ask Peter of Aragon for help against Simon of Montfort, leader of the Albigensian crusaders. Peter did come to help; but at the disastrous battle of Muret in 1213, the Occitan forces were defeated and Peter killed.

CHAPTER 10

Rhetoric and hermeneutics

Sarah Spence

Ever since Dante singled out the troubadours for their 'vernacular eloquence' the rhetorical artistry of these poets has been, on and off, in the spotlight. It has, in fact, become such a commonplace to speak of the rhetoric of troubadour poetry that a more compelling question is often overlooked, namely, why did the troubadours make their rhetoric evident at all? Why do so many of the poets draw attention to the fact that they are making poetry; why do many of them refer in explicitly technical ways to their 'razos' or the 'art d'escriure'? These poetic works are not, or at least not primarily, didactic tracts where one might expect to find overt mention or explicit use of rhetorical techniques and strategies. Rather, the poems of the troubadours contain some of the most beautiful and lyrical verse of all time. Why, then, 'spoil it' with the metalanguage of rhetoric?

Linda Paterson and, more recently, Nathaniel Smith have each addressed the question of troubadour rhetoric. In *Troubadours and Eloquence*, Paterson sets out to discuss the nature of the *eloquentia* of five troubadours who made explicit mention of style in their poetry. Her project is to consider the literary terminology used by the poets themselves and to relate this terminology to their 'methods of composition'. While she establishes clearly that many if not all five of these troubadours knew medieval rhetoric, she aims mostly to suggest that the classical tradition, as it was passed down into the Middle Ages, was a launching pad from which the troubadours developed their own sense of the term, one which focused, she argues, mostly on style. Paterson argues persuasively that classical rhetoric not only was adapted to troubadour needs but also varied considerably among the troubadours who use and acknowledge it.[1]

Smith, while continuing to focus on style as the fundamental concern of troubadour rhetoric, argues that their eloquence was aimed primarily at persuasion. By using figures of speech and thought they would have found readily available in handbooks such as the *Rhetorica ad Herennium* the troubadours, argues Smith, were able to make their works convincing to their patrons as they communicated 'self-satisfaction, public praise, and fame ... [as well as] a master[y of] language and song. In return, the troubadours ... received some access to the higher reaches of a hierarchical socio-economic system' (Smith, 'Rhetoric', p. 418). Smith concludes that it was precisely the troubadours' efforts to please the ruling noble class through conventional rhetoric that prevented them 'from expressing new political or social values' (p. 418). Yet troubadour lyric, especially when referring to its own style and purpose, frequently mentions its novelty. Perhaps by limiting the purpose of rhetoric to persuasion Smith has unnecessarily curtailed the possibilities that rhetoric in fact granted to troubadour poetry. What Paterson, by contrast, makes clear is that the troubadours' use of rhetoric was anything but conventional; her argument that each troubadour used rhetoric in a different way suggests that the tradition was seen as something malleable, useful, empowering.

Paterson's approach can be extended beyond *eloquentia* if rhetoric is understood not just as style but rather as the 'ars bene dicendi' (the art of speaking well) that it was defined as in antiquity. While style is indeed an aspect of most, if not all, rhetoric, it is clear from Cicero's works that rhetoric is a term that includes within it a social, or socialising, valence: rhetoric, for Cicero at least, is the means for ordering the passions, especially those related to the body. Before the first orator, man 'did nothing by the guidance of reason, but relied chiefly on physical strength'. It was

[a]t this juncture [that] a man great and wise I am sure became aware of the power latent in man and the wide field offered by his mind for great achievements if one could develop this power and improve it by instruction. Men were scattered in the fields and hidden in sylvan retreats when he assembled and gathered them in accordance with a plan; he introduced them to every useful and honourable occupation, though they cried out against it at first because of its novelty, and then when through reason and eloquence they had listened with greater attention, he transformed them from wild savages into a kind and gentle folk. (Cicero, *De inventione*, 1.2)

This myth suggests that rhetoric is the institution that transforms the savage into the civilised as it orders the bodily passions through reason and eloquence.[2] Significantly, it does this through the physical presence and speech of a 'man great and wise'; the orator is no different from the savage except in the way that he orders and controls his passions, and those of his audience. As a system that organises the passions through language, rhetoric situates itself at the source of desire's expression. It thereby offers a means – perhaps *the* means – for positioning the body at the site of persuasion. This is a critical fact which both unites all systems of rhetoric and gives an opportunity for possible reinterpretation; the definition of the body, and the valence granted its physicality, shifts with time. In fact, the difference between major rhetorical systems, and attitudes towards rhetoric, can be understood via the relative treatment granted the body: rhetoric is powerful for Cicero because it manipulates and controls bodily drives even as it was dangerous for Plato because it performed its transactions in the currency of eros. For Augustine, it is reconfigured to incorporate desire for God, even as it, skilfully, writes out the presence of the body. Charity and cupidity are the two poles of his rhetorical system, as he explains it in the *De doctrina christiana*, and charity is defined as 'the motion of the soul toward . . . God' while cupidity is 'the motion of the soul toward . . . *any corporal thing.*' Good rhetoric, like good living, steers you away from the body; bad rhetoric draws you toward it.[3] For the troubadours, this relationship is reworked so that the body can re-enter the field of rhetoric since desire is situated in the language of the body – or the vernacular – even as reason retains its connection to the tangible, visible world, for as I have argued elsewhere the use of the vernacular at this point may be marked by its differentiation from Latin, the language of the ethereal Word.[4]

While, then, I would agree with Paterson that rhetoric empowers the troubadours I would add that it does so by granting the weight of tradition to the language of the body. In other words, the problem central to the creation of troubadour verse is the ascription of authority to the language traditionally associated with commerce and the physical. As both the medieval treatises on rhetoric and the poems themselves demonstrate, the troubadours were able to grant authority, and with it literary value, to their vernacular poems by overtly emphasising rhetoric in terms of style, technical terms and the organisation of the poems.

In the following pages I will look at the treatment of rhetoric in rhetorical treatises of the time, in the poems themselves and in the organisation of the poems into subgenres using, as my conceptual framework, the relationship between rhetoric and the body that I have just outlined.

THE RHETORICAL TREATISES

There are no Occitan treatises extant from the time when the first troubadours were writing.[5] The extant texts derive from the late twelfth century onwards. While we can extrapolate from the treatises, then, they bear the same relation to the poems that Aristotle's *Poetics* bears to the tragedies it discusses, and the problems are comparable. For one thing, the treatises only hint at the rhetorical richness of the poems. All extant treatises are prescriptive, similar in purpose to Horace's *Ars poetica*. Of the few extant treatises that talk directly about troubadour rhetoric we will consider three: Dante's *De vulgari eloquentia*, dated between 1303 and 1305, the *Razos de trobar* of Raimon Vidal, dated between 1190 and 1213, and the anonymous *Doctrina de compondre dictatz*. We will then look briefly at a twelfth-century rhetorical text, Matthew of Vendôme's *Ars versificatoria*, which considers lyric in general.[6]

Dante's comment in the *Purgatorio* that Arnaut Daniel was the 'miglior fabbro della lingua materna' (the better craftsman of the mother tongue) perhaps did more for drawing attention to troubadour poetry than any other single comment. His treatment of the poetry of the *lingua d'oc* in the *De vulgari eloquentia* likewise suggests that the language and its poetic treatment by the troubadours offered a model for Italian poets of his time. Strikingly, when Dante goes on to describe the proper use of style he is careful to use terms drawn from a natural lexicon rather than an artificial one. For example, while style should not be 'glossy' or 'bristly' it should be either 'combed' or 'hairy'. The beauty, order and harmony of vernacular language will arise, he suggests, from an innate order, not one imposed from without. In this he suggests that vernacular poetics, which begins, he says, with the troubadours, is a rhetoric of natural beauty. The implications for the placement of desire are certainly different from those of Cicero, as Dante suggests that rhetorical beauty is affiliated with the body in both its natural and its manicured state.

Both the *Razos* of Raimon Vidal and the anonymous *Doctrina de compondre dictatz* are didactic in the extreme, lacking any discernible artistic nuance, the *Razos* discussing the oddities of vernacular grammar, and so reading more like the standard school texts of *grammatica*, the *Doctrina* discussing the division of troubadour song into subgenres. This treatise, whose dating is uncertain though it is found in manuscripts containing the *Razos*, is useful for its approach to these subdivisions. While 40 per cent of troubadour lyrics were love songs, or *cansos*, there exists ample testimony of more than eight other genres (the *Doctrina* lists seventeen), including *planh, pastorela, tenso, vers, sirventes, alba, descort, partimen*.[7] The *Doctrina* distinguishes the genres in terms of theme, so the *alba*, or dawn song, is a song about and sung at dawn, while the *planh* 'speaks in grief and weeps for something that is lost or lamented' (*Doctrina*, p.130). That the love song was the most popular can be seen in the *Doctrina*, as even some of the other subgenres are defined as love songs in different settings, e.g. *planh, descort, alba, gaita*.

A final type of treatise, and one with which the troubadours would have been familiar, is the stylistic handbook, such as the *Rhetorica ad Herennium* of Pseudo-Cicero or the *Ars versificatoria* of Matthew of Vendôme. While the *Ad Herennium* is indeed just a list that teaches the difference between figures of speech and figures of thought, the *Ars versificatoria*, while not necessarily known by the troubadours, is something much more interesting: a rewriting of the Ciceronian treatise that, in its innovations, suggests an interest in the role of the body in rhetoric. While initially reading like a Ciceronian treatise, with a proper *exordium, narratio, partitio* and so on, the treatise is interrupted roughly half way through by an allegorical dream that the author recounts in which Philosophy, Tragedy, Satire and Comedy all accompany Elegy, who comes to teach how lyric persuades. This persuasion depends, Elegy says, on three things: 'the charm of inner meaning, the inner honeycomb', 'the "attire" of words, polished words, the superficial gaiety of words', and 'the quality of speaking, way of speaking, color of speaking, rhetorical color'. The setting is in spring: 'when the nasty winter barrier has been broken', and Flora, the 'hostess of spring', has made the world look and smell beautiful for the benefit of the students of rhetoric. The allegory is derived, clearly, from Boethius and Martianus Capella. But given that its appearance is delayed, that it intrudes an unusual degree of narrative, and that it infuses with sensuality not only the fictional frame but also, by association, the rhetorical advice and terms ('charm', 'gaiety' and even 'colour'), it draws attention to the body and associates the body with the context of rhetoric specifically when discussing the creation of lyric. Moreover, when compared to the similar fictions of Cicero, the change in the role granted the body is striking since, as we have seen, Cicero exiles the passions at the start of his treatise. The rhetoric of twelfth-century lyrics, it would appear, is a rhetoric that embraces and extols sensual pleasure. While none of the treatises that focus on troubadour lyric per se states this explicitly, the *Doctrina* suggests that many of the subgenres have to do with love.

Handbooks on style, such as the *Ad Herennium* and the *Ars versificatoria*, speak to a strong interest in the twelfth century in style and eloquence, especially in the writing of poetry. Dante's later text suggests that that style is derived from nature; Matthew of Vendôme's work explicitly connects such style to the sensual pleasures of spring, a favourite thematic topos for the troubadours. As we have seen, Smith has demonstrated that the troubadours' interest in such style was unsurpassed, whether it be in terms of their interest in figures of repetition, of syntax, of description and argumentation, or those of transfer of sense. All of these techniques could have been learned from handbooks such as these. What is striking about all of these treatises, however, especially in comparison to Horace and Cicero, is the fact that the audience is not the main concern. Persuasion, in other words, is not as important as the process of construction; Matthew of Vendôme's treatise underscores this by placing composition squarely in the domain of desire and therefore in the realm of the poet's as much as his audience's pleasure.

THE POEMS

Turning to the evidence of the poems themselves we find that the troubadours' interest in rhetoric is clear. As with the treatises, however, their main rhetorical concern seems to be as much in creating a rhetorically interesting poem as in persuading the audience. For example, when rhetoric itself is mentioned it is usually in terms of the artist and his creation:

> Qu'eu sai be razon e chauza
> que posc' a midons mostrar. (Bernart de Ventadorn, XXVII, 33–5)

(I know well what explanations and arguments I can demonstrate to my lady.)

> Ben conosc ses art d'escriure,
> que es plan o que es comba. (Arnaut Daniel, IV, 41–2)[8]

(I truly know, without the art of rhetoric, what is flat and what is curved.)

Moreover, while figures of speech and thought, such as those listed by Smith, are indeed evident throughout the troubadour corpus the rhetorical effect seems to have been more to draw attention to the poem than to persuade the audience of anything. For example:

> En breu brisara·l temps braus
> e·ill bisa busin'els brancs. (Arnaut Daniel, XI, 1–2)

(Shortly the rough season will break through and the wind whistle through the branches.)

or:

> L'aur'amara
> fa·l bruoills brancutz
> clarzir. (Arnaut Daniel, IX, 1–3)

(The bitter breeze makes the branched trees bare.)

Each of these openings foregrounds the shape and sound of words through alliteration and assonance, rather than the communication of meaning.

A further way in which the poems show evidence of the rhetorical tradition and an interest in creation is in the discussion of their poetics. However, they approach this topic not in terms of grammar, as Raimon Vidal will, but rather in their descriptions of the product and the process of poetising, for example:

> En cest sonet coind'e leri,
> fauc motz, e capuig e doli,
> que serant verai e cert
> qan n'aurai passat la lima,
> q'Amors marves plan'e daura
> mon chantar, que de liei mou
> qui pretz manten e governa. (Arnaut Daniel, X, 1–7)

(In this little song, pretty and joyful, I create my words, and I plane and hew them, and they will be exact and certain when I've passed the file over them, since Love for me [at once] smooths down and gilds my singing, which emanates from her who maintains and governs Value.)

Or:

> Era si·m fos en grat tengut
>   preir'eu sens glut
> un chantaret prim e menut
>   q'el mon non ha
> doctor qi tan prim ni plus pla
>   lo prezes
>   ni miels l'afines
>   e qi·m creses
>   q'aissi chantes,
>   polira
>   forbira
>   mon chan
>   ses afan
>   gran;
>   mais a lor veiaire
>   qar no·n sabon gaire
>   fail, car non l'esclaire
>   d'aitan
> qe l'entendesson neus l'enfan. (Giraut de Bornelh, XXIX, 1–19)

(Now if anyone were to thank me for it, I would capture without lime the words of a delicate and finely worked little song; for there is no master in the world who could capture it in form so delicate and words more plain, or put on it a more perfect finish. And if anyone were to believe that I could sing in this way, I would polish and adorn my song without great effort; but according to those who know very little about it, I fail by not making it clear enough for even children to understand.)

Here there is the occasional echo of Horace as Giraut, like Raimbaut d'Aurenga and Arnaut Daniel, speaks of 'filing' his poem (even as Horace says in his *Ars poetica*) but, for the most part, the terms are *sui generis* and the emphasis is on creation not persuasion. Emphasis throughout is placed on the quality and craftsmanship required to produce such fine objects as these poems.[9]

A similar observation can be made of the terms the troubadours themselves used to discuss their style: *trobar clus, leu, brau, plan, prim, naturau* and *car*.[10] No extant treatise defines these terms, strikingly, and many are used without definition within the poems themselves. While Marcabru uses classical rhetorical terms such as *razo* and *argumens* he also coins his own term, *trobar naturau*, which refers to his anti-rhetorical stance (a rhetorical ploy as old as Plato) in which his poetry will derive its truth from nature. Peire d'Alvernha's use of the *vers entiers* (whole song) has been read variously as a moral comment, an aesthetic one or, most convincingly by Paterson (for example, *Troubadours*, p. 67), as a rhetorical ploy that suggests that all *vers* other than Peire's is unfinished and therefore imperfect while his is thoroughly finished and so perfect. Read this way, interesting resonances exist between Peire's assertions about good song and Cicero's notions of a good rhetorical speech that, when done correctly, is as finished and complete as a walled city. Peire also discusses *trobar braus*, which opposes the *vers entiers*, and which Marcabru sees as appropriate for discussions of rough themes.

But the troubadours' understanding of rhetoric is not limited to style. Rather, there is evidence of a full comprehension of the range of rhetoric. As Paterson has pointed out (*Troubadours*, p. 15), troubadour poems, such as Marcabru's satire 'Per savi·l tenc ses doptanssa' (XXXVII), demonstrate a clear rhetorical structure as well. Moreover, in this poem there is evidence that rhetoric is clearly linked, at least in Marcabru's mind, to morality:

> Trobador, ab sen d'enfanssa . . .
> . . . fant los motz, per esmanssa,
> entrebeschatz de fraichura.
> E meton en un'eganssa
> falss'Amor encontra fina . . . (XXXVII, 7, 11–14)

(Troubadours with but the sense of a child . . . put together, somehow, words interwoven with cracks and they put on the same footing false and true Love)

a theme which Marcabru continues in another of his satires, 'Pus mos coratges s'es clarzitz':

> Aicel cui fin'Amors causitz
> viu letz, cortes e sapiens,
> e selh cui refuda delis
> e met a totz destruzemens;
> car qui fin'Amors vol blasmar
> elha·l fai si en folh muzar
> que per art cuid'esser peritz. (XL, 8–14)

(The one whom pure Love has chosen thrives as happy, courtly and wise; the one she rejects is destroyed and subjected to utter ruin. For pure Love makes the one who attacks her act like a fool so well that he thinks he perishes by art.)

Marcabru's focus, here and elsewhere, is on the evil troubadours who lump true and false love together. In these two satires Marcabru establishes a moral code in which good poetry, true love and virtue are aligned against the works of bad troubadours and those who are vicious enough to burn in hell: 'Car fin'Amors o a promes, / Lai er dols dels dezesperatz' (XL, 34–5: for true love has promised that it will be so: there will be the lamentations of the hopeless). Marcabru therefore associates good and bad rhetorical with good and bad physical practices. Rhetoric, for Marcabru, has an inalienable relationship to the body.

Perhaps the most heated rhetorical discussion in troubadour poetry concerns the definition of *trobar clus* and *trobar leu*, terms that are, on the face of it, stylistic terms, yet include much more besides. The poets themselves not only use but discuss these terms, most notably in the following *tenso* between Giraut de Bornelh and Raimbaut d'Aurenga:

I   Ara·m platz, Guiraut de Borneill,
      que sapcha per c'anatz blasman
      trobar clus, ni per cal semblan.
        Aiso·m digaz
        si tan prezatz   5
      so que es a toz comunal;
      car adonc tut seran egual.

II   Seign'en Lignaura, no·m coreill
      si qecs s'i trob'a son talan.
      Mas eu son jujaire d'aitan   10
        qu'es mais amatz
        e plus prezatz
      qui·l fa levet e venarsal;
      e vos no m'o tornetz a mal.

III Giraut, non voill qu'en tal trepeil   15
      torn mos trobars. Que ja ogan
      lo lauzo·l bon, e·l pauc e·l gran:
        ja per los fatz
        non er lauzatz,
      car non conoisson (ni lor cal)   20
      so que plus car es ni mais val.

IV   Lignaura, si per aiso veil
ni mon sojorn torn en affan,
sembla que·m dopte del mazan.
   A que trobatz   25
    si non vos platz
c'ades o sapchon tal e cal?
Que chanz non port'altre cabtal.

V   Giraut, sol que·l miels appareil
e·l dig'ades e·l trag'enan,   30
mi non cal sitot non s'espan,
    c'anc granz viutaz
    non fon denhtatz;
per so prez'om mais aur que sal,
e de tot chant es attretal.   35

VI   Lignaura, fort de bon conseill
es fis amans contrarian!
E pero si·m val mais d'affan
    mos sos levatz,
    c'us enraumatz   40
lo·m deissazec e·l diga mal!
Que no·l deing ad home sesal. (Raimbaut d'Aurenga, XXXI) [11]

I   Now I should like to know, Giraut de Bornelh, why you go about finding fault with the 'obscure' style and for what reason. Tell me this: if you esteem so greatly that which is common to all; for then all will be equal.

II   Sir Lignaura, I don't complain if each one writes according to his desire. But I am of the opinion that if one makes [the poem] understandable and common to all, it is more loved and esteemed; and do not take me wrong in this.

III   Giraut, I don't want my compositions turned into such confusion; may the good and the small and the great never praise them henceforth! They will never be praised by fools, for they do not recognise (nor does it matter to them) what is most valuable and worthwhile.

IV   Lignaura, if I should lie awake and turn my pleasure into anguish, it would seem that I'm afraid of popular acclaim. Why do you write if you don't want all to understand it immediately? For a song has no other value.

V   Giraut, if only I prepare the best and say and bring it forth, it doesn't bother me if it is not spread abroad. A thing of great vileness was never a thing of great worth: for that reason one esteems gold more than salt, and with any song it is the same.

VI Lignaura, excellent adviser, you are a very argumentative lover! [However I would rather hear my song uplifted by a child than] a hoarse-voiced singer garble and sing badly my tune, as I do not judge it fitting for a person of a higher rank.

Michel-André Bossy has recently demonstrated, following Marianne Shapiro and others, that *trobar clus* refers to the deliberately artificial style of the *clus* poem. He concludes with the observation that 'poets employ obscurity first of all to foreground their medium, to endow their art language with opacity and texture' (Bossy, 'Trobar Clus', p. 215). Amelia Van Vleck has proposed that *clus* may refer to the relative difficulty of the 'process of memorization and transmission' (*Memory*, Chapter 6) with these songs; I would like to go further and suggest that the *clus/leu* debate refers not only to memory but also to different methods for turning the language of the streets, from the body, into art. The relationship between poet and poem in troubadour lyric can be seen as rooted in the body because of the fact that the troubadours are composing their songs in the vernacular which, among other things, is the language of the body.[12] In terms of the *tenso* quoted above, Raimbaut recommends using recherché, vernacular terms to accomplish this (*clus*) while Giraut argues, instead, that the use of a style that is *levet* (plain) and *venarsal* (simple) is what makes the language poetic (10–14). Each participant evinces a concern for his interaction with a physically present audience (4–7, 10–14, 14–21, 25–8), for the quality of performances of his work (29–30, 38–42) and for rank in the concrete hierarchical world of the court (7, 17–18, 28, 34–5). Rhetoric thus again becomes inextricably bound up with embodiment in the vernacular world of troubadour poetics.

All the views expressed in this poem converge in the perception that the troubadours who composed especially in the more obscuring styles were less concerned with the obfuscation of hermeticism than with their stance vis-à-vis language. In other words, the troubadours are fascinated by rhetoric because it offers a means by which a speaker can address his relation to language. This is borne out in rhetorical terminology itself. While Latin rhetorical texts speak of style in terms of levels – high, middle, low – troubadour poems refer to style in terms that foreground relationships between people. Such words as closed, open, broken, filed, rich, posit a strong interaction between poet and poem; at the same time they invite the participation of the audience with the physicality of the song.

GENRES

The generic subdivision functions in a similar way. The *Doctrina de compondre dictatz* does not attempt to explain why these topics and no others were chosen; yet it is possible to suggest that the genres are not randomly selected. A brief look at some examples will clarify this. There is little, if any, agreement on how the generic terms should apply.[13] For instance, after 1160 *canso* was the more common term than *vers* for love song, although even that distinction is not entirely precise (Raimbaut d'Aurenga, for instance, suggests that the two are interchangeable, see XXX; later satires as well tended to continue to use the term *vers*). *Cansos*, for example, are indeed about love, but not just any love. Rather, it is a love that has something in common with song:

> Chantars no pot gaire valer
> si d'ins dal cor no mou lo chans (Bernart de Ventadorn, II, 1–2)

(There is no use in singing if, from the heart, the song does not spring.)

And again:

> Quan lo rius de la fontana
> s'esclarzis si cum far sol,
> e par la flors aiglentina,
> e·l rossignoletz el ram
> volf e refranh et aplana
> son dous chantar et afina,
> dreitz es qu'ieu lo mieu refranha. (Jaufré Rudel, III, 1–7)[14]

(When the fountain's flow shines brilliantly as usual, and the wild rose appears, and the little nightingale on the branch varies, changes, smooths out and perfects his sweet song, it is right that I should rehearse mine.)

So, too, the *planh*, while indeed a lament, is also a lyric meditation on the way in which loss and lyric have much in common:

> Si tuit li doil e·il plor e·il marrimen
> e las dolors e·il dan e·il chaitivier
> c'om hanc agues en est segle dolen
> fossen ensems, sembleran tuit leugier
> contra la mort del joven rei engles,

don reman pres et jovenz doloiros,
escurs e tieins e negr'e tenebros,
sems de tot joi, ples de tristor e d'ira.

Dolen e trist e ple de marrimen
son remazut li cortes soudadier,
e·il trobador e·il joglar avinen;
trop an e Mort agut mortal guerrier,
qe tout lur ha lo joven rei engles,
vas cui eran li plus larc cobeitos.
Ja non er mais ni non crezatz q'anc fos,
vas aquest dol el segle plurs ni ira. (Bertran de Born, XIV, 1–16)

(If all the grief, the tears, and the distress, the suffering, the pain, and the misery which one had ever suffered in this grievous life were put together, they would all seem minor compared with the death of the young English king; merit and youth are left grieving, dark and sombre and gloomy, emptied of all joy, weighed down with sadness and sorrow.

Sorrowful and sad and weighed down with distress are left the courtly retainers, the poets and the pleasant minstrels: they have found in death a too-deathly foe who has taken from them the young English king, beside whom the most generous seem mean. There never more will be – and think not there ever was – compared to this loss, such tears or sorrow.)

Much like a negative nature opening that sings of winter rather than spring, this poem reverses *topoi* common to the *canso*: the death of the king has left the world empty of joy, and as with joy, such grief cannot be measured. As a consequence, while the poem indeed is an elegiac lament it is also, to all intents and purposes, a reverse *canso*, where the lack of joy, in its boundlessness, has replaced joy itself. Notice that the *trobadors* and *joglars* in stanza II are claimed to be full of grief as the *cortes soudadier*; yet, surely, the claim is ironic, for the grief continues to provide the singers with material for further song, if not with the immediate compensation for its performance, while the members of the court are indeed left empty-handed.

What we find with the subgenres, in short, is a generic taxonomy that is organised by desire and reflects a thematic preoccupation with the struggle between order and desire as it positions desire in the tangible medium of the spoken language and, in so doing, positions the speaker as the purveyor of desire in language. *Canso*, *alba*, *planh*, *tenso*, *pastorela* and *sirventes* all entail unresolved tensions that are either explicitly or implicitly about desire. Indeed, I would suggest that these genres can be distinguished in terms of the temporal trajectory of their desire: *planh*, for example, explores the tension between present and past, *alba*, present and future. This taxonomy therefore reflects concerns similar to those of rhetoric. It recalls, in fact, the rhetorical divisions of Aristotle, repeated by Cicero, into epideictic, deliberative and forensic, categories determined not just by theme (panegyric, political and judicial) but by the time of the event: present, future, past. With the troubadours, however, the subject is framed and defined precisely in terms of the tension that is created between the present of the speaker and the time of the event. The difference, in other words, between classical subdivisions and those of the troubadours is that the relation between the speaker and his subgenre is established first in terms of temporal setting and then in terms of the particular desire that that temporal or spatial distance evokes.[15]

CONCLUSION

In sum, the fact that the troubadours refer to rhetoric, specifically and in other ways, suggests their preoccupation not with persuasion but with the intersection between poet and poem (and, arguably, language and the body). This assertion is borne out by the fact that the most stylistically assertive texts – those of Raimbaut d'Aurenga or Arnaut Daniel, for example – foreground language and the lyric persona's relation to that language. The stylistic terms, likewise, speak to relational models between speaker and object, on-going processes that invite the positing of interpretation. Genres and subgenres as well each speak to an interest in the placement of the speaker in the world, and the relation of the body to language.

Recently Eugene Garver has demonstrated how Aristotle's concern in his *Rhetoric*, one of the earliest systematisations of the discipline, is not so much with oratory per se as it is with defining culture in terms of the ways in which language confronts reason and desire. Aristotle's rhetoric, Garver argues, serves to 'preserve and systematize the ambiguities between discourse and reality'. Unlike Cicero, whose rhetoric serves to control bodily passions through exile, Aristotle strikingly includes emotion in his system.

The appearance of rhetorical treatises such as this one corresponds to moments of cultural definition precisely, I would argue, because rhetoric represents an effort to coordinate the two opposing forces of reason and desire through language. What is striking about troubadour poetry is that its use of rhetoric and rhetorical terminology, new and old, recalls the systems of Aristotle and Cicero in its complexity and inclusiveness; it, too, tries to suggest a means for the interaction of body and language. Moreover, its use of rhetoric suggests a willingness to espouse the values of Cicero (and Horace after him) to the extent that they too celebrate the visual tangible world. But the troubadours engage at the same time in a deconstruction of classical rhetorical values as they suggest that the embrace of the visual and the tangible is also an embrace of the corporeal and therefore of the passions. They see, in other words, the tangible and visual as vehicles for desire, not (like Cicero) as threats to it or (like Augustine) as a means that is ultimately divorced from its end. Rather, the classical rhetorical tradition offers the troubadour a way to integrate the world with desire through the body-centred medium of the vernacular word.

NOTES

1 See particularly Paterson, *Troubadours*, p. 211, where she summarises her conclusions. My thanks to Bill Paden for help with an earlier draft of this chapter.
2 See Spence, *Rhetoric*, Chapter 1.
3 *De doctrina christiana* 2.1; emphasis mine.
4 See my *Texts and the Self*.
5 For an overview of the question of treatises and rhetorical terms in Occitan poetry see Gaunt, 'Occitan grammars'.
6 Excellent background, bibliography (including available translations) and introduction to all of these treatises can be found in Kelly, *Arts*. The first three of these can be found, in translation, in Shapiro, *De Vulgari*; the last in Faral, *Arts* (Latin and French summaries), Gallo, 'Matthew' (English translation of most of the treatise).
7 According to Paden ('System'), 40 per cent of troubadour lyric were *cansos*, 20 per cent *sirventes*, 20 per cent *coblas*, 20 per cent minor genres.
8 Translations of Arnaut Daniel are taken from Wilhelm.
9 Another facet of troubadour lyric that adds to the notion that the poems are to be perceived as beautiful, almost plastic, works of art

is the intricate rhyme schemes they employ. For more on this see Chambers, *Introduction*, and Chapter 9. For further on the poem as an *objet d'art* see Chapter 14.

10 Here, most notably, see Paterson, *Troubadours*.

11 Text and translation from Pattison with the exception of line 38, which has been emended to follow Sharman.

12 Spence, *Texts and the Self*, Chapter 4; see also Kay, 'Rhetoric'.

13 Here, most usefully, see Bec, 'Le problème'.

14 Translation from *Jaufre Rudel*, ed. Wolf and Rosenstein, p. 139.

15 For further on how the temporal relations map onto the subgenres of troubadour song see my 'The Subgeneric Division of Troubadour Lyric' (diss., Columbia University, 1981).

CHAPTER 11

Intertextuality and dialogism in the troubadours

Maria Luisa Meneghetti

Researchers into physiology, cybernetics, epistemology, linguistics and semiology over the past thirty years concur in positing at the basis of the development of creative thought – in the arts and even the sciences – mechanisms that are dialogic in nature. The concept of dialogue which they use, of course, is above all a metaphorical one. In the case of the literary work in particular, each text is seen as originating from a type of dialogue instituted between the poet and his predecessors, the novelist and the characters he wants to represent or, more generally, between the language of the writer and the language of the world in which he lives.

From this perspective, intertextuality, that is to say the close formal interdependence between a text and one or more of its antecedents ('relation de coprésence entre deux ou plusieurs textes', as Gérard Genette has succinctly defined it[1]), can indeed be seen as a fundamental nodal point of expression through which any literary 'dialogue' takes shape or, indeed, even as its principal vehicle. It is to a formidable scholar, Mikhail M. Bakhtin, that we owe the formulation and first use of the concept of intertextuality – according to which every text is constructed like an actual mosaic of the 'words of others', of more or less direct and explicit citations – together with the injunction to view dialogism as characterising many literary forms: that of the novel, in the first instance.[2]

I have spoken of intertextuality as *vehicle* of the dialogue, and this is without doubt Bakhtin's position. As he does not distinguish between the repetition of everyday language and actual citations from literary texts, he believes that the recuperation of 'another's word' lacks, or at least does not necessarily possess, artistic authority, but serves instead as the basis for a more open and dynamic dialogue into which the conceptual and the ideological can both be drawn.

In fact, however, when instead of looking at the web of relationships between ordinary statements, we turn to those between literary texts, in which the word, as deployed by the writer, already carries a certain weight in itself, it becomes clear that intertextuality and dialogism are phenomena which belong not only to the same category of communicative act – one which I would define as 'anaphoric communication'[3] – but to the same level, since neither is subordinated to the other. Within a given literary text there may in fact be intertextual re-production when the repetition works above all at the level of the signifier (that is, when what prompts recognition is an exact formal or verbal echoing of the source text), thus establishing a similarity between texts which may concern their use of *topoi*, or which may be lexical, syntactical-stylistic, structural or even, in the case of poetic works, metrical. However, within that very same literary text, on the other hand, there may be dialogic re-production. In such a case, the repetition works above all at the level of the signified, in that what prompts the interaction creates a solidarity through content, and sets up a discourse between the authors concerned, a weft of ideas that are homogeneous (though not necessarily harmonious) and that are developed through a series of exchanges.

I have said that the repetitions can relate either to the signifier 'above all', or to the signified 'above all'. It must be emphasised, however, that in actual artistic expression there cannot be a solely intertextual re-production, just as there cannot be one which is purely dialogic. The bridge flung between one text and another by the reiteration of a key expression, a structured *topos* or a certain rhyme scheme always enables some ideological, or conceptual, implications to pass between them as well. The second text may perhaps overturn these in order to construct a discourse which either attacks or just differs from the first. Conversely, dialogue has to be supported by some kind of mark at the level of the signifier which serves to point out that anaphoric communication is taking place.

Even when taking purely empirical data as one's point of departure, one may, however, propose that there are types of literature and/or genres which lend themselves more to the intertextual, and types of literature and/or genres which are more drawn to the dialogic. And if, thanks to Bakhtin's astute observations, the novel is now seen as the genre best suited to dialogism, it seems that the lyric should instead take the prize for the genre with the greatest capacity for exploiting intertextuality. One has only to flick through any edition with a good critical apparatus of the lyric output of any author – old or recent – to see how each poetic product feeds on allusions or references to previous texts, how each poem is founded on other poetry.

Once it has been said that the lyric genre appears particularly suited to the techniques of intertextuality, two clarifications are, however, immediately necessary.

In the first place, it is easy for the scholar to fall victim to what I would call 'le piège de la poésie formelle' (the formalist poetic trap). We know, in broad terms, that in a given language certain words rhyme only with one or two other words ('you do not avoid . . . certain couplets or tercets', observed Aldo Menichetti, one of the greatest authorities on metrical forms in the Romance languages, and especially in Italian).[4] More specifically, we know that in many cultural contexts the lyric was founded on a rigidly formulaic language of *topoi*, with the concept of 'variation on a theme' as its driving force and perhaps also its very reason for composition. One need only think of the production of the Old French *trouvères*, in relation to which Robert Guiette coined the expression 'poésie formelle'. In these situations, the problem is that of distinguishing the redeployment of a *topos*, or the reference back to a conceptual and expressive mode of a particular style, from actual intertextual recuperation. In other words, how is one to distinguish, in relation to an author's use of a given ideological and literary system, between reference to a specific text and a generic process of literary self-validation? I believe that an important distinction which makes such discernment possible lies in the fact that, in order for it to be significant at an intertextual level, the repeated form of a concept or of an element belonging to a *topos* should present itself as structured in the same way as in the source text, that is to say as possessing analogous stylistic elements, rhythmic or metrical similarities. The closeness of the syntactical constructions, lexical choices and metrical forms guarantees an interdependence of imagery that, in the absence of such markers, should be seen as determined by the tradition.[5]

Secondly, even if from a quantitative point of view, so to speak, the lyric genre's propensity for intertextual play beyond the dialogic appears indisputable, within the diachronic development of many poetic traditions there is no shortage of examples in which the reference back to the 'other's word' takes on a strongly dialogic value. For example, in the development of the Italian lyric between the Middle Ages and the Renaissance, the strand that tends to privilege a purely intertextual recuperation on the level of the signifier seems to dominate two periods. In the earlier period, there is that of the so-called Sicilian school, whose striking adoption of the form and *topoi* of Occitan models is not matched by any real harmonisation of content, such was the ideological distance that by then separated the world of the troubadours from that of the court of Emperor Frederick II.[6] More recently there is the strand of sixteenth-century Petrarchism in which, as its name indicates, the cult of Petrarch and Petrarchan form founds a sort of poetic monotheism, masking the extreme slightness of its practitioners' inspiration. In contrast, in the *dolce stil nuovo* period, the dense network of intellectual connections between the leading poets of the movement results in works in which the strictly intertextual element, which is not as apparent or at least not as extensive as one would expect in view of their Occitan and Sicilian antecedents, is of little importance in itself, serving rather sporadically to highlight a series of intentional and motivated dialogic trajectories between the authors.[7]

Two clearly distinct models of anaphoric communication can be isolated. The first, which I shall call linear, builds textual chains in such a way that the meaning of what is communicated does not change. Each new text derives from a pre-existing text and in turn can generate a further text, and so on, in an expansion which is theoretically infinite. At its extreme are more complex cases in which a single text produces different intertextual outcomes, all independent of one another. A second model, which I shall call alternating, instead constructs a system of textual relations in which the line of communication tends to turn back on itself, and can even do so with every new creation, so that the roles of author and addressee are continually being exchanged.

Obviously, the linear model presents wider opportunites for use. This is particularly because it can develop diachronically, whilst the alternating model does not have this capacity in any obvious way, since it necessarily entails control of the intertext on the part of all of its authors, throughout every phase of its creation. And it is, I believe, similarly evident that, whilst dialogic interactions may be borne as much by one model as by the other, intertextual relations can only lend themselves to the linear type of creative model. In fact, because of the intrinsic ideological neutrality of the structures of meaning at the level where every intertextual procedure takes place, even when a new piece is created broadly contemporaneously with its antecedent, the author of that antecedent rarely feels implicated in any possible antagonism on the part of the author of the new work.

Recourse to techniques of anaphoric communication in the Occitan lyric is extensive and, above all, has crucial consequences for the way troubadour poetry developed. Such an assertion is not in the least revolutionary, given that many scholars in recent years have systematically emphasised this fact, drawing attention to ever more numerous, and often persuasive, examples of sequences or constellations of compositions that are tightly interconnected through precisely these anaphoric links. They have spoken of an actual 'Dialektik des Trobar', of intertextual 'metamorphoses', or of 'dialogism' as an almost congenital tendency in the literary culture of medieval Occitania.[8]

However, the variety of formulations used by the various scholars to define the phenomenon shows that so far there seems to have been no place for a careful consideration of the nature of the phenomenon itself. It has not occurred to anyone to distinguish the different degrees of interaction, case by case, and whether they centre on formal composition, content or ideological slant. In other words, no one has thought to make a clear distinction between those cases in which intertextuality dominates and those which are instead inclined to make links of a distinctly more dialogic type.

In actual fact, both the intertextual and dialogic tendencies can be said to be present in all four of the most widespread genres of troubadour poetry: the *canso*, the *sirventes*, the *tenso* and the *partimen*.[9] They are found, however, in proportions which vary according not only to the genre involved but also to authors and period. To put it very schematically, it could be said that as far as the *canso* is concerned, whilst recourse to the various intertextual typologies seems to stay constant across the whole sweep of its development, transforming a vast sequence of works by different authors into a kind of unified formal web, the tendency towards dialogism gradually diminishes the further one moves away from the earliest poets. This decrease parallels the end of courtly 'militancy' in the Midi, as a consequence of the deep political and social disturbances resulting from the Albigensian Crusade, so harmful to the southern magnates. After the first or second decade of the thirteenth century, when we still find someone of the calibre of Aimeric de Peguilhan engaged in close dialogue with his predecessors, most notably Folquet de Marselha,[10] there are no more truly significant examples of *cansos* in which the courtly 'creed' is thrashed out via comparison with the preceding tradition.

Tensos and *partimens* display a relatively slight tendency towards intertextuality, probably because of the scant formal control which characterises them, as a result, no doubt, of their improvised composition; their significant feature is rather dialogism. This remains so even in the later period, persisting well after the beginning of the thirteenth century, for example in the two-hander 'N'Albertz, chauzetz' (III), in which Aimeric de Peguilhan and his partner Albertet are debating the satisfactions of love, and introducing a subtle 'dialogue' with the Jaufré Rudel of 'Belhs m'es' (V) and 'Quan lo rossinhols' (VI), and the Raimbaut d'Aurenga of 'Loncs temps' (XXVIII).[11] Indeed, this dialogism continues up to the end of the first half, or even right into the second half, of the thirteenth century, as confirmed by one doubtless very late example amongst others: a *tenso*, which has unfortunately come down to us only in a fragmentary form, between the two Genoese troubadours Simon Doria and Giacomo Grillo, 'Segne' n Iacme Grils' (PC 436.3). This picks up the metrical form and rhymes of a preceding debate between Peire Guilhem de Tolosa and Sordello ('En Sordel, que us es semblan', XIV) in such a way as to mock the latter.[12]

Finally, the genre of the *sirventes* (or the subgenres thematically connected with it, such as the *gap* for example) confirms that recourse to predominantly intertextual techniques is more recent than that to predominantly dialogic ones. For whilst the recourse to *contrafactum* (the derivation of the melody, rhyme scheme and metre from external sources, leaving out any identity of theme or thought) seems to be affirmed, and that not even standardly, only from the time of Bertran de Born,[13] Marcabru, in an exchange with N'Audric (del Vilar?), had already launched the model of the strongly dialogic reply. I refer here, of course, to the well-known 'Tot a estru' and 'Seigner n'Audric' (XX, XX bis), but also to Marcabru's so-called *gap*, 'D'aisso lau Dieu' (XVI). This likewise picks up the metrical form introduced by N'Audric so that Marcabru can offend his rival indirectly, while recycling coarse insults on the paucity of his possessions and, what is more, casting doubt on the legitimacy of his progeny. I thus postulate the order of composition of these songs as XX–XX bis–XVI, as opposed to the traditional ordering XVI–XX–XX bis.[14]

I shall now attempt to clarify some significant examples of anaphoric communication (significant in some cases because problematic), and try to draw from them conclusions with wider implications. I will present three instances, distant from each other in terms of period and context, and also of the motivations and implications which characterise them.

The first case involves the very beginnings of the troubadour lyric (or, at least, those beginnings known to us), since it concerns the interactions between the works of Guilhem IX and those of Jaufré Rudel.

Having gone back to that old identification of Jaufré's *amor de lonh* with the Virgin, Gruber had already corroborated, along the lines of what I call the dialogic, the points of contact, which had actually always been suspected, between two so-called *devinalhs*, namely 'Farai un vers de dreyt nien' (IV) by Guilhem IX and Jaufré's 'Non sap chantar' (I).[15] In the latter he saw an exact, polemical riposte to the sacrilegious banter of the Duke of Aquitaine's, who, being indifferent to the appeal of his unobtainable *amiga*, had declared his preference for a wholly earthly love.

But even leaving aside the hypothetical equation whereby 'amor de lonh' means the Virgin Mary, Gruber's reconstruction still left the not insignificant problem of the chronological succession of interventions. If Guilhem precedes Jaufré Rudel, but parodies the very convictions later espoused by Jaufré, such convictions must have been in circulation *before* Jaufré. Yet there is no evidence that such beliefs were in circulation, given the absence of contemporaneous vernacular lyrics to take as comparison and the lack of parallel material in what survives in medieval Latin. Bologna and Fassò have tried to resolve the problem, starting from a reinterpretation of the documented facts concerning Jaufré (according to which he would already be an adult in the years 1120–5)[16] and from an astute evaluation of the expressive and formal points of convergence between the two troubadours (although these are certainly not numerous). They have proposed, albeit cautiously, an account whereby 'Farai un vers' (V, a true *gap* in which Guilhem, a fake pilgrim 'en Alvernhe, part Lemozi', boasts of his sexual conquests) would be succeeded by Jaufré's 'Lanquan li jorn' (IV, a counter-*gap* playing on the theme of the 'true', or 'pious', pilgrimage to the holy places where lives an unobtainable *amor de lonh*), both then followed by – and at this point the sequence becomes more convincing – 'Farai un vers de dreyt nien' and 'Non sap chantar'.[17] If relations between the two troubadours are really as these scholars suggest, their dialogic communication takes on an unforeseen 'alternating' aspect, as distinct from the traditionally assumed linear one of Jaufré responding to Guilhem. Whatever the facts in the case, we are dealing with 'dialogic communication'. Indeed, as has been shown, within the complex network of connections linking the works of the two poets, the interactions that may be defined as intertextual in the strict sense of the word appear much less marked and unequivocal than those that are conceptual and ideological. The interweaving of their discursive duet emerges as even more sophisticated than had previously been thought.

The second case allows us to widen our geographical horizons beyond the Occitan domain, since here the anaphoric knot involves not just a handful of troubadours, but also two well-known *trouvères* from the North of France. There are five compositions, datable within the period roughly 1170 to 1260, which display considerable formal and conceptual links, even though these are concentrated within their respective introductory stanzas. They are: (1) a *canso* by Giraut de Bornelh (XXXIII, 'A penas sai'); (2) another *canso*, 'Leu chansonet' ad entendre' (PC 62.1) which two out of three MSS attribute to a mysterious Bernart de la Fon, whilst the third favours the much more famous Bernart de Ventadorn;[18] (3) a *canso* by the *trouvère* Conon de Béthune ('Chançon legiere a entendre'); (4) a *sirventes* by Uc de Saint Circ (XX, 'Chanzos q'es leus') that picks up the same metrical form and rhymes as the *canso* of Bernart de la Fon/Bernart de Ventadorn;

(5) a *canso* by the *trouvère* Raoul de Soissons ('Chançon legiere a chanter'):

> (1) A penas sai comensar
>   un vers que volh far leuger
>   e si n'ai pensat des er
>   que·l fezes de tal razo
>   que l'entenda tota gens
>   e qu'el fass' a leu chantar;
>   qu'eu·l fatz per pla deportar.

(I scarcely know how to start a *vers* that I wish to be easy and so I have been thinking since yesterday how I might compose it on a topic that would be easy for everyone to understand and easy to sing; and so I compose it to be enjoyed straightforwardly.)

> (2) Leu chansonet' ad entendre
>   ab leu sonet volgra far,
>   coindet' e leu per apendre
>   e plan' e leu per chantar,
>   quar leu m'aven la razo,
>   e leu latz los motz e·l so;
>   per so m'en vuelh leu passar,
>   quar de plan e leu trobar
>   nulhs hom no·m pot leu reprendre.

(I'd like to compose a song easy to understand with an accessible tune, elegant and easy to learn, and smooth and easy to sing, for the theme comes to me easily and I find that I lace the words and music together easily too. For this reason I wish to acquit myself of it easily for when it comes to straightforward and easy compositions, no one can make an easy case against me.)

> (3) Chançon legiere a entendre
>   ferai, car bien m'est mestiers
>   ke chascuns le puist aprendre
>   et c'on le chant volentiers;
>   ne par autres messaigiers
>   n'iert ja ma dolors mostree
>   a la millor ki soit nee.

(I shall compose a song that's easy to understand, for I need everyone to be able to learn it and sing it willingly; nor will my pain be communicated to the best lady ever born by any other messenger.)

(4)   Chanzos q'es leu per entendre
        et avinenz per chantar,
        tal qu'om non puescha reprendre
        los motz ni·l chant esmendar,
        et a douz e gai lo son
        e es de bella razon
        ed avinen per condar,
        mi plai e la voil lauzar
        a qi la blasm' e defendre.

(A song easy to understand and agreeable to sing, so that the words can't be criticised or the song improved upon, and which has a sweet and merry tune and a fine theme, agreeable to relate, that's what pleases me, and I intend to praise and defend it against anyone who criticises it.)

(5)   Chançon legiere a chanter
        et plesant a escouter
        ferai conme chevaliers,
        pour ma grant dolor mostrer
        la ou je ne puis aler,
        ne dire mes desiriers;
        si me sera grant mestiers
        qu'ele soit bone et legiere,
        pour ce que de ma priere
        me soit chascuns mesagiers
        et amis et amparliers
        a ma douce dame chiere.

(As a knight should, I shall compose a song easy to sing and pleasant to listen to, in order to communicate my great grief in the place where I cannot go myself, nor speak of my desires. And so it will be very useful to me that the song should be good and accessible, so that everyone can be the spokesman, ally, and advocate of my request to my sweet dear lady.)

In all five texts, the central motif, which takes up one of the key points of troubadour poetic thought – the communicability of the poetic message – is expressed through similar terminology and syntactical forms, starting with the incipits which are almost identical in four out of five cases, and continuing through the convergence or close resemblance of many of the rhyme words (*chantar/chanter* in 1, 2, 4, 5; *entendre* in 2, 3, 4; *razo/razon* in 1, 2, 4; *so/son* in 2, 4; *apendre/aprendre* in 2, 3; *reprendre* in 2, 4; *messagiers* in 3, 5; *leuger/legiere* in 1, 5; *mostree/mostrer* in 3, 5).

However, in looking at the contexts which, one by one, are invested with this motif, it becomes apparent that there is a progressive conceptual slippage effected by the various authors. In Giraut, already committed elsewhere to defending a poetic discourse which is clear and comprehensible to everyone (as in the *tenso* with Raimbaut d'Aurenga, 'Era·m platz'; see Chapter 10), the declaration of intent emerges from the opening lines, extending over a good three *coblas* out of seven (the four remaining ones are made up of generic expressions of love for the lady), and so takes on the value of literary polemic. This polemical-literary investment is undoubtedly lacking in Bernart de la Fon's (or de Ventadorn's) text as well as in those of the two *trouvères*: Bernart wishes, above all, to proclaim his own unshakeable desire to use the 'easy' style to glorify *midons* (note that the term *leu*, used in some cases as an adjective, in others as an adverb, appears without fail in each line). For Conon and Raoul likewise the transparency of poetic discourse seems to be the only route to harmony with the haughty object of their love, and, indeed, to attaining the 'miracle' of a more lenient bearing on her part. Uc de Saint Circ's starting point, however, marks a complete eradication of this motif, given that 'Chanzos q'es leus' is a violent *sirventes* against Ezzelino da Romano, vice-regent of Emperor Frederick II. So it is that the search for clarity of exposition concludes in an orientation towards political propaganda.

In this example, in short, the situation seems the opposite of that delineated in the preceding one: with a minimal investment in dialogism, it offers instead a maximal inscription of intertextuality.

The third example again brings us to the canonical beginnings of Occitan lyricism, or rather, even further back, towards origins that until recently were not even suspected. But it also shows us a cultural frame of reference that crosses over and beyond the literature of the troubadours, into the domain of the mythical and anthropological.

Perhaps one of the most famous passages of the poetic corpus of Bernart de Ventadorn is the beginning of *cobla* V of 'Tant ai' (IV):

> A! Deus! car no sui ironda
> que voles per l'aire
> e vengues de noih prionda
> lai dins so repaire?

(Oh God, why am I not a swallow that might fly through the air and enter, in the depth of night, the place where she dwells?)

A little strophe which was recently discovered in a manuscript copied in a German-speaking area, but whose Poitevin origin and very ancient date (the last third of the eleventh century) seem certain, not only presents the same motif of the lover who fantasises about being transformed into a bird so as to reach his beloved lady, who is far away or at least not easily reachable, but it also does so using a syntactical structure that, in the two opening lines at least, displays extraordinary affinities with Bernart's two opening lines:

> Las, qui non sun sparvir astur,
> qui podis a li voler,
> la sintil imbracher,
> se buchschi duls baser,
> dussir e repasar tu dulur.[19]

(Alas, why am I not a sparrow-hawk that might fly to her and embrace her and give her a sweet kiss to sweeten and lighten all pain?)

Furthermore the undoubted correspondence between the two texts (which can only reflect a chronology in which the anonymous Poitevin precedes Bernart) is inserted within a complex system of echoes of *topoi* that seems to embrace not only the lyric works of the troubadours, but also those from the French, medieval German, old Italian and even the Mozarabic domains; and not just lyric works either, but even some pertaining to the epistolary genre, as well as narrative (for example, the extraordinary narrative 'translation' of the motif in the first part of Marie de France's *lai* of *Yonec* in which the knight Muldumarec reaches his lady, imprisoned in a high tower by the jealous husband, by assuming the form of a goshawk).[20]

The cohesion of all these passages is, it must be stressed, unstable from an intertextual point of view: they share no formal structures – that is to say, metrical, stylistic or syntactical ones – given that the only feature truly common to all of them is the minimal narrative function assigned to the protagonist which can be formulated as: 'a bird–lover flies (hopes to fly) towards his beloved lady, or he goes away (has to go away) from her'.[21]

This does not, however, exclude the possibility that the set of texts in question may be criss-crossed here and there and even activated by closer connections, analogous to those already dis-

cerned between the little Poitevin strophe and the Bernart passage. For example, it has been strongly emphasised recently that
two of the less evident exemplars of the motif, namely the second
cobla of Jaufré Rudel's 'Quan lo rius' (III) and the sixth of Bernart
Marti's 'Bel m'es' (III), are connected to each other through a link
which is as strong formally as ideologically.[22] The case is interesting, not least because Jaufré's allusion to the motif of the bird–
lover is not apparent at first sight, but only becomes so if one
bears in mind the true meaning of the term *reclam* ('bait of meat,
fit to lure the falcon and sparrow-hawk back').[23] This is the central
rhyme word of the *cobla* of 'Quan lo rius', which reads:

> Amors de terra lonhdana,
> per vos totz lo cors mi dol.
> E no·n puosc trobar meizina,
> si non vau al sieu reclam,
> ab atraich d'amor doussana
> dinz vergier o sotz cortina
> ab dezirada companha. (III, 14–20)

(Love of a distant land, for you all my heart aches. And I cannot find
medicine unless I go to its summons, with the lure of sweet love within
the garden or beneath the bed-hanging, with longed-for companionship.)

The lover, embodying himself as a noble bird of prey accustomed
to soaring up into the pure heights, declares that he wants to
refuse the *meizina*, the balm for any nearby allurement of *amor
doussana*, so that he might instead follow the *reclam* of the much
more powerful 'amor de terra lonhdana'.

Let us now see how Bernart Marti reworks the image, or rather,
to put it another way, how he reworks the ornithological self-
identification, strikingly totemic indeed:

> En autr'amistat propdana
> m'amar mis, que·m fo dolsana:
>   ans la·m nei
>   que·m sordei,
> mas la meiller no·m vairei.
> L'esparviers, ab bel semblant,
> va del Pueg ves lei volant:
>   la longua trencada,
>   pren lai sa volada. (III, 46–54)

(I set my [bitter] love on another, nearby friendship, which was sweet to
me: I give it up before I degenerate, but I'll not change her who is best.

The fine-looking sparrow-hawk flies from the Puy towards her. With a long swoop it takes its flight there.)

There is no doubt that the sparrow-hawk–Bernart Marti, disdainful of an *amistat propdana* which by his own account degrades him, also stretches his wings to join a faraway *mielhs*. However, this lady *lunhada* does not seem to have any connotations whatsoever of the pure being, free from the constraints of sensuality, of Jaufré's *amor de lonh*. Instead she comes across as an extremely concrete object of lust: '. . . graile, grass'e plana, / sotz la camiza ransana' (slender, sleek and smooth beneath her embroidered shirt, 37–8). In short, the long journey of the sparrow-hawk ends yet again in that lukewarm intimacy created by the *cortina* that the Prince of Blaye appeared to have definitively rejected as a place of love.

Despite appearances, Bernart Marti's contribution, rather than being seen as a parody of Jaufré, should be considered as a sort of return, a polemical one certainly, to the true meaning of the *topos* which Jaufré himself had subverted so to speak from the standpoint of the object. In connoting his *amor de lonh* as utterly spiritual, Jaufré had in fact dimmed the powerful sensuality that characterised the bond between the predatory bird–lover and the object of his love in all the other examples of the *topos*. It is a subversion of the motif in the name of an increasingly triumphant ideology of the *amor purus* analogous to that undertaken, only a little later, although still perhaps prior to Bernart Marti's call to order, by Bernart de Ventadorn. Ventadorn's subversion was, however, from the standpoint of the subject, transforming the carnivorous goshawk into a gentle swallow.

Thus in the Occitan lyric, a relatively limited or tenuous hold on the intertextual develops into a much more vigorous dialogic contact between the positions of the various troubadours. In this poetry, as with the Italian *dolce stil nuovo*, the tendency to initiate dialogue about content seems, all things considered, stronger – and more productive – than that to institute a purely intertextual relation. And this is yet further proof of the massive ideological power characterising what can only be described as the most creative and original phase of that civilisation which found its finest vehicle of expression precisely in the poetry of the troubadours.

Translated by Katherine Brown

1 Genette, *Palimpsestes*, p. 8.
2 For Bakhtin see 'Discourse in the novel' (*Dialogical Imagination*), and 'Problem of speech genres' (*Speech Genres*). The term *intertextuality* is not Bakhtin's, but rather a later, serendipitous coining by Kristeva, *Recherches*, pp. 143–73.
3 The recourse to the term anaphora (a technical term in linguistics meaning: 'the repetition of one or more words at the start of consecutive or nearby clauses or lines') is justified since the constituent texts in a literary dialogue could be seen to form a construct which is ideally unitary.
4 Menichetti, *Metrica italiana*, p. 587.
5 See Meneghetti, *Pubblico*, pp. 74–5; Pasero, 'Cattivi consiglieri', pp. 133–42.
6 See Meneghetti, *Pubblico*, especially pp. 158–75.
7 See Avalle, *Ai luoghi*, pp. 38–55; Tanturli, 'Guido Cavalcanti', pp. 3–13; Malato, *Dante e Guido Cavalcanti*; Pasero, 'Dante in Cavalcanti'; Bologna, *Ritorno di Beatrice*.
8 See *inter alia* Gruber's important pioneering volume, *Dialektik*; Pasero, 'Pastora contro cavaliere', pp. 9–25; Meneghetti, *Pubblico*, especially Chapters 3, 4; Mancini, 'Aimeric', pp. 45–89; Bologna and Fassò, *Da Poitiers*; Lazzerini, 'Trasmutazione insensibile', pp. 153–205, 313–69.
9 As is well known, the works of the last two genres are dialogic in actuality (and not, or not only, metaphorically). I have not considered the purely 'internal' re-echoings as forms of intertextuality or dialogism.
10 See Mancini, 'Aimeric', pp. 59–62.
11 Ibid., pp. 51–2.
12 I see the seemingly generic outburst against the *cobes recrezutz* who destroy 'solatz e domneis' in the Genoese *tenso*, as, in fact, a covert polemical allusion to Sordello. Confirmatory evidence is presented in *Sordello: le poesie*, ed. Boni, p. 76, and pp. XCVI ff.
13 On this, see Chambers, 'Imitation', pp. 104–20.
14 For the text of XVI see also Roncaglia, 'Il *gap*', pp. 46–70. The relationship between 'Tot a estru' and 'D'aisso lau Dieu' has already been signalled among others by Appel ('Zu Marcabru', p. 425), Chambers ('D'aisso lau Dieu', pp. 489–500) and Spaggiari (*Nome*, pp. 45–68).
15 Gruber, *Dialektik*, especially pp. 200–9.
16 See Rosenstein, 'Années d'apprentissage', pp. 7–15.
17 Bologna and Fassò, *Da Poitiers*.
18 See *Bernart von Ventadorn*, ed. Appel, pp. 301–4.
19 This little strophe, followed by a second short text, whose interpretation is more doubtful, is on fol. 94v of MS Harley 2750 of the British Library. On its dating, see Bischoff, *Anecdota novissima*, pp. 266–8; on

its localisation, see Lazzerini, 'A proposito', pp. 123–34 (Lazzerini concentrates particularly on the form *imbracher* <IMBRACHIARE, with the outcome of a palatal *-er* + *à*, which is indeed genuinely Poitevin). The text transcribed here takes her suggested emendations into account.

20 See Ziltener, 'Ai Deus!', pp. 363–71, and Lazzerini, 'Trasmutazione insensibile', pp. 188–90.

21 I use the concept of function in the sense attributed to it by Propp: 'function is understood as an act of a character, defined from the point of view of its significance for the course of action' (*Morphology*, p. 21).

22 See Lazzerini, 'Trasmutazione insensibile', pp. 173–90. However, I do not agree with all her remarks, particularly those that reinstate a mystical interpretation of Jaufré's poetry.

23 See *'Donatz Proensals'*, ed. Marshall [Appendix 3, p. 298], 1679.

CHAPTER 12

The troubadours at play: irony, parody and burlesque

Don A. Monson

Although early research generally took troubadour poetry very seriously, the attitude of scholars subsequently changed considerably, in accordance with changes in the prevailing intellectual climate. In the second half of the twentieth century, scholars became much more aware of the textual dynamics operating within troubadour poetry as well as the dynamics of performance and reception at work between the poetry and its audience. In the process play, humour and related phenomena increasingly emerged as central elements of the troubadours' artistic creation.

The point of departure for the modern study of play is the work of Huizinga, *Homo ludens*, published in 1938. Huizinga shows how the element of play provides a common denominator for a variety of seemingly unrelated human activities, including law, war, philosophy, poetry and art. While contesting it and modifying it on several points, the 1958 book by Roger Caillois builds on Huizinga's analysis and extends it, especially with regard to the classification of games. Despite some cogent subsequent criticism by Henriot and Ehrmann, these two studies remain the fundamental works on the subject.[1]

Huizinga's description of play (*Homo ludens*, p. 13) as amended by Caillois (*Man*, pp. 9–10) lists six essential components. Play is seen as an activity: (1) engaged in freely; (2) circumscribed within definite limits of time and space; (3) uncertain as to its outcome; (4) unproductive, in that wealth is not created, although it may be exchanged; (5) governed by rules; and (6) accompanied by a special awareness of make-believe separating it from 'real life'. Completing the two-fold classification of Huizinga (p. 13), who distinguishes in play the functions of contest and representation, Caillois (pp. 12–26) breaks down the phenomenon into four fundamental categories: (1) *agôn* (competition); (2) *alea* (chance); (3)

mimicry (simulation); and (4) *ilinx* (vertigo). Superimposed on this typology is another based on a continuum going from *paidia* (spontaneous play) to *ludus* (controlled play).[2] It is the interaction between these two typologies, according to Caillois (p. 36), which accounts for all the varieties of play and games.

A number of scholars have considered the love poetry of the troubadours and their medieval emulators as play. The first was Huizinga (*Homo ludens*, p. 125), who devoted a paragraph to the troubadours and their 'courts of love' in the course of a discussion of play and poetry. In the 1960s, following the translation of *Homo ludens* into English in 1949, such interpretations multiplied.[3]

In his 1977 survey of scholarship on courtly love, Roger Boase accords to game theory a prominence which doubtless reflects his own interest in the subject as much as its importance in previous research.[4] Boase considers 'play phenomenon' among the five principal theories on the meaning of courtly love (*Origin*, pp. 103–7) and, indeed, in his conclusion he retains it, along with 'stylistic convention', as one of two complementary theories which he judges of primary importance (p. 128). Resuming the theoretical work of Huizinga, Caillois and Henriot, Boase suggests a number of ways in which their descriptions of play and games can be applied to courtly literature.

A recent article by Nathaniel Smith takes a somewhat different approach, applying to troubadour poetry the methods of 'transactional analysis' expounded in a work of popular psychology by Eric Berne.[5] A 'game', according to Berne (*Games*, p. 40), is an ongoing series of social transactions with a concealed motive proceeding to a well-defined, predictable outcome (the 'payoff'). Examining some of Berne's examples drawn from twentieth-century American life, particularly a game of flirtation labelled 'Cavalier', Smith shows how they can shed light on the psychological dynamics of medieval Occitan lyric.

From this brief survey, the play element in troubadour lyric emerges as a fruitful area of investigation which has only begun to be exploited. Often evoked but seldom pursued, this approach holds out the promise of elucidating aspects of this poetry which have remained matters of doubt and controversy. Moreover, it is reconcilable with and complementary to other approaches, such as the psychological or the stylistic. Nevertheless, the results achieved to date remain limited and fragmentary. A rapid sum-

mary of these will also indicate some promising perspectives for
further research.

The most obvious application of game theory to troubadour
poetry concerns the debate poems, the *tenso* and the *partimen*,
which are singled out for special mention in this connection by
Huizinga (*Homo ludens*, p. 125) and Smith ('Games', p. 5). The
game-like character of the *partimen* is indicated by the alternative
name by which it was known: *joc partit*. The essence of the *partimen*,
as with most games, is competition, in this case competition in wit
and poetic skill. Like other games, the *partimen* has its rules, such
as the regular alternation between contestants, it is circumscribed
within limits of time and space, those of the stanza established in
the first exchange, and it has no other possible outcome than a
victory of prestige. The artificial, non-serious nature of the debate
is underlined by the necessity of proposing for discussion a real
dilemma, a question both sides of which are defensible, for according to another rule of the game, the proposer must be prepared
to defend whichever side is left to him by his adversary.[6]

More loosely organised, the *tenso* does not share all of the formal
game-like properties of the *partimen*, yet it often participates in
the same playful spirit. This tendency is particularly clear in the
tensos with inanimate objects, such as that of Gui de Cavaillon
with his cloak, or in other fictive debates such as the Monje de
Montaudon's *tensos* with God. In Caillois' terminology, the *tenso*
occupies the pole *paidia* with respect to the *ludus* of the *partimen*.

Two other minor genres, the *gap* and the nonsense poem, also
participate quite clearly in the playful spirit of the *tenso* and the
partimen, but without the formal game structure which characterises the latter. The *gap*, or boasting song, is based, like the *partimen*,
on competition, albeit of a more diffused nature. As Guilhem de
Peitieu put it in 'Ben vuelh' (VI), the prototype of the genre (cf.
gabar, 43), the poet's implicit competitor is whoever, *li pluzor* (1;
cf. 'nulh mon vezi', 27). According to the rules of the game, the
boasting must be accomplished in a witty and humorous manner,
thus compensating for the social disapproval which normally
accompanies self-praise. Hence the *double entendre* between poetry
making and love-making maintained throughout Guilhem's poem,
relayed by such ambiguous terms as *mester* (4, 23, 39) and *joc/jogar*
(11, 25, 30), and culminating in the extended metaphor of the
gaming board (43–62), which formally thematises the poet's

gamesmanship. It is the manner of the *gap* at least as much as its content which is the subject of competition, as Guilhem indicates in calling on his poem to bear witness to his own superiority (6–7). The stakes are, once again, a victory of prestige, with the challenge of making self-praise socially acceptable providing scope for the display of poetic virtuosity.

The nonsense poem plays with the public's normal expectation of a logical, coherent discourse by offering instead a series of paradoxes and non-sequiturs. Here too the prototype is a poem of Guilhem de Peitieu, the 'Vers de dreit nient' (IV), which the poet claims to have composed while asleep, on horseback, for a beloved whom he doesn't know, etc. The challenge of making an aesthetically pleasing poem out of nothing, as Guilhem puts it, is once more the pretext for a facetious display of poetic virtuosity.

The amenability of the principal poetic genre cultivated by the troubadours, the *canso* or love song, to analysis in terms of game theory is somewhat less obvious but no less real. This most 'serious' of lyric genres presents a complex configuration superimposing different game structures at different levels. The troubadour love song constitutes, in fact, a game within a game, as can be elucidated by reference to a distinction made by Benveniste.

Benveniste sees play as deriving from the sacred, which he defines in terms of the consubstantial unity of myth and rite. There is play, according to his theory, when only half of the sacred operation is carried out – when the myth alone is translated into words, or the rite alone into acts. Thus play occurs in two forms: *jocus*, play in words, corresponding to the myth, and *ludus*, play in action, corresponding to the rite.[7] Leaving aside the vexed question of the relationship of play to the sacred, we can recognise in the *canso* the interpenetration of the two kinds of play distinguished by Benveniste, *ludus* and *jocus*.

At the thematic level, the troubadour love song presents an act of courtship, a common social situation, as Huizinga points out (*Homo ludens*, p. 43), surrounded in all cultures by game-like rituals. It is this act of courtship or flirtation which Smith, following Berne, analyses under the label 'Cavalier'.[8] The game opposes two players, a lover and his lady, each with a carefully prescribed role: communicating his romantic interest to the lady, the lover tries to advance as fast and as far as possible towards emotional and physical intimacy with her, whereas she resists his advances.

Between these two opposite poles of volition reign a constant tension and an uncertainty of outcome which are crucial to the main-
tenance of the game. Whatever the favours (described in the medieval tradition in terms of the 'stages of love') which the lover may
already have received from the lady, his immediate aim is to
obtain further concessions from her, but without offending her
by his forwardness, which could cause him to lose ground. While
minimising the concessions, the lady must try to avoid completely
discouraging the lover, unless she wishes to put an end to the
game. The lady's adamant resistance is countered by various ploys
on the part of the lover: he praises her, appeals to her pity or her
sense of justice, protests his own sincerity, disclaims (temporarily)
the desire for any 'reward', complains of suffering and 'death',
even threatens to leave the game, the ultimate gambit, as at the
end of Bernart de Ventadorn's 'Can vei' (XXXI, 49–60). Although
the game concerns primarily these two principal players, it can
also include competition with accessory players, namely rivals of
the lover for the favours of the lady, known in the *canso* as *lauzengiers*.[9]

Of course, a troubadour love song constitutes not an actual act
of courtship, but a fictionalised depiction of an act of courtship. It
is make-believe, mimicry (Caillois), illusion, representation
(Huizinga). The addressee of the poem is not a real lady but an
idealised abstraction, *la domna*. Her role in the game of courtship
as described above remains purely theoretical, except in so far as
it is reflected in the discourse of the poet–lover, the only one who
has a voice. The qualities ascribed to the *domna* are not the individual traits of an existing person but those superlative virtues which
any woman would presumably like to hear attributed to herself.
There is often an attempt to personalise the poem through the
use of nicknames, or *senhals*, but these remain general, laudatory
labels in which many women would be pleased to see themselves.
The sentiments expressed by the poet–lover are no less general
and conventional, and it is doubtless possible to apply to them
Diderot's paradox of the actor, who is all the more capable of
conveying emotion the less he actually feels it.[10] Nor is the poet's
goal to seduce his (fictitious) lady, but merely to depict the process
by which such a seduction might be accomplished, or at least
attempted.

It is at the level of representation that the *ludus* of flirtation and courtship is transformed into another game, the *jocus* of poetic invention and expression. The circumscribed time and place of this game are constituted by the six to eight metrically identical stanzas of six to eight lines each which normally make up a *canso*. The rules of the game are comprised of all the *canso*'s conventional generic features. An imperious tradition presides over every aspect of poetic creation, dictating the subject to be treated and the manner of its treatment, the themes and motifs to be developed, the words and phrases to be employed, the metrical and musical forms to be adopted. Within these constraints, the poet's challenge is to create 'un chan novel', a new song from old material. Playing with the conventional poetic elements handed down by the tradition, he must find a new angle, a new twist, a new configuration which will distinguish his song from those which have preceded, thus demonstrating his ingenuity, wit and poetic virtuosity. The amatory competition between rivals developed at the thematic level by means of the *lauzengiers* becomes at this level a poetic competition between colleagues, with social prestige primarily at stake, but also, for troubadours of humble birth, a livelihood. Needless to say, this poetic game incorporates and subsumes the psychological game of courtship embodied in the poem's thematics: as Bernart de Ventadorn declares in the opening of 'Non es meravelha' (I), it is the excellence of the song which confirms the sincerity of the poet's sentiments and which provides, consequently, the best possible grounds for clemency on the part of the lady.

The playful poetic innovation by which the troubadours place their individual marks on their *cansos* takes on many forms, corresponding to the many different levels of poetic creation. It may be the foregrounding and systematic exploitation of a relatively minor theme, as with the theme of physical separation developed by Jaufré Rudel in his poems of 'far-away love'. It may be the ironic inversion of a traditional motif, as when Bernart de Ventadorn converts the customary spring opening into a paradoxical winter opening in 'Tant ai' (IV). It may be the use of unusual comparisons and metaphors, as with the animal imagery deployed by Rigaut de Berbezilh in 'Atressi cum l'orifans' (II). For many, including the adepts of *trobar ric* and *trobar clus*, it may involve the search for rare rhymes and complicated rhyme schemes whose increased difficulty affords greater scope for the display of virtuosity. For some later poets, the desire to renew the genre may lead to the negation of some of its fundamental themes, as with the three songs of Bernart de Tot lo Mon addressed to unmarried women or the humorous poem of Gausbert Amiel in which he insists at length that he is not interested in courting women of higher birth.

If genre provides the rules of the game, the play itself can sometimes modify those rules, as these last examples illustrate. In extreme cases this process can result in the creation of new genres with new rules, just as bridge evolved from whist or canasta from rummy. It is such a development which accounts for the existence of the *descort*: playing on the common lyric theme of the lover's emotional turmoil, some poets transpose this confusion to the level of versification and music, changing the strophic structure and melody with each successive stanza. Threats to leave the intransigent lady, such as that of Bernart de Ventadorn mentioned above, give rise to a separate genre, the *comjat*, devoted entirely to leave-taking, as well as to the so-called 'chansons de change', in which the poet switches allegiance to another woman, thus carrying out the threat.[11]

Certain troubadours, such as Raimbaut de Vaqueiras in 'Domna, tan vos ai preiada' (III), go much farther, interspersing between the stanzas of their own *domnejaire* other stanzas purporting to be the reply of the lady, thus creating a small but significant variety of *tenso*. An even more radical transformation is carried out by Marcabru in 'L'autrier jost' una sebissa' (XXX): here the principle of reply and dialogue is combined with an ironic inversion of the social relationships of the *canso* – an unmarried peasant girl (*toza*), rather than a married noblewoman, is courted by a knight, rather than a low-born churl – to make a major new genre, the *pastorela*.[12] Each of these new genres sets up a new game with a new set of rules which may in turn be modified by the play of subsequent troubadours. In their *pastorelas*, for example, Gavaudan and Gui d'Ussel replace the recalcitrant *toza* of 'L'autrier jost' una sebissa' with a much more compliant shepherdess, thus 'recuperating' Marcabru's ironic inversion and transforming it into boastings of male conquest not unlike those of the *gap*.

Thus it emerges that the entire enterprise of troubadour poetry can be seen as a game. Representation at the fictional level of the psychological game of courtship, it is especially a literary game of poetic invention and expression. The rules of the game are the ensemble of poetic conventions embodied in the various poetic genres. Within those rules, the role of the poet is to play with the conventional material transmitted by the tradition and to transform it, sometimes minimally, sometimes radically, in order to produce a new song testifying to his wit and skill. This dual emphasis on tradition and play leads to a further possible conclusion, namely that all troubadour poetry tends more or less towards parody.

The definition of parody and its relationship to such related phenomena as burlesque and satire are thorny questions surrounded by scholarly controversy.[13] By all accounts, parody is a literary phenomenon involving two essential elements: (1) a conscious, recognisable imitation of the style and/or thematic content of another author, work, or literary movement; (2) a critical outlook, described variously in terms of a humorous perspective, a mocking attitude, an incongruous treatment or an ironic distance, with respect to the material imitated. The problems encountered in analysing parody include that of determining the degree to which the imitation is recognisable and thus may be assumed to have been conscious and intentional on the part of the author and that of assigning to the parody a precise tone or 'pragmatic force' within a range which may extend from the respectfully playful to the violently satirical.[14]

Sometimes defined as the generic concept of which parody is one form,[15] burlesque is more often viewed as a less refined variety or cousin of parody.[16] Burlesque often includes a grotesque element, and (as is indicated by its etymology, from Ital. *burla*, 'joke') it regularly takes on a broadly jocular tone, neither of which is necessarily present in parody. However, the distinction is one of degree.

Theoretically, the difference between parody and satire is fairly clear, for although they share a critical and ironic attitude towards their subject, they bring this attitude to bear in different domains.[17] Whereas parody is an internal, purely literary phenomenon applying aesthetic norms to authors, works, styles and movements, satire has an external, social focus concerned with moral norms and their application to human behaviour. In other words, satire mocks the social reality which is the *object* of its literary representation, whereas parody derides the *manner* of previous literary representations of that reality. Of course, these two dimensions are not always easy to separate, and historically parody and satire have often interacted with each other.

The two essential components of parody, imitation and critical distance, are present to a greater or lesser degree in all troubadour poetry, as we have seen. Whether it be described as a 'poésie du lieu commun' by the structuralist critics of the 1960s and 70s (Guiette, Dragonetti, Zumthor) or in terms of 'intertextuality' and 'dialectic' by more recent scholars (Meneghetti, Gruber), the imitative character of this literature is no longer in doubt. At the same time, this most recent research emphasises the dynamic, interactive nature of the imitation, thus calling attention to a playful, humorous dimension of the poetry which previous scholarship had largely ignored. In the wake of these latest studies, it is tempting to see a certain dimension of parody at work throughout the entire troubadour corpus.

No general study yet exists of parody in the troubadours, but a number of scholars have examined this phenomenon in particular poems or authors.[18] Two major recent studies devote a fair amount of discussion to parody in connection with other, related matters.[19] Interest in the subject has also been renewed by the recent publication of two anthologies calling attention to the importance of parodic texts in the troubadour tradition while also making available a large number of them.[20] Like the application of game theory, the study of parody in troubadour poetry appears to be a very promising area of investigation which has only begun to be exploited. Nevertheless, a few observations are in order about the problems raised by this line of research.

The general tendency of troubadour poetry towards playful and humorous imitation complicates the problem of identifying conscious, intentional parody. Since the entire corpus is vaguely parodic, it is not always easy to decide whether a given poem stands out sufficiently from the common textual practice of the troubadours to merit special designation as a parody. For poets such as Guilhem de Peitieu, Marcabru, Peire d'Alvernha, Raimbaut d'Aurenga, Arnaut Daniel and Peire Cardenal, the parodic intention can hardly be disputed, at least for certain of their poems, but in many other cases it may prove difficult to establish a firm demarcation between the 'serious' and the truly parodic.

A related problem concerns the identification of the target of

parody in a given text, which may be either a specific work/author
or the entire tradition. The parody of Peire d'Alvernha is aimed
specifically at Bernart de Ventadorn, according to Gaunt's analysis, while that of Marcabru and Raimbaut d'Aurenga has a much
broader target. 'Ar me puesc' by Peire Cardenal (I) is clearly a
parody, but of what? It takes its rhyme scheme, rhymes and
melody from a poem of Giraut de Bornelh, 'Non puesc sofrir'
(XXXVII), but the thematic and verbal reminiscences are minimal, suggesting a more general object.

The highly conventional and imitative character of troubadour
poetry, which an earlier generation of scholars condemned for its
uniformity, often makes it difficult to identify specific intertextual
references with any degree of certainty. The ascendancy of the
tradition means that the repetition of one or two words or images
will generally not be sufficient to establish a specific intertextual
reference; an entire nexus of verbal and semantic associations is
usually required. Because intertextuality is now fashionable, scholars can easily lose sight of that principle in their eagerness to
make connections between particular poets.[21]

Whatever the target, the coarseness of burlesque usually means
that its parodic intention is quite apparent, even 'overdetermined'.
In the troubadour tradition, burlesque is frequently, though not
exclusively, associated with obscenity, as Pierre Bec's anthology
makes clear. As such, it stands in opposition to the erotic ambiguity of the 'serious' love lyric, as a 'counter-text', to use Bec's
expression.

A hallmark of troubadour poetry is the ambiguity of its erotic
imagery, an ambiguity which has inspired widely divergent
interpretations among modern critics, ranging from the resolute
idealism of a Camproux to the frank sensuality of a Lazar.[22] This
ambiguity has an important function in the psychological game of
courtship of which the poem is a representation, for the poet–
lover wants to signal to the lady his erotic interest in her, failing
which he cannot expect to make progress, but he must do so in a
subtle and refined way, so as not to offend her, which would set
back his cause. Meanwhile, this same ambiguity offers the poet
ample scope to display his talent for witty allusion and innuendo
in the game of poetic creation.

Reducing the ambiguity, the burlesque text makes explicit the
veiled and diffused eroticism of the love song and thus 'demysti-

fies' it. Here again, the distinction between parody and burlesque is a matter of degree. Alongside the obscene and scatological, the Bec anthology contains a section of humorous and parodic texts and another devoted to poems in which *fin'amor* is 'marginalised'. Between the standard practice of the troubadours and the gross excesses of Montan (Bec, *Burlesque*, no. 34) stand such texts as Bernart d'Auriac's erotic chess game (Bec, *Burlesque*, no. 6) or the anonymous sexual grammar (Bec, *Burlesque*, no. 25).

Satire is amply represented in the troubadour tradition in the form of moral and political *sirventes*. This subject lies largely outside the scope of my inquiry, but not entirely, for there is considerable interaction between parody and satire in troubadour poetry, as the case of Marcabru shows. Gaunt (*Troubadours*, pp. 65–72) has demonstrated that a number of Marcabru's satirical *vers* begin by a parody of the conventional spring opening of the love song. Like many burlesque 'counter-texts', Marcabru also uses crude sexual language and striking erotic images, presumably to 'demystify' the erotic ambiguity of mainstream troubadour poetry. Moreover, the principal object of Marcabru's satire, the bastardisation of noble lineages through the granting of sexual favours by highborn ladies to low-born churls, may reflect the exploitation of this theme in the songs of his contemporaries as much as any social reality. That is at least the conclusion that one might draw from one of the most explicit and virulent of his poems, 'L'iverns vai' (XXXI), in which he associates this tendency with the poetry of the school of *N'Eblo*, 'Lord Eble' (73–6), apparently a reference to Eble of Ventadorn. With Marcabru it is clearly not easy to draw the line between satire and parody.

In terms of the means of poetic expression employed in the parody, burlesque and satire of the troubadours, two techniques stand out: wordplay and irony. Each has been the subject of significant recent scholarship. Neither is unproblematic.

Wordplay, usually punning, is often mentioned in passing in troubadour studies (for example, with regard to *senhals*[23]), but by far the most extensive investigation of the question is that of Laura Kendrick.[24] This study calls for a new, less restrictive reading of troubadour texts allowing for greater play with language. Citing ambiguities in the division of words in medieval manuscripts, as well as the existence of opaque, undecipherable manuscript variants, Kendrick sees in these phenomena a conscious invitation to practise such reading. On the basis of this method, Kendrick posits a medieval tradition of facetious wordplay, found especially in the songs of early troubadours such as Guilhem IX but also in those of the fourteenth-century Consistori del Gay Saber. The troubadours wrote down their poems, she contends, as an encouragement to such wordplay, and they intended their songs to be burlesqued in performance.

The seminal work on irony in the troubadours is that of Simon Gaunt.[25] Reviewing the medieval and modern theory on the subject, it defines irony as including not only statements which say one thing and mean the opposite, but also those in which the real meaning diverges from and is incongruous with the apparent meaning. The study examines irony in five early troubadours – Marcabru, Bernart Marti, Peire d'Alvernha, Raimbaut d'Aurenga and Giraut de Bornelh – focusing sometimes on detailed interpretation of individual poems, sometimes on more general aesthetic or thematic considerations, including rhetorical devices used as signals to irony, the role of irony in parody and intertextuality, ironic sexual innuendo, and suggestions of irony in the debate on style. It shows a fair amount of similarity and influence among poets, particularly the influence of Marcabru on his later colleagues, but also a remarkable variety in the degree and manner in which the five troubadours use irony in their poetry.

In the wake of Gaunt's study, Sarah Kay discusses irony in connection with the construction of lyric subjectivity.[26] Like Kendrick, she explores 'indeterminacy of meaning' in troubadour poetry, albeit of a more limited nature, and she accords an important role to irony in making meaning elusive. The definition of irony used is broader than Gaunt's, for it includes 'the capacity of a text to signal disengagement from its apparent meaning' (*Subjectivity*, p. 17), even when the abandoned meaning is not replaced by another. Kay also links irony closely with hyperbole, listing them together among 'the most characteristic tropes of troubadour composition' (p. 17). These theses are supported by an examination of hyperbole in a song of Bernart de Ventadorn and by an analysis of the ironic effects emanating from Marcabru's *pastorela* and from several poems developing 'narratives of two women'.

Extremely stimulating, the recent work on wordplay and irony has opened up new horizons for troubadour scholars. In its wake it now seems clear that these devices occur much more frequently in troubadour poetry than was previously imagined. Nevertheless, a word of caution seems in order, for the phenomena in question are among the most difficult and elusive in literary studies, and their investigation requires a discipline which is not always in evidence. We can not just assume, for example, as Kendrick seems to do, that the ambiguity of troubadour songs was systematically reduced in performance in favour of facetious and racy interpretations.[27]

No discussion of play and humour in troubadour poetry can be complete without some consideration of the dimension of performance and reception. Troubadour songs were performed publicly, and in performance they doubtless took on a dramatic quality, became small 'plays' in the theatrical sense of the word. (Since they were sung, we can perhaps think of them as tiny musical comedies, or *Singspiele*.) In performing them, poets and *joglars* were presumably conscious of playing a role; they must have tried, like any actor, to find the gestures, facial expressions and inflections of tone of voice capable of conveying to their audience the emotions of the dramatic characters whom they were representing. Their success in this regard must have been a significant factor in determining the reception of their songs by their public.

The dramatic character of the poetic texts is especially apparent in the poems which take the form of a dialogue: the *pastorelas*, of course, which were in fact dramatised by Adam de la Halle in the *Jeu de Robin et de Marion*, but also *tensos, partimens* and some *albas*. The drama of such texts could easily be reinforced in performance by the use of two performers or by the adoption of different voices by a single performer. Even the *canso* presents an implied or truncated dramatic situation, and the discourse of the poet–lover can be interpreted as a kind of dramatic monologue.[28]

The theatrical or 'play-like' quality of the poetry is closely related to the more jocular forms of playfulness which we often find there. The possibilities of reinforcing in performance the humorous or ironic effects of the text are obvious. Quintilian (*Institutio oratoria*, 8.6.54) lists 'tone of voice' (*pronunciatio*) among the signals to irony, and the thirteenth-century rhetorician Boncompagno of Signa cites 'gestures' (*gestus*) in this connection.[29] At least a rudimentary *mise en scène* of gestures and intonation must have played an important role in conveying to medieval audiences the humorous or ironic potential of a given poem.

Not surprisingly, recent studies on humour or irony in troubadour poetry often accord an important place to performance.[30] Unfortunately, our knowledge of medieval performance is limited, and much of what we can say about it conjectural. Nevertheless, the current tendency to take medieval conditions of performance into consideration is a very positive development, and the suggestions for performance which sometimes accompany the scholarly exegesis of individual poems can be very illuminating.

It is clear that play, humour, and related topics can claim an important place in contemporary troubadour studies. Long neglected by scholars, they have come into their own in recent years. This development includes a number of separated but related strands, including the application of game theory to the poetry, the study of the parody, burlesque and satire often found there, and that of the role played by wordplay, irony and performance in giving expression to these phenomena. A substantial body of scholarship has already been developed for each of these topics, obliging us to ask ourselves just how seriously we should take the poetry of the troubadours. This question in all its various ramifications constitutes one of the most exciting and promising areas for future research in troubadour scholarship.

NOTES

1 Huizinga, *Homo ludens*; Caillois, *Man*; Henriot, *Le Jeu*; Ehrmann, 'Homo Ludens'.
2 Caillois, *Man*, pp. 27–35. The latter distinction appears to correspond at least in part to that which obtains in English between the words 'play' and 'game'; both concepts are subsumed in French by the word *jeu*.
3 Stevens, *Music*, pp. 154–202; Howard, *The Three*, pp. 93–109; Wind, 'Ce jeu'; Manning, 'Game'; Singleton, 'Dante', pp. 47–8. Forty years before Huizinga, W. A. Neilson had already suggested that the participants in the medieval 'courts of love' were 'only playing a game' (*Origins*, p. 250).
4 Boase, *Origin*.
5 Smith, 'Games'; Berne, *Games*.
6 Neumeister, *Das Spiel*.
7 Benveniste, 'Le jeu'.

8 For Berne and Smith, Cavalier is not an act of serious courtship but rather a light-hearted game of flirtation, in which the goal of the male participant is not to seduce the woman but merely to express his appreciation for her attractiveness while displaying his own skill at expressing appreciation.

9 Monson, 'Les *Lauzengiers*'.

10 Boase, *Origin*, pp. 103–4; on p. 115, n. 11, he quotes the fifteenth-century Spanish poet Juan Alfonso de Baena to the effect that a poet who is not in love should at least be prepared to play the part. Cf. Stevens, *Music*, p. 156; Manning, 'Game', p. 22.

11 Kay, *Subjectivity*, pp. 26–37.

12 Some scholars have likewise seen in the boastings of the *gap* an ironic inversion of the theme of discretion developed in the *canso*. See Fechner, 'Zum *gab*'; Köhler, '*Gabar e rire*'.

13 Two recent, useful accounts are Hutcheon, *A Theory* and Rose, *Parody*. On medieval Latin parody see Lehmann, *Die Parodie*.

14 Hutcheon, *A Theory*, pp. 50–68.

15 Bond, *English Burlesque*; Jump, *The Burlesque*.

16 *Merriam Webster's*, p. 187: 'Burlesque is closely related to parody, although burlesque is generally broader and coarser.' For a brief history of the relationship between the two concepts, see Rose, *Parody*, pp. 54–68.

17 Two classic studies are Worcester, *The Art* and Highet, *The Anatomy*.

18 Nichols, '*Canso* → *conso*'; Jernigan, 'The Song'; Paden, 'A new parody'.

19 Kendrick, *The Game*, pp. 157–64, 176–81; Gaunt, *Troubadours*, pp. 65–72, 114–20, 134–8.

20 Nelli, *Écrivains*; Bec, *Burlesque*. Cf. Lazar, 'Carmina erotica', which is largely inspired by Bec's anthology.

21 For some less-than-convincing claims of intertextual reference in Gruber's otherwise excellent study, see Monson, '*Nadal*' .

22 Paden, '*Utrum copularentur*'; cf. Camproux, *Le 'joi d'amor*'; Lazar, *Amour courtois*.

23 Harvey, 'The satirical use', pp. 30–1; Gaunt, *Troubadours*, pp. 58–9; Monson, 'Bernart'.

24 Kendrick, *The Game*.

25 Gaunt, *Troubadours*; see also Monson, 'Andreas Capellanus', pp. 539–45.

26 Kay, *Subjectivity*, pp. 17–37.

27 Kay, Review; Paden, Review.

28 Sutherland, 'L'Elément théâtral'.

29 Monson, 'Andreas Capellanus', p. 540 and n. 2.

30 Kendrick, *The Game*, Chapter 8; Gaunt, *Troubadours*; Pollina, *Si cum*; cf. Kay, *Subjectivity*, Chapter 4.

CHAPTER 13

Desire and subjectivity

Sarah Kay

In his monumental *Essai de poétique médiévale* of 1972, Paul Zumthor represents medieval lyric poetry as a closed system of mutually referring formal elements. Each poem is now wholly defined in relation to that system, the human circumstances of its production being irrecuperably lost. For the modern critic, Zumthor concluded, there can be no subjectivity in the medieval lyric; it can only be seen as 'objectified' by the codes that shape it.[1] Zumthor's influence has been so great that subjectivity, and with it desire, have long been marginalised topics in troubadour studies.[2] This is ironic since modern conceptions of both desire and subjectivity position them in relation to language, and thus as dependent on precisely those verbal and rhetorical codes valorised in Zumthor's approach.

Desire and subjectivity have, of course, always been a key element in psychoanalytical criticism, but this too has tended to be marginal to the reception of troubadour poetry. The most commonly given reason for rejecting the psychoanalytical approach is its alleged anachronism. While this may have some plausibility where Freudian analysis is concerned, it is firmly rebutted by Lacan's insistence that language, which is what gives shape to everything we can apprehend, is subject to historical contingency and changeability.[3] Indeed, emphasis on what he calls the signifier (the material dimension of language) can provide a new impetus to the close reading of early texts.[4] Medievalists' dislike of psychoanalytical criticism stems rather, I think, from its relative inaccessibility as a critical discourse, and from its central concept of the unconscious which is alien to the prevailing positivism (whether historicist or formalist) of medieval studies. It is only with the rise of feminist and gender criticism in the 1980s that issues of desire and subjectivity attained any degree of critical prominence in our reading of troubadour poetry.

This chapter is about the way psychoanalytical and gender-based approaches can contribute to our understanding of the troubadour tradition. It starts by showing how well their songs bear out Lacan's account of 'courtly love',[5] before suggesting how this account might open new avenues of thought for gender criticism. I have taken as my corpus all the surviving troubadour songs to use a *senhal* involving the Occitan word for desire, *dezir*. Although of different authorship, date, quality and intent (some are satirical, others love songs), these songs all perform an address to desire. In approximate chronological order they are Marcabru V 'Al son desviat'; Bernart Marti III 'Bel m'es lai'; Gaucelm Faidit VII 'Razon e mandamen' and VIII 'Trop malamen'; Raimon Jordan II 'Ben es camjaz' and XI 'Vas vos soplei'; Arnaut Daniel XVIII 'Lo ferm voler'; Cadenet I 'Ab leyal cor'; Daude de Pradas X 'El temps que·l rossignols', XVI 'Del bel dezir' and XVII 'Ben deu esser solatz'; and Peire Bremon Ricas Novas IV 'Us covinens gentils cors'.

To speak of desire and subjectivity as positioned relative to language is to say that the 'I' of the text, its first-person subject, is produced within language (rather than that language 'expresses' a pre-existing self) and that the desires voiced by this 'I' are subject to language rather than springing, in some original and natural way, from the self. This regulating structure of linguistic (and other institutional) codes makes up what Lacan calls the symbolic order. It interacts with what he calls the imaginary order, in which we fail to recognise our subjection to the symbolic, but instead nurture the delusion of being whole and autonomous selves. From the interaction between the symbolic and the imaginary orders, Lacan infers the existence of a third order: that of the real, which lies outside the limit of either, and which includes much that is unconscious. The real is the site of all that resists symbolisation absolutely, all that has to be sacrificed or 'repressed' as the price of our becoming socially admissible subjects in the symbolic order.[6]

In troubadour poetry, the linguistic and social construction of the subject (that is, its dependence on the symbolic order) is especially obvious because of the restricted and repetitive vocabulary used to articulate it. The same key terms recur from one end of the tradition to the other, in both satirical and love poetry;[7] often they seem vested with a force beyond that of mere 'words', apparently dominating the first-person subject with their agency and power. The songs of Daude de Pradas, for example, describe how Amor (love), Merces (reward or pity), Joi (joy), and Desir determine the lover's state of mind. Amor does not let him rest, 'anz vol qu'ieu chant, o vuoill'o no' (X, 5, 'instead she insists that I sing, whether I want to or not,' and cf. XVI, 21). Having set himself to love a lady too high above him socially, the subject trusts that Merces will prevail over rank, and incline her to him (X,14-19; cf. XVI, 31). He has pursued Joi Novel to its very head-quarters, only to be snubbed:

> Cais que disses: 'E no i a pro,
> s'ab pessamen cortes e gai
> vos sai donar joi et esmai
> e·us fatz plazer vostre dampnatge?' (X, 24–7)

(As though she were saying, 'Isn't it enough that, together with courtly and cheerful thoughts, I give you joy and distress, and make you like the harm you suffer?')

Wretched and intimidated, he turns for assistance to Bel Desir (fair desire, X, 31, cf. XVI, 1). Marcabru's 'Al son desviat' deploys the same terms in a moralistic register to represent us as con-demned to live in a world of declining values (V, 37–48); he like-wise looks to desire for a solution (V, 55–6). Subjectivity belongs here to the group rather than the individual, and is associated with moral and emotional debasement.

The 'I' of the love lyric also often experiences subjection as debasement; he commonly sees himself as being at the mercy of a supreme, arbitrary and perverse power. This corresponds with Lacan's account of the symbolic order as a force which is inhumanly and traumatically alienating, what he calls 'the big Other'. In Daude de Pradas, for example, the lover eventually reaches Joi Novel in her fortress:

> on mi mostret tant gran orguoill
> cum si tengues del mon la clau. (X, 21–2)

(where she was so haughty with me as though she held the key to the entire world.)

This unendurable arrogance is like that of a lion, its powers a bestial parody of God's omnipotence, 'que so que·s vol fai e desfai' (X, 33–4, 'who makes and unmakes according to her whim'.) This sense of being faced by an inhuman adversary is a common one in troubadour song. For example, Cadenet (I, 33–5) says that his lady kills him in his imagination and may kill him in reality if she does not tame (*domda*) her attitude to him. Raimon Jordan feels placed in a no-win situation by his lady's arrogance (*erguelh*, II, 30) and begs her to relent:

> Qu'ab vos guerrei, a cui no m'aus tornar,
> ni sai fugir, ni puesc pro encaussar. (II, 35–6)

(since I war against you and yet cannot even approach you, and can neither flee you nor satisfactorily give chase.)

The fearful regime which these poets describe lies at the heart of Lacan's understanding of courtly love. The alienating force of the big Other – the symbolic order by virtue of which the subject *is* a subject – creates a pressure point which Lacan calls the 'Thing': a place of trauma, because it is the point just *outside* language on which is focused all of our resentment and dissatisfaction *with* language, our anguish and anger at being subjected to it. The 'Thing' is the point of the real at which the inhuman domination of the Other is sensed; it is the point where the pain of what we have sacrificed to the symbolic order is located.[8] Lacan sees the vein of horror running through courtly love as arising because the poetic code (the manifestation of the symbolic in the lyric) aligns the lady with the Thing, via a process which he terms sublimation. 'By means of a form of sublimation specific to art, poetic creation consists in positing an object I can only describe as terrifying, an inhuman partner.'[9] The Lacanian critic Jean-Charles Huchet puts the same point another way when he speaks of 'the unbearable which poetry transforms into song'.[10]

In the passages just quoted, then, both Daude de Pradas and Raimon Jordan sing about the sense of being gripped by, and exposed to harm from, a powerful Something which words cannot properly express. Much of the effort of 'courtliness' goes into attempts to police and regulate this Something, not only 'taming' it (as in the Cadenet example), but throwing up a complex legislative framework around it. Here too satirical and erotic traditions coincide; everyone has an interest in containing the horror, and wrapping it up in a consolatory morality. Bernart Marti in 'Bel

m'es' envisages unworthy lovers being made to gape like idiots
(III, 27) like the brash knight rebuked by Marcabru's shepherdess:
'bada, fols, bada' ('gape, idiot, gape,' XXX, 55). The pleasures
of discipline are keenly embraced by Gaucelm Faidit in 'Razon e
mandamen', a song dominated by the common image of the lady
as suzerain and the lover as her servant. The first-person subject
sternly enjoins respect for the obligations this imagined relationship entails and gloats over the punishments that await defaulters:

> Drutz c'ama falsamen
> deu, per dreich jutjamen,
> aver fals guizerdo. (VII, 46–8)

(A lover who loves falsely ought, according to a rightful verdict, to reap
a false reward.)

Women who transgress the moral code can be denigrated in the
vilest terms (Bernart Marti, for example, fulminates, 'es deslei-
ada / e puta provada', III, 17–18; 'she is a lawbreaker and a proven
whore') while jealous husbands and gossip-mongers are always
beyond the pale (Daude de Pradas XVI, 8–30). For Lacan, the
work of 'sublimation' is the mainspring of human moral activity –
that is why he devotes so much space to courtly love in his seminar
on *Ethics*. Legislation, regulation, and morality are designed to
transform horror into socially sanctioned behaviours, but they preserve all the rigour and inhumanity of the Thing they seek to
mask.

Inhumanity can present advantages, however, and medieval discourse, with religious pressures constantly upon it, generates sub-
limely benign and powerful objects as well as punitive ones. Cadenet, besides wishing to 'tame' his lady, reveres her as a supreme
source of illumination:

> Si que·l solelhs sobr' autr' alumnamen
> Nos ren clardat, ben puesc dir eissamen
> Qu'ilh es clardatz e rent alumenatge. (I, 26–8)

(Just as the sun gives us more brightness than any other source of light,
in the same way I can say that she both is brightness, and gives light.)

Such a quasi-divine creature, Cadenet considers, should be
inclined to mercy. Peire Bremon Ricas Novas also humbles himself
to an all-powerful lady, trusting that she will respond graciously
and accord him favour:

Sopley vas vos, cuy yeu am at azor,
e suy vostres liges e domesgiers;
a vos m'autrey, qar etz la genser res
e la mielhers qu'anc de maire nasques;
e, quar no·m puesc de vos amar suffrir,
per merce·us prec que no·m layssetz morir. (IV, 19–24)

(I bow down to you, whom I love and adore, and I am your liegeman and
your household servant; I yield myself up to you, for you are the noblest
and the best creature that was ever born of a mother; and since I cannot
help but love you, I beg you, for your mercy's sake, not to let me die.)

Whilst this passage uses the same vocabulary of secular service as
Gaucelm Faidit VII, the tone is altogether different. Gaucelm's
rhetoric was one of regulation and punishment whereas here the
relations of servant and lord are deftly subsumed into those of
worshipper and gracious deity. Far from being legalistic, Peire
Bremon's discourse relies on the affective categories of abasement
and exaltation. The more the lover gives himself over to this trans-
cendence, this passionate aspiration to union with a Supreme
Being, the more his desire is coloured with what Lacan calls the
'imaginary', whereas the legislative-punitive framework is more
characteristic of the symbolic. Thus for Lacan 'the element of ide-
alizing exaltation that is expressly sought out in the ideology of
courtly love ... is fundamentally narcissistic [i.e. imaginary] in
character' (*Ethics*, p. 151). Lacan here is scornful of the self-
deluding quality of troubadour poetry which suffuses the inhumanity of the Thing with a soft-focus, self-valorising haze. Kristeva's reading of Arnaut Daniel in *Histoires d'amour* is, in comparison, sympathetic to the way the medieval imaginary channels
emotional affect (such as exaltation) into the construction of personal value.[11]

However, Lacan does admire the Occitan lyric for seeing beyond
this imaginary harmony and for representing the lady not as the
object of desire who might provide beatitude and fulfil what is
lacking to the subject, but rather as a persistent absence drawing
attention to this lack. Troubadour poetry is not complicitous with
desire, according to Lacan, but transgressive; it does not pretend
to satisfy desire, but to map it by underlining the absence at its
core. 'There are ... detours and obstacles which are organised so
as to make the domain of the vacuole stand out as such. What
gets to be projected as such is a certain transgression of desire'

(*Ethics*, p. 152). Raimon Jordan's 'Vas vos soplei' (XI) illustrates
this, since it simultaneously demands a positive response from the
lady and justifies her in not making one; her very qualities explain
her unresponsiveness:

> Tan fai beltatz son <gen> cors ergulhos
> e son ric pretz fai pojar sobre·ls bos,
> per qu'ieu <n'ai mais> d'esmai e d'espaven
> tan sui duptos que m'o tengu' a follatge. (21–4)

(Beauty makes her noble person so haughty and merit makes her rise
high above the good and so I have more dismay and fear, I am so frightened she will take me for a fool.)

Even troubadours whose songs seem to celebrate a love already
consummated find ways of ensuring that desire remains thwarted.
Bernart Marti is happy to devote himself to *Na Dezirada* ('My
Desired Lady') apparently only when 'trop m'es lunhada' (III, 35–
6, 'she is too far away from me'). He indulges in erotic fantasies
about her (37–45) when she is a sparrow-hawk's flight away (51–
4) but intimacy is decisively renounced:

> En autr' amistat propdana
> m'amar mis, que·m fo dolsana,
>   ans la·m nei
>   que·m sordei
> mas la meiller no·m vairei. (III, 46–50)

(I devoted (bitter)[12] love to a nearby courtship, which was sweet for me,
but I repudiate it before I am corrupted, whereas I did not change
towards the best.)

The opposition Huchet sees in troubadour lyric whereby 'désir' is
preferred to 'jouissance' (bliss) would be another instance of how
the troubadours privilege the gap in desire.[13]

Psychoanalysis thus brings to troubadour poetry a highly complex account of how both desire and the subject are structured in
the texts. The complex knotting together of imaginary, symbolic
and real provides a powerful tool with which to unpack the different layers of the fantasised, the said and the unspeakable. The
interaction of these three orders helps us to explore the complex
relation of the first-person subject to the object of desire (the
lady), a relation both traumatic and paradoxical because it is at
the same time imaginary (aspiring to delusional exaltation), symbolic (a product of the poet's linguistic and institutional codes)

and real (powered by its relation to the Thing). In particular, this interaction is responsible for one of the major features of troubadour poetry: its combination of horror at the monstrous inhumanity threatened by the lady, and its submissive adoration of the gracious benevolence the poet tries to conjure in its place. This dichotomy pervades both satirical and amorous verse, with less difference of emphasis between the two than one might expect; for women (often, it is true, women other than the poet's lady) are not uncommonly vilified in the love lyric as well as in satirical invective, while satire does admit the obligation at times to promote a positive image of women. Indeed, of the songs considered here, Bernart Marti's 'Bel m'es lai' could be classed as either.

Recognising the splitting of 'woman' into two contrasting types, one negative, the other positive, has become a commonplace of troubadour feminist criticism.[14] Lacan too describes this split in the seminar *Encore*, which marks a return of his interest in courtly love more than a decade after the *Ethics* seminar. Here Lacan explores the unbridgeable nature of sexual difference, and the way it renders ultimately impossible a relationship between a man and a woman because woman is inevitably other to man: she is both an imaginary other, a fantasmatic complement to the self, and the radical Other of the symbolic order, incarnating the structure of difference to which he is subject. Punningly he contends of lovers that 'they' (*d'eux*) cannot be other than 'two' (*deux*).[15]

This fundamental *impasse* in the relation to the other/Other is the central preoccupation of Huchet's writing on courtly love.[16] In so far as she represents the symbolic Other, Huchet writes, 'the lady is above all a space towards which desire, and the song which sustains it, are drawn' (*L'Amour discourtois*, p. 35). Feminists have reproached Huchet with his indifference towards real historical women, his willingness to accept femininity as purely discursive.[17] Huchet's position, however, is that what is outside of language is literally indescribable: as the real, it exerts a terrible pressure on the symbolic order but by definition it remains outside it. It would be fairer to object that Huchet does not systematically distinguish fictional from non-fictional discourses of the feminine. (This, in turn, is less unreasonable the more one is prepared to admit that our perceptions are permeated by fantasy, making it hard rigorously to discriminate between the fictional and the non-fictional.) Huchet also thinks that men are better (or rather, less worse)

situated in the symbolic order than women. True, the central role
in signification which Lacan accords to the phallus means that the
symbolic order is tilted towards the masculine;[18] but the complaint
that Lacan's theory does not address 'real women' can equally be
reversed into the claim that the alienation of women is precisely
what it best explains.[19] In other words, if feminists find Huchet's
attitude unacceptably complacent, he in turn critiques feminist
criticism as self-deluding.[20]

Psychoanalysis has always recognised its 'othering' of women.
As Lacan has it, 'all desire is the desire of the Other': the
French construction, like the English, equivocates between positing the Other as the source or as the object of desire. Desire,
Lacan is asserting, is defined not by its origin or its goal but
by the dynamic of difference: the differential structure of language, and the sexual difference which founds it.[21] Huchet
alludes to this circulation of desire through the medium of the
Other – social, linguistic and sexual – when describing troubadour performance: 'chaque récitant parle à une femme de l'Au-
tre-femme, à une femme de "La Femme", non tant pour en
approcher le mystère que pour se donner à désirer à travers le
désir de/pour l'Autre' (*L'Amour discourtois*, p. 35: 'each performer
addresses a woman of the Woman-as-Other, the [symbolic]
woman of "Womanness", not so much in order to draw closer
to the mystery she represents as to offer himself up to the
desire of/for the Other'). The first-person subject is not the
point of origin of desire: not in fact, as one might think, the
subject *of* desire. Desire comes to him from the Other, with
woman as its support. Splitting the image of women into positive and negative at once acknowledges this alienating power of
the Other, and attempts to appease and contain it.[22]

Psychoanalysis can thus theorise a feature of troubadour poetry
often commented on by critics interested in gender, namely its
combination of misogyny with a concomitant effort to flatter and
cajole the women that inspire it. Another frequent observation of
gender criticism is that positive images of the lady tend to be
assimilated to the masculine, whereas negative ones rely on 'feminine' stereotypes such as sensuality, fickleness, deceit and so on.[23]
The matrix of desire in troubadour poetry (and nowadays too) is
biased as much towards the homosocial as the heterosexual: that
is, towards the privileging of same-sex social relations between

men. While the desire of the masculine subject is normatively directed to a feminine object, at the same time the gender hierarchy underwrites the value of masculinity, making men's perceived qualities more desirable than women's. As a result, the only woman worth loving is, paradoxically, a woman who can be represented as a man. Thus Gaucelm Faidit resolves, he says, to rejoice:

> q'en francha seignoria
> ai mes mon cor e me;
> pos so taing e·is cove,
> pois q'us seigner fai be
> a son bon servidor,
> q'el se meillur e cresca sa valor. (VII, 10–15)

(for I have placed my heart and myself under noble lordship and thus it is right and proper, given that a lord acts well to his good servant, that in return he should improve and increase his worth.)

By this imaginary detour, the troubadours try to elude the *impasse* on the sexual relation described by Lacan: the two 'men' come closer to unity than a man and a woman.

It seems to me now that most gender-based criticism (including my own) operates at the imaginary level. In accepting the subjects and objects of these songs as 'persons', as 'men' and 'women', we become complicitous with the fantasies they articulate. So seductive are these representations that we participate in them, even if mainly in order to critique them. In the remainder of this essay, I shall sketch a different approach. Rather than accepting the participants of the lyric as primary, with desire as a subordinate element linking them together, I shall start instead from desire as the structure within which the participants are located and defined. My corpus of songs all contain an address to *dezir*. To this extent, of course, they seek to personify it, and treat it as a part of the fantasy. Yet their insistence on the word *dezir* and on its use as a name is also a foregrounding of the symbolic structure on which poetry necessarily depends. Indeed, an obsession with the name is a striking feature of troubadour songs, so many of which culminate in the celebration of one or more *senhals*. Huchet identifies this focus on the name as a symptom pointing to the traumatic imposition of the symbolic on the real. The scenarios that expand the *senhal* are then the concomitant fantasy, whose role is to 'make sense' of the symptom, to repair the unease surrounding it.[24] On closer examination, the fantasy scenarios outlined in these songs of *dezir* betray their own flimsiness; they show how contingent, ultimately, are the positions of subject and object. While in some degree presented as 'a person', *dezir* makes the outlines of the 'person' (including gender) more difficult to grasp.

The *senhal* assumes both masculine and feminine forms. Bernart Marti III has *Desirada*. Arnaut Daniel XVIII, conversely, has *Desirat*, possibly a *senhal* for Bertran de Born.[25] Both these examples are unambiguous about the gender of the one the subject desires. None of the other songs is so straightforward, however. Thus in Marcabru V the *tornada* as edited by Dejeanne from the MSS presents two masculine forms:

> Desirat[26] per desiraire
> a nom qui·n vol Amor traire. (55–6)

(For the sake of (or by) the desiring one (m.), the name 'Desired-one' (m.) is given to the one who wishes to draw to him the Love found there [i.e. from the place of delight described in the previous stanza].)

The song's rhyme scheme, though, would lead one to expect a masculine and feminine pairing: 'desirat per desirada / a nom qui·n vol amor traire' ('the one who wishes to draw to him the Love found there is called "Desired" (m.) by (or because of) the desired one (f.)').[27] Whether in the MSS or the emended text, naming and desiring are intriguingly, but mysteriously, interrelated, and it is unsure who is desired by whom. Desire is a textual certainty, but its direction, gendering and articulation are not fixed.

All the other songs in my corpus present forms of *Dezir/Dezirier*. The possible interrelations between them have been much discussed (see most recently Asperti's edition of Raimon Jordan, pp. 48–57). Cadenet uses *Mon Dezir* (I, 43) as a *senhal* for the lady he has allegedly loved unrequitedly for seven years. The construction presumably means 'my desire for her, she who is the object of my desire'. In Daude de Pradas, however, the expression *bel dezir* refers ambiguously to the subject's desire for the lady, and her desire for him. The opening of song XVI suggests that *his* feelings have prompted him to sing:

Del bel dezir que Joys Novels m'adutz
farai un vers, qu'er luenh et pres auzitz ... (1–2)

(With the fair desire that New Enjoyment brings to me I'll compose a
vers that will be heard far and near ...)

But the end of the same stanza disqualifies *lauzengiers* from learning the song because they seek to crush the expression of desire
by women (9–10: 'quan dompna pros [...] vol far ni dir [...]
sas voluntaz'). Perhaps, then, the opening lines mean 'I'll compose
a song about the favourable desire which my Most Recent Joy
directs towards me ... ' The quasi-allegorical cast of song X lends
itself to the same double reading. *Joi Novel* having proved recalcitrant (that is, an affair only just started proving rather hard
going?), the subject looks to *Bel Desir* to provide 'protection against
the lion' (32). In an idealising reading, this might represent fidelity in the face of adversity, the bolstering of *his* desire; in the
light of Daude's other songs, it might more likely be a bid for an
improvement in his lady's attitude, i.e. in *her* desire. The same
ambiguity is discernible in both the Gaucelm Faidit songs, but I
will confine myself to 'Razo e mandamen' (VII). Legalistic though
this song is, Gaucelm is distinctly gingerly about referring to his
lady's kindnesses to him, and his emphasis on reciprocal obligation
stops short of specifiying exactly who owes what to whom. The
tornada, in which the address to *Bels Desirs* occurs, initially gives
scope for assuming he is referring to his desire for her, since her
desirable qualities are expatiated upon (76–9); its closing lines,
however, slyly acknowledge that he has been the recipient of
expressions of her favourable intentions towards him (81–2) and
thus point rather to her desire for him. Asperti, meanwhile, suggests (p. 52) that *Bels Desirs* in this song designates a patroness,
considering the eulogy not to have the amorous colouring here
which he finds in Gaucelm's song VIII.

These examples underline the supreme importance of desire in
troubadour songs, to the extent that its subject and object, and
their gender, appear to be merely of secondary importance: men
and women are subject and object, interchangeably, indifferently,
indeterminately. This second-order status of the person is
increased when we realise that in some of the songs we don't know
whether the *senhal Bels Desirs* relates to a female or a male
addressee. We cannot rule out, in Daude de Pradas' song X, that

Bel Desir could designate a male friend and confidant: someone who will come to his succour against the nasty lion his lady has turned out to be. The same phrase recurs in the *tornada* of his song XVII, a *planh* for the troubadour Uc Brunenc, where the text (preserved only in MSS *A* and *D*) is clearly insecure. The first two lines of the *tornada* in *A* are hypermetric, and in *D* the last line, the one most likely to lead us to identify *Bels Desirs* as female, is faulty:

> Bels Desirs, on q'ieu sia,
> a en mi seignoria
> per far e per dir qe·il plagues;
> et anc no·l vi, mes el cor m'es. (XVII, 45–8)

> 45-6] Bels desirs vas on qieu sia. a en mi la seignoria (*A*)
> 48] e anc nol mais en cor mes (*D*)

(Fair Desire has lordship through me wherever I may be to say and do his/her pleasure, and I never saw him/her, though he/she is in my heart [*D*: and I never again her/him in my heart ?placed].)

Stronski, meanwhile, believed that Gaucelm Faidit's *Bels Desirs* also designated a male friend, whom he identified as Raimon Jordan, seeing the latter's use of *Mon Desir* as a reciprocal *senhal* for Gaucelm (the two troubadours, who were contemporary, are reported to have paid court to two sisters);[28] and Asperti agrees that *Bels Desirs* might refer to a patron (p. 52). These examples leave a number of uncertainties, then. Does the male subject use the *senhal* to celebrate his desire for a male friend or patron (homosocial desire)? Where desire is qualified as 'fair', does the *senhal* imply its return towards himself ('your fair desire for me'), praising it because it gratifies him (also homosocial desire, but with the poet as beneficiary)? Or is the desire heterosexual, and thus integrated to the fantasy of the song, rather than providing a frame for performance? And to whom is desire directed, the lover or the lady?

In two cases, Raimon Jordan II and the song by Peire Bremon Ricas Novas, although the *senhal* is repeated in the course of the song, uncertainty about its reference is increased rather than diminished. Peire Bremon complains he has been looking for a lady for thirty months and not found any who pleased him 'tant cum vos faitz, cuy apelh Belh Dezir' (IV, 15; 'as much as you do, whom I call Fair Desire'). The assumption he now loves a lady whom he names *Belh Dezir* is, however, troubled by the *tornada*:

> Belhs Dezirier, ad Amor ren merces
> quar mon fin cor a del tot en vos mes,
> e quar m'a fag gent en dompna venir,
> sitot m'a fag trop ponhar al chauzir. (41–4)

(Fair Desiring, I thank Love for having set my sincere heart entirely on you and for bringing me nobly to a lady, even though she [Love] made me struggle long over the selection.)

It is possible, but not obvious, that Belhs Dezirier and the *dompna* are one and the same, and surprising that whereas previously the lover was explicit that he called his lady 'Fair Desire', he now represents himself as having his heart set on 'Fair Desiring'. Raimon Jordan's song II is likewise disconcerting. The opening lines speak of being unable any longer to resist the temptation to go to see his lady (II, 1–4). Then:

> Mas eras sai, si Merces non la vens,
> qu'a Mon-Dezir dei demandar ma mort. (5–6)

(But now I know that if she is not conquered by Mercy, I shall have to go to demand my death of Mon-Dezir.[29])

Asperti takes Mon-Dezir to be a female patron, and yet the syntax invites identification between Mon-Dezir and the poet's lady, and Mon-Dezir's power of life and death over the lover would seem to confirm it: it is love that is death-dealing, after all, not patronage. But again the *tornada* points another way:

> A ma dona fai la razon entendre,
> chansoneta, e pueis vai, e non len\<s\>
> a Mon-Dezir, que pens de mon conort,
> ....
> tot enaissi cum sap que·l tanh a far
> e·ls companhos sapchas me saludar. (46–51)

(Song, communicate your substance to my lady and then go, and not slowly, to Mon-Dezir, so that he/she may think how to console me as she/he knows is appropriate [line missing], and be sure to greet my companions for me.)

Now desire, as the addressee of song, seems distinct from the lady. So if initially it brings death at the hands of an implacable Other, here it invokes new directions and new objects, down an endless chain of signification.

While these *senhals* of desire involve some personification, a move to fix language in the imaginary as a fantasised 'person', their persistent indeterminacy also shows up the gap between the name and the being, and so points towards the Thing at the limit of language. In that sense they are symptomatic. The fantasy they conjure up, though, is a benign one. Desire features as lady or helpmeet, supporter or patron. *Bels Dezirs* figures along with other *senhals* used by these same poets (such as *Bos Espers*, 'Good Hope') like the comforters given to the lover by Amor in Guillaume de Lorris's *Romance of the Rose*: Dous Regard, Dous Penser, and so on. In thus solidifying their language as agency, the troubadours pay tribute to the power of the signifier. And in the ambiguity consistently associated with this *senhal* they signal the capacity of desire constantly to recreate and reposition subjects and objects. By seeing persons, gender and relations as products of desire, rather than the other way round, these songs suggest more dynamic and performative approaches for gender criticism. And by welcoming such desire as 'Fair', as a support and comfort, the troubadours show how the symptom can also be a solution: they certainly intended to enjoy it.[30]

NOTES

1 Zumthor, *Essai*, especially p. 192.
2 For arguments against Zumthor's 1972 position see Kay, *Subjectivity*, pp. 5–16, and Van Vleck, *Memory*, pp. 2–6. In his subsequent *Parler du moyen âge*, and *La Poésie et la voix*, Zumthor shifted away from his earlier views, but these works never exercised the same influence as the *Essai*.
3 Lacan, *Ethics*, p. 213; see also Brennan, *History after Lacan*.
4 The work of the Lacanian critic Cholakian is largely commentary-based; his readings of Jaufré Rudel are especially successful (*The Troubadour Lyric*, Chapter 4).
5 *Ethics*, pp. 139–54 and 161–4; see also the exposition by Žižek, 'Courtly Love', and Huchet, *L'Amour discourtois* and *Littérature médiévale*.
6 For introductions to Lacan's thought, consult Bowie, *Lacan*, and Leader and Groves, *Lacan for Beginners*.
7 See also Chapter 2 on linguistic codification of love and value.
8 Lacan defines the Thing as 'that which in the real, the primordial real ... suffers from the signifier' (*Ethics*, p. 118) .

9 Ibid., p. 150 and cf. Žižek, 'Courtly Love', pp. 89–91.

10 *Littérature médiévale*, p. 29.

11 Cholakian, likewise, though with less sympathy, traces what he sees as the troubadours' androcentrism to the pre-Oedipal phase: see *The Troubadour Lyric*, Chapter 7.

12 Marcabru likewise puns on *amar* meaning 'to love' and 'bitter'; see Chapter 3.

13 *L'Amour discourtois*, p. 52. Initially Lacan sees *jouissance* as release from and satisfaction of desire (as in orgasm), but he later emphasises its complicity with the deathwish (e.g. *Ethics*, p. 189) .

14 See e.g. Burns, 'Man behind the lady'.

15 *Encore*, p. 12.

16 See both *L'Amour discourtois* and *Littérature médiévale*.

17 Gaunt, *Gender*, pp. 125–35.

18 See Brennan, *Between Feminism and Psychoanalysis*, Introduction. More accurately, Lacan envisages sexual difference as a fantasy spun in response to the trauma of potential castration. The phallus which is crucial to the symbolic order is the phallus which, precisely, is lacking: the phallus of the mother.

19 For a feminist critique of the phallus in Lacan, see Rubin, 'Traffic in women'.

20 Review of Cholakian, *The Troubadour Lyric*, p. 191.

21 Cf. Žižek, *Metastases*, p. 160.

22 Brennan, *History after Lacan*, pp. 56–75.

23 Kay, *Subjectivity*, pp. 86–93.

24 *Littérature médiévale*, Chapter 2.

25 The attribution is in a note in MS *H* (see Chapter 15); it is accepted in *Bertran de Born*, ed. Paden, Sankovitch and Stäblein, p. 55.

26 Marcabru's form 'Desirat' may refer to Sancho of Castille, surnamed 'desiderabilis', but its significance is motivated by the poem's preoccupation with good love.

27 And is so edited by Roncaglia, 'Trobar clus'. Curiously, in Gaucelm Faidit VIII, 28, *Dezirier* is also emended to *Bel Dezir* on grounds of rhyme. Several of these *tornadas* are metrically irregular; cf. also Raimon Jordan II, discussed below.

28 *Folquet de Marseille*, ed. Stronski, 36*–37*.

29 Asperti offers several alternatives for *demandar*: 'ask to grant', 'ask account of', 'hold responsible for'.

30 Cf. Žižek, *Enjoy Your Symptom!*

CHAPTER 14

Orality and writing:
the text of the troubadour poem

Simon Gaunt

We know little about how troubadour lyrics were originally performed. They were songs set to music and they were 'courtly' in that they were composed for performance at court, but how they were performed and by whom is open to question: the refined nature of many *cansos* suggests an intimate setting, while the more raucous tone of many other genres suggests a more extended public. Whatever the context of performance, interaction with an audience is intrinsic to the rhetoric of troubadour poetry, as are allusions to known individuals and textual flourishes that lend themselves to dramatic exploitation.[1] While lyrics may have been performed by their composers, they were also undoubtedly performed by others: like the scripts of plays, they are the starting point for multiple and diverse fictional performances.

In the thirteenth and fourteenth centuries troubadour lyrics were gathered into elaborate manuscripts that are organised by troubadour or genre. The poor rate of survival of melodies suggests that when these *chansonniers* were compiled their reading public was more interested in texts than melodies, but the displacement effected by the *chansonniers* is not simply a transposition from song to script: there is a chronological gap of at least 150 years between the composition of the earliest lyrics and the *chansonniers*; furthermore although some *chansonniers* were produced in Occitania, the majority are Italian or Catalan.[2] In the *chansonniers*, each stanza constitutes a 'paragraph' and line-endings are marked by full-points (line-stops); this layout indicates that the stanza is the main unit of composition and gives rhyme less prominence than on the printed page. As is usual with medieval script, there is no punctuation as we would understand it, no regularised spelling or fixed conventions for dividing words (see Figure 1). Troubadour lyrics in the *chansonniers* therefore look different from the printed poems they become in modern editions. Modern editors transcribe and collate surviving versions of a lyric before recasting it into a form recognisable to us as a printed 'poem' with (often numerous) substantive 'variants' printed in a critical apparatus. Furthermore, whereas modern editions dedicate one volume to the surviving songs of a troubadour, the *chansonniers* are vast anthologies of a range of poets: the *chansonniers* thus value the tradition rather than the work of a single poet.[3]

A troubadour poem on the printed page has thus undergone a double displacement: first from song to book, then from script to print.[4] There are two main methodologies for effecting the second of these transpositions. Many modern editors produce a theoretical reconstruction of the poem they believe the poet composed; because of the temporal gap between the manuscript sources and the production of most lyrics and because it is generally agreed that texts were altered in transmission, these scholars often emend or conflate their sources in an attempt to retrieve a lost authorial version of the text. Other scholars stick close to what they believe to be the best surviving manuscript in order to reproduce a more authentically medieval text. My purpose here is not to offer a critique or defence of these two methodological camps, usually called Lachmannian and Bédieriste after the scholars most closely identified with the methodology in question; it is rather to invite reflection on the status of the texts of troubadour lyrics in modern editions and to draw attention to how the different modes of textuality through which they have passed might inform our reading.

What happened to troubadour poems between composition and transcription in the *chansonniers*? And were they composed and transmitted orally or in writing? It has been argued, notably by Rupert Pickens, not only that troubadour poetry was composed and transmitted orally, but that transmitters were invited, even expected to rework songs.[5] This textual instability – termed *mouvance* – would explain why, when troubadour lyrics are preserved in several manuscripts, they seem susceptible to so much variation: for Pickens, these texts are not fixed, there is no one 'authorised' version and they are not reliably the work of one person. Thus the text of a troubadour lyric, for some critics, is inherently susceptible to reworking (*remaniement*), while writing – with its relative fixity – only impacts upon the tradition at a relatively late stage.

(a)

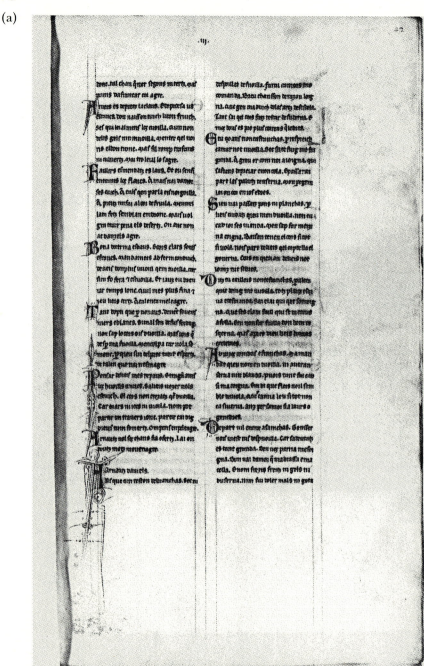

Figure 1a and b Arnaut Daniel's 'Ans que'; Rome, Vatican Library Latin MS 5232 (MS *A*), fol. 42 *r-v*. Reproduced by permission

(b)

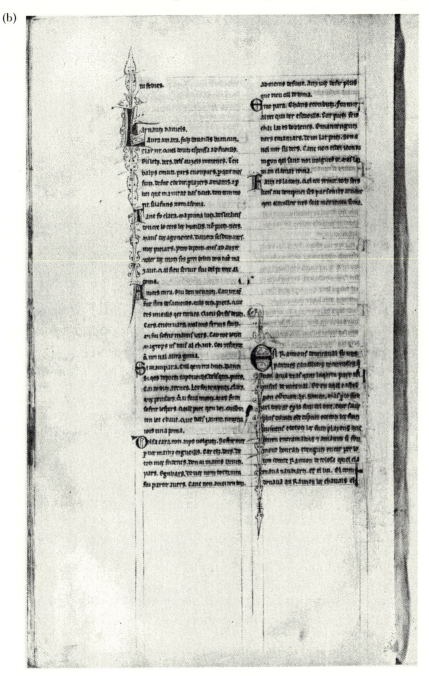

Pickens' argument, which has proved controversial, depends on the interpretation of a few crucial stanzas from the small corpus of Jaufré Rudel:

> Bos es lo vers, qu'anc no·i falhi
> e tot so que·i es ben esta;
> e sel que de mi l'apenra
> gart se no·l franha ni·l pessi.
> Car si l'auzon en Caersi
> en Bertrans e·l coms de Tolza, aa
>
> bos es lo vers, e faran hi
> calque re don hom chantara. Aa (I, 31–8)

(The *vers* is good, for I have not failed in it and everything in it is just right; and may the one who learns it from me be careful not to break or fragment it. For if Sir Bertran and the Count of Toulouse hear it in the Quercy, ah! ah! the *vers* is good, and they will do something there that will be sung about. Ah! ah!)

> Senes breu de pargamina
> tramet lo vers, que chantam
> en plan lengua romana,
> a·n Hugon Brun per Filhol:
> bo·m sap quar gens peitavina,
> de Beiriu e de Guiana,
> s'esgau per lui e Bretanha. (III, 29–35)

(Without parchment sheet I send the *vers* that we sing in the plain romance tongue to Sir Hugo Brun, by Filhol: it pleases me that the Poitevins, the people from Berry and Guyenne are happy for him, and those from Brittany.)

For Pickens, the transmitter of the first poem cited is enjoined not to change anything so that its *addressees* may do so, but he bases this interpretation on an isolated reading in line 38 from a notoriously unreliable manuscript (*C*, on which see below):[6] 'bos es lo sos, e faran hi / Quas que don mos chans gensara' (. . . the tune is good and they will do there whatever will improve my song).[7] Even in this second version, it is not clear that it is the text rather than the melody that the addressees are to improve, while in the text as transmitted by the other manuscripts, it is not clear that the thing (*re*) they are asked to do (or make) with the song is textual or even that they are asked to do (or make) it with the song. Similarly, the second stanza cited poses problems: is the song to be transmitted without parchment – that is orally – because this was the normal practice, or on the contrary is this mentioned because it is unusual?[8]

Evidence concerning oral composition and transmission is often susceptible to more than one interpretation and in practice most editors assume a high degree of written transmission. Whereas proponents of oral transmission believe troubadour poetry was committed to writing only when it ceased to thrive in Occitania and therefore that different versions of a song record different performances, proponents of written transmission believe that songs were composed through the medium of writing (on wax tablets), then committed to more permanent written record, on so-called song-sheets or in individual poets' personal song-books, finally in *chansonniers*. No song-sheets survive (naturally enough since they would have been loose bits of parchment or paper), but there are later medieval references to such sheets.[9] The evidence for song-books is more secure: the collections of Guiraut Riquier's *cansos* in *CR* (both fourteenth-century) derive from a single source that dated each song and arranged them in chronological order. As Guiraut is a late troubadour – indeed a near contemporary of these *chansonniers* – it is plausible that this compilation was author-ial, while Avalle thought it possible to reconstruct Peire Vidal's personal song-book from the surviving manuscript testimony.[10]

Of course, we plunge into the realm of conjecture here, but it is certain that we have lost written sources upon which surviving *chansonniers* drew. For example, comparison of *IK* (both fourteenth-century Italian) reveals that they must have been copied from the same (lost) source. Thus although we cannot be sure when writing intervened in the production and transmission of troubadour poetry, writing obviously did play a large role in the transmission of surviving texts. But it would be a mistake to assume that because texts were written down they became more stable, just as it would be to assume that if texts were composed orally this meant they were intentionally unstable. Scribes adapted texts as well as performers: furthermore scribes miscopy words, miss out chunks of text or fill gaps, which is why some editors discard what they read in manuscripts. Conversely, performers can learn mater-ial accurately by heart.

Among the troubadours themselves there was a range of

attitudes towards textual stability. If Jaufré Rudel (arguably) invites transmitters to improve on his work, Marcabru evinces a concern for his text's integrity:[11]

> Auias de chan com enans' e meillura,
> e Marcabru, segon s'entensa pura,
> sap la razo del vers lasar e faire
> si que autre no l'en pot un mot raire. (IX, 1–4)

(Hear how the song progresses and improves, and Marcabru, according to his pure intention, knows how to make and bind up the theme of the *vers* so that no one can erase a word from it.)

Indeed, Amelia Van Vleck has plausibly argued that there are two types of troubadour poem: those for which a degree of textual stability is guaranteed by form (because the rhymes are disposed in a pattern that makes only one stanza-order possible) and those for which the form encourages a degree of instability (in that the stanzas can be placed in any order without affecting the form).[12] If troubadours could choose between forms that offered varying degrees of textual stability, to polarise their work as either infinitely, but wilfully susceptible to *mouvance*, or as aspiring to fixity, but ruined by disrespectful transmitters, is misguided.

   Part of the problem in any analysis of textuality is that notions such as 'the text' and 'the author' are culturally specific and ideologically charged. For example, in medieval Occitan, an *autor* was not an 'author', but rather an 'authority', usually an ancient writer. The composer of a troubadour lyric was not an *autor*, but a *trobador*, one who 'finds', the implication being that the text preexists the poet and is an object that has somehow to be retrieved. The text does not emanate from the troubadour, but antecedes him or at the very least exists independently, a notion that is reinforced by the metaphors used to articulate troubadour poetics: the poem is an artefact that is bound up, planed, filed or polished.[13] The text then is not a unique utterance expressing the poet's essential being: it is rather an exquisite, inanimate, jewel-like object, fashioned from a resistant and challenging matter, language.

   Many modern editors invest heavily in notions of the 'text' and 'author' that are at odds with those that inform much troubadour poetry. The metaphors they use to talk about their relation to the manuscripts they work with are instructive: thus for William

Paden editing is a 'field of combat' governed by a moral imperative which makes the editor 'responsible' for reconstituting the poet's text;[14] or John Marshall warns against being seduced by an habitually *facilior* manuscript that he calls a *belle infidèle* (*C*, on which see below).[15] In both cases, manuscripts become an impediment to the editor's task: one feels he has a moral duty to battle heroically through a mass of hostile variants to rescue the text the poet produced; the other fears being seduced away from the real object of desire, again the elusive authorial text. The notion of authorship implicitly espoused by most modern editors is not so much anachronistic (since the idea of the authentic authorial text has some currency both among troubadours and transmitters)[16] as, rather, insensitive to alternative views of the text and its relation to its author; it denies the plurality and mobility of the medieval text and devalues the richness of its manuscript dissemination in favour of an absent authorial original. This monolithic view of authorship is also, significantly, out of step with many modern views of the 'author' and the 'text'.

Indeed, since the structuralist critical revolution, the position of the subject in language has been critically reassessed. As Barthes says, 'language knows a "subject" not a "person"'.[17] The subject (that is the 'I' who speaks) is constituted by his discourse and proceeds from it. He is as much an effect of his language as its point of origin and any agency he has is subject to the discourse in which he struggles to take up a subject position.[18] From this perspective a poem is not a privileged expression of an author's intentions and viewing it as such is a fiction which we use to make sense of it, but which occludes our understanding of how its discourse works to constitute its subject. Furthermore, the status of the 'author' in relation to his or her text varies over time and from culture to culture: thus whereas a medieval poet might vaunt the fact that his text is a reworking of traditional material, poets from later periods might value originality or rupture with past textual traditions. As Foucault argues, what he calls the 'author-function' varies historically.[19]

Indeed, in a tradition that derives much of its impulse from competitive imitation, where the dominant mode is citational,[20] the unique 'authorship' of any text, regardless of whether it has been subject to *remaniement*, is open to question. The poet emerges as an individual not because his songs reflect his individuality as a person in real life, but because they differentiate their subject from the subjects of similar songs. Text produces 'author' as much as 'author' produces text. But if the text (rather than the 'author') ought to be our starting point for reading a troubadour lyric, we nonetheless need to recognise the implications of textual instability when considering an 'author'. Thus I have argued elsewhere that our view of Bernart de Ventadorn as a desperate but respectful lover in his famous 'Can vei' (XXXI) derives from an idiosyncratic edition, the crucial features of which were confected by a gifted nineteenth-century German scholar (Carl Appel); a widely disseminated medieval version of the song offers us a different image of an angry and recalcitrant woman-hater. Because medieval versions of 'Can vei' did not conform to the expectations of its modern editor, he produced a version that was largely shaped by his own fantasy of what 'Bernart' must have intended: a modern fantasy of and about the 'author' and his song has, in other words, determined its reception in the twentieth century, occluding its medieval manifestations.[21]

Both the Lachmannian and the Bédieriste methods of editing require a value-judgement about what the poet may or may not have intended, to authorise either a hypothetical reconstruction of the 'original text' or, more modestly perhaps, the choice of 'best manuscript'. They therefore implicitly invoke a fantasy author and place him before the text, at its point of origin. Both methods – because of the notion of authorship they espouse – have a vested interest in subordinating the instability of the medieval text to one authoritative version: other versions are disseminated into a critical apparatus that seems to make them available, while in fact smashing them to smithereens. This critique of the premises of traditional editorial practices is not a plea for the production of editions that systematically offer multiple versions of every troubadour song. It is, rather, simply a cautionary note about the status of troubadour poems in modern editions and about the ideological and aesthetic wrapping in which these editions package their contents.

The critical apparatuses of modern editions are, however, informed by a good deal of meticulous research concerning the relationship of the *chansonniers*. Careful comparison of poems that have survived in large numbers of copies reveals that several main traditions in the transmission of the troubadour lyric can be dis-cerned (for example an Occitan tradition, represented by *CR* and an Italian tradition represented by *AIK*), and also that the compilers of *chansonniers* often worked from more than one source. Even putting aside the question of orality, the transmission of troubadour poetry is therefore a complex process and any attempt to reconstruct an 'original' is fraught with difficulty. For example, one of the main methods editors use to determine the relative quality of different manuscript copies is the imputation to two or more of them of a 'common error', that is, a 'mistake' that suggests that the manuscripts that contain it derive from a single source. This method presupposes that we can tell the difference between a 'correct' and 'incorrect' reading, which is not always easy, as we will see.

The remainder of this chapter is devoted to outlining some of the different types of textual instability, or *remaniement*, that are encountered in the *chansonniers* and to illustrating the problems *remaniement* poses for modern editors. If I use the term *remaniement* ('rehandling') rather than rewriting, this is because I do not wish to put aside entirely the question of orality. But I am wary of appealing to absent originals, whether oral or written, and so base my remarks on the texts that we have, rather than fantasmic archetypes or their fantasmic authors. In any case the opposition between the oral and the written is probably a false one if it leads us to imagine texts which were wholly one or the other. Written texts in the Middle Ages are 'voiced' in that they were usually intended for reading aloud and Laura Kendrick has highlighted the audio-visual aesthetic of troubadour songs in the *chansonniers*, which often appeal both to the eye and ear:[22] if truly 'oral' texts existed, they are by definition not the texts we know, whereas no vernacular medieval text from the twelfth and thirteenth centuries can be regarded as purely 'written'.[23]

A corollary of the assumption that the text is a unique, immutable utterance is that all departures from the 'absent original' are the work of transmitters. However, writers of all periods may revise their work after its initial publication and some 'variant' readings may result from authorial rehandling. One celebrated case is Marcabru's 'Al prim comens' (IV), which survives in two distinct versions.[24] To conflate them into a single text, as has been done recently by one Lachmannian editor,[25] masks the song's adaptation to different historical circumstances, possibly by

Marcabru himself, while to opt for a 'best manuscript' is equally
unsatisfactory.

The import of the content of most variants, however, is less
clear cut. To take another example from Marcabru, he mockingly
accuses his patron Audric of boasting in the following terms in
ADIKz (with signficant variants to the right):

> segon tas leis   *Dz* leis] les
> as plus conques   *K* conqueis
> que non fetz Cesar als Romans. (XXb, 28–30)

(According to you, you have conquered more than Caesar for the
Romans.)

In *CR* these lines read:

> segon las leys
> semblatz mielhs reys   *R* mielhs] pus
> que no fetz Cezars lo Romas.

(According to songs you are more like a king than was Caesar the
Roman.)

Superficially *CR* seems to offer the better text here: whereas the
apparently inexact rhyme between *leis* and *conques* troubled the
scribes of *DKz*, the corresponding rhymes in *C* are exact, while the
syntax of the last line seems more clearly marked in *CR* than in
ADIKz because of the inflection of the proper noun and the elimination of the preposition which, combined, clearly suggest that in
CR 'Caesar the Roman' is construed as the subject of *fetz*. *ADIKz*
might therefore seem peppered with errors: *les* and *conqueis* are
implausible forms; *Cezar* is uninflected. But the rhyming of *-es/-eis*
occurs elsewhere in Marcabru while the inflection of *Cezar* in Occitan is hypercorrect given its Latin derivation.[26] Thus *CR*'s text is
only 'better' if the highly normative assumptions about rhyme and
linguistic correctness that seem to inform this fourteenth-century
tradition are accepted as reflecting twelfth-century linguistic practice. Perhaps uncertainty about Marcabru's practice and a failure
to understand the syntax of Caesar conquering 'for' the Romans
led *CR*'s source (generally interventionist) to produce a *facilior*
text.

Transmitters did not, however, simply rework the material they
copied. Occasionally they made additions. This may have been a
widespread practice, but the more successfully it was done, the

less likely we are to notice. Sarah Kay has argued that apocryphal material in Jaufré Rudel's corpus offers valuable insight into near-contemporary responses to the lyrics.[27] Indeed extra, possibly apocryphal stanzas can radically reorient a poem. Thus, Marcabru's 'Pus mos coratges' (XL), a programmatic attack on sinners redolent with Biblical language, consists of six stanzas in *AIK* and ends famously with a prayer to *fin'amor*. *CE*, on the other hand, conclude as follows:

> Mon cor per aquest vers destrenh
> quar mi plus que·ls autres reprenh,
> que qui autrui vol encolpar
> dregs es que si sapcha guardar
> que no sia dels crims techitz
> de qu'el ieys encolpa e ditz:
> pueis poira segurs castiar.
>
> Pero si es asatz cauzitz
> sel que be sap dire e·l ditz,
> que pot si, si·s vol, remembrar. (43–52)

(With this song I master my heart, since I admonish myself more than I do others, for it is right that he who wishes to accuse others should know how to avoid being covered in the reproaches with which he himself makes accusations and speaks out: then he will be able to chastise in safety.

But he who knows how to speak well and does so is indeed among the chosen, for he can, if he wishes, regain awareness of himself.)

These stanzas use the rhyme-sounds of the first six stanzas, but a different rhyme-scheme. Since the first two stanzas use a different rhyme-scheme from stanzas III–VI, this may in itself not indicate that this last stanza and *tornada* are apocryphal, but they redirect the poem by focusing attention on the subject, so the poem becomes a meditation on *his* relation to the sins listed, rather than the sins of others. Is it then significant that *CE* attribute this poem not to Marcabru, but to Bernart de Ventadorn? The editor of this poem is confronted with confusing evidence. If this extra stanza is considered an integral, 'authentic' part of the poem, should the whole poem then be assigned to Bernart's rather than Marcabru's corpus and is the *AIK* version then a 'Marcabrunian' *remaniement* of a Bernart lyric? *C* – Marshall's *belle infidèle* – is not, as we have seen, necessarily a reliable witness. But rather than simply discarding its evidence here (which in any case is supported by *E*), it is perhaps more interesting to consider how it shows one poet's

dicourse being assimilated to another's. Marcabru goes to some
lengths to distinguish his style from courtly poets such as Bernart
de Ventadorn, but this does not prevent his work from being
assimilated to Bernart's here.

Apart from adding and rehandling material, the main form of
remaniement encountered concerns stanza-order. Many editors have
an ambivalent attitude towards stanza-order: on the one hand they
acknowledge that songs that have rhyme-schemes that do not fix
the stanza-order (notably *coblas unissonans* and *singulars*) evince a
good deal of *mouvance* in this respect; on the other they believe
there must be some logic in the progression of a poem. But such
logic is in the eye of the beholder and where editors fail to perceive
an amorous, aesthetic or rhetorical logic, they create one.[28] Thus
some lyrics appear in modern editions with a stanza-order that is
not attested in any medieval source. Such is the case with Arnaut
Daniel's 'Ans qe·l cim' (XVI), which is a striking example in that
Arnaut is possibly the most frequently edited poet in the tradition – there are to my knowledge six critical editions – and yet
this poem has never been edited using a stanza-order attested
from a medieval source. Here is Toja's text.

I   Ans qe·l cim reston de branchas
        sec, ni despoillat de fuoilla,
        farai, c'Amors m'o comanda,
        breu chansson de razon loigna,
    que gen m'a duoich de las artz de s'escola;   5
    tant sai qe·l cors fatz restar de suberna
    e mos bous es pro plus correns que lebres.

II   Ab razos coindas e franchas
        m'a mandat q'ieu no m'en tuoilla
        ni autra·n serva ni·n blanda   10
        puois tant fai c'ab si m'acoigna;
    e·m di que flors no·il semble de viola,
    qui·is camia leu, sitot nonca s'iverna,
    anz per s'amor sia laurs o genebres.

III   Ditz: 'Tu c'aillors non t'estanchas   15
        per altra qui·t deing ni·t vuoilla,
        totz plaitz esqiv' e desmanda,
        sai e lai qui qe·t somoigna;
    que ses clam faill qui se meteus afola,
    e tu no far failla don hom t'esqerna,   20
    mas apres Dieu lieis honors e celebres'.

IV   E: 'Tu, coartz, non t'afranchas
            per respieich c'amar no·t vuoilla;
            sec, s'il te fuig ni·t fai ganda,
            que greu er c'om no·i apoigna   25
        qui s'afortis de preiar e no cola,
        q'en passara part las palutz d'Userna
        con peregrins, lai on cor en ios Ebres'.

V   S'ieu n'ai passatz pons ni planchas
            per lieis, cuidatz q'ieu m'en duoilla?   30
            Non eu, c'ab ioi ses vianda
            m'en sap far meizina coigna,
        baisan tenen; e·l cors, sitot si vola,
        no·is part de lieis qe·l capdell' e·l governa.
        Cors, on q'ieu an, de lieis no·t loinz ni·t sebres.   35

VI   De part Nil entro c'a Sanchas
            gensser no·is viest ni·s despuoilla,
            car sa beutatz es tan granda
            que semblaria·us messoigna.
        Be·m vai d'amor, q'ela·m bais' e m'acola,   40
        e no·m frezis freitz ni gels ni buerna,
        ni·m fai dolor mals ni gota ni febres.

VII   Sieus es Arnautz del cim tro en la sola,
        e senes lieis no vol aver Lucerna
        ni·l senhoriu del renc per on cor Ebres.   45

I   Before the branches in the treetops become dry and denuded of leaves, I will compose, since Love commands me to do this, a brief song with a distant theme, for she has sweetly instructed me in the arts of her school; I know so much that I can halt the flow of the tide and my ox is swifter than a hare.

II   With sweet and pure reasoning, she has ordered that I not remove myself from her, nor serve or court another, since I succeed in attaching myself to her; and she tells me that I should not seem to her like a violet flower , which wilts quickly, even if it is not winter, rather for her love I should be laurel or juniper.

III   She says: 'You who do not remain elsewhere for another who deigns to love you or wants you, avoid and resist all suits, whosoever beseeches you; for he who confounds himself is destroyed with no appeal and do not commit a fault for which you might be mocked, but after God honour and celebrate her.'

IV   And: 'You, coward, do not free yourself in the expectation that she might not wish to love you; follow, even if she flees and dodges from you, for one can hardly fail to catch up if one persists in beseeching and does not give up until one has gone beyond the marshes of Luserna as a pilgrim, there where the Ebro flows to the sea.'

V   If I have passed bridges and beams for her, do you think this pains me? Not I, for with joy and without any other nourishment I know how to make sweet medicine for myself, kissing and embracing; and if my heart, although it departs, never leaves her who rules over and governs it. Heart, wherever I go, do not distance or sever yourself from her.

VI   Beyond the Nile and as far as Saintes, no fairer woman dresses or disrobes herself, for her beauty is so great that it would seem like a lie to you here. Love treats me well for she kisses and embraces me and neither cold nor frost nor fog chills me, nor do pain or gout or fever hurt me.

VII   Arnaut belongs to her from top to toe, and without her he does not wish to have Lucerne, nor the lordship in the land where the Ebro flows.

Toja (1960) follows the stanza-order first adopted by Canello (1883) as do Lavaud (1910), Wilhelm (1981) and Eusebi (1984). Although Wilhelm suggests more attention should be paid to the stanza-order in the manuscripts, only Perugi (1978) breaks ranks but to adopt an order that likewise is unattested in any medieval source (keyed to Toja's stanza-order: 1625347). The stanza-orders in the manuscripts are as follows (again keyed to Toja's stanza-order):

ABDN	145326
E	1453267
L	14526
IKN²	1425637
Uc	1453627
CT	1245367
V	124536
R	1645327

As *E* and *L* support *ABDN*, the majority stanza-order is clear, particularly since the sequence 1453 occurs in two other manuscripts, 453 in six, and 4536 in five. Canello asserted that the stanza-order in the manuscripts is 'very confused' (p. 250). He is then cited by later editors, but neither he nor they explain how the attested stanza-orders produce a garbled logic.[29] Before turning to an examination of the 'logic' of the poem in one set of manuscripts, what of its logic in most modern editions?

In Toja's text, the song is largely a dialogue between the poet and Love personified:[30] Love commands the poet to compose (stanza I) and to love properly (stanza II), then addresses him directly (stanzas III and IV), before the poet vaunts his constancy (stanza V) and his lady's worth (stanza VI), with the *tornada* recapping on the last two stanzas. This is perfectly logical, but is it less logical than what occurs in the manuscripts? And on what does this logic rely?

In *ABDELN*, the opening stanza is followed by stanza IV. When not preceded by stanza III, there is no reason to assume stanza IV is direct speech and the 'tu' addressed in the opening line, rather than being the poet addressed by Love, is merely an interlocutor upon whom the poet rounds didactically, picking up perhaps on the idea that he had been a star pupil in Love's school. Note that in the manuscript upon which all editors base their texts, *A* (see Figure 1), the stanza opens 'E tu q'o aus' (you who hear this) and it is supported in this by the majority of the other manuscripts; Toja's *coartz*, adopted from Canello, is not in any manuscript, but is suggested by *L*'s *coars*.[31] Note also that the verb in the sixth line of this stanza is first person in *all* manuscripts (*passarai*) rather than third person, so the last two lines become a statement of the poet's worthy intentions with regard to his lady ('I will go beyond . . . '), which is of course 'illogical' if the stanza is Love's direct speech.[32] The logic of Toja's text is enhanced then by nifty – but unnecessary – alterations to his base manuscript. This editorial procedure is solipsistic: the manuscripts are 'illogical' because they fail to acknowledge a logic that they cannot by definition have known; because the manuscripts are 'illogical' they require emendations that will enhance the 'right' logic, thereby demonstrating further the 'illogicality' of the medieval versions.

In the majority stanza-order, stanza IV is followed by V, so that the poet's protestations of constancy follow on neatly from his 'lesson' to his interlocutor. At the end of stanza V, the poet addresses his heart and it is this that immediately precedes the only clearly marked instance of direct speech in the manuscripts (Toja's stanza III): rather than being addressed by Love, the poet is addressed by his heart in this version.[33] Whereas for modern editors 'logic' derives from the poet being guided by an external force that inhabits him (Love), in this medieval version, the poet's guidance comes more clearly from within. As stanza III ends with the heart talking about the lady, the subject of the first verb of stanza II (which follows in this version) is either still the poet's heart, or his lady, rather than Love, and the end of the poem is devoted to praise of the lady and her powers: thus whereas Toja's text is anchored in the abstract (Love) and only focuses briefly on the lady, this text dwells insistently on the lady and the poet's agency.[34]

I have no idea whether the logic that informs this version of the text is the one Arnaut intended. As my two previous examples from Marcabru indicated, the displacement of troubadour lyrics from song to book could lead to their being transformed in the process so that the logic of a song in a *chansonnier* is not necessarily that of the troubadour to whom it is attributed. Just as the displacement of a lyric from song to book may lead away from the troubadour, so its subsequent displacement from script to print may lead away from the manuscript. This does not mean, however, that we are thereby necessarily led back to the troubadour! What this analysis of 'Ans qe·l cim' shows is the extent to which the texts of troubadour lyrics in modern editions are overlaid by others' preconceptions about the logic of medieval poetry. You will bring your own preconceptions to troubadour lyrics, as I do mine, but you might wish to bear in mind that these texts, in the *chansonniers* and in modern editions, always already bear the traces of other readers' responses. The scribes and compilers of medieval *chansonniers* sometimes wanted to confer on the absent voice of the poet a fixity and a regularity it may never have possessed in performance. And the modern editor's desire to reconstitute the poet's (absent) voice often leads him to lend reality to his own imaginary fictions of the song and its original singer even (or perhaps particularly) when these do not coincide with the manuscript evidence.

NOTES

1 See Sutherland, 'L'Elément théâtral'.
2 For Perugi, *Saggi*, pp. 7–8, the linguistic incompetence of transmitters is a crucial impediment to their understanding of the troubadours.

3 See Chapter 15.

4 I evoke, of course, the titles of two important studies: Chaytor, *From Script to Print* and Huot, *From Song to Book*.

5 Pickens, 'Jaufré Rudel'.

6 On the letters used to designate the *chansonniers* see Appendix 4.

7 Pickens, VI, 43–4; pp. 35–6 of his edition for analysis.

8 Avalle, *Manoscritti*, p. 28.

9 Ibid., pp. 61–2.

10 Ibid., pp. 62–5; *Peire Vidal*, ed. Avalle [Appendix 1, item 46], pp. lxxiv–xc.

11 Marcabru quotations from Gaunt, Harvey, Marshall and Paterson's forthcoming edition.

12 *Memory and Re-creation.*

13 For example Arnaut Daniel, II, 12–14 and X, 1–7.

14 'Manuscripts', pp. 324 and 326.

15 *Transmission*, p. 16. The term *facilior* is used of a manuscript reading when a scribe may have intervened to render a difficult text more comprehensible.

16 See the compiler's prologue to *a* in Gruber, *Dialektik*, pp. 28–9.

17 'The death of the author', p. 169.

18 See Kay, *Subjectivity* and Chapter 13.

19 See 'What is an author?'

20 See Gruber, *Dialektik* and Chapter 11.

21 'Discourse desired'.

22 See Kendrick, *Game*.

23 See Fleischman, 'Discourse'.

24 Avalle, *Manoscritti*, pp. 44–5.

25 Lazzerini, 'Un caso esemplare': she bases the last stanza on *A*, but follows this with the *tornada*; she emends all manuscripts unnecessarily in line 62 (*A* line 56).

26 Though analogical inflections are not uncommon. The term 'hypercorrect' describes a scribal practice that observes normative linguistic rules over-zealously.

27 'Continuation as criticism'.

28 See again my 'Discourse desired'.

29 Indeed, only Eusebi attempts an explanation of how the stanza-orders might have arisen through mechanical error.

30 For a commentary, see Kay, *Subjectivity*, pp. 37–40.

31 Wilhelm's, Eusebi's and Perugi's editions (Perugi line 36) adopt the majority reading.

32 Only Perugi (his line 41) gives a first person form here, though he emends in the next line, where Toja adopts a *facilior* reading only in *CT* (*con*).

33 Compare Lanfranc Cigala's fictive debate with his heart and understanding (X), discussed by Kay, *Subjectivity*, pp. 65–6.

34 The *tornada* is absent in *A*, but the poem is intelligible without it.

CHAPTER 15

The chansonniers *as books*

William Burgwinkle

The thirteenth-century troubadour manuscripts are among the earliest known collections of lyric poetry in a European vernacular and the first in Occitan to treat secular rather than religious works. With their large number and variety of songs, frequent emendations, attention to distinctions of genre and attribution, consciousness of literary history, and comprehensive plans for rubrication, they proclaim their double status as book, rather than mere compendium, and art object, worthy of collection. Prized from the outset,[1] multiple copies were often made from the same source (for example *AA'* and the Auvergnat *B*, or the important series *IKK'K"*) or sometime later in cheaper editions (such as *a*, a copy on paper of the Bernart Amoros *chansonnier*).[2] Both the Italian and slightly later Languedocian codices served as models for the Italian lyric collections of the fourteenth century and as source books for Italian poets, including Dante and Petrarch, and the Occitan anthologist-critic Matfre Ermengaud.[3] Indeed, Occitan poetry and French romances were in demand at the Northern Italian courts throughout the thirteenth and fourteenth centuries as badges of aristocratic legitimacy (Krauss, *Epica feodale*).

There are forty *chansonniers* extant.[4] The earliest of them (the group dated from 1254 to approximately 1300) were either produced in the workshops of Venice, Padua and Treviso, often by Occitan scribes (*AIKDD^aHST*), or brought to Italy shortly thereafter (as in the case of *V*, and the original from which *a* was copied).[5] More than 50 per cent of those dating from the fourteenth century were likewise made in Northern Italy.[6] In the wake of Napoleon's grand conquest and the nascent nationalism that followed, Romantic critics undertook the systematic study of these rediscovered treasures. The issues of provenance, sources and poetics that they raised served in turn to solidify the links being forged between linguistic identity and nationalist scholarship, philology and patriotism (Kendrick, 'Science').

How did the tradition develop over the course of the thirteenth and fourteenth centuries? The number of extant *chansonniers* indicates that interest grew with time. While there are nine extant from the thirteenth century and two from the cusp between centuries, twenty date from later in the fourteenth century. Contrast the Northern French *trouvère* manuscripts, of which twelve are from the thirteenth century (some earlier than the first known troubadour manuscript *D*); five are from the cusp and only three date from the fourteenth century (Bec, 'Troubadours et trouvères'). The notion that Occitan poetry lost its vitality and audience after the Albigensian Crusade (1209–29) is thus questionable. Instead we witness a rise in interest in the written forms of the songs and in the collections themselves.[7] The loss of independence and prestige that followed the Northern French invasion fuelled a taste for local poetry and a drive to record cultural history. In Italy, this foreign poetry became a status symbol for its benefactors as well as a model for vernacular lyrics and a medium for diffusing political propaganda over the tensions pitting the Lombard League and papal interests against Frederick II's imperial designs.

The earliest manuscripts from the Veneto indicate that the lyrics had by then already attained the status of what Pierre Bourdieu has called 'cultural capital'.[8] Their compilers did not see *chansonniers* as simple catalogues or compendia but rather as complex and encyclopedic, documenting not just the lyrics but also the lives of the poets, the development of the genres, and the courts which supported the practice and practitioners of song. This interest in the social and cultural conditions in which Occitan song developed is unusual for the time, especially since it concerns a near-contemporary literary phenomenon. It seems likely that in the late twelfth century, Occitan poets carried with them to Italy an enormous amount of lyric and biographical-cultural material gathered at the major courts and centres of learning where they had previously practised their art.[9] Especially in Venetian scriptoria, luxury manuscripts were composed on vellum to preserve this tradition and set it forth in a clear and highly organised form. These earliest manuscripts are often carefully indexed, organised by genre and poet (*ABDIKN*).[10] Songs are presented in the order

established by the index, sometimes under coloured rubrics indicating *cansos*, *sirventes* and *tensos* or *coblas*.[11] Others, though lacking
the index, are still organised (albeit less systematically) by genre
(*HE*). In many of these MSS (*ABHIK*), a *vida*, or biographical
introduction, figures at the head of a poet's works or immediately
after. Some of the most expensively produced MSS (*AIKM*) further
celebrate individual poets with illuminated portraits.[12] Monumental in size and quality, *I* and *K* alone contain 87 of the 101 *vidas*.
Most of the early compilers clearly favoured love songs over other
genres and musical notation is absent from their work. The finished product, expensively bound, is weighty in every sense of the
word: source-book, cultural repository and object of great beauty
reflecting the glory of the tradition and its patrons.[13]

Why are these thirteenth-century manuscripts so similar
despite their variations on a theme? Was there a model or were
there similar collections already in circulation in the Veneto?
Bernart Amoros' prologue to his now-lost manuscript offers some
clues. Laying claim to expertise through his Auvergnat origins and
poetic training, he states:

qe en bona fe eu ai escrig en aqest libre drechamen, lo miels q'ieu ai
sauput e pogut. E si ai mout eme̦ndat d'aq̦o q'ieu trobei en l'issemple,
don ieu o tiein e bon e dreig segon lo dreig lengatge (quoted in Zufferey,
Recherches, p. 80).

(in good faith I wrote things in this book correctly, the best that I knew
and was able. And though I did emend what I found in the model somewhat, I hold that it (*or* my copy) is right and just according to correct
language usage.)

Bernart goes on to warn future scribes not to alter his manuscript
in any way. Thus already in the late thirteenth century the compiler was aware of his role in cultural preservation, proud of his
accomplishments and respectful of his sources. Perhaps one or
more of his sources subsequently travelled to Italy, as did
Bernart's own copy, or perhaps Bernart himself was working in
Italy, from a source found there, when he took up his task.[14] In
any case, models like the one consulted by Bernart left their mark
on the Italian manuscripts, which, in turn, made their way back
to Southern France, probably in the form of copies, to instigate or
reactivate local manuscript production in Languedoc and Catalonia.

The extant Occitan manuscripts (*CEJR*), all from the early to mid-fourteenth century, are less numerous but equally important for different reasons.[15] Though indexed like the Italian manuscripts, they tend to list by author alone rather than genre (*CR*). *C* has two indexes: one by name of poet and the other alphabetical. *C* and *R*, both early fourteenth-century, are considerably more comprehensive than most: *R* contains almost 1,000 songs, *C* a staggering 1,206.[16] *C* has beautifully illuminated capitals and some miniatures of poets and heraldic beasts but no biographical prose texts. *R*, on the other hand, has *vidas* and *razos* and extensive illumination but nothing approaching the systematic portraiture of *AIK*. *R* is also distinguished by the inclusion of 160 melodies, being one of only two southern manuscripts to contain music.[17] Both *C* and *R* include a sequence of songs by Guiraut Riquier that the scribe probably copied from an authorial collection, and *R* closes with an important series of narrative and didactic texts, some of them in prose. When biographical prose texts (*vidas* and *razos*) figure in the fourteenth-century and later manuscripts, they appear together in a separate section (*EN²PRSg/Z*). Their narratives also tend to be longer and more developed. The Catalan *Sg/Z*, though clearly indebted to the Auvergnat/Italian model of *AB*, also features an important collection of texts by and about Giraut de Bornelh that is unavailable elsewhere, and the works of many later poets associated with Catalonia and Toulouse.[18] Thus, while its scribes consulted a source common to that used for *EPR*, they also had access to collections that seem to have been maintained locally.

The rapidity with which troubadour texts accrued prestige is reflected in these remarkable manuscripts, but their existence alone does not explain it. By the mid-thirteenth century, interest in troubadour poetry in Italy was apparently sustained largely through written transcription, while in Languedoc the lyrics were still supplemented by a more active oral tradition (Tavera, 'Chansonnier d'Urfé'). The collection and transmission of troubadour songs in book form surely played a major role in the preservation of the lyrics, both at foreign courts and at home, but in linking songs with individualised poets, the authors and scribes also outlined a cultural economy, established the use of Occitan, praised important dynasties and created a mythology of court practice. The result was a new form of cultural and literary history that advocated a political identity founded on cultural practices rather than geography, ethnicity or language use.

Much of what we know about troubadour lyric comes from these prose biographies. Ranging in length from twenty-seven words (Bertran d'Alamanon) to over two thousand (Guillem de Cabestany), the *vidas* are distributed rather unevenly throughout the early manuscripts. Increasingly, despite reservations about their unwieldy style and unreliable claims, the *vidas* are recognised as essential documents that offer much more than positivist historical accuracy, while also approaching that on occasion (Stronski, *La Poésie*). They provide an early example of an *esprit de classification*: a self-referentiality that establishes the power of the collected texts as social and cultural document, and a conscious effort to associate the lyrics, through rhetorical commentary, with the classical tradition of *accessus ad auctores*, biographical commentary on literary works (Egan, '"Razo"'). The *vidas*, and their manuscripts, indicate how literary material worked with biographical and geographical data to produce and inculcate a form of cultural memory that was at once foundational, nostalgic and self-serving.

Most *vidas* follow a set rhetorical paradigm that underscores their status as traditional, *ergo* historical. The format usually includes: name of poet, provenance, quality of talents, patrons, love story, success or failure, death. The authors were anxious to systematise and categorise the phenomenon of court poetry rather than simply record it and valorise its practitioners. Many of the *vidas* criticise poets for the quality of their work, and there is no effort to establish their nobility. The *vidas* reveal a deliberate effort to present these varied poets, genres and courts as part of an ideologically sanctioned system of training, thematics and patronage, while still claiming some individual qualities for the practitioners. Though not all poets and patrons are equally talented and respectable, the honour of the system in which they participate is not questioned.

The *razos*, a second, distinguishable sub-set within the genre of biographical commentary, raise other problems. To begin with, the dividing line between *vida* and *razo* is not absolutely clear. The word *razo* is used to refer to both types of texts, while *vida* appears only in fourteenth-century manuscripts. *Razo* is derived from the Latin *ratione(m)*, meaning introduction, explanation, reasoned commentary, subject matter, background or gloss. *Razos* are generally longer and may include citations from, or even the entire text of, the song(s) under discussion. Present already in some thirteenth-century manuscripts (*HIK*) but to a lesser degree than the generally shorter *vidas*, they appear to have gained in popularity as the institutionalisation of troubadour studies developed.[19] In some manuscripts from the early fourteenth century (especially *P* and *R*), the *razos* are longer and capable of standing alone as independent tales. There is no set rhetorical form as there tends to be for the *vida*. *Razos* sometimes even refer back to *vidas* with such expressions as 'As you have heard by now . . . ' before launching into a tale that purports to explain why the song under consideration was composed.

Both types of commentaries are essential to an understanding of the *chansonnier* tradition. By the time that the thirteenth-century Venetan manuscripts were commissioned, the songs and lore of the troubadours were clearly in demand at the courts of Northern Italy and the glosses/biographies came to serve as the founding texts of a form of collective cultural memory. In creating individual personae to match the lyric voices, the prose authors created the first vernacular literary history and an international 'star' system. Bertran de Born, Arnaut Daniel and Sordello went on to play major roles in Dante's *Commedia*. These and other poets wend their way proudly through Petrarch's *Trionfi*.

The rhetoric of the prose texts establishes them as essentially transitional and mediating: between the oral and the written, prose and verse, life and representation. The standard formulae used to close *razo* texts include such statements as: 'and here is song *x* and it goes like this . . . '; 'and for this reason poet *x* composed this *sirventes*' – statements that could lead directly into either an oral performance or a written version of the lyrics. Several of the *razos* have hybrid endings that point even more explicitly to both written and oral transmission: '(song *x*) . . . which is *written* here, as you shall *hear*' (Boutière and Schutz, *Biographies*, p. 314). Such language may reflect the early integration of written material into lyric performance, as in a case where the poet introduces his song before performing it to music, or interweaves his musical renditions with prose commentaries (Schutz, 'Were the Vidas'). It indicates that the *vidas* and *razos* were available in an early written form, that at least one author clearly intended that the prose commentary and lyric text should be linked, and that the *razos* were used early on to set up interpretative parameters for lyrics.[20]

The dating and transmission of the *razos* are thus central to the issue of how the *chansonniers* developed as books. Guido Favati's intuition that the *razos* were actually composed before the *vidas* is now generally accepted (Favati, *Biografie*; Poe, *'L'autr'escrit'*). Though the *razos* appear more frequently in later documents, none of the stories they tell refers to events that postdate 1219, the approximate date at which the poet Uc de Saint Circ made his definitive move to Lombardy and the Veneto. Elizabeth Poe has shown that Uc, originally from the Quercy, likely brought with him to Italy a collection of *razos* dealing with a diverse group of poets and another separate collection devoted primarily to lyrics by Bertran de Born (Poe, *'L'autr'escrit'*). All of these *razos* share some stylistic traits, thematic concerns and narrative structures, along with frequent cross-references one to another.

References within the *razos* to earlier *vidas* sometimes backfire, as in the two *razos* pertaining to Guilhem de Sant Leidier's songs VI and XIII (Boutière and Schutz, *Biographies*; pp. 274, 280). Both begin with an author saying that he has already told us who the poet is and where he came from, but in neither case is there a *vida* or *razo* in the MS that gives this information. Such contradictions suggest that some original, now lost prototype combining *vidas* and *razos* once existed. At whatever point the *razos* were split apart and copied as introductions to individual songs, more attention was paid to the integrity of the individual text than to how it would read in its new context. In one famous case, a reference back to another body of *razos* (referred to as *'l'autr'escrit'*) has been shown to refer to the whole separate collection of *razos* dedicated to the works of Bertran de Born, a collection which remained in large part intact in manuscripts *F*, *I* and *K*, but not in the manuscript (*N²*) in which the reference occurs (Poe, *'L'autr'escrit'*).

If Uc de Saint Circ arrived in Italy with a collection of *razos* and *vidas* and continued to accumulate additional biographical and geographical material during his stay, then we could postulate that the first impulse towards bringing together a unified and coherent body of texts in book form occurred in the first third of the thirteenth century. If Uc used previously composed material on the major troubadours that preceded him, material collected in an intellectual centre like Montpellier, then we might push that date back even earlier. Either way, this early impulse did not end with Uc's collection(s). The late thirteenth- and early fourteenth-century manuscripts include *vidas* composed for poets who outlived Uc or whose work he could not have known. Miquel de la Tor is mentioned within Peire Cardenal's *vida* as the author of that text; several other *vidas* referring to some of the Italian troubadours mention events that postdate Uc's supposed date of death, c. 1260. By the time that the Venetian manuscripts *AIK* were composed, their scribes and illustrators clearly had a plan to follow, perhaps a model from the Auvergne already known to the compiler of *B* and Bernart Amoros. The ambitious organisation of the material indicates that some one, or some scriptorium, had already seen to it that the collections were presented as part of a unified and impressively thought-out whole with the same tripartite presentation by genre (*cansos/sirventes/tensos* or *cansos/tensos/sirventes*).[21]

Even the innovative alternation of prose and verse within these manuscripts marks a distinctive moment in the evolution from simple lyric anthology to organised and functional compilation. Vernacular prose is found only rarely in manuscripts of the twelfth century and is largely limited to homilies, translations of the Bible, charters and juridical texts. The formal juxtaposition of commentary and lyric is an innovation that reveals a revolutionary attitude towards the truth value and referentiality of verse and prose. Though verse was the standard means of transmitting both history and fiction in narrative form in the twelfth century, by the early thirteenth century it was under attack as being mendacious. Prose, previously reserved for legal documents and civic registers, was now being valorised as the more appropriate medium for historiography (Spiegel, *Romancing the Past*; Kittay and Godzich, *Emergence of Prose*). Capitalising on such a distinction without ever explicitly acknowledging it, the compilers and scribes of early *chansonniers* established a double-tiered system in which the interplay between the verse and prose establishes the illusion of an extratextual reality which both supports and interprets the lyrical and personal. It is a tribute to the effectiveness of this structuring device that most critics continue to read the texts on the terms which these authors set for them, i.e. expecting the prose to be factual and the verse an expression of subjective emotion when, in fact, the external referent is as much a creation of the lyric text as it is a support. Using what Roland Barthes referred to as a 'reality effect' to suggest a grounding in fact, the *vida/razo* authors often manage to conjure up what seems to be a solid and infallible past out of nothing more substantial than the textual play in the songs themselves.

Some notion of the complexity and development of the thirteenth-century manuscript tradition can be gained by examining more closely two of the earliest manuscripts, the Venetan *D* and *H*. The former was the work of at least five scribes and can be divided into five sections (index, *D*, D^a, D^b, D^r). A notation at the beginning of the first section informs us that this portion of the collection dates to 1254, hence its reputation as trail-blazer. The same notation informs us that the index that follows will contain the names of the poets represented and a listing of their songs. Divisions in the manuscript are also reflected in the index. On folio 6*r*, for example, we find a notation indicating that what follows from that point on in the manuscript is the book compiled for Lord Alberico.[22] Since it can be assumed, given the date and provenance, that this is a reference to Alberico da Romano, Lord of Treviso, it would appear to have been compiled for a single major patron at a moment when interest in the art and political use of troubadour lyric was growing at the Italian courts and communes.[23]

Since most scholars also agree that this 'book' was the work of Uc de Saint Circ, resident poet at Alberico's court for close to forty years, it may well reflect the individual tastes of either one collector or one poet and tell us something about the practices of organising and presenting material in this milieu. Uc's presence in Treviso, the administrative centre of Alberico's court, is attested in 1255, contemporaneous with this collection (Zufferey, 'Un document'). A document from that date indicates that Uc was prosecuted on charges of heresy and usury the previous year. Scholars agree that this first portion of the manuscript was compiled in the Marca Trevigiana, probably in Treviso itself, as was the last portion, a *florilegium* of quotations compiled by Ferrari da Ferrara. Uc de Saint Circ's own name was added by a later hand to the index of poets at the end of the first column on folio 8*r*, perhaps an indication that Uc was responsible for the original compilation and had therefore inadvertently left out his own name.

The index notes carefully at which point each section of the manuscript begins and ends. The collection we have been discussing, the 1254 *Liber Alberici*, is found on folios 153*r*–211*r*. A collection of sixty-three French songs follows (noted in the index on fol. 8*r*). The preservation of separate, intact collections within the whole is an indication of the scribes' attention to historical and editorial distinctions. The organising schema is quite clear: *cansos* (fols. 1–129); *sirventes* and *tensos* (fols. 130–52); *Liber Alberici* (fols. 153–211); French section (fols. 211–31); Peire Cardenal collection (fols. 232–43); *Florilegium of Ferrari da Ferrara* (fols. 243–61); and finally an additional section on paper, as opposed to vellum, that includes Arnaut de Maruelh's *Ensenhamen*. The scribes, while maintaining the distinctions between their sources, are still attentive to the use of the collection as a manual. In this sense, it is already a book: to be consulted by specialists, compiled in the interest of artistic preservation rather than performance. It contains no biographical prose texts or illuminated portraits or melodies. The existence of a fragment from another *florilegium* (*C^m*) compiled at the same scriptorium indicates that this collecting impulse was not unusual (Allegri, 'Frammento', p. 327). The conscientious editing of the first section of manuscript *D* indicates that the scribe had several versions of some of the songs at his disposal and that he referred to all of them as he worked. Occasionally he incorporated variants, even marginal notes.

MS *H*, dating also from the third quarter of the thirteenth century and the same region of Italy, stands out in most scholars' discussions of textual transmission. In the nineteenth century it was already recognised as an anomaly, probably a privately prepared collection. According to Maria Careri's recent and magisterial study, four scribal hands are discernible. The first was from the Veneto and worked somewhere between Treviso and Padua. According to Careri, the manuscript was prepared in sections: three are complete, two are partial. This first hand (Careri's 1^a) wrote most of the text. A second (1^b) retouched his predecessor's work, adding marginal notes and corrections. A third, independent hand (2), worked on the rubrics, and a fourth, perhaps that of a later owner (3), added only one final text on the last page, a song by Uc de Saint Circ. Careri notes that the original scribe was a jack-of-all-trades: an artisan who had to prepare the manuscript, even erasing an earlier Latin text, then calligraph it; a scholar who had to know and select his material; and a philologist who had to interpret his sources, making corrections and notes. The second hand was more scholarly than artistic, glossing and writing over, privileging absolute fidelity to the text over any overarching aesthetic sense. It was the third scribe (Careri's *mano* 2) who decided to overhaul the collection by adding further corrections, rubrics and a comprehensive illumination project. He rebound the diverse sections and united them as an artistic whole.

H most memorably distinguishes itself in its idiosyncratic choice of texts. Two-thirds of the songs and several of the *razos* are *unica*, texts found only in that one manuscript. The emphasis is on little-anthologised parodic *tensos*.[24] So striking is this characteristic that it has even been suggested that the manuscript was meant to serve as a footnote or appendix to the more canonical Venetian collections – a repository for short, comic, satirical songs that were either considered unfit for the major manuscripts or indicative of a scribe/collector's personal tastes. Furthermore, many of the major troubadours are either absent (Peire d'Alvernha, Peire Rogier, Bernart de Ventadorn) or displaced from their customary position at the head of the collection.

Equally distinctive is the large number of songs by *trobairitz* and the singular fact that these *trobairitz* are the only poets to have miniature portraits. Many of their songs, too, are *unica* and in several cases the only evidence of the existence of the poet. Unlike *D*, *H* includes *vidas* and *razos*, though the distinction between the genres is particularly cloudy here. Written in red ink to distinguish them from the songs that follow, most of the texts are either *unica* or linked to other versions found in the *EPR* manuscript family. One indication, however, that *H* belongs to an earlier tradition is that unlike *EPR*, it presents the *vidas* as introductions to a poet's song(s) (as do *ABIK*) rather than grouped together in a special section. The *razos* found in *H* generally concern parodic or satirical songs unique to this manuscript. In the case of Uc de Saint Circ, for example, ten of the twelve of his songs included in *H* are unica.

There is one final and peculiar feature that marks some of the *razos* in manuscript *H*. In one section (fols. 47*v*–49*v*), there are twenty-six generic *razos*, written in red ink, which serve to introduce not any one song or poet but rather a whole group of songs that treat the theme announced in the rubric; for example:

Aquestas doas coblas son qel fis amics repren la follas dompnas qe cre qeill don prez so qeil tol e qe si cre enriquir qant ue ni aug qe sei faiz menut entron en rumor (47v)

(These two *coblas* are about true lovers who criticise foolish ladies who think that what diminishes their reputation enhances it and who think that they gain something when they see or hear that their every move is being talked about).[25]

In all, there are thirty-seven *coblas* in this section, twenty-six of which were composed by well-known troubadours (including Peire Vidal, Raimon de Miraval, Folquet de Marselha, Uc de Saint Circ). This series, essentially another type of *florilegium*, is also an extended commentary on recriminations against treacherous women. A similar collection in *J* suggests that both *florilegia* might be indebted to an earlier collection which was similar to that of the *Liber Alberici*, but which specialised in songs that presented a satirical view of love.

As in *D*, the scribes of *H* knew their troubadours and showed great respect for the texts. The treatment of Arnaut Daniel is instructive. In what amounts to an embedded anthology of his works, the single most important collection of his songs, the scribe/editors included marginal glosses and references to extra-textual material not found in this manuscript. In one example, the *senhal* or code-name (*Dezirat*) used by Arnaut in 'Lo ferm voler' is identified in the margin as referring to Bertran de Born, though nothing in the texts themselves would provide such information (Meneghetti, *Il pubblico*). In three other glosses to Arnaut's works there are references to *cansos* by Bertran de Born and even to a *sirventes*, none of which are found in *H*. Throughout the manuscript marginal glosses identify which original songs are being parodied or rewritten by the *sirventes* anthologised in *H*. Arnaut's works are annotated to show variants; word choice is highlighted. The care with which this section is edited is a clear sign that Dante was not alone in valuing Arnaut's work.

The power of *H* to evoke the complex processes of textual trans-mission, generic development, patronage and linguistic pride that led to the literary canonisation of troubadour song in Italy is unrivalled. In no other manuscript does one sense the incredible

richness of the tradition – the heteroglossia, gender politics, interplay of verse and prose, oral and written variants, that secured for
troubadour song both its spot in the Western canon and its resistance to any one canonical interpretation.

Some *chansonniers* also include non-lyric texts in Occitan. The
Italian manuscript *P*, for example, a portion of which is dated
1310, includes two manuals on Occitan usage and a collection of
longer and more elaborate *razos*. The first of these is the *Razos de
trobar* (fols. 79–83), composed by the Catalan Raimon Vidal de
Besalù in the early thirteenth century. It is the oldest known
grammatical treatise on a Romance language (Marshall, *Razos*;
Poe, 'Problem') and also includes a discussion of Limousin morphology. The second, dated to 1240, is the *Donatz Proensals* (67–
78). Signed by Uc Faidit, it is another treatise on grammar and
poetry, peppered with Uc's own original texts as examples. It
includes also a brief glossary of Occitan terms and their Italian
equivalents as well as a dictionary of rhymes.[26] MS *O* also closes
with a glossary of Occitan vocabulary and Italian equivalents. *N*
and *L* contain sections that include non-lyric texts in Occitan:
largely narrative and didactic poetry such as excerpts from *Jaufre*
and Raimon Vidal's *So fo el tems* (Fleischman, 'Non-Lyric'; Lavaud
and Nelli, *Les Troubadours*, vol. I; Huchet, *Nouvelles*).

Zufferey's linguistic studies (*Recherches*) of Italian and Southern
French manuscripts only confirmed what others had intuited: that
both traditions are intimately bound in a complex network of borrowing made possible by itinerant scribes and transplanted source
books. Philologists have shown, for example, that the Langtiedo-
cian manuscripts *R*, *E* and *J* all show some common reliance on
the Italian manuscript *P*. Manuscript *V* appears to have been composed in part in Catalonia, then transported to Italy, where it
was completed by Italian scribes (Zufferey, *Recherches*, p. 231). The
scribe of the *florilegium* excerpt from the Veneto (*C^m*) mentioned
earlier relied upon a source also used by the Languedocian Matfre
Ermengaud in composing the *Breviari d'Amor* (Allegri, 'Frammento', p. 343). All of the *razo* texts are found in the collected MSS
EHPR except for the separate Bertran de Born collection, but
there is no clue as to how that grouping occurred: *H* and *P* are
Italian; *E* is Languedocian but includes *vidas* and *razos* marked by
Italianisms (Boutière and Schutz, *Biographies*, p. XL); *R* is Langue-

docian but incorporates a massive amount of material gathered from Italian collections as well as local sources.

We will close by returning to the first two sections of MS *R*. The first is a meticulous index in four columns over three pages that organises the material by *incipit* under authors' names. Immediately following that we find a special section dedicated to *vidas* and *razos*. The last *razo* in this section glosses a song by Savaric de Maulleon in which Uc de Saint Circ acknowledges his own participation in the action being chronicled: 'E sapias per ver que ieu . . . que ay escrichas estas razos, fuy lo mesatje que lay aniey e·l portey tots los mans e·ls escriz' (Boutière and Schutz, p. 224: And let it be known that I . . . who have written these *razos*, was the courier who went there and delivered those messages to him). This simple statement is dazzling in its implications. It suggests that Uc wrote all of the *razos* in this section, perhaps even all of the *razos* in an original collection that served as the basis for the prose introductions found throughout the manuscripts. His self-consciousness as author and director emerges behind the biographical edifice that supports, perhaps even created, the notion of a collective, if widely dispersed, poetic sensibility and cultural practice.

The troubadour manuscripts tell us that from the inception of what we know about the written vernacular literary tradition there existed already an idea of what a lyric collection should represent. An artistic plan involving rubrication, illumination, and indexes offered one means of presenting the texts as signs of a larger cultural practice, incorporation of the *vidas* and *razos* was another. In the best-known manuscripts, the two are combined to brilliant effect. As Uc implies, and Bernart Amoros and Raimon Vidal state explicitly, scribes and compilers are conscious witnesses to the process by which troubadour poetry became cultural capital. Bernart Amoros vaunts his dual role as clerk and 'scriptors d'aqest libre' (copyist of this book). Raimon Vidal, in the prologue to the *Razos de Trobar*, is clear on his motives: 'Vull heu far aquest libre per dar a conexeres a ssaber qual trobar han meyls trobat . . . ' (I want to put together this book to make it known which troubadours composed the best . . .). Never simple random collections of transcribed oral texts, these manuscripts reflect their compilers' interest in shaping their material. Our knowledge of the poets, even our own critical judgements on their talents and art, is formed within the ingenious presentation of what these scribes and authors were already calling, as early as the thirteenth century, books.

1 Gröber ('Die Liedersammlungen') hypothesised early collections by individual poets (*Liederblätter*) and larger collections containing several poets (*Liederbücher*) that have since disappeared but which formed the basis of the extant thirteenth-century manuscripts. See also Chapter 14.

2 Were certain manuscripts produced in the Auvergne region or in Venice or the Veneto using Occitan scribes? According to Zufferey, MS *B* was probably composed in the Auvergne by a scribe who worked from the same source that underlies MS *A*. Others postulate that *B* was also a Venetian production, like *AIK*, that only later made its way to France (Folena, 'Tradizione', p. 460). The Bernart Amoros MS, probably late thirteenth-century, is now known only through the 1589 copy on paper (Zufferey, *Recherches*, pp. 33–101). See Appendix 4 for the *sigla* that are used to designate the MSS.

3 Several *florilegia*, collections of citations from a variety of songs organised by poet or theme, exist from the late thirteenth and early fourteenth centuries (D^cFC^m), e.g. Matfre Ermengaud's didactic *Breviari d'Amor* from Languedoc (Béziers).

4 Zufferey has refined Brunel's count of ninety-five by eliminating exact copies and French and Catalan manuscripts which only incidentally include lyric texts in Occitan. Of the forty, thirty-four are on vellum (and ten of these are only fragments), two are on paper, and four are copies on paper of now lost manuscripts (*Recherches*, p. 316).

5 MS *V* was produced in Catalonia but carried to Italy where it was added to by Italian scribes (Zufferey, *Recherches*, pp. 228–33). The traditional dating of *T* to the fifteenth century has been challenged by Brunetti ('Sul canzoniere', p. 68), who considers it a late thirteenth-century Italian production.

6 The ten from the thirteenth century to which I refer are *ABDHIKSTV* and the lost original of *a*.

7 See Chapter 6.

8 Bourdieu, *La Distinction*.

9 The court of Dalfi d'Alvernhe may have served as one such centre, Montpellier another.

10 Occasionally the attributions in the index are contradicted by the attributions in the body of the manuscript (Riquer, *Los trovadores*, I, p. 14) but there seems in general to have been a serious attempt at accuracy.

11 Zufferey (*Recherches*, pp. 33–4) speculates that one of the differences

between MSS copied by Occitan scribes and those copied by Italians is whether their organisational structure is *cansos/sirventes/tensos* (Italian) or *cansos/tensos/sirventes* (Auvergnat). Another is the presence of Peire d'Alvernha or Giraut de Bornelh at the head of the collection.

12 MS *B*'s scribes left spaces for an illumination project that was never begun. Other less expensively produced Italian manuscripts (*DFP*) forgo portraits altogether.

13 This does not necessarily mean that all the manuscripts were produced for noble court patrons. *H* and *T* were both made for private collectors (Careri, *Il canzoniere H*; Brunetti, 'Sul canzoniere').

14 See notes 2 and 5 above.

15 *E*, though generally considered to be of Southern French origin (Zufferey, *Recherches*, p. 168), has also sometimes been assigned to Northern Italy (Bertoni, *Trovatori*, p. 191; Folena, 'Tradizione', p. 460).

16 The largest of the Italian MSS (*A*) has 626, by comparison.

17 The others are the Italian MS *G* and two French manuscripts, *W* and *X* (van der Werf, 'Music').

18 Zufferey changed the siglum of the Catalan manuscript traditionally known as *Sg* (indicating Saragossa) to *Z*. I therefore refer to it as *Sg/Z*.

19 There are c. 101 *vidas* and 81 *razos*. Manuscripts *IK* each have eighty-seven *vidas* but the *razos* to only one poet, Bertran de Born (nineteen in all). The other *razos* all appear somewhere in the *EHPR* grouping.

20 The Clemencic Consort has recorded a song by Peire Vidal in which they interweave the song with the spoken *razo* that explains it (*Troubadours*). English translations of all the *razos*, followed by the songs they cite, are collected in Burgwinkle, *Razos*.

21 Several MSS also dedicate a section to anonymous texts or to a pot-pourri of texts from a variety of genres (*GHLNQSg/ZT*). Vernacular French manuscripts of the same period also show signs of authorial and scribal agency and may have served as models for the Venetan and Auvergnat scribes (Huot, *From Song to Book*).

22 'Hec sunt inceptiones cantionum de libro qui fuit domini Alberici et nomina repertorum eorundem cantionum' (Here are the beginnings of the songs from Lord Alberico's book and the names of the authors of these songs).

23 In the Veneto, personal tensions between the da Romano brothers, Alberico and Ezzelino, were aggravated by political alliances. Ezzelino (Verona) became Frederick II's ally, while Alberico (Treviso) was a supporter of the Guelph cause.

24 *G* and *Q* (both from Lombardy) contain a similarly idiosyncratic selection of texts that favours *tensos*, *partimens* and other genres (*G* contains thirty anonymous *coblas*) over *cansos*.

25 The language of this generic *razo* echoes that used by Uc de Saint
Circ in song X.

26 Many critics identify this Uc 'Faidit' ('in exile/banished') with Uc de
Saint Circ, who in 1240 was in the middle of his forty-year career in
the Marca Trevigiana (*'Donatz Proensals'*, ed. Marshall [Appendix 3,
p. 298], p. 62; Burgwinkle, *Love*, p. 136).

CHAPTER 16

Troubadour lyric and Old French narrative

Sylvia Huot

This chapter will examine the absorption of lyric motifs into Old French narrative poetry. Northern French and Anglo-Norman poets could certainly have encountered troubadour lyric at the courts where vernacular literature flourished, such as the Plantagenet court in England or that of Marie, Countess of Champagne.[1] Two thirteenth-century manuscripts of Northern French lyric contain substantial groupings of troubadour verse, and two of the earliest French romances with lyric insertions, Jean Renart's *Roman de la rose (Guillaume de Dole)* and Gerbert de Montreuil's *Roman de la violette*, include citations of troubadour songs.[2] But while some narrative poets would have had direct knowledge of troubadour verse, others would have known only its reception and recasting by Northern French lyric poets, or *trouvères*. The corpus of *trouvère* lyric, heavily influenced by that of the troubadours, established a first-person discourse of desire in the Northern French vernacular and articulated a courtly ideology of love.[3] The following discussion will examine the reception of the troubadour corpus as a genre, whether direct or mediated by the *trouvères*. Without attempting to identify specific sources and lines of dissemination, I will focus on ways in which constructions of courtliness, subjectivity and affective experience explored by the troubadours are reworked by Northern French narrative poets.

The transposition of lyric into narrative requires certain changes: the advent of a narrator who speaks from a vantage point outside the fictional frame, the creation of a linear progression governed at least minimally by a logic of space, time and causality. A narrative text cannot simply present images in the manner of a strophically constructed lyric, but must account for its movement from one stage to the next. Narrative raises expectations that the poetic image will be contextualised – a character will not exist in isolation but as part of a social network, with which he or she will engage in at least some fashion. Narrative exposition allows the meaning of lyric images to be questioned and their implications examined. As such it may result in comedy, as lyric motifs are subjected to narrative scrutiny and exposed as fundamentally irrational; or it may result in tragedy, when the fragile lyric construct is overcome and undone by the encroachments of the surrounding narrative world.[4]

The movement from lyric to narrative can be effected either by taking the songs and setting them in a narrative context that explains their composition or performance, or by projecting standard lyric motifs into a narrative format. The passage from lyric to narrative might be accomplished through recourse to allegory, generated through the personification of attributes associated with the lover, the lady and their respective allies or enemies, or through the elaboration and concretisation of imagery drawn from the lyric repertoire. Narrative action might also be generated by exploring the relationship between the lyric self or couple and the world at large. In the latter case, lyric conventions are generally associated with a private experience of desire, joy or pain, contrasting or conflicting with the public domain in which the narrative is set. The following examples – far from exhaustive – will illustrate a range of possible approaches to this interaction of genres.

My analysis will focus in particular on certain motifs that function to express the fantasy of contact with the beloved. One is the nightingale, a pervasive image in medieval love poetry.[5] Often the nightingale figures as an emblem of erotic desire endlessly voicing itself, and thus as inspiration for the lyric persona, as in this song by Jaufré Rudel:

> Quan lo rius de la fontana
> s'esclarzis, si cum far sol,
> e par la flors aiglentina
> e·l rossinholetz el ram
> volf e refranh ez aplana
> son dous chantar e afina,
> dreitz es qu'ieu lo mieu refranha. (III, 1–7)

(When the streamlet of the fountain runs clear, as it is wont to do, and the flower appears on the eglantine, and the little nightingale on the branch warbles and modulates and smooths out its sweet song and refines it, it is fitting that I modulate mine.)[6]

The nightingale can act as a messenger between the lyric persona and his lady, as in this song by Peire d'Alvernha:

> Rossinhol, el seu repaire
> m'iras ma dona vezer,
> e diguas li·l mieu afaire
> e ill digua·t del sieu ver,
>   e man sai
>   com l'estai. . . (I, 1–6)

(Nightingale, go see my lady at her home, tell her how it is with me, and let her tell you the truth about herself, and send back word of how she is.)

The other motif on which I will concentrate is the heart, which similarly functions both as the seat of desire and affective experience, and as a figure for the lyric persona himself, which can be sent to the lady or captured and retained by her. As Bernart de Ventadorn states in 'Lancan vei la folha':

> Domna, mo caratge,
> ·l melhor amic qu'eu ai,
>   vos man en ostatge
> entro qu'eu torn de sai. (XXXVIII, 85–8)

(Lady, I send you as hostage my heart, the best friend I have, until I return here.)

Both the heart and the nightingale are key elements in the carefully orchestrated dynamics of presence and absence, desire and resistance, possession and loss, that are fundamental both to the lyric tradition and to its narrative reworking.

THE HEART AND THE NIGHTINGALE: CONSTRUCTING NARRATIVITY

I begin with the mid-thirteenth-century poem *Le Roman de la Poire*, which is less a romance than an early version of what would later be known as the *dit amoureux*.[7] Though less well known than some of my other examples, the *Poire* is a good starting point because it illustrates the technique of producing narrative scenarios from a series of standard lyric images. In this poem, the first-person narrator's lyrical evocations of love are subjected to repeated questioning by an unidentified interlocutor, whose questions and frequent objections to the logical impossibility of the lover's claims generate narrative efforts to explain the motifs. Unlike many *tensos*, in which points of love casuistry are explored from within a shared framework of courtly ideology, the *Poire* introduces an external perspective that challenges the narrator's use of conventional rhetorical tropes and poetic motifs.

The narrator's account of his love affair begins with a description of a pear given him by the lady, from which he derived much joy and much sorrow. The oxymoronic qualities of the love experience are a standard feature of courtly lyric; as Bernart de Ventadorn says in 'Non es meravelha s'eu chan',

> cen vetz mor lo jorn de dolor
> e reviu de joi autras cen.
> Ben es mos mals de bel semblan,
> que mais val mos mals qu'autre bes. (I, 27–30)

(A hundred times a day I die of grief and I revive from joy another hundred times. My pain is so fair that it is worth more than another's pleasure.)

The interlocutor of the *Poire*, however, challenges this account, complaining 'Max et biens, ce sunt .II. contraire, / et vos lé metez en commun' (Ill and good, those are two opposites, and you place them together (*Poire*, ed. Marchello-Nizia, 507–8)). Under pressure, the narrator reverts to allegory, first describing an internal battle between Love and Hope and then announcing hyperbolically that Love assailed him with 'hundreds and thousands of knights and sergeants' (778–89). This claim is met with fresh objections from the interlocutor, who dismisses it as delusion brought on by excessive drink. The narrator's response recounts his interactions with a series of allegorical personifications singing refrains – Beauty, Courtesy, Nobility, Frankness, Love and Sweet Glances – and culminates in the removal of his heart, which is sent to the lady. Subsequent episodes present further personifications, also singing, who bring the lady's heart to him. A final exchange of refrains beween lover and lady introduces references to a nightingale to which both address their declarations of love, and which acts as a kind of go-between.

Personification allegory is thus fundamental to the generation of narrative action from lyric discourse in the *Poire*. The technique is already present in embryonic form in the works of some troubadours, as in Arnaut Daniel's evocation of a castle of Love in 'Lanquan vei fueill' e flor e frug':[8]

Ar sai ieu c'Amors m'a condug
el sieu plus seguran castel,
[...]
non ai poder ni cor que·m vir' aillors
qu'Ensenhamens e Fizeutatz plevida
jai per estar. . . (V, 8–9, 12–14)

(Now I know that Love has brought me to her most secure castle. . . I have neither the power nor the wish to turn elsewhere, since Upbringing and sworn Fidelity remain there permanently.)

As in Guillaume de Lorris's *Roman de la Rose*, an obvious influence on the *Poire*, narrative is produced when the lyric construction of courtly subjectivity is fragmented into a series of attributes, each of which takes on the status of an independent character. The lyric associations are clearly indicated both by the amorous framework in which the personifications act, and by their performance of song and dance. In the *Rose* the allegorical participants in the carol stand at the threshold of lyric and narrative. Initially they seem eternally suspended in the repetitive, circular motions of the carol. Yet their timely interventions are crucial to the advancement of the narrative, since it is they who encourage the dreamer to join the dance and penetrate the Garden, and they who mediate between him and the guardians of the Rose.[9]

The singing personifications of the *Poire* similarly retain a lyrical aura while serving as a vehicle for the projection of amorous sentiment and courtly ideology into narrative form. Their liminal status is particularly evident at certain key moments, as when Loyalty accuses Moderation of singing an immodest refrain, exclaiming 'E encor est la foleur pire / por ce que tu as non Mesure' (And the folly is even worse because you are named Moderation (*Poire*, 2513–14)). Loyalty's criticisms and Moderation's self-justifications test the boundary between true narrative and lyrical personification allegory: are these actual characters, capable of transgression and susceptible to psychological analysis? Or are they simply the representation of a single attribute which exclusively determines their identity? Again, one is reminded of the *Rose*, where in a similar moment of slippage between strict allegory and narrative psychology, Resistance (*Danger*) is accused of showing more courtesy than befits the role defined by his name: 'Il n'afiert pas a vostre non / que vos faciez se anui non' (It is unfitting to your name for you to be anything other than annoying (*Rose*, ed. Lecoy, 3677–78)).

The central event of the allegorical narrative in the *Poire* is the exchange of hearts. This, too, is subjected to narrative scrutiny, as the lover and his interlocutor discuss the relationship between heart and body and debate the logic of their separation. Again, a conventional lyric trope is reified into a narrative construct, with the heart now functioning as an independent character that speaks and moves about on its own. The humour is reminiscent of Chrétien's use of this *topos* in *Le Chevalier au lion*, where the narrator marvels at the separation of heart and body when Yvain departs from Laudine:

> Des que li cors est sans le cuer,
> Comment puet il vivre a nul fuer?
> Et se li cors sans le cuer vit,
> Tel merveille nus hom ne vit. (ed. Hult, 2647–50)

(Once the body is without a heart, how can it go on living? And if the body lives without a heart, no man ever saw such a wonder.)

The discussion in the *Poire* similarly generates humour by questioning the narrative logic of the motif and, more generally, by examining the interactions of the lover, the lady and their respective hearts. The narrative becomes more intricate as the text goes along: his heart was an inanimate object, but the lady's heart is personified and indeed quite talkative. Though clearly intimate with the lady and able to report on her innermost feelings, the heart nonetheless cannot be completely identified with her: it is masculine, in keeping with the grammatical gender of the word *cuer*, and it always refers to her in the third person. Thus the *Poire*, like the *Rose* before it, remains true to the conventional lyric model of the distant lady who is less a real female subject than a sort of reference point around which the male subject articulates his desire, and with regard to whom he interacts with various male allies, rivals and interlocutors.[10]

Through the constant mediation of songs, allegorical personifications, disembodied hearts, and finally the nightingale, the lovers, though physically separated, achieve a kind of mutual presence. As in the lyric, there is no final resolution: desire remains suspended and the lovers do not interact directly with one another. Although lyric discourse is constantly challenged and forced to transmute into narrative, it is not defeated; it creates its own space for the elaboration of desire. But the dangers of narrative are clearly present in the *Poire*. The exemplary figures cited in the opening passages – Tristan, Cligès, Pyramus, Paris – herald the constant threat of misunderstanding, persecution, warfare, death. It is difficult for lovers to maintain their private world, and implication in a larger world spells trouble. It is to these dangers that I now turn.

THE BIRD ENSNARED

One image that evokes the entanglement of the lyric subject in a narrative world is that of the songbird trapped in snares. A relatively straightforward treatment of this motif appears in the anonymous thirteenth-century *Lai de l'Oiselet*. The poem describes a lovely garden animated by the song of a bird, where knights and ladies gather to talk of love. But the garden is sold to a *vilain* (a peasant or other person of low birth) who captures the bird in his snares. The bird escapes by promising to impart useful knowledge to the *vilain* but, after reciting a series of platitudes, flies away; once it is gone the fountain dries up and the garden withers.

The bird, in effect, is the very embodiment of courtly lyricism, singing 'lais et noveaus sons/Et rotrüenges et chançons' (lais and new tunes and rotruenges and songs (*Oiselet*, ed. Wolfgang, 89–90)). Any man who hears it is not only granted joy, but also made to feel young, handsome and worthy of love. It is this eternal song that feeds the fountain and keeps the garden verdant: 'Car du chant issoit li humors/Qui en vertu tenoit les flors' (for from the song issued the humours that kept the flowers growing (117–18)). And it is the intervention of the *vilain*, a character more appropriate to the *fabliaux* than to the courtly lyric tradition, that shatters the lyric idyll. Unable to appreciate the refinements of courtliness, the *vilain* perceives the bird as property, subject to commercial exchange and private ownership. He first hopes to sell it; then plans to cage it and make it sing exclusively for him; and finally threatens to eat it. His behaviour transforms a magical and potent image into an ordinary object of narrative manipulation. Where courtly lyric celebrates the prolongation of desire, the contemplation of beauty and the exquisite pain of absence from the beloved, the *vilain* prefers immediate sensory gratification, financial gain and absolute ownership.

The disruption of the lyric idyll, effected through its entanglement in the world of the *fabliaux*, is here treated humorously and
used as a vehicle for social commentary: the *vilain*'s misapprehen-
sion of the bird figuratively represents his overall inability to grasp
the subtleties of courtliness. His encounter with pure lyricism generates narrative action, but of a type that destroys the lyric construct by objectifying it out of existence, thereby arriving at a
dead end. An even more complex treatment of the bird ensnared
appears in Marie de France's *Laüstic*, which dates from the mid to
late twelfth century. Though nothing is known of the poet now
called Marie de France, it is assumed that the *lais* were composed
at the court of Henry II and Eleanor of Aquitaine, and were thus
produced by a poet, and for an audience, familiar with troubadour
lyric.

Laüstic is constructed around the figure of the nightingale,
which becomes a magnet for linguistic and literary associations.
The story is simple: a knight falls in love with his neighbour's wife,
who returns his affections. Unable to consummate their passion,
the lovers converse at night from their respective windows. When
her husband asks about these nightly vigils, the lady claims that
she is listening to the song of the nightingale. Undeceived, he
responds by snaring the nightingale. Announcing that she will now
sleep undisturbed, he hurls the bird at her, staining her dress with
its blood. The heartbroken wife embroiders a cloth to tell her lover
what happened and sends it to him along with the bird's body,
which he enshrines in a casket of gold and jewels.

Most explicitly, this short tale is announced as an explanation
of events giving rise to a Breton *lai*:

> Une aventure vus dirai
> Dunt li Bretun firent un lai.
> *Laüstic* ad nun, ceo m'est vis,
> Si l'apelent en lur païs;
> Ceo est 'russignol' en franceis
> E 'nihtegale' en dreit engleis. (*Laüstic*, ed. Rychner, 1–6)

(I will tell you a story from which the Bretons made a *lai*. I think it is
called *Laüstic*, thus they call it in their land; that means 'russignol' in
French and 'nihtegale' in proper English.)

Since the nightingale is always referred to as 'le laüstic', it can be
seen as an emblem of the Breton world; and by additionally

naming the bird in both French and English, Marie alerts us that this figure is a focal point for different cultural contexts.

For one, the nightingale carries associations with the Ovidian tale of Philomela (*Metamorphoses* 6: 424–674). Raped by her sister Procne's husband and silenced by the loss of her tongue, Philomela tells her story by weaving a tapestry; Procne takes revenge by killing (and cooking) her own son. The tale reaches a climax of mounting frenzy – Philomela bursts in and flings the child's severed head at her attacker – and as the participants endeavour to kill one another, they are changed into birds. Philomela becomes a nightingale, bird of passion. Though quite differently constructed, *Laüstic* too is a tale of violence and erotic passion in which the nightingale plays a central role as the victim of male aggression, silenced forever, whose story can be told only through the medium of a tapestry. Other Ovidian tales have also left their traces. Like Pyramus and Thisbe (*Metamorphoses* 4: 55–166), the couple in *Laüstic* fall in love because of the proximity of their dwellings; they find a way of communicating across barriers; and their story ends tragically, with bloodshed, death and a funereal monument. There is also an echo of the tale that follows that of Pyramus and Thisbe: the adultery of Mars and Venus, caught in a snare set by an angry husband (*Metamorphoses* 4: 169–89). Marie adapts her Ovidian sources, however, in such a way that the action is consistently diverted onto the nightingale. It is the bird, not the lovers, that dies, sheds its blood and is entombed. It is the bird, not the lovers, that is snared by a jealous husband. It is even the bird, and not a child, whose dead body is flung about. Thus the nightingale, in addition to being an emblem of the Breton tradition, also becomes a repository for Latin mythological associations, which adhere to it in a sort of layering process.

The nightingale, indeed, can be seen as the very emblem of love itself, and hence as the focus for the elaboration of poetry. The lady creates it as a symbol of erotic passion in response to her husband's query: when she says that she is up nights listening to the nightingale, she means that she is listening to the desire that speaks in her own heart and absorbed in the pleasures and yearnings of illicit passion. The way the bird is introduced, moreover, serves to highlight its associations with vernacular lyric. The nightingale is announced as follows:

Les nuiz, quant la lune luseit
E ses sires cuchiez esteit,
De juste lui sovent levot
E de sun mantel s'afublot;
A la fenestre ester veneit
Pur sun ami qu'ele saveit
Qu'autreteu vie demenot
E le plus de la nuit veillot.
Delit aveient al veeir,
Quant plus ne poeient aveir.
Tant i estut, tant i leva,
Que ses sires s'en curuça
E meintefeiz li demanda
Pur quei levot e u ala.
'Sire, la dame li respunt,
Il nen ad joïë en cest mund
Ki n'ot le laüstic chanter.' (69–85)

(At night, when the moon shone and her husband had gone to bed, she often arose from his side and put on her cloak; she would go to the window for the sake of her beloved, who, she knew, led a similar life and stayed awake most of the night. They took pleasure in seeing each other, since they could have nothing more. So much did she stand there, so much did she get up, that her husband grew angry, and asked her many times why she got up and where she went. 'Sir', the lady replied, 'he has no joy in this world who does not hear the nightingale sing.')

The fourteen lines leading up to the lady's declaration – the first instance of direct discourse in the poem – present an interesting use of the couplet rhyme scheme. The repetition of rhymes, which does not occur elsewhere in this *lai* and is unusual in general, suggests the intricate rhymes of a lyric strophe. It is as though the stanzaic rhyme scheme *ababcdd* has been recreated in couplet form: *aabbaabbccdddd*.[11] In the opening couplets the stage is set: the lyric setting of moonlit nights and of lovers physically separated but united in desire. A single couplet intervenes with a different rhyme, stating both the pleasure and the frustration of the lovers, followed by four lines with the same rhyme. The repetition of rhymes, all verbs narrating events in the simple past, creates a sense of urgency, of precipitous events overwhelming the lovers. This evocation of lyric versification thus also encompasses a movement from lyric static description of an unchanging and ongoing situation, to a narrative description of events unfolding and changing uncontrollably. And significantly, it occupies the lines leading up to the precise midpoint of the poem (80).

At the moment that the nightingale enters the text, then, it is overdetermined with both narrative and lyric associations and participates in a complex set of transformations. One might say that the lady names it from within the lyric idyll that she inhabits, one in which jealous husbands, though troublesome obstacles, have little impact on the pleasurable prolongation of desire and the joys of listening to the nightingale. The husband, however, stalks the bird from the perspective of the narrative world in which he lives, one determined by Ovidian tales of violence and jealousy, vengeance and death. Caught in this web, the self-contained lyric world is shattered. The voice of the nightingale – the voice of love, of song – is silenced forever. The bird has ceased to sing and become instead the marker of absence and desire around which art is fashioned.

Marie thus suggests that Old French poetry might be, in part, a sort of tomb or reliquary for dying or linguistically incomprehensible oral traditions; that written narrative is an elaborate and ornate artifice constructed to preserve the memory of lyric voices now silent and irretrievable.[12] And if the lyric nightingale is silenced by writing, strangled by the web of narrative action, if the living tradition of Breton song is reified and displayed as an artefact in its new textual setting – nonetheless this silencing is not an end but a new beginning. A saint's body, placed in a reliquary, retains a potency that allows it to act as intermediary to the divine and to intervene directly in human affairs. Similarly, the relics of Breton or Occitan song enshrined in French texts exert a profound influence on their audience; they retain a very real power to entertain, admonish or inspire; they will give rise, in turn, to future artistic and literary enterprises.

In *Laüstic* Marie establishes associations linking the subjective experience of desire, the lyric tradition in which this desire finds expression, and the Breton *lai*, all of which are incorporated into narrative structures reminiscent of Ovidian motifs, through the medium of French narrative poetry. Lyric subjectivity, the voice of pure desire, is the centre around which narrative is elaborated. Marie's poem has a tragic dimension that distinguishes it from the *Oiselet* or the *Poire*, but it is also a much more profound meditation on literary creation. In *Laüstic* the core subjectivity so strongly associated with the lyric tradition is not merely a foil for humorous banter or for the generation of allegory, or a convenient trope for social commentary; rather, it is shown to be the very stuff of poetry. Transforming subjective experience into poetry entails a certain violence, a loss of immediacy and restriction of meaning; but it gives rise to an ever-changing process of literary creation.

THE EATEN HEART

The image of the lover's heart sent to the lady takes on a grisly literalism in the narrative motif of the 'eaten heart'.[13] This motif intersects with Occitan lyric in the *vida* of the troubadour Guillem de Cabestany. There we are told that Guillem was murdered by his lady's husband, who removed his heart, had it cooked and served to the lady, and then revealed to her what it was; at this shocking disclosure the lady committed suicide. Among the other texts in which the 'eaten heart' appears is another pseudo-biography of a lyric poet, this time a Northern French *trouvère*: the *Roman du Castelain de Couci*.[14] This late thirteenth-century romance, quite possibly influenced by the *vida*, incorporates six songs traditionally attributed to the Châtelain de Couci, along with a virelai and three rondeaux unattested outside the romance, and recounts the love affair with the Lady of Fayel that supposedly gave rise to their composition. When the Châtelain dies on crusade he has his heart sent to the lady; her husband intercepts the gift and serves it for dinner. The lady initially exclaims over the delicious meal, but when her husband reveals its identity, she dies of grief.

Although the technique of incorporating songs into a narrative text dates from the early years of the thirteenth century, the *Castelain de Couci* is innovative in focusing on a specific poet and purporting to explain the genesis of his oeuvre. The effect is somewhat reminiscent of troubadour manuscripts in which each corpus of songs is preceded by a *vida* and, in some cases, includes intercalated *razos* providing further narrative context.[15] The romance transposes the conventional lyric motifs, present in the songs, into narrative form. Unlike the *Rose* or the *Poire*, it does not resort to allegory, but rather grounds the lyric formulations in a concrete world of social interactions and bodily experience. The infamous spies and slanderers of lyric tradition, for example, are incarnated as the lady's husband and a woman spurned by the Châtelain, who conspire to thwart the love affair, while the conventional 'pains' and 'wounds' of love manifest themselves as actual bodily illness and injury.

The episode of the heart, then, is only the most striking example of a technique pervasive throughout the romance of literalising the conventional lyric expressions of affectivity. The motif of the disembodied heart is already present in the crusade song 'A vous, amant, ains qu'a nule autre gent', traditionally attributed to the Châtelain de Couci and incorporated into the romance (*Castelain*, ed. Matzke and Delbouille, 7347–98). Here the lyric persona, lamenting his forced departure from the lady, exclaims, 'Comment me poet li coers el corps durer / Qu'il ne me part? Ciertes trop est mauvais' (How can my heart remain in my body and not part from me? Certainly this is too dreadful (7367–68)). The Châtelain of the romance employs the same motif in his final meeting with the Lady of Fayel before his departure, telling her, 'Car jou yrai en corps sans coer' (for I will go away in body, without a heart (7249)). The physical removal of the heart from the body and its return to the lady can thus be seen as the logical narrative consequence of this lyric-based language of desire. Indeed in the letter dictated by the dying Châtelain, the literal heart can scarcely be distinguished from the figurative: 'Et pour cou que je sai et croi / Que vo coer emportai o moi / ... / Vous envoie jou mon coer ore' (and since I know and believe that I carried your heart away with me. . . I now send you my heart (7661–2, 7668)).

As in *Laüstic*, the actions of the husband in the *Castelain de Couci* represent the narrative appropriation of a lyric image. Like the nightingale in Marie de France's *lai*, the Châtelain's heart is the vehicle through which the various characters vie for narrative control: the Châtelain designates it as a memento of his love; his messenger uses it to barter for his life when confronted by the angry husband, who in turn makes the heart an instrument of vengeance; for the lady it is emblematic of the entire love experience, being a source first of pleasure, then of pain. The movement from lyric to narrative is effected by means of a movement from the realm of sentiment to that of the body. The figurative heart, metaphor for the Châtelain's love, is replaced by the fleshly heart which figures him by metonymy, and which becomes an object of exchange and manipulation within the larger narrative world.

The narrative ends with the Lady of Fayel's dying lament for her beloved. This closing scene, with its lyrical expression of impossible desire, presents a paradoxical fusion of presence and absence, fulfilment and despair. Having consumed her lover's heart, the lady is complicitous in his effacement from the narrative world; yet she has also achieved a perfect union, an absolute integration of his body into hers. Any further erotic coupling is impossible both because the two bodies can never come together, and because they have already been inextricably merged. The lady recognises that she possesses her lover's heart both literally and figuratively:

> Ha! com dolereus envoi a
> De son coer que il m'envoia!
> Bien me moustra qu'il estoit miens. (8143–5)

(Ha! what a grievous gift he made of his heart which he sent me! He showed clearly that he/it was mine.)

Her only possible action, however, is non-action, as narrative dissolves back into an expression of pure love: 'Car pour soie amour finnerai' (thus I will end my life for love of him (8148)).

As she lies dying, forever separated from the lover whose body she contains within her own, the lady is reminiscent of the dying Narcissus, a figure often associated with the expression of *fin'amor* in courtly lyric and romance. In contrast with modern interpretations, the medieval Narcissus was less a figure of self-absorption than one of frustrated desire: the crucial point was not that he fell in love with an image of himself, but that his desire was for something unattainable, indeed phantasmagorical. Thus he appears in the *Rose* as a figure for the Lover's unfulfillable desire for the ever-receding rosebud. Narcissus is also cited in one of the most famous of all troubadour songs, Bernart de Ventadorn's 'Can vei la lauzeta mover'. There the lyric persona, recalling the moment when he gazed into the mirror of his lady's eyes, exclaims: 'aissi·m perdei com perdet se / lo bels Narcisus en la fon' (thus I lost myself as the fair Narcissus lost himself in the fountain (XXXI, 23–4)). Still, if the love object desired by Narcissus is unattainable, this is due not to its absence but to its all too immediate presence. The Ovidian Narcissus recognises this keenly:

quod cupio mecum est: inopem me copia fecit.
o utinam a nostro secedere corpore possem!
votum in amante novum, vellem, quod amamus, abesset.
(ed. and transl. Miller, *Met.* 3:466–8)

(What I desire, I have; the very abundance of my riches beggars me. Oh, that I might be parted from my own body! and, strange prayer for a lover, I would that what I love were absent from me!)

The Lady of Fayel thus resembles Narcissus in her realisation that the love object is both forever unattainable and yet fully possessed. Her death, which brings the love story to an end, represents a return to lyric stasis, in which the tension of absence and presence, desire and despair, is forever held in balance. The dying Châtelain, composing one final song with his last breath, abandons all hope of a narrative 'happy ending' and attempts to turn his very body into a lyric metaphor. Withdrawing into herself, in turn, the lady likewise recognises the impossibility of narrative resolution, and rejects any further involvement with the social world within which the love story had unfolded.

Though each of the above examples treats the interaction of lyric and narrative somewhat differently, one can draw certain general conclusions from this brief survey. Narrative texts generate action by turning lyric images and aspects of the lyric subject and his field of desire into material objects and characters in the narrative world. This may be accomplished through allegorical personification, through the literalisation of poetic figures, through a passage from metaphor to metonymy or from abstract sentiment to corporeal reality.[16] As it is cast in narrative texts, the lyric tends to be identified with a private, indeed often secret or forbidden realm of affective experience. The relationship of this private lyric world to its narrative context is always in some sense problematical, and it is from the ensuing interaction and juxtaposition of conflicting perspectives that narrative is produced. This dialogue, this tension, this constant interplay of frustration, resolution and renewal, is an endless source of literary experimentation.

NOTES

1 For example, on possible ties between Chrétien de Troyes and the troubadours, see Meneghetti, *Pubblico*, pp. 138–44.

2 See Paden, 'Old Occitan'. The manuscripts in question are Paris, Bibl. Nat. fr. 844 and fr. 20050.

3 See Meneghetti, *Pubblico*, pp. 196–211.

4 On the treatment of the lyric in narrative texts, see Kay, *Subjectivity*, pp. 171–211; Stone, *Death*; Boulton, *Song*; Huot, *From Song to Book*.

5 See Pfeffer, *Change of Philomel*.

6 Unless indicated otherwise, this and all other translations are mine.

7 See Cerquiglini, 'Clerc'.

8 On allegory in this poem and in the troubadours generally, see Kay, *Subjectivity*, pp. 50–80.

9 On the interplay of lyric and narrative in the *Rose*, see Hult, *Self-fulfilling Prophecies*, pp. 186–262; Baumgartner, 'Play'.

10 See Gaunt, *Gender*, pp. 122–79.

11 István Frank lists two songs, by Giraut Riquier and Guillem de Cabestany respectively, that use seven-line stanzas with the rhyme scheme *ababcdd*, as well as numerous other songs with longer stanzas using that same rhyme scheme for the first seven lines; see his *Répertoire*, I, pp. 82–6.

12 See Bloch, 'Voice'.

13 For an overview of the 'eaten heart' in literary history, see Matzke, 'Legend'.

14 The historical Châtelain responsible for the lyric corpus transmitted under that name is presumed to have been Gui de Thourotte, Châtelain of Couci from 1186 to 1203. On the 'eaten heart' and other bodily imagery in the *Castelain*, see Solterer, 'Dismembering'.

15 See Chapter 15.

16 For an examination of manuscript illumination as an analogous response to lyric texts, comparable to the production of sentimental or allegorical narratives, see Huot, 'Visualization'.

Major troubadours

Simon Gaunt and Sarah Kay

1. Aimeric de Belenoi (... 1216–43 ...) PC 9: *Poésies du troubadour Aimeric de Belenoi*, ed. Maria Dumitrescu, SATF (Paris, 1935). A native of the Bordelais, he was a cleric turned *joglar*, and composed some fifteen (perhaps as many as twenty-two) surviving songs (one with music) dismissed by Dumitrescu as 'banal' but well received by medieval audiences, especially in Italy, and offering interesting combinations of religious, moral and amorous themes.

2. Aimeric de Peguilhan (... 1190–1221 ...) PC 10: William P. Shepard and Frank M. Chambers, *The Poems of Aimeric de Peguilhan* (Evanston, IL, 1950). Born in Toulouse of bourgeois family, but made most of his career in the Iberian peninsula and then Italy, and author of c. fifty poems (five with surviving music), mainly limpid *cansos*, plus a number of occasional pieces and exchanges with other troubadours (including Albertet and Sordello).

3. Albertet (... 1194–1221 ...) PC 16: Jean Boutière, 'Les Poésies du troubadour Albertet', *Studi Medievali* N.S., 10 (1937), 1–129. Troubadour from Gap (Hautes-Alpes) who began his career as a *joglar*, with twenty-one (perhaps twenty-five) surviving poems (three with music), mostly conventional love songs, one *descort*, and a number of debates, including one with Aimeric de Peguilhan.

4. Alegret (... 1145 ...) PC 17: Alfred Jeanroy, *Jongleurs et troubadours gascons des XIIᵉ et XIIIᵉ siècles*, CFMA (Paris, 1923), pp. 4–11. Referred to by Marcabru, Raimbaut d'Aurenga, and possibly Bernart de Ventadorn, but has only two songs surviving.

5. Arnaut Daniel (... 1180–95 ...) PC 29: Gianluigi Toja,

Arnaut Daniel: Canzoni. Edizione critica, studio introduttivo, commento e traduzione (Florence, 1960). Originally a cleric from the Perigord, he composed eighteen (possibly twenty) songs (with two surviving melodies) characterised by intricate rhyming and unusual vocabulary. One is an obscene *sirventes*, others draw on so many discourses (including the religious) that their meaning is ambiguous. Arnaut was influenced by Marcabru and Raimbaut d'Aurenga, and in turn influenced Dante and Petrarch – also Ezra Pound.

6.   Arnaut de Maruelh (. . . 1195 . . .) PC 30: R. C. Johnston, *Les Poésies lyriques du troubadour Arnaut de Mareuil* (Paris, 1935; repr. Geneva, 1973). Like his contemporary Arnaut Daniel a Perigordian cleric turned *joglar*. Twenty-five (twenty-nine?) songs survive (six with music) which, on Johnston's account, form a single cycle recording the poet's love for Adelaide of Béziers.

7.   Azalais de Porgairagues (. . . 1173 . . .) PC 43: Angelica Rieger, *Trobairitz. Der Beitrag der Frau in der altokzitanischen höfischen Lyrik. Edition des Gesamtkorpus* (Tübingen, 1991), pp. 480–504. One of the earliest *trobairitz*; her only surviving song refers to the death of Raimbaut d'Aurenga.

8.   Bernart Marti (mid twelfth century) PC 63: Fabrizio Beggiato, *Il Trovatore Bernart Marti* (Modena, 1984). Rather marginal in the manuscripts, with only nine surviving songs, which are by turns enigmatic, ironic and satiric. Bernart, who may have been a painter, addresses himself to his contemporaries Peire d'Alvernha and Marcabru but has no known following among later troubadours.

9.   Bernart de Ventadorn (. . . 1147–70 . . .) PC 70: Moshé Lazar, *Bernard de Ventadour, Chansons d'amour* (Paris, 1966). The most glitteringly successful of the troubadours in staging the intensity, refinement and controlled sincerity of *fin'amor* in a style that influenced not only the subsequent Occitan tradition but also French and German courtly love poetry. Despite the 'rags to riches' account of his Occitan biographer, Bernart was probably of noble birth, from the vice-comital family of Ventadorn in Limousin. He enjoyed patronage from the Plantagenets as well as the court of Toulouse. Some forty-five songs survive, including a debate song with Peire (d'Alvernha?), all on the subject of love. Nineteen melodies of his songs have been preserved.

10.   Bernart de Venzac (... 1195 ...) PC 71: Maria Picchio Simonelli, *Lirica Moralistica nell'Occitania del XII secolo: Bernart de Venzac* (Modena, 1974). A shadowy figure even by troubadour standards, his slim *œuvre* comprises five moralising lyrics in the manner of Marcabru (with whose corpus they are sometimes confused in MSS), and a religious *alba*.

11.   Bertran de Born (... 1159–95, d. 1215) PC 80: Gérard Gouiran, *L'Amour et la guerre. L'œuvre de Bertran de Born* (Aix–Marseille, 1985). A Perigordian nobleman, Bertran comments rumbustiously in his forty-seven or so surviving songs (only one of which has the melody preserved) on the political misadventures of his Plantagenet overlords and on the social and amorous interests of a self-styled warrior-poet. In contact with numerous other troubadours and Northern French *trouvères*, Bertran is also – with Arnaut Daniel – one of the troubadours most influential on subsequent poetry, his readers including Dante, Eliot and Pound.

12.   Bertran Carbonel (... 1252–65 ...) PC 82: ed. Michael J. Routledge, *Bertran Carbonel: Cansos e Coblas* (London, 1998). Wrote eighteen lyrics, but best known for his seventy-two isolated *coblas* on edifying themes. Not everyone's favourite troubadour.

13.   Cadenet (first third of the thirteenth century) PC 106: Josef Zemp, *Les Poésies du troubadour Cadenet* (Bern, etc., 1978). Takes his name from his place of birth, Cadenet (south of Apt, Vaucluse), but it also means 'juniper grove' from *cade*, 'juniper'. His twenty-five songs include an *alba*, a *pastorela*, a *partimen* and a religious lyric, the remainder being *cansos*, whose only particularity is Cadenet's repeated praise of the *lauzengiers* for surrounding love with a tissue of deceit. One melody only survives.

14.   Castelloza (first half of the thirteenth century) PC 109: Rieger, *Trobairitz*, pp. 518–69 (see no. 7). One of the two most important of the *trobairitz* (with the Comtessa de Dia). Came from the Auvergne, and may have been in contact with Peirol. Only three (or four?) melancholy love songs survive.

15.   Cercamon (... 1137–49 ...) PC 112: Valeria Tortoreto, *Il Trovatore Cercamon* (Modena, 1981). Alleged in a *vida* to have been Marcabru's teacher, but probably his contemporary. Cercamon's corpus comprises a *planh* for Guilhem X, who was probably his patron, plus a further seven or eight songs on themes explored by other early troubadours: love, marriage, court life and crusade.

16. Cerverí de Girona (... 1259–85 ...) PC 434: Martín de Riquer, *Obras completas del trovador Cerverí de Girona* (Barcelona, 1947). Prolific Catalan troubadour whose real name was Guillem de Cervera, under which he also wrote a book of Proverbs for his son. Cerverí composed some 114 lyrics in a wide variety of genres including *pastorela* and *sirventes*, his overriding preoccupation being the complexities of the role of court poet.

17. Comtessa de Dia (second half of the twelfth century)[1] PC 46: Rieger, *Trobairitz*, pp. 585–626 (see no. 7). Dia is in the Drôme, but it can also be a forename, and there is no agreed historical identification of this important *trobairitz*; her four surviving songs echo Azalais de Porgairagues and Bernart de Ventadorn. One melody only survives.

18. Dalfi d'Alvernhe (... 1160–1235 ...) PC 119: no published edition of the whole corpus of ten songs exists; details of the whereabouts of individual poems are in Chambers, *Proper Names*, p. 21, supplemented by Taylor, *Littérature occitane*, p. 67 (see Appendix 3, p. 301). Count of Auvergne; amateur poet, composing mainly dialogues with other troubadours plus two *sirventes joglaresc*; and major patron of the troubadours of his day, with known contacts including Giraut de Bornelh, Gaucelm Faidit, Elias de Barjols, Perdigon and Peirol.

19. Daude de Pradas (... 1214–82 ...) PC 124: A. H. Schutz, *Poésies de Daude de Pradas* (Toulouse–Paris, 1933). Said to be a canon from the Rouergue; also wrote a treatise on falconry and a didactic poem on the four cardinal virtues. There are twelve surviving love lyrics, a religious lyric, a *planh* and three rather risqué songs about sexual conquest. One melody has been preserved.

20. Elias Cairel (... 1204–22 ...) PC 133: Hilde Jaeschke, *Der Trobador Elias Cairel* (Berlin, 1921). Went from his birthplace of Sarlat in the Perigord to an international career in the Byzantine empire (Thessalonika), Spain and Italy. Fourteen songs survive, mostly love songs characterised by refrain rhyme and/or *cap-finidas* structure, but with isolated examples from other genres: a *tenso* (with Isabella), a *sirventes*, a *descort* and a crusade song.

21. Elias de Barjols (... 1191–1230 ...) PC 132: Stanislaw Stronski, *Le Troubadour Elias de Barjols* (Toulouse, 1906; repr. New York and London, 1971). Author of thirteen surviving songs written in an accessible style. They include two *descorts* and a song describing the composition, using attributes of his contemporaries, of a model knight, the *cavalier soissebut*, in imitation of a song by Bertran de Born about an imaginary lady (*domna soissebuda*) made up of the best features of contemporary noblewomen.

22. Falquet de Romans (... 1219²–33 ...) PC 156: Raymond Arveiller and Gérard Gouiran, *L'Œuvre poétique de Falquet de Romans, troubadour* (Aix-en-Provence, 1987). Described by his *vida* as a *joglar*, Falquet seems nonetheless to have achieved considerable recognition at the court of Frederick II of Germany. His surviving corpus consists of a *salut*, three exchanges of *coblas*, and ten lyrics, including two *cansos*, one religious *alba* and the rest *sirventes*.

23. Folquet de Marselha (... 1178–95, d. 1231) PC 155: Stanislaw Stronski, *Le Troubadour Folquet de Marseille* (Cracow, 1910; repr. Geneva, 1968). Born into a merchant family in Marseilles, Folquet carried on a career as a troubadour alongside his family business. He took orders soon after 1195 and eventually became bishop of Toulouse, participating with the Inquisition during the Albigensian crusade. He composed fourteen *cansos*, two crusade songs, a *tenso*, a *planh* and the odd *cobla*, all in a rather ponderous style. A high proportion of music survives: thirteen melodies.

24. Gaucelm Faidit (... 1172–1203 ...) PC 167: Jean Mouzat, *Les Poèmes de Gaucelm Faidit, troubadour du XIIe siècle* (Paris, 1965). Prolific Limousin troubadour influenced by Bernart de Ventadorn, and in contact with Raimbaut d'Aurenga, Dalfi d'Alvernhe and Maria de Ventadorn, all poet-patrons; he was further associated for a while with the court of Toulouse, and the Plantagenets, writing a fine *planh* on the death of Richard Lionheart and a debate poem with his brother Geoffrey, Count of Brittany. Gaucelm composed crusade songs for both the Third and the Fourth Crusades, and probably participated in the latter. Sixty-five (?sixty-eight) songs survive (fourteen with their music), mostly *cansos*, but also a significant number of *sirventes*, and debates with, among others, Raimbaut (d'Aurenga) and Uc de la Bacalaria (PC 449). A major figure of his generation (he is mentioned in the

Monje de Montaudon's satire), he has been rather neglected since.

25.   Gausbert de Poicibot (... 1220–31 ...) PC 173: William
P. Shepard, *Les Poésies de Jausbert de Puycibot*, CFMA (Paris, 1924).
This author of fifteen songs, all *cansos* except for a *tenso* and a
sirventes joglaresc, is notable mainly for his *vida*, which tells how he
left his life as a monk for an ill-fated love.

26.   Gavaudan (... 1195–1211 ...) PC 174: Saverio Guida, *Il
Trovatore Gavaudan* (Modena, 1979). Connected with the court of
Toulouse under Raymond V and VI, and author of ten surviving
poems, all moralistic: two *pastorelas*, a *planh*, and songs on religious,
moral and political themes.

27.   Giraut de Bornelh (... 1162–99 ...) PC 242: Ruth Verity
Sharman, *The Cansos and Sirventes of the Troubadour Giraut de Borneil:
A Critical Edition* (Cambridge, 1989). Said by his biographer to
stem from 'Essidolh' (= Excideuil, in the Limousin) and, with tan-
talising lack of explanation, to have been 'master of the troubadours', Giraut is undoubtedly one of the major figures in the tradition. His output, at seventy-seven surviving lyrics, is the largest
of the twelfth century, but above all is remarkable for its variety
in style, verse form and genre. Several pieces belong in a debate
over *trobar clus* and *trobar leu* conducted, in particular, with Raimbaut d'Aurenga. Many display a particular rhetorical device. The
relations between love poetry and *sirventes*, humour and earnest,
are explored. Giraut's greatness was more acknowledged in the
Middle Ages – e.g. in Raimon Vidal de Bessalú's *Abrils issia* and by
Dante – than in modern criticism. Only four melodies survive.

28.   Gui d'Ussel (... 1195–96 ...) PC 194: Jean Audiau, *Les
Poésies des quatre troubadours d'Ussel* (Paris, 1922). The most prolific
of a family of three brothers (Gui, Eble and Peire) and their cousin
(Elias) who were lords of Ussel in the Limousin. Wrote eight love
songs, two *pastorelas* and a considerable number of debate poems,
many with other members of his eccentric household. Four melodies survive.

29.   Guilhem Ademar (... 1195–1217 ...) PC 202: Kurt
Almqvist, *Poésies du troubadour Guilhem Adémar* (Uppsala, 1951).
Impoverished noble from the Gévaudan; frequented the courts of
Albi, Toulouse, Narbonne and Spain. Figures in the Monje of Mon-

taudon's satire; ultimately entered holy orders. Fourteen *cansos*, a *partimen* with Eble (probably d'Ussel) and a *sirventes* survive. His *cansos* are often humorous; several are delicious spoofs of Arnaut Daniel.

30. Guilhem de Montanhagol (... 1233–68 ...) PC 225: Peter T. Ricketts, *Les Poésies de Guilhem de Montanhagol* (Toronto, 1964). Fourteen songs survive: a *partimen* with Sordello, *cansos* and *sirventes*. Of humble origin; probably from Toulouse (*pace* his *vida*); often sings about contemporary Toulousain and Spanish politics. A ponderous love poet, Guilhem extols the virtues of *mezura*, striving to emulate earlier troubadours; no heretic, he is nonetheless hostile to the Inquisition.

31. Guilhem de Peitieu (... 1071–1126 ...) PC 183: Nicolò Pasero, *Guglielmo IX d'Aquitania: poesie* (Modena, 1973). Earliest known troubadour; seventh Count of Poitou and ninth Duke of Aquitaine. The most high-ranking Occitan troubadour, his life is well documented. Eleven songs survive (though authorship of PC 183.6 is disputed); several are crude in versification and expression, but all are infectiously high-spirited.

32. Guilhem de Sant Leidier (... 1165–95 ...) PC 234: Aimo Sakari, *Poésies du troubadour Guillem de Saint-Didier* (Helsinki, 1956). Lord of Sant Leidier de la Selva (now Saint-Didier-en-Velay, Haute-Loire); the first troubadour mentioned in the Monje de Montaudon's satire. Thirteen songs survive (one with music), mostly routine *cansos*, but also a *planh*, and an interesting *tenso* in which Guilhem interprets the allegorical dream of an anonymous interlocutor.

33. Guillem de Berguedà (... 1138–92 ...) PC 210: Martín de Riquer, *Guillem de Berguedà. Edición crítica, traducción y glosario*, 2 vols. (Abadía de Poblet, 1971). Viscount of Berguedà; played an important role in Catalonian politics. Some *cansos* survive, but his corpus of thirty-one poems is dominated by violent, obsessive, often obscene *sirventes* that reflect a turbulent life. Had a *penchant* for unusual verse forms.

34. Guillem de Cabestany (... 1212 ...) PC 213: Arthur Långfors, *Les Chansons de Guilhem de Cabestanh* (Paris, 1924). From the Roussillon; nine *cansos* survive, but he is principally known for the 'eaten heart' story (later retold by Boccaccio) that became attached to his corpus both as a *vida* and as a *razo* to PC 213.5.

35. Guiraut de Calanson (. . . 1202–12) PC 243: Alfred Jean-roy, *Jongleurs et troubadours gascons des XIIe et XIIIe siècles* (Paris, 1923), pp. 26–74. Gascon troubadour; frequented the courts of Northern Spain. Ten lyrics survive: five *cansos* that make extensive use of allegory, a *congé*, a *planh*, a *vers* that imitates Arnaut Daniel and two *descorts*. Also the author of *Fadet juglar* (see Pirot, *Recherches*, pp. 563–95), a mock *ensenhamen* that chastises a *joglar*'s ignorance.

36. Guiraut Riquier (. . . 1254–92 . . .) PC 248: Ulrich Mölk, *Guiraut Riquier: Las Cansos* (Heidelberg, 1962); Jean Audiau, *La Pastourelle dans la poésie occitane au moyen âge* (Paris, 1923); Joseph Linskell, *Les Epîtres de Guiraut Riquier* (London, 1985); some poems unedited or available only in anthologies. Prolific troubadour from Narbonne. His 101 surviving compositions include *cansos*, *sirventes*, epistles, six *pastorelas* forming a narrative stretching over more than a decade, devotional lyrics, and poems from minor genres. MS *C* apparently copied its collection of his accomplished, but sententious lyrics from his own autograph song book. MS *R* has all forty-eight surviving melodies along with the corresponding texts, together with rubrics providing dates and in one case, instructions for performing the song.

37. Jaufré Rudel (. . . 1125–48 . . .) PC 262: Giorgio Chiarini, *Il canzoniere di Jaufre Rudel* (Rome, 1985). Prince of Blaye; probably died on the Second Crusade. The famous *vida* says he died overseas after falling in love with the Countess of Tripoli before seeing her; Marcabru (PC 293.15) suggests he is *outramar* in 1148. His corpus of lyrical, but often banal songs includes two that had a wide medieval dissemination, no doubt because of the allusive *amor de lonh* theme, and the success of his musical compositions: four melodies for just seven surviving poems have been preserved.

38. Lanfranc Cigala (. . . 1235–57 . . .) PC 282: Francesco Branciforti, *Il canzoniere di Lanfranco Cigala* (Florence, 1954). Genoese bourgeois; ambassador to the court of Provence in 1241. His thirty-two surviving poems include *cansos*, *sirventes*, devotional lyrics, crusading songs, a *planh* and *tensos*. Ostensibly values poetic transparency, but often seems to practise a more hermetic style.

39. Lombarda (... 1217–26 ...) PC 288: Rieger, *Trobairitz*, pp. 242–54 (see no. 7). *Trobairitz* from Toulouse; known only from her *vida* and an exchange with Bernart Arnaut d'Armagnac. Her allusive *coblas* have been interpreted alternatively as political satire and as a deconstruction of Bernart's courtly discourse.

40. Marcabru (... 1130–49 ...) PC 293: Jean-Marie-Lucien Dejeanne, *Les Poésies complètes du troubadour Marcabru* (Toulouse, 1909). Forty-two surviving poems (four with melodies), mostly satirical *vers*, but his corpus includes a *tenso* and the earliest Occitan *pastorelas*. Probably a Gascon clerk; thought to have frequented the courts of Poitiers, Toulouse and Spain. Marcabru's difficult, but gripping poetry mixes dense opacity, learned allusion and obscene tirades while obsessively attacking the immorality of courtly society. Profoundly influenced subsequent troubadours, both stylistically and morally.

41. Monje de Montaudon (... 1193–1210 ...) PC 305: Michael J. Routledge, *Les Poésies du Moine de Montaudon* (Montpellier, 1977). Auvergnat troubadour; apparently abandoned holy orders (*Monje* = monk) for courtly life; died in Spain. His seven *cansos* make extensive use of feudal metaphors, but he is primarily known for his *enuegs* and *plazers* (genres he probably invented), his fictional *tensos* with God and his satire (imitating Peire d'Alvernha) on a host of contemporary troubadours. Said to have been the lord of the *Cour du Puy*, possibly a 'court' devoted to the appreciation of poetry. Two melodies survive.

42. Peire d'Alvernha (... 1149–68 ...) PC 323: Alberto del Monte, *Peire d'Alvernha: liriche* (Turin, 1955). Little is known of his life, but he certainly travelled to Spain and Bernart Marti accuses him of having abandoned holy orders. His twenty-one surviving poems include *cansos*, *vers* (in which Peire indicates he admired Marcabru), a *tenso* with Bernart (probably de Ventadorn), a satire of twelve other troubadours, and devotional lyrics. Two melodies only survive. Peire cultivated an allusive, formally complex style; his *vida* accords him pre-eminence among the early troubadours and he is the earliest troubadour cited by Dante.

43. Peire Bremon Ricas Novas (... 1230–41 ...) PC 330: Jean Boutière, *Les Poésies du troubadour Peire Bremon Ricas Novas* (Toulouse and Paris, 1930). Provençal troubadour; thirteen unre-

markable *cansos* survive, but also a series of apparently acrimonious *sirventes* attacking Sordello.

44. Peire Cardenal (... 1205–72 ...) PC 335: René Lavaud,
Poésies complètes du troubadour Peire Cardenal (Toulouse, 1957). From
the Haute-Loire, but clearly lived in Toulouse (where he probably
worked as a scribe) and Montpellier. Notable for his longevity and
for the volume of his output. His ninety-six surviving poems,
influenced by Marcabru and Bertran de Born, are mainly satirical
or moralising pieces, though some are devotional. Only three melodies survive. An engaging poet, Peire's satirical register ranges
from subtle irony to acerbic invective. Hostile to the French in the
post-Albigensian crusade period.

45. Peire Rogier (third quarter of the twelfth century) PC 356:
Derek E. T. Nicholson, *The Poems of the Troubadour Peire Rogier*
(Manchester, 1976). Auvergnat troubadour, mentioned in Peire
d'Alvernha's satire; his *vida* says he left religious orders to become
a *joglar*; thought to have frequented the courts of Narbonne, Toulouse, Orange, Castile and Aragon. Seven, possibly eight *cansos* and
a poem addressed to Raimbaut d'Aurenga survive. The earliest
troubadour to use the technique of internal dialogue, he was imitated by Giraut de Bornelh and in *Flamenca*.

46. Peire Vidal (... 1183–1204 ...) PC 364: D'Arco Silvio
Avalle, *Peire Vidal: poesie*, 2 vols. (Milan and Naples, 1960). Toulousain of humble origin, but seems to have frequented influential
courts, travelling widely in Europe and the Holy Land. An
accomplished poet with a wacky sense of humour, his forty-nine
lyrics include delicate *cansos* with an impressive variety of metres,
outrageous *gaps*, delightful parodies, crusading songs and *sirventes*.
The Monje de Montaudon comments on Peire's mischievous spirit
in his satire. Peire was an impressive musician, and twelve melodies survive.

47. Peirol (... 1188–1222 ...) PC 366: Stanley C. Aston,
Peirol: Troubadour of Auvergne (Cambridge, 1953). Impoverished
knight in the service of Dalfi d'Alvernhe; figures in the Monje de
Montaudon's satire. Thirty-two pieces survive, mainly seemingly
anecdotal *cansos*, but also an exchange with Blacatz (PC 97; see
Riquer, *Los trovadores*, III, pp. 1257–60), *partimens* with Gaucelm

Faidit and Dalfi d'Alvernhe, and two crusading songs. The music survives to more than half of his corpus (seventeen melodies).

48. Perdigon (. . . 1192–1212 . . .) PC 370: Henry J. Chaytor, *Les Chansons de Perdigon* (Paris, 1926). A *joglar*, thought to be from the Ardèche. Twelve pieces survive (three with music), mainly conventional *cansos*, but also *partimens* with Gaucelm Faidit and his patron Dalfi d'Alvernhe and a three-way *tenso* with Raimbaut de Vaqueiras and an Aimar.

49. Pons de Capduelh (. . . 1190–1237 . . .) PC 375: Max von Napolski, *Leben und Werke des Trobadors Ponz de Capduoill* (Halle, 1880). Auvergnat; probably a poor knight; knew Folquet de Marselha. His twenty-seven surviving lyrics (four with melodies) are largely accomplished, but unremarkable *cansos*, but there are also some notable crusading songs.

50. Raimbaut d'Aurenga (. . . 1147–73 . . .) PC 389: Walter T. Pattison, *The Life and Works of the Troubadour Raimbaut d'Orange* (Minneapolis, 1952). Count of Orange; died young, but left an impressive corpus of forty poems (though only one melody), mainly *cansos* marked by his strong personality. Seems to have known a wide circle of poets: Bernart de Ventadorn, Peire Rogier, Giraut de Bornelh, Peire d'Alvernha, Gaucelm Faidit, Azalais de Porgairagues, possibly Chrétien de Troyes. A key figure in the *clus/ leu* controversy, Raimbaut revelled in formal complexity and had an extravagant sense of humour.

51. Raimbaut de Vaqueiras (. . . 1180–1205 . . .) PC 392: Joseph Linskill, *The Poems of the Troubadour Raimbaut de Vaqueiras* (The Hague, 1964). Provençal knight who worked for his living at a variety of courts in Italy and Provence. Appears, if his songs are to be believed, to have had a raucous friendship with his patron, Boniface of Montferrat. His twenty-six poems include *cansos*, but also some more quirky compositions such as the remarkable bilingual *tenso* with a Genoese woman, a multi-lingual *descort*, dance songs, a burlesque 'tournament of ladies', and an epic letter, addressed to Boniface. Eight melodies survive.

52. Raimon Jordan (. . . 1178–95 . . .) PC 404: Stefano Asperti, *Il trovatore Raimon Jordan* (Modena, 1990). Viscount of Saint-Antonin; second troubadour in the Monje de Montaudon's satire; probably also knew Guillem de Berguedà. His twelve surviving *cansos* are limpid and graceful, though obsequious. Two melodies survive.

53. Raimon de Miraval (. . . 1191–1229 . . .)[3] PC 406: Leslie T. Topsfield, *Les Poésies du troubadour Raimon de Miraval* (Paris, 1971). Prolific troubadour from near Castre who features in the Monje de Montaudon's satire; apparently well-known among his contemporaries. His corpus of forty-five surviving songs includes a few *sirventes*, but is dominated by *cansos* in which he presents himself as an anguished and fawning courtly lover. Specifically rejects the *trobar clus* for a lighter style. Notable also for the large proportion of surviving music: twenty-two melodies (see Switten, *Miraval*, for edition and discussion of these).

54. Rigaut de Berbezilh (. . . 1141–60 . . .) PC 421: Alberto Varvaro, *Rigaut de Berbezilh: liriche* (Bari, 1960). Probably a knight from Barbézieux; the date of his career is disputed, but he was probably a relatively early troubadour. His nine surviving *cansos* are best known for their heavy-handed use of simile. Four survive with melodies.

55. Sordello (. . . 1220–69 . . .) PC 437: James J. Wilhelm, *The Poetry of Sordello* (New York, 1987). Important Italian troubadour active in Northern Italy and the courts of Provence. Some forty-three pieces survive. These include *cansos* admired by Dante, *sirventes*, debates (with, *inter alia*, Guilhem de Montanhagol), a series of seemingly scathing attacks on Peire Bremon Ricas Novas, and a lengthy *Ensenhamens d'onor*.

56. Uc de Saint Circ (. . . 1217–53 . . .) PC 457: Alfred Jeanroy and J.-J. Salverda de Grave, *Poésies de Uc de Saint-Circ* (Toulouse, 1913). Of humble origin, Uc came from the Lot and composed *vidas* as well as poetry. Some forty-four poems (three with melodies), many bearing the mark of his clerical education, survive: some pedantic, mildly truculent *cansos*, but also *sirventes* and *tensos*, some ostensibly with patrons.

NOTES

Spellings and dates (usually of known activity, those of birth and death being unknown except in the case of a few aristocratic troubadours) are taken from Riquer, *Los trovadores*, unless otherwise specified.

1 Rieger, p. 614, refutes Riquer's dating of 'late 12th – early 13th c.'.
2 Riquer has 1215, but this earliest date of known activity is argued for by Falquet's editors, pp. 5–6.
3 See also Topsfield and Switten on the dating of Raimon's activity.

Occitan terms

alba	dawn song
amor de lonh	distant love
canso	love poem; used after c. 1160
cansoneta	diminutive of *canso*
cauda	second half of a stanza
cobla	stanza
coblas alternadas	stanzas have same rhyme scheme, but sounds alternate
coblas capcaudadas	last rhyme sound of first stanza becomes first rhyme sound of second stanza, e.g. Bernart de Ventadorn IV
coblas capfinidas	first line of each stanza contains last rhyme word of previous stanza, e.g. Bernart de Ventadorn XXXIX
coblas doblas	stanzas have the same rhyme scheme, but sounds change every two stanzas
coblas esparsas	single, free-standing stanzas
coblas retrogradadas	stanzas in which the rhymes change position according to a fixed pattern of permutation
coblas singulars	stanzas have same rhyme scheme with different rhyme sounds
coblas ternas	stanzas have same rhyme scheme, but sounds change every three stanzas
coblas unissonans	stanzas have same rhyme scheme with same rhyme sounds
cortesia	courtliness
descort	poem in which stanzas are not metrically identical
devinalh	riddle poem
domna	lady

enueg	poem listing unpleasant things
estampida	a dance song
estribot	a minor genre associated with *joglars*
fin aman	true lover(s)
fin'amor	pure love; main term for what modern critics call 'courtly love'
frons	first half of a stanza
gap	boasting poem
joglar	minstrel, performer
joven	youth, but also a courtly virtue
largueza	generosity; an important virtue for a patron
midons	my lady; grammatically masculine; of disputed etymology
partimen	debate poem in which a specific problem is posed
pastorela	poem narrating an encounter with a peasant woman, often a shepherdess
planh	lament for a dead patron or friend
plazer	poem listing pleasant things
razo	the argument of a poem; prose text explaining a poem
rima derivada	not strictly speaking rhymes: words from the same root are placed at the rhyme in patterns, e.g. *folh/folha, colh/colha, dolh/dolha*, e.g. Bernart de Ventadorn V
rim derivatiu	see *rima derivada*
rim estramp	a rhyme sound that occurs only once in each stanza
salut	greeting poem in rhyming couplets
senhal	a code name for a lady, friend or patron; ladies are often designated with masculine *senhals*
sestina	a form that moves six rhyme-words in a structured sequence through every possible position in six six-line stanzas
sidons	his lady; see also *midons*
sirventes	poem with a political or satirical theme
sirventes joglaresc	a poem that insults a *joglar*
soudadier	a hired man; either a knight or an

	administrator
tenso	a debate poem
tornada	a final shorter stanza; often addresses a patron, friend or lady
trobador	troubadour; poet
trobairitz	woman troubadour
trobar	to compose poetry; literally 'to find'; often qualified to designate a style
trobar brau	a style of poetry characterised by harsh sounds
trobar car	a style of poetry characterised by rich sounds or rare words
trobar clus	the 'closed', or hermetic style of poetry
trobar leu	the 'light', or easy style of poetry
trobar naturau	Marcabrunian term to designate a style in harmony with nature
trobar plan	a style of poetry characterised by smooth sounds
trobar prim	a style of poetry characterised by smooth, clipped sounds
trobar ric	possibly the same as *trobar car*; exhibits an abundance of poetic resources
vers	term used for all poems before about 1160
vida	prose text recounting the life of a troubadour

Research tools and reference works

Catherine Léglu

The language of the troubadours is thought to have evolved into a *koiné*, a standardised literary idiom. Treatises were composed in the thirteenth century to teach it to aspiring poets in Italy and Catalonia; by the mid-fourteenth century, it was necessary to compose one for the benefit of Occitan-speakers in Toulouse.

Old Occitan in its lyric usage is a difficult language to read. The restricted size of the surviving corpus and the lack of a substantial body of non-lyric literary texts mean that our grasp of vocabulary and syntax is often imperfect; much of the poetry is formulaic, and depends on a consensus over meaning which may not be immediately apparent. The chronological gap between composition and written transmission may compound linguistic difficulties.

This Appendix attempts to set out the essential research and reference tools for learning to read the language of the troubadours, followed by an outline of other important manuals.

LANGUAGE

Dictionaries

Lexique roman, ou dictionnaire de la langue des troubadours, ed. François Raynouard, 6 vols. (Paris, 1838–44). (*LR* or Raynouard)
Definitions in French. Intended to complement a selection of poetry. Precise sources and quotations are provided for each item. Often vague and poorly organised, this dictionary is still useful as the springboard for the *PSW*.

Provenzalisches Supplement-Wörterbuch, Berichtigungen und Ergänzungen zu Raynouards 'Lexique Roman', ed. Emil Levy, 8 vols. (Leipzig, 1894–1924; repr. Hildersheim, 1973). (*PSW*)
Definitions in German. This is the (almost) definitive dictionary for Old Occitan. Intended as a supplement to *LR*, Levy's definitions become

more assured as he moves down the alphabet. Quotations and precise references are given for all items. Earlier vols. often feature the succinct statement 'Unklar'. In such cases, consult the *Petit Dictionnaire*.

Petit Dictionnaire Provençal–Français, ed. Emil Levy (Heidelberg, 1909). (*PD*)
Definitions in French. A pocket version of the *PSW* with one-word definitions. It is very useful for earlier parts of the alphabet, where the *PSW* is less complete. The *FEW* may give explanations and sources.

Index inverse du Petit Dictionnaire Provençal–Français, ed. Mervyn Roy Harris (Heidelberg, 1981)
This Index offers all the words featured in the *PD* listed by last, rather than first, letter, without definitions. Used primarily by editors to locate possible rhyme-words.

Complément bibliographique au Provenzalisches Supplementwörterbuch de Emil Levy: Sources-Datations, ed. Kurt Baldinger with the assistance of Doris Diekmann-Sammet (Geneva, 1983)
Identifies sources and gives datings for the examples cited in the *PSW*; it also provides sources for *LR*.

Französisches Etymologisches Wörterbuch, ed. Walther von Wartburg, 22 vols., 3 supplements and 15 unbound parts (Bonn, 1925–83). (*FEW*)
Definitions in German. A thorough source for a wide range of Romance languages, with a vast number of examples. All entries are classified by Latin stem. Difficult of access at first, it proves an invaluable aid.

Dictionnaire onomasiologique de l'ancien occitan, ed. Kurt Baldinger with the assistance of Inge Popelar, 6 vols., 5 vols. of the *Supplement* published to date (Tübingen, 1975–94)
From French into Occitan. Still in progress, this is a thesaurus of Old Occitan vocabulary, classified by concept (see the index at the back of each volume). The main vols. (*DAO*) combine words from the *PSW*, the *FEW* and *LR*, while the *DAO Suppl.* vols. comprise words found by Baldinger's research team. Useful when seeking to establish the range of synonyms possible for a given term.

Dictionnaire onomasiologique de l'ancien gascon, ed. Kurt Baldinger with the assistance of Inge Popelar, 8 vols. published to date (Tübingen, 1975–95). (*DAG*)

From French into Gascon. Still in progress.

It is also worth consulting an Old French or Medieval Latin dictionary, principally:

Altfranzösisches Wörterbuch, ed. Adolf Tobler and Erhard Lommatzsch, 10 vols. (Berlin, 1925–76). (TL)
Definitions in German. This dictionary gives quotations and sources for Old French words up to the end of the thirteenth century; headings are in Old French.

Glossarium ad scriptores mediae et infimiae graecitatis, ed. Charles du Fresne du Cange (Graz, Austria, 1958). (Du Cange)
Reprint of the edition of 1688. Still the essential reference book for medieval Latin vocabulary.

Mediae latinitatis lexicon minus: lexique latin médiéval–français/anglais: A Medieval Latin–French/English Dictionary, ed. Jan Frederik Niermeyer, 2nd edition (Leiden, 1993)
For quick reference-hunting.

Modern Occitan dictionaries may also be useful, especially when dealing with technical vocabulary, the names of trees and plants, and so on. See especially:

Lou Tresor dóu Felibrige, ed. Frédéric Mistral, 2 vols. (Aix-en-Provence, 1882 and 1886; repr. Aix-en-Provence, 1979)
A compendium of vocabulary for the eastern Occitan regions. Mistral's aim was to provide a stable linguistic base for the Félibrige, which has led to accusations of artificial standardisation.

Lou Pichot Tresor, ed. Rodolphe Rieux Xavier de Fourvières (Avignon, 1902)
A condensed version of the *Tresor*, which can be useful for quick reference.

Dictionnaire Occitan–Français: d'après les parlers languedociens, ed. Louis Alibert (Toulouse, 1966)
A dictionary of modern Languedoc usage, with a good range of examples. Alibert was a 'purist' who excluded terms he perceived to be Gallicisms, and preferred expressions which brought Languedoc dialects closer to Catalan.

Dictionnaire Français–Occitanien: donnant l'équivalent des mots français dans tous les dialectes de la langue d'oc moderne, ed. Louis Piat, reprint (Aix-en-Provence, 1970)
This dictionary gives Languedoc forms, basing itself on the modern French *Littré*, and is useful for comparison with the *Tresor*.

Grammars

Many would now question the rigidity of the rules, for example concerning inflexion or form-levelling, presented by modern grammars. Whereas earlier scholars tended to correct medieval texts in the light of their grammatical certainties, it is more frequent now to respect and to analyse these 'mistakes' as evidence of freer linguistic usage.

The first attempts at a grammar of Old Occitan were made in the *Donatz Proensals* of Uc Faidit and the *Razos de Trobar* of Raimon Vidal de Besalú, both probably from the mid-thirteenth century. These and other related texts are interesting for the links they establish with the lyric, and are available in modern editions with translation:

The 'Donatz Proensals' of Uc Faidit, ed. John H. Marshall (London and New York, 1969)

The 'Razos de Trobar' of Raimon Vidal and associated texts, ed. John H. Marshall (London and New York, 1972)

Las Flors del Gay Saber, estier dichas las Leys d'Amors, ed. A. F. Gatien-Arnould, in *Monuments de la littérature romane jusqu'au XIVe siècle* (Toulouse, 1841–3)
A fourteenth-century treatise, composed for use in poetry competitions in Toulouse.

Las Leys d'Amors: Manuscrit de l'Académie des jeux floraux, ed. Joseph Anglade, 4 vols. (Toulouse, 1919–20)

Modern grammars
The following list is selective.

C. H. Grandgent, *An Outline of the Phonology and Morphology of Old Provençal* (Boston, 1905; repr. New York, 1973)
Still useful.

Edward Larrabee Adams, *Word Formation in Provençal* (New York, 1913)
Still useful.

Joseph Anglade, *Grammaire de l'ancien provençal, de l'ancienne langue d'oc* (Paris, 1921)
Concise and accessible, but dated.

Carl Appel, *Provenzalische Chrestomathie: mit Abriss der Formenlehre und Glossar* (Leipzig, 1930)
Has an introduction on the language which is still invaluable.

Aurelio Roncaglia, *La Lingua dei trovatori: profilo di grammatica storica del provenzale antico* (Rome, 1965)
A solid introduction.

Frank R. Hamlin, John Hathaway and Peter T. Ricketts, *Introduction à l'étude de l'ancien provençal: textes d'étude*, 2nd edition (Geneva, 1985)
A concise and clearly-presented grammar and morphology with a good glossary, this volume aims to introduce the reader to the troubadour lyric via a selection of lyric texts.

Frede Jensen, *From Vulgar Latin to Old Provençal* (Chapel Hill, NC, 1972)
Intended as a 'teach-yourself' manual for students of Provençal linguistics, this is not a systematic grammar, but a continuous linguistic commentary on selected texts.

The Syntax of Medieval Occitan (Tübingen, 1986)
An essential linguistic introduction.

Q. I. M. Mok, *Manuel pratique de morphologie d'ancien occitan* (Muiderberg, 1977)
Clearly presented, but – as it states – only concerned with morphology.

Nathaniel B. Smith, Thomas G. Bergin, *An Old Provençal Primer* (New York and London, 1984)
An excellent teaching primer based on classroom handouts.

José Ramón Fernández González, *Gramática histórica provenzal* (Oviedo, 1985)

A thorough manual for Old and Modern Occitan grammar, with a historical preface and maps.

Pierre Bec, *La Langue occitane*, 5th edition (Paris, 1986)
A short, concise and instructive introduction to the language; not a teaching manual.

William D. Paden, *Introduction to Old Occitan* (MLA, 1998), 600 pp. plus Audio CD.
Appeared while this book was in preparation.

OTHER RESEARCH TOOLS

This section presents the research tools which should be used to situate, classify and discuss any song, *vida*, *razo* or attribution.

The transmission and composition of the troubadour corpus

Karl Bartsch, *Grundriss zur Geschichte der provenzalischen Literatur* (Eberfeld, 1872)
For Bartsch's classification of troubadour manuscripts, see Appendix 4. Bartsch also classified all named troubadours in alphabetical order, and all attributed songs, listing them alphabetically by first line (*incipit*) under each name.

Alfred Jeanroy, *Bibliographie sommaire des chansonniers provençaux* (Paris, 1916)
Jeanroy's reworking of Bartsch's classification, including the changing of certain *sigla*, has not enjoyed much success.

Clovis Brunel, *Bibliographie des manuscrits littéraires en ancien provençal* (Paris, 1935)
Provides the fullest list of troubadour MSS.

François Zufferey, *Recherches linguistiques sur les chansonniers provençaux* (Geneva, 1987)
Zufferey's proposed alterations to Bartsch's *sigla* have been accepted by many recent editors; it is worth consulting, in order to avoid confusion.

Bibliographie der Troubadours, ed. Alfred Pillet and Henry Carstens (Halle, 1933; repr. New York, 1968). (PC or P.-C.)
The key reference work for all troubadour research. Pillet adopted

Bartsch's classification of troubadour names and songs, and inserted omitted items. Each song is assigned a number; all manuscripts are noted, with folio numbers, and any editions available then are included. The text is in German, as is some of the classification. This bibliography has not been re-edited; as a result, there is no single reference book available for the editions, changes to attributions or discoveries made since the late 1920s, but the second volume of Frank's *Répertoire métrique* (see below) added further material; see also the following items.

Eleonora Vincenti, *Bibliografia antica dei trovatori* (Milan, Naples, 1963)
Covers works published about the troubadours between 1525 and 1804.

Robert A. Taylor, *La Littérature occitane du moyen âge: Bibliographie sélective et critique* (Toronto, 1977)
This update includes reference works and bibliographies.

Marcelle D'Herde-Heiliger, *Répertoire des traductions des œuvres lyriques des troubadours des XIe au XIIIe siècles* (Béziers, 1985)
Gives access to individual translations of complete troubadour poems.

A CD-Rom project is under way which aims to offer full texts of all extant Old Occitan songs and non-lyric works. The MLA bibliographies, the IMB and the Occitan literature and language sections of *The Year's Work in Modern Language Studies* are also useful resources.

Specialist repertories

István Frank, *Répertoire métrique de la poésie des troubadours*, 2 vols. (Paris, 1953, 1957)
Text in French. This repertory classifies each troubadour song by rhyme scheme, with differences in metre noted but not subdivided. Rhyme endings are given for each item. It has separate sections for the *descort*, and for non-lyric pieces. There is also a summary (II, pp. 89–192) of each troubadour's corpus of metrical structures.

Jean Boutière, A.-H. Schutz, *Biographies des troubadours*, 2nd edition (Paris, 1964)
An edition with French translations of all the extant *vidas* and *razos* of the troubadour *chansonniers*.

Wilhelmina M. Wiacek, *Lexique des noms géographiques et ethniques dans les poésies des troubadours* (Paris, 1968)

Text in French. A lexicon of all proper names in the texts of troubadour songs.

Frank M. Chambers, *Proper Names in the Lyrics of the Troubadours* (Chapel Hill, NC, 1971)
Text in English. A similar compendium.

Frank M. Chambers, *An Introduction to Old Provençal Versification* (Philadelphia, 1985)
 A useful critical introduction to the study of techniques of versification.

MUSIC

Recent studies of the troubadours tend to acknowledge the importance of musical performance in the texts. Only 315 melodies survive for troubadour songs, which compares unfavourably to over 2,000 melodies for the *trouvère* lyric and amounts to only a small percentage of the extant corpus of texts. However, some studies and editions have been made of the troubadour melodic corpus on its own.

Friedrich Gennrich, *Der musikalische Nachlass der Troubadours*, 3 vols. (Darmstadt and Langen-bei-Frankfurt, 1958–65)
An edition of all the extant melodies; Gennrich's approach is now considered dated.

Hendrik van der Werf, *The Extant Troubadour Melodies: Transcriptions and Essays for Performers and Scholars* (Rochester, NY, 1984)
An edition and study of the extant melodies, intended for use by performers as much as for research, and published by the author.

Margaret L. Switten, *Music and Poetry in the Middle Ages: A Guide to Research on French and Occitan Song, 1100–1400* (New York, 1995)
An essential research tool.

Samuel N. Rosenberg, Margaret L. Switten, and Gérard Le Vot, *Songs of the Troubadours and Trouvères: An Anthology of Poems and Melodies* (New York and London, 1998)
Accompanied by a compact disc.

The chansonniers

Reference works disagree as to the number of extant *chansonniers*: those that give a higher number include fragments and manuscripts that are collections in other languages, but which include some Occitan lyrics. For the fullest list, see Brunel, *Bibliographie*. The following list draws on Pillet-Carstens, *Bibliographie*, pp. x–xliv, Riquer, *Los trovadores*, I, pp. 12–14 and Zufferey, *Recherches*, pp. 4–6; it does not include fragments, which are usually classified in relation to the *chansonniers* they are thought to resemble most closely (see Zufferey, *Recherches*, p. 5 for details).

The *sigla* with which the *chansonniers* are conventionally designated were first assigned by the nineteenth-century scholar Karl Bartsch (*Grundriss*, pp. 27–81). He used the letters of the alphabet to rank the *chansonniers* in order of merit: thus MSS assigned letters at the beginning of the alphabet in his view constituted good sources for the poems they contain, whereas MSS assigned letters towards the end of the alphabet were deemed inferior or corrupt. But as John Marshall has argued (*Transmission*), when a MS seems to offer a clean copy of a poem this does not necessarily mean that it preserves what the troubadour composed: it may in fact indicate that a scribe has intervened in order to make his source understandable to a later (often Italian) readership (see Chapters 14 and 15). Bartsch's classification has probably influenced editors unduly, particularly those using a 'best manuscript' method of editing (see Chapter 14).

PARCHMENT *CHANSONNIERS*

Bartsch used upper-case letters for parchment MSS. In the following list BN f.f. = Bibliothèque Nationale fonds français. Because Zufferey does not accept all the French *chansonniers* into his corpus of Occitan *chansonniers*, he reassigns or does not use some letters towards the end of the alphabet. Notably, he uses Z to designate the MS that is conventionally referred to as *Sg*, which is why it is called *Sg/Z* here and in Chapter 15.

A	Rome, Vatican Latin 5232; Italian; 13th-c.
B	Paris, BN f.f. 1592; Occitan; 13th-c.
C	Paris, BN f.f. 856; Occitan; 14th-c.
D	Modena, Biblioteca Estense α, R.4.4; Italian; 1254
E	Paris, BN f.f. 1749; Occitan; 14th-c.
F	Rome, Vatican Chigi L.IV.106; Italian; 14th-c.
G	Milan, Biblioteca Ambrosiana R 71 sup.; Italian; 14th-c.
H	Rome, Vatican Latin 3207; Italian; late13th-c.
I	Paris, BN f.f. 854; Italian; 13th-c.
J	Florence, Biblioteca Nazionale Conv. Sopp. F.IV.776; Occitan; 14th-c.
K	Paris, BN f.f. 12473; Italian; 13th-c.
L	Rome, Vatican Latin 3206; Italian; 14th-c.
M	Paris, BN f.f. 12474; Italian; 14th-c.
N	New York, Pierpont Morgan 819; Italian; 14th-c.
O	Rome, Vatican Latin 3208; Italian; 14th-c.
P	Florence, Biblioteca Laurenziana XLI.42; Italian; 1310
Q	Florence, Biblioteca Riccardiana 2909; Italian; 14th-c.
R	Paris, BN f.f. 22543; Occitan; 14th-c.
S	Oxford, Bodleian Douce 269; Italian; 13th-c.
Sg/Z	Barcelona, Biblioteca de Catalunya 146; Catalan; 14th-c.
T	Paris, BN f.f. 15211; Italian; late 13th-c.
U	Florence, Biblioteca Laurenziana; XLI.43; Italian; 14th-c.
V	Venice, Biblioteca Marciana fr. App. cod. XI; Catalan; 1268
W	Paris, BN f.f. 844; French; 13th-c.
X	Paris, BN f.f. 20050; French; 13th-c.
Y	Paris, BN f.f. 795; French/Italian; 13th-c.
Z	Paris, BN f.f. 1745; Occitan; 13th-c.

PAPER *CHANSONNIERS*

Paper was used less frequently than parchment and is more fragile so there are fewer surviving MSS. However, *a* and *a*[1], which are two parts of a later copy of an early *chansonnier*, are an important

source. The following list is selective and does not include fragments.

a　　　Florence, Biblioteca Riccardiana 2814; Italian; 1589
a[1]　　Modena, Biblioteca Estense, Campori γ.N.8.4; 11, 12, 13;
　　　　Italian; 1589
c　　　Florence, Biblioteca Laurenziana XC 26; Italian; 15th-c.
f　　　Paris, BN f.f. 12472; Occitan; 14th-c.

Bibliography

EDITIONS NOT GIVEN IN APPENDIX 1

Andreas Capellanus: *On Love*, ed. and trans. P. G. Walsh (London, 1982)

Arnaut Daniel: *La vita e le opere del trovatore Arnaldo Daniello*, ed. Ugo Angelo Canello (Halle, 1883)

Les Poésies d'Arnaut Daniel, ed. René Lavaud (Toulouse, 1910)

Le Canzoni di Arnaut Daniel, ed. Maurizio Perugi (Milan and Naples, 1978)

The Poetry of Arnaut Daniel, ed. James J. Wilhelm (New York, 1981)

Arnaut Daniel: il sirventese e le canzoni, ed. Mario Eusebi (Milan, 1984)

Arnaut de Maruelh: Mario Eusebi, 'L'*Ensenhamen* di Arnaut de Mareuil', *Romania*, 90 (1969), 14–30

Augustine: *On Christian Doctrine*, trans. D. W. Robertson, Jr. (Indianapolis, 1958)

Bernart von Ventadorn: seine Lieder mit Einleitung und Glossar, ed. Carl Appel (Halle, 1915)

Bertran d'Alamanon: *Le Troubadour Bertran d'Alamanon*, ed. J.-J. Salverda de Grave (Toulouse, 1902)

Bertran de Born: *The Poems of the Troubadour Bertran de Born*, ed. William D. Paden, Tilde Sankovitch and Patricia H. Stäblein (Berkeley, Los Angeles and London, 1986)

Blacatz: in O. Soltau, 'Die Werke des Troubadours Blacatz', *Zeitschrift für romanische Philologie*, 23 (1899), 201–48 and 24 (1900), 33–60

Chanson de la Croisade Albigeoise, ed. Eugène Martin-Chabot, adapted by Henri Gougaud (Paris, 1989)

Chrétien de Troyes: *Le Chevalier au lion*, ed. David F. Hult (Paris, 1994)

Cicero: *De Inventione*, trans. H. M. Hubbell (Cambridge, MA, 1949)

Dante Alighieri: *The Divine Comedy of Dante Alighieri*, ed. and trans. John D. Sinclair, 3 vols. (New York, 1961)

La vita nuova, trans. B. Reynolds (New York and London, 1969)

'De vulgari eloquentia', in *The Literary Criticism of Dante Alighieri*, trans. R. Haller (Lincoln, NB, 1973)

Garin d'Apchier: *I Sirventesi di Garin d'Apchier e di Torcafol*, ed. Fortunata Latella (Modena, 1994)

Guilhem de Peitieu: *Les Chansons de Guillaume IX, Duc d'Aquitaine (1071–1127)*, ed. Alfred Jeanroy (Paris, 1927)

The Poetry of Guilhem IX, Count of Poitiers, IX Duke of Aquitaine, ed. and trans. Gerald A. Bond (New York, 1982)

Guilhem de la Tor: *Le poesie di Guilhem de la Tor*, ed. Ferruccio Blasi (Geneva, 1934)

Guillaume de Lorris and Jean de Meun: *Le Roman de la Rose*, ed. Félix Lecoy, 3 vols. (Paris, 1973–4)

Guillem Augier Novella: in Johannes Müller, 'Die Gedichte des Guillem Augier Novella', *Zeitschrift für romanische Philologie*, 23 (1899), 47–78

Guiraut Riquier: *Werke Guiraut Riquiers*, ed. S. L. H. Pfaff, in *Die Werke der Troubadours in provenzalischer Sprache*, directed by C. A. F. Mahn, 4 vols. (Berlin, 1846–53)

Jakemes: *Le Roman du Chastelain de Coucy et de la dame de Fayel*, ed. John E. Matzke and Maurice Delbouille (Paris, 1936)

Jaufré Rudel: *Les Chansons de Jaufré Rudel*, ed. Alfred Jeanroy (Paris, 1915)
The Songs of Jaufré Rudel, ed. Rupert T. Pickens (Toronto, 1978)
The Poetry of Cercamon and Jaufre Rudel, ed. G. Wolf and Roy Rosenstein (New York, 1983)

Lai de l'Oiselet, ed. Lenora D. Wolfgang (Philadelphia, 1990)

Leys d'amors: Las Flors del Gay Saber, estier dichas Las Leys d'Amors, trans. d'Aguilar and d'Escouloubre, revised and completed by Adolphe-F. Gatien-Arnoult (Toulouse, 1841–3; repr. Geneva: Slatkine, 1977)

Marcabru: *Marcabru: A Critical Edition*, ed. Simon Gaunt, Ruth Harvey, John Marshall and Linda Paterson, forthcoming (Woodbridge, 2000)

Marie de France: *Lais*, ed. Jean Rychner (Paris, 1973)

Matfre Ermengaud: *Le Breviari d'Amor de Matfre Ermengaud*, ed. Peter T. Ricketts vol. V (Leiden, 1976), vols. II and III (London, 1989 and 1998), others forthcoming

Nouvelles occitanes du moyen âge, ed. and trans. Jean-Charles Huchet (Paris, 1992)

Ovid: *Metamorphoses*, ed. and trans. Frank Justus Miller (Cambridge, MA and London, 1971)

Palaizi: István Frank, 'Tomier et Palaizi: troubadours tarasconnais (1199–1226)', *Romania*, 78 (1957), 46–85

Paulet de Marselha: Isabel de Riquer, 'Las poesías del trovador Paulet de Marselha', *Boletín de la Real Academia de Buenas Letras de Barcelona*, 38 (1979–82), 133–205

Peire Raimon de Tolosa: *Le poesie di Peire Raimon de Tolosa*, ed. Alfredo Cavaliere. Biblioteca dell'Archivum Romanicum (Florence, 1935)

Petrarca, Francesco: *Trionfi*, intro. G. Bezzola (Milano, 1984)

Quintilian: *Institut oratoire*, ed. Jean Cousin, 7 vols. (Paris, 1976)

Raimon Vidal de Besalú: *The 'Razos de trobar' of Raimon Vidal and Associated Texts*, ed. John H. Marshall (London, 1972)
Obra poètica, ed. Hugh Field, 2 vols. (Barcelona, 1989–91)

Rambertino Buvalelli: *Le poesie*, ed. Elio Melli (Bologna, 1978)

Rhetorica ad Herennium: Rhétorique à Hérennius, ed. Guy Achard (Paris, 1989)

Roland à Saragosse, ed. Mario Roques (Paris, 1956)

Saint Bernard: *Sancti Bernardi Opera*, ed. J. Leclerq and H. Rochais, 8 vols. (Rome, 1957–77)

Sordello: le poesie, ed. M. Boni (Bologna, 1954)

Tibaut: *Le Roman de la Poire*, ed. Christiane Marchello-Nizia (Paris, 1984)

Tomier: *see* Palaizi

Torcafol: *see* Garin d'Apchier

Trobairitz: Chants d'amour des femmes-troubadours, ed. Pierre Bec (Paris, 1995)

> *The Women Troubadours*, ed. Meg Bogin (New York and London, 1976)

> *Songs of the Women Troubadours*, ed. Matilda Tomaryn Bruckner, Laurie Shepard, Sarah White (New York and London, 1995)

> *The Minor Trobairitz: An Edition with Translation and Commentary*, ed. Deborah Perkal-Balinsky (DAI 47, 1987)

> *Die provenzalischen Dichterinnen*, ed. Oskar Schultz-Gora (Leipzig, 1888)

> *Les Poétesses provençales du Moyen Age*, ed. Jules Véran (Paris, 1946)

Uc Faidit: *The 'Donatz Proensals' of Uc Faidit*, ed. John H. Marshall (London, 1969)

Vidas: Biographies des troubadours: textes provençaux des XIIIe et XIVe siècles, ed. Jean Boutière and A.-H. Schutz, 2nd edition (Paris, 1964)

SECONDARY WORKS

Akehurst, F. R. P. and Davies, Judith M., eds., *A Handbook of the Troubadours* (Berkeley, London, Los Angeles, 1995)

Alcover, A. M. and Moll, F. de B., *Diccionari català–valencià–balear*, 10 vols. (Palma de Mallorca, 1980)

Allegri, Laura, 'Frammento di un antico florilegio provenzale', *Studi Medievali*, 27 (1986), 319–51

Alvar, Carlos, *La poesía trovadoresca en España y Portugal* (Madrid, 1979)

Antonelli, Roberto, 'Politica e volgare: Guglielmo IX, Enrico II, Frederico II', in *Seminaro Romanzo* (Rome, 1979), pp. 9–109

Appel, Carl, 'Zu Marcabru', *Zeitschrift für romanische Philologie*, 43 (1923), 403–69

Arlt, Wulf, 'Zur Interpretation zweier Lieder: *A madre de Deus* und *Reis glorios*', *Basler Jahrbuch für historische Musikpraxis*, 1 (1977), 117–30

> '*Nova Cantica*: Grundsätzliches und Spezielles zur Interpretation musikalischer Texte des Mittelalters', *Basler Jahrbuch für historische Musikpraxis*, 10 (1986), 13–62

Asperti, Stefano, '*Flamenca* e dintorni: considerazioni sui rapporti fra Occitania e Catalogna nel XIV secolo', *Cultura Neolatina*, 45 (1985), 59–103

> 'Sul sirventese "Qi qe s'esmai ni·s desconort" di Bertran d'Alamanon

et su altri testi lirici ispirati dalle guerre di Provenza', in *Cantarem d'aquestz trobadors. Studi occitanici in onore di Giuseppe Tavani*, ed. Luciano Rossi (Alessandria, 1995), pp. 169–234

Carlo I d'Angiò e i trovatori: componenti 'provenzali' e angioine nella tradizione manoscritta della lirica trobadorica (Ravenna, 1995)

Aubrey, Elizabeth, *The Music of the Troubadours* (Bloomington, 1996)

Aurell, Martin, *La Vielle et l'épée: troubadours et politique en Provence au XIIIe siècle* (Paris, 1989)

Avalle, D'Arco Silvio, *La letteratura medievale in lingua d'oc nella sua tradizione manoscritta: problemi di critica testuale* (Turin, 1961)

Ai luoghi di delizia pieni (Milan and Naples, 1977)

I manoscritti della letteratura in lingua d'oc, new edition by L. Leonardi (Turin, 1993)

Bakhtin, Mikhail, *The Dialogical Imagination: Four Essays*, trans. Caryl Emerson and Michael Holquist (Austin, 1981)

Speech Genres and Other Late Essays, trans. Caryl Emerson and Michael Holquist (Austin, 1985)

Ballestros-Beretta, Antonio, *Alfonso X el Sabio* (Barcelona, 1963)

Baratier, Eugène, 'Marquisat et comtés en Provence', in *Histoire de la Provence*, ed. Eugène Baratier (Toulouse, 1969), pp. 123–67

Barber, Malcolm, 'Catharism and the Occitan nobility: the lordships of Cabaret, Minerve and Termes', in *The Ideals and Practice of Medieval Knighthood III*, ed. Christopher Harper-Bill and Ruth Harvey (Woodbridge, 1990), pp. 1–19

Barthes, Roland, 'The reality effect', in *The Rustle of Language*, trans. R. Howard (New York, 1986), pp. 141–8

'The death of the author', in *Modern Criticism and Theory: a Reader*, ed. David Lodge (London and New York, 1988), pp. 167–72

Bartsch, Karl, *Grundriss zur Geschichte der provenzalischen Literatur* (Elberfeld, 1872)

Baumel, J., *Histoire d'une seigneurie du Midi de la France*, 2 vols. (Montpellier, 1969)

Baumgartner, Emmanuèle, 'The play of temporalities; or the reported dream of Guillaume de Lorris', in *Rethinking the Romance of the Rose: Text, Image, Reception*, ed. Kevin Brownlee and Sylvia Huot (Philadelphia, 1992), pp. 22–38

Bec, Pierre, 'Le problème des genres chez les premiers troubadours', *Cahiers de Civilisation Médiévale*, 25 (1982), 31–47

'Troubadours, trouvères et espace Plantagenet', *Cahiers de Civilisation Médiévale*, 29 (1986), 9–14

Burlesque et obscénité chez les troubadours: le contre-texte au Moyen Age (Paris, 1984)

Beltrami, Pietro G., 'Ancora su Guglielmo IX e i trovatori antichi', *Messana*, 4 (1990), 5–45

Benveniste, Emile, 'Le jeu comme structure', *Deucalion*, 2 (1947), 161–67

Berne, Eric, *Games People Play: The Psychology of Human Relationships* (New York, 1964)

Bertoni, Giulio, *I Trovatori d'Italia* (Modena, 1915)

'La poesia provenzale nell'Italia superiore', in *Storia letteraria d'Italia, II: Il Duecento* (Milan, 1930), pp. 13–37

Bezzola, Reto R., *Les Origines et la formation de la littérature courtoise en occident*, 5 vols. (Paris, 1958–63)

Billy, Dominique, *L'Architecture lyrique médiévale: analyse métrique et modélisation des structures interstrophiques dans la poésie des troubadours et des trouvères* (Montpellier, 1989)

Bischoff, Bernhard, *Anecdota novissima: Texte des vierten bis sechzehnten Jahrhunderts* (Stuttgart, 1984)

Bisson, T. N., *The Medieval Crown of Aragon: A Short History* (Oxford, 1986)

Bloch, Marc, *Feudal Society*, 2 vols. (London, 1962)

Bloch, R. Howard, *Etymologies and Genealogies: A Literary Anthropology of the French Middle Ages* (Chicago and London, 1983)

'The voice of the dead nightingale: orality in the tomb of Old French literature', *Culture and History*, 3 (1988), 63–78

Bloch, R. Howard and Nichols, Stephen G., eds., *Medievalism and the Modernist Temper* (Baltimore and London, 1996)

Boase, Roger, *The Origin and Meaning of Courtly Love: a Critical Survey of European Scholarship* (Manchester, 1977)

Bologna, Corroda, 'La letteratura dell'Italia settentrionale nel Duecento', in *Letteratura italiana: storia e geografia, I: l'età medievale*, ed. Alberto Asor Rosa (Turin, 1987), pp. 101–88

Il ritorno di Beatrice: simmetrie dantesche fra Vita nova, Petrose *et* Commedia, forthcoming

Bologna, Corroda and Fassò, Andrea, *Da Poitiers a Blaia: prima giornata del pellegrinaggio d'amore* (Messina, 1991)

Bond, Richard P., *English Burlesque Poetry, 1700–1750* (Cambridge, MA, 1932)

Bonnet, Marie-Rose, 'Le clerc et le troubadour dans les *vidas* provençales', *Senefiance*, 37 (1995), 65–78

Bossy, Michel-André, 'The *trobar clus* of Raimbaut d'Aurenga, Giraut de Bornelh and Arnaut Daniel', *Mediaevalia*, 19 (1996), 203–19

Bossy, Michel-André and Jones, Nancy, 'Gender and compilation patterns in troubadour lyric: the case of manuscript *N*', *French Forum*, 21 (1996), 261–80

Boulton, Maureen Barry McCann, *The Song in the Story: Lyric Insertions in French Narrative Fiction 1200–1400* (Philadelphia, 1993)

Bourdieu, Pierre, *La Distinction, critique sociale du jugement* (Paris, 1984)

Bowie, Malcolm, *Lacan* (London, 1991)

Brennan, Teresa, *Between Feminism and Psychoanalysis* (London and New York, 1989)

History after Lacan (London and New York, 1993)

Briffault, Robert, *Les Troubadours et le sentiment romanesque* (Paris, 1945)

Bruckner, Matilda Tomaryn, 'Fictions of the female voice: the women troubadours', *Speculum*, 67 (1992), 865–91

Brundage, James A., *Law, Sex and Christian Society in Medieval Europe* (Chicago and London, 1987)

Brunel, Clovis, *Bibliographie des manuscrits littéraires en ancien provençal* (Paris, 1935)

Brunel-Lobrichon, Geneviève, 'Images of women and imagined trobairitz in the Béziers chansonnier', in Paden, ed., *Voice of the Trobairitz*, pp. 211–25

Brunel-Lobrichon, Geneviève, and Duhamel-Amado, Claudie, *Au Temps des troubadours, XIIe–XIIIe siècles* (Paris, 1997)

Brunetti, Giuseppina D. B., 'Sul canzoniere provenzale *T* (Parigi, Bibl. Nat. F. fr. 15211)', *Cultura Neolatina*, 50 (1990), 45–73
   'Per la storia del manoscritto provenzale *T*', *Cultura Neolatina*, 51 (1991), 27–41

Bull, Marcus, *Knightly Piety and the Lay Response to the First Crusade* (Oxford, 1993)

Burgwinkle, William E., *Razos and Troubadour Songs* (New York and London, 1990)
   Love for Sale: Materialist Readings of the Troubadour Razos Corpus (New York and London, 1997)

Burns, E. Jane, 'The man behind the lady in troubadour lyric', *Romance Notes*, 25 (1985), 254–70

Burns, Robert I. (ed.), *Emperor of Culture: Alfonso X the Learned of Castile and his Thirteenth-Century Renaissance* (Philadelphia, 1990)

Butler, Judith, *Bodies that Matter: On the Discursive Limits of 'Sex'* (New York and London, 1993)

Cabré, Miriam, '"Ne suy juglars ne·n fay capteniments": l'offici de trobador segons Cerverí de Girona', in *Actes du Vème Congrès International de l'Association Internationale d'Etudes Occitanes*, forthcoming
   Cerverí de Girona and his Poetic Traditions (Woodbridge, 1998)

Caillois, Roger, *Man, Play, and Games*, trans. Meyer Barash (Glencoe, IL, 1961)

Camproux, Charles, *Le 'joi d'amor' des troubadours: joie et jeu d'amour* (Montpellier, 1965)

Careri, Maria, *Il canzoniere H: struttura, contenuto, e fonti* (Modena, 1990)

Cerquiglini, Jacqueline, 'Le Clerc et l'écriture: Le *Voir Dit* de Guillaume de Machaut et la définition du dit', in *Literatur in der Gesellschaft des Spätmittelalters*, ed. Hans Ulrich Gumbrecht *et al.* (Heidelberg, 1980), pp. 151–68

Chailley, Jacques, 'Les premiers troubadours et les *versus* de l'école d'Aquitaine', *Romania*, 76 (1955), 212–39

Chambers, Frank M., 'Imitation of form in the Old Provençal lyric', *Romance Philology*, 6 (1953), 104–20

'*D'aisso lau Dieu* and Aldric del Vilar', *Romance Philology*, 35 (1982), 489–500

Proper Names in the Lyrics of the Troubadours (Chapel Hill, NC, 1971)

An Introduction to Old Provençal Versification (Philadelphia, 1985)

'*Las trobairitz soiseubudas*', in Paden, ed., *Voice of the Trobairitz*, pp. 45–60

Chaytor, Henry J., *From Script to Print: an Introduction to Medieval Vernacular Literature* (Cambridge, 1945)

Cheyette, Fredric, 'Women, poets and politics in Occitania', in *Aristocratic Women of Twelfth-Century France*, ed. Theodore Evergates (forthcoming, Philadelphia, 1999)

Cholakian, Rouben C., *The Troubadour Lyric: A Psychocritical Reading* (Manchester and New York, 1990)

Cingolani, Stefano, 'The *sirventes-ensenhamen* of Guerau de Cabrera: a proposal for a new interpretation', *Journal of Hispanic Research*, 1 (1992–3), 191–200

Cluzel, Irénée, 'Princes et troubadours de la maison royale de Barcelone-Aragon', *Boletín de la Real Academia de Buenas Letras de Barcelona*, 27 (1957–8), 321–73

Cots, Montserrat, 'Las poesías del trovador Guillem de Cabestany', *Boletín de la Real Academia de Buenas Letras de Barcelona*, 40 (1985–6), 227–330

Cropp, Glynnis M., *Le Vocabulaire courtois des troubadours de l'époque classique* (Paris, 1975)

De Bartholomaeis, Vincenzo, *Poesie provenzali storiche relative all'Italia*, 2 vols. (Rome, 1931)

Denomy, A. J., '*Fin'amors*: the pure love of the troubadours: its amorality and possible source', *Medieval Studies*, 7 (1945), 139–207

'Courtly love and courtliness', *Speculum*, 28 (1953), 44–63

'Concerning the accessibility of Arabic influences to the earliest Provençal troubadours', *Medieval Studies*, 15 (1953), 147–58

De Rougement, Denis, *L'Amour et l'Occident* (Paris, 1963)

D'Heur, Jean-Marie, *Troubadours d'oc et troubadours galiciens-portugais: recherches sur quelques échanges dans la littérature de l'Europe au Moyen Age* (Paris, 1973)

Dragonetti, Roger, *La Technique poétique des trouvères dans la chanson courtoise: contribution à l'étude de la rhétorique médiévale* (Bruges, 1960)

'*Aizi* et *aizimen* chez les plus anciens troubadours', in *Mélanges Delbouille*, ed. J. Renson, 2 vols. (Liège, 1964), II, pp. 127–53

Dronke, Peter, *Women Writers of the Middle Ages: Critical Texts from Perpetua to Marguerite Porete* (Cambridge, 1983)

Dufournet, Jean, *Le Registre d'Inquisition de Jacques Fournier, évêque de Pamiers (1318–1325)*, 3 vols. (Toulouse, 1965)

Duhamel-Amado, Claudie, 'L'Etat toulousain sur ses marges: les choix politiques des Trencavels entre les maisons comtales de Toulouse et de Barcelone (1070–1209)', in *Les Troubadours et l'état toulousain avant la Croisade (1209)*, ed. Arno Krispin (Bordes, 1995), pp. 117–38

Egan, Margarita, ' "Razo" and "Novella": a case study in narrative forms', *Medioevo Romanzo*, 6 (1979), 302–14

Ehrmann, Jacques, 'Homo ludens revisited', *Yale French Studies*, 41 (1971), 31–57

Evergates, Theodore, 'The feudal imaginary of Georges Duby', *The Journal of Medieval and Early Modern Studies*, 17 (1997), 641–60

Faral, Edmond, *Les Arts poétiques du XIIe et du XIIIe siècles* (Paris, 1924)

Favati, Guido, *Le biografie trovadoriche, testi provenzali dei secc. XIIIe e XIVe* (Bologna, 1961)

Fechner, J. U., 'Zum *gab* in der altprovenzalischen Lyrik', *Germanisch-Romanische Monatsschrift*, 14 (1964), 19–34

Ferrante, Joan, 'Notes toward the study of a female rhetoric in the trobairitz', in Paden, ed., *Voice of the Trobairitz*, pp. 63–72

Fleischman, Suzanne, 'Philology, linguistics and the discourse of the medieval text', *Speculum*, 65 (1990), 19–37

'The non-lyric texts', in Akehurst and Davis, eds., *Handbook*, pp. 167–84

Folena, Gianfranco, 'Tradizione e cultura trobadorica nelle corti e nelle città venete', in *Storia della cultura veneta I* (Vicenza, 1976), pp. 453–562

'Tradizione e cultura trobadorica nelle corti e nella città venete', in *Culture e lingue nel Veneto medievale* (Padua, 1990), pp. 1–137

Foucault, Michel, 'What is an author?' in *Modern Criticism and Theory: a Reader*, ed. David Lodge (London and New York, 1988), pp. 196–210

Frank, István, *Répertoire métrique de la poésie des troubadours*, 2 vols. (Paris, 1953–7)

Gallo, E., 'Matthew of Vendôme: introductory treatise on the art of poetry', *Proceedings of the American Philosophical Society*, 118 (1974), 51–92

Garver, Eugene, *Aristotle's Rhetoric: An Art of Character* (Chicago, 1994)

Gaunt, Simon, *Troubadours and Irony* (Cambridge, 1989)

'Poetry of exclusion: a feminist reading of some troubadour lyrics', *Modern Language Review*, 85 (1990), 310–29

'Marcabru, marginal men and orthodoxy: the early troubadours and adultery', *Medium Aevum*, 59 (1990), 55–72

Gender and Genre in Medieval French Literature (Cambridge, 1995)

'Discourse desired: desire subjectivity and *mouvance* in *Can vei la lauzeta mover*', in *Desiring Discourse: the Literature of Love, Ovid through Chaucer*, ed. Cynthia Gravlee and James J. Paxson (Cranbury, NJ, 1998), pp. 89–110

'Occitan grammars and the art of troubadour poetry', in *Cambridge History of Literary Criticism II: The Middle Ages*, ed. Alistair Minnis, forthcoming

Geertz, Clifford, *The Interpretation of Cultures: Selected Essays* (New York, 1973)

Genette, Gérard, *Palimpsestes: la littérature au second degré* (Paris, 1982)

Gennrich, Friedrich, *Der musikalische Nachlass der Troubadours* (Darmstadt, 1958–60)

Ghil, Eliza Miruna, *L'Age de Parage: essai sur le poétique et le politique en Occitanie au XIIIe siècle* (New York, 1989)

Gillingham, John, *Richard the Lionheart*, 2nd edition (London, 1989)

Goddard, R. N. B., 'The early troubadours and the Latin tradition' (D.Phil. diss., Oxford, 1985)

Godzich, Wlad and Kittay, Jeffrey, *The Emergence of Prose: An Essay in Prosaics* (Minneapolis, 1987)

Goldin, Frederick, *The Mirror of Narcissus in the Courtly Love Lyric* (Ithaca, 1967)

Gouiran, Gérard, 'L'opinion publique au moyen âge: Bertran de Born', in *Actualité des troubadours. (Ventabren, 21 juin 1987)* (Marseilles, 1988), pp. 20–5

  Lo Ferm Voler. Les troubadours et l'Europe de la poésie (Montpellier, 1990)

Gouiran, Gérard, ed., *Contacts de langues, de civilisations et intertextualité: IIIᵉ Congrès International de l'Association Internationale d'Etudes Occitanes*, 3 vols. (Montpellier, 1992)

Gravdal, Kathryn, 'Metaphor, metonymy and the medieval women *trobairitz*', *Romanic Review*, 83 (1992), 411–26

Grier, James, 'A new voice in the monastery: tropes and *versus* from eleventh- and twelfth-century Aquitaine', *Speculum*, 69 (1994), 641–60

Gröber, Gustav, 'Die Liedersammlungen der Troubadours', *Romanische Studien*, 2 (1875–7), 337–670

Gruber, Jörn, *Die Dialektik des Trobar* (Tübingen, 1983)

Gubar, Susan, '"The Blank Page" and the issues of female creativity', in *Writing and Sexual Difference*, ed. Elizabeth Abel (Chicago, 1982), pp. 73–93

Guida, Saverio, *Jocs poetici alla corte di Enrico II di Rodez* (Modena, 1983)

  Primi approcci a Uc de Saint Circ (Messina, 1996)

Harvey, Ruth E., 'The satirical use of the expression "sidons" in the works of the troubadour Marcabru', *Modern Language Review*, 78 (1983), 24–33

  The Troubadour Marcabru and Love (London, 1989)

  'Allusions intertextuelles et les *lengua-forcat* de Bernart Marti', in Gouiran, ed., *Contacts de Langues*, III, pp. 927–42

  '*Joglars* and the professional status of the early troubadours', *Medium Aevum*, 62 (1993), 221–41

Henriot, Jacques, *Le Jeu* (Paris, 1969)

Highet, Gilbert, *The Anatomy of Satire* (Princeton, NJ, 1962)

Higounet, Charles, 'Un grand chapitre de l'histoire du XIIe siècle: la rivalité des maisons de Toulouse et de Barcelone pour la prépondérance méridionale', in *Mélanges d'histoire du moyen âge dédiés à la mémoire de Louis Halphen* (Paris, 1951), pp. 313–22

Hoepffner, Ernest, *Les Troubadours dans leur vie et dans leurs œuvres* (Paris, 1955)

Hölzle, P., *Die Kreuzzüge in der okzitanischen und deutschen Lyrik des 12. Jahrhunderts: das Gattungsproblem 'Kreuzlied' im historischen Kontext*, 2 vols. (Göppingen, 1980)

Howard, Donald R., *The Three Temptations: Medieval Man in Search of the World* (Princeton, NJ, 1966)

Huchet, Jean-Charles, *L'Amour discourtois: la 'Fin'Amors' chez les premiers troubadours* (Toulouse, 1987)

    Littérature médiévale et psychanalyse: pour une clinique littéraire (Paris, 1990)

    Review of Rouben C. Cholakian, *The Troubadour Lyric*, *Revue des Langues Romanes*, 95 (1991), 186–91

Huizinga, J[ohan], *Homo ludens: A Study of the Play Element in Culture* (Boston, 1955)

Hult, David F., *Self-fulfilling Prophecies: Readership and Authority in the First Roman de la Rose* (Cambridge, 1986)

Huot, Sylvia, *From Song to Book: The Poetics of Writing in Old French Lyric and Lyrical Narrative Poetry* (Ithaca and London, 1987)

    'Visualization and memory: the illustration of troubadour lyric in a thirteenth-century manuscript', *Gesta*, 31 (1992), 3–14

Hutcheon, Linda, *A Theory of Parody: The Teachings of Twentieth-Century Art Forms* (New York and London, 1985)

Irigaray, Luce, *Speculum de l'autre femme* (Paris, 1974)

    This Sex Which Is Not One, trans. Catherine Porter with Carolyn Burke (Ithaca, NY, 1985)

Jaeger, C. Stephen, *The Origins of Courtliness. Civilising Trends and the Formation of Courtly Ideals, 939–1210* (Philadelphia, 1985)

Jeanroy, Alfred, *La Poésie lyrique des troubadours*, 2 vols. (Toulouse, 1934)

    Bibliographie sommaire des chansonniers provençaux (Paris, 1966)

Jensen, Frede, *The Syntax of Medieval Occitan* (Tübingen, 1986)

Jernigan, Charles, 'The Song of Nail and Uncle: Arnaut Daniel's Sestina *Lo ferm voler q'el cor m'intra*', *Studies in Philology*, 71 (1974), 127–51

Jump, John D., *The Burlesque* (New York and London, 1972)

Kasten, Ingrid, *Frauendienst bei Trobadors und Minnesängern im 12. Jahrhundert* (Heidelberg, 1986)

Kay, Sarah, 'Rhetoric and subjectivity in troubadour poetry', in *The Troubadours and the Epic: Essays in Memory of W. Mary Hackett*, ed. Simon Gaunt and Linda Paterson (University of Warwick, 1987), pp. 102–42

    'Continuation as criticism: the case of Jaufre Rudel', *Medium Aevum*, 56 (1987), 46–64

    Review of Laura Kendrick, *The Game of Love*, *Medium Aevum*, 58 (1989), 331–2

    'Derivation, derived rhyme and the trobairitz', in Paden, ed., *Voice of the Trobairitz*, pp. 157–82

Subjectivity in Troubadour Poetry (Cambridge, 1990)

'The contradictions of courtly love: the evidence of the *lauzengiers*', *Journal of Medieval and Early Modern Studies*, 26 (1996), 209–53

Kelly, Douglas, *The Arts of Poetry and Prose* (Brepols, 1991)

Kendrick, Laura, *The Game of Love: Troubadour Wordplay* (Berkeley, 1988)

'Jongleur as propagandist: the ecclesiastical politics of Marcabru's poetry', in *Cultures of Power, Lordship, Status and Property in Twelfth-Century Europe*, ed. T. N. Bisson (Philadelphia, 1995), pp. 259–86

'The science of imposture and the professionalization of medieval Occitan literary studies', in *Medievalism and the Modernist Temper*, eds. R. Howard Bloch and Stephen G. Nichols (Baltimore and London, 1996), pp. 95–126

Klein, Karen Wilk, *The Partisan Voice: a Study of the Political Lyric in France and Germany, 1180–1230* (The Hague and Paris, 1971)

Köhler, Erich, *Trobadorlyrik und höfischer Roman* (Berlin, 1962)

'Observations historiques et sociologiques sur la poésie des troubadours', *Cahiers de Civilisation Médiévale*, 7 (1964), 27–51

'Marcabru und die beiden "Schulen"', *Cultura Neolatina*, 30 (1970), 300–14

Sociologia della fin'amor, trans. M. Mancini (Padua, 1976)

'*Gabar e rire*: Bermerkungen zum *gab* in der Dichtung der Trobadors', in *Mélanges Wathelet-Willem* (Liège, 1978), pp. 315–28

Krauss, Henning, *Epica feodale e pubblico borghese: per la storia poetica di Carlomagno in Italia* (Padua, 1980)

Kristeva, Julia, Σημιοτικε: *Recherches pour une sémanalyse* (Paris, 1969)

Histoires d'amour (Paris, 1983)

Tales of Love, trans. Leon S. Roudiez (New York, 1987)

Lacan, Jacques, *The Ethics of Psychoanalysis. 1959–60. The Seminar of Jacques Lacan Book VII*, ed. Jacques-Alain Miller, trans. Dennis Porter (London and New York, 1992)

Le Séminaire livre XX: Encore (Paris, 1975)

Lafont, Robert, and Anatole, C., *Nouvelle histoire de la littérature occitane*, 2 vols. (Paris, 1970–71)

Lavaud, René and Nelli, René, eds., *Les Troubadours*, 2 vols. (Bruges, 1960, 1966)

Lazar, Moshé, *Amour courtois et 'fin'amors' dans la littérature du XIIe siècle* (Paris, 1964)

'Carmina erotica, carmina iocosa: the body and the bawdy in medieval love songs', in *Poetics of Love in the Middle Ages: Texts and Contexts*, ed. Moshé Lazar and Norris J. Lacy (Fairfax, VA, 1989), pp. 249–76

Lazzerini, Lucia, '*Cornar lo corn*: sulla tenzone tra Raimon de Durfort, Truc Malec e Arnaut Daniel', *Medioevo Romanzo*, 8 (1981–83), 339–70

'Un caso esemplare: Marcabru IV, *Al prim comens de l'ivernaill*', *Medioevo Romanzo*, 17 (1992), 7–42

'La trasmutazione insensibile. Intertestualità e metamorfismo nella lirica trobadorica dalle origine alla codificazione cortese (I parte)', *Medioevo Romanzo*, 18 (1993), 153–205 and 313–69

'A proposito di due "Liebesstrophen" pretrobadoriche', *Cultura Neolatina*, 53 (1993), 123–34

Leader, Darian and Groves, Judy, *Lacan for Beginners* (London, 1995)

Lehmann, Paul, *Die Parodie im Mittelalter* (Stuttgart, 1963)

Lejeune, Rita, 'Formules féodales et style amoureux chez Guillaume IX', in *Littérature et société occitanes au moyen âge* (Liège, 1979), pp. 103–20

Leube-Fey, Christiane, *Bild und Funktion der 'dompna' in der Lyrik der Trobadors* (Heidelberg, 1971)

Lewis, Archibald R., 'La féodalité dans le Toulousain et la France méridionale (850–1050)', *Annales du Midi*, 76 (1964), 247–59

Lewis, C. S., *The Allegory of Love* (Oxford, 1936)

Liebertz-Grün, Ursula, *Zur Soziologie des 'amour courtois'* (Heidelberg, 1977)

Mairs, Nancy, 'Carnal Acts', *Triquarterly*, 75 (1989), 61–70

Malato, E., *Dante e Guido Cavalcanti: il dissidio per la Vita nuova e il 'disdegno' di Guido* (Rome, 1997)

Mancini, Mario, 'Aimeric de Peguilhan "rhétoriqueur" e giullare', in *Il medioevo nella Marca: trovatori, giullari, letterati a Treviso nei secoli XIII e XIV. Atti del Convegno (Treviso, 28–29 settembre 1990)*, ed. Maria Luisa Meneghetti and Francisco Zambon (Treviso, 1991), pp. 45–89

Manning, Stephen, 'Game and earnest in the Middle English and Provençal love lyrics', *Comparative Literature*, 18 (1966), 225–41

Marshall, John H., 'Le *vers* au XIIe siècle: genre poétique?', *Revue de Langue et Littérature d'Oc*, 12-13 (1962-3), 55–63

The Transmission of Troubadour Poetry (London, 1975)

'The isostrophic *descort* in the poetry of the troubadours', *Romance Philology*, 35 (1981), 130–57

'Textual transmission and complex musico-metrical form in the Old French lyric', in *Medieval French Textual Studies in Memory of T. B. W. Reid*, ed. Ian Short (London, 1984), pp. 119–48

'Une versification lyrique popularisante en ancien provençal', in *Actes du premier Congrès International de l'Association Internationale d'Etudes Occitanes*, ed. Peter Ricketts (London, 1987), pp. 35–66

Martel, Philippe, 'Vers la construction de l'Occitanie', in *Histoire d'Occitanie*, ed. A. Armengaud and R. Lafont (Paris, 1979), pp. 179–255

Martindale, Jane, '*Cavalaria et orgueill*: Duke William IX of Aquitaine and the historian', in *The Ideals and Practice of Medieval Knighthood*, ed. Christopher Harper-Bill and Ruth Harvey, 3 vols. (Woodbridge, 1986–90), II, pp. 87–116

'Eleanor of Aquitaine', in *Richard Cœur de Lion in History and Myth*, ed. Janet L. Nelson (London, 1992), pp. 17–40

Matzke, John E., 'The Legend of the Eaten Heart', *Modern Language Notes*, 26 (1911), 1–8

Méjean, Suzanne, 'Contribution à l'étude du *sirventes-joglaresc*', in *Mélanges Boutière*, ed. Irénée Cluzel and François Pirot, 2 vols. (Liège, 1972), I, pp. 377–95

Meneghetti, Maria Luisa, *Il pubblico dei trovatori: ricezione e riuso dei testi lirici cortesi fina al XIV secolo* (Modena, 1984), 2nd edition (Turin, 1992)

'Uc de Saint Circ tra filologia e divulgazione', in *Il medioevo nella Marca: trovatori, giullari, letterati a Treviso nei secoli XIII e XIV. Atti del Convegno (Treviso, 28–29 settembre 1990)*, ed. Maria Luisa Meneghetti and Francisco Zambon (Treviso, 1991), pp. 115–28

'Aldric e Marcabru', in *Studi in onore di Bruno Panvini*, forthcoming

Menichetti, Aldo, *Metrica italiana: fondamenti metrici, prosodia, rima* (Padua, 1993)

Merriam Webster's Encyclopedia of Literature (Springfield, MA, 1995)

Milá y Fontanels, Manuel, *De los trovadores en España*, in *Obras de Manuel Milá y Fontanels*, II, second edition (Barcelona, 1966)

Mölk, Ulrich, *Trobar clus: trobar leu* (Munich, 1968)

Monson, Don A., 'Andreas Capellanus and the problem of irony', *Speculum*, 63 (1988), 539–72

'Bernart de Ventadorn et Tristan', in *Mélanges Pierre Bec* (Poitiers, 1991), pp. 385–400

'Les *Lauzengiers*', *Medioevo Romanzo*, 19 (1994), 219–35

'*Nadal* chez Bernart de Ventadorn', *Revue des Langues Romanes*, 98 (1994), 447–55

'The troubadour's lady reconsidered again', *Speculum*, 70 (1995), 255–74

Murphy, James J., *Three Medieval Rhetorical Arts* (Berkeley, 1971)

Muschamp, Herbert, 'Student center as mall and visionary jukebox', *New York Times* (10 February 1998), section B, 1–2

Neilson, William Allen, *The Origins and Sources of the Court of Love* (New York, 1899)

Nelli, René, *L'Erotique des troubadours* (Toulouse, 1963)

Les Ecrivains anticonformistes du Moyen Age occitan, 2 vols. (Paris, 1977)

Neumeister, Sebastian, *Das Spiel mit der höfischen Liebe* (Munich, 1969)

Nichols, Stephen G. Jr., '*Canso → conso*: structures of parodic humor in three songs of Guilhem IX', *L'Esprit Créateur*, 16 (1976), 16–29

'Medieval women writers: *Aisthesis* and the powers of marginality', *Yale French Studies*, 75 (1988), 77–94

'Why material philology? Some thoughts', *Zeitschrift für deutsche Philologie*, 116 (1997), pp. 10–30

Nylk, Alois, *Hispano-Arabic Poetry and its Relations with the Old Provençal Troubadours* (Baltimore, 1946)

Oroz Arizcuren, Francisco J., *La lirica religiosa en la literatura provenzal antigua* (Pamplona, 1972)

Ourliac, Paul, 'Troubadours et juristes', *Cahiers de Civilisation Médiévale*, 8 (1965), 159–77

Paden, William D., 'The troubadour's lady: her marital status and social rank', *Studies in Philology*, 72 (1975), 28–50

'*Utrum copularentur*: of *cors*', *L'Esprit Créateur*, 19 (1979), 70–83

'The role of the *joglar* in troubadour lyric poetry', in *Chrétien de Troyes and the Troubadours. Essays in Memory of Leslie Topsfield*, ed. Peter Noble and Linda Paterson (Cambridge, 1984), pp. 90–111

'A new parody by Arnaut Daniel: *Mout m'es bel el tems d'estiou*', in *Poetics of Love in the Middle Ages: Texts and Contexts*, ed. Moshé Lazar and Norris J. Lacy (Fairfax, VA, 1989), pp. 187–97

Review of Laura Kendrick, *The Game of Love*, *Studies in the Age of Chaucer*, 11 (1989), 256–63

'Bernart de Ventadour le troubadour, devint-il abbé de Tulle?', in *Mélanges Pierre Bec* (Poitiers, 1991), pp. 401–41

'Old Occitan as a lyric language: the insertions from Occitan in three thirteenth-century French romances', *Speculum*, 68 (1993), 36–53

'The troubadours and the Albigensian crusade: a long view', *Romance Philology*, 49 (1995), 168–91

'Manuscripts', in Akehurst and Davis, eds., *Handbook of the Troubadours*, pp. 307–33

'The system of genres in troubadour lyric' in *Historicising Genre in Medieval Lyric*, ed. William D. Paden (forthcoming)

Paden, William D. *et al.*, 'The poems of the *Trobairitz* Na Castelloza', *Romance Philology*, 35 (1981), 158–82

Paden, William D., ed., *The Voice of the Trobairitz: Perspectives on the Women Troubadours* (Philadelphia, 1989)

Page, Christopher, *Voices and Instruments of the Middle Ages: Instrumental Practice and Songs in France 1100–1300* (Berkeley, 1986)

The Owl and the Nightingale. Musical Life and Ideas in France, 1100–1300 (London, 1989)

Pasero, Nicolò, 'Pastora contro cavaliere, Marcabruno contro Guglielmo IX', *Cultura Neolatina*, 43 (1983), 9–26

'Cattivi consiglieri: ancora sui rapporti intertestuali fra Guglielmo IX e Jaufré Rudel', in *Literatur: Geschichte und Verstehen. Festschrift für Ulrich Mölk zum 60. Geburtstag* (Heidelberg, 1997), pp. 133–42

'Dante in Cavalcanti: ancora sui rapporti fra *Vita nuova* e *Donna me prega*', *Medioevo Romanzo*, forthcoming

Paterson, Linda, *Troubadours and Eloquence* (Oxford, 1975)

The World of the Troubadours: Medieval Occitan Society c. 1100–c. 1300 (Cambridge, 1993)

'Marcabru's rhetoric and the dialectics of *trobar*: "Ans que·l terminis verdei" (PC 293.7) and Jaufre Rudel', in *Conjunctures: Medieval Studies in Honour of Douglas Kelly*, ed. Keith Busby and Norris J. Lacy (Atlanta and Amsterdam, 1994), pp. 407–23

Payen, Jean-Charles, 'A propos du "Vocabulaire courtois des troubadours": problèmes méthodologiques', *Cahiers de Civilisation Médiévale*, 21 (1978), 151–5

Peron, Gianfelice, 'Trovatori e politica nella Marca Trevigiana', in *Il medioevo nella Marca: trovatori, giullari, letterati a Treviso nei secoli XIII e XIV. Atti del Convegno (Treviso, 28–29 settembre 1990)*, ed. Maria Luisa Meneghetti and Francisco Zambon (Treviso, 1991), pp. 11–44

Perugi, Maurizo, *Saggi di linguistica trovadorica* (Tübingen, 1995)

Pfeffer, Wendy, *The Change of Philomel: The Nightingale in Medieval Literature* (New York, 1985)

Phillips, Jonathan P., *Defenders of the Holy Land: Relations between the Latin East and the West (1119–1187)* (Oxford, 1996)

Pickens, Rupert T., 'Jaufré Rudel et la poétique de la mouvance', *Cahiers de Civilisation Médiévale*, 20 (1977), 323–37

Pirot, François, *Recherches sur les connaissances littéraires des troubadours* (Barcelona, 1972)

Poe, Elizabeth W., 'The problem of the prologue in Raimon Vidal's *Las Razos de Trobar*', *Res Publica Litterarum*, 6 (1983), 303–17

 '*L'autr' escrit* of Uc de Saint Circ: the *Razos* for Bertran de Born', *Romance Philology*, 44 (1990), 123–36

 'The *Vidas* and *Razos*', in Akehurst and Davis, eds., *Handbook of the Troubadours*, pp. 185–97

Pollina, Vincent, 'Troubadours dans le Nord: observations sur la transmission des mélodies occitanes dans les manuscrits septentrionaux', *Romanistische Zeitschrift für Literaturgeschichte / Cahiers d'histoire des littératures romanes*, 9 (1985), 263–78

 Si cum Marcabrus declina: Studies in the Poetics of the Troubadour Marcabru (Modena, 1991)

Pollmann, Leo, *Trobar clus* (Münster, 1965)

Press, Alan R., 'The adulterous nature of *fin'amors*: a re-examination of the theory', *Forum for Modern Language Studies*, 6 (1970), 327–41

Propp, Vladimir, *Morphology of the Folktale*, trans. Laurence Scott (Austin and London, 1968)

Raby, F. J. E., *A History of Secular Latin Poetry in the Middle Ages*, 2 vols. (Oxford, 1957)

Ricketts, Peter T., '*L'estribot*, forme et fond', in *Mélanges Pierre Bec* (Poitiers, 1991), pp. 475–83

Rieger, Angelica, 'Was Bieiris de Romans lesbian? Women's relations with each other in the world of the troubadours', in Paden, ed., *Voice of the Trobairitz*, pp. 73–94

 'Beruf: *Joglaressa*. Die Spielfrau im okzitanischen Mittelalter', in *Feste und Feiern im Mittelalter. Paderborner Symposion des Mediävistenverbandes*, ed. D. Altenburg, J. Jarnut and H. H. Steinhoff (Sigmaringen, 1991), pp. 229–42

Rieger, Dietmar, *Gattungen und Gattungsbezeichnungen der Trobadorlyrik* (Tübingen, 1976)

Riquer, Isabel de, 'Giraut de Bornelh en las obras de Ramon Vidal de Besalú y Jofre de Foixà', *Boletín de la Real Academia de Buenas Letras de Barcelona*, 42 (1989–90), 161–84

'Giraut de Bornelh chez les grammariens et les troubadours catalans du XIIIe siècle', in Gouiran, ed., *Contacts de langues*, III, pp. 1089–103

Riquer, Martín de, 'Un trovador valenciano: Pedro el Grande de Aragón', *Revista Valenciana de Filología*, 1 (1951), 273–311

'La littérature provençale à la cour d'Alphonse II d'Aragon', *Cahiers de Civilisation Médiévale*, 2 (1959), 177–201

'Els trobadors catalans', in *Història de la literatura catalana: part antiga I* (Barcelona, 1964), pp. 24–1096

Los trovadores: historia literaria y textos, 3 vols. (Barcelona, 1975)

'Els *Verses proverbials* de Cerverí de Girona', *Revista de Catalunya*, 54 (1991), 115–33

Roncaglia, Aurelio, 'Il *gap* di Marcabruno', *Studi Medievali*, 17 (1951), 46–70

'*Trobar clus*: discussione aperta', *Cultura Neolatina*, 29 (1969), 5–55

'Le corti medievale', in *Letteratura italiana, I: il letterato e le istituzioni*, ed. Alberto Asor Rosa (Turin, 1982), pp. 33–147

'Guillaume IX d'Aquitaine et le jeu du trobar (avec un plaidoyer pour la déidéologisation de *Midons*)', in Gouiran, ed., *Contacts de langues*, III, pp. 1105–17

Roquebert, Michel, *L'Epopée cathare*, 3 vols. (Toulouse, 1970–86)

Rose, Margaret A., *Parody: Ancient, Modern, and Post-modern* (Cambridge, 1993)

Rosenberg, Samuel, Margaret Switten and Gérard le Vot, *Songs of the Troubadours and Trouvères: An Anthology of Poems and Melodies with accompanying CD* (New York and London, 1998)

Rosenstein, Roy, 'Les années d'apprentissage du troubadour Jaufre Rudel: de l' "escola n'Eblo" à la "segura escola"', *Annales du Midi*, 100 (1988), 7–15

Rossi, Luciano, 'Per l'interpretazione di "Cantarai d'aquests trobadors" (323. 11)', in *Cantarem d'aquestz trobadors. Studi occitanici in onore di Giuseppe Tavani*, ed. Luciano Rossi (Alessandria, 1995), pp. 65–111

Roubaud, Jacques, *La Fleur inverse: essai sur l'art formel des troubadours* (Paris, 1986)

Rouche, M., *Histoire générale de l'enseignement et de l'éducation en France. I. Des origines à la Renaissance* (Paris, 1981)

Routledge, Michael J., 'The monk who knew the ways of love', *Reading Medieval Studies*, 12 (1986), 3–25

'Troubadours, trouvères et la cour du Puy', in Gouiran, ed., *Contacts de Langues*, III, pp. 1133–44

Rubin, Gayle, 'The traffic in women: notes on the political economy of sex', in *Toward an Anthropology of Women*, ed. Rayner R. Reiter (New York and London, 1975), pp. 157–210

Runciman, Steven, *The Sicilian Vespers: A History of the Mediterranean World in the Later Thirteenth Century* (Cambridge, 1958)

Saffioti, Tito, *I giullari in Italia* (Milan, 1990)

Salvatorelli, Luigi, *A Concise History of Italy* (London, 1940)

Sapegno, Natalino, *Compendio di storia della letteratura italiana, I: dalle origini alla fine del Quattrocento* (Florence, 1989)

Schmitt, Jean-Claude, *La Raison des gestes dans l'Occident médiéval* (Paris, 1990)

Schutz, Alexander H., 'Were the *vidas* and *razos* recited?', *Studies in Philology*, 36 (1939), 565–70

Segre, Cesare, 'Le forme e le tradizione didattiche', in *Grundriss der romanischen Literaturen des Mittelalters*, VI/1, ed. Hans Robert Jauss (Heidelberg, 1968), pp. 58–145

Shapiro, Marianne, 'The Provençal *trobairitz* and the limits of courtly love', *Signs*, 3 (1978), 560–71

'*Entrebescar los motz*: word-weaving and divine rhetoric', *Zeitschrift für romanische Philologie*, 100 (1984), 355–83

De Vulgari Eloquentia: Dante's Book of Exile (Lincoln, NB, 1990)

Showalter, Elaine, 'Feminist criticism in the wilderness', in *Feminist Criticism: Essays on Women, Literature and Theory*, ed. Elaine Showalter (New York, 1985), pp. 243–70

Singleton, Charles S., 'Dante: within courtly love and beyond', in *The Meaning of Courtly Love*, ed. F. X. Newman (Albany, NY, 1968), pp. 43–54

Smith, Nathaniel B., 'Games troubadours play', in *Poetics of Love in the Middle Ages: Texts and Contexts*, ed. Moshé Lazar and Norris J. Lacy (Fairfax, VA, 1989), pp. 3–15

'Rhetoric', in Akehurst and Davis, eds., *Handbook of the Troubadours*, pp. 400–20

Soldevila, Ferran, *Pere el Gran*, 2 vols. (Barcelona, 1950–62)

Solterer, Helen, 'Dismembering, remembering the Châtelain de Couci', *Romance Philology*, 46 (1992), 103–24

Spaggiari, Barbara, *Il nome di Marcabru* (Spoleto, 1992)

Spence, Sarah, *Rhetorics of Reason and Desire: Vergil, Augustine, and the Troubadours* (Ithaca and London, 1988)

Texts and the Self in the Twelfth Century (Cambridge, 1996)

Spiegel, Gabrielle, *Romancing the Past: The Rise of Vernacular Prose Historiography in Thirteenth-Century France* (Berkeley and London, 1993)

Stevens, John, *Music and Poetry in the Early Tudor Court* (Lincoln, NB, 1961)

Words and Music in the Middle Ages: Song, Narrative, Dance and Drama, 1050–1350 (Cambridge, 1986)

Stone, Gregory, *The Death of the Troubadour: The Late Medieval Resistance to the Renaissance* (Philadelphia, 1994)

Stronski, Stanislaw, *La Poésie et la réalité au temps des troubadours* (Oxford, 1943)

Sutherland, Dorothy R., 'L'Elément théâtral dans la *canso* chez les troubadours de l'époque classique', *Revue de Langue et de Littérature d'Oc*, 12–13 (1962–3), 95–101

Switten, Margaret, *The Cansos of Raimon de Miraval: a Study of the Poems and Melodies* (Cambridge, MA, 1985)

'De la sextine: amour et musique chez Arnaut Daniel', in *Mélanges Pierre Bec* (Poitiers, 1991), pp. 549–65

Music and Poetry in the Middle Ages: a Guide to Research on French and Occitan Song, 1100–1400 (New York and London, 1995)

'Music and words: methodologies and sample analyses', in Samuel Rosenberg *et al.*, eds., *Songs of the Troubadours*, pp. 14–28

Tabacco, Giovanni, 'La storia politica e sociale: dal tramonto dell'Imperio alle prime formazione di stati regionali', in *Storia d'Italia, II: dalla caduta dell'Imperio romano al secolo XVIII* (Turin, 1974), pp. 5–274

Tanturli, G., 'Guido Cavalcanti contro Dante', in *Le tradizioni del testo: studi di letteratura italiana offerti a Domenico De Robertis* (Milan and Naples, 1993), pp. 3–13

Tavera, Antoine, 'Le Chansonnier d'Urfé et les problèmes qu'il pose', *Cultura Neolatina*, 38 (1978), 233–50

Thiolier-Méjean, Suzanne, *Les Poésies satiriques et morales des troubadours* (Paris, 1978)

La Poétique des troubadours: trois études sur le sirventes (Paris, 1994)

Topsfield, Leslie T., *Troubadours and Love* (Cambridge, 1975)

Treitler, Leo, 'Medieval lyric', in *Models of Musical Analysis: Music Before 1600*, ed. Mark Everist (Oxford, 1992), pp. 1–19

Troubadours, Clemencic Consort, directed by Reñé Clemencic, LP, *harmonia mundi*, HM 396–8 (1977)

Ugolini, Francesco, *La poesia provenzale e l'Italia*, 2nd edition (Modena, 1949)

Utley, F. L., 'Must we abandon the concept of courtly love?', *Medievalia et Humanistica*, N.S. 3 (1972), 299–324

Van Vleck, Amelia E., *Memory and Re-Creation in Troubadour Lyric* (Berkeley, 1991)

Vatteroni, Sergio, 'Peire Cardenal e l'*estribot* nella poesia provenzale', *Medioevo Romanzo*, 15 (1990), 61–91

Viscardi, Antonio, 'I trovatori italiani', in *La letteratura: storia e testi, I: le origini: testi latini, italiani, provenzali e franco-italiani* (Milan, 1956), pp. 985–1043

Vitz, Evelyn B., 'Chrétien de Troyes: clerc ou ménestrel? Problèmes des traditions orales et littéraires dans les cours de France au XIIe siècle', *Poétique*, 81 (1990), 21–42

Wakefield, Walter L., *Heresy, Crusade and Inquisition in Southern France, 1100–1250* (London and Berkeley, 1974)

Werf, Hendrick van der, *The Chansons of the Troubadours and Trouvères: a Study of the Melodies and of their Relation to the Poems* (Utrecht, 1972)

The Extant Troubadour Melodies: Transcriptions and Essays for Performers and Scholars, with Gerald A. Bond, text editor (Rochester, NY, 1984)

'The "not-so-precisely measured" music of the Middle Ages', *Performance Practice Review*, 1 (1988), 42–60

'Music', in Akehurst and Davis, eds., *Handbook of the Troubadours*, pp. 121–64

Wettstein, J., *'Mezura': L'idéal des troubadours: son essence et ses aspects* (Zurich, 1945)

Wieruszowski, Helene, 'La corte di Pietro d'Aragona e i precedenti dell'impresa siciliani', in *Politics and Culture in Medieval Spain and Italy* (Rome, 1971), pp. 185–221

Wilhelm, James J., *Seven Troubadours: the Creators of Modern Verse* (University Park and London, 1970)

Wind, Bartina, 'Ce jeu subtil, l'Amour courtois', in *Mélanges offerts à Rita Lejeune*, 2 vols. (Gembloux, 1964), I, pp. 1257–61

Witthoeft, Friedrich, *Sirventes Joglaresc: ein Blick auf das altfranzösiche Spielmannsleben* (Marburg, 1891)

Worcester, David, *The Art of Satire* (Cambridge, MA, 1940)

Ziltener, Werner, 'Ai Deus! Car no sui ironda?', in *Studia Occitanica in memoriam Paul Rémy*, ed. Hans-Erich Keller, 2 vols. (Kalamazoo, 1986), I, pp. 363–71

Žižek, Slavoj, *Looking Awry: an Introduction to Jacques Lacan through Popular Culture* (Cambridge, MA, 1991)

    Enjoy Your Symptom! Jacques Lacan in Hollywood and out (New York and London, 1992)

    'Courtly love, or, Woman as Thing', in *The Metastases of Enjoyment: Six Essays on Women and Causality* (London, 1994), pp. 89–112

Zufferey, François, 'Un document relatif à Uc de Saint-Circ à la Bibliothèque Capitulaire de Trévise', *Cultura Neolatina*, 34 (1974), 9–14

    Bibliographie des poètes provençaux des XIVe et XVe siècles (Geneva, 1981)

    Recherches linguistiques sur les chansonniers provençaux (Geneva, 1987)

    'Toward a delimitation of the trobairitz corpus', in Paden, ed., *Voice of the Trobairitz*, pp. 31–43

Zumthor, Paul, *Langue et techniques poétiques à l'époque romane* (Paris, 1963)

    Essai de poétique médiévale (Paris, 1972)

    Parler du moyen âge (Paris, 1980)

    La Poésie et la voix: de la littérature médiévale (Paris, 1987)

Index

NON-LYRIC POEMS, AND OTHER VERNACULAR WRITERS AND TEXTS

CHANSONNIERS

Married Women
Who Love Women

Second Edition

Carren Strock

Routledge
Taylor & Francis Group
New York   London

Routledge
Taylor & Francis Group
270 Madison Avenue
New York, NY 10016

Routledge
Taylor & Francis Group
2 Park Square
Milton Park, Abingdon
Oxon OX14 4RN

Printed in the United States of America on acid-free paper
10 9 8 7 6 5 4 3 2 1

International Standard Book Number-13: 978-1-56023-791-4 (Softcover) 978-1-56023-790-7 (Hardcover)

Library of Congress Cataloging-in-Publication Data

Strock, Carren.
   Married women who love women / Carren Strock. – 2nd ed.
     p. cm.
   Includes bibliographical references.
   ISBN-13: 978-1-56023-791-4 (soft 13 : alk. paper)
   1. Lesbians. 2. married women. 3. Wives. I. Title.

HQ75.5.S77 2008
306.76'5082--dc22
                                      2007046354

Visit the Taylor & Francis Web site at
http://www.taylorandfrancis.com

and the Routledge Web site at
http://www.routledge.com

Dedication

This book is dedicated to
Noel,
Ian and Kit,
Laurie and Joel,
for their unconditional love and acceptance,
and to
Braden Robert and Bailey Rebecca,
who make my heart sing.

Epigraph

Whether women who love women are born or
choose to be is not the issue. It is that we are.
—Joanne Luellen

Poem

THE LIGHT
Jeanne Ferg
July 13, 1940–February 11, 1990
  in the plainness
  of her words
  i hear the echo
  of women calling out
  in their darkness
  listening for answers
  to questions never voiced
  touched by feelings
  newly felt
  and i laugh in recognition
  within myself, ah yes!
  the secret place
  where i once lived alone
  without answers
  and only loud questions …

Contents

Preface

I never imagined the first edition of *Married Women Who Love Women* would touch so many lives so deeply. Since its initial publication, I have received numerous letters from women with long-unanswered questions and from women struggling with feelings of guilt, shame, and isolation.

Many have shared their own poignant stories. One woman, sobbing and clutching my book, approached me at a reading: "I came to thank you. I thought I was the only married woman ever to have fallen in love with another woman," she said, pausing often to regain her composure. Finally she told me, "I was so terrified, I decided to kill myself. Then I found your book, and it saved my life."

I have also received mail from single lesbians thanking me for helping them gain a better understanding of the women they love; from straight women thanking me for helping them to better understand what their sisters, daughters, mothers, or friends are going through; and from husbands, also searching for answers and understanding.

My original purpose in writing *Married Women Who Love Women* was to let other women going through their own discoveries know they were not alone and to help families and friends to understand them and to be less judgmental. Judging from some of my many e-mails such as, "I felt like you were reading my mind, and feeling my heart. ... I smiled, cried, and chuckled through all of your book. ... I felt it was 'my' book. ... I felt a part of every woman in there," and "I inhaled your book and painted it with a yellow highlighter as I read, related, and absorbed every last word," and "I still love my emerging-lesbian wife and am struggling to find a graceful way to let our relationship evolve into a friendship that will last longer than any union or marriage," I know that I have succeeded.

For more information, or to contact me, please access my Web site at www.carrenstrock.com.

Acknowledgments

I would be remiss in not thanking, once again, those who helped the first edition of *Married Women Who Love Women* to be birthed because, without them, there would have been no second edition. I wish to thank the courageous women who entrusted me with their secrets—speaking to you was an enriching experience. And the women who called but were too frightened to follow through with interviews—your fear and silence kept me focused on the importance of the book. And the husbands and children who came forward—I applaud you for your openness and honesty and for choosing paths of understanding and acceptance rather than rejection and anger.

Thank you to Hannelore Hahn and Elizabeth Julia for the International Women's Writing Guild (www.iwwg.org) and my guild sisters, who believed in me and encouraged me to keep on when I faltered, and especially to Liz Alshire, guild member and teacher, who taught me the "nuts and bolts" of writing a book; to reference librarian Susan Levy of the Grand Army Plaza branch of the Brooklyn Public Library for being so accommodating; to the Greater New York Mensa Writers' SIG, especially Ed Pell, Bruce Kent, and Ian Randal Strock—your critiques forged the direction that *Married Women Who Love Women* would take; to the Second Thursday Networking Group and to Doris, who understood the importance of this book and insisted that I spend my time writing it rather than working on her committee; to my cronies from Stoney and to Connie Kurtz and Ruth Berman for showing me how to "make my own kind of music."

Special thanks to Toni, who started me on my journey; to Becca Ritchie, who encouraged me from the beginning—and offered clear-headed advice as well; to Rita Montana, who was never too busy to listen when I needed to vent; to Henny Weiss, whose spelling abilities I availed myself of when my children were unavailable; to CeCe, a stranger who opened her home to me so that women in her area could tell me their stories; and to the numerous other women who touched my life along the way.

In addition to being blessed with special friends, I am blessed with a special family. I thank them all; my dad, Robert Wagner, who taught me, "If you have a mouth to ask directions, you'll never be lost"; my mom, Bobbe Wagner, whose voice I'd hear saying, "It doesn't pay to be lazy," whenever I looked for shortcuts or wanted to procrastinate; my brother Sam, for his tremendous praise after reading my synopsis and for say-ing, before he had, "It doesn't make any difference; you're my sister and I love you"; and my sister Melody, who said, "I'm only sorry I didn't know sooner so I could have been there for you when you were going through the pain."

My very special thanks and love go to my son, Ian, whose invaluable critiques, editorial expertise, and spelling prowess moved my early drafts along; my daughter, Laurie, who transcribed hours of tapes and served as my grammar consultant and number two spell-checker; and my husband, Noel, who said, "I'm not comfortable with this book, but I know how strongly you feel about it, so I'd never ask you not to do it."

Special thanks to Carol Mann, my agent, and to Betsy Lerner, my editor at Doubleday. The first edition would not have been possible without all of you.

Special thanks to the Author's Guild and Anita Fore, Esq., who understood the importance of the second edition, and special thanks to Kathy Rutz, who made it a reality.

Writing the second edition of *Married Women Who Love Women* has enabled me to meet more unique women: wonderful, caring, honest, and sincere. Thank you to the single lovers of married women who came forward with their stories to give the second edition an important added dimension. Thank you to all of the women for putting words to your dis-coveries and for sharing them with me; I applaud your bravery. I also applaud the courage of those of you who were willing to trade society's approval for the chance to lead authentic lives in redefined marriages or with new beginnings. Every day, I continue to feel humbled as I learn from you.

I remain indebted to Jeanne Ferg, my friend the poet. Her favorite expression, "Use it and defuse it," was in part responsible for the birth of the first edition. Jeanne also said, "The more you talk about this subject, the less frightening it will become." She was right.

My gratitude and love for my incredible family and friends, who continue to give me their unconditional love and support, knows no limits. Every day, I feel blessed to have you in my life.

New Introduction

In 1990, after 25 years of marriage, I discovered my own same-gender sexuality. Desperate to understand more about this strange new world I'd entered, but afraid to come out, I decided to write a book. Gathering information to write *Married Women Who Love Women* would lend credibility to my interest without revealing my own secret. Over dinner with a writer friend, I timidly broached the idea. "I don't think there would be much of an audience for a book like that," she said. "I don't know anyone in that situation."

Shortly after I returned home that evening, the phone rang. "Carren, write that book," my friend said. I asked what had happened to make her change her mind. "When I got home, my husband was on the telephone. A family friend had just called to tell us that his wife had left him for another woman!"

Much has changed since I made my own discovery and embarked on my research for *Married Women Who Love Women* in 1993. Locating women to interview for the second edition a decade and a half later has been considerably less complicated thanks to the Internet, which has become a standard fixture in most households and libraries. Originally, many of the women who came forth to share their stories were in their mid-thirties to their mid-fifties. Now, I'm hearing from more women in their sixties and women in their early twenties as well.

For some of these women, like those I interviewed for the first edition, the new discovery came after marriage and the start of families. Like those in the earlier group, some knew about their leanings but believed that marriage and motherhood would blunt their feelings for women. One young wife and mother said, "I wanted to be one of those women who could put away her feelings and continue with my normal life with this wonderful man, but in the end, I couldn't."

Today—although women are still making similar discoveries—thanks to the media, few can say they have never heard the word *lesbian*. According to a study being done by David Wyatt, between the years of 1961 and 1970, one gay character was documented on a television show. From 1991 to 2000, gay characters numbered 306.

In 2006, Cybill Shepherd joined the cast of *L Word*, Showtime's drama about a circle of gay women friends and lovers who move in the trendiest of Los Angeles circles. She played the president of a college and a married woman with two grown children who begins questioning her sexuality.[1] *Brokeback Mountain*, a movie about two married men in love with each other, made all kinds of headlines in 2006. The term *brokeback marriage*— a marriage of mixed orientation in which one partner is straight and the other bisexual or gay—was coined from this movie.[2]

When New Jersey's Governor Jim McGreevey, a married man, came out publicly in 2004, the *Oprah Winfrey Show* immediately produced a segment devoted to this topic. But it was a biased program: All of their guests were people who had left marriages once they came out. This gave only a part of the picture. In an age when lesbians and gay men can live openly in some parts of the country, one might think that brokeback marriages would begin to disappear, but that is not happening. Many individuals still want to preserve the facades, and in some cases, the actual workings of the domestic lives they had in their heterosexual marriages before making their discoveries. They are redefining their marriages or changing their family structures to make them work.

In the early 1990s, most books about lesbians, or on the subject of lesbianism, were published by small presses. For the general public, chances of buying a book from one of the large chain bookstores in which a lesbian was realistically portrayed were slim. Except for the books of Rita Mae Brown, Lisa Alther's *Other Women*, Margret Erhart's *Unusual Company*, and biographies about celebrated women who loved women (such as Vita Sackville-West, Virginia Woolf, Margaret Mead, and Eleanor Roosevelt), there was little chance of finding books with lesbian content. The few that were available were relegated to women's New Age and independent book stores. These small, independently owned shops also served as information centers. Their bulletin boards brimmed with women-related happenings and available resources for women in transition. As the major chain stores realized how lucrative the gay market was and made gay theme books more available, many of the small establishments could not make enough money to remain open.

Unfortunately, once these chains cornered the market, fewer gay and lesbian backlist books could be found on their shelves. Now, however, online book stores can offer far more titles, and these books are becoming available once again.

The ways in which we communicate have changed even more drastically than the ways we shop. In the early 1990s, women—worried about making phone calls their spouses might question—used pay phones instead of their home phones. Then, phone cards and disposable cell phones took the place of those public phones. While these are still readily available, e-mail is becoming the primary source of communication for many women.

Before the Internet, few national publications could be found that listed resources for people discovering, or coming to terms with, their same-gender identities. To find support groups, I searched through telephone directories looking for anything that began with the word "women." I also turned to professional associations such as the Women's Health Care Services and the National Organization for Women in my search for support groups. Now, thanks to everyone's easy access to the Internet, you only have to search for "married lesbians" and you can find thousands of sites. If you broaden your search by using just the word "lesbians," the number goes into the millions. Although many are porn sites, you will find numerous online support groups, counselors and counseling services, legal advice, personal sites, and chat rooms. There are sites for married women who love women (MWLW), single lovers of married women, men married to lesbians, and wives of gay men, to name a few. But be aware. Not all sites that call themselves "support sites" are. Some are conduits of negative energy.

I remember how difficult it was when I told that first woman about myself. Intellectually, I knew she was a lesbian, but my knowing that did not make my personal revelation any less emotional or painful for me. We, as a society, have come a long way since then. Talk of gay rights is now splashed all over the media. Literature is available. Television actors are out as gays and lesbians or are portraying gay and lesbian characters. (When asked how she did her research for the part of a middle-aged woman discovering her lesbianism, Laura Innes, who played Dr. Kerry Weaver on *ER*, said, "I read a book called *Married Women Who Love Women*.")[3] Gay and lesbian issues are no longer whispered about or giggled over but are front and center in the national news and national debates.

Still, life is a continuum of change, and not everyone is aware of their true sexuality early on. As one reader said, "I greatly appreciate your book because it gives support to the idea that we don't necessarily have our orientation all figured out by a certain age and that we could still be surprised." Many women making their discoveries today, regardless of the media exposure in the last few years, continue to be fearful. The stakes are high, as an admission of homosexuality—when one is married and especially when children are involved—can, and frequently does, change a comfortable and secure world.

The e-mails I receive from women currently reading my book, or finding my Web site, www.carrenstrock.com, are as poignant as those I received in the 1990s, their cries for help and understanding as loud. Women write things like, "I find myself drawn back to your book again and again. If it wasn't for it, I'd be a lost soul." "I find your book to be a place of safety." "I just finished *Married Women Who Love Women*. I couldn't turn the pages fast enough. It eased my panic faster than even Xanax could. It was a clear connection over the white noise in my head."

I have also received mail from women who had no idea about their own sexuality until hearing me speak. One woman said, "My coworkers and friends see me as well-balanced, joyful, loving, and with inner peace. But I've noticed that, although I wanted a happy marriage and children, I never felt attracted to men as other women were. Seeing you those few brief moments on the *Sally Jessy Raphael Show*, I went through a multitude of emotions. I realized that what you were saying applied to me, and everything became clear. I want the connection—the closeness—I can have only with a woman. I can't explain it any better than this. I just feel it inside of me."

It isn't only women in the United States who are making their voices heard. Women from Australia, Brazil, Colombia, England, Germany, Hong Kong, Indonesia, Ireland, Israel, Mongolia, New Zealand, the Philippines, Slovakia, South Africa, and Switzerland have e-mailed me as well.

The Internet has also become an invaluable aid for researchers and writers like myself. To gather respondents for my research while working on the first edition of *Married Women Who Love Women*, I left fliers in women's clubs, university women's centers, and theater and restaurant restrooms. I left them in bookstores and libraries and even put them on supermarket bulletin boards. And, I put notices in the few newspapers I could find that had lesbian content. I came to learn that women were helping to spread the word by photocopying my fliers and sending them to friends around the country. This time around, for the second edition, I e-mailed my request for subjects to a few women's groups with which I was familiar. Women again stepped in to help, but instead of making photocopies and snail-mailing, they now e-mailed my requests to other group lists and to friends both nationally and internationally. Within a day or two, many women were responding.

When I originally wrote *Married Women Who Love Women*, I focused primarily on the women who were in marriages and how they dealt with husbands and children and coped with double lives, but there was another very important part of the picture that I had inadvertently left out—the single lovers of married women. By the time I realized this, it was too late to add that chapter. I was not the only one to catch my omission. Many readers called this to my attention, and I realized that I could not ignore them while trying to grapple with this complex issue from multiple perspectives. Still, I was surprised at the large response I got when I put out a call looking for these women to interview for the second edition. Thanks to their generosity, both in time and in the information they willingly shared, this edition rectifies that omission with its chapter, "The Single Lovers of Married Women."

While the entire book has been updated, another completely new addition is the chapter "Redefined Marriages." There were only a few women I interviewed for the original edition who told me of harmonious relationships between their husbands and girlfriends. One woman had been contemplating divorce until her husband became ill. She stayed in her marriage to tend to him, and he, knowing her feelings for her woman friend, suggested that she invite her lover to move in and join their family. Another woman talked about how she and her husband decided to lead separate lives but live together to co-parent their children. Since finances were tight, he built a separate living area in the basement. Today, those families would not be unique. People no longer need excuses to create the unusual living arrangements that work for them.

The society in which we grow up plays a major role in our socialization. From infancy, messages received, overtly or subliminally, have told us that heterosexual sex and marriage are normal, and everything else is not. And, rightly or wrongly, until recently, when the issue of same-sex marriages came to the political forefront, that socialization has been toward heterosexual union, although a great percentage of heterosexual marriages end in divorce.

While we tend to think of our culture as a monogamous one, in which people have relationships with only one person, other alternatives—such as group marriages and plural marriages—also exist. Free love, prevalent with the flower children of the 1960s and 1970s, led to the term *polyamory* in the 1980s.

Some married women, lesbians and bisexuals, have been creating various types of polyamorous relationships to meet their needs and those of their families. In some, married women share their houses with their spouses and their lovers. While the husbands are a vital part of the group, only the women share physical intimacy. In other cases, physical affection is shared by all three. The 2006 television hit *Big Love* is an example of a polygamous relationship that includes one husband and three wives. Although the female characters have not shown a sexual attraction to one another, they have a strong commitment to each other and to making their unusual marriage work.

While certain rules in our society are necessary for the safety and protection of each individual, as our world continues to evolve, perhaps we may one day reach a point at which we no longer feel the need to judge and are no longer hurt by the judgment of others.

Original Introduction

My weight plummeted, and my clothes hung sloppily over my body. I could not have cared less, but at the insistence of my family I found myself at Macy's. I had been instructed to buy some things that fit. Indifferently I pulled a blouse over my head. Suddenly I found myself sliding to the floor of the dressing room, choking back loud, anguished sobs. I sat with my back hunched over and my knees drawn to my chin, rocking back and forth, trying to muffle the cries I could not control.

These involuntary outbursts were coming more frequently. I had to find help. I had to find someone to tell. Where could I turn? Whom could I trust with this horrible secret?

In the space of six months my mind had become completely disordered. My value system had failed me. Suddenly I, who had been so sure about everything, knew nothing.

I had fallen in love with another woman!

My sister used to call me Pollyanna. I lived in a secure world protected by an invisible white picket fence. Mine was the "perfect" family.

My husband and I were married in 1964 after we had dated for three years. I was nineteen and he was twenty-one. We felt certain enough of our maturity to take on the responsibilities of raising a family. Our babies came as we had planned. Two and a half years after our wedding, our son arrived, and then two years after him, our daughter. We moved to our house in the suburbs.

Our door was open, and friends and neighbors dropped in all the time. I was great at stretching meals to accommodate unexpected guests. I was the one called when last-minute brownies were needed for the Girl Scout sale or when a chairperson was needed for a charity drive. While my kids were growing up, I was active in the parent-teacher association, the Junior Women's Club, and Hadassah.

I was so preoccupied with my husband and children and their needs that I was oblivious to my own, or to what was happening in the larger world. Eventually, my children grew up, and my husband and I moved to the city.

And then I met Toby.

With my new friend came the beginnings of my awareness of women's liberation. Toby had been divorced and raised two sons while putting herself through college and graduate school. She was a published author working on her second novel while supporting herself and her family. I was impressed by her accomplishments. I had always taken my own talents for granted, thinking that if I could paint and do craftwork, so could everyone else. But Toby was impressed with my abilities; she called me "the Renaissance woman."

We became fast friends, and soon I couldn't imagine Toby not being a part of my life. We might phone each other five times a day to share some silly story or go for a week without talking. It didn't matter; each of us knew we were there for the other. We shared long walks and heavy conversations about intimate parts of our lives. We felt free in each other's kitchens and comfortable with each other's families.

One evening, while we were sitting and talking, I found myself looking, really looking, at Toby. She smiled at me from across the room, and a strange and powerful feeling rushed through my body. My heart began to race. I realized I was in love with my best friend.

I didn't say anything at first, but my feelings grew daily. Each time I saw her, my stomach fluttered. Just being in her company, colors became brighter, sounds clearer. I had never felt like that before.

Toby and I had always hugged each other hello and good-bye, but now these hugs took on new meaning. I couldn't wait to see her, and then I couldn't wait for her to leave for those brief moments when we would be in each other's arms.

Our friendship had always been based on honesty, and now, given the intensity of my new feelings, I felt compelled to share them with her. It felt so natural and so wonderful to love her as I did that it had to be all right. We arranged to meet for dinner, and I picked her up at the station. Toby chatted animatedly about her week as we drove toward the shore. Her voice was comforting, and it felt so good to be with her. Still, the pounding in my chest was growing louder. I swallowed several times and took a deep breath. Without taking my eyes from the road, I said, "Toby, I'm in love with you."

"I love you, too, Carren," she said.

"No. You don't understand. I've fallen in love with you."

An uncomfortably long pause replaced Toby's laughter of minutes before. "Carren, you're in love with the idea of sisterhood, of feminism, I've opened your eyes to—"

"Toby," I cut her off. "I'm in love with you."

We drove on to the bay in silence and parked the car. I turned toward the dock where we usually walked before eating.

"I'd rather go right to the restaurant," she said. "I'm cold." The weather was mild and her coat was open, so I knew it was a different kind of cold she was feeling. Suddenly, I was terrified. What had I done? I was filled with turmoil. What if my confession made her mad, or she thought I was sick and never wanted to speak to me again? Could my being in love with Toby destroy our friendship? Then I thought, no. That's absurd. We'll work it out. I ordered wine with my dinner, something I rarely did, then left my meal untouched, another thing I rarely did. I felt an awkwardness growing between us. I had never seen Toby at a loss for words, yet now she seemed to consider each one carefully before it left her mouth. Why had I been so insensitive? How could I have been such a fool? Why had I never anticipated her rejecting me?

Maybe it was the wine, I'm not sure, but by the end of dinner our customary way of bantering seemed to have returned. I drove her home, put the car in park, and we hugged as usual. After a brief second, however, I pulled away, suddenly shy.

For a while, we continued to speak several times a week. Only now I found myself fumbling over words and having trouble keeping my voice steady. Toby was guarded and spoke only in generalities. Each time I lifted the receiver to call her, my hands trembled and I began to hyperventilate. Our conversations lost their fun and spontaneity. Their main theme became my obsession with her. I could talk of little else. Out of fairness to Toby, I must say that she did try to remain my friend. She listened kindly, but over the following months the frequency of her phone calls dwindled until she stopped calling altogether. She didn't feel toward me as I did toward her, and she had had enough of the crazed woman I had become. Our friendship ended.

At home, with great difficulty I functioned as though nothing had happened. After all, I was the nurturer and the caregiver—others depended on me. I had to be strong. If my husband or children saw any changes in my behavior, they never acknowledged them. Privately, in great pain, I mourned the loss of my best friend. There was no one to offer comfort, no one with whom to share my sorrow. I lay awake night after night, replaying all that had happened, thinking of Toby. I began walking for hours at a time, needing to force myself into exhausted sleep.

I remember Toby asking me during one of our last visits if it was sex with her that I wanted. I had been shocked at her question. I realize now that I had no frame of reference for such an idea. I'd never thought of having sex with her, only about being with her, holding her, having her hold me. Sex was something I had with my husband. It had nothing to do with this passion I was feeling for her.

While I mourned, the question she had put into my head kept repeating itself. Was it sex with her that I wanted? Did I want to have sex with a woman? Did that make me a lesbian? I could hardly even say the word at first, but the more I thought about it, the less absurd it seemed. I began to wonder. Although my husband was always considerate about satisfying me, I had never had a strong sex drive with him.

Now I had to contend not only with the loss of my best friend, but the shock of discovering my possible new sexuality. I searched but found no reading material, no affirmation that I wasn't insane or that other women had had the same experience; the more alone I felt, the more terrified I became.

Eventually, without telling my family, secretly skimming money off the food budget to pay for it, I went into therapy. I had no idea of how it could help me, but I knew that I desperately needed to find someone I could talk to. I would not understand for several years that I had been going through a process of discovery. It is only now, looking back, that I can appreciate the strength it took as well as the courage to move forward, accept myself, and, eventually, come out to my family. Along the way I have also come to learn that my story is not unique.

Through the self-help groups I sought out during my transition period, I met numerous other married women who had also discovered their previously hidden sexuality, or were trying to come to terms with long-denied feelings of being different. They were trying to make sense of their lives, to preserve their marriages and families and, in some cases, their very sanity. Finally, I had connected with women who were like me. We talked on and on until everything began to make sense.

According to *The Hite Report*, 87% of all married women have their deepest emotional attachments with other women, usually their best friends.[1] While it doesn't happen to every woman, sometimes these friendships unexpectedly burst into passionate romantic and physical love.

Due to the clandestine way in which MWLW often live, few people have been aware that we even exist. Consequently, it is understandable that researchers might conclude that these women tend to divorce immediately on learning about their sexuality.[2] And who would contradict them? None-theless, I knew that not all MWLW leave their marriages, and I set out to explore all the ways in which women who love women lead their lives.

Having accepted their culturally sanctioned roles as caregivers and nurturers, some women believe they have no choice other than to remain in their marriages and keep their feelings and needs repressed. Fear of repercussions—having their children taken from them, being shunned by family and friends, even becoming destitute—makes other women decide to stay married. All these women silently endure the guilt and anguish brought on by the frightening discovery of their new sexuality. At the same time, many have affairs outside marriage to discover who they are and what they crave. For the first time in their lives, they do what they need to do for themselves.

Married Women Who Love Women is the result of open and truthful dialogues with more than one hundred women who had the courage to acknowledge their same-sex preferences. It addresses issues that have never been freely discussed before: Why do women turn to other women for emotional fulfillment? What would make a married woman cross that invisible line that turns her best friend into her lover? Why do some women struggle with identity while others easily embrace their sexuality? What do married women do when they realize that a large part of themselves has been missing? Why might they choose to remain in a marriage after hav-ing discovered their sexual preference? What kind of men are they mar-ried to? Why would men remain with wives who love women? How are these women and their husbands redefining their marriages to make them work? How are children, parents, and friends affected? What about the single lovers of married women? Do relationships ever include more than two? And finally, where do straight women fit into the picture?

It also answers intimate questions that have crossed the minds of all women, although few have had the courage to say so. What is it like for a woman who has believed herself heterosexual to come together physically with a woman for the first time? How is making love with a woman differ-ent from making love with a man? How does a woman know whether she is a lesbian or bisexual? What are the distinctions, and why do they matter?

I have compiled my evidence from the courageous women who have stepped forward to speak with me. Their stories present an eye-opening picture of a growing population that has been silent too long.

In my search, I found MWLW at women's groups and gathering places. Sharing my story made others comfortable enough to share their own. Con-sequently, while many women had never told even their therapists about their sexual preference, for me, finding MWLW to interview was relatively easy. The women I spoke to referred me to their friends. Others identified friends but, because of the sensitivity of the subject matter, were hesitant to give me their phone numbers. I gave them fliers to pass along instead.

Although the fliers specifically requested married women for the book, divorced women—who had discovered their lesbianism either before or after their divorces—also came forward to share their stories. In addition, I placed ads in lesbian publications and in newsletters that served lesbian communities. And, knowing that not all MWLW have access to those papers or are even aware of their existence, I placed an ad in *National NOW*, the newspaper of the National Organization for Women. In the *NOW* ad I revealed my same-sex feelings. This brought a response from women who lived in rural areas and had felt especially cut off.

I mailed fliers to feminist bookstores across the country and to women's centers at colleges and universities. I posted fliers on supermarket bulletin boards and left them in the ladies' rooms of restaurants and theaters.

I have received calls from women who said they had picked up my fliers in places I was unfamiliar with, and I later learned that other women had taken it upon themselves to make additional copies and further circulate the fliers.

Women told me things they said they had never been able to tell anyone else before. They expressed relief at being able to share their feelings openly and honestly. Long-pent up frustrations spilled out along with angry or sad feelings about their husbands, marriages, families, and lives in general. At times it was difficult for me to hear about their pain and isolation without reliving my own. Many of the women I interviewed thanked me, saying that for the first time, they didn't feel alone. One woman echoed the feelings of many when she said, "Your ad jumped off the page for me. Until now no one had seemed to care about married women who must live with their secret."

Through the course of my research, which grew to include husbands and children of MWLW and their single lovers as well, the majority of people, both men and women, responded to the subject matter with a mixture of relief and gratitude.

The MWLW interviewed ranged in age from twenty-one to seventy. Thirty percent were thirty-five or younger, 60% were between the ages of thirty-six and fifty-five, and 10% were over fifty-five.

Because the subject of lesbianism is no longer taboo as it once was and the average age at which women marry had risen from 20.3 in 1950 to 24 by 1990,[3] younger women in general are growing up with an increased awareness and, having more time to explore, a better understanding of their own sexuality and available life choices. Yet some young women, aware of their preference for women, still elect to marry men. Their reasons may be as basic as medical coverage for spouses or fear of rejection by family and friends since societal pressures still restrict many young women, especially those outside of urban areas.

The majority of women interviewed initially in the early 1990s were between their mid-thirties and their mid-fifties when their same-sex feelings became apparent. For the most part, middle-aged women grew up knowing that they were "supposed to" marry a nice man who would be a good provider and a good father. The unspoken message was: "A woman cannot take care of herself." Furthermore, sex outside marriage was considered taboo, and so, nice girls married. The single career woman was still an anomaly.

Only 23% of the MWLW interviewed knew or had a feeling about their same-sex orientation before they were married. Twelve percent realized in hindsight that they had same-sex orientation, and 6% couldn't recall exactly when they made the discovery. However, the majority, 59%, had no idea of their same-sex orientation before they were married.

Married women discovering or reawakening their dormant sexual awareness generally fall into four categories. The first consists of women who, as young girls, sensed a difference between themselves and their peers but didn't have the words to describe their differences. They had no knowledge that there was any such thing as lesbianism. The second consists of women who knew positively, early in life, that they had lesbian tendencies. However, because they had been indoctrinated by society's teachings into believing that lesbianism was a sickness or evil, or because they simply wanted to fit into mainstream society, they tried to conform. The third is women who knew what lesbianism was, did not deny their feelings, and had even been involved with other women, but thought they were different. They were in such strong states of denial that they never characterized themselves as lesbians. And the fourth consists of women who totally believed they were heterosexual ... until they fell in love with another woman.

Apparently, not all married women are happy. According to Carol Botwin's book, *Tempted Women*, "twenty-one million women in America—40 percent of the married population—are having affairs."[4] Other books such as *The Erotic Silence of the American Wife* by Dalma Heyn,[5] and *Secret Loves* by Sonya Friedman,[6] also discuss the extramarital affairs women have, though all three mainly focus on heterosexual affairs, thereby missing a very large slice of the issue.

This book fills that gap. And in so doing, I hope, sheds both light and understanding for MWLW, their married or single lovers, and their families and friends.

PART **ONE**
The Discovery

CHAPTER 1

Awakening

Until I was forty-three, I would have said with absolute certainty, "I am not, nor could I ever become, a lesbian. I know exactly who and what I am."

One year later I fell in love with another woman. I was to experience more passion, pain, isolation, and turmoil than I had ever thought possible. Through it all, my life was to become clearer and brighter ... and I was to grow wiser from my experience.

Although I felt totally alone at the time, I am not the only woman who has stumbled onto the path of sexual discovery and growth. My experience is not uncommon. Some women make a sudden discovery as I did. For others, it is a compilation of occurrences and a slow realization and awakening. This new awareness, brought on by the gradual synthesis of ongoing incidents and old recollections, can change an entire life.

Is there any woman, heterosexual or homosexual, who can truly say that she cannot remember having been especially fond of a particular woman in her life, maybe a teacher she admired, a girlhood friend, a special family friend? Women who knew or sensed that their sexual preference leaned toward women easily recalled crushes on schoolmates and female teachers. For me, it wasn't so simple.

When I finally had the courage to talk about my same-sex feelings, most women asked if I had ever suspected or had an inkling that I was attracted to other women. Some simply wanted to satisfy their curiosity; others wanted to reinforce in their own minds that they were not like me and they were, therefore, safe from any possibility of ever becoming lesbians.

Sometimes the questions felt like accusations. "How could you not have known?" And I felt forced to deny any knowledge, as if there must be blame, and I am not to blame. I would answer, "No. Definitely not. Not me. I never felt attracted to another woman." What I was saying was: I'm innocent. I had no idea. It's not my fault. All of which was true.

It was not that I consciously lied about any feelings I might have had for women. The specific incidents I recalled seemed insignificant and innocent. I remember the older girl in Hebrew school, assigned to be my "buddy" when we went on a class trip: I must have been seven at the time, and I remember thinking that she was beautiful and feeling glad that the teacher had chosen her to team up with me. Then there was my camp counselor when I was nine. She was so pretty that I would rush to the front of the line so she would hold my hand when we took nature walks. But hadn't all of the girls in my group done the same thing?

Did having these feelings as a young girl mean I was destined to walk a different path? Not necessarily. Appreciating beauty in others is natural. Forming attachments to older women, wanting to emulate them, is also a natural process of growing up. Besides, I never went looking for a woman to fall in love with. At first I felt only anger. Why me? I didn't want things to change. I was married, had a husband, a family. I hadn't even known feelings like this existed.

The anger was followed by a period of deep grief. Initially, I thought I was mourning the loss of my best friend because she withdrew from me and our friendship dissolved. The pain of not having her as a part of my life was excruciating. We had shared everything. She had been my confidante. Now she was not there to help me through the most difficult road I had ever traveled. I realized I was also mourning the changes in myself. This newly acquired knowledge about my sexuality could never be forgotten. I would no longer be content, naive, … or innocent.

There was also blame. I had to blame someone. It had to be someone's fault that all of this was happening to me. So I blamed my husband: he should have been more understanding, more perceptive, more supportive. I lost sight of the fact that we had other issues we had never dealt with, issues having nothing to do with my sexuality.

All of this was going on in my head, and he had no idea I was harboring these thoughts. I was living my life on a seesaw. On one side, with family and friends, I felt forced to go on as though nothing had changed. And I was a good actress, keeping everything inside until the last person had left the house in the morning; then I would collapse, sobbing, against the nearest piece of furniture. Or, when the family was home and my feelings became overwhelming, I'd run out on some fictitious errand, get in the car, and bawl. I spent many hours walking. Only when I was with women who knew about me did my vulnerability surface. Someone need only ask, "How are you doing?" and the tears would flow. This went on for more than a year.

Slowly, these steps did lead to acceptance and growth. But these were not clear-cut periods in my life. My feelings vacillated between denial, grief, and anger. Although I visited old friends and extended family, until I began therapy and started connecting with women I could talk to, I felt as though I were living in total isolation.

Shari

Shari, a forty-year-old wife and mother, says, "I'd pulled the van over because I was crying too hard to drive. ... I thought I was crying about my intense physical and emotional feelings for a new friend (who I knew was a lesbian), when 'it' very suddenly hit me—right in the middle of my forehead, like a hammer.

"I was crying about myself, not about my friend and the fact that she was in love with someone else. I became aware that I was absolutely starving in a place I'd never known existed, and starving in a way I'd never known before: the need to be with others of my own kind.

"The next awareness, coming minutes later, was the revelation: 'I'm gay!'

"The sensation that immediately followed was falling backward into a bottomless pit: forever lost to an alien and yet completely known 'other life.' ... I was taking in, all at once, the complete awareness that I was gay and that this was going to totally change the rest of my life.

"I simultaneously felt terror (What does this mean for me and my family?) and the purest euphoria of total relief. For the first time in my life, 'I' filled me from my core to the outer edges of my skin."

Shari is an educated woman, yet she was totally confused at the intensity of her emotional feelings for another woman. The only way she could explain her feelings was by deciding that on an emotional level, she must be bisexual. She wanted that to be the answer.

"That felt like the answer for about a day and a half," Shari says. "But when I pictured myself telling my longtime best friend that I was bisexual, the imaginary conversation was always interrupted by this inner voice that said, 'You're a fuckin' dyke.'

"I replayed this 'conversation' of voices for a couple more days—and on that night, in the van, somehow was able to let the last of whatever was holding me back go ... and now, here all of me is!"

Shari had never questioned her sexuality, although she admits to thinking of herself as "strangely unique." She identified her uniqueness only as "I'm clumsy, clunky, not feminine." But what woman can't identify with having those same feelings at some time in her life?

Today's youth can turn on a television and find a talk show on any kind of sexuality or go to a school counselor or the library to obtain information. Women raised prior to the late 1960s often had limited sex education. Although they may have sensed differences between themselves and their friends, they often had no understanding of these differences.

Most of the women, like Shari, never understood the significance of their feelings. Those who did have questions had no place to go for information. They put their feelings on hold and did what society expected them to do: marry and have children.

Martha

Martha went to an all-girl Catholic high school. She had a large circle of friends and found herself caring about them emotionally … and physically. When she realized that none of her friends seemed to feel the way she did, she began to feel "unusual."

In her senior year Martha and Roxanne became very close. Martha says, "We started hanging out together and going places together. It was incredible. It felt so natural. When we sat together in the movie theater and our elbows touched, it was wonderful.

"All we did was kiss. We were both young and naive. We knew we weren't satisfied with just kissing each other, but we didn't know what else to do. Anything else would have felt dirty. We were extremely Catholic. Roxanne was going into a convent. She was consecrated to God."

The day that Roxanne entered the convent, Martha was there for the ceremony. "I watched my friend walk down the aisle in a white dress and wanted to die. Roxanne went behind a door and came back in her habit." Martha remembers fighting back her tears because she was with Roxanne's family and it wouldn't be right to show how disappointed she was.

Both girls were so inexperienced that they were incapable of understanding their feelings, much less putting them into words. At the time, neither girl knew what a homosexual was. Even after Martha fell in love with Roxanne, she thought they were unique, that what happened to them didn't happen to other girls. Never did she identify herself as a lesbian.

"I remember a joke I heard at sixteen," Martha says. "'Let's be lesbo and go homo.' I laughed because everyone else did, but I had no idea what it meant. If I knew at all, I wasn't sure that it had anything to do with women."

Since all of her friends had married, she realized it was time for her to do the same. She dated halfheartedly, and when the man she had been dating asked her to marry him, she rushed home to call her girlfriends before giving him her answer. "Should I feel a tingling when he touches me or see skyrockets going off when he kisses me?" she asked.

"No," her friends assured her. "That only happens in the movies." How could she tell anyone she had experienced those feelings with her friend Roxanne?

It wasn't until she was in her early forties that Martha realized she was a lesbian. Meanwhile, Roxanne had died in the convent at thirty-three. Martha still grieves for the untried chance at happiness she and Roxanne might have had if they had understood what their feelings were all about.

Rifka

"Since I was four years old, I would identify more with women than with men. ... I had crushes on boys and girls through my adolescence and adulthood, but I knew where I would go. I would get married. I would have babies. At twenty-one, I did.

"My sexuality could be satisfied with my husband because I wanted it to be. But emotionally there was always something missing. There was nobody in my life who could fill that. I had dozens of friends, but that didn't help. When I tried to talk to my husband about my needs, he said, 'Physically I can give you anything, but don't ask for anything emotionally.'"

Rifka was teaching a mental health course at a college and her students came to her and told her how their lives were changing. She says, "I listened to them and at forty, decided it was time to take care of me. Prior to that I was in a consciousness-raising group.

"That had helped me to realize I could make my life not my mother's, my husband's, or my children's, but entirely my own."

Rifka didn't know how she was going to take back her life. "I was not making a conscious decision at forty to become a lesbian," she says. "I was very homophobic, so when I fell in love with Fran, the shit hit the fan. The best and worst time of my life. My internalized homophobia was externalized as well. I'm grateful to Fran because she wasn't homophobic, and her patience as a friend helped me."

Roberta

Roberta, on the other hand, had been sexually abused by her father from the time she was a little girl until he died when she was twenty-three years old, and felt a tremendous distaste for men from early on. She could have left home, but she believed that by being there, she was saving her younger siblings the same fate with their father. Years later, she found out that they were being abused despite her sacrifice.

Whether or not Roberta would have had same-sex tendencies had she not been sexually abused by her father we can't tell, but psychotherapist Arlene DiMarco believes that women who have been incest victims and have had "no bonding with the father, the person they were supposed to be able to trust, would be more apt to try to find a constant with another woman ... women view other women as being kinder and gentler, sensitive and more understanding than men."[1]

Had she been aware that lesbians existed, Roberta would probably have made other life choices early on. Unfortunately, even with the abhorrence she had for men, she knew of no alternative.

Roberta says, "I lived in West Virginia, and all of the women I worked with were always looking for men, so I would go with them on their outings. I wasn't interested but I had to do that. First of all, I couldn't let any of them know about my father ... or that I even knew about sex. So I had to be this totally naive virgin. I pretended I didn't know anything about anything. We went to Myrtle Beach, South Carolina. They would be picking up guys. I remember thinking, 'I don't want to pick up anyone so I'm going to eat onions.' Then this cute guy came over. He was in the army, so he used to hitchhike three hundred miles every other weekend just to see me. I would sort of lead him on, but I wasn't about to have sex with him. I was scared to death to have sex.

"Still, I knew I had to get married. I didn't know what else a woman could or would do.

"Then, at a club, I met a much older man, a traveling salesman. He came over and wanted to dance with me. He started courting me, and eventually I agreed to go to bed with him. I was twenty-five. So that was my first real sexual experience, not counting what happened with my father. I had sex with this man for about a year until I found out he had lied to me. He was married, not divorced as he had told me.

"At twenty-eight I met Jay, my husband-to-be. I actually met four other men before I met him at sort of a pickup place. They were all awful, absolute beasts. My friend was supposed to go with me that night, but she changed her mind. I had said to her, 'I'm going by myself, and if I don't meet a nice man here I'm through with men forever.' And I went and I met those four awful men and I was raped and I thought I was pregnant, so when I met Jay and he was really nice and he seemed different … I felt, 'Jay would be a nice man to marry.'

"When I went into labor, I couldn't give birth. I didn't know if my daughter was Jay's or one of the other men's. It was absolute terror. They had to do a cesarean. But I never told Jay. I carried the secret on my own, like everything. Everything was a secret. In the meantime, I tried to be the best mother and the best wife in the whole world, and I did that for twenty-four years."

Roberta sighed. "When I listen to my life, it sounds so awful.

"Probably about fourteen years ago I started struggling to claim myself. I started going to therapy and women's support groups."

Roberta fell in love with one of the first women she shared her story with. "When it happened I was startled, but that lasted for about five seconds, then I began to remember that I had always been in love with women. I could remember this little girl, Ann; we were in the first grade. I don't remember an erotic aspect to it, but I loved her madly. Then I remember working at the telephone company, and there was a woman working there. I was really in love with her, and I'd have these erotic thoughts, and I'd say to myself, 'Cut that out. You're not supposed to be thinking that. She's a woman.'"

Eleanor

"My husband and I went to his childhood home to celebrate a family event. I met the daughter of my in-laws' friends. I had an immediate attraction to the way she talked, walked, looked, everything, but I didn't acknowledge this to myself. She was married, and yet something seemed different about her. I blurted out, 'Is Darlene a lesbian?' My husband assured me that she wasn't. During the course of the week, I learned that Darlene and my husband had been intimate years before we married. I was hurt that he hadn't told me and went through a whole range of emotions. Then, suddenly, it hit me. I wasn't jealous of her for being with him; I was jealous of my husband for being with Darlene. Suddenly, my whole world didn't make sense any more. How could I be jealous of my husband for sleeping with a woman?

"Later, through e-mails, I found out that Darlene was divorcing her husband because she realized that she was a lesbian. We have been corresponding ever since."

Other women knew positively, early in life, that they had lesbian tendencies. But, because society had told them that to love a person of the same sex was wrong, they feared being ostracized by their families and peers and tried to conform to society's accepted standards. It was very natural for these women to do everything possible to put their feelings to rest. They made themselves "well" through therapy and by choosing the traditional roles of wives in heterosexual marriages.

Helen

Helen, a sixty-four-year-old grandmother, was reunited with Bernice, who had left a convent, four years ago at their fortieth-year college reunion. When the two old friends met, the forty years they had spent apart slid away. The women, then sixty, were immediately drawn back to each other.

"I had plenty of best friends when I was growing up. I was very attracted to one in particular but didn't know I was gay. I just thought I loved her.

"Then I went away to college. The girl I roomed with, Bernice, had seen a picture of me and wrote on it 'wait and see.' I found out I was gay when she started making love to me.

"We were together for two years. Then Bernice went on to become a nun, and I went out to find someone to marry. I was engaged three times before I did that because I just never felt anything."

Why hadn't the two women remained together after college? Helen says, "Bernice wanted to be normal, and I wanted to be normal. We did what we were supposed to do back then. We didn't talk about it. It was make love every night and then just kind of act like nothing was going on. We hated to leave one another, but we felt like in society that was the thing we should do.

"Before Bernice reappeared, every time I'd be attracted to somebody I'd run away from them. It was a part of my life I'd just tried to ignore and hide since I had four children and all these grandchildren. When we got together [after the reunion] we were running back and forth from her city to mine.

"I was going to get a divorce, but with the state laws, I would end up without anything. I wasn't willing to have that happen. I'm too old to do that."

Had Helen and Bernice met in college in the nineties instead of in the fifties, they would have known that more than one lifestyle option existed and might not have chosen to hide their natural sexual inclinations. They made their decisions based on the limited knowledge of their day.

Estelle

"I was always painfully aware that being a lesbian was sick," Estelle says. "During my twenties, I played the part of the single heterosexual woman in every phase. The only place it wasn't true was in my heart and gut. I didn't come out, but when I saw a movie or was in a social situation, I knew where my preference was. It wasn't toward the men on screen, but toward the women. I was very unhappy. After college I went into therapy, both individual and group, for several years. I picked a male father figure as my therapist to make me right. I believed that my therapist was going to cure me of my disease. When I was twenty-eight I met Jim. It was the therapist who encouraged me to see him because he said it sounded like wonderful therapy for me.

"I listened because I had paid him to get rid of my disease. I dated Jim and became infatuated with him. He was one of the first males I met who knew what to do sexually and did satisfy me and that was it for me. I thought that meant I was in love. I was thirty and Jim was thirty-four when we married.

"In the beginning, I felt that I was cured. So for quite a few years I put my lesbianism—which I'd never really experienced—in remission.

"I never had a maternal desire and Jim called the shots. I was just very content to be his wife. To support him, follow him, and let him make every decision. For the first time in my life, I felt normal. I became his slave as repayment.

"The first ten years he satisfied me sexually, but then, as problems crept into our marriage, I realized my husband was not really fulfilling me emotionally in terms of conversation or interaction with problems. I found, in the last few years, that my urges started coming back.

"I began wandering the streets of Greenwich Village, watching people. My parents had died when I was young, and I was used to living on the periphery of life, so wandering the streets and looking at bookstores was not something I found lonely. It was a natural state. I was very curious, seeing how this world lived. I remember wandering into a mixed bar [gay and lesbian] and being absolutely thrilled. I was like a kid being let loose in a candy store." Estelle never took a phone number. "Just talking to gay women was thrilling after so many years of denial."

Estelle was almost fifty before she shared her lifelong secret at a twelve-step program for overeaters. Glenda, also attending the Overeaters Anonymous meeting for her own issue with food, heard Estelle speak.

Glenda

"The things Estelle shared brought flashbacks of my own private sexual torments. For the first time, I was able talk to another woman who had gone through what I had been going through. Finally, I told someone who I really was and what had been plaguing me for years."

Estelle and Glenda connected, becoming friends, and then lovers.

Glenda, like Estelle, thought she was attracted to women when she was a young girl, but she could find no information to help her explain her feelings, so she put them aside, opting for a traditional marriage. She is now in her mid-fifties and has two grown children who are on their own.

"My very best friend was beautiful, and I had a crush on her. My emotional attachment to women was always stronger. I knew, but I was ashamed of it.

"When I was little I remember adults didn't talk to children. But, I would listen, and I would hear them saying things. I heard that it was very normal to have a crush on a teacher or a girlfriend. 'Kids outgrow it.' But I kept thinking about my girlfriend, and I didn't outgrow my feelings.

"As a child, nobody talked about it [lesbianism]. It was an embarrassment. So I looked in all the books I could find. I couldn't even find the word in the dictionary. I didn't know how to spell it. At the same time, having my hormones raging, boys certainly did the trick. And there was a certain satisfaction, but I went to therapy. In the fifties, if you went to therapy, you got out of it [lesbianism].

"I dated a lot of guys. In 1961 I got married. I was physically attracted to my husband, and thoughts of women went by the wayside, but I never felt quite right.

"I lived a fantasy life after I got married. In the fantasy I was in love with a very good friend, but I was a good girl, and I would never say anything to her. She was just a darling person. It was a whole complicated matrix of friendships.

"I wanted to tell her everything, be with her, touch her, kiss her. Anyway, I was very busy with my children for years. Children, careers. But, on my fiftieth birthday and going into menopause I think the urge—I don't know if it was my hormones changing—but it became an unbearable problem. I got to the point where I felt I was going to die from this, and I had this middle-aged urgency pushing me along, and I had no children at home and financial matters had eased up.

"When you hit fifty-one, fifty-two, you see that time is short, and there are all the things you still want to do, so I started to think about me for a change. I started to do things independently. It just became imperative. I had made my mark, and what was next? My emotional life. I couldn't put it on hold anymore. I couldn't sublimate with smoking. I couldn't sublimate with food. The desire to have an experience became intense."

Susan

"As a little kid I liked both boys and girls. I'm sure it was as sexual and emotional as a child could feel at eight or nine. But I felt freer to have a little girl hug me. I saw women hugging and kissing all the time, and I got the message from my family that that was all right. I also got the message from them that it was not acceptable for me to have boys touch me, so I fantasized about having boys hug me or kiss me, and I thought it would be very romantic. I made a very strong association of being swept off my feet by a male person. So my sexual identity as it continued was definitely toward men.

"I realized, however, at fifteen or sixteen that there was a constant thread of having an eye for women. I looked at them, sometimes I felt a little turned on by them. It felt strange, but I didn't know I was excited—it was not clearly identified for me. But I was aware that I had crushes on other women my own age. I felt romantic about them. If anyone hugged me, I would push away those feelings of pleasure. I found this distressing and disturbing. ... I repressed all my sexual feelings. That's what part of my upbringing was. A lot of denial. I didn't know what these feelings were called, but I hoped I'd get over them real quick.

"I was spending a lot of time denying whatever sexual feelings I was having. 'I have to get home,' I'd say when I dated. I couldn't let them touch me in any way. It felt inappropriate. I was frightened of losing myself.

"When I turned twenty-one, I made up my mind that I had been a virgin long enough. Now I decided it was inappropriate not to have an experience. And I wanted to know what my sexuality was all about. I was walking around feeling pretty passionate most of the time, a state of having hot pants.

"My husband happened along at that time. I went on a trip, and I was not looking for a husband and my husband was not looking for a wife, so we both clicked. In a short span of time, it got very serious. He was kind and not pushy. I allowed myself to feel things, and it was pretty good, and I thought that was wonderful. He said he loved me, and I took it in, and we planned a marriage."

For Susan, it was a brush of an arm by a close friend that triggered an electric current and forced her female-focused sexuality to surface.

Both women were living in suburbia, where they met as young marrieds. Each had small children, and they became fast friends. Susan remembers Cynthia driving her somewhere: "Cynthia said something, and I touched her arm, in a very innocent way, I thought. She pulled away and asked me not to touch her again because she had a funny reaction. I realized I had also had a feeling from her of a particular pleasure."

Susan laughs. "I thought this would be a good time for shock treatment. One time in my house, the babies were napping, and we were sitting on the couch and watching television, and she did that thing that boys sometimes do in the movies. She draped her arm around my shoulder and then kissed me. And we were both stunned. I don't know which of us was more surprised."

Most of the women who knew about their feelings for other women believed that if they kept active, their feelings would go away. Marriage did serve as a temporary antidote. Children, school, homework, dance lessons, Little League, parent-teacher associations, and weddings were wonderful distractions ... until eventually their pent-up frustrations drove them to find a recipient for their love, or that special someone came along, making it impossible to deny their true selves any longer.

Yet, not every woman who loves women knows automatically whether or not she is a lesbian. Having experimented physically with another woman does not necessarily make one a lesbian, and the converse, never having an intimate encounter, does not discount her from being one. Then, there are the women who remain in total denial, so terrifying is the thought of same-sex love. Although many are familiar with the term and may be intimately involved with other women to some degree, these women choose to see no connection to themselves and lesbianism.

Maggie was one of these women. The mother of four, she says she never loved sex with a man but accepted the fact that it was part of life. Still, she had never identified her sexuality.

Maggie

"For a long time I had wondered, was it normal to check out women? I was always noticing wonderful things about them. She looks nice. She looks soft. I like the way she speaks. But I had no idea this was homosexuality. I had thought you were born knowing, and I didn't know therefore I was not. I was in a good state of denial.

"As a matter of fact, I was in a two-year relationship with my friend, and I never put a name to it. It was sensual, but we never actually had sex.

Although close. We would make out, caress, dress each other, but I was still straight. I was in love with her but I thought as long as I didn't …

"Then I got a new job, and I clicked with the person I was working with. She had a son in the service and so did I. One day, it was past closing, and she was on the phone with her son. She hung up and said, 'My son is gay.' I said 'So?' She said, 'So am I. I knew my son was gay from the time he was a little fellow, but I didn't realize my own sexuality until I was twenty-nine.'

"It was like a ton of bricks hit me when she said that. I thought, oh, my god, so that's what's wrong with me. That's what it is. I said, I have to leave now. Abruptly in the middle of her talking, I got up and left and went to my car and hyperventilated for fifteen minutes. My body shook, and thoughts went racing through my mind, and everything became so clear. Hindsight is always twenty/twenty. I had been a lesbian all my life and never knew!"

Sylvia

Even though she was physically active with a close girlfriend, Sylvia says, "We never really went to bed. We just kind of fooled around. I wasn't particularly attracted to her, but she was to me, and I didn't mind." And even when she found herself being drawn to the lesbian and gay crowd at college, and spending all her free time with them, she says, "I guess because I never stopped being attracted to boys or dating boys, even though I knew about my sexuality, I never felt that I was … you know.

"I got married quite young [in college]. On some unconscious level I must have realized that if I didn't get into a 'safe place,' I might end up getting more involved with a woman than I was comfortable with. I think I was flirting with the whole thing, and I was scared. Anyway, my girlfriend got married, too, and we continued being friends, typical couples going out for dinner. … Every now and then, she and I would just get together and do our thing: necking, cuddling. We didn't actually go to bed together. Then, finally we did. It was a long time coming."

Her denial was so strong that still, at that point in her life, Sylvia had no idea she might be a lesbian.

"Then," she says, "I became very attracted to another close friend. I thought she would be horrified if I told her what I had done [with my other friend], but I took the chance. … She wasn't horrified, … and we just started. We were so happy. Our intimacy enhanced our relationship. I was married and she had this guy in her life, but we had this great thing and it was wonderful.

"Here I've had two relationships with two good friends that have become physical, and I still was not saying that makes me anything. I'm saying I'm still just a married woman with a child, but I continued to be fascinated by gay life and gay people.

"Five years ago I went to a [work-related] conference. It was the kind of conference where you really did a lot of soul searching and stuff, and at one point I had to stop and say … my marriage isn't doing well. We're not meeting each other's needs. We're going in opposite directions.

"At the conference, there were a bunch of gay people, and I found myself hanging out with them a lot." It was there that Sylvia acknowledged this part of herself for the first time. "I guess I'd been too afraid to really look at this part of me. So I sort of came out to the woman I was at the conference with."

While she had been in therapy previously, it was only after the conference that Sylvia decided to explore her gender preference. "Although my marriage had not caused this [sexual confusion], the fact that it was dissolving enabled me to take a look at the sexual part of me."

Sylvia has finally been able to admit to herself who she is. She has also chosen to leave her marriage.

Lynn

Lynn had been married twice, the second time for twelve years. "I was very much in love with my husbands, especially my second husband. The first seven years were wonderful, but then we started having some trouble. I have to be honest. I had an affair with a man.

"Then I met her. In the beginning I wasn't consciously aware that we were dating. It was like, 'I can handle this. It's fun. I'm just flirting.' But we did go to bed."

Even after she had been going to bed with her woman friend for six months, the denial part was so strong that Lynn was still saying, "I'm not a lesbian."

Lynn was studying to be a therapist, and for her, like Sylvia, the realization hit while she was away at a training course, seven months after her affair had begun.

"There was a lot of recovery stuff going on: AA, drug, and alcohol. As they announced all the different workshops, they announced a gay and lesbian meeting. I thought, no one knows me here. I could walk into this room.

"That was the first time I experienced a panic that maybe I was a lesbian. I went late and left early so I didn't get to talk to anyone, but I said to myself, 'Okay, everyone looks kind of normal.' I went back the next day. For those two weeks I made friends. And now I was afraid that they would reject me for not being a real lesbian. 'You're married. You don't even call yourself a lesbian. You're just dabbling.' I had thought that being a lesbian meant you grew up being one.

"Then I got up and told my story, and so many women stood up and said, 'I was married' or 'I am married.' And I realized that every lesbian doesn't start at thirteen.

"Even when my husband and I walked together and I'd look at women and say doesn't she have nice hair, or breasts, or legs, I never thought I was a lesbian. I thought all women looked at other women.

"My dearest girlfriend was a lesbian. She never told me she was, but she dated only women. I loved being around her. I had this dream that maybe she'd invite me to a gay bar. I wasn't a lesbian, but I wouldn't mind seeing this. She never did. And I had always dated boys.

Lynn says, "My husband said it came as no surprise to him when I told him, although I had never thought of myself as a lesbian ever, ever, ever."

Cynthia

Cynthia was a young bride in the early 1950s. She had never heard lesbianism discussed and had no idea that a woman could love other women like a man and a woman could love each other. She especially had no idea she could love another woman until Susan set off feelings of passion in her that she never knew existed.

"I remember when I was a youngster, my girlfriends were very important to me. There was nothing sexual about it except that we all had a common frame of reference. There was a thread of understanding that didn't seem to exist in boy–girl relationships. I did date very extensively. I was engaged once before I got married. Somehow as I look back I see the relationship didn't have the same validity as my feelings with girlfriends.

"I'm not sure if I was in love with my husband when I married him. As I think back, I think maybe I was performing as I was supposed to. At that time I may have thought I was in love with him. I remember evaluating him in a way that was rather cruel—as someone who seemed like he would be reliable to earn a living. That was a serious consideration in 1954 because at that time it was pretty standard that women who were married did their work in the home, and their husbands earned the living.

"I met Susan shortly after we were both married. At that time, I was living in a Long Island suburb. We became acquaintances when she and her husband moved to our development. My sister and Susan had worked together, and she introduced us.

"We were together a lot during our first pregnancies. I had stopped working. She was also not working. We were together a lot with our children. It seemed perfectly natural seeing how close in age they were. We had so much in common.

"We didn't socialize much as couples though. Our husbands' interests were very different. I remember it happening a couple of times. More often than not, Susan invited me and my children to have dinner at her house, and I would invite her and her children to have dinner at my house.

"My husband got sick when I was pregnant with my third child. At the time I didn't have a driver's license, but I had been driving him, and sometimes Susan drove." Then he had to be hospitalized. "While he was in the hospital, I gave birth to my third child.

"Meanwhile Susan was very caring for him as well as for me. Every time there was a crisis where I would need help, I would turn around, and she would be helping. And I became more and more fond of her. I don't know exactly what happened, but I did know it was very important for me to touch her. If I touched her arm I felt a particular pleasure, different from the pleasure I felt when I touched a baby."

These feelings that neither woman knew what to do with caused a great deal of stress on their friendship. They tried to have a physical relationship but at the time couldn't handle it and wound up in therapy.

"Still," Cynthia says, "There was no way I was going to let go of Susan if I had that choice. I found her adorable then, and I do now. We were both thoroughly wacky. I was very abrasive, very angry a lot of the time. She was very timid, unsure of herself, demanding, and obsessive. As time went on, the relationship continued to blossom. We are not the same people now that we were then."

It took several years before Susan and Cynthia, once realizing they were in love with each other, came to understand their differences, learn to accept themselves, and live with their alternative sexuality. That was when they became sexually intimate. They have remained best friends and discreet lovers for more than twenty-five years.

Jackie

"I thought I was in love with my husband. I thought we had the perfect marriage. My husband was absolutely wonderful, and I loved my family." Yet Jackie admits, "I don't remember my sexual life with him at all. I have no memory of it.

"Then he had an affair with my best friend. I don't know why, but he told me about it. It was one of the lowest points of my life. I had had no idea. Up until that time he was my best friend and lover ... though infrequently. And I trusted him with every single thing in the world. I never didn't trust him."

Jackie's husband's affair was a turning point for her. "It didn't mean I loved him less, but why it's important is, up until that point, I didn't look at people sexually at all. That part of me was closed down.

"This whole life opened up. It was so weird. I don't understand what happened. After he told me, I started to look at people differently, in a sexual way. Men and women. That's all I did, and I went on with my life. I noticed that I was looking at women more than at men, but I couldn't talk to anyone about it.

"For years I didn't do anything with these feelings. I just sat and looked at people.

"Several years before I realized what I was, I was visiting a friend who was a lesbian. She had a magazine with letters from married lesbians. I remember being surprised. I had never known that women who were married could love other women. I was so stupid. I never knew that people could change. I thought someone was a lesbian or not.

"Anyway, I went to college for a semester to take a teaching course, and I fell in love with my teacher. In the beginning I had no idea I was falling in love with her. I remember the first night of class being shocked that the teacher was my age, smart, interesting, and had a good sense of humor. I had avoided education courses in college, finding them boring. Now I was taking the history of education and really loving the course.

"There was some attraction on her part, too, although she wasn't a lesbian. Neither of us knew what to do with this. I thought it was that she was this really great teacher. At one point I got a very short haircut. She put her hand on my head to feel it like you would do with a kid, and I was amazed. There was an electric charge. I didn't understand it at all. I had no idea where it came from. Neither of us knew what was happening.

"During the course, we both found reasons to stay with each other ... in a professional manner. We went for coffee, always with other students. When the course ended, we arranged to go to a state park for the day. It was raining, but we went and sat in the car and suddenly we were making out like two teenagers. That was our beginning."

Anna

Anna, a wife and the mother of an eight-year-old, returned to college and learned more than she ever imagined she would. She was taking a course and became friendly with the woman sitting next to her. One day while waiting for the class to begin, the woman shared with Anna that she was bisexual.

"Somehow that knowledge freaked me out. I couldn't believe what I was thinking. I was shocked, terrified. It made thoughts I must have been harboring subconsciously jump into my consciousness. It was like she was me, only more honest."

Anna's classmate's words had served as the catalyst, triggering an awareness of something that had been buried.

Edith's awareness was triggered when she read the first edition of *Married Women Who Love Women*. She'd picked it up out of curiosity, she said, but shortly into it, found herself sobbing in recognition. "I remember shaking, laughing, finally allowing myself to feel. Suddenly, I knew who I was."

Many married women who love women (MWLW) did not discover their attraction to women until they reached midlife. When their children were grown or almost grown and their hectic lives revolving around children's schedules had slowed, they felt a sense of loss. They turned to their husbands for the companionship and communication they desired, only to find the men emotionally unavailable.

To fill the void, they returned to school or to the workplace or joined organizations. In these new situations, they connected with other women who were able to offer the warmth and understanding denied them at home.

A powerful emotional love can emerge from these feelings of being nurtured and cared for after years of doing the nurturing for others. Sexuality, not generally planned, becomes a natural extension of that love.

Gracie

Married for thirty-two years and the mother of five, Gracie was active in her church and community and never felt an attraction for women until Fern set off feelings of passion she never knew existed. "In no way would I ever have believed that I could be enticed by or interested in a woman. I thought I was in love with my husband.

"When I met Fern, I knew she was a lesbian. We live in a small, artsy town, and she was out. She'd never made any bones about it. I have many gay friends and many straight friends. There are a tremendous number of women that I am in contact with. There are probably at least sixteen women whom I associate with weekly, and I'm very close to them, but not in a way that I would ever consider any kind of sexual behavior. And to this day I am not turned on by just anybody. So I didn't think about her sexuality. I liked her as a person.

"I had seen Fern on the street; she was in a wheelchair. I asked her if she'd like to come into my shop. I'd heard about her reputation for being a spunky, free-spirited woman, and I liked that.

"In fact, the first time she came into my shop she made a funny little remark. I said, 'I left the door open hoping you'd come in. I'm freezing.'" Fern said, 'Well, I'll warm you up.' She chuckled and winked. Then she blushed and said, 'I can't believe I said that.'"

Gracie says, "I didn't know what to say, but I knew where she was coming from, and I just thought it was kind of funny, and we laughed. That's the first time we really spoke. She became my very good friend. We talked, and we compared our lives: They paralleled each other in so many ways. The more we talked, the more we realized how much we had in common. Soon I was just so eager to see her and talk to her.

"Then there was a town party. I went with my husband and Fern was at the party. There was a lot of dancing and a lot of loud music. I danced and danced for about two or three hours straight. I started out dancing with my husband and then he was tired, and I danced with other people and then by myself, and I danced across the room over to where Fern was, and I asked her to dance, and she danced wonderfully in her wheelchair. She was all over the place, and I was laughing and smiling, and I just felt so free and my arms were in the air, and I was having a wonderful time.

"At three in the morning my husband and I went home, and in bed that night I couldn't stop thinking about dancing and the music and Fern in her chair. It was that night that I sort of dreamt about maybe snuggling up to her. Smelling her hair was the thing I wanted to do more than anything else. The next day when she came into the store, we chatted. I wrote her a little note. She had a way with words, four letter words in particular. I'm sort of straitlaced and proper, and I think my note said something like 'you fucking knocked me off my feet,' and she laughed and roared, and we talked some more."

Like Gracie, I, too, felt as though I had been knocked off my feet. For a few brief weeks after I fell in love with Toby, my initial feelings were so overwhelming they nullified any other thoughts. I walked around apart from the rest of the world. I might have been from another galaxy. Before entering a room I'd have to remember to clear my face of the huge grin that kept appearing involuntarily. At the beginning, while I believed that Toby being a woman had little to do with my feelings for her, I soon realized I was deluding myself. I was attracted to her womanliness, and I did love the woman in her. What did that mean? What did that make me?

CHAPTER 2

What Am I?

Initially, on the discovery of my true sexual identification, I felt like a leaf on a current: flowing along, being tossed about, and then being trapped in a whirlpool and swirling in circles. Why didn't I know about myself before? Was it my environment? Genetics? Both? My feelings were of total desperation and, at the same time, overwhelming longing. An act as simple as sitting in a cafe and watching other women laughing or walking together, arm in arm, brought excruciating pain.

Yet, when asked, "If you had it to do over, would you choose the kind of anguish you went through, or would you prefer your old life?" I would have to say, "I couldn't *not* do it again. To not know who I really am would be worse."

Still, married women who love women (MWLW), feeling forced to balance the roles society imposes on them, remain one of the most clandestine groups in our society. The total secrecy within which the phenomenon exists prevents researchers not only from finding MWLW who are willing to talk about their lives, but from knowing how widespread their presence actually is.

Citing the lack of studies on the subject of homosexual women in heterosexual marriages and the unavailability of appropriate subjects to interview, Dr. Eli Coleman turned to bisexual, divorced bisexual, and single lesbian women to complete his research article, "The Married Lesbian." Of the forty-five participants involved in his research, only four were currently married.[1]

Amity Pierce Buxton, PhD, writes that the general understanding seems to be, "Once they [married lesbians] discover and admit their homosexuality [to themselves], most seem to come out to their husbands quickly."[2]

To assume, as Dr. Buxton did, that *most* women who discover their female sexual orientation come out quickly or, as Dr. Coleman did, that married women who discover their lesbianism simply leave their marriages is misleading.

As one woman wrote in response to my ad, "I will make the assumption that your phrasing of 'we' is an indicator that you have experienced what it is like to be married, lesbian, and in the closet."

After receiving my assurance, she felt comfortable enough to write, "I just celebrated my twenty-fifth anniversary, five years after I finally admitted to myself I was in the closet. Probably some fifteen years of knowing, but just compartmentalizing it for a long time."

She ended with, "You are certainly right about the loneliness ... even during the periods when I've tried to be in *both* worlds. Now I stay in one [the heterosexual one], but it is so hard" (emphasis added).

While 20% of the MWLW surveyed did leave their marriages and 8% separated, as in many heterosexual marriages, it was the general incompatibility between husband and wife that finally brought about the divorce or separation. Those women who had contemplated divorce before learning about their gender preference, but did not have the courage to take that first step, did note that it was the personal growth they experienced while coming to terms with their own sexuality that gave them the confidence to act on their previous desire to leave.

Seventy-two percent of the women I interviewed were currently married. Like all minorities, MWLW come from all ethnic and religious groups and from a large cross section of the United States and other countries as well. They come from low-income city housing projects and sprawling suburban homes set on manicured lawns. They have attended public and private schools, day and boarding schools, coed and all-girl schools. They can be found at supermarkets and grocery stores, the cleaners, Little League games, and PTA meetings. Besides being wives and mothers, they are daughters, sisters, classmates, friends, and neighbors. MWLW are students, clerks, and lawyers. They are blue-collar and white-collar workers, executives with large corporations, artisans, and actresses struggling to survive. They are members of the workforce and educators.

The diversity of MWLW interviewed reflects that of any heterosexual group of women in our society. The most common experience recounted by those women who were consciously aware of their true sexual inclinations through their youth was dating boys despite being uncomfortable so no one would know they were different, and drinking heavily or abusing drugs to get through evenings out with friends they could not confide in.

All MWLW related the initial feelings of stress, isolation, and despondency they secretly lived with once they acknowledged themselves.

"Imagine having a secret and never being able to share it with even your best friend," one woman said. "I grew up trying to be who I was 'supposed' to be, always acting a part. Sometimes I lost sight of who the real me was—both of me were so unhappy."

Of course the idea of women loving women is not new. In contrast, though, while same-sex love between women was not viewed as the equal of heterosexual love, it was not always viewed in the same negative light as today.

In the seventeenth and eighteenth centuries, romantic friendships (the term used to describe the love relationships between two women) were considered noble and virtuous. Lillian Faderman, in *Surpassing the Love of Men*, goes on to say that by the nineteenth century, terms such as "sentimental friends," "the love of kindred spirits," and "Boston marriage" had replaced romantic friendships to describe the love relationships between two women.[3]

"Boston marriage" described long-term monogamous relationships between two unmarried women, generally financially independent of men. They were usually feminists and often involved with culture and social betterment. These shared values formed a strong basis for their lives together. Mark DeWolfe Howe, the nineteenth-century *Atlantic Monthly* editor who had contact with many of these women in the New England area, described their involvement as "a union—there is no truer word for it."[4] According to Faderman, "What surprised me most about these romantic friendships was that society appeared to condone them rather than view them as disruptive of the social structure."[5]

Such relationships were considered threatening to society only in a specific instance. If a woman dressed in attire that was termed masculine, she acted masculine because she was a man trapped in a woman's body, and all her instincts were inverted, including her sexual instinct. "If she dressed in clothes suitable for her sex, it might be assumed that she was not sexually aggressive, and two unaggressive females together would do nothing to violate men's presumptive property rights to women's bodies."[6]

Although she might be one, a woman dressed in feminine attire was often excluded from the category of lesbian, while a straight woman wearing men's work clothes was suspect. Nevertheless, in the early 1950s, significant numbers of lesbians were coming together and searching for a social identity. Since there were few lesbian models to follow, the community adopted the heterosexual patterns of masculine and feminine roles within marriage and assumed the parts of butch (the male version of a lesbian) and femme (the female counterpart), mandating appropriate masculine and feminine dress and role behavior for each partner.

Women who are turning to other women now, especially MWLW, have little desire to emulate the heterosexual relationships that did not work for them. They are choosing to create more equal types of relationships instead.

As early as the 1800s, when women's colleges began to multiply, conservative writers, interested in what they believed to be the proper functioning of society, feared "race suicide" and prophesied the decline of the country. Their rationale was that since the best (female) blood of American stock went off to college and probably would not marry, the mothers of America would eventually all be from the lower orders of society. Worse, some writers came to fear that higher education for females, especially in all-woman colleges, not only "masculinized" women, but also made men dispensable to them and rendered women more attractive to one another.

Statistics confirm that those who were interested in maintaining women in the narrow prison of heterosexuality as it was experienced by females in the nineteenth century were quite right in fearing the spread of higher education. In *Odd Girls and Twilight Lovers*, Faderman points out that females who attended college (with newfound opportunities in education and the professions) were far less likely to marry than their uneducated counterparts.[7]

Today, as in other eras, as long as feelings for women by women are nonthreatening to men, the significance of their relationships is trivialized.

When asked why so few data could be found on MWLW, one male psychologist, who preferred not to be named, responded: "Because we live in a patriarchal, or male-oriented, country, female homosexuality is not as threatening to the male ego as is male homosexuality. Therefore, the subject of women who love each other is viewed as not terribly important."

In 2003, the New Hampshire Supreme Court ruled that a sexual relationship between a married woman and another woman did not constitute adultery.[8] In that state, adultery is not defined in the state's divorce laws, so the court based its ruling on the dictionary definition of adultery: "voluntary sexual intercourse between a married man and someone other than his wife, or between a married woman and someone other than her husband." Although the definition did not specifically state that the "someone" with whom one commits adultery must be of the opposite gender, it does require sexual intercourse.[9] The plain and ordinary meaning of *sexual intercourse* is "sexual connection esp. between humans: COITUS, COPULATION" (*Webster's Third New International Dictionary*). *Coitus* is defined to require "insertion of the penis in the vagina."[10]

Even as far back as the writing of the Bible, intimate relationships between women were not considered seriously. "Homosexual intercourse is not labeled *tebel* (improper) mixing, but the extreme prohibition of homosexuality by the death penalty (*Leviticus* 20:13) … is best explained as a desire to keep categories of 'male' and 'female' intact. … *Lesbian interaction, however, is not mentioned possibly because it did not result in true physical 'union' (by male entry)*" (emphasis added).[11]

"Samuel Tissot, a Swiss doctor whose work *Onania: A Treatise Upon the Disorders Produced by Masturbation* (1758) was translated into English in 1766, was one of the few writers who recognized the possibility of manual clitoral stimulation in female/female sex. 'The act,' he says, 'is even worse than masturbation because it sometimes causes women to love other women with as much fondness and jealousy as they did men.'"[12]

In the earliest societies, families were composed of extended groups, with everyone sharing equally in the upbringing of children; the mother did not particularly "own" her child, and there was no concept of "father" as we know it today. According to Shere Hite in *The Hite Report*, "The male role in reproduction was not understood for quite a long time, and intercourse and male orgasm were not connected with pregnancy."

When the connection was made regarding the man's part in reproduction, men like Aristotle used their misogyny, parading as science, to elevate the importance of the father. According to Shari L. Thurer, author of *The Myths of Motherhood*, Aristotle, in his treatise *Generation of Animals*, was aware of the role the male seed played in reproduction by "cooking" the female residue and thus converting it into a new being. While he credited the male with having an active role, he decided that the female blood had a passive one. Aristotle then used this female passivity in reproduction to justify her social inferiority.[13]

Nancy Marvel, in her 1971 article, "The Case for Feminist Celibacy" (prior to the advent of DNA identification), said that while under normal circumstances a man was needed to provide sperm for the conception of the baby, it was practically impossible to determine which man had done so. As individuals, a man's claim to any particular child could never be as clear as that of the mother, who demonstrably gave birth to that child. With the changeover to a patrilineal or patriarchal society, sexuality became a crucial issue. A man could prove with absolute certainty that he was the one to have contributed the sperm only if he took control of the sexual conduct of the woman. "Beyond all of the symbolic aspects of the sexual act (symbolizing the male's dominance, manipulation, and control over the female), it assumes an overwhelming practical importance."[14]

Religious and civil laws gave men the authority to control the sexuality of the woman. This was done by keeping them monogamous. In the Middle Ages, women were made to wear chastity belts, straplike devices of leather or metal fastened on a woman to prevent sexual intercourse with men other than their husbands. Women were taught to believe in purity above all else. In the 1930s, writer Margaret Mitchell, who was considered radical for her time, would not allow *Gone with the Wind*'s Scarlett O'Hara to make love with any of the men she loved until she had married them.[15] In her earliest book, *Lost Laysen* (the manuscript was found among Mitchell's papers sixty years after her death), the heroine commits suicide rather than allow herself to be dishonored.[16]

There are African and Arab countries today that sanction genital mutilation to lessen a woman's sexual desires. In the heterosexual United States today, according to Marvel, the most commonly used method for controlling a woman's sexual conduct is to "convince her that sex is the same thing as love, and that if she has sexual relations with anyone else, she is violating the sacred ethics of love."[17]

Male sexual dominance continues today to be very strongly felt, especially by women who were brought up to feel that marriage validates their worth as women and that their lifework should be serving their husbands and children. These women will go to almost any length to make their marriages work.

Before the nineteenth century, homosexuality may have been viewed as a misdeed, but those who "committed the crime" were not categorized as criminals. This changed in the nineteenth century, when modern medicine, particularly the science of psychiatry, came to view homosexuality as a form of mental illness. By the 1940s, homosexuality was discussed as an aspect of psychopathic, paranoid, and schizoid personality disorders.

"James Harrison, a psychologist who produced the 1992 documentary film *Changing Our Minds*, notes that the medical profession viewed homosexuality with such abhorrence that virtually any proposed treatment seemed defensible. Lesbians were forced to submit to hysterectomies and estrogen injections, although it became clear that neither of these had any effect on their sexual orientation."[18]

In 1969, the gay community took a stand and fought for their recognition and rights at the Stonewall bar in New York City's Greenwich Village. "By the late sixties ... human sexuality became a respectable subject for academic study, trade publications, and individual therapy. ... In 1974, the American Psychiatric Association voted to remove homosexuality from the list of pathological diseases, lessening the stigma attached to gay persons and activities."[19]

Eighty-six percent of the women interviewed in the early 1990s had been married only once and 14% twice. Still, being raised to believe what our patriarchal society has presented as doctrine, many women had less difficulty giving up their marriages or becoming involved in affairs with men than giving up their heterosexuality, even when they knew it was not working for them.

While the majority of women had sexual experience only with their husbands until they became aware of their need for women, one woman told of having had six extramarital heterosexual affairs before acknowledging to herself that no man could give her what she was missing and had been searching for. Others, like Evie, were running away from themselves. Evie went from marriage to marriage, refusing to stop long enough to acknowledge that she was a lesbian, until finally she could run no more. She says, "I have gone from a lost little girl to a woman of emotional substance. This is something I have never been able to claim before. I am free and happy at last."

When Nicole, gloriously happy for the first time in years, confided to her friend Sandra that she was involved with another woman, Sandra was horrified. "You're married," she said. "How could you do this to your husband?"

"What about you?" Nicole asked. "You've had two extramarital relationships with married men!"

"That's different," Sandra said. "They were men."

"The origins of human sexuality, and of homosexuality in particular, have puzzled philosophers, theologians, and ordinary people for thousands of years. In a few scattered cultures, homosexuality has been regarded as a normal part of life or even as a special talent or gift from the gods."[20]

Many psychotherapists believe that gender preference is something we are born with. "Wilhelm Stekel, a co-worker with Freud, stated in his book *Bisexual Love* 'All persons originally are bisexual in their predisposition. There are no exceptions.' ... At the age of puberty, however, the heterosexual represses his homosexuality, sublimating it to the more acceptable proprieties of friendship, nationalism, social endeavors, and gatherings. The homosexual, on the other hand, somehow pushes the 'wrong' button and represses his or her heterosexuality instead."[21]

Still, the debate of nurture versus nature continues. Psychiatrist Richard Pillard points out that "as fetuses, human beings of both sexes start out with complete male and female 'anlages,' precursors of the basic interior sexual equipment—vagina, uterus, and fallopian tubes for women, and vas deferens, seminal vesicles, and ejaculatory ducts for men. At conception an embryo is given its chromosomal sex, which determines whether it will develop testes or ovaries. In females, the female structures simply develop, without any help from hormones and the male parts will shrivel up."[22]

Molecular geneticist Dr. Dean Hamer and a team of scientific colleagues, in a 1993 study, reported finding a genetic link to homosexuality among men. He says, "We didn't isolate a 'gay gene'; we only detected its presence through linkage."[23]

Dr. Hamer and his colleagues found a high rate of homosexuality among men on the mother's side of the family. This pattern showed consistency with the transmission of a gene through the X chromosome. Unfortunately, unlike eye or hair color, which can be readily seen and categorized, the only way to know a person's sexual identification is to ask about his or her behavior. Since people come out at different ages, their responses can differ from one year to the next, causing carefully researched data to go askew.

Hamer believes that "female sexual orientation is as likely to be inherited as male sexual orientation, but narrowing the role of individual genes will require more effort than did the male project. A complicating factor was that even if the X chromosome were involved in female sexual orientation, the expected pattern would not necessarily show an excess of either paternal or maternal gay relatives, because the woman inherits one X chromosome from her mother and one from her father."[24]

"There is no way to be sure yet," Dr. Hamer concludes, "but it is unlikely the same version of Xq28 associated with male homosexuality also is associated with lesbianism."

"Research on the population percentages for homosexuality has begun only recently, and the figures are still extremely inexact since political, social, and religious pressure has always dissuaded homosexuals from identifying their sexual orientation."[25]

Molecular geneticist Angela Pattatucci "confirmed in the end that women do something men virtually never do: They move among straight, bisexual, and lesbian."[26]

The genetic concept of expression for the trait sexual orientation could be posed as the following question: If a homosexual is homosexual, just how homosexual is that homosexual? It turns out that the answer is different for men and women. For men, the answer is usually completely. For women the answer is: sometimes not as homosexual as homosexual men. And straight women are not as straight as straight men, either.

"While most women are stable in their orientation, Pattatucci determined that it is not unusual for a small portion of women to report feeling themselves to be straight at age sixteen, perhaps lesbian at age twenty-four, maybe bisexual at age thirty-eight, and straight again at fifty-five. With men, Hamer says flatly, 'This sort of movement is very, very rare. It's pretty much a phenomenon we see exclusively in women.'"[27]

Pattatucci goes on to explain that if you ask men, gay or straight, if they have ever wondered about their sexual orientation, they almost always say no. It's not at all rare for women to say they've wondered. "A large number of straight women and almost as large a percentage of lesbians have wondered about their sexual orientations." She adds, "I think few people want to say what the real answers are because it's too politically sensitive."[28]

Psychotherapist Gwenn A. Nusbaum, board certified diplomat in clinical social work with certification in psychotherapy and psychoanalysis, also believes that while there may be a genetic predisposition, family environment plays a significant role in the development of homosexual choices and lifestyles. She says, "If a genetic component exists, it tends to interact with and be further influenced by family dynamics and attachment patterns, though other contributing factors may be operative as well."[29]

Lillian Faderman, who characterizes herself as "primarily a social constructionist," considers heredity theories too simplistic. "They don't account for the fact, as Kinsey pointed out, that people often move in and out of sexualities; they could be heterosexual for one period of their lives and homosexual for another. They don't account for the fact that in other cultures, same-sex relationships are ubiquitous. If they're given up, it's in order to procreate, and very often they are carried on even while one is married. It seems to me," she concludes, "the essentialists don't deal with the complexity of human sexuality."[30]

Society, through the family, communicates the norms and values for all its members. Thus, it is understandable that even a woman with a predisposition toward other women, not wanting to be seen as an anomaly, might consciously or unconsciously deny anything that would keep her from slipping quietly into the role of a "normal" heterosexual female. Betsy, a married lesbian, confesses that the time she was most attracted to her husband was when she was trying to mold herself to society's ideal but beginning to question. "He made me feel safe, even though there was no sexual attraction involved. Does that make me bisexual?" she asked.

Louisa

The general consensus among the women I interviewed was that men are not as capable of having as intimate a relationship as women are. Louisa sees this inability as something positive. Now involved again with Pattie, her first love, but otherwise in a monogamous relationship with her husband, Louisa says, "It's so different, being with men and being with women. There are things I get from men that I wouldn't expect to get from women. There is a certain kind of distance that I always have with men. I really like that distance.

"I tend to always want my space. Men can't come into me the way a woman can, especially Pattie. We just read each other so fast. For me, if Pattie and I lived together, it would almost be too much. Right now, the space that's there works very well for me.

"My very closest friends are in lesbian relationships. What works for them is that they're very close, very together. They share everything. That doesn't work so well for me. So that's one of the things I like about being with a man."

Still, Louisa says, "If I didn't have a woman who could read me, I would miss that terribly. I really missed it when I was only with my husband. Being with my husband and being with Pattie, it's like they're two separate experiences. I certainly have gone back and forth and thought, 'Well, am I really more gay or am I really more straight?' and that's when I finally came to say I'm really bisexual."

At twenty-five, Louisa had been involved with Pattie. When that didn't work out, Louisa felt herself drawn to other women. "But I always knew I had a very strong attraction to men and wanted men in my life. I never identified myself as a lesbian, although my feminism was very radical. I felt that my sex life had to be bisexual. That's been incredibly hard." When she met her husband, the first thing Louisa told him was that she was bisexual.

Now forty, Louisa is struggling to sort out what has been going on. She had been married to her husband for six and a half years when Pattie came back into her life. That was almost two years ago.

According to Louisa: "If you want your life to be more in synch and you want to avoid dealing with a lot of conflict, it is easier to bring it all together."

Maryann

"Looking back, I realize that women have always been an important part of my life, but I hadn't recognized it. During college, I started admitting to those feelings. My husband knew before we were married, and he has no problems with my being bisexual. It is a turn-on to him to some degree, but not an overwhelming thing.

"I had a real problem in the beginning, trying to sort through how I wanted to define myself; how we, as a couple, wanted to define our relationship. There really was a whole process of trying to work out, 'Well maybe what culture has to say about monogamy really isn't right for me as a person or us as a couple.'

"When I first came to the realization that I was bi and was interested in having a relationship with someone else, I wasn't the one who wanted to pursue that. I thought it wouldn't be fair to my husband. I'm not sure if I have a need to be with two people, but it's a need to not stifle the part of me that loves women. My husband actually encouraged me because, I think, he didn't want to deny me a part of myself.

"Sex is a big part of my relationship with my husband, but it's nowhere near the most important part of our relationship. I identify as a bi because there really isn't any other label. That's the best of it. Most of my activities are very feminist in nature, and while I'm in a wonderful relationship with this man, I've never found any other men who interest me.

"So, at this time, it's necessary to satisfy both sides: the need to be with my husband and not deny the fact that I also have the desire to be with women. I think one of the things society tries to convince people of is that you can love only one person. I don't believe that that's true … in some ways, being in two relationships is easier than being dependent on one person for all your needs."

According to early investigations by Alfred Kinsey, people exhibit a range of sexualities. Still, those who are not exclusively heterosexual in their sexual feelings and behavior have usually been considered homosexual, say Martin S. Weinberg, Colin J. Williams, and Douglas W. Pryor, authors of *Dual Attraction: Understanding Bisexuality*. As a result, a great deal of attention has been paid to explaining the differences between heterosexuals and homosexuals. "This tendency has reinforced the belief that there are two natural classes of people whose sexual desire is fixed. Bisexuals, who do not fit either category, have generally been seen as confused, dishonest, or in transition to becoming homosexual."[31]

Another common perception that Anastasia Toufexis, author of the article, "Bisexuality: What Is It?" brings up is that "bisexuals are basically straights with a taste for exotic adventure or essentially gays who are unable or unwilling to acknowledge their true orientation. To growing numbers of bisexuals, however, as well as therapists and researchers, this is nonsense. They insist that bisexuality is not a walk on the wild side or a run from reality, but has a legitimate identity of its own."[32]

Masters and Johnson argue that "all people initially learn the desirable aspects of both genders and can produce gendered pleasure in both directions. Becoming conventionally heterosexual, however, mandates that people unlearn or repress the attractiveness of their own gender.

"Following this line of thought, bisexuality emerges as the result of the failure to repress (or as the result of rediscovering) same-sex pleasures; those pleasures are then added onto opposite-sex attractions. Instead of connecting sexuality with gender in the conventional way, bisexuals seem to untangle gender and sexual preference, so that the direction of sexual desire—be it toward the same or the opposite sex—operates independently of a person's own gender."[33]

Bisexuals, more open and accepting than heterosexuals or homosexuals, break down cultural rigidities about sexual and emotional closeness. The complexity of human sexuality makes trying to come to any conclusions or put labels on people a temporary measure at best. "Instead of learning directly to eroticize one gender or the other," say Weinberg, Williams, and Pryor, "we learn to act as a woman or to act as a man. A woman learns that, to be an adequate woman in our society, her sexual feelings and behaviors should be directed toward men, because this is 'what women do.' Gender, not sexuality, is the encompassing framework through which we learn and process this information."[34]

A majority of the women I spoke with initially labeled themselves bisexual, and yet many also agreed that if their husbands were no longer a part of their lives, it was unlikely that they would be intimate with another man. Given a choice, these women would now prefer to be exclusively with women. While some still enjoyed the sexual intimacy they shared with their husbands, and could therefore be labeled as bisexual, others felt no physical attraction toward men. They were being intimate only to maintain their marriages, having sex with their husbands either as an accommodation or because "it is easier to give in to his demands." For this reason, many women had mistakenly defined themselves as bisexual. Eventually, they recognized that, by choice, they would be lesbian and redefined themselves accordingly.

Of the women I spoke to, 78% identified themselves as lesbians, while only 22% identified themselves as bisexuals. The major difference between the women drawn only to women and those drawn to both men and women seemed to be their initial reactions. Almost all women who classified themselves as lesbians said they initially felt an emotional attraction to the other woman that eventually led to a physical one. The majority of women who classified themselves as bisexual most often talked about being physically attracted to that other woman and then later developing an emotional attachment.

Lana

"When I participated in your questionnaire, I was still living with and married to my husband. In the early stages, he was one of my biggest supporters, bringing home lesbian movies and documentaries, and hooking me up with open-minded social groups. Because of our care for each other, and our serious feelings about the commitment of marriage, we tried to make it work, even though there was much tension due to our pulls outside the relationship. We sought a marriage counselor, who suggested separation since we didn't have any children. I think what flushed me out was the growing interest in our peer group in 'threesomes,' two women in bed with one man. Whenever my husband brought up such an arrangement, I'd say, 'that would be fine with me as long as you leave after five minutes, leaving me with the other woman for a while.'

"Yet in the face of the most obvious clues, I still fought against my true identity; leaning toward bisexual and very uncomfortable with the term lesbian. It finally took an actual experience with a lesbian to bring me to the point of full acceptance. Partnerless for the time being, I am ready either way—for a future with or without a female partner. At least I know who I am, and that is a relief beyond description."

Years ago, I would have said, "I have no doubt. I am a heterosexual woman," yet when I discovered my true gender identity, the label was so frightening that I could not have said—although it was true—"I have no doubt, I am a lesbian." Today, while I can comfortably say "I am a lesbian," I no longer have the need for a label. I see myself as a whole. Still, my journey was a frightening one, and I kept asking myself: "What now?"

CHAPTER 3
What Now?

It takes a tremendous amount of strength for a married woman who discovers she loves women to explore what is happening to her. And even more courage to acknowledge that she does have options and begin her search for them.

Some women seek self-help groups or therapy. Others secretly devour every book on lesbianism in the library or apprehensively cross the threshold into their first "women's bookstore." Women's bookstores had once been the only places to find the kind of information women were searching for. Now, however, gay and lesbian titles are more readily available in all bookstores.

I will never forget the anxiety I experienced as I journeyed to my first women's bookstore. Initially, I had scoured the libraries. The catalogue listed books about lesbianism, but they were not to be found on the shelves. I could not bring myself to ask the librarian for help, so I searched through all the local libraries. I returned often for several weeks hoping the books would magically reappear.

Finally, someone told me about a woman's bookstore uptown. It took me more than an hour on the subway to reach the store. All the while, sitting on the train, I wondered if the other passengers could read my discomfort. It took every ounce of strength I possessed to enter that feminist bookstore for the first time—and all I wanted to do was to browse the shelves for information that might help me to understand who or what I was and what I was going through.

When I reached Womenkind Books, I pretended to be browsing and walked past the section on lesbianism several times. Why was this section so open, why wasn't it hidden in the back of the store? I wondered. Finally, I stopped and grabbed the first book that caught my eye with the word lesbian on the cover, *Lesbian Passion*.

I put a twenty-dollar bill on the counter and fumbled in my purse so I would not have to meet the eyes of the cashier. Had she given me my book first, I probably would have run from the store without my change. Anyway, I never counted the money, just stuffed it into my pocket and made a fast exit.

On the train home, I held my package tightly to me while different scenarios popped into my head. What if the train lurched, the book slid from its brown paper bag and everyone saw the word LESBIAN? What if I left it on the train, and someone picked it up and ran after me calling out, "You left your LESBIAN book!"? Then, I began to worry, where could I hide this book when I got it home? I almost tossed it into the trash can when I got off the subway.

Before accepting the new sexuality that married women who love women (MWLW) have discovered is truly theirs, women go through a kaleidoscope of emotions. Those lucky enough to have the support of the woman they have fallen in love with often report feelings of elation and rightness. Those forced to deal with this issue of unexplored sexuality alone frequently find themselves on a different path, filled with anxiety and terror.

Nearly all MWLW experience an initial anger toward their husbands, wondering, "Why didn't he do something about my unhappiness, about his inability to communicate with me?"

Those women who had acknowledged their tendency toward lesbianism, yet had concealed the information in favor of a traditional marriage, believed that if the communication with their spouses had been better, those feelings would not have surfaced again. They initially blamed their husbands for not meeting their needs and for letting them down.

Most women believed they had no choice but to marry. Still, for the women who knew about their sexuality early on, the decision had been a difficult one. Whether they went into marriage to try to "make themselves right" or to please their families, remaining in the marriage once they committed themselves became an all-consuming job.

Marion

Marion, one of those women who had known about her desire for women and gone into therapy before marriage to "make herself right," says, "I spent my energies and time pleasing him, moving from state to state as he changed jobs, being the dutiful housewife, supporting his efforts, caring for his children by a previous marriage."

When Marion joined a twelve-step program for overeaters, she realized that her problems with food were only a cover under which she had been hiding her deeper distress, her true sexual leaning. She was aware that she had been feeling a general unhappiness but had no idea why. Eventually, working through her food issues forced her to acknowledge for the first time that she had needs of her own. After this awakening came the truth: Her needs were not being met. She realized that she had never been satisfied with the conversation or any sort of interaction within her marriage and had turned to food for comfort.

Eventually, she felt comfortable enough in the group to bring up the issue of her sexuality.

"Before I realized I had needs, I had no expectations of my husband to fill them. Sometimes, when I tried to talk to him, he would leave the house, or he'd say, 'You don't know what you're talking about.' And I had accepted that. But now, as I was allowing my feelings to surface, I wanted him to acknowledge them, too. It really didn't matter what they were.

"When I understood my reason for overeating was frustration because he wasn't satisfying me emotionally, my previous inclination started coming back."

Problems in Marion's marriage became apparent only after she discovered that she had feelings. This is not uncommon. Many marriages initially work because women, taught to be the caregivers, do not acknowledge their own needs.

Being unaware that we have needs is a problem that has been prevalent in our society. My parents survived the Depression and World War II by hiding their feelings—being tough. They wanted my siblings and me to be strong, too. And I found myself following their lead. When my young children fell or scraped their knees and came to me crying, I often caught myself saying, "You didn't get hurt. Stop crying. You're okay." I realize now the message they were receiving was: "I'm not important, what happens to me doesn't matter," or "It's not all right to have feelings."

Some women go through two or three marriages or numerous heterosexual affairs trying to find the "something missing" in their lives. Others, not understanding why, try to fill themselves with food or alcohol. Many sublimate their own needs by investing all their time and energies in their husbands and children, becoming the perfect wife and mother, or putting all their energy into their work, never making time for a husband or family.

Bella

Bella, a free spirit of the 1960s, became a devout Christian woman. She says, "My husband and I were just kids in the sixties. We'd get high, get a little wine, play strip poker with friends, and just do it. We never called it anything other than 'having a good time.' A bell didn't go off that I shouldn't be able to be with women. It was so natural. No one told me that it was bad, wrong, or evil. My own inner self didn't tell me not to do it. I didn't know I had enjoyed being with other women. I just knew I could be with them. It was a kid thing we did before we grew up. It wasn't until 1989 that I found a label for it [making love with women].

"In a Christian home a wife is dutiful," Bella says, "so I did the Christian thing, I practiced being a good wife, and I am a very good wife. In those early years I just did what was scripturally correct. The Bible didn't say I was supposed to get anything out of this [making love]. It never occurred to me that I should. But I felt an incompleteness, an inadequacy, compared with my picture of what a family was supposed to be like. In our intimate moments, I felt I should be relating to my husband in a certain way. I should be more nurturing and caring toward him than I was. So, I learned how to act. I didn't pretend orgasms; I really had those. But anything else...

"I went to church with my problem. The nuns said, 'Go home and submit to your husband.' I went home and got pregnant. I still felt something was wrong. I went back to talk to the nuns again. Again the same advice. Again another baby. Eight babies later, it suddenly came to me. I was a lover of women."

While none of the MWLW interviewed said their relationships with their husbands had been perfect at the time they discovered their preference for women, they were divided regarding whether a better marriage would have made a difference in the long run. Some believed that, eventually, their true sexuality would have emerged regardless of their marital situation. Others felt it had come about only because of the conflict within their marriages. Still, the common feeling among many of the women interviewed was that if their spouses had been more sensitive, they would not have had a need to turn to their women friends for the verbal closeness and emotional intimacy lacking at home.

The belief that a lack of communication caused them to look elsewhere for validation and fulfillment, thus leading them to discover their preference for women, is a strongly debated topic among MWLW and among therapists as well.

Girls and boys grow up differently because, while they are both mothered by women, for boys, that first love object is of the opposite sex, whereas for girls it is the same sex. "Because the child's first intense emotional/libidinal love object is a woman, it is the smell and feel of a woman to which both sexes are primally drawn, and according to Freud, feel the first sexual attraction."[1] Freud, in his "Theory of Female Sexuality," and many other psychoanalysts since have struggled with this question. Heterosexual sons never make a transition. Their first love object remains female throughout their adult lives. Why would girls, then, "pull away from the same-sex attraction with their mother to develop an 'inferior,' passive heterosexual attachment to men? Nancy Chodorow contends that indeed, women do *not* give up their primary attachment to their mothers, but add secondary heterosexual attachment to men later in life primarily because of the internal and external taboos against lesbianism and the deep ambivalence of this first love. Chodorow maintains that in heterosexual relationships women recreate the primary mother bond by intense attachment to their children, and particularly their daughters, rather than with their husband or lover. Because a man's masculinity is tied to being unemotional and therefore less connected than a woman often wants, a mother is inclined to see her child/daughter as a reflection of her own mother in order to bring the emotional connectedness to her life that she is missing with her husband."[2]

A typical Oedipal configuration, even for heterosexual women, Chodorow suggests, is bisexual. Thus, when a girl turns toward her father she is not necessarily turning away from her mother. "When a girl's father does become an important primary person, it is in the context of a bisexual relational triangle. A girl's relation to him is emotionally in reaction to, interwoven and competing for primacy with, her relation to her mother."[3]

According to Chodorow, while a girl retains her pre-Oedipal tie to her mother, she builds Oedipal attachments to both her mother and father on it. "From this perspective it is much easier to understand that object choice for many women may be a more flexible matter, with much room for later developmental factors to have a significant role. Interactions with siblings, peers, and teachers may play their part. Social and cultural attitudes about sexuality from schools, churches, and the media also contribute. Finally, the circumstances of life can tip the balance. Sexual identity may shift accordingly over a lifetime."

"The traditional explanation of lesbianism is that it is founded on a psychic love affair with the mother, which the daughter never outgrows." Beverly Burch suggests that "because the psychic love affair with the father is either never experienced or is closed off for defensive purposes, the basis for romantic and sexual relationships with men has been foreclosed."[4]

Although much has changed since the women's movement, in general women have been taught to be dependent and passive, to seek attention and approval from other people, and to attend to and respond to the needs of others. Where assertive behavior is rewarded in the male, an assertive female is viewed negatively as pushy or aggressive. Women are taught that to be unassertive and care-taking of others is to be appropriately female. Since female behavior and characteristics are less valued than their male counterparts, to be gender appropriate, women must accept a status that makes the development of a positive self-image difficult. This often leads to low self-esteem or depression.[5]

Communication is difficult for women whose self-esteem is low. They may have trouble carrying on a discussion if someone disagrees with them. They may become flustered or shut down, especially if it is a man doing the disagreeing. Having been brought up to feel inadequate and defenseless, believing that taking care of themselves or being assertive is unfeminine, women fear being criticized, saying no, and stating their needs clearly and directly.[6] In the latest backlash against female advancement, some young women disdain the label of feminist altogether, fearing it labels them as either man-hating or lesbian.[7]

Some accept being one down from men. Others attempt to redefine their position in society by glorifying traditionally female roles. The isolation in which MWLW exist, however, makes their growth even more difficult because they are different from other women. To build positive self-images, they must resolve the conflicts of gender difference.

For many women, those conflicts were exacerbated by hypocritical aspects of the churches in which they had been raised. Disheartened, many no longer attended services. Here, too, they found they were no longer welcome members. Several women did, however, enthusiastically report changing affiliation to the Unitarian Church, which they said was more accepting of their lifestyles.

Gail

From an Irish-Catholic family, Gail, at thirty-five, is not certain if she considers herself bisexual or lesbian. She recalls being attracted to both boys and girls at a very early age. But she married and had babies—because she was supposed to.

As Gail began to come to terms with her own sexuality, however, she became more disenchanted by the Catholic church. "It disturbs me greatly," she says, "because basically I've realized it [the Church] is homophobic and patriarchal. It's sad because I've been raised in the religion, had twelve years of Catholic school, and have been educating my sixteen-year-old daughter through Catholic traditions. Now, I face a dilemma. I have another child at that age where he should be enrolling in grammar school. I don't know if I want to perpetuate this [the Church's] negative way of thinking.

"I love my church, and I was disappointed with the Church's stand on homosexuality. It's very hypocritical because there is so much homosexuality in the priesthood.

"But I don't think I would reject God because I don't think God rejects me. I don't think he rejects gay people. I think a bunch of men are making these silly rules and imposing their values on people."

Gail went on to say: "I read *Lesbian Nuns Breaking Silence*. It was so poignant, the way the women describe their relationships with the other women, very intense, very touching. I cried from cover to cover."

The women who were most strongly tied to their churches while growing up, the Catholic women, were the ones who most often cut the ties when they began to deal with their sexuality. As their consciousness rose, they could no longer be forced to follow the rigid rules of the Church. Some attributed their leaving to the lack of support and understanding offered by their religious institutions. Others believe it was the Church-imposed morality that caused them to turn toward women.

Maria

A parochial school graduate, Maria says, "I am a Puerto Rican. I was a Catholic, raised to be a virgin and get married. They [the nuns] said getting pregnant out of wedlock was a sin. Nothing was discussed in school about birth control. Around me, all I saw were girls getting pregnant and nobody with them. I was afraid to get close to a guy because I didn't want to end up with a baby and alone. So it was safer to be with a girl.

"I lived with my female lover for three years, and then we watched a friend's baby for the weekend. Being raised Catholic, you grow up, get married, and have kids. That's when I decided I wanted to marry a man so I could have a baby of my own. This was in the early sixties. I got involved and thought I fell in love with the first man I was with. I didn't take into consideration the kind of insensitive man he was. I married him to have my babies."

Maria's husband abused her, yet she remained in the marriage for the children … until he turned his abuse toward their eldest daughter.

Then she took her children and left. Needing help to raise her young family, she married again.

"With my second husband I tried to recapture the intimacy I had shared with my lover. It was impossible. I became promiscuous, finding male lovers outside my marriage. They couldn't satisfy me either. I was so frustrated. Eventually I found another woman lover. I think if I was getting the emotional stuff I needed from my husband, I wouldn't have looked."

Arlene DiMarco, MSW, CSW, certified psychotherapist, feels that women turn to women for romantic love in lieu of support from their husbands. She believes that for MWLW "even if their husbands were more sensitive, eventually they [the women] would begin to feel that something was missing. Regardless of how good and how sensitive the man is, there is always that void. It needs to be filled by another woman."

She believes that "the need to be with women is something women are born with. By and large many women, afraid of the ramifications, will ignore this need. As uncomfortable as they are, they're not about to make any changes. It is only the women who are more in touch with their feelings who will search."[8]

Religious persuasions, subtly instilled or more blatantly coerced, can strongly affect the lives of many women who have not yet come to separate themselves from their families and form their own identities.

Maryann

Although most women, once enlightened, chose to leave their churches, Maryann, raised in a middle-class community in upstate New York, was an exception. She remained within the Catholic church, which had always been important to her.

"While growing up, homosexuality was never discussed—in a positive or negative way," she says. "But when I found out about myself, it was painful, especially when people I cared about were telling me that it was awful and wrong [to feel the way I did]. What got me through was my faith. I knew deep inside me that it was right for me ... and I found people around me who accepted me for who I was. My husband for one. I feel comfortable with myself and my church."

Maryann continues to be active in her church. She met another woman there, and the two became friends, then lovers. Involved in the same activities, church allows them to spend time together. People don't question their relationship, and her husband does not have to cover for her.

Those women who had strong religious upbringing had the most difficulty breaking with their childhood teachings. Some never did.

One sixty-six-year-old from an Orthodox Jewish background talked of having had her marriage arranged for her when she was a young girl. She lived with her husband for several months without being able to consummate the union. Eventually, the marriage was annulled.

For years, the woman lived with the shame she had brought to her family, believing something was wrong with her—until she heard there was such a thing as women who loved women. She finally understood that was the kind of woman she was born to be.

She was not alone. The more I talked with women, the more similar I found their stories and sentiments. I also received several notes such as this one: "I don't have a story to tell since it is impossible to act on my feelings, but your words literally leaped off the page. For the first time, I realized I was not alone. Someone cared about me and women like me and the secret we are forced to live with."

Leslie

Leslie, in her twenties, grew up in a small town in North Carolina. She describes her childhood home as being very homophobic.

"My Baptist upbringing made me nervous and uptight with sexual things. I thought that's why I hadn't really been interested in boys in high school. But as soon as I went to college, my life changed. I realized there was a whole world out there other than what I had been brought up to believe in. My friends talked about the wild things they had done with guys. That was all new to me. So while in college I went out and fucked a lot of guys, thinking, 'Eventually, I'm going to like it.' But that never happened.

"Then I found a guy I actually thought I loved. I blame my parents for forcing me to marry him though. He and I were together, but I still had this feeling that something was missing. My mother would call constantly and be in tears, accusing us of living together in a house of sin. She ranted on and on. As much as I didn't believe those things [about sin] from my religious upbringing anymore, it still made me crazy because it was part of my background, and I didn't want to lose my parents. So we made plans for our wedding.

"Two weeks before the wedding, I had an affair with a woman. I guess I was curious, but afterward I knew who I was. I was honest with my fiancé and it made him a little nervous, but we had planned a big wedding and we didn't know what else to do. We got married."

In the sixties, the first wave of feminism brought about an internal revolution as well. The prevalence of support groups for women who had become isolated from family and friends in our mobile society increased dramatically. The word *share* replaced the word *tell*. Terms such as *codependent* and *self-help* began to pepper our vocabularies.

Economics forced women back to the workplace. Others began to attend or return to college. Women were becoming part of the larger world outside the home. They were becoming aware that they had rights and privileges.

The feminist movement brought attention to women's problems and new ways of seeing and addressing issues relating to them. Self-esteem grew. As women began to share their frustrations with one another, they became aware of their own needs—learning that it was all right to have them. Feelings and emotions, once denied, were now being acknowledged.

Consciousness-raising groups became popular. The groups provided safe environments where women could discuss personal roles, issues, attitudes, and needs. For the first time, women began to talk about marital concerns they had kept repressed. Sharing their secrets helped them to realize that their problems and thoughts were not unique, and that they were not alone.

Open dialogue brought increasing awareness, helping women to see that others shared the same frustrations as wives, mothers, and daughters. Taboo subjects, such as sex and intercourse, were no longer forbidden topics of conversation. Women discovered that not everyone had experienced an orgasm—although each had believed she was the only one who hadn't. For the first time, women began to feel good about their sexuality.

Nine percent of the women interviewed admitted to having been sexually abused as children. While they did not agree regarding whether or not the violation made them turn to women, it is probable that while most women reject lesbianism because of cultural taboos, an incest survivor—who has been forced to live outside of society's rules since childhood—has the freedom to make that choice more easily than a traditionally raised woman.

"I observe in my practice," says Karin Meiselman, "that virtually all of the lesbian father–daughter incest survivors reveal an intense longing for a nurturing, positive relationship with a woman, which I see as a distinctly separate issue from the survivor's anger at and difficulties with men."[9]

Psychotherapist Eileen Starzecpyzel sees a correlation between the choice of women as a sexual object for both men and lesbians who have been victims of incest by their fathers. "A woman's relationship with her sons is different from that with her daughters and produces significant personality differences in her male child … her son, having a penis, will grow up to be more like his father than like her. Under the influence of powerful cultural and patriarchal pressure, the mother subconsciously relinquishes the boy to his father, who must teach him manhood. At the same time, her relationship to her son takes on strong Oedipal (sexual) overtones, because she begins to relate to him as a sexual 'other' or 'little man,' while her own husband remains distant and absent from her daily life, as is customary in this culture. This new, sexually charged interaction with the mother frightens the boy, who gives up the emotional link with his mother in favor of masculine identity and power. Until he gains a wife/mother substitute later in life, he loses the warmth with mother that girls retain."[10]

Starzecpyzel hypothesizes that "the early loss of mothering, or severance of pre-Oedipal connectedness to mother, not only happens to boys in normal development, but also happens to girls who have been victimized by father–daughter incest. The loss of and longing for the early sexual pre-Oedipal bond with mother may be a significant factor in creating for the boy and the incested girl an unsatisfied longing for mother."[11]

While Belinda, a Southern Baptist from Kentucky, feels that the abuse she suffered at the hands of men played a major role in determining her sexual preference, Joan, a Catholic from New Jersey, insists that her sexuality had already been determined before she was sexually violated by a woman when she was five years old. "It was a painful and confusing experience," Joan says. "Given that in my case it was a woman, it might have turned me away from women—and it didn't. If I really think back," she says, "I can recall instances even prior to that where the inclination was already there."

Belinda

Belinda believes it was the sexual abuse she endured as a young girl, as well as her mother's desertion, that made her turn to women.

"My mother took off when I was four. My father slept with me, then he sold me and my brothers and sisters. The people who bought me took me to church every Sunday. Then the man slept with me every Monday. I was six when that started. How could I have trust in God? He represented men, and look what they had done to me.

"I married a man at sixteen to escape the abusive situation at home," Belinda says. "But I left a short time later. I kept being drawn to women. I'm forty now, and I'm not certain what I am. I could make love to women, and I love them to pieces. I would do anything to please the other woman, but I don't like anyone making love to me. I can't let anyone touch me. I only recently learned through intensive therapy that I have spent my life seeking the mother figure I never had."

For an incest survivor, whether a lesbian or a heterosexual woman, psychotherapist Starzecpyzel says, "Sex is never just sex, and it is rare to experience pleasure, good feelings, and the vulnerability of orgasm." Sex brings with it difficulties with trust and a struggle to believe that letting someone be close will not result in humiliation, degradation, betrayal, and rejection as well as feelings of badness. While the paternal seduction is bad, "the primary wound of incest is the loss of the mother bond, which is damaged severely by the father's sexual appropriation and misuse of the child."[12]

In father–daughter psychological/sexual incest, the father initiates incest consciously or subconsciously by appropriating his daughter as his "special" child, his possession. The father may actively keep the mother from having a relationship with the child.

For the child, Starzecpyzel says, a sense of being unconnected to and stolen from her mother—the feeling of being a motherless child—is what results. Through his seduction, the father forces the girl into a tight father–daughter bond that replaces the normal mother–daughter bond needed for a girl's secure development. This replacement bond causes the child to develop an identity, not like the mother's, but similar to a boy's psychosexual development. Then, like the traditionally raised heterosexual male, she may have a sexual response toward females.

If the father's intrusive disruption of the mother bond occurred early, the girl may be aware only of her rejection of mother as a worthy object to identify with, and she may be more conscious of having never wanted to be like her mother. While the core issues, as Starzecpyzel sees them, are identification with the father, protectiveness toward the mother, rejection of the mother, intense longing for the mother, and feelings of abandonment by the lost mother, the lesbian victim may initially enter therapy hating women and identifying primarily with men.

According to Starzecpyzel, despite the sexual abuse, it frequently occurs that the relationship with the father was the most available to the child. As a result, the child is inclined to value the power of masculinity as the healthier model of adaptation. A turning away from identification with the mother and a preference for the identifying with the father is sometimes an important factor in the formation of lesbian sexual identity.

Many women who had accused their husbands of not fulfilling them emotionally came to the realization that the men had not changed. It was they who had changed. They realized that as their own self-regard and awareness grew, their expectations of their husbands had also grown—and so did their unhappiness at the men who were not fulfilling those expectations.

This new understanding led them to connect with other women who could fulfill their needs, and for some, that meant sexually.

According to psychotherapist Hedda Begelman, CSW-R, board-certified diplomate in clinical social work and director of the Gay and Lesbian Counselling Center of Long Island, "Even after discovering their sexual preference and connecting with women who make them feel complete, some women come to therapy with their issue being 'How can I stay in this marriage and not explore this woman–woman relationship any further?'

"They have been disciplined by society's definitions of what is right and what is not," Begelman says. "Being a lesbian is one of the great prohibitions."[13]

Many MWLW initially began therapy to suppress their feelings.

Martha

"I started therapy and told my therapist, 'I am thirty-two, married six years, and very unhappy. I can't communicate with my husband.' Not knowing I had other choices, I said to her, 'And I want to stay married.' My therapist took that as her marching orders. I didn't hold anything back. I told her how I'd felt about women all my life. She didn't say much.

"I spent twelve thousand dollars and eight years in therapy with a homophobic therapist, trying to make my marriage work. Still, none of this stuff [my preference for women] was obvious.

"Then a friend suggested I join a women's consciousness-raising group to get more in touch with my sexual orientation. When I told my therapist what I had done, she said that was ridiculous."

Martha says, "When I look back now, it made lots of sense. If I had followed my friend's advice, I would have gotten in touch with who I was long before now. Finally, I changed therapists and started to figure my life out."

Not every MWLW will consider therapy to help her through her transition. Indoctrinated with society's attitude against same-sex feelings, some women perceive themselves as deserving of punishment for the crime of having fallen in love with another woman. They feel unworthy of help from a therapist.

Lucy

Lucy, married and the mother of a twelve-year-old son and fourteen-year-old daughter, was active in the PTA of her children's school when, suddenly, she realized she had fallen in love with her best friend of eighteen years. Needing an outlet for those new feelings, Lucy began to write poetry. When her husband accidentally found her writings, she was mortified. He said, "You're a foolish woman. Forget this nonsense. Forget your friend. Stay home, and I'll buy you a new car."

She says, "I was so grateful to him for not throwing me out when he found out what a disgusting person I was. I sat home, buried my face in the refrigerator, and proceeded to gain almost one hundred pounds. It was easier and safer to eat than to think about the strange, unnatural feelings I had for my friend. I don't want to think about that time in my life anymore."

Almost too obese to leave the house now, Lucy will still not consider therapy. She continues to believe that she is detestable.

In the beginning of my discovery period, I thought maybe I was just in love with my best friend. Maybe the fact that she was a woman was insignificant. I could no longer talk to her, and I desperately needed to find someone who could answer my questions.

I went to a meeting for women who were dealing with the issue of loving women. It was at the Gay and Lesbian Center in New York City. As difficult as it had been for me to go to a woman's bookstore for the first time, my discomfort was nothing compared to what I felt walking into this redbrick building. My heart was beating so hard that I was afraid if I looked down I would see it straining against my shirt. I became slightly paranoid: Was anyone watching? Would they think I was like "those women" if they saw me go into this place? I walked around the block three times before I could get up my courage to climb the two steps.

In the assigned room, I quickly took the nearest available chair. Afraid of any eye contact, I studied my shoes. Eventually, though, my curiosity got the best of me, and I slowly raised my eyes. My first reaction was one of surprise. The other women looked so "normal." I could stand next to them in the supermarket or at a school meeting, and I'd never know they were lesbians. I briefly shared my story with the woman sitting beside me, and she invited me to join her for coffee the next day.

In my naïveté and ignorance, I assumed, as do many uninformed people I speak to, that the only thing lesbians do is have sex with other lesbians. Period. I remember feeling uncomfortable but determined to do what I had to so that I would know the truth about myself. I felt absolutely no attraction toward this woman, but to put my curiosity to rest, I thought, if this is what lesbians do, I will do it to find out if I am one or not. I actually went out and bought new panties and a new bra.

We met at a diner. She ordered coffee and a Danish, and I ordered tea and a large cookie. Like any two women would, we talked about our families and our jobs. We talked about ourselves and the newly discovered feelings we both had for our respective friends. Then we said good-bye, and each of us went home to prepare dinner for our families. That was all that happened.

Months later, when we had become friends, I told her what had crossed my mind that afternoon, and we laughed together.

When I began therapy soon after my trip to the bookstore and the open center, my mouth moved, but the words wouldn't come out. I trembled as I tried to talk. At the time, I believed I was the only woman in the world to ever have fallen in love with another woman.

Married women who love women begin therapy for various reasons. Some, as I did, begin because they feel they are heading for a breakdown. Some start to deal with what their new sexuality means to them and continue to decide whether they can accept themselves as MWLW. Often, a client is in therapy for a long period of time before revealing her proclivity. Other women have already accepted what they have discovered—that they are lesbians—and now need to decide if they want to remain in their marriages or begin new lives altogether. They need to find out how to act on this new dimension of their lives.

Some of the women I interviewed were specific about what they wanted in a therapist—although some admitted that after being in therapy for a while, their requirements for a therapist had changed. Some preferred a male therapist, feeling a male perspective would be more detached. Some needed it to be a woman—their discomfort in sharing their secret with a man being too great to deal with. Others wanted only a heterosexual woman, fearing a lesbian might influence them when they were still unsure or confused about their sexuality. Yet, once an internal frame of reference has been developed, many women are less fearful of being influenced and often seek a lesbian-identified therapist to gain further support or to use as a role model.[14]

One homosexual therapist I spoke with is of the opinion that although heterosexual therapists can be objective, many do not have enough experience with lesbians to help these women. Often, a client is in therapy for a long period of time without revealing her same-gender sexuality.

The power of our heterocentric society is so strong that some therapists still believe no normal woman could want to be a lesbian. Viewing homosexuality as a disease, they are still trying to convert their patients to heterosexual lifestyles rather than dealing with the actual issues these women are facing with relation to their true sexuality.

Pamela

Pamela says, "After realizing I was attracted to women, I became depressed and went into therapy." Her male therapist refused to accept the truth regarding her sexual preference. "He was convinced that I was not gay, that I was just unhappy and should work on my marriage, which I found difficult," she says. "My husband was into fads and toys, beautiful cars, and women. He was into sex scenes, which made me uncomfortable."

Eventually Pamela's therapist acknowledged that maybe the problem was with her husband and suggested she try an affair with a man. "But the question of my preferring women kept coming back, and I'd say to my therapist, 'We're not dealing with this issue.' And he'd say, 'It's not a problem. You're seeing a man. Continue seeing men.'

"I remained very depressed. I had rashes all over my body, hemorrhoids—any psychosomatic thing that could happen to my body was happening.

"Finally I left my marriage, my therapist, and my male lover, and I came out to myself. All of my physical problems went away."

Psychotherapist Hedda Begelman says, "A woman who begins to feel that she loves women has to accept that that's an okay way of life and there's nothing wrong with that. She's not perverted and not crazy, and she doesn't have a disease, but for some reason, probably, she was born this way.

"A woman in transition should be going to a sympathetic therapist to help her deal with her situation," Begelman says. "Half of the women I see in my practice, which is primarily gay and lesbian, are married." She adds, however, that "whether a woman chooses a straight or a gay therapist, one of the same sex or the opposite, the most important issue to be dealt with is learning how to accept herself."[15]

Not all MWLW have an immediate need to seek therapy or written information when they discover their differences. When love between two women is reciprocated, sometimes the close and intimate relationship they share is enough to give each of them the support she needs. The completeness each feels can also make her respective marriage work more smoothly.

Joanna

Joanna says, "I loved my husband, and I never wanted to hurt him. He was a very good man who always treated me fairly and with tremendous respect. I felt he didn't deserve this, yet he couldn't fulfill my needs. I needed to be able to communicate with somebody. I needed to have somebody know me one hundred percent. I needed to have somebody listen to and hear me. As wonderful as he was, he really couldn't do that for me. Because of this, I felt that it was okay to be with my best friend and lover.

"Actually, I believe he was relieved when I stopped nagging him to go out with me or to listen to me. Here I was, for the first time in my life, taking care of my needs, and it was making the rest of my world better, too."

Women who experience the deep emotional level they can reach with another woman can no longer settle for the contentedness they may have accepted as their lot in life before. Across the country, many of the same words were repeated as women described their newfound feelings. One said, "I never realized how two-dimensional my life had been until I discovered that third dimension within myself."

I would have to describe the new depth of feelings I experienced as "drawing back a curtain and having my dull gray world flow into a full spectrum of beautiful color." When I told others of this sense of leaving a black-and-white existence and entering one of brilliance, they said, "Yes. That's it. That's how I would describe it, too."

Women talked about having lived with insatiable emptiness. Only in retrospect did they realize that they had been trying to fill that void by keeping occupied with work in organizations or in their communities. Others kept busy with adult education courses and workshops.

I was constantly busy and constantly eating, but I never felt satisfied. When I fell in love with Toby, it was as though my whole life and my whole system changed, even though the feelings were one-sided. Suddenly, I didn't have to be busy anymore. I could sit in a chair and daydream, and that was all right. I had no desire for food. I found I was losing weight for the first time in my life without consciously dieting.

Most MWLW who become awakened to their new sexuality do not see divorce as the obvious solution. Frequently, they say, "I wish my husband weren't such a nice guy." The overwhelming sense of guilt and duty coupled with the fear of living a gay lifestyle make staying in a marriage preferable for some women. Many of those I spoke with echoed each other with the following wish: "If only he drank or gambled away our money or hit me, then it would be easy to leave him." Yet, even women in abusive relationships have a difficult time making the break. The idea of suddenly being alone, especially for those women who went directly from their parents' home to their husband's, is difficult. The need of a man has been so ingrained in the education of most women that some even remain in marriages that are absolutely unbearable.

In *Codependent No More*, Melody Beattie describes a marriage in which the man spends his days lying on the couch, drunk and abusing his family. The wife works, pays the bills, maintains the house, and cares for the children. When asked why she doesn't leave her husband, the woman says, "Then who would take care of me?"[16]

Geri

"I felt like sex was his payment for taking care of me. Sometimes I felt like I was prostituting myself. It was the woman I fell in love with who made me realize that I was, and had always been, an equal partner in my marriage. I had been the budgeter and manager, and I had been responsible for raising three terrific kids. All of these years, my husband had made me feel as though I had been living off him."

Our society equates marriage with legal sex, and women used to be taught, even if they were not interested, that they did not have the right to say no when their husbands approached them. Sex came as part of the package. However, this notion, even among heterosexual couples, is changing.

Women taught to equate marriage with monogamy believe that if they do not choose to be monogamous, something is wrong with them, their partner, or their relationship. With education and growing self-esteem, women are beginning to realize that they can alter what society has mandated. Patsy, a MWLW and the mother of an eight-year-old daughter, has modified her life to meet her needs as well as the needs of her family.

Patsy

"What I've often seen in marriages are two people who are together forever and ever, bored stiff with each other, dull and uninteresting but together anyway because of the big pressure: 'If you don't stay, you're a failure.'

"I want my marriage to work because I am happy and therefore happy in it, not because society says if you leave it you are a failure.

"No one person can be expected to fulfill another person totally. Why can't I have my husband who I love and care about and also a woman who can give me what he cannot. To include Cheryl in my life is to make my life complete. For that, I have had to change my whole perspective of the world.

"Society has set up certain guidelines, and the people who don't fit into its predisposed rules, like me, are made to feel different," Patsy says. "For a long time, I thought there was something wrong with me. But the more I grew educationally and emotionally, the more I liked me and the more I saw other people liked me, too. The way people responded to me became much more positive. So I thought, 'How could it be me? I must be all right.'

"That's when I started to question. I questioned the whole system, including all those definitions of a marriage, a husband, a wife. And I stopped wearing a wedding ring. I don't like all the connotations that come affixed with that."

Most people can live comfortably within society's established guidelines—but for women who have discovered that third dimension in themselves, the world must be redefined.

Patsy says, "Taking charge of my life and changing the rules was the critical turning point for me. I no longer bemoan the fact that I couldn't have the kind of marriage I was 'supposed' to have. Regardless of whether it's proper by society's definition or not, I have to feel good and happy about myself.

"When I come home feeling good, I can be open to my child and my husband. I can be open to the stranger I bump into on the bus. My guide is 'How do I feel about myself?' If I feel good about me and the interactions between the people that I care about in my life, then I'm happy—my life is working. I'm not hurting anyone and society can take its rules to someone else.

"I think society limits us, and I think it's done intentionally. I want my life to be wide open enough that I can make any decisions based on what feels right for me and the people in my life. I don't want to be stuck into 'Well, I'm a mother so I can't do this,' or 'I'm a wife so I can't do that.'"

Shelly

Married six years and the mother of a five-year-old daughter, Shelly, unlike Patsy (who considers herself a lesbian), had been in relationships with men and women before she was married. "I never viewed monogamy as something I particularly wanted," she says. "It's not a style that really suits my nature, and it's not a value I hold. But when I met my husband, he felt it was important for him, so I said I'd try. For two years it worked. My life felt all right, but in a certain way I felt like a part of me was dying. I was living a life that was not me."

Today, it is common to find in alternative weekly newspapers personal ads that attest to the void many MWLW feel. "Female, caring, nonsmoker, married, seeks kindred woman for unending friendship," and "Married female with children seeks same for discreet correspondence, friendship." Another adds "Only therapied women need apply." In one center for gay men and lesbians, a MWLW started a support group for women like herself, and within a few months the group had grown to more than sixty members and is still growing.

The process of a MWLW becoming comfortable with who she is and of defining new boundaries and understandings in her relationships is an ongoing one. There are highs and lows and periods of frustration and confusion. Hours are spent trying to understand the question, "Why can't I just be happy?" Once I realized who I was, I was able to accept the fact that there was nothing wrong with me. A feeling of liberation and a tremendous sense of relief at being able finally to acknowledge my gender preference replaced my initial anger and frustration, and all the pieces seemed to fit into place.

I had been shocked when I realized I was a lesbian. I certainly didn't know when I married. I knew I wasn't very interested in sex, but I thought my low sex drive was the result of a thyroid condition. Over the last few years, I found myself getting up earlier than my husband and going to bed after he was asleep. Only after I found out about myself did I realize I had gotten into this sleep pattern to avoid physical intimacy with him. I realized I would need more space for our marriage to endure. For this to happen, I would have to tell him about myself—but how?

PART **TWO**
A New Life

CHAPTER 4

Do I Tell My Husband or Not?

Although she may think she knows her husband well, no woman can accurately predict his response should she choose to disclose her preference for women, and once the words are out, they can never be taken back. Therefore, to tell or not to tell is one of the most difficult decisions a MWLW must make, and one for which there is no easy answer.

When I learned about myself, I didn't believe I'd ever tell my husband. The whole thing came as such a shock to me. It was something I had never contemplated.

I agonized over my decision to come out to him, and then, when I decided to, over how I would tell him and when. I chose a time when the kids were away for the weekend, but I couldn't find the right words. Friday passed, then Saturday was almost over. I couldn't say anything. I knew Sunday would be too late. It wasn't fair for him not to have time to digest this news.

We had gone to a street fair, but I was so uptight about wanting to tell him and not being able to get the words out that I can't remember what we saw that day. He led the way to an ice cream parlor, and we sat down. He commented innocently on the amount of money I was spending in therapy, which I had finally told him about, and I just began to cry. Then all the words poured out. I told him I had been in therapy for months before I mustered the courage to tell him. I told him how I felt about Toby and how she had stopped talking to me when I told her how I felt. I told him about the pain I had endured and the isolation I had lived with since the loss of my best friend.

It was a lot for him to take in, and we drove home in silence. Normally, we'd go our separate ways once we got home. Today, we sat together on the couch and cried. "Now each time you go out I'm going to wonder if you are looking for a woman," he said.

"Did you wonder if I was looking for a man each time I went out before?"

Darkness came, and we remained in our places. Neither of us moved to turn on a light. After a while I asked if he'd like something to eat. "No," he said. "I need to take a walk."

That night was long and filled with sorrow. As I waited for my husband to return, I recalled the two innocent young teenagers we had been when we met, and my pain intensified. Still, the anguish I had lived with for the past two years began to lessen. My secret was finally out.

It seemed like hours before he returned. Exhausted, we went up to bed, but neither of us slept. We lay side by side, talking and crying into the early morning.

I think my telling my husband everything helped him to have a little more understanding for me and what I was going through, but it didn't lessen his shock or the grief that soon replaced the first numbing blow. I tried to help him to see that there was nothing he could have done to change what had happened.

After a while, I got used to being who I was and realized it was easier to live with the new me than with the detachment I originally felt from my family. They had been living with someone they didn't really know—and I had been feeling very incomplete.

My husband still went through periods of grief mixed with anger and for a while had days when the slightest upset could bring on uncalled-for fury. But, those days grew father apart, and I kept remembering that it took me several years to come to terms with who and what I am, so it was only fair to give him the time he needed.

To his credit, he began therapy and learned a lot about himself. When he talks now, it's with a deeper level of understanding. I'm finding him more interesting than I have in years. I don't know what will become of our marriage, but I think eventually we'll be better friends than would ever have been possible before.

While homosexual men have been the forerunners in leading the way out of the closet, women are only now beginning to feel the same freedom to be who they are. This may be due, in part, to society's begrudging acknowledgment of lesbianism, brought on by the shift in society's supposition that the cause of one's sexual persuasion was a personal choice and therefore could be changed.

Chandler Burr, author of *Homosexuality and Biology*, says, "Homosexuals have long maintained that sexual orientation, far from being a personal choice or lifestyle (as it is often called), is something neither chosen nor changeable; heterosexuals who have made their peace with homosexuals have often done so by accepting that premise. The very term 'sexual orientation,' which in the 1980s replaced 'sexual preference,' asserts the deeply rooted nature of sexual desire and love. It implies biology."[1]

Prior to the sixties, it was not uncommon for a woman to grow up never having heard the word *lesbian*. Even when the word did begin to surface, it was generally in whispered conversations and in the most derogatory manner.

Then, between June and October 1993, *Newsweek*, *Vanity Fair*, and *Cosmopolitan* featured lesbians on their covers and as their top stories. *New York Magazine*'s May 10, 1993, issue featured singer k.d. lang on its cover with the title "Lesbian Chic." Now it is common to see national magazines with articles on gay issues.

By 1996, top television series such as *ER* and *Roseanne* had announced shows with lesbian content. Then, on *Roseanne*, to boost ratings, Roseanne's mother announced that she was a lesbian. The series *Friends* and *Mad About You* introduced lesbian characters as regulars, and in 1997, a landmark in American television was reached when Ellen DeGeneres came out in both in her private life and on her eponymous television show.

Because lesbians are finding a voice and making themselves seen and heard, the isolation each MWLW has felt living with her own "terrible secret" is slowly lifting.

Younger women, once they have identified their own sexuality, seem to experience less difficulty coming out to their spouses, even when they have children. Perhaps this is because they have not yet been conditioned by our culture to see alternative lifestyles as taboo or spent years being taken care of and possibly losing their sense of self. They therefore have more confidence in their ability to survive without a mate than do older women.

The process of telling is one many older women do not know how to handle. They don't want to remain in their marriages on bad terms or to leave on bad terms. They want everything to remain intact. The internal turmoil they feel leads to ambivalence or tremendous difficulty with decision making. The idea of deceiving someone else is so overwhelming that these women often fail to recognize that they are deceiving themselves.

Even when a woman has made the decision to tell her husband, her words are often met with disbelief or denial because a common misconception is that if a woman was a lesbian, she would be incapable of having a heterosexual sexual relationship. Yet, according to clinical psychologist and sex therapist Margaret Nichols, "The vast majority of lesbians have had some sexual involvement with men before coming out: More than ninety percent have had sex with men, and one third have been married."[2]

Most of the MWLW interviewed believed that if they hadn't discovered their same-sex preference when they did, their preference would have eventually made itself known anyway. Initially, however, many of these MWLW who had recently learned of, or come to terms with, their new sexuality admitted to being extremely angry with their spouses, blaming the men for causing them to turn to women. If the woman is in the accusation stage, it may be better to wait until she has gone through her own exploration and composed herself before sharing this information.

There are no specific guidelines for MWLW and no right or wrong solutions to this marital predicament. Each woman has her own agenda in choosing if, when, and how to come out to her husband. What works for one may not work for another. While disclosures often seem to come about gradually, the timing of the "official disclosure" in relation to business or financial pressures, family illness, or problems with a child has a lot to do with how the husband will react.

One woman says, "We were married eleven years before I finally felt I was in a place in our marital relationship where it felt safe enough for me to share who I was with my husband."

Another says, "I waited two days. Then I couldn't keep it to myself anymore. It made so many other things so clear."

Whether the couple decide to continue in their marriage, if there is to be peace, the way a MWLW tells her spouse about herself and the way he is able to listen to her are very important. Often, sharing what she is going through serves to create a greater understanding and a closer bond between husband and wife.

When she tells her husband, the MWLW should keep in mind that it is she who has changed. He has not. Every man's reaction is going to differ depending on his own security. Even a man secure in his own sexuality will experience a variety of reactions. Shock, anger, rage, and denial are common feelings. Some men go through depression. Even men who are compassionate and sympathetic to their wives' plights will experience hostile feelings at some time. The confirmation of suspicions, an explanation or excuse for sexual incompatibility may bring relief to others. Being as honest as possible without being hurtful will help.

The ease with which a MWLW has been able to communicate with her husband is one important aspect in determining whether she will share this information with him. The negative or positive feelings she has about her own sexuality—often related to her upbringing, education, and level of self-confidence—are another. The agony brought on by the deception of not telling causes other women to come out. Women who have never acted on their impulses to be with another woman but who know they are more attracted to women than they are to men face the same turmoil. They would like to share the truth about themselves but cannot.

Pat

"I had gotten to the point where my feelings just weren't going anywhere," says forty-five-year-old Pat. "They weren't changing, they weren't disappearing, and my husband and I knew something was wrong. In a fit of honesty and openness, I told him that while I'd never had an experience with another woman, I always knew there was something 'different' about myself.

"He never believed me," she says. "In his mind, if I were gay I would be incapable of having a heterosexual relationship."

Frustrated after various unsuccessful attempts to broach the topic, Pat simply decided to let it drop.

"It's a subject now that's avoided," she says. "We don't talk about it, but anytime we have a fight or a disagreement, it's simmering in the background. I regret having said anything, and I can't take it back."

Pat, brought up to put the feelings and needs of her family first, has been living unhappily in this "stuck" state for the past eighteen years.

Norma

Norma fell in love with a woman who was going to die. She says, "I had never felt this way about another woman before, and I didn't think I could feel this way again. I was very happy with my husband. I wasn't looking to get out of my marriage. I wasn't looking for 'it,' but 'it' found me. Marcia would have liked me to come out of the closet, leave my husband and family, and join her in her life, but I was afraid.

"My husband knew her. He knew that she was my best friend. He also knew that she was a lesbian. I had even told him that I loved her. He asked me how I meant that, and I said, 'Like I love a lot of people.' I never told him that we had a physical relationship, so he was tolerant.

"I told my husband that she was sick, and I wanted to be all the friend I could be to her while she was alive. He seemed to understand and allowed me the time I wanted with her. Whether he knew or not, I don't know. I think when she died, it was a relief to him. I know that he had been very jealous."

Janette

Janette never had any sexual experience with another woman but always knew she was different. Her friends in high school had posters of male actors covering their walls. She remembers thinking, "Why would they want to look at these?" She married a man who was her friend because, like so many others, she thought marriage was something she was supposed to do.

"My husband knew but didn't know," she says. "We joked about my feeling anxious and scared. I thought I was going crazy. I loved him, but I wasn't in love with him. I had two children and another coming, a house, and a dog. All that and it wasn't me.

"Three years ago, I thought I could be married forever. Then a feeling of 'it's not fair' started growing. I know now I can't spend the rest of my life faking something I don't feel. I needed to share my feelings with my husband.

"Recently, I went to a store and picked up a few books," Janette says. "One was *Call Me Lesbian*. I showed it to him. He took it as a joke and wouldn't talk to me about it. I asked if he wanted to know what page I was up to and what the book was about. He wanted no part of it. He said he was going to call Howard Stern, a New York talk show host known for insulting his listeners.

"Then a program, 'In Bed with a Secret' aired about straight spouses. I asked him to watch it with me. I said to him, 'I don't know what to do. Am I supposed to act on my feelings? Am I supposed to suppress them? What should I do?' He got very mad. He said I could do what I wanted, but his kids would never be in a house with women like on that program. Then he wouldn't talk about it anymore.

"That night, afraid he'd call me an unfit mother, I got rid of the books. Now he seems to have forgotten the whole thing like it is no longer an issue."

Open communication might have saved Janette's marriage, but her husband's refusal to deal with the truth has stopped any chance of that possibility.

Janette has started therapy alone. "My husband knows I'm in therapy and says to me, 'Did you tell her [the therapist] how good you have it? What a good husband you have?' I say, yes, of course, and I save my money and plan for my future without him."

Within a marriage, it might come to light that sexual preferences differ, but lesbianism alone is rarely the only problem a couple faces. Each partner enters the relationship with his or her emotional baggage. The sexual issue, however, is often the catalyst through which other problems are identified.

Liz

Liz, thirty-seven, was brought up in an independent, female-headed household where the women did everything. She never imagined herself in a subordinate position to a man. She and her husband both had careers in the theater; they spent much time traveling and living in hotels on the road, which they both loved. But then Liz's career began to outdistance her husband's. He grew negative and withdrew. She, not able to break through his shell, began to feel isolated. Unconsciously, although she had always believed herself to be heterosexual, she was drawn to a woman employee who traveled with them, and she initiated an affair with her. Liz describes the woman as "vivacious, energetic, and, most important, incredibly supportive."

"When my husband asked me what was going on, I fessed up. It was a loud, horrible dialogue. But I felt what I had done to him was pretty horrible, so that whatever he wanted to dish out to me, I should just take. He became really angry more at my friend than at me. Now he basically thinks all lesbians should die.

"He's throwing 'you don't need anyone' at me, but that's not the point. I didn't need him when I married him. I married him because I wanted him. If I had had to be a spineless female just to prove to him that I loved him I wouldn't have grown in my profession as I've done. He feels women should be weak, and that he, as the man, must always be in control and take care of the woman.

"All he can see is that my friend ruined everything for him. He'll take no responsibility for his actions and the behavior that pushed me away from him. He chooses instead to pass the blame and responsibility rather than look at the underlying causes that turned me from him. He's got so much misplaced anger now I don't know if he would ever be able to bury the hatchet."

At times, the decision to tell is taken out of the MWLW's hands. Some husbands suspect that their wives are no longer interested in them sexually and sense that their feelings for women are powerful, perhaps even sexual. Several women were "outed" accidentally when their husbands overheard phone conversations. One husband found a letter inadvertently left out, and another came home to find his wife embracing her woman friend.

David

"Ellen got pregnant, and we married, so you can't say we started off our relationship in love with each other, but it's something that has grown. As far as our sex life is concerned, I've never questioned any of that. I believe the man ought to satisfy the woman in a sexual relationship, so she's always been satisfied on that part."

Now the father of two and an educator at a midwestern college, David said, "I had been to a meeting and walked into the house. Our children were away at camp. I saw my wife, Ellen, with a young woman from the neighborhood. They had lost track of time and were actually making love.

"I'm not the kind of person who gets real angry and screams and yells. I'm the kind who wants to talk situations out, and I guess I wanted an explanation more than anything else. The other woman left, and Ellen explained that it was a complicated thing. She didn't think it was something women went out looking for. It was just something that happened. She said she had these feelings.

"I could understand when she said she didn't know what they were all about. I could accept that. Now I'm not only trying to learn about Ellen's life, but I'm trying to understand my fascination with her life.

"We're not doing anything [sexually] more frequently, but ... there is definitely more emotional intimacy because we've both been so open with each other. She has begun to confide in me in terms of her relationships and the way she feels about other women and who she's attracted to."

David hesitantly admitted that after recovering from the initial blow of seeing his wife in the arms of another woman, "I was more intrigued watching the women than shocked by the idea of them together. I'm turned on by the fact that Ellen is with another woman. What intrigues me is not that it's two women but that it's *Ellen* and someone else. I don't think I would enjoy literally being in a three-some, but I did enjoy the watching part. If she were with another man, I can pretty well predict that my response would not be positive."

David is not unique. Human beings, by nature, are sexual beings. While society would try to repress this notion, it was not uncommon for men to relate an increase of their own sexual appetites after learning that their wives were attracted to women. The idea of two women together excites a great many men. We need only to look at billboards or glance through magazine ads to see beautiful women in intimate poses with other women. Popular rental choices for men at video stores are movies of two women making love. As one man explained, "Because there is no man performing on the tape, no comparisons need to be made, and I can visualize myself in whatever capacity I choose."

It can take some women years to discover and then accept their own sexuality before even beginning to consider sharing who they are with their husbands. While that is not unusual, it is also not unusual for a perceptive husband to discern what is happening between his wife and a woman friend before the women are aware of the sexual component of their friendship.

Shari

"My husband saw things before I did—noting that my friend and I were getting very close, he asked me if we were in love with each other—so the groundwork had been laid by him to have this discussion. Our relationship and my own style are such that I would be open with him on any matter—as he is with me—so this was no exception. Knowing I had the understanding and support of my husband was an incredible load off my shoulders.

"When I finally admitted to myself what was happening, I first ran it by my therapist for some guidance. Then I sat down with my husband one night and told him pretty straightforwardly that I'm gay. He said, 'We'll work it out.' His response set the course for all the work we've done since."

While the majority of men take their wives' preference for women as a personal affront to their own manhood, men with a strong sense of self understand that the preference doesn't necessarily reflect on them. Because of her husband's self-confidence, Shari felt comfortable sharing her discovery with him. She was able to go through the agonizing questions, trauma, decisions, and changes brought about by her breakthrough with him at her side.

Still, a husband's emotional support does not guarantee that the marriage will endure because it isn't always the man who chooses to end the marriage when he learns about his wife.

Luann

"I was married to my first husband for seven years. When he accused me of being a lesbian, I thought he was crazy. My second marriage lasted twelve years. I was very much in love with my husbands, especially my second husband, and when I was walking in the street with him, I'd look at women and say, 'Doesn't she have nice hair or breasts or legs.' I thought all women looked at other women. I still had no idea about my sexuality. Sometimes before we had sex, we'd look at porno films. I was always watching the women. The first seven years were wonderful, but then we started having some trouble, not getting along.

"I began spending more time with my girlfriend. In the beginning I thought, 'I'm just flirting with her. This is fun.' Even after we had been going to bed for six months I believed I was doing it because I was really pissed at my husband.

"When I realized eventually that I was a lesbian, I told him. He said, 'I always thought it was so innocent the way you used to look at women and comment on them. I never really thought you found them attractive, but I guess I'm not surprised.'"

Once she came to the realization that she was a lesbian, it was Luann who chose to end her marriage.

Women who know about and discuss their sexual predilection with their husbands in advance of their marriages and truly believe that they will be able to honor the contracts they have created—having families, working together, caring about each other—also find that open communication and understanding are not always enough make their marriages work.

Florence

Florence, thirty-three, says, "I knew I was a lesbian and was scared that even if I married, my life would be difficult. But I thought I had to get married. When I married my first husband and kept my secret, the marriage fell apart. I believed it was because I had not been honest with him. When I met my second husband, I told him that I was gay the day we met. I still thought getting married would take my gayness away from me.

"My husband didn't take this information as a threat to our marriage. He just thought it was one of my attributes, like having brown hair. So I was gay. I was able to be with women when I was married to him. As long as I didn't flaunt what I did, it was all right with him. I'd tell him I was going away for a weekend, and he was comfortable with that as long as I came home again.

"We were married for three years when I ended our union. He would have liked me to remain, but I couldn't. As time went by, I became more strongly attracted to women and less comfortable living with a man. Although he accepted who I was, and I cared about him, I still felt that I was living a lie. Finally I couldn't do that anymore."

Some men hadn't fully comprehended the ramifications of their wives' lesbianism or bisexuality when they said they could stick it out. Some confessed that, at the time, they had chosen not to believe it, while others made it clear that they didn't want to talk about it or even to hear their wives' stories. Others, who continued to have a physical relationship with their wives, related an increase in their sexual appetites after hearing about their wives' true sexuality.

The bottom line is that having your wife tell you she is a lesbian is a lot of information for anyone to process. While there is no way to predict how any husband will react, it became clear that those women who hadn't become alienated from their husbands in the process of discovering their sexual preference were more likely to maintain an intimate partnership, if not a sexual one. In rare instances, a husband might even help his wife explore her new identity.

Faye

Faye's husband was one of those men who tried to help his wife by inviting another woman to their bed. "My husband saved me from a terribly abusive childhood," Faye explains. "He is an amazing and wonderful person. I owe him my life, but I am killing all that I loved in him because I can't seem to keep the lesbian from spilling out of me. I am so lost. I don't want to lose him or hurt him, but my life is nonexistent. I am all work and no blue sky. I keep attaining one degree after another trying to take the focus off my lack of fulfillment. Meanwhile, he continues to look for a cure for me. He thought inviting another woman to our bed would be the answer."

Although Faye's husband realized he was having trouble dealing with it and called off the arrangement before it became too intimate, Faye has had an emotional affair with the woman ever since.

Paula

"We were married fifteen years," Paula, the mother of three, explains. "My husband is one of my best friends and has always known about my struggles with sexuality and my strong feelings for particular women in my life. He supported me lovingly when my journey finally brought me to recognize myself as a lesbian. Believe it or not, he helped me to write this ad to place in a local women's newspaper:

Married lesbian wants to join or form a lesbian support group for friendship, conversation, and understanding.

"I don't think either he or I ever expected that this realization could have much of a practical impact on our lives. After all, I had no intention of leaving my marriage or breaking up the family. Instead, I simply embraced the newfound internal peace that had come to me with this ultimate self-acceptance, and I began to explore ways to feel comfortable in the lesbian community without turning my back on my world as it was."

Paula's husband was sensitive to her needs and knowingly helped her to learn of her sexual identity. But lesbianism can also be extraordinarily threatening to some men. There are husbands who are simply incapable of understanding their spouses' needs and pleasures. Others can imagine women together only as a sexual turn-on for their own fantasies. In Melinda's case, it was only when her husband expressed a desire to see his wife with another woman that she finally acted on feelings she had secretly harbored.

Melinda

"When my husband told me he wanted to see me with a woman, I thought I would do it as a gift to him for his birthday. And at the same time, I could explore my own sexuality. A friend put me in touch with a woman who helped me to make his fantasy come true. It was a very positive, wonderful experience," she says. "What I really want to do now is to be with another woman without my husband present."

After her experience, Melinda told her husband of her feelings for women. "He said it would be fine with him if I was involved with a woman as long as it was not a relationship that took up the amount of time and energy that my relationship with him does. He doesn't want to be pushed aside. He wants to be the main focus of my life. But, maybe because he is turned on by the idea of two women together, he is not opposed to my being with a woman."

Melinda's husband is fairly accepting, and he doesn't want to lose her. Other men, however, can neither stand to have their wives have outside relationships with women nor leave them. They cannot cope with any aspect of their wives' new sexuality.

Martha

When Martha told her husband about herself after having been in therapy for eight years, his response was "I thought so."

She says, "He had figured that because I didn't respond to him sexually, there must be something wrong with me. So now it was, 'Okay, so you are. That explains things.'

"He was thinking that what I told him solved the mystery of my not being physical. He still figured that I was going to stay with him forever and was very upset when I told him I was thinking of leaving him. He hadn't considered that fact.

"We went through months of crying together, and he would hate me, then he would try to get me to feel sorry for him and not change his life. I realized that the bottom line was he didn't care that I was in pain. He only wanted me to continue keeping things the way they were for him."

Martha's husband's reaction is not uncommon. No one wants to be embarrassed, to have his life changed, to have his job affected. Human beings become comfortable in their worlds; it is human nature that people try to maintain the status quo. For some, the threat of change can be devastating.

Realistically, women must be aware that their revelation may provoke outrage. Some men have become physically violent. Others started withholding money or using it for revenge. One husband told his child, "Mommy doesn't love us anymore." MWLW who divulge this information must understand that they may be faced with consequences not of their choosing. Even for those who have shared open channels of communication with their spouses, or believed their husbands to have surmised their true sexuality, the actual admission can come as a shock.

Likewise, the MWLW who believes she has her husband's support and understanding when she gives this information to him must understand that although his reactions may be delayed, at some point he will likely experience a sense of bewilderment and loss. This time of transition differs for each individual. Even those men secure in their own identity must recognize that their world is going to change, and that change may mean the dissolution of their marriage.

CHAPTER 5

The Husbands

One particular question that never fails to arise when the subject of MWLW comes up is, What kind of men are these women married to?

Just as there is no common denominator among MWLW, their husbands also come from a wide variety of backgrounds. Their occupations range from factory workers to professors and from civil service employees to chief executive officers; their hobbies range from motorcycles to botany. Like any diverse group of men, some were described as virile, others not. While some were intuitive and knew their wives' preference before their wives realized it themselves; others preferred to live with their heads in the sand, even after full disclosure. Depending on their level of self-awareness, the men saw their wives' same-gender choices as threatening or stimulating.

One man said he saw his wife's relationships with women as a prelude for more stimulating sex. "I was the one who brought it up," he said. "I started asking her questions, purely sexual and descriptive, not emotional. I thought, 'If we could be honest, it could be a good relationship.' And I found she was excited by it. It improved the sexual part of our life together."

Another man has looked the other way while his wife has been in a relationship with her best friend for more than thirty years, nearly as long as she has been in her marriage. She vacations with and spends weekends and every spare minute with her friend.

"My husband is glad I have Cynthia and I don't bother him," Susan says, "since he chooses to live with blinders."

Not all men wear blinders or see their wives' announcements in terms of their own sexual fantasies. For some men, it was their wives' coming out that caused them to look at themselves analytically for the first time. Not every husband felt the need, but several went to therapy as a means of working out marital issues. Admittedly, the decision to see a therapist was a difficult one for most to make. One husband, who went only twice, talked about probably going back "some other time." Another spoke of developing a greater awareness of his own problems, unrelated to his wife's sexuality. He said part of the reason he was going was to gather the courage to make changes for himself.

Michael

Michael had always resisted the idea of therapy. It wasn't until after his wife had started seeing another woman that he finally decided to go. However, he remained adamant that therapy could not help his marriage. "There is nothing in it for me anymore," he said bitterly. He agreed to go only because he was in a bad way and was desperate to find some help. What came to light during his therapy sessions was his own baggage. He had refused to acknowledge or deal with any of the problems that had accumulated since childhood. He began to focus on himself, working on long-buried childhood issues instead of his floundering marriage.

Michael began to understand how his problems were related to his slow withdrawal from his wife. He stopped blaming her for his anger and hurt and began to accept responsibility for his share in the way things had gone between them. He came to realize that the marriage, although altered according to society's general definition regarding the sexual component, still held much for him. Barbara and Michael have been working at renegotiating and stabilizing their new relationship.

Tom

Tom, like Michael, was finally able to see and understand that problems with his marriage began long before his wife made her discovery and may even have affected her discovery.

"My wife, Frances, knew there was something bothering me and wanted to talk to me about our situation, about how I was feeling, what I was thinking, and what was happening with us long before she turned to her friend for the comfort she wasn't getting from me. But I was in my own world. She kept pleading with me to talk," he says, "but, like always, trying to talk to me must have been frustrating as hell for her. I was brought up to keep my emotions in check, and I am a pro at that.

"I told her that I was indifferent to the situation and it didn't matter to me what she did, but that's not true. It does matter. What's really bothering me is me. I'm down on myself. She's doing what she wants to and I feel like I'm stuck. I'm jealous. I know it's my fault for not being able to communicate. She says she probably would have discovered her identity sooner or later anyway, but I wonder about that. Our marriage was going bad before she found out about herself. Maybe if it wasn't … I know it was my fault. I think it started when I lost my job and I took the one in the city. I was miserable with the commute. No. I think it started before that. I was withdrawing: from her, from life. I was submerging myself in my work, in the television, in books.

"I feel real unhappy about myself. Frustrated, like I missed something my whole life, and I don't know why. Basically I've given up on everything. Now I'm very lonely. I have no friends. She goes out with her women friends, and I have no one to do anything with. I have a hard time making friends on my own. I always expected her to take care of the entire social part of my life.

"Since I couldn't talk about my feelings or show my feelings in any other way, sex was my only way to get really close to her, and now that's gone, too. How should I feel?"

It is not surprising that most of the men who agreed to be interviewed seemed secure in their sexual identification. Their wives' same-sex orientations didn't threaten their sexual identity and the idea of homosexuality in general did not seem frightening to them. They were open and able to talk about it. Perhaps more noteworthy, these men were also able to step back to see and appreciate their wives as separate individuals.

Howard

"I love my wife and want what's best for her. The fact that she loves women, I think, is something important to her, and I want to respect that. If this is a part of who my wife is, I have no right to tell her to be different. That would be like denying her a part of what makes her her."

Asked if her revelation made him question his own sexuality, Howard said, "I guess I'm not particularly attracted to gay men. I had an offer to play around with an older male cousin of mine when I was younger. It just didn't interest me. If the same situation was to come along today, I don't think I'd be interested.

"Actually, I think I'm more attracted to women than I have been. I realize now they have another dimension that they're struggling with and working with and trying to be accepted for.

"I think, had my wife said, 'I want a divorce,' when I found out, it would have been painful, but I think after the initial shock and adjustment was over with, I would still have walked away with a deeper appreciation for women."

Nathan

Nathan, like Howard, explains his unusual marital situation philosophically. "Whatever makes a person happy is what that person has to do. My wife has certain needs. She's not a happy person, but she strives to be happy."

Eighteen years ago, while his children were small, his wife told him of her need for women in her life. He nevertheless chose to remain in his marriage. "I'm a creature of habit and convenience. I didn't want to have to go out and start a new life all over again, so I made the necessary adjustments so as not to rock my existing boat.

"When I first realized I was never going to be able to fill her emotional need, that was a tough time. I was also a little bit angry because she never told me that she had had sexual feelings for women earlier," Nathan says about the timing of his wife's coming out. "I resent that I didn't know in the beginning. I should have been told right off the bat. I think it would have made a difference.

"I can't deny that's what I'm mad about, but the fact that this is what she is, I can't take that away from her. Once I knew about her, I chose not to change my life.

"After I realized I had to make my own settlement, everything was fine. We went on normally for a long while; then we sort of arrived at our own lives."

Jack

Jack was attracted to his wife Rosalie because he sensed something different in her than in other women.

"At thirty-five, I got to the point that I was ready for marriage," Jack says. "There was something in Rosalie that wasn't the female touch I felt in other women. There was nothing girlish or whiny about her. There was something different that I couldn't identify. We complimented each other's personalities, and I needed what was in her.

"Rosalie had no great desire to be a mother. We would have had children if it had been important to her, but it wasn't. Besides, I had been the diaperer for my younger siblings, and I didn't mind being relieved of that burden.

"When Rosalie identified her feelings and came out to me, it made me feel lost for a while, until I realized that that part of her had always been there. I wasn't angry, but I felt lonely at times.

"I'd rather have this woman be able to sit down and talk to me and relate to me than cater to me and cook for me. There was an honesty about her. This was one of the things I always admired about her."

Jack believes that lesbianism is more about the emotional support derived from another woman than strictly sexual issues. "For some, sex may be more important. But I think most important is that you've got to be able to talk and sense and feel for each other.

"I couldn't fulfill all of her needs. I had sensed that for quite a while, but I didn't know what they were. She had to take the necessary steps before I could understand. I feel more secure now knowing that there is another person, Brenda, who also cares about the person I care about."

Rosalie's friend Brenda lives nearby. Jack and Brenda each have a separate physical relationship with Rosalie but not with each other. Jack and Brenda have, however, become good friends. Brenda was even invited to stay at Rosalie and Jack's house while her house was under construction.

Admittedly, this new arrangement was not always easy. A lot of dialogue went into creating the open and honest rapport they now share. Jack admits, "At times there was resentment in the beginning that Rosalie had someone else to talk to, but knowing how important Brenda was to her, I wanted to make it work.

"There were times I'd sleep alone at night and curl up with a pillow because she wasn't there. That was hard. At times I resented Rosalie for this. But it wasn't important as far as affecting the way I felt about my wife. It was just time to say, 'Damn it, what's this all about?'

"I was able to tell Rosalie how I felt. Sometimes she cried a little. I'm sure she felt she was letting me down, and I'm sure she still struggles with it, but I'll help her in any way I can."

Jack's acceptance was not arrived at overnight. Much time was spent in thought, and then discussing and evaluating the situation, before coming to the realization of their individual needs. "I know that as a man I can't give Rosalie everything she needs, and as a woman she can't give me everything I need either."

Society would have us believe that marriage makes for completion. This places a tremendous burden on both partners: the one who believes that there is something wrong with him or her as an individual if his mate occasionally turns to another—whether for physical, emotional, or spiritual connection—and the one who does not feel complete but agonizes over the possibility of hurting a mate if he or she finds someone else who can help to fill the void. If one mate feels content but the other doesn't, the stress can be even greater. Yet, it is almost impossible for one person to be able to fill all of another person's needs.

Frank

"There was always a sexual problem between us," Frank, married for eleven years, says. "And why we stayed together this long I don't even know. Maybe there's a bond or sense of security. Anyway, I had a feeling, so when she told me, I didn't really think anything of it. It wasn't like she said, 'I have a girlfriend, and I'm in love, and I'm leaving you.' She just said, 'I like girls.' I sort of knew already. I wouldn't call her a feminist, but she had always been sort of antimale.

"So even when she presented it to me it wasn't like it was a big thing. But as time went on, she progressively got more and more obsessed with the idea of lesbianism. It was like she was searching for something that's never been. Every minute, every chance, everything revolved around that. She was on America Online eighteen hours a day, like 'til four in the morning with these women.

"We work together, we're partners in a small manufacturing business, and we also have a son. So very quickly, things started to fall apart. From the America Online, she started talking on the phone. There were all kinds of calls, and then she started meeting people.

"I was livid. Really mad. The lesbian part didn't make me as angry as what she was doing to my life, to my son's life, and to the business. Probably that's where I had the most anger. I was getting up at five in the morning, getting the kid and doing everything for him, working all day 'til seven o'clock, and at nine I was like beat. She totally neglected my son, totally neglected the business, and everything was just in a complete upheaval. We had lots of fights, or I would go for a week and not say a word to her."

While Frank admits to constant conflict, he also acknowledges that during the early months of his wife's coming out, their sex life was good. "That was the strange thing," he says. "As far as sexuality goes, there had always been something lacking, and now, sexually, she was charged. So sex was better than it ever was. And more often, and more frequent. But at the same time she was also flipping out.

"After about three months the sex was cut off. There was a lot of lying going on, things behind my back. She was meeting people and telling me she was going someplace else.

"I got really, really mad and at that point said, 'Why don't you move out,' but I felt really bad kicking her out like that. She suffers from depression, which was compounded by her feelings of guilt. She wouldn't get out of bed and was constantly crying. It took more than a year. Anyway, once she got off the antidepressant, she got much better. She got an apartment, and she is moving out, but now we talk. We made a joint decision for her to leave my son with me. At first she wanted him, and I finally talked her out of it. Our workshop is at the back of our place. I wouldn't have felt comfortable coming to her house to work if she stayed and I left. I'd be subjected to her lifestyle with her phone calls, etc. Now I see us being friends and jointly raising our son.

"I still care for her a lot. I'm not in love with her anymore, but I still love her. We have a bond, married for eleven years, a kid. That just doesn't go away."

Eddie

Married for sixteen years and the father of one, Eddie says, "I look at our relationship like a giant organic thing. It's part of both of us. We've been together sixteen years. We have a son. We have a history, and our lives are built around this history. Anyway, Shari was always very open communication-wise, and she came out to me within a day of her realizing it herself. She had been working through issues of abuse as a child, reliving them. So my reaction was, 'We'll work it through.' I wasn't really shocked until I realized it was fairly serious stuff. I guess I thought it was just something else to put on the pile."

Shari describes Eddie as "a man with high energy and sometimes high tension. He is enthusiastic and has strongly expressed opinions that can also be tossed to the wind. He is distant emotionally in some ways and very loving and supportive in others. He throws himself full tilt into a successive series of hobbies, but always finds one more to move on to. Always being involved in one project or another is one of the things that attracted me to him at the beginning. I was in love with him when we married, and I love him now."

Still, Eddie and Shari led very different lives. Eddie says, "We hadn't always done everything together. We have very distinct tastes, our interests aren't parallel, and our hobbies don't coincide. We both have our own releases. She's into horses. I like motorcycles. We allow each other to grow in many different directions."

Although their sex life had diminished over the years to "a rare event," Eddie initially believed they should remain monogamous when Shari told him about herself. "At first it bothered me." Eddie explained, "I didn't want her to be with another person, male or female. I was jealous that she might take her sexuality elsewhere and that became an issue.

"In the back of my mind I was hoping I could change this," Eddie says. "Then I realized that was very unrealistic, and I had to somehow cope with it and kind of weave that into our marriage, hoping that our marriage could survive. Still, just because I'm understanding, it isn't easy to deal with. I wish it wasn't this way."

"I've thought of divorce," Eddie said, "but I didn't want that. I saw the pain my sister went through with a divorce ... get a machete and chop it in two.

"We had to work it through," he says. "Eventually, I realized that this was something society had put upon me: 'You make your wife loyal to you.' But it wasn't something I really felt inside. So I kind of let that go, and it really changed things. It lifted this burden off Shari's shoulders, too."

It is not uncommon when a wife brings her new sexuality out into the open for her husband to wonder whether he is to blame, to question his manliness. In Woody Allen's film *Manhattan*, the wife, played by Meryl Streep, leaves him for another woman. To prove his manhood, he enters into a physical relationship with a seventeen-year-old girl.

One woman said, "In reexamining my relationship with my husband, I realized that it was not that he loved me, but his ego and his manliness were at stake. Here he is, a CEO, making over six figures a year. He handled all of our money, controlled my whole life, even decided what we would and wouldn't eat. He had me cleaning the house, shopping, cooking, and taking care of the children. But he couldn't change my feelings.

"If it was another man I was in love with he could beat the hell out of him, but it was a woman. He couldn't touch a woman. He felt deflated. He didn't feel anger or rejection. He felt resentment."

It is also not uncommon, when a wife comes out to her husband, for him to question his own sexuality.

"Sometimes I wondered if I could be gay," admits one man after his wife's disclosure. "When I saw men who were attractive, I'd think, 'Maybe I could have an affair,' but then I really thought about it. I never questioned my sexuality before, but I did recently. And it's cut and dry. I am a heterosexual. I am not attracted to men, and I don't consider myself bisexual, although I see men as potentially attractive. I can't see myself wanting a man as I do a woman. But then, I don't want to be married to a lesbian, but I am. It's a difficult thing."

Another woman wondered if her husband might be gay years before she had any clue that she was a lesbian. "When we were young marrieds," she says, "we were at a picnic with friends. The guys were tossing a ball around and running to catch it. For a fleeting instance I thought my husband looked effeminate as he ran, but I didn't give it much thought. After all, we had three children.

"The more I thought about it, though, the more I wondered. Although he was generally a kind and considerate man, he made ridiculing comments about 'fags' and 'queers' whenever the opportunity arose. He sort of talked about them too much, like he was trying to show how different he was from them.

"When our sex life dwindled and came to an end, he never said anything about it. Neither did I. I think we both felt relieved. Looking back, I realize it had never been anything to boast about. Never any experimentation, a little foreplay, him always on top. It was sort of like, okay, we did it. I made you come, and I came. Good night.

"After twenty-seven years of marriage, I realized that I was a lesbian and told him. Even though I had no intention of leaving, it was real hard for him. He was not in the habit of making phone calls, so he couldn't talk to anyone about it. He saw his male friends only when we went out as couples. So he was really alone. I felt so sorry that I had told him but I needed to talk about me.

"We don't talk about my sexuality now but we do talk more about general things. Other than where the topic of gays and lesbians is concerned, he's a very good and gentle man and a wonderful and involved father, and I care about him a lot.

"I really believe that one of the reasons he's so homophobic is because he's afraid to deal with his own sexual issues. Recently, in conversation, I said to him, 'If you find people you truly care about, gender shouldn't matter.' He jumped down my throat, shouting, 'I'm not queer.'"

Not every husband struggles with the question of his manhood or his sexual identity when he learns of his wife's predilection. One husband talked of feeling relief. "I had felt constant pressure to be 'sexual.' There is this thing in our culture which equates masculinity with being aggressive and with wanting frequent sex, and that's not what I'm about. I would describe myself as being passive sexually. I was willing to do whatever it took to please my wife in the bedroom department," he said. "But that was really never my thing. I was always more interested in the companionship part of our marriage. I think I must be basically asexual. I know I'm not gay. I'm not attracted to men at all.

"Now that my wife came out, I don't know if my marriage is going to last. I'd like it to, but it's not up to me alone. I would feel very bad if it broke up, because I care about her and I'm comfortable with her. And while I would describe myself as being sensitive to women's needs and most of my friends are female, the thought of having to prove my sexual prowess with women in the dating scene all over again is very uncomfortable."

According to Robert T. Michael's book *Sex in America, A Definitive Survey,* "American society is structured to reward those who play by the marriage rules. You are likely to gain the approval of your friends and family and colleagues at work by being happily married by an appropriate age."[1]

Still, Michael and his associates, relying on a survey of 3,432 randomly selected people, found that "Americans fall into three groups. About a third have sex with a partner at least once a week, a third have sex with a partner a few times a month, and the rest have sex with a partner a few times a year or have no sexual partners at all."[2]

This finding concurs with findings of Masters and Johnson in their book *Masters and Johnson on Sex and Human Loving.* They say, "In the last few years, celibacy has become more talked about as a sexual alternative."[3]

The general public assumes that something may be wrong with a man who chooses to remain in a marriage that becomes celibate or in one that offers reduced sexual activity, but "for people who get no pleasure out of sex, celibacy may be a welcome relief, like being released from imprisonment."[4]

According to the *Almanac of the American People,* while 86% of the people surveyed listed having a "traditional marriage" as a "most important life goal," when asked what they looked for in a relationship, the majority said love or companionship. Only 1% said sex.[5]

Charlie

"The sexuality part of it is really secondary. It's not even secondary, it's probably like ten on the list," Charlie says in speaking about his marriage of fourteen years. "It's the whole social aspect of it, like a complete change of lifestyle. Over the years, single friends kind of drifted off. All our friends were basically married, and she doesn't want to hang out with straight people all of the time anymore, so I've been doing tons of lying. If she didn't go to an event or birthday party, everyone would say, 'Where's the Mrs.?' I would say, 'Oh she's working' or 'Oh, she had to do this, or she had to do that.' My biggest problem with my wife's disclosure was how it would reflect on me if others found out.

"I was in pain for two years. My stomach was killing me. It was the lying, being lied to, having to lie. I had no one to talk to. Then my wife joined this support group for women like herself. She met a woman there, and we went out with her and her husband a few times. It's funny. Men don't talk much. They're closed. The guy never said a word to me about any of this when we got together.

"Then my wife told me about a support group for spouses of gay men and lesbians, and I went. It was mostly women and four men. These people were really really angry. At this point, I had been starting to get over my anger a little bit, and I didn't want to surround myself with such angry people, so I never went back.

"The hardest part of my wife's announcement was knowing that people might find out. I tried to hide it from my family especially. The whole thing made me very uncomfortable. I was always conscious of who she would tell. When I was with people, I'd think, 'Do they know?' I felt that people would ostracize me, or they would think it was my fault or I did something wrong.

"My stomach was getting so bad that I knew I just *had* to tell someone what was going on. Finally I told my brother. He was very understanding. Then, one at a time, I told a few other people. They were compassionate and understanding about it, too. They basically said, 'Look, it's not your fault. You didn't do anything.'"

Anthony

Anthony, in his mid-fifties, has been married to Claire, his second wife, for twelve years. He believes the reason she turned to other women was that he shut down and stopped listening and talking and was unable to sustain the intimacy they had shared in their early marriage.

"I think Claire was trying to let me know that she needed someone, and I was unavailable. She had asked me to go with her a few times on business trips, but I didn't have the time. So that's when she met this woman. That's over now, but she wants to live on her own for a while. She told me she wants to go to every lesbian workshop, meeting, and movie she can find to see who she really is, but I'm hopeful that we may get back together again.

"We talk all the time and see each other every other week or so. She's trying to find herself, and I'm willing to wait.

"Claire had said I was physical but not intimate. It was hard for me. I started thinking about myself and what I was doing wrong. I've been celibate since she left. I'm a very flirtatious guy. I bullshit a lot, I talk a lot, but that's about it. Sex isn't number one on my hit parade priority anymore. At this point in my life, I'm looking for someone to mellow with. I just want compatibility. It doesn't have to be sexually great, and it doesn't have to be active sex. I want to have a comfortable relationship, a walk in the park.

"Claire came over to help me put the Christmas tree up and then to take it down. She comes and stays overnight sometimes, and we're building up a new comfortability. While we have been sleeping together again and there has been no sex, there has been more pleasurable holding and cuddling. I'm not pushing anything. Tender kisses. I'm giving her space. Not getting angry. She appreciates me showering in the morning and shaving and then coming back to bed to cuddle."

While none of the men who remained in their marriages liked the idea of their wives needing women to make their lives complete, and would not have chosen the situation given a choice, most came to understand and accept that another woman might be able to fill a specific need that they, as men, could not. The husbands who left, once their anger had subsided, also came to understand this. And eventually, all the men came to realize that their wives' female-oriented sexuality was not an affront to their own manhood.

Barry

"My wife left me for her childhood friend, another woman. We went to a therapist to make the separation easier, and I broke down and cried. For me, the saddest part was not that I was losing my wife, but that I was losing my best friend. I told her how I felt, and she cried, too. She said, 'No, you're not. We'll still be friends. We have two children we have to raise together.'

"I was very angry for a while, until I started getting my life back on track. Now we see each other on the holidays. We raise the kids together. I even send her Mother's Day cards telling her that she's a wonderful mother, because she is. We've remained part of each other's lives."

I found that the husbands and ex-husbands of the MWLW who consented to be interviewed all became more actively involved in their children's worlds following their wives' disclosures, taking on their share of child care, feeding, and chauffeuring, some for the first time. Those who had a strong desire to keep their families intact, now aware of the kinds of problems they faced within their redefined marriages, were working with their wives to resolve them.

"It's funny," one man said, "a lot of people tell me I've grown since this experience. I guess you're just forced to. Sort of an enlightenment. Just living it. Now I have more understanding of the communication problem between men and women and what makes a woman happy. I don't think the sexual part was our main problem. It was an emotional connection that I never filled with her and that she just had to search for in other places. I think the next relationship I have will be better because of that."

CHAPTER 6

What Do the Kids Think?

A woman who discovers that she is a married woman who loves women (MWLW) has a tremendous number of issues to work through. Whether she chooses to share her new identity with her family or not, changes in the household will be inevitable. She will often find that children are intuitive. Even children too young to have the words to describe what they feel nevertheless have insight.

"It was kind of confusing," one young woman said, remembering back to the time when she was nine and began to sense that her household was different from those of her friends. "From what I would see on television, the mothers didn't have women friends really, and when they did, they played cards or they exchanged recipes. They didn't have big fights; they didn't have big emotional anythings. I knew my mother's friendships were different."

Should we try to hide our true identities from our children? Are we protecting them if we practice duplicity rather than honesty? Can being open hurt them? Each woman must come to her own decision.

The decision to tell my children, Ian and Laurie, twenty-four and twenty-six at the time, was not one hastily reached. I deliberated at length with myself, my husband, and friends who shared my secret.

At first my husband was uncomfortable with them knowing, but I felt strongly that it was really about me and who and what I was, and I needed them to know. He finally agreed. I decided to tell them separately, and one evening, when my son and I were alone, I reminded him of an article I'd written on this topic and told him that my interest was actually a personal one. I told him how I had made my discovery and then handed him the introduction that I had just finished for this book. He read it as I sat quietly and waited. When he finished, he looked up at me. "What about Dad?" he asked.

"Dad knows. We've talked about it, and we're dealing with it. Neither he nor I is walking out the door."

"Okay," he said, accepting what I had to tell him at face value, neither evaluating it in the context of pain or pleasure nor seeing it as an emotional thing. To him it was a piece of information.

A while later I asked him if he felt any anger or resentment toward me or his father.

"No," he said. "You haven't done anything to make me angry. You haven't done anything to make me resentful either. The first three things that went through my mind when you told me were: Are you breaking up? Are you moving out? Do I have to find another place to live? But my life continues pretty much as it has before. The way you and Dad dealt with this has enabled me to think about it less. Neither of you has changed much. You've both become a bit more of a pain in the ass about needing separate space, but I can accept that. I need my space, too."

When I asked him how he would feel if his friends knew about me, Ian responded with questions of his own: "Does it make me a different person? Do you respect me any less? Do you like me any less because you know? Does it change your opinion of me? If knowing a fact about my life, or your life, since it affects my life, will change someone's opinion about me for the worse, then I don't consider that opinion to be worth anything. With a few notable exceptions, I don't care what other people think."

Ian is a writer and as such has done research on a variety of different topics, so he had not connected a previous article I had written on MWLW with my personal story, but Laurie had, so my disclosure to her didn't come as a surprise.

"I kind of figured something since your friendship with Toby began."

"But that was a year and a half before I realized I had fallen in love with her," I said.

"I could tell from the way you talked about her. It was kind of like the way I would talk about my boyfriends, just casually slipping her name into conversation and stuff like that. You acted different with her, in a way that you never acted with any of your other friends. And then you wrote that piece about married women, so when you told me, it was just kind of confirming what I thought."

Still, Laurie's first concern was very much like Ian's. "What about Dad?"

I assured her, as I had Ian, that her dad knew, and he and I were dealing with it.

"How did knowing about me make you feel about your own sexuality?" I asked after she had gotten used to the "other me."

"I know how I feel toward men and women, so it didn't scare me like 'Am I going to be that way now?' You are you and I am me, and your sexuality isn't going to change my life."

While I'm certain Laurie would have preferred me to remain my old self, she was glad that I had shared with her. "I don't like to be kept in the dark," she said. "And I want you to be able to tell me anything, just like I tell you anything about my life."

Still, she made it graphically clear what she didn't want to know. "I'm not ashamed of who or what you are, Mom, and I don't resent it or anything like that, but if you were to have an affair, I wouldn't want to know about it. I don't know of many kids who want to hear that their parents are screwing around on each other. What you do with your sex life and what Daddy does with his is your business. Just like I wouldn't want to hear the details of the sex life you and Daddy had before and just like I wouldn't tell you the details of my sex life.

"I want you to be happy, and if this will do it, great. Just remember, I'm your friend, but I'm your daughter first, and there are some things left better unsaid."

Ian had no need to share this information, saying, "It's your life, Mom, you can tell who you want." Laurie, on the other hand, has talked about it with her friends. She confided that she told a new boyfriend, too. "I guess I was sort of testing him," she said. "If he's close-minded about you, he'll be close-minded about other things, and I don't want those kinds of people in my life."

While I had spoken to my children of tolerance and understanding, by hiding the real me I had denied them the chance to put these thoughts into practice in their immediate world. Being honest and straightforward has led to more open communication and a stronger family bond. They have learned to think independently and to stand up for what they believe in, and we have all developed a stronger awareness and sensitivity for others.

One of Laurie's friends had been going through much distress in regard to his own hidden homosexuality. His relief after hearing about me enabled him to talk about himself for the first time.

This announcement to one's children will not always be met with acceptance, however. Various factors affect the way children of any age respond to the disclosure: the comfort level with which the mother deals with her situation, the emotional maturity and sexual security of the child, the relationship between the parents, the relationship between child and parents, and the level of tension the child feels in the home. Initially, every child's biggest concern, regardless of age or independence, is not the parent's sexuality, but what will happen to *our* family? How will *my* world change? How will *I* be affected?

"If children feel loved and secure, they adjust," says psychotherapist Lois Wadas. "They are much more resilient than we give them credit for being. What hurts them is not telling them the truth when they have ears to hear and eyes to see. Children are intuitive, and when you discount the reality, you do more damage than talking about it.[1]

"Naturally, telling is a whole different scenario for each age group," Wadas cautions. "All ages require a special approach, but with an adolescent, you definitely should have outside help. Adolescents are volatile. They are moving into their own sexuality and to be confronted with their parents' is very unsettling. Because they are in the process of forming who they are, they need things to be steady and predictable."

June

June had four children who were married and on their own. Facing a terminal illness, she made the difficult and painful decision to, at last, acknowledge her true sexuality, a part of herself she had rejected for more than forty years. Although she could not predict the response her loved ones would have or how her disclosure might alter her own life or theirs, June believed she had to come out. She did this, not for her family, but for herself because she needed to be who she was. She could not die peacefully knowing she had lived a lie.

First, she told her husband. Aware that being on her own would be difficult because of her disease, yet wanting to be fair, she offered him his freedom. He opted to remain nearby. While they chose to reside in separate units in the multifamily dwelling they owned together, they remained caring and supportive of each other throughout the remainder of her life.

Admission to herself and then to her family brought her closer to her daughters. One daughter said, "Mom had always seemed so strong, so unapproachable. Even after her disease was diagnosed, she was like a rock. Then she told us about herself, and we were able to see her as a woman with human frailties."

But June's married son, ignoring the fact that his parents' separation had been a mutually acceptable agreement and that they still cared for each other, could only see his mother as having abandoned his father. He developed a growing fear that if she could leave his father, his wife could do the same to him. He became an angry, suspicious, and abusive husband, and eventually his wife did leave him.

Arlene

Arlene relates the difficulty one particular son had with her disclosure, of taking it as a personal affront.

"He's a yuppie: makes excellent money, lives downtown. He's up and coming ... and I stigmatized him. I've associated negativity with his perfect self. It's like I came up with a bruise on his ego.

"I am the person he loved the most, who gave him his life, his mom, and now he could not live with me. We are a very God-oriented, loving family," Arlene says. "He needed that bond back. He could not continue to get prosperous unless he came back to his family. That's exactly what he learned. Eventually he came back to me and said, 'Mom, I was wrong to turn away.'"

While not all children are straight, children raised by gay or lesbian parents or couples are no more likely to grow up to be homosexual than are children raised by heterosexual parents. According to *The Kinsey Institute New Report on Sex*, "There is evidence, in fact, that parents have very little influence on the outcome of their children's sexual partner orientation."[2] *Reinventing the Family*'s author, Laura Benkov, concurs. Study after study revealed no essential differences between children raised by heterosexual parents and those raised by gay or lesbian parents. These children were "no more prone to confusion about their gender identities or to emotional disturbance of any kind."[3]

When gay parents face custody or visitation battles in court, legal precedent usually deems gay parents unfit. The irony of this is that "children of gays are most often born to parents in heterosexual marriages who subsequently come out." Because today's gay father or mother is much more apt than those of a generation ago to be honest, however, a larger percentage of today's children who have gay parents will grow up aware that they do.[4]

Still, children of MWLW have generally grown up with little exposure to lesbians or gay men and have absorbed some of mainstream culture's homophobia. "The Bank Street study tapped into the fact that many teachers, and educational administrators, like everyone else in our culture, harbor subtle or blatant homophobic views—views which are reflected in the classroom in a variety of ways, ranging from a lack of sensitivity to specific children's families, to exclusionary curricula, to rigid ideas about the role of gender in children's lives ... often even the least homophobic teachers and administrators are ill-prepared to address issues lesbian and gay families raise.[5]

"For these children," says Benkov, "the revelation of a parent's homosexuality requires a total shift in perspective. Coming to terms can be complicated if there is an acrimonious divorce, an atmosphere of threat, or homophobic family members. Traversing this territory can take years, and is sometimes never accomplished. But many children—even those steeped in homophobia—are readily moved by love for a parent to reconceptualize their world."[6]

Although living with a mother who is a MWLW does not necessarily cause a child to feel that his or her sexuality may also be out of the norm, having a parent, sibling, or child who is gay may trigger the question, Could I be gay, too?

Roberta

Years before Roberta identified her own sexuality, she knew that her teenage son was gay. Confiding this to her daughter, who had known about her brother for some time, made the young girl comfortable enough with her mother to say, "I once experimented with another girl to see if I was a lesbian. I'm not."

Living with a sibling who is gay or with a mother who is a MWLW does not inevitably necessitate wanting to explore alternative sexual choices. The close exposure, however, to a person who lives outside of the conventional norm, makes these children more aware that options other than the traditional male–female relationships do exist, and they are often more able to put same-sex relationships in proper perspective. As a result, lesbianism eventually loses its taboo status; it becomes not bad or good, just different.

Carla

Carla, the twenty-one-year-old daughter of a MWLW, experienced her mother's disclosure differently. She says, "I had all kinds of questions about my own sexuality because that's how I am. ... I read a book in one of my women's studies classes about coping when you're a lesbian. Some essays were sexual and some totally emotional, so I've had exposure to diversity as far as their philosophy of it is.

"I have one really good friend who is a lesbian. While I don't consider myself a lesbian and I don't have my primary relationships with women, this friendship has allowed me to be even more open and questioning about how I feel."

Carla remembers that she was seventeen when she first began to talk about her mother's gender choice. "I wasn't comfortable with my body. I was in relationships with men, but I wasn't comfortable with them sexually. I wasn't comfortable with any sexuality at that point. So when I started to think specifically about the sexual part, I thought it was disgusting. I started to picture it in my mind, and I started to think that it was really gross."

"You mean with women?" I asked her.

"Women with women, but for some reason women with men also seemed pretty gross at that age. It also had to do with the fact that it was my mother. You know, it's a parent thing. Picturing my mother having sex with anyone was weird."

Now comfortable with her own sexuality, Carla realizes that what had made her ill at ease about her mother's was that she had no prior knowledge that two women might be both emotionally and physically attracted to each other. "You didn't usually see two women being together on TV. I don't mean seeing two women together in a porno movie, to turn on a man, but seeing them in a respectful way. I think if I had been more used to seeing women with women, I would not have been so uncomfortable."

From the time she was nine, Carla had surmised that her mother's relationships with women were unconventional. She remembers sensing emotional changes in her household. "I don't know if I had the words then, but I definitely knew something. My mom and dad weren't fighting so much. There wasn't anything there really. The fighting was going on between my mom and different women friends, which, to me, showed more of an investment. The emotional intensity she had with women affected her more."

She was able to remember the specific friendship her mother had that had given her a sense that something was going on. It was with another married woman with whom her mother worked. "From a business relationship, all of a sudden it became very personal, and our families did everything together. Then my mom and the other woman had a fight or something, and my mom was totally depressed."

Carla felt that in her household, the roles of mother and daughter had been reversed. "My mom was in bed all day long for like a couple of years. I was around ten, and I had to do a lot of things for her. She was very sensitive, and it was important for me to be a good girl and make Mom happy."

Although she had had suspicions, since she couldn't formulate her thoughts, Carla believed that there was nothing to talk about, and so did her mother, until Carla was getting ready to leave for college.

"I started to get a sense that my mother wanted to tell me something. I couldn't even say, 'I think my mother's a lesbian.' I could have notions about it, and feelings, but to put the word on it, that was something different. I started to feel that if my mom talked to me without me being ready, I would freak out and be really unsupportive. I didn't want that to happen. I knew it would destroy her."

When Carla felt she was ready, she and her mother talked. Carla says, "I think my mother has a lot of internalized hatred from society, like this is dirty, this is disgusting. She's so closeted, and this keeps her trapped in a circle. I don't really know what she should do; it's her choice. But I feel that while there are, on a practical level, a lot of intelligent reasons for being secretive, this perpetuates the 'well, there is something wrong with what I am and so I can't tell anybody' idea. It leaves her closed off to other women who might find her and connect with her and help her as well as them."

Carla's concern for her mother and her desire to help her has fostered her own interest in women's issues. She attributes her strong feminist tendencies to the women's studies classes she attended while in college as well as to her voracious reading, which began as a way to understand better what her mother was going through: "If it wasn't for the pain I saw my mother living with, I think I might have had internalized hatred or oppression toward people who are different. I've learned a lot of things through this. I've become more aware about being who I am rather than being who I'm supposed to be."

The ability to reason can be temporarily affected by the stress and anxiety MWLW frequently feel during their transitional period. For Carla's mother, it was her own internalized hatred about what she was that affected her physical health and, without realizing it, put extra pressure on her children.

Allison

"My mother specifically said, 'Don't tell your roommate, your best friend, your father.' I felt a tremendous conflict of loyalties. Because I was not supposed to know, I could not show support for my father, and therefore, the only person I could be supportive of was Mom.

"I was very torn. I was very angry at her for making me choose. Probably more so than because of the actual information about herself. She was putting me in an impossible position. I was getting angrier and angrier. When I get angry, I have to talk. I felt like I was betraying her, but as soon as I got off the phone I told my friend. I had to tell someone.

"In some ways, my mother was like a brand-new baby discovering things for the first time. For a couple of years I really felt like I was raising her. No kidding. I was living it, and I've got the labor pains and stretch marks to show it. She lost her inhibitions, and it was difficult for me to deal with. In one way she was a woman and having these great, wonderful, mysterious feelings ... and, at the same time, she's my mother."

Initially on hearing that the mother is a MWLW, children often see their father as the wronged parent. After a while, they may become angry with him for choosing to remain in a compromising situation in the marriage.

Stacy

"I felt like my father was a martyr. I felt like he was the best person in the world. He was giving everything to everyone else, doing everything for me and my brother. ... We were his life because he didn't have any outside friends. Here Mom is, changing her whole lifestyle, investing time and energy elsewhere, and he's totally flexible. My mom is bringing home women she's involved with, and my dad continues to be not only flexible, like 'I won't see what's going on,' although that is part of it, but engaged with these people and helping do things for them and really bending over backward.

"I got to a point where I felt I had to do everything to make my father happy because he's doing everything to make everyone else happy. Now, I have this immense pressure on me."

Stacy's compulsion to ensure her father's happiness caused her to assume a parenting role, taking on responsibility for him, until therapy changed her way of thinking. "I started getting the point, like, 'Wait a minute. This is my father's choice to remain in this relationship, and it's his choice to be flexible about things. For some reason, it's worth it to him to be bending over backward. Not because he's a martyr but because it's his choice.'"

She has suggested to him that he not necessarily seek a divorce, but "get a life." He said, "I have a life. This is what I choose."

Although Stacy thinks she now understands her parents' relationship more fully, she still gets angry with both her parents. "I get angry at my mom for putting my dad in this position, and I get angry with him for staying in this position or putting up with it.

"Sometimes I feel that he has contributed by not being emotionally supportive. There are so many different levels. I feel like they shouldn't be together, and my mom should be out, but it's their lives."

Stacy knows she doesn't want what her parents have for herself and has struggled to find the relationship that will meet her own needs. She says of her old boyfriends, "I went out with someone like my mother, meaning he was really emotional, and then I went out with someone like my father, really distant and unemotional. Now, I'm working on a place in between."

Lisa

Lisa also acknowledged anger at her father's inability to be there for her mother emotionally. She describes him as being "emotionally dormant," and while she believes that the issue of her mother's sexuality still would have come about had her father been more in tune emotionally, "it wouldn't have felt so desperate."

Having examined the possibility of a separation for her parents, she says, "I would feel great for my mom because she would be free and happy, or happier or more capable of being happy. I'd want to be supportive of her as a person, but apart from her being a person, she is my father's wife. Her happiness would be to some extent at the expense of someone else I care about, so it would be very difficult.

"I love my father dearly, but I think the important thing is they both have to acknowledge that they deserve to have a life, and this doesn't have to be with the person they've been with. They also have to realize that they can stand on their own and be whole people. I think my mom can do it. She's capable and ready. My dad's the one I'm concerned about."

Her dad was not the only one Lisa expressed concern for. "I have concerns for myself," she said. "Because my dad doesn't have much of a life, I can see him on my doorstep, so as great as it could be for my mom, I'd like my dad to have a playmate or a distraction or something so I don't have to be his entertainment center, his hand holder."

Lisa sighs. "My parents love so differently. They care so differently. They're both good people, but they need different things so they have to be allowed to be different, and they can't do that together.

"I certainly want my mom to feel fulfilled and know what being in love is like, and I don't think she knows with my dad."

All the adult children of MWLW I interviewed said they were glad they knew the truth about their mothers' lives even though it had been difficult information to take in and deal with. The only studies that corroborate this information, however, involve single lesbian mothers, not MWLW. While one study done by Hanscombe and Forster in 1982 did not describe how the children were told, it did report that when lesbian mothers were open with their children, the children felt closer to their mothers emotionally.[7]

Another study on mental health in single lesbian mothers done by Rand, Graham, and Rawlings in 1982 did not record the family's reaction to disclosure but reported that admission to ex-husbands, children, and employers positively correlates with the psychological well-being of the lesbian mother.[8]

While some women who wanted to tell their children about their gender preference talked about waiting until the children were certain ages to begin their dialogue, others found age to be of no concern.

Louisa

Louisa had been married to a man for over six years and had a five-year-old daughter when she came across the woman who had been her lover fifteen years earlier. "I fell in love with Pattie, but for many reasons we ended up not staying together." On meeting again, they reconnected.

"I wasn't looking for this to happen when it happened," Louisa says. "I was not expecting the intensity that I did feel. Pattie and I have been struggling to sort out what's been going on for the last year and a half, and we're both very committed to being in this relationship."

Louisa, who considers herself bisexual, is out to her husband and endeavoring to make her marriage, as well as her same-gender relationship, work. She and her husband have chosen to raise their child in an open environment.

"My daughter is seven now, and she's grown up around all kinds of people. Her godmother is a lesbian. She knows women can be married to men, women can be married to women, and men can be married to men. That's normal for her because this is her world. I'm not particularly physical with Pattie in front of my daughter, but we are demonstrative. She isn't at a point where she realizes it isn't common for everyone."

Louisa, encouraging her child to form ideas with openness, says, "I don't say gay, straight, bisexual and define those terms because I think, in some way, giving her this language would limit her to thinking in categories.

"So right now, she just assumes that people love each other in different ways. When she asks me more, like she asked me if my two very good [women] friends were married [to each other], I said yes. And that was it. That was her question, and I answered it. When she wants to know more, she will ask me, and I will give her truthful answers."

The desire to bring together all the people they love is not uncommon among MWLW, regardless of whether they are out to their families or not. If that special other woman is single, the MWLW may try to incorporate her into her family by including her, as a good friend, in family functions and activities. If both women are MWLW and have children of similar ages, their families may become close, and they may share their lives while keeping their relationship secret.

Cynthia and Susan

Cynthia and Susan have been intimately involved with each other for more than thirty years. Between them they have six children. While they have chosen not to tell their respective families about their committed relationship, because they have been best friends since their children were infants, their families have grown up sharing birthday parties, holidays, and special occasions. Recently, one of their daughters was married in an orthodox Jewish wedding in which men and women dance separately. "Something I had dreamed of happened," Cynthia said. "Susan and I were able to dance together at a family wedding."

On occasion, if the other woman is unmarried and occupies much of a mother's time, rivalry between the lover and the MWLW's children might result.

Penny

During Penny's high school years, her mother formed an attachment with a single woman. Penny remembers feeling resentful when this particular friend entered her mother's life. "I was away at camp, and I got a letter from my mom. She told me that she had met a new friend, and I could tell from her letter that she was happy, so I was happy for her. But then, as I saw their friendship progress, I didn't like her anymore. This woman wasn't married. She came over alone, and she wanted all of my mother's time. My mom was buying her things, doing things for her. My younger brother thought she was pretty, and he loved her. He had a very simple relationship with her. They played ball together. But I definitely felt some kind of competition and jealousy. She had all of my mother's attention.

"And then, at some point, this woman got engaged, and that was the last time I saw her, and my mom never saw her again."

Penny's mother did not consciously try to ingratiate her lover, but other women work very hard at making the special woman in their lives become special to their children, too.

Gerry

Unlike many MWLW who went through their discovery period alone, Gerry's husband, aware of her inner turmoil, was supportive and understanding of her needs from the beginning. He was even glad for her when she found Cathy.

"When I became involved in a relationship that finally brought me to the new awareness of my sexual orientation, my husband and I made integrating Cathy into our family a priority. We agreed that our fourteen-year-old daughter should be informed of my relationship with Cathy, although we felt our sons were too young to understand.

"My news elicited a loving but questioning response from my daughter. Her major concern was about the future of our marriage. She expressed satisfaction and relief when I explained that her father and I were very committed to each other and intended to keep the family intact. Still, she was obviously struggling with the very idea of homosexuality, and I can't say she was pleased for me in any way.

"Cathy, also married, but childless, has participated in important family events with us and has scheduled outings with each of the children, and they have been to her home. While my daughter knows what my relationship with her is all about, the boys simply understand that she is an important person in my life, and I hope they are beginning to recognize that she is truly an honorary family member.

"As for my daughter, my relationship with her is excellent, and the subject of my sexuality is one of many serious issues that we work on together. She seems to have gotten used to the idea to the extent that it is not one of the major issues in her life, and by all evidence she is a lovely, well-adjusted young lady."

Gerry had no intention of discussing her sexuality with her eight-year-old son until one day when they had been in a bookstore near a display for Gay Pride Month.

Jarret said, "Oh, this is a lesbian book."

Later in the car, Gerry asked, "Do you know what a lesbian is?"

"No. But you are one!"

"How do you know?"

"Because you listen to that lesbian music."

"Oh, yeah! Well, what do you think the word *lesbian* might mean?" Gerry asked him.

"Maybe women who like to march in Washington?"

"A good guess, but you're still not right," Gerry said.

"Well, what is it?"

"A lesbian is a woman who is in love with another woman instead of in love with a man. Or she might be in love with a man, too, but the point is, she can be in love with a woman."

"Oh, weird."

"You think so? Some people do think it's a little weird. But I think it's pretty great." Gerry said.

After a long pause, Jarret asked, "Well, what woman do you love?"

"I love Cathy."

"I'm not surprised."

Later, Gerry said, "There's one more thing I have to tell you about my being a lesbian. It's kind of private. It's nobody's business but my own, so it's not the kind of thing to talk to your friends about or anything, okay?"

"Hmm, I don't really think much about it, to tell you the truth."

"That's fine, great, but I still want you to understand about privacy."

"Okay. Well, I really do hate that music you listen to!" Jarret said.

"Well, I hate that music you listen to, too!"

Gerry says, "We laughed together then, and that was that. I'm pleased that my second child can now understand more fully just how important my woman is to me. I'm proud of this interaction with my son and the special relationships I enjoy with each of my children."

A tiny minority of MWLW said that because of the difficulties gay people face, they might have reconsidered having children had they known about their true sexuality before becoming parents. Most, however, were happy they had families. Yet, some women voiced feelings of guilt in regard to difficulties their children might encounter owing to society's intolerant attitudes.

One MWLW said, "My daughters were watching a talk show on television. Two women declared their marriage and kissed. My seven-year-old said, 'Yuk,' but my ten-year-old said, 'Wow, cool.' She thought it was wonderful that two women could love each other. I'm glad that my girls are learning that they have other options, that their choices aren't as limited as mine were. Still, I hope that neither one chooses this lifestyle. I would not have chosen it for myself, not in the conditions gay women are forced to live in now. It's hard, bigoted. I'm living the lie of heterosexuality. It's driving me crazy."

Some women believe this information is too challenging for their children. Others believe in being honest because, while it is easy to monitor a young child's environment, the increasingly social nature of children's lives as they grow will present them with constant threat of exposure: overhearing adult conversations or hearing from other children. In Bea's case, it was her lover, in an angry moment, who let the secret out.

Bea

Bea, the mother of two, had been married for seven years, then divorced. Not yet aware of her true sexual identity, she had three unfulfilling relationships with men before she connected with another woman at a Little League baseball game. "Marcy was married, and I was engaged. We hit it off, becoming friends. We were friends for a year and a half before we became lovers, the first for each of us. It just happened very suddenly."

While the women were together for fifteen years, they maintained separate households. "I knew I wanted to be with her and she with me, but with five kids between us, we had the need for separate households. I never told my children. I thought Marcy and I had this tremendous secret," Bea says. "They saw my lover constantly, at holidays, etc. We were a family, she and her three kids and me and my two. Although we didn't live together, we practically raised our five kids together. Then we had a tremendous argument, and she told her children about us, and they told mine. My oldest son knew I was in pain, so it made it easier to discuss things with him. I admitted that Marcy and I had been more than friends for fifteen years. He said, 'I know.' I asked how he felt about it, and he said he didn't want to discuss it right then. After a time, though, he said, 'I know you would accept anyone who would make me happy, and I will accept anyone who will make you happy.'

"But my younger son and I had always had trouble communicating, and when the other kids told him about me and Marcy, he got so angry that my relationship with him became totally estranged."

Most MWLW discover that there is no perfect time to come out to their children. The process of discovering and outing oneself is an ongoing one.

Once told, children of MWLW face the dilemma of whether to keep their mothers' inclinations secret or seek friends to confide in. Teenagers, especially, worry about telling their friends, not only because of what their reactions might be, but also because those reactions might reflect and reinforce the hidden anxieties and fear in themselves. According to Laura Benkov in *Reinventing the Family*, adolescence is the period in a child's life that generally poses the most significant challenges. Children are struggling to separate themselves from their families and at the same time to establish themselves in friendships. It is a time when they are intensely focused on their own personal identity, especially sexuality. It is also a time when homophobia in the environment can be the most intense.[9]

When a MWLW remains in her marriage, regardless of the renegotiated contract she and her husband may have agreed to live with, her children have the option of keeping their mother's lifestyle a private matter. When the parents are separated, however, and the mother has a female lover in her life, keeping the circumstances from friends becomes more difficult for a child.

Angela

Angela had left her husband and was living with her seventeen-year-old daughter. Her daughter knew she was gay and accepted it. Still, it was uncomfortable at first for the teenager to tell her friends about her mother.

Angela says, "My daughter tried to keep it secret, and that was very difficult because her friends were always here, and I had a lover who was out and had lived her whole life out and resented being asked to be closeted in the house she was now living in.

"So it was necessary for my daughter to come out about me to her friends, and she did, one by one in whatever way. First, she came out to the people she felt safest with, her camp friends who don't live nearby. They were wonderful. She didn't have any negative feedback. Then, she came out to her other friends. The kids were just wonderful, too. They liked me before, so they like me now.

"The difficulty was my daughter hated my lover, who had tattoos, very dyky. I guess she would have been more comfortable with my lover looking like a schoolteacher."

The mother's true sexuality was not a major issue in most children's lives, and most MWLW reported building stronger, more open relationships with their children in the long run. Three women who had left their marriages, however, reported having children who no longer spoke to them. They believed that the children's anger and resentment came because of the breakup and not because of their own gender preference.

Evelyn

Evelyn and her husband had appeared to have the perfect marriage: affluent home, three nice children, respect of the community and of the corporate world the husband inhabited. But, neither could communicate with the other. His ambition drove him further and further from the family, leaving Evelyn with emotional problems.

"I knew my marriage was dead before I met Katie. Visiting her only confirmed it. It was one of the few times I got in touch with myself, and I realized I had to leave my husband."

Having no money of her own, and seeing no way to support her teenaged children, she made a painful choice, one she says was the only one she had. She left them behind in their large and familiar home.

Although our laws have some equity of marital property, Evelyn felt that demanding what was rightfully hers might have meant long, drawn-out court battles, and she refused to put herself or her children through this.

Over the last twelve years, while two of her children have come to understand and forgive their mother for what she had done, the third child never did. "I haven't seen or spoken to my middle daughter for about ten years, and she lives blocks from me. It makes me feel terrible. She is living with a cult group and blames me for all her pain and unhappiness."

All the women who had decided on separation or divorce said it was more difficult to tell the children about the dissolution of their marriage than about their sexual inclination. Dr. Lee Salk said that, "Although there is little stigma to divorce these days, studies have shown that next to the death of a loved one, divorce is the most stressful situation an individual can face."[10]

Judith Wallerstein and Berlin Kelly, in their study "Surviving the Breakup," found that "more than half the women were better off by psychological indicators and by their own judgment. ... Somewhat fewer of the men seem to have used divorce as a device for changing the course of their lives for the better. Their most important finding in regard to children is that the children's development and the way they view the divorce depends directly on what happens to the adults after the divorce—on how successful the divorce is for the parents ... when one or both parents cannot achieve a successful divorce, the children pay a high price. In particular, if the parents continue to fight and blame each other, the children have a hard time."[11]

Jackie

On returning to college in her early forties, Jackie fell in love with her female professor. She says that once she realized her true sexual inclinations, she wanted a divorce. Fond of her husband and concerned about his well-being and that of their children, she suggested couples therapy. She felt this would be a good way for him to slowly get used to the idea that things were going to change.

After several months, they decided together that it was time to tell their children. Piece by piece, they prepared their sons, who were home from college, for the announcement of their coming separation. "We formed a united front and told them we had pulled apart," says Jackie.

"We didn't tell them about my feelings for women at the time because I wanted to tell each of them about that separately.

"Because we had seemed so happy on the outside, when we told our children that we were going to separate, one son broke out in tears in the middle of the restaurant, saying, 'I thought we were perfect.'

"I wanted to say, 'But we're still perfect. This doesn't mean we're any less perfect.'

"When we separated, our children were devastated." As a result, Jackie was very concerned about how they would deal with her other announcement a short time later. She needn't have worried.

Her oldest son said, "You know, Mom, maybe it's for the wrong reasons, but I'm glad." Jackie said, "I think what he meant was, 'I'm glad you're leaving Dad because you're a lesbian and not because he did anything wrong.'"

Jackie's sons have adjusted well. While they are protective of both parents and try hard to steer a middle course, her oldest son talks about his family situation openly and even kids about it.

"While he was in college, my son wrote a play," Jackie says. "He said to one of his friends, 'This is a heavy weekend. My play is going to be produced, and both of my parents are coming up—with their girlfriends.'"

While shaken, Jackie's children were able to adjust to their parents' divorce and then to Jackie's announcement because of the relationship they had with their parents prior to the change in family structure. I believe that was why my kids were able to deal with my announcement. When I came out to them, I wasn't thinking: Are they going to reject me, be angry, resentful? We had always had open communication, and my kids had always been involved in family matters. I felt this is just another hurdle, and we'll make it through. While I was a little anxious about how they would receive my news, my thoughts were, I need to tell them and we'll deal with it.

CHAPTER 7

Coming Out to Friends and Family

Realistically, I knew that it was my feelings for Toby that had made her uncomfortable and caused her to pull away, but I also knew that it was being truthful with her that had ruined our friendship. And so, sharing sensitive issues had become more and more difficult for me. It was only after I found the courage to confide in other women that I was able to break through my established patterns of isolation.

Occasional evening walks with a neighbor, Lorraine, had become an enjoyable daily routine, and we'd recently begun to become friends as well. Our conversations covered a wide range of topics. Once, I tentatively mentioned that I was working on a book about MWLW.

"Why?" she had asked.

About to tell her, I lost my nerve. "Because I'm a writer," I answered. Several times I came close to telling her about myself, but I was afraid. So, she remained another person to keep my secret from.

One evening, Lorraine stopped by for some help with an embroidery piece she had begun. I was so pleased with the pages I had just completed, that in my excitement, without considering possible consequences, I asked if she'd like to hear a few. She listened as I read to her from across the room. We were alone in the house, but she said, "I don't want to ask you this question out loud. Come sit next to me on the couch."

She said, "Once you told me there had briefly been someone very special in your life." I nodded.

"Was that someone a woman?"

Normally one to blurt things out, I was suddenly silent. Was it right to tell Lorraine? Would I be burdening her with this information? Frightening her away?

"Yes," I said quietly.

There was a pause, then she said, "I don't think you're really a lesbian."

I had to keep from smiling. I knew she was trying to make me feel better, but I actually felt fine. By this time, I had realized that having same-gender feelings was not the horrible thing society portrayed it to be.

"I work with some of those women, and you're nothing like them. You don't dress like them or look like them," Lorraine said with the authority of one who knows.

Then awkwardly, she said, "I have to ask you something. Do you like me ... like that?"

"No," I reassured her. "I like you as a friend."

"But if you're a les ... ," she began.

"Lorraine, are you attracted to every man you see in a sexual way?"

"No," she said.

"Well, it's the same with me."

She breathed a sigh of relief, but things between us had changed. In the past, she would stop by for a brief chat when she'd see me coming home from work. Now, she began to wave from her doorway instead. She stopped calling. When I called, she rejected my invitations to walk as we used to. I felt saddened. I missed Lorraine's company.

A couple of months passed before she called me again. She said she had missed our chats and asked me if I'd like to join her that evening. Still, through our entire walk she kept a noticeable distance from me. I could sense her nervousness. Each time we passed a man, she would comment. "Nice buns" or "great ass." And, while she never had before, now she talked incessantly about how good sex was between her and her husband, until finally I found it difficult to constrain my laughter. "Lorraine, it's all right. You're safe with me," I told her.

"Was I so obvious?"

"Yes," I said, and we both laughed like we used to before the *L* word interfered with our growing friendship.

Lorraine asked numerous questions, and I shared some of my findings with her. One letter I received from a MWLW about her own discovery was so poignant that I read a part of it to Lorraine.

After I'd finished, she said, "Wow, this is very scary."

"What?" I asked.

"This whole thing. How do I know I won't wake up one day and realize I love women? If you don't look like one but turned out to be one, could that happen to me, too?"

For Lorraine, the jolt of my announcement was compounded by the similarities she saw in us. Besides both of us being married, we shared similar child-raising philosophies, had comparable homes, and before this surfaced, shared similar frustrations about our husbands.

No woman is automatically exempt from the frightening possibility that she, too, might sometime realize she is a lesbian. Suddenly, Lorraine had to face the same realization that countless others have struggled with. Being married was no guarantee that she or her husband couldn't realize a new sexual preference.

Most people simply need time to process the surprising information when a friend comes out, unless they suspected all along. For others, the disclosure may bring hitherto unresolved sexual or social issues to the surface. People who have difficulty dealing with their own sexual uncertainties are less likely to be able to accept this type of disclosure.

One woman realized that her inability to come to terms with her daughter's same-gender preference stemmed not from her daughter's revelation, but from her own inability to deal with the sexuality she had repressed since childhood.

Only after years of therapy, while going through her menopause, could this woman finally acknowledge her own preference for women. And only then was she able to make peace with her daughter.

Several women told me of friends who deserted them on learning of their sexual orientation. They also told me that years later, some of these same women, once horrified, sought them out to tell them of their own enlightenment when they, too, discovered or acknowledged their attraction to women.

Lois

Lois was tormented by the belief that she had done a horrible thing to her husband by discovering her true self. She was unsure of what her future with him would be. While the people she worked with knew of her relationship with her woman friend, she had not told her good friend, Gina, in whom she confided almost everything via phone calls or letters. Lois was afraid that sharing her same-sex preference might affect their friendship and kept her problem to herself.

Even when Gina came for a visit and asked how her marriage was, Lois lied and said fine. Then Gina said, "Mine broke up. I went away and met a woman."

Lois laughed. "I had known Gina since high school, more than twenty years. For the last ten years she had been too afraid to say anything to me that might affect our friendship, and here I was doing the same thing.

"The only reason Gina told me now was that in our business the rumor mill is very active, and a mutual friend I worked with let my secret out."

Finally, Lois confided in Gina. "It was great, and it made me feel like I wasn't such a two-headed monster because Gina was like me, yet she was the nice, sweet person I always knew."

While telling does get easier with time, initially it feels like an earth-shattering event. We choose the recipients of this information carefully.

Early in my discovery process, I had received a Christmas card from an old friend. We had each moved, and our correspondence had dwindled, then ceased. Still, her card brought back fond memories of long, chatty visits. I decided to confide in her. Although at the time it was still difficult for me to tell anyone, I sent her a four-page letter telling her what had happened to me.

Why did I choose her? Something in me wanted her to know who I was. Maybe it was because she was living halfway around the world. Maybe because I'd always admired her, I wanted her validation.

Time passed without acknowledgment to what I then believed was a huge confession. Had I been wrong to tell? Did she think I was awful? Was she rejecting me? More than a year later, I received a letter from her. There was no judgment, only curiosity regarding how I was getting on with my life. She filled me in on hers, the busy life of a mother with young children and a husband often traveling for business. I could feel the warmth of our old friendship.

I realized that while I was working my way through a major trauma in my life, it was not a major priority in her life, which was moving along its own track.

Even though we got together two or three times a year, I also felt the need to share my concerns and feelings with my two oldest friends, Beth and Sherry. But, we had all double-dated since junior high school and then married at about the same time, and our husbands were friends, too. This weighed heavily on my decision regarding whether to tell the women about myself. Even if I asked them not to, they might tell their spouses. This could affect my husband. Would it be fair to him? Would he be comfortable with the other men knowing? Would he feel ridiculed? Blamed?

I thought about consulting him, then decided that my sexuality was not about him; he was neither the cause nor the catalyst. It was about me and who I am, and I needed the support of my friends.

Over the years, due to distance, family priorities, and busy schedules, our visits had dwindled to a few times a year. Our deep, endless girlhood talks had evolved into quick phone calls for updates on the kids or occasional evenings spent as couples. And then, except for the few minutes we would find ourselves together in one of our kitchens, cleaning up after having shared a meal, all conversations, as they had for years, took place in the presence of the men.

On one such visit, I had driven to the store with Sherry while the men prepared the barbecue. This was at the time when my husband and I were talking separation. "What's wrong?" she asked. "You seem so unhappy." I was uncomfortable talking about my revelation and what had been going on at home, but at the same time, it felt like such a relief to be able to talk. Sherry listened, nodding from time to time. "You weren't having your needs met, and the person who gave you what you needed just happened to be a woman. I never thought of being with a woman—but that doesn't make it wrong, it just makes it different. I guess you can't help your life circumstances," she said.

Before we got out of the car, Sherry assured me that she still loved me, and that this didn't change her old feelings of friendship toward me. During a phone conversation afterward she said, "I was surprised about your gayness. I thought, where did that come from? In all of the years we've been friends, I didn't see that in your life at all. I don't think it was something you thought about. I think it just happened."

A few weeks later, I told Beth what was going on. Beth was my very oldest friend. She, like Sherry, assured me that this didn't change her feelings of friendship toward me.

While I feel the same old warmth and caring each time we speak, our lives are presently taking different paths. I don't know for certain if they ever told their husbands. No one has ever brought up the subject in front of me, but invitations to their homes have become fewer. I understand their discomfort with our situation and their fear of dividing their loyalties.

Jan

"My best friend and I met through our husbands at a company dinner, and because neither of us lived near our families, we became surrogate families for each other. We celebrated holidays and birthdays together, and we had gone with our husbands on some business trips, too. Now, her husband had changed jobs, and they had moved to a different state. We spent hours on the phone. Still, it took a long time for me to build up the courage to tell Emily my secret. I thought I was past the emotional part, but as soon as I started talking, I started crying. Through tears I told her what I was and how I knew and everything that had happened to me since she moved and how I felt, etc. Emily didn't know what to say after 'oh.' There was a pause, then she said, 'I have to go now,' and hung up. I was devastated.

"Normally we took turns calling each other. But when she missed her turn, I called her. 'I'm sorry if I said something to offend you. I thought you would understand.'

"'No,' she said, 'you didn't offend me. You just hit home. I've been going through hell for the past few years wondering about myself, but I never had the guts to find out for sure. And, I was afraid to say anything to anyone, even to you.'

"It was my turn to say, 'Oh.'"

Carol

When friends are intuitive, coming out to them is not always necessary. Carol, married and the mother of two small children, works in the film industry. Between her private life and her work life, she balances a very busy schedule but has always made time for her friends. Until, while working closely on a special project with another woman, she felt an odd sort of pull. She had never consciously thought about her sexuality and kept telling herself the feeling was only because they worked so well together. Still, she says, "When our project was completed, I was afraid she would go out of my life, and I couldn't bear that. I asked her to join me for dinner, and that was the beginning of us together."

Carol laughed. "One old friend said, 'What's been going on with you?' I said, 'I've been working incredibly hard.' She said, 'You've worked long hours before, but you've returned my phone calls. You're having an affair with a woman, aren't you?' She said she knew because, if it had been a man, I would have confided in her. She was right.

"All of my friends know now, and every one of them has been very supportive."

Carol's mother also intuitively knew. Carol says, "Before I told my mother about us, I told her there was stuff going on in my marriage, and I didn't know how long I could stay in it. She got really upset about the kids and what would happen to them.

"I realized she was bringing up her own fears, and eventually I began to retreat from her. But she was so concerned that finally I said, 'Mom, I'm really happy, but I'm going through a difficult period.'

"Although we don't fit the traditional stereotypes of lesbians, once she met my friend, my mother had a feeling. She told me she felt a tremendous energy between the two of us. She's been really terrific about it. She hasn't told my father, nor have I. I never had a terrific relationship or communication with him, so if my mother is comfortable with him not knowing, that's okay."

While I had a need to be known and accepted by my mother, I once told a friend, "I tried to tell my mother about myself, but she just doesn't get it."

"Your mother doesn't get it because you didn't give it," she said. I knew she was right. I had been sidestepping the topic. I had told my mother about the book I was working on, about going to Washington to join the march for gay rights, and even about two of my friends who had played a part in bringing about domestic rights for same-sex partners, but I had never said, "Mom, I recently found out that I am a lesbian."

Telling my mother was not easy, especially over a long-distance phone line, but I was tired of the shallow chitchat that had begun to pass for conversation between us. I needed to know that she loved me unconditionally, not based on an image she had created of me.

There were pauses, and I could hear her quiet sobs as I told her about my feelings for Toby and how they had caused me to lose her friendship, of the pain I had endured and the isolation I had lived with since making my discovery.

"I knew you were unhappy," my mother said. "But I had no idea why. I'm glad you told me. I wish I could have been there to help you." She said she was sorry that I was a lesbian because she knew how hard being different could be. She would have preferred my life to be less difficult. And, while she was saddened by how my being a lesbian would affect my husband and the security of the life I had created with him, by the end of our phone call I felt closer to my mother than I ever had in my entire life, and I believe she felt the same toward me.

For many MWLW, the decision to come out to their mothers is one of the most difficult. Still, Sherry Zitter, MSW, LICSW, says that a daughter's coming out to her mother can be a positive step. "For a mother, a daughter's coming out may revive her own early same-sex attraction; it may feel like abandonment, rejection, sexual intrusion, or affirmation and validation; it may precipitate a mourning process for the wished-for heterosexual daughter, and it may induce altruistic satisfaction that her daughter has the opportunity for sexual and emotional reciprocity.[1]

"From a family systems perspective, coming out often creates a clearer boundary between mother and daughter. ... The coming-out process rejects cultural norms, proclaims a woman's sexuality, and challenges the heterosexual assumption. ... Coming out to one's mother, as an appropriate and well-informed decision, can be a vital and life-affirming developmental task."[2]

The reluctance to tell a mother, for most MWLW, stems from their societal upbringing, in which different often equates with unacceptable. Fear of losing the "good girl" status women hold within their family is often enough to warrant their silence. These fears are not unfounded.

"A son is yours till he finds a wife, but a daughter is yours for the rest of your life. This proverb succinctly describes what many mothers expect of their children. When a mother raises a son, she generally expects to lose him to another woman someday. When she raises a daughter, however, she usually anticipates that even if that daughter marries a man, Mother will always be the most important woman in her daughter's life. This myth, which runs deep in our culture and our psyche, may be primary in a mother's reaction to her daughter's coming out."[3]

One reason some women initially keep their sexual preference from their mothers is the fear that they will be consumed with guilt and assume responsibility for their daughter's homosexuality.

Robin

"My mother did so much for us kids that I didn't want her to think this is something she fucked up about. She would blame herself. When we were growing up, although my father had left us, she never trashed him. She had every opportunity and every reason. She let us grow up to be rational adults and to make up our own minds about our father and to establish our own relationships with him.

"I thought, if I tell her, she'll go through her own mind thinking, 'Did I do something to make it seem like men were horrible? Was I too strong?' She would blame herself."

Eventually Robin realized that her reasons for not telling her mother were not as selfless as they first appeared to be.

When Robin told her mother she was having marital problems, her mother said, "I hope you're not being influenced by your homosexual friends. Are you?"

"'Oh, no, Mother. God forbid,' I said. I was nervous as hell. Later in the conversation, I took that back. I'm thirty-seven years old. Why should I be nervous in front of my mother?"

While some families open their arms with absolute acceptance and love on receiving the information that their daughter or sister is a MWLW, others totally reject their own children.

These parents fail to see their children, even their adult children, as individuals. They view their offspring only as extensions of themselves and are interested in the persons their children are supposed to be, while their true identities are discounted.

Parents are not the only ones to discount their daughters' true sexual inclinations in their need to keep their own world unaltered. MWLW often have a strong need to conform to what they believe are their parents' perceptions of how things are supposed to be. Trying to be the daughters they are supposed to be causes them to stifle themselves or to develop two different personas, one for the family and one for themselves.

Juanita

Juanita had never considered her sexuality, although she remembers being frustrated with her friendships as a teenager. Though they were intense, they never seemed intense enough. She felt like she wanted more, but she didn't know what. She knew she was supposed to get married and have a baby, and that's what she did.

"I was connected to the me that other people wanted me to be," Juanita says, "and that was connected to my sexuality. Because to be the daughter my mother wanted, my father wanted, my sister wanted, I needed to play certain roles, and in order to fulfill these roles it was critical that I suppress my sexuality. Looking back, I think that was a big part of it."

While Juanita has now learned who she is, and is able to feel powerful and positive about herself, she still has problems dealing with her family. "I still turn to my family, and it scares the shit out of me to ever say to my mother, 'Mom, I'm a lesbian' or 'Mom, this is the person I love, and she makes me happier than anyone in the world ever did.' She would have a heart attack and drop dead, and I would feel like shit, so even though I feel great about myself, I'm Latina, and in my family it would be such a major shock. Forget it."

Because Juanita's strength and confidence have grown and she is now able to accept herself, she is able to accept her family with their limited ability to understand. While she may or may not ever tell them about the secret she lives with, she does say they have noticed a positive change and commented on the "new Juanita."

Miriam

Miriam speaks for many women when she voices this common complaint. "I have felt for years that my parents don't know me, and that was long before my sexuality. They see what they want to see, and they are very limited, so I decided long ago not to waste my breath. It's a shame though. I am out to almost all of my friends. Although I would like who I really am not to be so jarring to them, I don't think I could ever sit with my mother and swap confidences.

"I feel, under the circumstances, that I am a mythical being. I hate the myth my parents have constructed about what my life is and who I am. They have the constant assumption of heterosexuality. They don't love me but some construct."

Still, for this need of family approval, Miriam, a grown woman with a child of her own, leads a pretend life, always being "the good little daughter." Presently, Miriam's bedroom remains as it always has, with one large bed the focal point. While she or her husband sleeps on the couch, Miriam ponders, "How could I explain separate bedrooms to my mother?" Although they have the space for another bedroom, the other room remains the den. She says, "I find it painful and annoying that I have to accommodate for that all of the time. It makes me wish I lived nowhere near my parents."

While coming out created discord for some, the majority of MWLW felt that revealing themselves almost invariably strengthened whatever bonds already existed between themselves and close friends or family members.

Josie

Josie remembers the day she told her mother. She had only recently discovered her feelings and found herself crying throughout the long drive from her home to her parents' in a neighboring state. "When I got there, I took my mother out for lunch. My dad didn't want to join us. After lunch I just cried, telling her that I was in love with two people. She listened. I wasn't going to tell her that the second person was a woman. She brought it out.

"It was very relieving. She said something beautiful. 'Look how lucky you are that two people love you. Most people go through life never knowing that even one person loves them.'"

At some time, Josie's mother told her father. "He knows but he doesn't talk about it much," Josie says.

Amber

The majority of women who were out to their parents said that they communicated primarily with their mothers, and that their fathers didn't talk much. Amber, on the other hand, says, "I was raised in

Texas by a very racist Catholic family. My mother was awful. She and my husband felt it was their duty to notify all my relatives when they found out about me. She sees my relationship as dirty and has referred to it as 'rolling around on the floor having sex in front of your children.' You can see how uneducated and homophobic she is. But my father's and brother's reactions were wonderful. 'Amber needs someone to love,' they said."

Antoinette

Antoinette came from a very privileged home in the South. While in college, she spent a lot of time photographing women, clothed and unclothed. She had overnights with friends. "I remember I touched one of my friend's breasts, and she stiffened up. I thought, oh, this is not going to work. I apologized and felt ashamed and guilty."

Antoinette was in denial and never realized that she might be attracted to women. "These are things I sort of put away," she says. "Still, I always had a sense of being different. Maybe that's why I dated the people I dated." Antoinette entered into an interracial marriage, even though both her parents and her in-laws were opposed. She looks at that decision, in retrospect, as a stepping-stone to coming out.

Eventually, she connected with a woman and privately acknowledged her sexuality. Before she was ready to make the news public, however, her mother guessed. They were driving together, when her mother said, "Are you attracted more to men or to women?"

"I thought I'd drive off the road," Antoinette says. "I wasn't ready to tell her, but I had to." She gave her mother *Loving Someone Gay* and *The Other Side of the Closet*, which she had also given to her husband.

"My mother had picked up on a comment I had made during a visit. She had told me of a young man they knew who was gay. 'So?' I had asked.

"'His parents don't know, and he doesn't acknowledge it.'

"I said, 'That's really too bad that he can't share that important part of his life.'

"My mother said, "That was something overly sensitive for you to say, and it started me wondering.'"

Antoinette's mother told her father. He said he wasn't surprised. "I knew things were not going well with your marriage, and when you had come to visit us and got a call from your girlfriend late at night, I thought, 'Why would a friend be calling so late. It must be more than friendship.'"

Still, Antoinette says, "My father was very upset when he found out … not because his daughter liked women, but because he didn't want the neighbors to know."

Antoinette had the rector at her church send her parents a book called *Now That You Know*. She says that since then, her mother has bought and passed out five copies to family and friends. Now, her father is reading the book, and they are working it through.

Not all parents are concerned with what the neighbors will think or how same-sex relationships reflect on the family. For most parents, the primary concern is, "If you leave your marriage, who will take care of you?" They want their children to be safe and cared for.

Charlene

Charlene is another woman who has confided in her father. He is one of her most staunch supporters, although that was not always the case.

When she came out to her parents, everything came out, including the incidences of abuse she had lived with: having been molested by a cousin when she was three and having been raped at seventeen. While she does not feel that these events made her a lesbian, it was only after her father learned of them that he was able to accept her for who she was. Charlene says, "I got total restitution. My father then wanted to protect his daughter; he wanted to champion my cause. He said, 'So that's why you turned to women. It all makes sense now.' That's the way he thought, so I said, 'Okay Daddy, that's fine.' I was just glad to have my parents back."

Once family and friends learn to ignore labels and see people for who they are, most women report fondness on the part of their families for their special women friends, even to welcoming them into the family with open arms.

Letty

Letty had been attracted to women before she married, but because she also liked men, she felt marriage would work. Yet, when her first lover reappeared in her life, she couldn't bear to lose her again or give up her husband or child. "I had to step away from the prevailing culture and really claim my right to define what's right and wrong in my own value system. That is what I have tried to do." While Letty still lives with her husband and child, Rebecca has become another family member.

"It's taken a while for my family to take to all of this. It was funny, because it was like coming out all over again. I came out years ago, before I got married. It was no longer an issue, and then I thought, oh, God, I have to go through this all over again. Still, everyone in my life is incredibly supportive of what I am doing. I am fortunate. My mother knows Rebecca, and she thinks she's bright and really likes her. She also loves my husband. My brother also really loves Rebecca and gets along with my husband. We all have mutual friends, and basically everyone knows and is supportive."

Rosa

Rosa never came out to her family but simply went about the business of incorporating her lover into her life. She believes that her family sensed the importance of that other woman to her and to her husband.

"Since my father has been in a nursing home, my mother has been preoccupied with the whole subject of homosexuality. She read Rock Hudson's story as soon as it was published and seems to expound on the subject a lot of the time. I don't know if it's because my father's absence creates a less-oppressive atmosphere or if it is a natural interest of hers or she senses the relationship that Lillie and I have and wants to project her understanding.

"When Lillie arrived, she lived with my husband and me until her house nearby was built. She began attending most family gatherings with us. My family accepted her as if she had always belonged, never asking how we'd gotten to know her or why she moved in with us. My parents had never included 'outsiders,' and I found this immediate acceptance interesting."

While Rosa has never explained explicitly to her mother the part that Lillie plays in her life, she believes that her mother knows how important Lillie is to her.

Often, hearing that a daughter is considering divorce is more distressing for her parents than hearing that she is a lesbian. The fact that the secure world they have envisioned for their daughter might be toppling can take precedence over discovering her new sexuality, especially when children are involved.

Martha

"I'm a better mother since finding out about myself. Therapy has helped me to experience all of the pain that I'd held back. I'm much more compassionate toward my son and toward my friends. It's helped me to be able to relate to people better.

"For my family, though, I have no desire to be more understanding. My mother doesn't want me to be divorced. She is upset that I have changed everything, and it's not even the issue of my sexual orientation. It's the fact that I've changed everybody's lives by saying I don't want to be married anymore. She condemns me, so there is no support from my family. My brother, who was on my side, has taken my mother's side. He's not judging me; he's not against me for coming out or for wanting to get divorced. But he thinks I should be treating my mother differently. That I should be making peace with her."

Leslie

Leslie, although not out to her family, is facing the same kinds of accusations and rejection from them as Martha because of her announcement of divorce.

Throughout college, Leslie had been able to deny her suspicions about her same-sex attraction. Her suspicions were confirmed, however, when she was intimate with another woman two weeks before her wedding. She thought her feelings for the woman, and women in general, would go away at that point, but she wasn't certain, so she discussed them with her husband-to-be. He believed he could deal with her inclinations, and they proceeded with the wedding as planned.

Nevertheless, after the wedding Leslie realized she had made a mistake. She really cared about her husband, and didn't want to hurt him any more than she already had, so she decided to leave him.

Leslie then realized where she fit within her family's priorities. Their need to maintain status quo, as well as their need for acceptance within their small community, took precedence over her happiness.

"My family is very nonsupportive," Leslie says. "They're so upset that I'm leaving my husband that they can't deal with anything else. My brother thinks I'm crazy and callous and that I traumatized my husband. I really am not these things. I've been honest with my husband the whole time, but how honest could I be with my family? They say they're so humiliated about my wanting to leave my marriage that they're talking about moving out of town.

"Divorce is not something that happens in our family. I don't want to be cut off from my family, but I'd almost rather be cut off than be treated like I'm being treated now: all of their phone calls telling me what an awful person I am, my mother crying all the time, my dad screaming at me that I didn't go to church.

"Can you imagine how they would behave if they knew the real reason for my divorce?"

A MWLW can give her parents the information about herself, but she must understand that there is no guarantee of acceptance. How parents choose to process it or to reject it is based on their own resolved or unresolved issues. While some parents choose to become estranged from their daughters, others choose a path of understanding, acceptance, and unconditional love, and still others choose denial as a way of dealing with, or not dealing with, the information they have been given.

Darcie

"I am a WASP," Darcie says. "My family is very straitlaced. I remember calling my mother and telling her that I was moving in with Melissa after my divorce.

"My mom said, 'Are you taking a two-bedroom apartment?'

"'No,' I said, 'One.'"

Her mother said, "Twin beds?"

"No," Darcie said.

"Is there any hanky-panky going on?" her mother asked.

Darcie said, "Mom, do you really want to know?"

She said, "Yes. That's why I'm asking."

Darcie said, "Okay. There is hanky-panky going on."

Her mother said, "Oh. I have to turn the vacuum cleaner off," and she hung up.

Although her mother had been in the habit of calling several times a week, she didn't call for three weeks. When Darcie resumed the phone calls, her mother's conversation began as though nothing out of the ordinary had happened. Darcie took her cue from her mother and since then has not discussed her sexuality. "This 'if we don't talk about it, it doesn't exist' attitude works for us."

Initially, the two major concerns parents seem to have on discovering that their married daughters are gay are morality and the survival of their family. However, the reasons that cause people to accept or reject a situation are far more complex.

Family dynamics are likely to change as a result of the information a MWLW gives to her parents, and deep psychological issues may come to a head.

For instance, "In a family where a father has had an overclose relationship with his daughter, a mother may view her daughter as a rival," says Sherry Zitter in her article, "Coming Out to Mom." "Coming out as a lesbian in such a family may actually engender a sense of relief in the lesbian's mother, who might see her daughter as less threatening to her own marital relationship. Father, however, may feel quite rejected by his daughter's choice of women as sex partners. Possibly his own repressed incest fantasies must be given up, as well as feeling a fantasized sexual rejection. This may be a factor in a family in which a mother has accepted the lesbianism much more easily than a father. (In view of high incest statistics, we must confront the reality that in many families, a father has had an actual incestuous relationship with his daughter. His reaction to her coming out could then involve anger at her rejection of sexual involvement with him as well as some guilt at 'causing her lesbianism.')"[4]

In-laws don't have as much of a personal investment in the MWLW as her own parents do. Their primary concern is with their son, who is being affected by his wife's sexuality, and with their grandchildren, who they may see as being harmed by their mother's lesbianism and a split within the family. Some women spoke of support and understanding from their mothers-in-law, while others had stories such as that of Phyllis.

Phyllis

Before they were married, Phyllis had confided in her husband that she thought she was bisexual. He said he didn't think it was a problem. Still, aware of the prejudices of others, she was always careful about revealing her secret further. She especially had no intention of telling her in-laws about herself, and he agreed.

Seven years later, what had at first appeared to be of little consequence in their marriage grew into a major problem as her husband's angry moods and drinking escalated. "While I was at the gay pride parade, my husband, drunk, told my in-laws I was out trying to find myself. So my mother-in-law called me to ask if I was a lesbian. She was asking questions and answering them for me: 'You can't be a lesbian because you have two children,' 'I know you're not,' and on and on. So I let her rant and rave and when she was finally done, I said, 'I choose not to discuss my sexuality with you.'

"It's never been a great relationship. I felt, in spite of that, I had done everything I could to make it better. But this news rocked their world, and for a while they didn't want to kiss me when they saw me. It was a bombshell."

Just as a MWLW may choose to come out to one parent and may not necessarily feel the need to come out to the other, likewise, anticipated negative consequences may prevent her from sharing her identity with all of her siblings. The bond she shares with each individually will usually determine who she decides to confide in.

Shari

Although they don't see each other often or talk much on the phone, Shari describes her relationship with her brother as open and intimate. Still, she was amazed at how easily he accepted her disclosure.

She says, "When I came out to him, about a month after I came out to myself, his reaction was really surprising—even more so considering that he belongs to a fairly strict Christian denomination. He actually laughed and said, 'I was wondering when you were going to tell me!' That felt great—that he had for some time been aware of my sexual orientation and accepted it as part of the whole me."

When I decided to tell my siblings, I wasn't actually involved with anyone. There is a big difference between confiding your sexuality to someone and introducing them to a lover. It was easier for me to tell them in the abstract, and it was probably easier for them to get used to the idea.

The very close relationship I share with my sister, four years my junior, emanated from my disclosure to her. While we had always been devoted—and I would have done anything for her—other than a biological connection I felt as though we had little in common. We saw the world from different perspectives. Once, before coming out to her, we had been walking in the city, and I led the way into a gay bookstore. "Let's check this out," I said, wanting to get some sense of how she felt. She said she'd wait for me outside. She was so uncomfortable that not only did she wait outside, she waited down the street. So, I couldn't imagine her being able to understand or, more importantly, accept the truth about me. I needn't have worried. I put off telling her until one day when she called, I was feeling so overwhelmed that I just had to let it all out. Although we had never been able to express our emotions openly before, I found myself crying as I recounted everything that had led to my discovery. My sister listened quietly. When I had finished, she said, "I'm only sorry you didn't feel comfortable enough to tell me at the beginning, so that you wouldn't have had to go through so much pain alone."

My older brother, although he tends to hide his feelings, was equally supportive. "You're my sister," he said simply when I told him. "Nothing can change that." Then, kind of gruffly, because he wasn't comfortable voicing his feelings, he said, "I love you."

Both my brother and sister were concerned about my husband, who has been like their brother for so many years. "You're both special people," my sister said, "I don't want to see either of you hurt, but you are different. I want you both to be happy."

When I told my sister-in-law about me, she said, "I love you and would like you to continue to be my sister-in-law, but even if your marriage doesn't work out, I'd like you to continue to be my friend."

For me, the greatest moment of acceptance came when I broached the subject of going to the gay pride parade with my mother. I had hesitated because she was visiting with my aunt Gertie, whom I hadn't told.

"Aunt Gertie knows," my mom said. "I told her, and we'd love to go."

Both women, one sixty-nine and the other seventy-nine, came with me to the parade. We all marched carrying signs. Theirs read: PROUD OF MY GAY DAUGHTER and PROUD OF MY GAY NIECE. Mine read: PROUD OF MY STRAIGHT MOM AND AUNT.

My mother and my aunt were awed by the thousands upon thousands of marchers: young and old; men and women; doctors, lawyers, teachers, mechanics—productive members of society. "These people aren't monsters. Just people like us," my mother said.

CHAPTER 8

The Reality of Marriage

I am grateful every day that my husband and I can communicate, that he is understanding and supportive, that we have a sense of caring for and about each other, and that there is peace and respect in our household because this was not always so. Recently, I picked up an old journal and was reminded of those bitter struggles that almost led to divorce at the beginning.

Those first few months after coming out to him had been hell. While I felt relief that I no longer had to be deceitful, he went through total mental chaos.

It was during a sailing trip with my brother and his friends that I made my decision to leave my marriage: not because of my sexuality but because of the growing bitterness and hostility between us. Even attempts to be civil failed. I'd say, "Here's the sunscreen," and he'd grab it from me snapping, "I am perfectly able to take care of myself." My stomach was in a knot. He spent his time swimming and snorkeling with the others. I spent my time thinking about what would be.

The way we were going on was not healthy for either of us. Until then, I had been considering everyone else: how the kids and my mom would feel or what others would say or how his family would react. Now, for the first time, I thought of myself and my frustration. I would tell him I wanted a separation.

Rather than speak up, however, I chose to avoid my husband instead. When we docked for the night, everyone scattered, and he and I wound up walking together. Eventually we sat down on a bench in a town square. Almost immediately, he said, "I've been giving it a lot of thought, and I can't see any other way. I want a separation."

I breathed a sigh of relief. I didn't have to be the one to say it. We talked quietly about how and when things had started going bad in our marriage. There was no blame or fault. We both realized it was over. I did feel a sadness, though, thinking that neither of us had ever really shared the kind of passion that I had learned was possible within a relationship. I wondered how I would feel if he were to discover it with another person. We talked of him moving out. It made sense since he could be happy with a comfortable chair and a television, while I was the collector and needed my things around me. Our daughter, Laurie, was in the process of finding a job and her own apartment, and so, we decided to wait until she had before we told the kids. I didn't want her thinking she had to change her plans or look for a larger apartment so that she could take care of her father. He agreed.

That night I lay awake. Surprisingly, my thoughts were not of finances, logistics, or losses, but of how I would redo my bedroom with the large downy quilt, fluffy pillows, and the ruffled edges I'd always wanted.

It is only in today's modern marriages that we have come to expect the perfect state of being, derived purely through the love of a man and a woman for each other. In some cultures, until recently, young people were generally paired in arranged marriages. "You'll learn to love each other" was as common a mandate as terms such as "marriage broker," "matchmaker," and "arranged marriage."

In the 1960s, Dr. John F. Cuber, a former marriage counselor turned sociologist, along with his wife, delivered a paper known as the Cuber Report. "Cuber and Harroff interviewed 437 highly successful Americans in depth, to discern the real quality of their marriages. Fewer than one in four had unions that could be described as intimate and loving and that in any way resembled the ideal which most people hope to attain.

"This is not to say that all of the others were actively unhappy. In many of these enduring marriages a *modus vivendi* [manner of living]—sometimes comfortable and sometimes not—had been achieved. Husbands and wives made their own lives and went their own ways, often avoiding each other, devoting their real attention to work, to children, and (sometimes) to other sex partners. These marriages were described as 'utilitarian.'"[1]

While the ultimate state of marriage would be the perfect union, in reality, marriage is a working arrangement that serves, or should serve, the mutual benefit of both parties involved. The reality is that most people do what they are "supposed" to do. They search for security, stability, and respectability within society's social constraints.

Before the idea of feminism and equal rights for women in the workplace took hold, women commonly married with economic reasons foremost in their minds.

"For many women, marriage [was] one of the few forms of employment that [was] readily available. Not marrying could easily mean becoming a domestic or factory worker or going on welfare."[2]

In the early 1970s, the University of Pennsylvania's Dr. William Kephart asked one thousand college students, "Would you marry a person you did not love if he or she had all the other qualities you desired?" Most of the men said no. Most of the women said maybe. One woman explained, "If a boy had all the other qualities I desired and I was not in love with him—well, I think I could talk myself into falling in love."[3]

The Kephart study showed that American girls were trained to approach marriage with practical considerations. College women could not afford the luxury of genuinely free choice because, according to the studies, they knew that their station in life would depend almost entirely on their husband's status.

While today's women are generally becoming more educated, more independent in respect to their earning powers, and more focused on what they want in a life-partner, many, like Sally, still feel the need to be taken care of, as women did twenty-five years ago. Some, however, do change their minds and leave their marriages.

Sally

Sally knew of her attraction for women at sixteen, when she fell in love with her best (male) friend's girlfriend. When she met a much older, well-to-do man, she was totally open about her earlier experience with the other woman and her feelings for women in general. She was also honest about her economic needs. He married her.

"When I sent for your questionnaire, I was intending to remain with my husband," Sally wrote. "Prior to our marriage he was kind, generous, and seemingly open-minded. Upon moving in, I discovered a variety of restrictions—those of money and freedom. He limited the friends I could have. He became very controlling, and I felt as though I were being smothered.

"There was a significant age difference between me and my husband, and he often used that to treat me like a child, and override the validity of my knowledge, learning, and experience. I was coming to hate him."

Still, Sally says she would have kept her part of the bargain, except that he changed. "Within three or four months, the conditions became intolerable.

"To not leave would have assured me of life-long income, land, and a comfortable large house. It would have meant enduring unpleasant sex, the degradation of myself, and my beliefs, dreams, and desires, and infliction of pain on myself, selling myself for material goods.

"I left because I was hurting inside. I was being controlled, manipulated, and used. And I had sold myself."

Dianna

"My husband and I met when we were sixteen years old in high school, got married when we were twenty-one. Church wedding, High Mass. Our first two children were born two years apart and then three years later, our third. We hadn't discovered who we were sexually or otherwise. When did we have time to do that? We just evolved. My evolution was into being a gay woman and owning it, confronting whatever had to be confronted.

"I think I knew I was gay when I married him. I told him, 'I really care very much about you, but I'm in love with Nina.' And he said, 'No. That's not possible.'

"I told him about how soft she was and how her smile made me feel alive, and he said he understood what I was feeling for her. We shared the same love object, you might say.

"'But you want to have a normal life, don't you? You want to have children, and I love you. I want to marry you,' he said.

"I was weak. I had an unhappy family situation and wanted to get away from home, and I didn't see many alternatives in terms of how else I could do it. So I focused myself on getting married and setting up a household, and there really wasn't another woman in my life for the first nine years. Then I did meet someone, and I couldn't repress it. What actually happened was that my husband started having an affair. Our relationship had grown very cold and bitter and withholding sexually on both of our parts, and I think I was depressed and repressed at that time. Sexually, I was very unhappy and feeling probably guilty and a whole bunch of negative things, and I used his affair as my excuse, my ammunition to say it's over. I was twenty-nine at the time.

Sylvi

I met Sylvi on the subway going to New York City's Gay and Lesbian Pride Parade. She was easily identified, not only by her rainbow-colored suspenders over her white T-shirt, but by the exuberance and excitement she gave off on that day.

"Going to the parade?" I asked. She smiled, and we began to talk.

Sylvi, it turned out, had known she loved women when she was sixteen but married anyway. "It was my only choice. I was so concerned with society's rules. I had the desire to maintain something relatively stable."

To do this, Sylvi became an avid churchgoer. She laughed. "It was at church, over the years, that I met my lovers. Some of the women I became involved with were straight when we met. Others, like me, knew they needed to be with women.

"Eventually, I realized that it was possible to be true to myself, and I left my marriage," Sylvi says. "It took some time for my husband to understand and accept who I was, but now we are friends and truly care about each other's well-being."

That marriage serves as a camouflage for the "unacceptable" lifestyles of gay men and lesbians is evidenced by the number of men and women who stay in their marriages as well as by those who seek its protection. It is not uncommon to read personal ads that say: "Gay male seeks gay female for marriage of convenience." One woman said, "I sought safety in a heterosexual marriage because I was terrified of how I had been treated when my family found out I was gay." Being able to fit into "traditional" society brings acceptance and simplifies the lives of lesbians by providing an acceptable partner to take home to Mother, a readily available escort for office functions and parties, or a date for Cousin Sal's wedding.

Not every lesbian who marries a gay or straight man does so as a smoke screen, however. Marriages of convenience are often warm and companionable. They can alleviate loneliness, offer unconditional friendship, and be a source of security for both partners as well.

Honey

Honey, an out lesbian who married a gay man, was encouraged to do so by her mother. While her mother accepted Honey's sexual preference, she was concerned that her daughter was alone. Suggesting that Honey consider her childhood friend as a possible mate, she told her daughter, "You'll have someone to take care of you, someone you truly care about in your life. You both understand each other, and you'll both be free to be who you are."

After actually analyzing their respective financial situations, Honey and Carl decided marriage made a lot of sense. They don't intend to raise a family, but they do intend to take advantage of all the tax benefits offered to married couples.

MaryBeth

MaryBeth says, "My hubby and I have a mutual understanding. Since we're both gay, it makes it easier to live as friends. We are celebrating our twenty-fifth anniversary with a big party and looking forward to it. I love him deeply as a person and vice versa. He fulfills many of my needs as a companion and co-parent. But, we are both free to date whomever and wherever. For the sake of the children, who know about our relationship but have asked us not to come out until they are out of the house, we are each other's 'beard.'"

The economic and sexual union of man and woman, the very nature of the institution of marriage through the ages, has been to serve the interest of society, not to ensure a couple's personal happiness. Marriage has often been used as a political device or to better the family's holdings with little regard for the woman's needs or desires. And so, throughout history, married women who love women (MWLW), especially those born to influential families, have been forced to create separate lives of their own. Two examples of such married women in the public eye were Eleanor Roosevelt and Vita Sackville-West.

While we know now that Eleanor Roosevelt was a MWLW, any private correspondence that even hinted of the sexual being within her has been suppressed or destroyed. Most of what we have learned has come from oral interviews, says Blanche Wiesen Cook, author of *Eleanor Roosevelt*. Until the 1970s, when the papers of Lorena Hickok, Roosevelt's longtime friend and intimate companion, were opened, her life was obscured by closed archives and court biography.

"Over the years, in Greenwich Village and at Valkill, Eleanor Roosevelt created homes of her own, with members of her chosen family, private, distinct, separate from her husband and children. Even as First Lady, ER established a hiding house in a brownstone walk-up that she rented. ... Away from the glare of reporters and photographers, she stepped outside and moved beyond the exclusive circle of her heritage to find comfort, privacy, and satisfaction. ...

"She never considered her friends or her friendships secret or shameful. Her family and her friends lived in one extended community. For decades, there was Eleanor's court and Franklin's court, which included Missy Lehand, his live-in secretary and companion. After ER's death, her friends might deny one another, in private or in print. But during her lifetime they had to deal with one another. They sat across from one another at Christmas and Thanksgiving. They were invited to the same parties, and the same picnics.[4]

"Until recently, historians and literary analysts have preferred to see our great women writers and activists as asexual spinsters, odd gentlewomen who sublimated their lust in their various good works," says Cook. "But as we consider their true natures, we see that it was frequently their ability to express love and passion—and to surround themselves with like-minded women and men who offered support, strength, and emotional armor—that enabled them to achieve all that they did achieve. The fact is that our culture has sought to deny the truths and complexities about women's passion because it is one of the great keys to women's power."

Vita Sackville-West was another highly visible woman. She was a prolific writer, wife, mother, and lover of women, Virginia Woolf among them. In 1920, she wrote: "I believe it will be recognized that many more people of my type do exist than under the present-day system of hypocrisy." *Portrait of a Marriage*, written by her son, Nigel Nicolson, is the story of West's marriage, which not only survived infidelity, sexual incompatibility, and long absences, but grew better and stronger as a result.[5]

Reasons for leaving a marriage are rarely as simple as "I realized I was a lesbian," although that knowledge helps to magnify other deficiencies in the marriage. MWLW, on deciding to leave their marriages, either act on their decisions quickly or remain on a temporary basis while they prepare for the economic responsibilities they will face as single women and mothers. Usually, because children are involved, there is much to work out, often lengthening the amount of time it takes to make the transition.

Some of the women I interviewed who opted to remain temporarily in their marriages were in the process of completing their educations, reentering the job market, finding positions in which they could advance, or working on upgrading their present job skills while planning for future needs such as housing, finances, and medical benefits.

The consensus of opinion was that there was no one perfect time to leave a marriage. Each woman decided according to what felt right for her. Some chose to wait until the last child had finished high school or began college, or until they felt that the youngest child could better handle the change.

Other MWLW—who initially planned to remain in their marriages until they could leave without jeopardizing their financial security as well as their children's—found that the escalating stress caused by hostile and bitter husbands took a physical and emotional toll and wound up leaving their now-intolerable relationships before they were ready.

In other situations, such as Joy's, the opposite was true. Joy and Frank truly felt they would be getting divorced.

Joy

"Almost a year ago, Frank moved to a nearby apartment," Joy explains. "However, when the time came to legally dismantle our long-term relationship, which up until three years ago was considered a perfect marriage, recognizing the complexities involved, we reversed our decision.

"I do love my husband, and he is deeply in love with me. While I now know that many parts of our relationship are not perfect, we are trying, with the help of a counselor, to figure out a way to explore our compatibility. I offer no guarantees to him. I don't know what tomorrow will bring. In part, due to the financial strain, as well as my belief that he has a right to be in his own home, he is returning to our house, where we will have separate bedrooms.

"I am generally seen as a strong professional woman, but now there are days when I think I'll crack up trying to reconcile my values with my need to fully feel, to express those emotions to another, and to just be me."

For many women who came of age before the sexual revolution, living in their parents' homes and then going directly to the ones they would share with their husbands made the idea of moving out, and being totally alone for the first time, frightening. More often than not, these women left their marriages only when they knew another woman was waiting for them. Shelly, however, felt the need to give up her lover to be able to eventually make that move.

Shelly

"When I met my husband and he satisfied me sexually, I thought I was in love with him. We were married for nineteen years. Over that period of time, he became more and more abusive. He wanted me to participate in bondage and other sex games, which made me uncomfortable. He cheated on me openly, and I remained silent. It was quite a few years before I could even admit to myself that I wasn't happy ... sexually or emotionally.

"Eventually, I became friendly with the mother of a child in my class. We became best friends, then lovers. I wound up in therapy. My therapist convinced me that I wasn't gay ... just unhappy. Even when

I told him about the kinds of things my husband wanted me to do, he said I should leave my lover and work on my marriage.

"As a result of my mixed-up feelings and depression, I was willing to do anything. I left her and tried to go straight because that's what the shrink told me to do. That didn't work."

Shelly began an affair with another man. "That didn't work either," she says. "I knew my therapist was wrong, and I reconnected with my woman lover.

"Eventually, I decided to leave my marriage, but the only way I could leave mentally and physically was to leave because it wasn't working. I couldn't leave for her. I didn't want to put that responsibility on anyone. I didn't want to ever say 'Look what I did for you.' So, actually, in order to leave my husband, I also left my lover."

The same economics that might liberate one woman might keep another in her marriage. In some cases, women who had enjoyed a higher standard of living found it less frightening to leave their marriages, while others remained because of their financial security.

Aware that leaving her marriage would cause a tremendous decline in her economic status and would also mean losing old friends, a large home, an affluent lifestyle, and an unlimited bank account, Elaine nevertheless opted to leave.

Elaine

The wife of an influential and prominent man, Elaine says, "For twenty-three years my husband took care of the bills, handled the money, and gave me everything I wanted. In return I spent my entire married life decorating homes and finding friends and then leaving them behind as my husband's growing success necessitated one move after another." She says, "With each promotion, I went into therapy to fix me so we could move again.

"My husband had an inability to see what was going on, and I had an inability to talk about what was going on, so we politely ignored it.

"I had been unhappy for a long time, and so lonely at this point. I took a part-time job for something to do. And I met Hilary. She was a friend of my boss's, and she'd visit with me while I worked in the store and we'd talk. There was a strong emotional, mental, and then physical attraction.

"When her vacation was over and Hilary left the city, I told her I'd go to visit her. And I bought a plane ticket and went. It was something I absolutely needed to do."

After the visit, staying in her marriage was no longer an option Elaine could live with. "I felt tremendous guilt and nothing at all. I was so cut off from my own feelings."

With barely more than her clothes and personal things, she moved in with Hilary while she temporarily sought public assistance. Eventually, she found a job and a small place of her own.

Elaine believes that she was able to leave not because she was confident and worldly, but because she was so naive in money matters. Her husband had always taken care of things such as health insurance, and she gave no thought to life's necessities.

Elaine explains that the failure of her marriage was due to a lack of communication, not sexual incompatibility. She believes that it was the ease with which she was able to communicate with Hilary that led to their love and union. "I went into marriage with a whole package of expectations colored by my childhood experience," she says. "A wife stays at home and is cared for physically. The house is provided, money is provided. Material things are provided by the male. The female partner makes the home, raises the children, makes the social arrangements, provides the artistic touch, plays the piano, cooks.

"When I met Hilary, I didn't have expectations. I could meet her on a one-to-one level. We explored ideas and attitudes and feelings. From that grew love and caring."

Unlike Elaine, who would have been financially secure but still chose to leave her marriage, Helene talked about the high standard of living she enjoyed and the status she held within her community. She admitted that as much as she would like to leave her husband, she could not give up her material comfort or the large circle of friends and activities she enjoyed by virtue of her financial circumstances.

Helene

As a young bride, eager to do her part, Helene spent her time and energy being the perfect helpmate, wife, and hostess. Her activities revolved solely around her husband. She acclimated herself to his needs and desires, until he grew to assume that her only purpose in life was to serve as an adornment to him.

Never able to communicate her growing frustrations, she grew apart from him, and over the thirty-five years of their marriage, her feelings for him gradually diminished. In search of the missing element in her life, she became involved in several heterosexual affairs. They proved to be unsatisfactory. Eventually, she acknowledged her attraction to women. Still, having learned so well to hide her own needs and feelings, she has found it difficult to become emotionally intimate with anyone.

While she prefers to spend as little time alone with her husband now as possible, she is not willing to change her marital status because of the lucrative lifestyle it affords her. Helene is aware that she uses her unlimited financial resources as a buffer. She describes her life: "I go from one activity to another and one friend to another: tennis, golf, theater, luncheons, dinners, movies. I travel constantly. I have two homes. I immerse myself totally in each activity, so as not to have the time to think of anything else."

Living on a treadmill serves a twofold purpose for Helene. It keeps her from being alone with her husband, and it makes it impossible to establish more than a superficial level of friendship with any of her numerous acquaintances or her female lover.

Although there is a widely held misconception that all MWLW, once they identify their lesbianism, leave their marriages, many choose to stay. Seventy percent of the women who responded to my self-selecting survey have remained in their marriages, some for more than thirty years and one for more than forty. One therapist I interviewed asked not to be identified because "half the women I see in my practice, which is primarily gay and lesbian, are married women."

The reasons women marry in the first place play a large part in why they remain in their marriages. The need to be loved, wanted, approved of, and taken care of is of primary importance. The conflict between wanting to be free and wanting to be protected paralyzes them. Most MWLW remain in marriages, even unsatisfying ones, for the same reasons that discontented heterosexual women do. They are tightly woven in their established lifestyles and families and cannot bring themselves to change everything. Protecting children and keeping the family together are priorities. Another reason, according to Dalma Heyn, author of *The Erotic Silence of the American Wife*, is that "the average income of women of all social classes who are divorced in this country decreases by roughly 30%.[6]

"Data from a study of 5,000 families by the University of Michigan panel Survey of Income Dynamics found that married women averaged 744 work hours a year. In the year before a separation, however, the hours of work jumped to 1,024 because women sought to protect themselves economically from the effects of divorce."[7]

Especially in states with new "no-fault" divorce laws, divorce had a catastrophic economic affect on women. While the standard of living for divorced men went up an average of 42% in the year following the divorce, that of divorced women plummeted 73%—even counting alimony and child support.[8]

Some MWLW cite love for their spouses as their primary reason for remaining. However, these same women frustratingly describe that love as platonic. Also operative, of course, is the fear of change that keeps most people from taking a risk—especially if their security is concerned.

Gail

For Gail, being in an unemotional involved relationship felt safe. Gail, thirty-five, has one child from her previous common-law marriage and one with Ralph, her current husband. She always had a sense that she liked women. After her separation from her first husband, which came about because of his violent outbursts, she dated women for several years.

"In the four years I was single again, I dated a lot of unstable people, and I didn't want to deal with that anymore. Then I met my second husband."

Gail chose to marry a second time because she craved a stability that she didn't see in her lesbian community. Her choice of a lifestyle was influenced more by our culture and her personal priorities than it was by her sexual identity.

"I wanted the whole nine yards," she says. "I wanted another baby. I wanted to correct all the wrongs. I wanted to have my cake and eat it, too."

In describing the relationship between herself and her husband, Gail says, "We used to get stoned together and really have fun. Our relationship was loving, kind, communicative, we were on a roll. We were the same age, we had a lot in common, we both came from a working-class background. And he knew about me.

"We had been very heavy drinkers when we met, frequenting the same bar, smoking a lot, partying. We thought, 'This is going to be a fun, modern marriage.' Then, after we married less than a year, all of the responsibilities of home buying brought a tremendous financial burden. He didn't have a clue as to how to write a check. He was very inept in financial matters. I had to take on that burden. Then I got pregnant, and we had a mortgage and a baby. I thought it was time we settled down and made an attempt at a mature lifestyle. He continued to smoke and drink and do all of those wonderful things, and I was at the point where I was hardly getting high at all because I had to keep my head about me. He maintained a working-class mentality while I strove to become professional." Ralph has a GED. Gail has a BA and hopes one day to have her MA.

"It's complicated, why I have chosen to remain in my marriage," she says. "Part of it is financial, but there is also a lot of love there. It's a crazy relationship. I tend to take on the male role; he tends to take on the female role, which is very much to my liking because I am somewhat androgynous. I have a lot of male hormones, and he has a lot of female hormones, and it seems to be a very natural thing."

Being a lesbian does not necessarily mean that one wants to live in a gay community. Choices are influenced as much by cultural and personal priorities as they are by sexual identity. Several of the women who had had every intention of eventually leaving their marriages but had opted to remain temporarily found different ways to "reinvent" their marriages and make them work instead of leaving.

This "holding period" created an opportunity to begin open communication for both spouses. For the first time in their marriages, they were able to achieve a clear understanding of what was going on for each partner. Some MWLW reported mutual growth. This led to a new or awakened respect. And in a few cases, a decision to remain within a redefined marriage became a possibility. They said they related better as friends in their newly redefined marriages than they had as sexual intimates. In several instances, after disclosure, it was the husbands who suggested that their wives remain.

Maggie

Not wanting to be considered an old maid, Maggie had married at twenty-one and had a baby at twenty-two. Then, she divorced at twenty-four. "When I met my second husband, several years later, I was past looking for love," Maggie says. Now forty-three years old, she has one grown child and three small ones.

Before she knew about her own sexuality, Maggie knew that sex with men repulsed her. She told her husband this, and he accepted that fact. "He was a good provider and a good person, and still is ... and I had no idea I liked women.

"I decided to come out to my husband before my ex-lover's husband, who knew because he had put a tap on her phone, told him. Now he knows I'm a lesbian."

Maggie admits things didn't go smoothly in her marriage when she first told her husband. "He told me he loved me, and he'd never stop loving me. I told him I was really sorry for that. I said I'd like him to get into a relationship with someone who could love him back.

"At first, he wanted to kill himself. For two months, my life was in total upheaval. He had an outing party. He called all of my friends and told them I was a lesbian. He didn't do it to be nasty. He was crying. He didn't know what else to do.

"I said I wanted a divorce. He's a corporate vice president, and he convinced me that divorce would not be beneficial for me or the children. I'd end up losing part of my house, health insurance, everything. I realized I'd be living at poverty level if I left because although I could get a job that paid more money, that would keep me away from my children, and I wouldn't do that. So I said okay.

"He's past the point of telling everyone. Now he wants to keep it a secret.

"I would leave him with the kids and go spend the weekend with my lover, and he would do the scrubbing and cleaning. We don't have sex, but we share the responsibility of raising the children together."

When Maggie's lover wanted a full-time relationship with her, Maggie felt forced to break off their relationship. Now, she feels frustrated and trapped, although the decision was hers. "I still get weak knees when I see her, but I can't give her what she wants. I can't pack my bags and show up on her doorstep with three little children."

Melinda

Melinda also chose to remain in her marriage. "There's a shared history, which, as I'm getting older, seems to feel really warm to me. Like putting on an old slipper. Financially, things are better than they've ever been, which offers us the freedom to do the thing I really enjoy: travel."

Then, she confesses, "There isn't a day that goes by that I don't imagine myself being with a woman, whether going on vacation or lying next to one another or talking or cooking dinner. There is nothing I could see in my life where I wouldn't include a woman and don't sometimes think of that happening. *It's definitely an 'and' situation to me, not an 'or.'*

"The only thing that scares me is: What does it mean in the long term in my lifestyle? I know what I have now and it's comfortable, yet I don't want to give up the other part, which is clearly part of who I am. That part doesn't scare me. What scares me is the potential disruption of my life as I know it."

For many people, family serves as an insulation against the world. The idea of it "collapsing" is frightening. "Who is going to take care of me when I get old?" "Who is going to be there when I'm needy?" are constant worries.

According to Catherine Whitney in her book *Uncommon Lives*, "The family has not collapsed so much as it has expanded in context to reflect who we are at the end of the twentieth century: A population whose average life expectancy stretches to seventy and eighty years, a society where nearly seventy percent of women work outside the home, a people whose technological advances expand our options for movement and communication. ... But many couples are afraid to risk change and instead they watch their twenty-five and thirty-five-year marriages cease to hold any meaning or give any joy. In this context, divorce might be the only way some people know how to move from one stage of life to another."[9]

Not all of the MWLW remaining in their marriages have been able to make their lives work for them. Some have resigned themselves to living a lonely existence, forgoing their own needs, bemoaning the fact that their lives are so flat.

Pearl

Pearl, a young woman with one small child, remembers being sent to a Catholic boarding school. "I thought I really liked this one person a lot, in a different way, but I never told her. She was one of the sisters. We were really good friends, and we could talk about a lot of things, so I thought of becoming a nun. Then I went back to a regular high school, pretty much a normal teenager."

Pearl had her first experience with a woman as a teenager at a party. "I really got stoned out, and there was this woman. ... I thought I was rebelling, then I put it to an emotional thing because I had attended an all-girls' Catholic boarding school. I put it on the back burner.

"I married about three years ago. After a while, it seemed like my husband wasn't connecting with me emotionally, then physically. Eventually I realized that I really was attracted to women."

While she acknowledges her feelings to herself, Pearl believes that she has no choice but to suppress them.

"I am very lonely in my marriage, but I will remain because I still care for my husband and because of my child. There is a lot of pressure. A woman is automatically expected to do so much. I work and have a child and keep house and organize and cook, while all he has to do is work. No strain. He feels everything is perfect the way it is."

When asked what she was doing about her unhappiness, Pearl said, "Nothing. I think of what could happen if I met another woman and we became close. ... I'm not putting myself in that situation.

"I have to be the strong person. I've always had to prove that I could be strong and handle [everything]. Now, it really doesn't matter. I'm used to that place. My needs are not being met, but I don't know what

I can do about that. My husband's needs come first. That's just how it is. I'm not as important as him. That's why there is a problem in my relationship. But I know it's not his fault."

Barbara

Barbara, like many MWLW, vacillates between wanting to remain in and wanting to leave her marriage. "I wonder how things would have been if I had had the courage to leave when I was so angry and frustrated with my husband initially. I also wonder if that was what led me to fall in love with Jill in the first place.

"Had Jill been in love with me, might I have given up thirty-two years of marriage for her? I don't know. I often think about what might have been. But the reality was that Jill chose instead to exit my life.

"I made myself believe I could not leave my marriage because I wouldn't be able to support myself. Then I got a job, and I still used finances as a reason for remaining. Then Michael lost his job, and I became the sole supporter, and that was why I couldn't leave. I don't know why I am staying. At times, when we're alone, I shudder to think of our empty future together, yet when the family is around, everything feels right.

"After four years of becoming acquainted with the real me, I came out to my husband. He went through a lot of emotional stuff. Finally, we decided to separate. What relief I felt, like a heavy weight had been lifted from my chest. We decided to go to therapy to ease the separation, and we began to talk. Sometimes, he is so sweet now, I think, why should either of us leave? Then, I can say something as innocent as I'm meeting a friend for dinner, and he'll blow up and scream, 'You have time for everything you want to do, but you never have time for the house.' And I think to myself, let it be over. I can't live with his yo-yo reactions. I feel like I'm on a roller coaster. ...

"But I still don't have the courage to make the final decision, nor am I certain that I want to."

Barbara believes, "I have been able to remain in my marriage primarily because I never felt the passion for Michael that I did later on for the women in my life, and I never felt the highs and lows that come with that passion. So, actually little had changed in our marriage except that we slowly ended the sexual part."

It is possible to have a strong desire to keep a marriage together and make it work and also to protect children from divorce, yet still have an equally strong desire to grow fully as a person and a sexual being. For some women, this requires going beyond their marriages.[10]

Betty

Betty had been in a relationship with Joan, also a MWLW, for two years without her family knowing. She says, "All the while I was with Joan, I was so happy that my relationship with my husband was better. Although we had stopped having sex several years before, we were more comfortable with each other. I had Joan to talk to so I wasn't at him all the time to listen to me and to talk to me. I stopped accusing him of not understanding me. I enjoyed spending time with my family because I knew I'd have special time with Joan. My children were happier sensing my peacefulness."

The relationship between Betty and Joan might have continued indefinitely if Joan's husband had not been transferred. Joan and her family moved across the country.

"Neither of us had ever considered leaving our families. Suddenly, I was desperate for the kind of closeness and companionship we had shared," Betty says.

"At women's bars, I was shunned because I was married. I realized how fortunate I had been to have Joan in my life. More than a year has passed without my being able to find another special woman to take her place, a woman who is also married and understands family obligations and therefore limitations. At home, surrounded by my family, I feel totally alone."

As some MWLW grow more aware of their own feelings and needs, they also become more aware of their rights to make their own choices. Sex within marriage often becomes less frequent or stops completely for both the lesbian-identified women who have come out and those who have not. For those who consider themselves bisexual, coming out often improves the sexual aspect of their marriage.

Within the group of women I interviewed and who have chosen to remain in their marriages, 39% have come out to their husbands. For them, the term *marriage* began to take on different meanings. Often, although celibacy replaced sex, the relationships became more solid as lines of communication opened and understanding deepened.

Andrea

"I had an affair with a woman in college, and I wanted to marry her, but she turned totally against me, so I married the first man who didn't try to jump into bed with me on the first date. I was convinced I was in love with him and was married for five years. When we separated, I was convinced I was in love again and married again.

"I looked at lesbian books, but I didn't pursue anything. I guess there was a fear of the unknown. After memories of incest surfaced and I read *Wild Fire Igniting* and *Ship That Sailed into the Living Room*, I realized that I did not want to be physically married.

"I told my husband I wanted separate bedrooms. He wasn't particularly happy about it, but I had been telling him I didn't want to be sexual with him, and he was denying it. So I moved into another bedroom, and he went into a period of anger.

"I came out to him several months later," Andrea says. "I had started seeing someone, and she was not willing to spend time with me until he knew. I was really nervous about telling him because of all I had read about the man taking the children away, etc., but it finally got too painful not to tell him.

"By that point, he wasn't really shocked. He had to go through a lot of grief and denial, but we co-parent. Now we consider ourselves friends. We support each other emotionally, and we share everything. We did peer counseling, taking turns listening to each other to give emotional release, which has helped us.

"I would like to go back to school to be able to get a job. Marriage right now is being a full-time mother to three children. I don't have a job history, and I'm not making enough money to support myself, and he's fully willing to have me stay here indefinitely.

"I didn't have a lover when I came out to my husband, but I do now. I bring her here. She likes my kids and my husband, and he wants to be friends with her.

"He's not in a relationship, but I think he would like to be. He's seeing someone who he's becoming a little more intimate with. He's taking control of his life. I've seen him grow tremendously."

Andrea concedes that "my husband would like more family time with me. I don't choose to, although I know, when we sit down and compare notes and recommit ourselves to the family and communications, we definitely get along better.

"We are more equally sharing the family and household chores than we ever did. He's doing things around here that he never would have done two years ago, not to please me, but because he's shifting his values. He never thought of me leaving and taking the kids, but he values their presence in his life more than before. He wakes them in the morning and helps them get dressed and cooks for them and sees that they have clean clothes."

While bringing up the issue of sexuality initially causes resentment and anger, it is often the starting place from which other old baggage is dragged out, aired, and then discarded. While spouses may no longer be sexual partners, with sexual issues and accompanying tensions out of the way, friendships may eventually develop.

Andrea and her husband have chosen to remain in their marriage because they have gotten it to work for them. "We share everything. Neither of us wants to be a single parent. He loves the kids.

"Actually, I have it pretty good because I know a lot of single parents don't get the freedom that I do because he's there. I was a single mother after my first marriage, and I remember what it's like. The emotional support isn't there when you're shuffling children back and forth. I'm very committed to my kids. I've got responsibility. I think if money were no object, I'd like to turn the garage into a room of my own. It would be easier to let the kids live here and have another apartment, where we could take turns going to.

"Our kids know how our family functions. There is no side taking or having to defend one parent or the other. We don't fight. There is no hostility. We get along better now."

Rosalie

Rosalie responded to my ad with this note: "I live in a rural setting in a midwestern state and have been married for twenty-five years. For the last five years, my husband and I have shared our lives with my friend. We consider ourselves a family. My husband helps her with many things. She spends time at our house.

"My family accepts her as part of the family, and she attends most functions, although no questions about the nature of the relationship have ever been asked."

Rosalie has since sent holiday greetings, information on concerts, and photographs of her country home, herself, her husband, Jack, and Brenda, the woman in her life.

I felt privileged to have been afforded insight into the life of this family who, against odds, has expanded its household and created an atmosphere of love and acceptance that works for them.

In a child-free marriage for twenty-five years, Rosalie and Jack, who had sensed something different about his wife when he married her, are totally open and honest with each other. And Jack and Brenda, Rosalie's special friend, are friends now. "Brenda is a very enlightened person," Jack says. "She has a brain. She's an independent woman. There is a lot of similarity between this woman and myself. ... It's a very comfortable thing."

When the truth came to Rosalie that she was a lesbian, Rosalie says, "I was concerned that I would remain lonely in that particular aspect of my life since I knew I had the life I wanted and was not interested in a divorce.

"There has always been a personal freedom in my marriage, and I have been able to pursue my interests without guilt. With that comes responsibility, and I had no desire to ruin what we had built. I would never be willing to hurt my husband or others to satisfy my own need."

While traveling for business, Rosalie met the friend of a business acquaintance. She was attending a dance and invited the other woman along, thinking she might meet someone. "The someone turned out to be me," Rosalie says. "The next day she came to my house, met my husband, and began coming down every weekend.

"Jack had been aware that this friendship was different, and when he discovered Brenda and me in the kitchen, hugging, he asked us not to be afraid to talk to him. The three of us talked a lot about this situation. I actually believe that Jack was the one who began to talk about a life that included all three of us. He did not want to lose me, or have the life we had together ruined, and knew that Brenda had become important to me.

"Jack chose to accept Brenda because he realized that she truly loved me. ... He also saw that I loved her and needed her. And it became evident during her early visits that Brenda sought a similar sort of life to the one we had built.

"When Brenda got a job nearby, it was Jack who made the offer to rent to her until she bought property down the road and built her house. We have rarely been separated since.

"That we have been able to achieve this family of ours is due to Jack's willingness to confront and accept the situation. In return, we have been given an extended family. Brenda and I can attend lesbian events and be open in that community, which gives us a needed outlet. Occasionally, Jack comes along, but generally these times are ours alone."

Rosalie says that her marriage to Jack works well. "We talk more about things than we did before, and I am able to be open about things I never would have talked about before.

"Brenda sometimes has more trouble with our arrangement than Jack. While she and he are friends, she does regret that she will never have me to herself; at times, she feels we aren't alone together enough, but we have always been able to work through that by taking a weekend regularly to attend a concert or function somewhere else."

While Rosalie continues to be sexually active with Jack, she says, "I don't consider myself bi ... but I didn't want to change what I had that was working for me. I also know my primary attraction is to women. If something happened to Jack, I would never look for another man.

"Changes in our sex life have more to do with Jack's being older than with my coming out to him. He has said that it has taken the pressure off him to try to perform more than he is able. Brenda is his gift to me since he is sensitive to the fact that I am younger [more than ten years] and might like sex more often than he can provide it.

"We have a 'three-cornered hug' that we engage in with each other in the morning and before retiring at night. That has become a family practice. There is no other physical intimacy between Jack and Brenda or the three of us together.

"I am sure there are times when Jack feels left out. He says, however, that he is genuinely happy that I have found someone with whom I can express my feelings for women, and I believe him. He seems glad when we are together, and when he has to be gone for several days to care for his mother, he says he is glad I do not have to be alone. Being alone has never been a particular concern of mine, but Jack has always worried that I would be left behind.

"Jack is more of a feminist than I am in many ways. His support has enabled me to accomplish things [create a business] I would never otherwise have had the freedom to do. When all four of our parents became ill, he was the one with the skill and willingness to give up his career to take care of them. That resulted in a role reversal we had not planned. I became the sole financial supporter of our household, and since my traveling job gave me no time, he assumed household duties.

"For many years, I had so little vacation time that Jack and I did not do much. We might travel for a few days, but mostly we would be at home. When Brenda entered our lives, he and I did not change that practice. Brenda has a greater need to get away and to be alone with me. Jack claims not to mind. He traveled the world while he was in the navy, and he is glad that I can do some of those things without his having to go himself.

"I try to be especially considerate of Jack and to try to express appreciation for the many things he does for me and for all of us. Now that I am home more, I try to do more of the work that he has normally done for some time. When Brenda and I are going to be gone for a weekend, I try to buy a special card or gift and leave it under his pillow so that he'll know that I'm thinking of him.

"There are times that I feel I am shortchanging Jack. I express it to him and do have guilt feelings and feelings of low self-worth. He does not feel that way and does not like it when I beat myself up. I feel the same about Brenda. While she cares for Jack, I know that her dream would be for there to be just the two of us. However, Brenda knew from the beginning that I was married, and that it would not change.

She chose to come; I never felt I had the right to ask either of them to accept this. She wanted to stay, and while it bothers her more to have to share, she also knows that we truly are her family. ...

"I feel caught in the middle sometimes, and sometimes I feel like the one shortchanged. My own friendships and activities have suffered to some degree because I always feel like any time I have belongs to either Jack or Brenda. I rarely plan anything alone or with another friend since I must accommodate their needs for time with me."

Initially, after my husband and I had talked on our trip, I thought a lot about our separating. But of late, the bickering and arguing that had been the constant source of irritation since my announcement had been replaced by a calmness, and now, with the Jewish holidays approaching, my thoughts were on the dinner we were preparing for the following evening. So I wasn't expecting it when, while peeling potatoes beside me, he said, "I've been looking for an apartment."

My eyes, already tearing from the onions I was dicing, felt an additional sting. I had expected to feel relief, but I wasn't feeling that. A jumble of emotions ran round my brain. Suddenly I felt overwhelmed by everything. Saddened. Here we were, side by side, preparing for our traditional Passover seder, for people we both loved, and talking about changing our lives. Then he continued. "But I've been going over our finances, and I can't move. We can't afford to pay a mortgage and a rent."

I didn't say anything. We continued working side by side.

I had come to terms with my female-oriented sexuality and now was also coming to terms with my marriage, which I decided I'd rather redefine than leave. For many years, my marriage had been a traditional one. I saw myself as the hub from which my husband and children ventured forth into the world and returned again to its safety and comfort. Now I, too, wanted to be free to venture forth and return again.

But, what kind of man would agree to this? What kind of man would want to stay with a MWLW?

CHAPTER 9

Redefined Marriages

On more than one occasion I have been asked, "Do you ever wish that all of your feelings for women would go away and your life could go back to being normal?" Early in my discovery, when I was distraught and lost my best friend because of my new feelings for her, I did think, "What if I could be hypnotized and not remember any of these feelings?" But then I thought that, even if it meant losing her friendship, I never wanted to forget the gift of being able to feel with such tremendous passion.

Other questions I have often been asked are, "Do you ever want to live happily ever after with the woman you love?" and "Are you more inclined to want to go back to living in your heterosexual world with your husband?"

These questions assume you must accept one or the other; heterosexual marriage or lesbian divorce. I refused to do either.

I used to live my life believing that things were either good or bad, right or wrong, or black or white. But when I discovered—and came to terms with—my true sexuality, after being married for twenty-five years, I realized that life is not that simple. I didn't believe those who told me, "You have to leave your marriage." It was true that, once I realized I was a lesbian and came out to my husband, we were on an emotional roller coaster for a while, and our marriage was temporarily fraught with anger and bitterness. But through it all, I remembered the love and the caring we had once had for each other, and I refused to throw away those things I held dear. Also, I realized that it was me who had changed and not my husband. So, I set about to find another way to make my marriage work. I am glad I did not fold to peer pressure and leave it.

Although some women may choose to believe that I have remained for the privilege and perks that come with a heterosexual marriage, I have remained because I have a deep love and great respect for this man who accepts and loves me knowing that I am a lesbian. I have done what many women in the same situation have done. To the best of my ability, I re-created my reality, and I feel comfortable with who I am.

Being married and gay is not easy. Some marriages remain intact because no disclosure is given or because the woman is afraid of the unknown or fearful of what her children might think of her if she were to leave their father. More and more women who have come out to their husbands are redefining their marriages and remaining in them. It might be a codependency issue, but at the heart of most redefined marriages there is something that each party feels is important enough to preserve, possibly the friendship that has grown over the years or the good co-parenting skills they've developed together. It might be economics or the love of a home neither wants to give up.

Remaining in a marriage may seem like a cop-out to some who have left their own, but often redefining a marriage can be as difficult as leaving one. While some husbands continue to go about the business of living together and parenting their children with little else ever being said after their wives' initial revelations, for others, the telling leads to immediate dialogue or to the process of digesting this new information. Deciding whether to remain in their marriage may take months or even years.

Practical issues such as sleeping arrangements, financial obligations, and division of child care and work responsibilities need to be worked out. What is each party willing to do to make this revised marriage work? What is each party willing to give up? What kind of united front would they like to present to their children?

Some women see remaining as a "temporary fix" or the "best they can do for now." I complimented Celeste, who, with her husband's support, had rearranged their shared home so that they could each have their own bedrooms.

Celeste

"I don't deserve to be praised," Celeste said. "I'm staying only because I don't have the courage to leave." Celeste hadn't realized how much courage she'd had just to come out to her husband and then to be able to communicate with him so that he could understand what she was going through and they could make the necessary adjustments for their marriage to function.

Maybe one day Celeste will leave or maybe during this period she'll discover that other options are available, as Lydia did.

Lydia

Lydia and her husband had agreed to share their home and have separate sleeping quarters temporarily—until they could work something else out. She laughed as she told me, "That was twenty years ago. Our long-term marriage has evolved into its own unique style. Both of us work and share household duties. We also share a caring friendship, and we are free to be our authentic selves."

Annie

Annie told me that she had decided to remain in her marriage and live her life as a wife, the mother of three preteens, … and as a lesbian. "It's complicated, but we're doing it," she said. A few years later she called me again. "After a brief illness, my husband died. The complications of leading a double life were nothing compared to what I need to deal with now."

Not every woman who has redefined her marriage is out to her husband. Michele, at 65, is such a woman.

Michele

"I've been in a relationship with Suzanne for the past eighteen years," Michele says. "Suzanne moved in with my husband and me temporarily twelve years ago, until she could establish herself after her move to our town. She has remained under the same roof ever since. The matrix of my life is exponentially complex. We live, on a daily basis, lives that few can even begin to comprehend. To simplify, my therapist, in a fit of laughter, once said, 'You pulled it off.' We're still pulling and pushing, compromising and comforting, listening and learning, laughing and loving, weeping and wishing that our lives could go on forever.

"I am not explicitly out to my husband, but implicitly. The words have never been spoken, but he is a smart man and knows and accepts what he chooses. We had our last intimate encounter on our twenty-fifth anniversary, about fifteen years ago, and he has never approached me again, nor has he spoken of the absence of intimacy. Each of us has our own bedroom and bathroom, and at home, Suzanne and I share an office.

"We had been childhood friends and, as young marrieds, lived in the same town. We moved, and she and I lost contact for many years. When we ran into each other as adults, she was divorced with grown children. She confessed that she had thought of me every day for the last 30 years and had loved me for all that time. I had always loved her as a friend, but the physical intimacy catapulted me into a world I'd only imagined. And my love grew and is still growing. There are not enough words to convey the comfort and joy that having her in my life brings. Suzanne is not out to her family and having to adapt to a household and routines established over many years of my marriage to my husband has been a major issue for her. But all of us have made adaptations and compromises. She misses her children and grandchildren, who are a distance away, while I am sometimes overwhelmed by mine, who all live close by.

"My husband talks a lot, and though he doesn't demand an audience, he appreciates one. I'd like to spend time with her when she gets home from work and that's the time of day he's usually winding down and wanting company. That's probably my biggest issue."

According to Helen Fisher, a research anthropologist at Rutgers University, human partnerships are shaped by three independent neurochemical brain–body systems, responsible respectively for sexual attraction, romantic yearning, and long-term attachment. These three systems can act together or separately, which would explain why people can be wildly sexually attracted to those they have no romantic interest in and romantically drawn to, or permanently attached to, people who elicit no sexual interest.[1]

As I grow older, I appreciate more and more the man who has stood by me as I ventured forth into my new world of special women friends and loves. We have both grown as individuals and are constantly changing, as is the world around us. Seventeen years after coming out to him, our friendship is stronger than ever. Both of our children are married now, and at their weddings, I danced with my husband and with the special women in my life. Now, together, we are immensely enjoying our first grandchild.

Other gay women have said, "You are blessed," and made observations such as, "Your family is unique, truly authentic." I have to agree with them. My family is special. But it didn't just happen. I worked hard to make their world, and mine, work.

When I first dealt with my feelings, I was overcome with sadness. I wondered if I was going to spend the rest of my life in a house with no warmth or love. Then, I realized that I had been the one who created that warmth. I had been the one who stopped doing those little things that brought that warmth and comfort to my home—buying fresh flowers, using pretty place mats, lighting scented candles. My husband and children really didn't care about those things. I was the one who enjoyed them, so who was I punishing by denying myself pretty flowers and the other things? Only me. I had also enjoyed having a neat home, yet I had allowed the clutter to grow in my living room. I was going through a difficult period emotionally, and I was making it worse on my own. I was giving myself a real pity party. Then, one day, it dawned on me: I couldn't change my entire situation overnight, but I could do something positive instead of brooding about it. When I set about bringing back the old warmth, I began my own transformation.

While women are beginning to realize that there are various options open to them, some still believe that, once they make their discoveries, they have no recourse other than to immediately tell their spouses and move out. I try not to give advice, as every woman's situation is different, but when women tell me that they *have to* tell and move out immediately because they've realized they are gay, I do tell them that they are putting the cart before the horse.

That should not be the first step in their process. There are many things to be taken into consideration, especially when children are involved. Finances, child care, and housing are three biggies. Overwhelmed with feelings of guilt for leaving, being lesbians, or taking their children from their husbands, women often agree to unrealistic, and unfair, arrangements. I have heard countless stories of women who left their homes unprepared to face the world as single mothers and, because of their impulsive actions, have lost a great deal.

One reader suggested that I just do a book with four stories, each having its own unique components:

1. A wife tells husband and children about her relationship with another woman.
2. Wife falls in love with another woman, and they have an affair without disclosure to anyone.
3. A married woman falls in love with another married woman. One woman divorces. The other does not.
4. Two women, wives and mothers, meet, divorce their husbands, and build a life together.

I thought about her suggestion and remembered a fortune cookie I'd once read. It said, "Genius is the ability to reduce the complicated to the simple." In this case, however, the simple proved to be a lot more complicated.

Depending on the confidence levels, the temperament, environment, family, and friends of those people involved, each scenario would be different. For example, in number one, do the children know or not? Does one know and the other(s) not know? Are the children angry or supportive? Is one child supportive and the other angry? Is one angry with the father for putting up with the mother? Are the children angry with each other because they are supportive of opposite parents? Is the husband one who buries his head in the sand and refuses to see? Is he in denial? Is he supportive, caring, and loving? And, what about the lover? Is she married or single? With her husband or living separately? Is one woman able to communicate with her husband and the other not? Is she jealous of her lover's children? Does she get along with the lover's husband? Does she resent him and any time his wife spends at home? Each shuffle of these possibilities would result in a completely different story.

Women who redefine their marriages often crave their own space, and sleeping arrangements are a key issue. Changes are needed in homes to accommodate these new situations. If an extra bedroom is not available, some simply make a dining area, or den, into sleeping quarters to allow for privacy. For some, conditions such as sleep apnea, back problems, conflicting work schedules, or colicky babies necessitate temporary shifts in sleeping arrangements, and those arrangements simply become permanent without a need for dialogue. But for other women, like Jessie, moving to a different bedroom is like making a final break.

Jessie

"I didn't want my husband to feel any more rejected than he already did, but I knew I couldn't share a bed with him once I realized who I was," Jessie said. "One night, before I could get up the courage to talk about having separate rooms, I fell asleep on the couch. My husband came downstairs the next morning and said, 'I slept better than I have in a long time. Much more space to turn in.' I asked him how he'd feel about us sleeping in separate beds, and he said, 'Let's try it.'"

Rikki

Rikki said, "Making love had become uncomfortable for me even before I told Joe about myself. After I told him, because of our kids, we decided to try to stay together anyway—in separate rooms. We're great at parenting together, and we're great as housemates, and now that sex isn't hanging over our heads, we're much better friends, too. The problem was that I love having my own room, but I missed watching the morning news with Joe and discussing it before going off to work. He never said I couldn't watch it with him, but I was uncomfortable going back into the room I'd given up. Then something major broke on the news, and I hurried into his room without stopping to think. He motioned to my old side of the bed, and we watched the news together. And we have, each morning since.

"The truth is, we can now share a bed with no discomfort. When the house is filled with overnight guests and it makes the most sense, I'll move back into his room for the weekend, and if we're traveling to family functions or whatever, we'll share a room rather than go for the expense of two, and we're both comfortable. My lover was uncomfortable with this at first, but once she got to know Joe, she felt differently."

Some women in celibate and redefined relationships continue to share their beds with their husbands, as Rachel has.

Rachel

"When I open my eyes in the morning," she says, "I'm glad to see my husband beside me. He's so dependable, and his presence in my life is comforting—very different from my feelings when I am with my lover. When I wake beside her, my hand immediately goes out to touch her, if we're not already in a spooning position."

Separating and remaining together is an option and not all that uncommon.

Goldie

"We've been separated for more than a year, and I've had a girlfriend for almost that long," Goldie says, "But my husband and I and our three small children still live together. This works for the sake of our children, and we both love our house. At times, I do have mixed emotions about my whole situation. What does my future hold? My husband still has hopes for the two of us being together again, even though he's dating right now. But I don't think that will happen."

Dana and Melanie had been friends for some time. When Melanie was laid up, her husband, not the best at dealing with illness, asked Dana if she'd come and stay with his wife.

Dana

"I was just coming out of a sexless relationship and thinking about trying sex with men again. Years before, to please my parents, I'd been close to marriage but hadn't been able to go through with it. In a no-strings-attached way, I liked the dynamic of a threesome with a committed married couple. I had actually been flirting with a couple with whom I had a long-standing invitation. And I actually wondered about Melanie and her husband as well. I have no particular attraction to him, although I do like him very much, but I had always thought she was one of the most beautiful women I know. Anyway, I told her how I had been flirting with this other couple.

"After I told her, I was surprised that she seemed a bit put off because she always struck me as very sex-positive and somewhat adventurous. I thought I had misjudged her and the idea offended her, so I backed off the subject. The next day, I got an e-mail from her apologizing for her odd reaction. She told me that she had feelings for me herself, and that she'd like to take me out on a date. I was floored and flattered and told her so, but I also told her that I was inspired by the [good] relationship she had with her husband and was very wary of treading anywhere that might harm that.

"A few hours later, I got an e-mail from her husband telling me that it was fine with him, that they had an open marriage and he had no problem whatsoever."

Some marriages do end in divorce once a woman discovers her same-sex sexuality. Still, it is also not unheard of for the ex-wife and ex-husband to continue to live in the same dwelling. Pro-marriage forces are fuming over this, but a new trend in family life is calling for the normalizing of divorce and accepting living together as a lifestyle because, according to an article in *USA Today*, while most marriages used to end in death, many more now are ending in divorce. The prevalence of divorce is cause for accepting different options, and living together should be seen as a legitimate end state in itself.[2]

Feelings of isolation often lead women to join support groups. These groups become substitute families, and wanting the approval and acceptance of their new "families," some women make decisions based on what the others in the group have done rather than what is right for them at that time. Women also rely on therapists to help them when contemplating the decision to remain or leave a marriage. Unfortunately, many therapists, like the women they counsel, are either not aware that other options exist or are counseling from their own agendas.

Milly

Milly said, "I believe my therapist is prejudiced against me because she left her husband within a year of coming out and feels I should do the same. She tells me I am in denial because I have chosen to stay married. This is not the case. I am in an intimate relationship with another woman and have come out to my family and friends. I am very open about my sexuality, but because I am not 'single' and going to community centers and political rallies, she regards me as homophobic.

"I don't believe that it is necessary for every woman to choose divorce in order to be true to herself. Indeed, if I am to be true to myself, then I have to realize that I am also a mother and wife, and I made this life for myself, too."

Penny

Penny wrote to say that, "It has been my experience in my journey with therapists that they never consider or talk about the possibility of staying married. This causes a great deal of depression for people who do not wish to change their family life along with their personal life. I just recently joined a coming-out group and found myself the only married woman in the group. I felt pressure from the other women to choose between my husband and being gay, but the reality is, he is my husband and I am gay. I had a husband and a family first, and that is also a large part of my life."

Whether a woman remains in her marriage or leaves, she may come to resent those who have chosen a different option—until she has made peace with herself. Linda had left her marriage.

Linda

"I had to come to terms with who I was before I could put my resentment for my friend aside—until I could make peace with myself." Linda says, "I looked down at my friend who chose to remain in her marriage. I realize now that part of my judgmental attitude came from a little resentment and jealousy. I guess I'm still working on forgiving myself for leaving my husband. I'm not yet at a place of closure in my own life. I have lived with such guilt and remorse for the past three years but, little by little, have been able to forgive myself."

Kimmy

Kimmy says, "My husband knew about my feelings for women years ago. He knew they had returned, but he thought that meant I was bisexual. Once I realized that I was interested in women far more than I'd ever been interested in men, I had to tell him. We have always been honest with each other and communicate to the best of our abilities. He was very upset and cried. When I said I was sorry because I do love him and because hurting him was not something I wanted to do, he said, 'Don't ever be sorry for who and what you are.' At that moment, he became my best friend, and he is that to this day. That is not to say that he doesn't have his ups and downs accepting the new me.

"We co-parent better than either of us would single parent. We live in the same household at present, sleeping separately. I have made the back hall area into an impromptu living space for myself, and we plan on buying a two-family house in the next year or two so that we will both be in the same building as our children. If the time ever comes when I live in a domestic partnership with a woman and am not married to my husband, I believe it will happen with minimum drama, pain, and anxiety for all involved. For now, I am feeling newly empowered and proud and deeply happy."

When a woman comes out to her husband, his reaction may be based more on whether another woman is in her life than on her desire to remain in or to leave her marriage. Men are often better able to deal with their wives' revelations in the abstract. If someone else has already taken their place, it becomes much more difficult to accept their changing world.

Myra

When Myra fell in love with Kate, she came to the realization that she was going through not a transformation, but a midlife epiphany. "Despite the fact that I had never had an awareness of my lesbianism prior to my marriage, I never experienced a moment of any shame, doubt, or remorse. Rather, I felt immediately liberated. I felt as though I had come home after decades of unknowingly wearing the skin of another woman."

Wanting to somehow merge her "new identity" with her previous status as suburban wife, homemaker, and mother, Myra says, "I have tried to maintain the integrity of my marriage by coming out to my husband and, with the guidance of a professional, to my children as it is my intention for us to share our lives with Kate as well as with my husband."

"While Gene was originally shocked, he was supportive of my 'discovery.' He has gone through a year of coming to terms with the painful realization that the future that he had envisioned for his family will never come to pass. Nonetheless, he has come to the initial stages of realizing that although I have found my true soul mate, I have never ceased to love him or to genuinely value him, and I have no desire to eliminate him from my life or the lives of our children."

Myra's husband has gone from not allowing Kate to enter their home to allowing her to become an integral part of not only Myra's life but also the lives of their children. Myra says, "The light in our children's eyes when they are in Kate's company speaks for itself, and Gene has been courageous enough to acknowledge and accept that."

Myra and Kate, along with Gene, have begun a long journey toward planning a future together. They have discussed alternatives that would allow Gene to be an ongoing daily presence in the kids' lives, including building an addition onto their home with separate living arrangements for either Gene or the women, but thus far Gene has not come to terms with living in such close proximity to the two women.

"For now, Kate will be moving to our area in order to allow us to spend more time together as well as to determine whether she, a single woman, really does want to rise to the challenge of sharing her life not only with me, but with three children and their dad as well. I wish I could say that Gene is happy about the arrangement, but he is living with his own concerns about the future."

Patricia

Patricia says "I have a husband whom I love and am emotionally intimate with. We've adapted a kind of sexual intimacy that works for him and that I can deal with. I also have a woman lover. They both know about one another and accept each other in my life. I view this as polyloving. For me, being a part of a triple is not unusual. We are in a stable, committed marriage of the heart and spirit, if not the law. The world is a complex place, and we have simply taken a more creative way to develop a relationship form that meets its challenges in a better way than the accepted norm does."

Not all redefined marriages work out. One wife, wanting to be fair, encouraged her husband to find a girlfriend since she had one. He did find someone, only the woman he found was not understanding of his home situation, and his wife found herself on the wrong end of a divorce.

While working on the first edition of *Married Women Who Love Women*, I came across few situations in which a single woman was living with her married lover and her lover's husband. Now, however, women are telling me about different types of relationships that include more than two individuals. Such relationship are called *polyamory*, although not all polyamorous relationships are identical. One relationship may take priority over the others, as in a relationship that allows partners to include outside lovers. Two or more relationships may be of comparable weight, but one person's partners may not have a strong relationship with each other. Or, an interrelationship of three or more people, in which there is a strong relational commitment between all members—which may or may not include sex—may exist.

Emma

Emma lives in a Mormon community. She had her first encounter with another girl when she was fifteen.

"Although polyamorous lifestyles were common among the closely knit community," Emma says, "I decided to follow the norm and married a man when I was eighteen. After my children were born, my feelings for women became stronger. I felt really bad when I first shared a bed with another girl after marrying, but soon my guilt began to vanish when I realized how happy and content I could be after each adventure. Now my relationship with my husband is mostly celibate with occasional sexual encounters, more as a routine thing to maintain our relationship and avoid any suspicions."

Doreen's evolution into polyamory was a gradual one.

Doreen

"Had you asked me years ago, I would have told you that I was definitely bisexual. But the older I get, the more lesbian identified I become and the stronger my need to be with my woman. Still, my husband is a good man; he has stood by me through thick and thin and pretty damn close to the gates of hell, and he has always known and understood this need of mine. I care about him and feel loyal to him and to our family. He does, too. And so, although there is now a woman in my life, and in our family, we try to look at the big picture as much as we can, and I try to make it clear that I still love him. We all have dinner together, and even though the food may be simple, it's a pleasant time. When we have appropriate leftovers, I pack them up for his lunch ... he loves 'food from my hand.' And I still remember to call him at work every afternoon.

"Some qualities ripen well and some don't, and some things just shift, like me being closer to lesbian now than I was at twenty or thirty or even forty, but my husband and I believe in each other and support each other in so many ways. If he could ever find a lover who would understand that she could be, on some level, a part of this family, if she wanted to, I wouldn't have a problem with that. But I don't think he's got the drive to want it enough."

Nydia's coming into polyamory was also transitional. She was bi when she married, and halfway into her marriage, which lasted fifteen years, she and her husband thought that bringing another woman into their relationship might strengthen it, but that didn't work. Nydia's desire to be with a woman grew. Her marriage broke up. She dated women and men.

Nydia

"I always had a problem identifying with one category or another. I knew I was bisexual but was completely monogamous to my husband the whole time I was married. I am now living with a straight male partner who supports my bisexuality. We have a common philosophy about polyamory. I have a woman lover who is married to a bisexual man. We had been friends for years before. She and I both have children, and all of our lives intermingle quite a bit. We are each other's support network.

"Having a polyamorous lifestyle is not about having casual sex. We all know each other. We take the time to learn about each other. We know each other's histories. It's not about lying, but about being one hundred percent open. It's about having integrity. You can't be selfish and go off and do what you want because it has a ripple effect. It's based on integrity, open communication, honesty, respect, and accountability."

After Wendy's second marriage broke up, she decided to explore a part of her sexuality that she had never looked into before. She began a correspondence with Sara, a woman she met through a lesbian chat room. They corresponded for several weeks before Sara told Wendy that she was married. Still, Wendy thought they had a lot in common, and they arranged to meet for coffee anyway.

Wendy

"My story began as a lesbian story, but turned into a polyamorous one. I met my wife, a married woman, five years ago. We three—me, her, and him [the married woman's husband]—live together in one union.

"Before our first date, I made sure her husband was aware of our seeing each other. I was not interested in lies or deception. I met Dan when I came to pick Sara up. He was supportive. It was not my intention to get involved with another woman's husband, and for a couple of months, it was just me and Sara. Although the three of us did spend a lot of time together, there was never anything physical between Dan and me. Sara and I fell in love, and Sara told me the dream that she and Dan had had about finding another woman to join them in a triad. Things happened quickly after that. I realized how deeply I felt for Dan. We shared a melding of the minds and were constantly involved in deep intellectual conversation. It was truly life altering for me to spend hours and hours with these intelligent people, exchanging ideas and philosophies. I was certainly attracted to him, but in my mind, he was off limits.

"Then things changed, and I realized I could have the best of two worlds. Within six months, we were all living together. At one point there were also five kids (my two and their three), and a dog. Now we're down to two full-time kids and two part-time. The fifth has left the nest. And of course, we still have the dog. This is the hardest thing I've ever done, and also the most rewarding."

Amber, like Wendy, also came to know Janet via their correspondence in a chat room—and her husband met Janet the same way.

Amber

"My husband and I were married for nineteen years when we both fell in love with Janet. She has been living with us in a committed relationship for the past nine years. We are pretty closeted in terms of the general public and introduce her as our 'roommate.' She plays a great independent spinster to the general local world. We met on the Internet. She'd had a tragic childhood, and something I wrote triggered a bunch of abuse memories for her. We'd been corresponding for a month or so when my husband began corresponding with her, too. Both he and I developed very strong feelings for her very quickly. She called so strongly to our hearts, and her life had been so difficult and her situation so precarious."

I received the following letter from one woman who had been on the verge of divorce when she realized she was a lesbian. "After a lot of honest communication, my husband and I decided to redefine our marriage. We are living authentically now. We're doing what we want to be doing. We're together because we choose to be, and things worked out for us because we didn't make rash decisions. I will be forever grateful to you for that."

Whether in a redefined marriage or divorced and in a relationship with another woman, children learn what a good relationship can be from seeing the adults in their lives respectful of, caring about, and communicating with each other.

CHAPTER 10

The Single Lovers of Married Women

The first bit of advice I was given by a friend when I came out to her was, "Don't tell anyone you're married. Single lesbians will run from you like you had the plague." She was right, and she was wrong. Some women, on hearing about my marital status, broke off their conversations midstream, but others did not.

Like their married sisters, single lesbians come from a wide spectrum. Some of the women I interviewed were lifelong lesbians, others had been married to men and divorced, and still others had been in partnerships with other women that had dissolved. And, I came to find out that many single lesbians are involved with married women.

Relationships are difficult to maintain even when women come from similar backgrounds and all things are equal. So, why would a single woman choose to be in a relationship with a married woman? There are many different reasons. We don't always get to choose who we fall in love with. Sometimes it makes no sense at all, but suddenly serotonin, that feel-good chemical, kicks in.

For some, it just happens, as in a chance meeting like Julie's or Renee's.

Julie

Julie had signed up for a three-day seminar. It turned out that most of the people attending were married. Allison was there with her husband, but she and Julie both felt an instant rapport. Julie never considered Allison, a married woman, as anything but a friend. "There is just the most amazing sense of trust and the most wonderful open communication between the two of us," Julie said. "She had her life set up: a house, a husband, a child, her whole life was in place. Then, shortly after we returned to our respective homes, she invited me to visit—and we became lovers."

Renee

Renee was attracted to Joanie when they first met on a hiking trip, but knowing Joanie was married, did not think being in a romantic situation with her was an option, so she ruled it out.

"Our love grew from a friendship, but I knew she was special from the very beginning," Renee said. "Then she showed her interest in me. We were lying next to each other, getting ready to go to sleep. She asked me if I wanted her to kiss me. I did want to, but I didn't. We talked about it because I was concerned with her being married. And once we talked about it, we kissed, and the rest is history."

Renee and Joanie are temporarily living a distance from each other. On her visits, about once a month, Renee stays with Joanie's family. She loves her children and spends time with them and with Joanie's husband as well. "I really like him a lot, and he told Joanie that he likes me, but it can be awkward when I'm visiting or when I talk to Joanie about how her husband is feeling. I have not actually talked with him about the relationship, but I hope to get to spend more time with him one-on-one as Joanie and I move forward with our relationship. Still, because she is not available all of the time, our situation is not ideal. It can be hard when I want her to be able to be with me for special events in my life, but I knew what I was getting into when we started this relationship."

Renee sums up the main problems in her relationship like this: "Joanie is trying to protect herself from the possibility that I may find someone who can commit to me one hundred percent. Her husband is trying to figure out if he can be happy sharing his wife with me, and I'm trying to figure out if I could be happy not having a full-time partner in her. And we are all defining what our relationships will be in the future."

For other women, old friendships blossom into love, as Tiffany's did.

Tiffany

"Christine, a married woman, and I had been friends for a long time. We'd met at work. I realized several years ago that I was falling in love with her, but to maintain our friendship, I was completely content to love her from afar. The acknowledgment of my sexuality had ruined many friendships throughout my school years, and I wasn't about to risk losing her by revealing my feelings. She meant too much to me. It took me forever to tell her about myself. When I did, she kissed me, and we haven't looked back since. She is everything to me. Everything a woman could want in a lover/partner/friend."

Unlike Julie, whose meeting was accidental, or Tiffany's whose relationship grew from a friendship, Camilla's decision to find a married woman had been a conscious one.

Camilla

"I was terrified of being outed at my job or to my family. I believed that no one would suspect me of being a lesbian if my 'best' friend was married, so I actually tried to meet and to partner with a married woman for that reason. Love and family were something I had dreamed of my whole life, and now I could play the stereotypical male spouse role with Jodi and her kids. I finally felt comfortable in my own skin."

Bethann, like Camilla, was also afraid of coming out, and although she did not purposely set out to meet a married woman, when she did meet someone she was attracted to, she did not hesitate to become involved.

Bethann

"It is easier to stay in the closet with a married woman. I didn't have to deal with the fear of coming out to myself, my friends, and my family, and I was providing understanding, comfort, and love to someone in a terribly unfortunate situation until it could be fixed with the least amount of impact on the kids."

Both Camilla and Bethann became involved with married women to protect themselves from being outed. But their reason is not the only one. Single women seek out married lovers for a variety of reasons.

Allie said, "I feel less performance anxiety being with a married woman as opposed to being with an experienced lesbian."

Rochelle said, "I need my space. I can't be with someone 24/7. Every single lesbian I've become involved with has eventually wanted to live with me."

Veronica said, "I chose a married lover because I value my 'singlehood.' My lover gives me companionship and affection, yet she also gives me space. I appreciate the time I am able to spend alone to pursue my own interests. I love that I can do what I want to at the spur of a moment. I pride myself on being able to face life on my own terms."

Lynnette had yet another reason for connecting with a married woman. "I'm 68 years old and attracted to women of my own age group. Many of them are married or have been married. I'm not out in my community and not involved in any local groups where I could meet single women. I'm currently very much involved with an unavailable married woman. We met online, and what attracted me to her was her love of animals."

Dora, divorced thirty years ago, says, "There is little fear of a married woman showing up on my doorstep with a U-Haul." Dora is extremely involved in her work and was totally up front about wanting to remain independent when she met Faith, a married woman. But, their friendship blossomed into an intoxicating love. "Our relationship will never be a 'living together' one, but we both understand this. We both have families and responsibilities, and we each understand and respect that mine come first with me and hers come first with her. Still, I could not be in a secret relationship, so Faith told her husband. He has been supportive and understanding, and her honesty with him has made our relationship a better one. I'm happy for her. He does not yet feel comfortable around me, but someday, I hope he will."

While there are women who like their own space, many single women involved with married women concede that during the holiday season, they get to feeling a little low. While they may have only themselves to think about, they understand and accept that their lovers' first responsibilities need to be to their children, especially during the holidays.

Some women work through this awkward season by choosing their own special dates for celebrating holidays such as Christmas and New Year's. They create their own traditions and find other special dates to celebrate: when they met, when they became lovers. But for Phoebe, who would love to become more a part of Faith's family, these times are especially difficult.

Phoebe

"There are restrictions being with Faith," Phoebe says. "It depresses me that I can't wake up beside her every day. Some days I curse myself for falling in love with her. Some days I'm glad. I love this woman with my soul. There is no one else I can talk to about my emotions. My friends have abandoned me. They think I'm nuts to want to be with a married woman. Even my therapist doesn't understand. I've learned to express my emotions through poetry. Throwing my feelings all out, helter skelter, and then putting them into meaningful thought in poems has been therapeutic."

Other women do become integral parts of their lovers' families. Some have actually found that they enjoyed the company of their lovers' husbands, too. That is not as surprising as it may seem; often, there are similarities in temperaments between husbands and lovers.

Still, families can cause major stumbling blocks in relationships.

Julia

When they met, Julia and Val were both married. Julia left her husband a short time after she met Val, but Val chose to remain in her marriage until she could get her college degree. "This woman pleases me in every way," Julia says. "Our lovemaking is out of this world, but that isn't everything. We have a wonderful time whenever we're together. I spend every weekend at her home with her husband there. He is okay with us being together. He never interferes. I'm not complaining, but I feel like I contribute more to the relationship than she does. I'm the one driving the long distance between our homes every weekend. I'm the one spending money on occasional hotel stays so she can be more relaxed and we can have the kind of lovemaking that we want. I'm the one who pays for our meals, the gas, the fun things we do. I don't mind all of that, but I am *very* jealous of her husband. I want what he has! I hate the idea of him touching her or being around her while she is naked. I can't get those issues out of my head. I'm afraid that my worry will destroy us. She claims it won't and says I need to get over it.

"My family would rather not talk to me because I left my husband. My finances are getting tight because of me spending so much money on us. I want her to myself and can't have her right now. It is killing me inside. She says everything is all right. She says she loves me but needs to wait a few years to clear some issues before leaving. Why can't she understand how difficult this is for me?"

Some never-married lesbians, like their divorced sisters, are mothers or guardians with full-time responsibility for children. At times, their schedules are more limiting than those of their married partners, who have spouses to relieve some of their child care duties. Other women share custody, either with ex-partners or ex-husbands, and their time with their lovers is determined by the "child-free" weekends penciled in on their calendars.

In addition, it is not unusual for women who identify as single, and are legally separated or divorced, to share residences with ex-husbands or ex-partners for the sake of their children, economics, or health benefits. These situations factor into the kind of relationships they can have with married women.

Single lesbians, like their married lovers, fall into different categories. Some knew early on that they were lesbians. Others had no idea until they happened to fall in love with that first woman. And still others had a sense that they were but did all in their power to hide their sexuality—other than marrying a man.

Simone

Simone was one of those women who didn't have a clue about her sexuality. "The whole situation took me by surprise," she said. "I never thought of myself as someone who would be fulfilled by a relationship with another woman—as opposed to one with a man—until an advance by my best married friend turned into a really special, loving, sexual relationship. Now, I'm struggling with the fact that I feel doomed to be the second string. I know she is struggling, too, trying to be everything to everyone. I am confused, excited, frustrated, and most certainly in love with a woman who tells me that our relationship is very special and important to her. Yet, I find myself childishly jealous and terrified of the path that she's afraid to veer from: buying a house with him, perhaps having kids, etc."

While Regina's relationship is strained, she is determined to hold on to the woman she loves.

Regina

"I am single, but I have been married," Regina says. "I got divorced after I discovered my sexuality. Now, as a now single lesbian mother of two, I have been in a three-year relationship with a married woman. I am the only woman she has ever been with, and I am very much in love with her. Unfortunately, because of work and family commitments for both of us, we only see each other for about four hours a week. Mobile phone messaging is our main source of communication. I don't know her home telephone number; she has never given it to me. I've never been to her house, and I've never met any of her friends or relatives. She comes to my house every other week. And yet, if I go out with other lesbian friends, she gets very jealous and possessive. I do the same, on occasion, with her about her married situation. Our relationship is very strained, but we have so much love for each other. She says she could never leave her husband, and I accept that, but I do feel hurt and rejected at times, although I know not everyone can just walk away from a heterosexual existence as I did. To combat the loneliness I feel when we are not together, I keep my life full, and I try not to rely on her exclusively for my happiness.

Connie is another woman whose relationship is strained. When she heard I was looking for the single lovers of married women to interview, she contacted me without first consulting her lover, a married woman. The married woman, who was not out, became very upset that Connie had called me. Connie called back to apologize and say that she had changed her mind about being interviewed. "My woman and I have a lot at stake that we would lose should anyone find out about our relationship," she explained. "So anything that could potentially threaten that cover scares her to death."

I could well understand that feeling. Intellectually, near the beginning of my own journey, I knew that the first woman I told about myself was a lesbian and still, I remember being terrified, thinking, "What if others find out about *me*?"

Not everyone is as determined as Regina or Connie are to keep their relationships intact. Often, it is the stress of having to be deceptive that destroys the relationships between single lesbians and married ones.

Charlotte

"I had dated other women—been in other relationships—but there was something different about the way I was feeling for my straight friend, and I told her that I thought it best not to hang out together as much as we did. She took my hand. Her touch was electric, so consuming that it was overwhelming. Instantly, I knew she was the one. I had never felt happier or more terrified in my life. Our relationship lasted four years.

"We saw or talked to each other daily. She didn't think it would be fair to leave her husband after more than twenty years with him. 'He didn't deserve to be left,' she said. I promised I'd never ask her to, but the whole idea of always being second, always being left, and always missing her was too much. One day she told me we couldn't be lovers anymore, and I told her I couldn't take seeing her and not being her lover. It's been more than two years now. Not a day goes by that I don't see her face, hear her voice, or feel her hand in mine. I haven't dated, and still haven't the desire to.

"When you truly love someone, the desire to be together—to plan, to share the ups and downs, the morning coffee, to quarrel about taking out the trash, or doing the laundry—that is all part of the package. I thought if I did enough, loved her enough, was enough, that one day there'd be reciprocation or appreciation or support.

"Loving her was the most destructive and selfish thing I've ever done. Truly loving her would have been to refuse to compromise her integrity or mine by having the affair. The worst part of it was the death of a dream. In the end, I lost a dear and wonderful friend."

Jennifer actually took over the role of Nettie's absent husband. She had been attending college evenings, and at the beginning of one course, Nettie walked into the room. Each time Jennifer saw her, her heart flipped.

Jennifer

"On breaks, Nettie and her friend saw that I stayed pretty much to myself and started talking to me. We all hit it off, and started hanging out to review notes. One night, Nettie wanted to go out after class, but her friend didn't. She asked me if I wanted to, and if I could drive her home afterward. She started confiding in me about her difficulties with her husband and, in essence, being married but a single parent. Her house and yard were neglected, and she was just falling apart. I started helping her around the house, taking on a spouse-like role. Her three sons were often disappointed because their father wasn't home to do father/son things, so I stepped in and taught them how to throw a football. I took them sailing and helped them with their homework.

"One day, while we were watching a movie, Nettie massaged my aching back and shoulders. Before long, she started kissing me. She rubbed my crotch. I was petrified but took over from there. Neither of us had thought we were lesbians. I had been in denial all these years, and Nettie confessed she was never into sex. Her husband called her a cold fish. She definitely was not. She loved our sexual intimacy. I was in the stereotypical male spouse-type role with her, and the dad role with her kids. I finally felt comfortable with myself. Love and family was something I had dreamed of having all my life."

Unfortunately, Jennifer's dream faded after about six years. Having been raised in the Bible Belt, Nettie's fear of exposure played a major role in the demise of their relationship. Jennifer believes that when they graduated from college, Nettie became more fearful of exposure because they no longer had school as an excuse to be spending so much time together.

"She became increasingly distant," Jennifer says, "even forbidding her children, who had become like my own, from contacting me. She wouldn't tell me why her attitude had changed, but I believe her husband realized how strong our friendship was and threatened her with losing her kids."

Beverly, a single woman, had always shied away from married women. She knew she required a large amount of contact and of time. With her past lover; there were daily phone calls, midweek visits, weekend trips. When her lover died, her friends introduced her to several women. None could replace the lover she had lost, and she preferred to remain alone. Then someone introduced her to Betty, a married woman. When she met Betty, all of that changed.

Beverly

"Betty is a very busy person. I know she's overextended, but she works hard to carve out free time to be with me. Sometimes, I resent her not being more available, but I think, even if she weren't married, she'd be the same. She has so many interests. I am willing to accept having less time with her because I find her so very interesting. With her encouragement, I'm learning to enjoy my own free time. I've learned to express myself through poetry, something I'd only thought about doing before."

Most of the single women I interviewed were understanding of the stresses on their married lovers and solicitous of their needs. I had e-mails that read:

> I bought your book [first edition of *Married Women Who Love Women*] so that I could understand better what my married lover must deal with.
> I know how hard it is for her when we're not together.
> I read your book to help me see and understand her point of view.

I loved her and would have done anything for her, but I wanted her to stay with her husband because I was unable to provide for her and her young son the way he was. Also, I knew that he would always take care of her.

Eva was one of the few single women I spoke to who had little understanding of what it was like for a woman who made the discovery while in a marriage. Her reason for being with married women was strictly the illicitness of it.

Eva

"I think an investment such as having children together, or owning a house together, helps a relationship to last, but living together is a bitch," Eva says. "I think having a secret makes a relationship exciting. I don't put a great emotional investment in if I meet a married woman. I establish parameters of what I will and will not accept. Sometimes, you need your fantasies satisfied. I saw one woman and I cared for her, but she wasn't everything. Some people are only good at certain things. I guess I wanted someone to be in complete wonder of all my stories. She was someone who didn't know me well and loved hearing me talk."

Iris

While Iris was not like Eva, she came to feel that her lover, Georgia, was using her. "We were together for three years. We probably could have been together longer than that. I had strong feelings for her almost as soon as we met, but because she was married, I was afraid to say anything. "She flirted with me. She'd say 'I love you,' then quickly throw in, 'like a sister.' She'd say, 'Did you ever hear of down low?' or 'Did you ever dream that you were kissing someone and it felt so real?'

"If she was single, I would have told her what I was feeling and let the cards fall where they would, but I was afraid of losing her friendship. With her, I couldn't tell if she was coming on to me or teasing me until one evening. We came from seeing a movie. I went to give her a peck on the cheek good night, and she turned and kissed me on the lips. At that instant, we both knew, and we haven't turned back since.

"We were just looking for a relationship with harmony and balance, one that would be okay for all involved, especially the children.

"Our relationship was fine all the while we kept it secret, but my lover wanted to tell her husband. Once she did, he didn't cause the marriage to end. Being with me was making her marriage tolerable. I felt as though I was being used, so I would no longer be her lover.

"I want the waking up together, the morning coffee, the getting each others' dry cleaning—all of the things she is sharing with him. She must really want it with her husband. Other side, she sees her marriage as a commitment for good or bad. It's a contract. You don't break one when another comes along. The ideal would be adding another commitment, constructing a new family from two households."

On the opposite side of the coin, Meryl knew that her married lover was using her "for fun." She told her so when they met through an Internet personals service.

Meryl

"I hadn't expected to fall for this woman. She was up front about being married, and we met and engaged in sexual intimacy the first date we had. 'For fun,' she said, and I agreed. As we spent more time together and she opened up to me, my love for her grew. She told me that her husband had been physically abusive. She'd left him once but then gone back. He had never repeated his physical abuse, although he threatened to kill her if she ever left him again. She made it very clear that she was not going to leave him for fear she would lose her children if she tried.

"We could both feel the closeness between us growing. I think she was beginning to feel frightened. She said I'd gone too far by making her fall in love with me, and she totally broke things off. She said she didn't feel comfortable with not being able to provide what I wanted, and because I loved her the way I did, she couldn't be with me anymore. It made things too hard.

"Several months later, she called. She apologized for the way she had acted and told me how much she had missed having me in her life. We are back together again. Sometimes, I feel that she is using me for emotional and physical benefits, things her husband never gives her, but I have fallen so completely in love with this woman that I couldn't even begin to think about having a relationship with anyone else."

In the gay community, friendships are not taken lightly. One single lesbian with a married lover said, "Among my friends, I feel that there is another closet I'm in now because of the taboo regarding getting involved with a married woman."

Many women are estranged from their families of birth or living far from home, and it is their friends who see them through difficult times and help them through intimate aspects of their lives. This mutual support may expand the boundaries of friendship until these friends become family. And so, when I spread the word that I wanted to interview single lovers involved with married women, I was not surprised that their friends contacted me as well.

Several voiced concern that their friends might be hurt by being involved with a married woman. For a few, the distinction between friend and lover had blurred, and the anger they voiced came from a more personal place.

Others had political reasons for rejecting the married women involved with their single friends, such as

> I resent married lesbians because they are pulling from a limited pool of available women.
>
> Through their silence, these married women do nothing to further causes important to lesbians and gays.
>
> Married lesbians are getting the best of both worlds. They're not out on the front line of the gay brigade, taking the heat.

When a single lesbian becomes involved with a married woman, most often it is she who has to be the more accommodating. And sometimes, that is just what she wants to happen.

Amy

Amy says, "She has her life set up; she has a house, a husband, and a family all in place. If I want to be part of that, then we have to figure out how I can fit into the picture that her family has created and make sure it is a picture I want to be in. So far, it is a picture I would love to be in.

"Friends told me that I must not be the right one for Mary because she doesn't want to leave her husband. But I see the love they have for each other, and I wouldn't want to take that away from either of them. My friends say, 'If you remain with Mary, you'll never be open to finding the right woman.' I love Mary too much to ask her to make a choice. I see how that would tear her apart, and I am happy to be with her whenever we can be together. I tell my friends, 'As far as finding the right woman, she is the right one for me.' For me, learning to honestly love one another is the ultimate truth."

While a major issue for many single women was the lack of time available to be with their married lovers, Karen enjoys the anticipation of each visit.

Karen

"My lover and I don't have to deal with daily routines that living together would entail: whose turn is it to clean the bathroom, do the dishes, take out the trash. I always have something to look forward to, and just knowing that I am going to see her fills me with joy. When she visits, I put everything else out of my mind just for our special time together.

"Being single, I have more free time than my lover, and I have to constantly remind myself that she is the one who has to juggle so many things. There are her children, her husband, her home. But in a way, because she is so busy and yet she makes time for me, she is more exciting to be with."

Ina

Ina says, "I was at a point in my life like, 'I'm done. I don't want to be in a relationship. I don't want to have to deal with the consequence of having to answer to someone anymore.' I was only looking for friendship, but now I'm in a relationship with a married woman. It's a weird situation, but we do what we can. We take it day by day. I'm very drawn to her.

"She has a powerful, sweet, comfortable personality. She's caring. She's the flower that bloomed in the trash. She makes my heart sing. She's so precious to me. But it drives me crazy that I'm the last person she talks to at night, and then she goes to sleep with her husband. And it makes me insane when I'm the second or third person she speaks to in the morning because she wakes up next to him. I try really hard not to think about that. I'd be lying if I said it was all right because God knows I want her to be all mine. She's out to her husband. I'm going to be meeting him soon, and I'm scared to death because what if I like him? What if we get along? What would I do with that?"

"My married partner's availability is not what bothers me. We've come to the understanding that if we nurture our friendship, the relationship will take care of itself. And part of nurturing the friendship requires spending time doing things as individuals. If we spent all our time attached at the hip, we'd have very little to talk about at the end of the day. What does frustrate me is not being able to call her and talk about the things we just spent the day doing. Her husband is quite possessive, and when he's around, I have no access to her whatsoever. He'd keep an ear on her conversation, which would require us to keep everything on such a superficial level that the conversation would be pointless."

Shannon

"As you've no doubt heard, frustration is the word," Shannon says. "Sometimes I just stare at myself in the mirror thinking, 'What the fuck are you doing with a married woman?' I have always been a person who looked down on cheating. Somehow, I've rationalized that this is not cheating. Her husband knows, and we've met, and he likes me. He's okay, too, but I don't want to be pals with him. She told him that she's a lesbian and is in love with me. He says he's known about her curiosity toward women for years and is working on accepting our relationship, but he wants things to stay the same. She is in the midst of fear—wanting to be with me only, but apparently fifteen years of patterned living is a bitch to break from.

"My big challenge right now is trying not to pressure her. Sometimes, I want to shake her and tell her to leave him. I also want to ask him why the hell he'd want to stay with a wife who admits she's a lesbian and is in love with another woman.

"There is quite a bit of support for MWLW [married women who love women], but little, if any, for those single women. I would like to find other single lesbians to talk to. I wonder how they deal with this. All this said, I really think she's worth waiting for."

Marie is a single lesbian in her mid-fifties. She believes that culture has a lot to do with her not being out. She also believes that she is bisexual, yet she said that she never met a man who responded the way she would like to be responded to, so she turned to women.

Marie

"Gail was in the process of getting a divorce. She came on to me. I responded. She had experimented before, but I was her first long-term relationship. I was attracted to her attraction for me. Our connecting had nothing to do with her being married or getting divorced. It had to do with intense chemistry. The way she looked at me, I could see me in her eyes. She had such love and devotion for me. I responded to that and I gave it back. Sexually, I made her a woman.

"Gail introduced me to her family, and they welcomed me. We could be open about our relationship in front of them. Culture plays a big part. It does impact. Gail's family was extremely open and tolerant. Maybe they were like that because they were Jewish, possibly because of what they went through in the war. But my parents are Hispanic and very clear on their feelings about homosexuality. It is not acceptable.

Period. So they ignored our relationship. The fact that Gail had been married helped them to do that.

"Life is hard enough as it is without bringing in family, children, jobs—all of these conditions play a big part in any relationship. But, I think that the cultural aspect is the biggest. Hispanics have a macho mentality that filters through everything.

"Our relationship worked for eight years because of who Gail was. I wonder if it would have been better if my family been accepting, and I could have come out. We didn't have a full relationship because I was closeted. I was looking for someone to hold and to love, but because I was always hiding, our connection was a lie. I could not have an openly gay relationship because of my parents. There was no freedom to be who we were. Eventually, we became more like roommates, like sisters who fuck each other. Then, she met a man who did for her what her husband had never been able to do. She lied to me about her meetings with him for a year. I would have been fine if she had told me. I don't want to have anyone around who is not happy with me."

After Gail left, Marie just stopped looking. "If you're going to go with one person and lose your family because of it, it isn't worth it," she said. "I love my family, but they don't know me. I can't be really myself when it comes to my sexuality. Right now, I'm just worn. I don't want it anymore. It's sad. I want to come out and can't because I'm not strong enough to make the choice of my family or lover. I lose out, and my family loses out.

"I realize now that I've never been looking for 'that one,' I've been looking for someone who would love me unconditionally. Now I'm at a point where I want to give my life priority."

While Marie has chosen to remain in the closet, she has developed a comfortable and convenient relationship with another married woman. She sees the woman when she can. No pressure, no strings. Total acceptance on both sides.

Every situation is different. Georgette loves a woman who lives with her husband and children. He is well aware of his wife's feelings for women. He is kind and considerate and treats Georgette like one of the family. When she visits, Georgette spends time with her lover's family. She sleeps in the guest room with her lover. "My problem," she says, "is my family. I keep hearing from my mom and my sister about how weird my situation is. They say 'situation.' They can't even call our connection a relationship. None of them will acknowledge that, for the first time since I came out to them sixteen years ago, I am happy. I've had a number of relationships with single women, but this is the first one that has lasted longer than five years."

Wanda

Unfortunately, there are instances even today, depending on the husband, when a woman's same-gender sexuality is enough to keep her from her family. Wanda's story would make a good argument for the positive side of coming out.

"I was married, but my husband left me after having me followed and finding out that I was a lesbian. Now, he has me blackmailed. I pay extremely high child support and see my two sons only rarely. I also pay all insurance and medical bills. I am a schoolteacher and this is so hard, but making my family understand and accept me would be even harder. He has promised not to tell as long as I keep my end of the bargain."

Wanda's lover is still married. Unlike Wanda's husband, her lover's husband has a sweet, almost feminine, disposition. He either does not know or chooses to ignore the women's relationship.

Long-distance relationships seem to work for some women. Ginger said, "My lover is able to take care of her home responsibilities and her kids, and I have time to focus on my job and see my old friends. When we are together, our time with each other is very special. The biggest challenge is when one of us is sick, and we aren't able to be right there for each other. We take our love a day at a time."

A great many lesbians, especially those born before the 1980s, have been married. There were not a lot of other choices prior to the 1990s. Mandie wrote, "I am a lesbian (always been). I never look for married women to be in relationships with. It just happens. Married or divorced. I don't understand how they find me ... or how I find them. What is the attraction: me to them and them to me?"

The woman who comes to terms with her sexual identity after being married is often like a teenager going through her first adolescence. Her wide-eyed innocence and excitement can be an attractive quality.

Each person who enters our life plays a specific role—but it isn't always the role we would chose.

Louise

"After an extremely close friendship of eleven years, I became physically involved with my best friend. Our relationship went on for several months, until she told her husband about us. Our affair has now ended. She is struggling to renew her commitment with him and still reassuring me of her love for me. I have fallen in love with her, and even though she wants me in her life in a platonic way, I am so confused about where this leaves me. I cannot imagine life without her. I have been living on a roller coaster of highs and lows.

"For the last two years, before our physical affair started, we had been emotionally intimate. Now, I feel betrayed, used, alone. And I struggle with the question of what kind of friend am I that doesn't want her marriage to work? She had told me that she loves him, although not to the degree that she loves me. She also told me that if she left him for me, she would be miserable because of the hurt she would cause him and her family."

Lulu

"I am deeply in love with a married woman. I want to spend more time with her and, when she's ready, be with her for the rest of our lives. Right now, she isn't ready to deal with all of the 'stuff' she needs to deal with. I know she's not ready to leave her husband and kids. I know she may never be. And I don't want to do anything to lose her. I know I have to be patient, but she's driving me nuts. She pulls the 'come here I want you, go away you confuse me' game."

Although Ruth and Stephie are both married, and relationships can work with less stress when both women are in marriages, that is not always the case. Extenuating circumstances do change the equation.

Ruth

"I might just as well be single. I spend very little time with my husband. I come and go as I please and haven't had a sexual relationship with him in years. Stephie, my love, is a happily married, country club wife. She has family meals, weekends, and vacations. While she doesn't especially enjoy sex with her husband, she is a willing participant and has little free time.

Tonya

"I have acknowledged to my lover that having a married woman as a girlfriend was hard. I needed to say that, and she acknowledged that she understood. I am sensitive to the feelings of her husband and children and have no desire to replace them or to cause them any distress or pain. Because they are a part of her, I would like to get to know them and to have them accept me. To that extent, I have been chatting with her son.

He and I are both Red Sox fans. Her daughter has been less accepting of me, but she did get on the computer recently and 'chat' with me. I am glad that they are willing to let me get to know them a bit."

Mindy

"My lover is a 40-year-old married woman. She had no overt or conscious gay impulses previously, but told me that she was open and curious. I kissed her, and she said that she felt as though she had been hit by a thunderbolt. Maybe it wasn't an accident. We believe we are soul mates, and maybe we were supposed to come together just this way. She was one hundred percent sure that she wanted to leave her husband until they began working on the larger issues such as child custody and housing. Now, she is having second thoughts, doubts. She keeps hoping that the answer will come to her, and I tell her I'll be here waiting when she is ready to make a decision."

Unlike Mindy's lover, who keeps hoping that the right decision will fall into her lap, Reva has given much thought to her predicament.

Reva

Reva had had several prior lovers, but when she talks about Jenna, she lights up. "I am so in love with her, and we share this incredible connection that I've never experienced with anyone before. There is an amazing sense of trust and the highest level of open communication between the two of us. We don't ever have to sit down and 'have a talk' because we talk about everything and anything all the time. She inspires me and wants to take care of me and protect me.

"The main issue we have," says Reva, "is how to keep us all happy. Jenna is trying to protect herself from the possibility that I may find someone who can commit to me one hundred percent. Her husband is trying to figure out if he can be happy sharing his wife with me and trying to not be hurt by this expression of love. I'm trying to figure out if I could be happy not having a full-time partner in her, and we all are defining what our relationships will be in the future."

Some of the single women said they had simply been drawn to women who happened to be married. Some liked the idea of an instant family. Others were dissuaded by it. And most were frustrated by their situations. So why did they remain? The word I heard most often as I interviewed each of these women was "love."

CHAPTER 11

Labeling: Lesbian or Bisexual

It is not uncommon for a woman at the beginning of her enlightenment to identify as bisexual and then, with her growth, come to realize and accept that she is a lesbian. It is also not uncommon for a woman to know all along what she is. Still, many women refuse to accept labels.

Lori

"Bethany was the first woman I was ever with. We were both married, and she didn't want us to tell our husbands that we were loving each other and therefore, lesbians. I became obsessed with labeling myself, and I felt it would be lying to my husband if I didn't tell him what I was. Bethany felt threatened by my need to come out not only to him, but to myself as to who I was. She refused to take on any label and wanted us just to call each other friends who shared something more."

Lori's need to define herself in regard to society's labels for sexuality drove her and Bethany apart, and it drove her husband—who felt threatened by her love for Bethany—to leave her. Lori lived alone for some time. Spending time with herself enabled her to see a broader picture and to understand how her self-imposed rigidity had ruined her relationship with Bethany. Lori said, "I'd heard that eighty percent of the human brain's capacity is not used, and I'd come to realize that the spiritual and emotional side of our beings, like the brain, is largely unexplored and unused. If it weren't for fear, I think our society would be filled with love to overflowing. Eventually, I eased up on my own, self-imposed rigidity."

Emilia

Emilia defines herself as gay but living the life of a bisexual. "I've chosen that lifestyle because, in my situation, I view myself as predominantly heterosexual and occasionally homosexual. But I don't like labels. I think when you start labeling yourself, you put yourself in a box and become a nonperson. I'm a person whose sexuality is liquid. I mold it for my relationships. I don't see the world as black or white. I believe that all people fall somewhere along the heterosexual-homosexual scale at different times."

Emilia has remained in her marriage and, with her husband's consent, has had a female lover. "I needed to experience what I was missing. I was like a fourteen-year-old boy, completely focused on sex and needing to know what it was like to make love to a woman," she says. "When I experienced my first relationship with another woman, it was incredible. And then, after almost two years, when the skyrockets stopped going off, I realized we didn't have anything in common other than sex. We had nothing to grab hold of.

"I had felt passion for the first time and run with it, forgetting about all of the other stuff I had, and I became very uncomfortable with my situation—my woman's and mine. For my entire life," Emilia says, "I was used to having the stronger part of my relationship with my husband be the camaraderie, doing things together, having the same sense of humor. It made me realize how much else I had with my husband, although sex was always a small part of our relationship.

"I never felt like doing it as much as he did, and we've gotten into a mechanical groove where we schedule sex. It's not spontaneous because it takes a lot more for me to get interested, but we at least carve out that space for us, because I know it's really important for our relationship. If we had no sex at all, there is no way my husband would stay with me.

"Our sex begins with oral, and then intercourse comes, because I have to have something to get into it, but once I am, I'm fine with it. This works for us. That's not to say that I never want to have another woman in my life again, but I did get over that pubescent part of my life."

Not every single lover of a married woman is a lesbian.

Cora

"I am a woman who loves women and loves men just as much. I am comfortable with either sex and enjoy intimacy equally. I know that being only with men makes me crazy. Being only with women would do the same. Therefore, I have concluded that I am not lesbian but bisexual."

Some women who consider themselves bisexual believe that things are more difficult for them because of their orientation.

Terry

"The hardest thing about being in the lesbian community is that as a bi, you're looked at as someone who just can't make up her mind. They want you to choose. But I love men and women equally. I don't have more of an emotional attachment to one or the other. I have different attachments. And neither is better than the other."

Evelyn

"I considered myself a straight woman and liked to date men until about age 30, at which point I met a woman and completely fell in love with her. We have been together for seven years, and I am still deeply in love with her, but there is a problem. I still have an attraction to men. I feel like the women in your book—but in an opposite way. I am in a constant struggle of wanting to keep the woman whom I love and am committed to and can't imagine my life without—but also feeling a yearning to be with a man. Is it that complacency in my relationship is making things on the outside seem more exciting?"

Cherise

Cherise is one of these women whose actions contradict her true feelings. She is very definite about what is lacking from her life, but negative stereotyping of lesbians and fear have kept her from searching for the missing piece.

"When I first dreamed about romance with boys," Cherise says, "I saw them as soft and gentle, but sex never entered my mind. Then, when I started going out with boys, I found them forceful, clumsy, slobbery. In general, they just didn't meet my expectations. I wanted to have a partner who was soft, cuddly, close to my size, and reactive."

Still, Cherise ruled out women from her life. "When I was in high school, I heard bad things, and I'd get an icky feeling about the word *lesbian*."

Knowing there was something missing, she married anyway, thinking she would be able to satisfy her longings through fantasies of women.

During her first two years of marriage, Cherise had been searching for an identity. "Eventually," she says, "by the process of elimination, I came to regard myself as bisexual. I am married to a man but secretly yearn to love women—what should I call myself? I wouldn't know where to put myself on a Kinsey scale because I consider myself in the closet and latent, and I am still not totally sure of my identity. I am not willing to call myself lesbian until the time comes that it is my lifestyle one hundred percent."

The declaration of lesbianism is so difficult for some that they choose to adopt a bisexual tag instead or use one as a transitory stopping point, to help them to avoid that initial, frightening lesbian identity, which seems so diametrically opposite to societal norms. Declaring oneself bisexual, which at least has overtones of heterosexuality, offers a person a chance to resist categorization or to avoid making decisions.

Unlike Cherise, who came to the conclusion that she was bisexual because of her circumstances but still isn't really certain, Nanette has always known that she is bisexual.

Nanette

"I had been in a traditional marriage. I knew I was bisexual, and my husband knew, but I was completely monogamous with him. Halfway into our marriage, we thought about bringing another woman into our relationship but didn't do it. I could only be in a relationship with one person at a time. After fifteen years, our marriage broke up—not because of my bisexuality, but because the marriage was not a strong one."

Now, Nanette is a divorced woman in a relationship with a married woman, but that is only the beginning of her story. Both she and Janice, her lover, are polyamorous. Nanette says, "I connect differently with men and women. For me, it's not about one being better than another. I have to have an emotional connection first, before I embark on a physical. The physical connection is an extension of the emotional connection.

"When I first divorced, I only dated women, but I felt like something was missing. Likewise, if I only dated men, my desire for a woman was missing. Because I don't prefer one or the other, I started dating both women and men. And I started to question my philosophy about monogamy. I knew that with the right people, I could be with both. So, you might say that my becoming polyamorous was a transitional process.

"Having an emotional and physical connection with more than one person at the same time works for me. But it isn't easy. Complications grow proportionately depending on the number of people involved because everyone is different, and there are more things to take on. It takes a lot of time and dialogue. In a polyamorous relationship, you're accountable to more than one person. If something affects one of us, it affects us all. We try to troubleshoot and work through problems as a group, although we work through things as separate families as well. My separate family now consists of a straight man, Tom, who shares my home, and a child whose custody I share jointly with my ex-husband. Janice's family consists of a bisexual husband, Brad, and four children."

Nannette says, "My situation is complicated. We could all actually be in the same bed, all physically connecting, although Tom and Janice don't have intercourse, by mutual choice. But they're being loving and supporting and things of that nature. It's not about sex. It's more about everyone sharing energies. Whatever I do is going to have a chain effect, so I have to be accountable, and it's the same for everyone. Because we take so much time to be considerate of each other's feelings, there is never a time when someone will say, 'that's not cool.'

"Its not about lying, or being deceitful. It's about having one hundred percent open communication and everyone being on the same page. You can't be selfish and just go off and do what you want because there is a ripple effect. It's more important to have integrity."

"Because lesbianism is itself inevitably a value-weighted categorization," Beverly Burch, author of *On Intimate Terms*, says "individual lesbians and the communal norms of lesbianism could make either designation more desirable to one woman, less desirable to another, depending on her own political and emotional biases. For example, some lesbians do not consider bisexual women or women with heterosexual histories 'real lesbians' regardless of what they call themselves. Therefore, some women might hesitate to name themselves bisexual. Others may feel that being a lifelong lesbian is admitting to some limitation, or that being a 'real lesbian' is more stigmatizing than being a lesbian with bisexual potential."[1]

According to Loraine Hutchins and Lani Kaahumanu, coeditors of *Bi Any Other Name: Bisexual People Speak Out*, "Bisexuality shakes up the rigid assumptions that people have about sexuality, that there is only heterosexuality and homosexuality when, in fact, sexual behavior is fluid. … The fluidity of bisexuality is scary for most people."[2]

"We are taught we have to be one thing," says Elias Farajaje-Jones, a divinity professor from Howard University. "Now people are finding out that they don't have to choose one thing or another. Nobody knows how many bisexuals there are in this country, or how bisexuality should be defined. Its existence alone makes many people uncomfortable."[3]

Often, bisexuals are assumed to be promiscuous, but the women I spoke with rejected that assumption. They told me about falling in love with individuals and being in monogamous relationships—with one male or one female—that lasted for years. The difficulty they found was when their chosen partner was of the opposite sex: They still considered themselves bisexual and wanted to be a part of the gay community—participating in activities, dances, and the like—but the gay community saw them as heterosexual.

While the idea of bisexuality is uncomfortable for some, there are men who are titillated by the idea that their wives may be bisexual.

Gloria

"My husband didn't know about my love for women when we married. When I told him, he was thrilled. He just assumed that my revelation meant I was bisexual, and he liked the idea. Even though I hadn't acted on my feelings, the thought of my being bi aroused his sexual interest. Because I didn't understand fully myself, and was not so certain about the label, I didn't say anything to change his assumption. I suppressed my own needs, and our family grew. But, as our four children grew, so did my need to explore my feelings. After fifteen years, I could no longer restrain them. I told him. He said he was ready, assuming I meant having a threesome. I finally said, 'No. This is about me, not us.' I told him we had to renegotiate our marriage contract because I didn't want to leave him, but I felt like I was dying on the inside.

"We went through a rough period. Finally, he accepted me for who I was and allowed women to come into my life. We have remained married, and I love and respect him more than ever. He's been absolutely wonderful."

Are people essentially either straight or gay, with bisexuality being merely the unnatural by-product of confusion and repression among some homosexuals? Or, is bisexuality a third, distinct orientation? Is sexuality governed by biology or culture? Is it fixed, an identity that is set early and endures through life? Or is it fluid, shifting with time and temptation? asks Anastasia Toufexis, author of "Bisexuality: What Is It?"

According to Toufexis, "Avowed lesbians sometimes sleep with men, and men who describe themselves as straight engage in sex with other men. In many Latin societies, men do not consider themselves bisexual or gay unless they take the passive-receptive role during sex. Moreover, sexuality is as much a state of mind as an act of body. People may be attracted to someone but unwilling to act on their desires out of guilt or shame; conversely, others may act contrary to their true feelings."[4]

Whether straight or gay, discovering our true sexual identity and feeling comfortable in our skin is a challenge.

Sexual identity is not set in stone and may not remain fixed throughout our lives. Patterns of sexual behavior evolve according to personal circumstances. Some women describe their marriages as always having been empty of emotional attachment. Others describe them as once having been a positive experience. Some women talked of previously feeling "in love" with their husbands, although they no longer felt an attraction to men.

One woman considers herself to be bisexual not because she's married, but because she remembers how it once was with her husband. "When we first got married, there was definitely a sexual attraction for each other, and we had a great sex life.

"Right now, I'm not enjoying the physical aspect of being with my husband because I'm not in love with him. For me, sexual pleasure has to do with my being in love with another individual."

Another woman considers herself sexual rather than bisexual, but, as she says, "in this society, at this time, bisexual is what would be applied to me. I'm attracted to women and men. The gender doesn't matter much to me, rather who they are, how comfortable I am with them, etc. I've aligned myself with lesbians, but I've never ruled out the possibility of attraction to a man. Loving a man, as I do currently, does not, equally, rule out my loving a woman again, or a purple creature from outer space, for that matter. It's who they are and not what they are."

While many people equate bisexuality with promiscuity, according to the *Stylebook Supplement on LGBT* [Lesbian, Gay, Bisexual, and Transgender] *Terminology* created by the National Lesbian and Gay Journalists Association, the definition of *bisexual* is clear: "As a noun, an individual who may be attracted to both sexes. As an adjective, of or relating to sexual and affectional attraction to both sexes. Does not presume non-monogamy."

Georgene

In the past, Georgene had resented bisexuals who insisted on calling themselves lesbians even while in heterosexual relationships. Then, after twelve years of being an out lesbian, she found herself in a three-month relationship with a man. When that ended, she was left desperately confused regarding what she was. Since she had the capacity to be with someone of the opposite sex, she supposed that she must be bi. She wondered if she would have to give up her membership in the lesbian organizations she belonged to. Now that she is single, she is wondering if and when she will have the right to call herself lesbian again.

Some women, like Audrey, feel that their lovers are not replacements for their husbands, but extensions.

Audrey

"It took nine years for my trust to break through the walls and for me to let out my secrets and fears. It was that release that made me fall in love with my husband all the more," Audrey says. "The second time I fell in love, I needed him to help me trust. I needed him to tell me that the love I share with my woman was all right.

"The love I share with both is so completely different. With him I share trust, companionship, home, health, life. His touch sets me on fire. It doesn't come as frequently as it once did, and it sometimes seems mechanical, or like a chore to be completed, but I know he still loves me. With her, I share a background, a love so serene it feels like a dream. Her touch also sets me on fire. The caresses are deliberate and slow. Each breath on my skin makes my soul light up. We make love together, just in our embraces.

"I feel he resents my second love. He tells me he wants to be included in it, but I cannot explain that to include him changes it. I try to explain how his love is different, and that it doesn't take away from the love we share—but it does. Time spent with her is time I once spent with him."

Constrained monosexual environments, such as prison or the military, can also lead to same-sex liaisons, yet the participants continue to think of themselves as heterosexual. Also, since it is possible to love someone of the opposite sex, then fall in love with someone of the same gender, and then, years later, to fall for someone of the opposite sex again, assigning labels or categories to individuals solely on behavior at one period in a lifetime can be difficult.

Still, we as a society seem to have a need to stereotype people and their behavior, sexual or anything else. By putting people into carefully defined boxes, we feel we create some kind of order.[5]

Beverly Burch, author of *On Intimate Terms*, concurs. "In the case of sexuality, we think that we are either heterosexual or homosexual, straight or gay. We may resist new scientific findings for fear that they will disturb our comfortable preconceptions."[6]

While there are people who resist the idea of labeling, feeling that labels are constricting, for some having a sexual identity can be stabilizing. If you can fit into a category, you can find a support group with others who identify themselves the same way.

At a discussion titled "Married and Wondering," several women who attended spoke of being in celibate marriages and having same-sex relationships, yet they referred to themselves as bisexual. When asked to explain, one woman said, "I needed to find a support group. I tried going to a lesbian gathering but was shunned because of my marital status. Then I found a bisexual group. This group welcomed me. They were open and accepting. So I stayed. I may never be interested in men again, but by using the term bisexual, I am keeping my options open."

Laurel

Laurel attended an all-female high school, where she fell in love with a classmate a couple of years her senior. Her love was unreturned. At the same time, she answered an ad in *The Village Voice*. "It wasn't that I was looking for a man, but I happened to see his ad, and I liked it," she says. "It was charming, with a quote from *The Merchant of Venice*." After high school, Laurel married the writer of the ad.

She describes her husband, twelve years older than she, as her soul mate. "I guess we're so much alike that there isn't a lot of sexual passion. I think that passion sometimes comes from tension, and we don't have any tension.

"My husband knew about me when we married, and it was okay. I think it sort of fascinated him. And he's sort of interested. He always asks me who I'm going out with, and he's very supportive."

Laurel continues to think of herself as bisexual and has had very intense friendships with men—both gay and straight—but believes that, at this time, if she had not met her husband, she would probably be with women exclusively. Still, she says, "There is no way I am going to leave my husband. That is not an option. I want a relationship where I can spend a lot of time with my husband, and I don't know where I can find a woman who could put up with this."

Although not presently in an intimate same-sex relationship, Laurel belongs to a support group for bisexual women.

Miriam

Miriam and her husband had decided early in their marriage that their commitment to each other would not be based on sex. "I had been burned with romantic love and wanted a relationship that worked—sex was just not that important—and we kept hoping it would get better."

In the beginning, Miriam's only clue to her latent bisexuality was feeling heartbroken when her best friend got married, but she had no idea why she felt that way for some time.

Then, the stress of her husband's graduate school studies created a rupture in their marriage. The terms under which they had gotten married were no longer working, yet it never occurred to either Miriam or her husband to break the commitments they had made to each other. After much discussion, Miriam convinced her husband of the intellectual integrity of an open marriage, although it was not something he wanted. "It hasn't worked out great," she concedes. "But my husband is very good at intellectual abstractions. On some feeling level, he doesn't like it at all, but he doesn't discuss it with me."

Eventually, it became clear that Miriam was attracted to women. Still, she says, "For a long time, I was bi in my head but not in my living. I had no desire to move in lesbian circles. To the extent that I went to women's dances, I felt biphobia. It was too much to explain that I had a husband and all this stuff. People acted like I had the plague.

"I had a strong need. Something was missing or empty. I knew I really wanted it, but I was tied down at home with a small child and a career, and I went to school full time.

"I went to a group for bi women, but they were different than me," Miriam says. "They were leading secret lives, cheating on their husbands, not telling them. This was not how my spouse and I were dealing with this thing. It seemed to me," Miriam initially said, "that their married lives were completely hollow. I was in an open relationship which was very different from sneaking around."

Eventually, Miriam broke down as she further described her life. "I'm lonesome, sexually unfulfilled. My husband is resentful and angry. I feel like I'm living someone else's life. Sometimes, I think if I didn't have a kid, I might try out another lifestyle, but now I don't see anything changing.

"After ten years of nothing, walking around with a strong bi identity, I finally had an ongoing relationship. I went to a national bisexual conference in San Francisco in 1990. I went expecting to be an anomaly, but I fit in fine. It wasn't weird that I was married, that I was nonmonogamous. It wasn't weird that I identified positively in a Jewish way. None of it was weird. There were people with sexual experience and people without."

Miriam says, "Now I have a clear and overwhelming sense of just how much easier and more natural sex is for me with a woman. I've done a lot of wrestling with myself once I realized that was true. I think it's common with bi women to have different kinds of sexual feelings with different people. You don't have to have the same sexual response to both men and women to be bi. They can be qualitatively different responses."

Grace

For Grace, her first connection with a woman was a physical attraction. "I am definitely bisexual. I have great sex with my husband, but I crave having sex with a woman, too. My lover insists that she's also bisexual, but I think she's more gay. She's always looking at women. I don't do that. I might look at a woman who I think is attractive, but I don't fantasize about her. Our sex is great, but it has something missing on an interpersonal level. I can come almost immediately. What's wonderful is that it's sort of like not connected to anything else. There's no attachment whatsoever. It's not connected to what you did this morning, and how you spoke to me last night, and was the checkbook balanced.

"Homosexuality is in some ways a paradoxical issue when it comes to societal acceptance. We wish people to perceive us as 'just like everyone else,' leading quiet, responsible lives. But when we do that, we become the 'hidden minority,' and it is only the more outrageous members of the community who grab the attention."

While labeling is commonly used in our society for classification and identification purposes, it is still difficult for many women to say the words lesbian, bisexual or homosexual. At the beginning of my journey, I could only whisper those words. I didn't realize just how comfortable I had become until one evening, while at a restaurant with a friend. I was discussing a gay-related issue and suddenly my voice dropped to a whisper—as the word "heterosexual" came out.

CHAPTER **12**
Sexual Intimacy

I had spent months searching for information: reading, questioning, feeling completely disassociated and isolated. And then, I met a woman, and we connected. We talked for hours and hours over pasta and bread sticks in a small village cafe. Neither of us wanted to say goodbye when it was time to part. A few days later, we went for a walk along the shorefront and talked some more. The third time we saw each other, we came together, and I knew that I was a sexual human being.

Whether women were able to come together at once or whether tremendous fears and insecurities dogged their attempts and delayed their sexual coming of age for years made no difference. What I learned as I interviewed women from across the country was that their first physically intimate relationships with other women were almost identical. They spoke of an immediate sense of well-being and rightness that came over them. They felt a new freedom when they connected with that other woman. Those who considered themselves heterosexual for most of their lives equated their first same-sex experience to an adolescence they now realized they had missed. I could identify with them.

While the women described sex with their husbands in mechanical terms, they spoke about their lovemaking with other women as being emotional, passionate, and all-inclusive. They reported a loss of the inhibitions that had been associated with their heterosexual relationships. They reported new feelings of acceptance and completeness.

Riva sums up her feelings: "With a man, I always felt that the physical aspect was expected. With a woman, there was a much richer and fuller kind of relationship. The physical aspect was just a component and not the totality of it."

While some women described their first same-sex experience in intimate sexual detail, for others the coming together was childlike and innocent.

Margaret

Shortly after she married, Margaret was working in an office. "Carolyn walked in and I saw her. I would say the weather changed in my whole body. I don't even know what season it was. It looked like springtime; she looked like springtime. There could have been a snowstorm, but I doubt it. A part of me held in reserve suddenly woke up. It was a full-blown crush on sight. Everything at once ... I felt enthralled. I didn't know what she was about. Nothing. All these things about love at first sight. I didn't think I was in love. I didn't know what I was. There was such a strong attraction. My eyes were truly riveted to her. And I thought: 'This is a momentary thing. She'll go away, and I'll never see her again.'

"In the beginning, I thought I was being unfaithful to my husband, but I really didn't have much of a marriage to preserve. I had realized that and tried to work on it with him. I thought we should go for marriage counseling. He refused. I asked him if the sexual part of our relationship was important enough to save, and he said it was fine the way it was. It was diminishing. He had become impotent, tired, disinterested.

"I felt very uncomfortable, and I wanted to straighten it out because I felt responsibility for him and the union, but he wasn't willing. I tried again, and when he refused, I said, 'The sexual part of our marriage is coming to an end. If you won't come to counseling with me, than I can't sleep with you.' And he said that was okay with him.

"After that I had more energy to be free in my sexuality.

"It got to be that Carolyn became more and more affectionate in a natural, loving, wonderful way, decent and normal. I felt my reaction was not normal. I brought my feelings to her attention with apologies, while we were driving together, certain I was going to get over it. But in the meantime, I told her, it would be a good idea if she wasn't so affectionate.

"Carolyn said to me, 'I have similar feelings.' When she said that, I thought my car had gone into a 180 degree spin. I was overwhelmed. It made me feel very sexual for the first time in my life. And very appealing and attractive. I felt I had come home. I felt wonderfully alive."

Shortly after their conversation in the car, the two women were watching television. "I remember Carolyn saying, 'I would really like to kiss you.' I remember looking straight ahead and saying, 'Why don't you?' Then I wondered who had said that. Was that me? And I turned toward her, and she kissed me. Very sweetly, very lovingly, very softly, very wonderfully. A six-dimensional kiss for me. Everything rolled into one. I didn't know what it meant or what you call it, but it was just so wonderful for me. It was a very mild, young, innocent, beautiful kiss."

That was not the beginning of their physical relationship, however. Neither woman could deal with the demands that her feelings were making on the other or with what she was feeling physically. For more than five years they fought, alternately breaking off communication, then reuniting.

"I behaved like I was twelve years old," says Margaret. "I was very unsure of myself, very bashful, very backward. I needed to be egged on and encouraged, and I perceived Carolyn as behaving like a woman of the world. Sexy, alluring, sure of herself.

"I was so shy the first time we went to bed together. We planned on having some sort of sex, but we didn't know what. I lay down beside Carolyn, and she said, 'Do you want to take your shoes off? How about your coat?' I behaved very jerky every step of the way. Almost like I didn't understand the English language."

"I didn't see myself as worldly," Carolyn said. "Neither of us quite understood what was going on or what we were getting involved in."

Eventually, Carolyn divorced her husband, not because of her sexuality, but because he was abusive. Although Margaret remained in her marriage, she never came out to her husband, and neither woman has come out to her children. Now in their late sixties, the two women are still in a loving relationship, and Carolyn says, "Looking at Margaret still brings the same rush of joy."

According to Shere Hite, for generations "female sexuality has been seen essentially as a response to male sexuality and intercourse. There has rarely been any acknowledgment that female sexuality might have a complex nature of its own which would be more than just the logical counterpart of [what we think of as] male sexuality."[1]

In the fifties, women were given little or no sex information. Boys at least had all sorts of ego-enhancing appellations for their penises, from given names to titles such as "The Monster" and "Mr. Wonderful," whereas girls simply referred to their genitals as "down there" or "privates."

Dalma Heyn writes in *The Erotic Silence of the American Wife*, "Daughters do not hear a great deal about sexual pleasure, from their mothers or anyone else—and how can silence beget anything but more silence? With no expression of girls' erotic feelings, no discourse of pleasure and desire passed from mother to daughter, no narratives of a girl's coming into sexual awareness, there exists no language for them in which to speak about their own experience. And because they do not speak, it is easy to assume girls' desire does not exist—for why wouldn't they say so, if it did?"[2]

If women were given any sexual information, they were taught that after marriage, their sexual pleasure *should* come from their husband's penis. This frequently did not happen, yet silence kept each woman believing that this sexual inadequacy was hers alone.

Sexual surveys such as *The Hite Report* have done much to dispel this myth, as have sex counselors or experts like Betty Dodson, author of *Sex for One*. Dodson finds that while women are now willing to talk about their sexual fears and hang-ups, men are less open. "Somehow men were supposed to have gained enough sexual expertise to teach women about sex. But having to project a masculine image at all times kept them from learning. If you already know all the answers, you can't ask questions."[3]

Women are attracted to women for all the same reasons that men are. As Nancy Friday, in *Women on Top*, explains, "There is something uniquely satisfying in a woman's body that cannot be had with a man. As sexually exciting and elegant as a male body may be, it lacks the obvious physical attributes of our first source of love, mother. It isn't just the breasts, it's the texture of the skin, the smell, the whole mysterious aura of that first body we lay against, which fed, warmed, and overwhelmed us with its power. ... How could any of us, male or female, forget that relationship?

"Whatever sexual pleasure women may find with a man, they cannot get this primitive physicality with him ... even the most tender of men cannot offer the unique satisfaction found in a woman's body."[4]

Psychotherapist Hedda Begelman said, "Women have always been nurturers. When women connect with one another, they have a chance to know what it is like to be nurtured. They learn that making love is more than sexual intercourse. Their new knowledge is frightening to men like Freud, who have taken it upon themselves to tell women how they are 'supposed to' feel."[5]

Women had been led by Freudian theory to believe that orgasms caused by clitoral stimulation were adolescent, and that, on puberty, when they began having intercourse with men, vaginal orgasms would naturally replace clitoral ones. Before Shere Hite's *The Hite Report* came out and dispelled this belief, women believed that if this did not happen, they were at fault, either being immature or needing to resolve sexual conflicts.

In the early 1990s, "Sex in America," a survey designed by academics at the University of Chicago's National Opinion Research Center, questioned 3,432 men and women and found that, while 75% of American men experience orgasm every time they have intercourse, only 29% of American women experience orgasm every time. If intercourse were the only "natural form of sex," the percentages of orgasms for men and women ought to be more equal.[6]

In 2001, in answer to a woman complaining about the lack of sexual interest from her husband, Dr. Joyce Brothers wrote, "You might be interested and somewhat surprised to learn that after all this time and money spent on advertising, films, talking and writing about sex, it doesn't rank as a top-priority leisure activity in this country. Gardening, visiting relatives, and going to and playing athletic games (including golf, tennis, and skiing) were in the top category."[7]

While gay rights opponents might argue that homosexuality is unnatural, they might need to consider using other arguments to support their views.[8] In 1997, *Bonobo: The Forgotten Ape* unleashed a huge discussion about animal sexuality, and then in 1999, Bruce Bagemihl's book *Biological Exuberance: Animal Homosexuality and Natural Diversity* provided an overview of scholarly studies and said that same-sex behavior in animals had been documented in some 450 species.[9]

Renee

By the time Renee was twenty-three, she had had four children. While she had no idea of her true sexual identity when she married, she knew that sex wasn't one of the things she married for. "But," Renee says, "I thought I could put up with it because I wanted a normal life."

Renee's husband made many sexual demands on her, and she soon discovered that "when I am pregnant, I could say no to him. When I was nursing I could say no, too. That's why I have so many kids."

There was very little to their relationship, but the routines and responsibilities of the household and young family kept the couple too busy for the first few years for them to realize this. It was only after she started therapy to trace the source of her unhappiness that Renee was able to identify herself as a married woman who loves women (MWLW).

Lauren

While Lauren identifies herself as being sexually attracted to both men and women, she rejects most of the physical attributes of men. Quite graphically, she explains, "In no way do I enjoy as much the taste, the smell, the sight, the touches. When I reach out to touch or taste a man's body, it can't hold a candle to how I feel in relating to a woman's body. No contest." Still she says, "I actually like intercourse, standard, plain vanilla vaginal intercourse, and I enjoy receiving oral sex. But it's absolutely beyond me to enjoy giving oral sex to a man. And, I don't really like holding a penis in my hand. I don't like how it looks or how it feels, and I hate how it tastes. I don't like how the whole area smells, even on someone who practices good hygiene. I have no particular desire to grapple with their genitals. I don't really have any interest."

With all these negatives, Lauren is equally clear about what she likes in a man. "I enjoy a man's physical strength and size. I love being picked up and carried, Clark Gable style, up the stairs. I like a lot of things about the male energy. Nonverbal stuff that comes across. Their humor, their comfort; when they have comfort in their bodies I respond to that. I still think a lot of guys are cute, and I can have some satisfying, although limited, sex with a man. I can have very nice kisses and embraces and intercourse.

"Still, I'm not interested enough in the male body to get off on just the sex. It has to have all sorts of other trappings associated with it. Whereas, with a woman, I think I could have all different kinds of sex: passionate, romantic, fuck-buddy, but I'm still not much of a casual sex person, even with a woman. I guess my feeling is that it's still important to me to be drawn to a person's mind.

"I have a friend that I'm occasionally lovers with, and the sex has become a texture in our friendship. It feels real good, and nice on the friendship plane, a nice sharing."

Lauren says, "I think bi women are more honest about what sex is about. Bisexual women seem to be less conservative about sex than heterosexual women or lesbians, willing to celebrate sex for sex and to feel that it's not dirty even when you're doing it and not madly in love with somebody. I think it's a wonderful energy to share with other people, and it can be valid even if you're not preparing to move in together. That's why I identify with the bi world and will continue to do so even if I end up engaging in nothing but lesbian sex."

Coitus has been set up to be the norm, and as most therapists would have us believe, any deviation from it is a sign of sexual dysfunction and, as such, abnormal. What is deceptive is trying to limit physical relations between humans to intercourse alone. Women who are with other women know that having intercourse and making love are not necessarily synonymous. When women connect, because there is no need to culminate their lovemaking with the physical act of genital penetration, there is more of an equality.

Lynn

"Men have always been conditioned to define themselves more through how much they make and what they do for a living; relationships are not *sooo* terribly important to them, not like to a woman.

"I had an affair with a man, and I didn't feel I had to leave my marriage. But when I was with her, it was just so synchronized.

"When I was dating her, I didn't have to say to myself, 'Is she going to call tomorrow?' She called tomorrow. With her, I didn't have to wonder, 'Are we talking too much?' With a guy, I always wondered. With her, I felt so much more welcome. My body wasn't an issue. With guys it was 'Am I skinny enough?' With her, I didn't worry. I always felt welcome. I felt like it was just right. I didn't feel lacking or wanting. I felt she intuitively understood me much better than men did.

"And, I also had no power struggle with her because she was a woman. With men I'd get into, 'What do you mean by that? Are you trying to put me down?' I became more defensive with men, feeling I'd have to explain myself more to be understood. I didn't have those issues with her. I felt more loved, more safe, more comfortable.

"Maybe it was my own issues with men. Men need you to take care of them emotionally. They feel very entitled to many things from women. To talk first, to talk most, their day is harder than your day, what they go through is harder than what you go through. You do all this nurturing for men. We do it, and we do it so naturally that we don't even know we do it, so when you're with a woman who's been taught to nurture, it was interesting to get that nurturing back. Not that I did anything differently. I did the same thing I did with men, but I got so much more back. So it felt so much more complete."

Lois

"Trying to understand and communicate with a man is so much work. I think it's a genetic thing, like men have selective vision. When women are fixing a meal together, they just go out there and do it, and they work side by side. They put something in a pan, and someone stirs it, and someone puts a lid on, kind of like a ballet. When you're in the kitchen with a man, you're each just trying to stay out of each other's way. Women just fit. The steps work out. ...

"I have a lot of lesbian friends, but it never even entered my mind that I would ever be that way," Lois, thirty-seven, married for five years, and positive about her heterosexual orientation, says. "Initially, when we first got married, there was definitely sexual attraction between my husband and me. We had a great sex life. But the longer we were married, the more and more infrequent it became."

For years, Lois had traveled on the road with her husband and fellow entertainers. Because of a change in her status to manager, Lois felt cut off from him and the other men who had been her friends.

"The feeling of isolation I had grew so strong," she says, "that I turned to another woman on tour for friendship. She was vivacious, energetic, and intellectual and all those wonderful words. She'd had a history as a lesbian, but she wasn't the one who initiated our relationship. I was.

"It started as a friendly relationship between us, and then it became more emotional. Then physical things were happening with me.

"I know if it was strictly sex I needed, I certainly could have gotten that from my husband. No. That wasn't the reason I turned to her. Emotionally, I had a need that was not being filled. Things were evolving with my husband and me and not in a good direction.

"Sexually, everything with her felt right from the start. Wonderful and right. I don't know what came first, if it was that emotionally I was not getting what I needed from my husband so I went someplace else, or if it was because there was so much great energy coming from her that I was drawn like a magnet.

"Ever since I'd been with her ... the pleasure [with my husband] definitely seemed to wane in comparison. My body didn't respond the same way. I was definitely more excited with her, and it was more from touch. The feeling of her skin was better than the feeling of his skin. The way he touched me was not the same.

"Making love with my husband became really stilted. It was almost like I would see how long I could hold my breath and hope that it would get over soon. With her, if it went on for hours, that was terrific with me."

The fallacy that a woman cannot be made love to without a man is shared by educated and uneducated people alike. Dr. David Reuben, the author of *Everything You Always Wanted to Know About Sex But Were Afraid to Ask*, in response to the question, "What do female homosexuals do?" quips, "One vagina plus another vagina equals zero."[10] Contrast this sexist response with that of Dr. Earle M. Marsh, assistant clinical professor of obstetrics and gynecology at the University of California Medical Center. At a 1968 series of lectures on sex, Dr. Marsh was quoted as saying: "It's too bad that every male cannot have instruction from a female homosexual prior to marriage. Only a female homosexual really knows how to make love to a woman. We, as men, are kind of duds along those lines."[11]

One woman and her female friend had been physically intimate for several years. When I asked her if she ever experienced feelings of guilt or betrayal toward her husband while with her friend, she was surprised. "Neither of us has a penis, so we're not really having sex."

As Hite wrote, "The role of women in sex, as in every other aspect of life, has been to serve the needs of others—men and children. And just as women did not recognize their oppression in a general sense until recently, just so sexual slavery has been an almost unconscious way of life for most women ... our model of sex and physical relations is culturally [not biologically] defined, and can be redefined—or undefined. We need not continue to have only one model of physical relations—foreplay, penetration, intercourse, and ejaculation."[12]

Helene

"It wasn't until ten years after I started having affairs with men that I fell in love with my best friend. I realize now I was seeking intimacy. With men, there had always been a challenge and a thrill, but intimacy and romance were lacking.

"When I fell in love with my best friend, I suddenly realized that love and sex could be very much the same. Loving her made me want to love and have sex all in one, and I realized that maybe that's what passion is. It supersedes everything. It was the first time I felt love and sex were entwined."

Shari

"In the context of marriage, having an affair with a man is very different than an affair with a woman. Having an affair with a man is seeking something outside the marriage that should be obtained within the marriage. Having an affair with a woman is seeking something outside the marriage that could never be obtained within a marriage.

"The first time I held my special friend's hand was a sexual as well as an emotional experience. So was the first time I hugged her. That felt wonderful and true—like a dream coming to life. Skipping to the more intense stuff—clothes off, skin to skin, sucking her breast—felt amazing, mind-blowing, and so incredibly natural.

"The first time I put my hand between her legs I was so shocked, all I could say was 'Oh, my God.' I was totally stunned at the warmth and wetness and softness between the sturdiness of her legs. The simultaneous thought was that I had actually touched heaven and the sea/origin of all life. Metaphysical concepts turned real in my hand.

"I was totally blown away. When she briefly licked me between my legs, the warmth and softness of her breath caught me so off guard that I could hardly talk. What I did manage to tell her—between gasps—was that this was like starting to pass through the gates of paradise. I couldn't pass all the way through, because if I did, I might never come back, meaning there would be nothing that could hold me to my family."

Long before she had her first experience with a woman, Shari's sex life with her husband had become intermittent. "It had become such a rare event that we actually forgot about it. From time to time, we wondered why, but it didn't feel like an especially serious problem.

"As soon as I came out, I had an amazing surge of sexual energy and an intense desire to solidify our bond as a couple. So we started having sex again—maybe once a week or every two weeks—and it was more intense and pleasurable than I recalled it having been for a long time.

"As the months passed, the frequency has again dwindled. … Eddie is concerned that we might never have it again. I told him that over the years, my feelings about sex have changed so that now it's primarily an act of emotional bonding.

"While I try to help him to see that it is not a matter of personal rejection, I'm sure it has pretty much the same effect on him. In some ways, it's a relief not to be active sexually with him because I feel there are many ways to bond with him on an emotional level. However, I'm also fearful that he will emotionally move away from me because sex is currently not a part of our bonding."

Barbara

"I believed that our society equates sex with marriage. The benefits of being in a marriage—legal rights, medical and insurance plans— are rewards for having legal sex. And I believed that even if I wasn't interested in sex, I didn't have the right to say no when my husband approached me.

"Still, I was shocked when I realized I was a lesbian. I certainly didn't know when I married. I knew I wasn't very interested in sex, but I thought I just had a low sex drive.

"I began doing different things to avoid sex with my husband: claiming headaches, creating additional periods or pretending they had lengthened, falling asleep on the couch rather than going into the bedroom.

"By the time I found out about myself, we had settled into a celibate marriage."

While some marriages become celibate at the time of the woman's announcement, often celibacy comes about, as it did in Barbara's marriage, before the woman actually identifies herself. In other marriages, while the sexual component is still in evidence, eventually it dwindles.

Barbara is not the only woman who has taken the path of a sexless marriage. Many heterosexual marriages continue long after the sexual component is gone.

On June 25, 1990, in a column called "Sex and Marriage," Ann Landers printed a letter from a woman in her late fifties who said that she and her husband had given up sex while in their forties and were content and happily married. They wondered if they were "oddballs." She asked, "How many other married couples live together happily without sex?" Ms. Landers conducted a poll and received over thirty-five thousand pieces of mail on that subject in two weeks.

Based on those responses, Landers wrote: "More than 65% of the couples over 60 years of age who wrote, and 75% of the couples over 70, have little or no sex, and they don't miss it."

According to Landers's mail, "Men of all ages are far more interested in sex than women and an amazing number of women in all age groups consider sex a duty or a nuisance. They pretend to enjoy it and fake orgasms to keep their men happy. Some couples gave up on sex in their early 30s while others were still enjoying it in their 80s."[13]

Diana Waltz, author of *Celibate Wives*, has found that the reasons for celibate marriages range from infidelity, boredom, loss of respect, alcoholism, illness, spiritual growth, and verbal abuse to simply incompatible sex drives.[14]

As women grow more sexually astute, they are beginning to question the quality of their marital sex lives. Self-help books on improving marriages flood the market. Articles on making marriages work appear regularly in women's magazines. Some downplay sex, telling couples that all they need to do is lower their sexual expectations. Others offer suggestions for refining their sexual techniques.

Dorothy

Dorothy, believing she had a low sex drive, never questioned her sexuality—until she fell in love with her friend. Because her love was not returned, and her friend was gone, all that remained for her was a haunting question: "Am I a lesbian?"

Searching for a confidante, Dorothy eventually met Tanya at a center for gays and lesbians. As a young girl in Russia, Tanya had had a physical relationship with a close girlfriend. Yet, when she grew up, she was not able to accept the fact that she preferred women. Wanting and trying to fit into her closely knit community, she married twice. Neither marriage worked.

Dorothy smiles. "We exchanged stories immediately. We spent a day walking in the park. Then, we went up to her apartment to hear some tapes. When it was time for me to go, she gave me a hug good-bye. From somewhere deep inside my body a huge sigh escaped, and I felt a sudden discharge between my legs. Confused, I stepped away and looked at her. Then, awkwardly, I came closer for another hug. The same thing happened.

"I walked downstairs bewildered, wondering about the wet-ness in my panties, eager to see Tanya again. I had been married for twenty-two years and had never experienced anything like this before.

"The following week she invited me over for the evening. I felt like a little kid getting ready for a party. I told my husband I was going to see my new friend, never realizing that she would be much more to me when I left her apartment later that evening.

"We sat and talked. Each time one of us shifted positions, our bodies came nearer. But we didn't touch. Then she got up and leaned against the back of a chair. I leaned against the piano facing her. We smiled at each other. She took my hands in hers and pulled me into her arms. Our lips touched. She cupped my face in her hands and whispered, 'When the time is right, I want to make love to you.'

"My legs turned to rubber, and I held on to her so I wouldn't fall. 'The time is right,' I said. 'It's right. ... But I don't know what to do.'

"Tanya said, 'Do anything that you'd like to do.'

"I touched her face, running my fingers across her cheekbones and over her eyes, her lips. My fingers tingled. It felt like electricity jumping from her to me. I put my hand against her back and timidly inched my fingers under her sweater. Her skin was so warm and soft and smooth.

"The two of us being together, what we were doing, it all seemed so natural. She led me to her bedroom and made love to me while I lay there touching her face, her breasts, her back, and saying over and over again, 'Oh, my God, oh, my God. Thank you, thank you.'"

There is a scene in Fanny Flagg's *Fried Green Tomatoes* in which the women have brought mirrors to class to study their private parts: Tawana is so uncomfortable, she can't look at her own body.[15] Unfortunately, many women have been socialized to feel shame and embarrassment in regard to their bodies. When women experience physical intimacy with other women, however, they become freer and more comfortable with their bodies and are able to reexamine their old negative feelings and to form more positive attitudes toward themselves. Some women report that the initial experience of being with a woman, and the comfort level with their own bodies derived from it, stimulates their marital sex life.

Angela

Angela, strongly tied to her Italian roots, says, "For years I felt like I was going through the motions sexually. I wanted kids. After the first, I had no interest. I liked and cared about my husband, but we didn't have an emotional sharing. Men are raised not to express their feelings. Women are taught to be more expressive and more emotional, so I turned to women. I always turned to them emotionally. I always told my best friends more, much more than I did my husband because he's not a feedback person. I can connect with women emotionally in a much more satisfying way than I can with men.

"When I started loving women, I began to look in the mirror and began to like myself. I guess I felt since I wasn't a size six and I didn't look like the women in magazines, I must not be beautiful. But somehow, when I connected my sexuality with women, I began to feel beautiful from the inside out.

"Once I took the pressure off myself and allowed me to love me, I felt more beautiful, sensual, and sexual than I ever had in my life. Because I feel better about me, I feel better about being physical with my husband.

"I enjoy sex with my husband much more since I discovered I love women."

Even those men willing to read marriage manuals about how to please their wives have difficulty understanding that it is the total psychological situation to which many women react. While men often see hugging as a precursor to sexual intercourse, often, between women, there is much hugging, touching, and kissing outside a sexual scenario as well as within one. Tenderness, nurturing, and caring are part of an intimate life that goes on all the time, not just when it is time to go to bed.

Ellen

"With my husband, Dave, intercourse was never anything special, but not boring. He got off, and that was fine with me. After a while, we realized I could get off better on top, so we did that regularly. And, I usually came that way, too, but I never compared it to coming through masturbation. I have multiple orgasms in masturbation. Also, after he would come he would stop, and that would leave me wanting more. I usually finished in the shower or tub.

"I don't think that before I met my lover I was aware that something was missing in my marriage. But once it happened, I knew. It was the passion, tenderness, and softness of another woman."

Still, while some MWLW were, or became, completely turned off by male bodies, Ellen, who identifies herself as a lesbian, continues to have a sexual relationship with her husband.

She says, "I have always liked Dave's cock. Somehow, we discovered anal intercourse. I am most satisfied when I give myself to him this way. To his way of thinking, no change has taken place since I have been involved with women. Actually, there is one change. We have never done oral sex where he goes down on me. Now that I've been with women, this will never happen. That is reserved for women only."

Gaby

Having been sexually indoctrinated in our heterosexual society, a small minority of women, coming together with another woman for the first time, remembered feeling great stress. Gaby, like other women, had spent her life judging her body against those she saw on billboards and in magazines. She says, "I was not young anymore. I was fifty-three. I was just so nervous about, 'Would she like me? Was my body going to be pleasing to her?'"

A highly successful executive in the corporate world, Gaby was a woman who needed total control in every aspect of her life, in the workplace and in bed as well.

Gaby says, "Actually, I was totally bewildered about the love aspect that grew out of our relationship because I had never thought beyond the physical.

"For many years, I never really thought about anything more than hugging and kissing another woman. I could imagine more, but it was not important. Then, two years ago, the desire to have an experience became very intense. Still, I don't think I would have had the nerve to go looking for another woman if I hadn't met my lover.

"We met at a twelve-step program. I had shared some of my feelings. We began to talk. It was very strange. A friendship didn't really have time to build up, but we had something in common. We were both married and in the same state of needing to have this experience. We were both conscious of each other's sexual inclinations, so from the beginning it was like a flirtatious friendship.

"We talked, and I invited her to my office, and we had dinner out, and I began to realize that I was trying to impress her and there was an attraction. I think it began more as an experiment. I urged her on by asking her where the relationship was going. She looked at me like I was crazy.

"It took months. We were both shy. She finally just came over, took me in her arms, and kissed me. We began doing natural things, touching, caressing. We ended up in the bedroom.

"I remember saying, 'This feels so good, it can't be wrong.' I wanted to tell the whole world. I was so pleased, proud. I finally had found the courage to do something for myself. I experienced myself. I grew up.

"The first time we were together, my lover had a tremendously natural orgasm," Gaby says. "I was very hot, but it didn't happen for me for the first couple of months because I am a control freak. I was aroused, but I was afraid to let go. I could satisfy my lover, but I couldn't let anybody make me vulnerable. Then, she told me I was a fantastic lover. After that, it got easier for me to let go.

"Still," Gaby confides, "when the first time was over, I cried. It was such a relief. It was so beautiful. I think it was the emotional thing of being with someone I trusted so much. It was a whole package, not just the physical thing I had thought it would be."

Ellie

An account executive, Ellie met her first lover while working on a large ad campaign. For her, the experience was completely absorbing, and for the first time in her life she opened herself up completely. "We worked on a project together. There was an emotional draw. Although we didn't have much in common, I found myself attracted to her in a way I had never felt before. I found myself making excuses to call her after we had finished the project. I began to obsess about her and attributed it to wanting some sort of a kick. I invited her to join me for dinner.

"When we finally got together, I knew it was not a kick. I didn't want to stop. I knew there was more to this. I became a lunatic; I was crazed. After we slept together, I felt like I was on another planet. I couldn't concentrate. I'd find myself reading the same line over and over because nothing would sink in. I had to summon every ounce of concentration to work, to listen to someone, to do anything. Either I wanted to be with her or I wanted to be alone. I felt like I was on another planet, or I felt like I was an alien who had dropped on this planet. I had no idea what was going on around me. It was incredible. I found myself walking miles in the freezing cold, just totally lost all track of time. It was pretty intense.

"We saw each other the following weekend. This went on for a while. After four or five weeks, she called me and told me she thought she was falling in love with me. 'No,' I told her, frightened. 'We're both having an infatuation, but it's not love. It can't be. It has nothing to do with that.'

"I was a mess, a total wreck. I, of course, could not tell anyone about this. No one knew at all. I'd go away with my family on weekends and wait until my husband was out of the house so I could sneak a call to her. I'd be afraid he'd look at the bill and ask who I was calling. I became terrified of everything, and the big thing was having no people to talk to. I started to retreat from people. My friends would call me for dinner, and I'd think of an excuse not to join them. How could I sit and pretend I was having an intimate conversation when this was what my life was totally about now."

Fran

Now sixty, Fran was married for seventeen years and had two children before realizing her love of women. In retrospect, she realizes she had not been in love with her husband, "But I would never have known, as I didn't know about my sexuality and my sensuality. I certainly did not know what being in love was. I would have assumed that I thought that I loved him. I still certainly care for him at this time in my life. My relationship with my husband is null and void seventeen years already. But my caring for the person is still there.

"I've done my homework, and I'm able to identify now that I have feelings of anger ... of growing up in a time when he was supposed to teach me, and he didn't. I was told, 'He will show you.' And I'm certainly talking about sex. 'He will give you what you're supposed to have.' He was supposed to be the sexual one, the aggressive one. What I'm angry about is that he didn't fill that role. It wasn't his fault either. We had both been duped."

Fran and her family had moved to Israel. Her best friend, Rifka, was living in the United States. Their friendship continued through letter writing. "The connection was always there," Fran says. "The caring was always there, and I didn't know that more was involved, or that I could even be more involved with another human being. I was a married woman. When I talk about my relationship with Rifka, and going outside my marriage, I had to deal with the right and wrong of it and the morality.

"But what happened was, once I gave myself permission to be physically sexual with her, I was free. I never felt freer in my life. I never felt more like a woman. Everything changed. Before, I had no femininity, no sexuality, no sense of who I was. It wasn't the thought of being in love with her, it was the act of allowing myself physically to love her, and even then I wasn't aware that I wasn't experiencing the best of what could be there for me, and I'm referring to an orgasm.

"I had been married for more than fourteen years and never experienced an orgasm with my husband. I didn't have an orgasm when I first came in contact with Rifka either. Sexually, I thought I was doing what I was supposed to do, until she told me, 'No, there's more for you. You're settling.' The exciting thing was not only to be in on it but to have it and the it was totally for me.

"I was still married at this time, visiting back and forth. It was very difficult." Yet, Fran, like the majority of women interviewed, spoke of experiencing an immediate feeling of rightness and well-being.

Fran was nearly forty before she divorced her husband to live in domestic partnership with her best friend, Rifka. The women have now been together for almost twenty years.

Regardless of whether marriages continued or ended after the revelations, very rarely did the women blame their husbands for their turning to women. They realized that not only they but the men as well had been raised with and given false information about sexuality.

Men were told that a man is not "a man" unless he wants intercourse, and so, maintaining an erection during sex became the focus for many men. This forced the timing and sequence of events to revolve around the erection, eliminating the possibility of more spontaneous feelings and actions. While it was known that women could masturbate to orgasm clitorally, they were told that the right way to orgasm was only from vaginal penetration by the penis. When this did not work, they were told they were to blame. Men felt that there was something wrong with them or their penis if the woman didn't orgasm. According to Hite, these oppressive expectations have led to needless suffering.[16]

While the sexual difficulties a couple experiences are not always due to the wife's revelation, her discovery may suddenly become the husband's convenient answer for all the couple's old and unresolved sexual problems. And conversely, it is these same unresolved problems that often lead a woman to discover her true sexual preference in the first place.

Tami

"My marriage was more of a friendship. He was ten years older than I was. I let him take care of me. He was very gentle, a good father. We had a house in the suburbs. We were very traditional. He went out to work; I raised the children. I was very unhappy but didn't know why. No matter what he would do, I was unhappy. We had no sex life whatsoever. He had a real big problem. To this day, I don't know why. But I'm grateful that he had a problem because I didn't have to act on it.

"He'd say, 'It's me, not you.' There were times I wondered if he was a latent homosexual. I don't think he could have acted on it. He's very homophobic. He has a sister who has been gay since she was a young teenager. He didn't talk to her for a year.

"I watched my sister-in-law's gender preference grow. I was very interested in her sexuality, but I didn't understand why."

When Tami began work, a coworker came in, and Tami felt a sudden connection with her. A year and a half later, they became lovers. Then Tami realized why she had identified so strongly with her sister-in-law.

Miriam

"Marriage started out okay, not because I was attracted to him, but because he was able to turn me on. But it was really all wrong. I never looked at him and said, 'God, this is someone whose body I desire.' I had sexual feelings and enjoyed doing sexual things and having orgasms, but I had never had a desire to really stimulate a man, to stimulate his organs, to reach out and touch them. I thought that was normal, the way women were, the low sex drive. I was aware that I had feelings of sexual pleasure in myself, but I didn't see anything odd about my lack of sexual desire for him. I understood that men were more mechanistic, into fondling genitals, and women were into tenderness, that this was normal."

Before they were engaged, Miriam says, "The only reason I had sex with him was because I was a horny thing, and he was a horny thing, and he knew how to turn me on. I was also tired of him nagging me, and I decided what am I protecting here? What is virginity anyway? It all went sour before we got engaged.

"At that point, there got to be an unwritten rule about the nature of our commitment. That was that sex was not going to be a make-or-break issue for our relationship. The commitment was not based on sex. Sex was just not that important, and we kept hoping it would get better. There was lots wrong with our sexual connection. It wasn't connected with his emotions. It always felt very mechanical to me; press this button, wiggle this knob."

Betty

"I was never really in love with my husband. I was twenty-three years old. Everyone else had already married and had a first baby and was working on a second. We were great pals and good friends, so we figured, 'Let's do this.'"

Betty has since divorced her husband but says, "We're still on friendly terms because of our son. But we went and fucked up a very good friendship. After we were finally separated permanently, we started becoming friends again because we didn't have unrealistic demands on each other any longer."

Betty's discovery came as an evolutionary process after her divorce. "As a teenager, my girlfriends were more important to me than boyfriends, but for certain occasions you needed a date, so I had one. I didn't know anything about gay people. After my marriage broke up, I still wanted to have sex, but I didn't want involvement. That was in the early seventies, when swinging was a big thing. I tried it. At first it was with men that I was getting my sexual needs taken care of, but then I started getting closer to women, and I realized, for the first time, I was really enjoying sex, and in a very short period of time men were pushed aside."

Cherry

"I grew up in a rigid Protestant, Waspy suburban family with fifties and sixties Anita Bryant-type values. The only thing I ever heard about homosexuality was that I'd never have to worry about it. It didn't apply to me.

"In high school, other girls called me a 'dyke' or 'lez' if I didn't have a boyfriend. It sounded like the most dirty, low-life thing in the world. I proved I could date boys just like them, but I never felt bad about the feelings I had toward girlfriends, even though they were unreturned. I wanted to hug, hold hands, snuggle, wrestle, massage, etc. Sex was not on my mind. Just affection in a situation where I didn't have to worry that sex was expected, as it would be with a guy."

Married for two years, Cherry says, "I married the man who I could 'tolerate' most sex-wise, but I am failing at forcing myself to be straight.

"I have remained in my marriage because I love my husband as a person and also because I want to have a child. We went to a marriage counselor, but she focused on our individual wants and needs, which made us pull away from each other, so we stopped going. There is a lot of stress on my husband, Burt, since I don't satisfy him sexually, and he doesn't satisfy me.

"We have talked about it [my feelings for women] extensively, but whenever we talk it into the ground, I get stressed. I like things better when they are quiet and mellow. I got him *The Other Side of the Closet*, but the book stressed him out because every couple he read about either broke up or had affairs. So, I avoid the subject with him as much as possible and try to concentrate on being friends.

"Burt considered my unresponsiveness to be a result of neglect I received from my parents and a couple of date-rape experiences as a teen. He thought if he were gentle and not forceful, he could make me enjoy sex. I felt if I forced myself and put a lot of effort into it, I could make myself like it. But I didn't know that my mind was going to continue to rebel. I expected when we got married that he would just do what he wanted in bed, and that I could get away with just lying there until it was over. It became more and more clear to me that I couldn't do this for the rest of my life, but we continue to look for new, creative ways to make it different and tolerable for me.

"We have compromised on one time per month, and we both masturbate. We fight about that because he feels he has to do it because he can't control the urge, and I feel I should be able to do it because he doesn't satisfy me. We compromise by doing it only when the other isn't around and not letting the other know about it.

"I feel the only way I can have a sex life with him for good is if I can also find some enjoyment on the side, including an occasional experience with a woman if that turns out to be what I like."

Cherry, fearful, has yet to act on her feelings for women.

Carmen

"My husband has always known everything about me. He was obviously quite present throughout my struggles with our sexual relationship, and he was aware of the confusion I experienced and the longing and frustration I felt. He was surprisingly supportive of my mental exploration of homosexuality; I'm afraid he found the idea a bit of a turn-on, but rather than getting perturbed about that, I chose to focus instead on his cooperative attitude and necessary flexibility. When

I finally came to the long-awaited, life-affirming conclusion of my own lesbianism a year and a half ago, he shared my joy and elation as a true friend would.

"However, since my relationship with my woman has become so all-encompassing and intense, more powerful than my husband or even she and I could have anticipated, his supportiveness has, not surprisingly, become tainted with hurt feelings, jealousy, anger, resentment, and concerns about issues of practicality like management of time, money, and energy resources.

"Before, sex was about his power and his pleasure and his entitlement, at my expense—a constant source of pain throughout our marriage. Once I claimed my own sexuality, I was able to forgive him these hurts and discover a sense of peace and self-acceptance and sexual enlightenment I hadn't known before.

"So far, he tells me the lack of sex in the marriage is not a problem, saying if it ever becomes a problem, we will deal with it then. Because I prefer to avoid that problem, and because I do love my husband dearly, I have occasional and minimal sexual contact with him. Because I now enjoy a sense of peace and self-knowledge, I no longer feel forced, and I no longer feel powerless and angry. Happily, he is extremely considerate and giving. Our occasional sexual encounters usually involve unadorned mutual manual contact; aside from these encounters, though, we regularly express our love for each other, as close friends do, through caring embraces and playful touches."

While current television shows and magazines have lifted some of the negativity associated with lesbianism and the word is becoming heard more often, women who love women have always been around. In the early 1900s, author Vita Sackville-West, a wife and mother, began a passionate love affair with another woman. "Her marriage not only survived infidelity, sexual incompatibility and long absences, but it became stronger and finer as a result." According to Nigel Nicolson, the son who found West's autobiographic journal after her death, while his father sought diversion with other men, his mother found her passion with women. For West and her husband, devoted to each other, marriage and sex were separate things, and being in love with someone of the same gender had little to do with the felicity of their marriage. "They achieved their ideal companionship only after a long struggle ... but once achieved, it was unalterable and lifelong, and they made of it ... the strangest and most successful union that two gifted people have ever enjoyed."[17]

Little did I know when I realized my sexuality that everything I went through would be more about my long struggle toward selfhood and a successful union than about having a same-gender sexual preference. It would be about discovering who and what I am and being honest with myself and with those who matter most to me. It would be about having the courage to go beyond the limited place society had dictated was mine and reaching a new level of growth and understanding. And, it would be about being able to reconstruct my marriage in a realistic light.

By reexamining feelings and attitudes instilled in me since childhood, and understanding society's motives behind them, I was able to break through the silence that had kept me from being able to acknowledge my own needs as a woman.

Recently, having freed myself of the embarrassment, shame, and discomfort I was taught to feel in regard to my body, I was able to take off my clothes, and, in the moonlight, with the exuberance of a child, roll naked down a grassy hill covered with sparkling dew.

My journey to selfhood has not been an easy one. Yet, I would gladly go through the same pain and suffering all over again to be able to reach my new beginning.

CHAPTER 13

New Beginnings

The admission of my true sexual identity was the beginning of a journey fraught with agony, isolation, pain, and panic. Not only did I have to live with the knowledge that I had violated one of society's imposed social mores, but I now felt forced to live a deceitful existence within my marriage as well.

Having been taught the value of honesty and openness, I desperately wanted to tell my husband why I felt unable to meet his needs. Having also been taught not to hurt others, I initially chose silence instead to shield him from any additional suffering. The internal conflict I lived with is one that most married women who love women (MWLW) have to resolve to live a full life instead of a double one.

Often, people ask, "Why couldn't you just keep your sexual identity to yourself?" While some women can and do, I felt as though I were on an emotional roller coaster and saw coming out as something I had little choice about. I felt as though it were a life-or-death situation, a fight for my sanity. I was feeling invisible, like part of myself was dying, because no one knew who I was. I would run to women's bars, not to drink, not to talk to anyone in particular, but to sit in a place where others would know I was a gay woman. Once I came out to my family and friends, the desperate need to run disappeared.

Jackie

"I'm basically an honest person, and although I have a rule that I would never lie to my husband, I told him half-truths. I don't have a moral compunction against lying, but I have a terrible memory, so I don't lie because I can fuck myself up. These half-truths were getting to me, and I didn't like living two lives, the life with my family, which I loved and never thought of leaving, and the life with my lover, who I loved but couldn't share with anyone."

Gracie

"At first I didn't feel guilt. It didn't feel like I was even cheating. I loved somebody, and it felt like there couldn't possibly be anything wrong with loving somebody the way I loved her. I still feel that loving somebody is not a bad thing. Later on, I did feel guilt, not so much for what I was doing—actually, it wasn't really guilt. It was fear, I guess, that I was going to hurt him, that the knowledge was going to hurt or destroy him or my children."

Dianna

Women are often brought up to believe that conflict is terrible and must be avoided at all costs. Still, some confront their internal conflict by coming out. Dianna, forty, the mother of a five-year-old, is in a committed relationship with another woman yet feels strongly about remaining in her marriage. She felt the only way to deal with her dual identity was by being open and honest about it, and she told her husband about herself. "My husband has been everything," Dianna says. "He's been furious, he's been suicidal, he's felt totally betrayed. But I guess still, for him, there is enough in the relationship and there is enough we have created together that makes it worth it for him to hang in. He struggles, and he certainly knows there are huge areas, emotionally especially, where he cannot meet me.

"I used to be bitchy. I used to feel so deprived, so hungry, so needy. In some ways, I think it's almost easier for him now because I'm getting my needs met."

While I am very fortunate to have the support of my family, for many, the coming-out process is often fraught with pain, rejection, and disappointment. Coming out often involves the loss of family and friends—the loss of their approval, love, and understanding—and might also involve the loss of children's respect.

Women who choose to remain in their marriages are often accused of "taking the easy way out." Yet, remaining is often more difficult. The

MWLW who is hiding her identity from her husband and yet has a need to be with women faces the possibility of accidental or deliberate exposure. One woman said she had heard that several women had been blackmailed.

Most women, whether they are out or not, deal with feelings of guilt and anxiety whenever they take time from their husbands and children for themselves. This is especially true if they choose to spend that time with a lover. One woman said, "I look forward to being with my woman friend and going away with her, and we have a wonderful time whenever we're together, but I find myself getting irritable and starting arguments, especially when it's time to return home. I hadn't been aware that I was doing this and that it had become a pattern until my lover brought it to my attention. I realize now that I feel so torn, wanting to be with her—I truly feel freer to be me when I'm with her and we have so much fun together—yet I also feel, at the same time, that I am supposed to be responsible and be with my family. Maybe it sounds crazy, but creating friction before we part must be my way of separating myself from her to be able to go back to my family."

When a woman feels obligated to spend time with her husband rather than with her lover, she also suffers the same irritability. Additional tension arises if the other woman is a single lesbian who wants her to leave her husband when she'd rather not have to choose. As one woman put it for many, "It's so hard to be everything for everyone."

Those women who had come out to their husbands, and then decided to separate, also faced a multitude of uncertainties. For some, depression and sadness followed the dissolution even though that's what they thought they wanted. Fear of finality made one woman unable to sell the house she had shared with her husband. One, missing her husband, kept coming up with excuses to go back to her house until he finally said, "You don't need excuses to come to see me," and they cried together. Another talked of going home to bring the kids for a visit and seeing her ex-husband helping his new girlfriend with laundry and shopping, things she'd always wanted him to do with her. Although these women were happy with their lovers, and it would have made no difference in their decision to leave, the pain was there nonetheless. What added to their sadness was their inability to share these particular feelings with lovers who might not understand.

Often, MWLW are ostracized by both the straight and gay communities. While we are used to seeing women hugging and kissing and dancing together in our society, in many people's minds the idea of women being truly intimate with each other upsets the "natural order," procreation being the one acceptable end to sexual function. Consequently, in the heterosexual community, a woman having an affair with a woman is viewed as a perversion. Yet, having an extramarital affair with a man is accepted as nearly normal.

In the lesbian community, there is resentment against those women who are a part of "the other world." One woman, aware of her lesbianism since the age of nine, said, "You [MWLW] know what it's like to feel normal, to feel fully accepted. I never felt that acceptance."

Felice

Felice, the mother of four, felt excluded from the lesbian community because "the only lesbians I know have no children. They're not married, and that's a whole different world. I was out with my friend one day, and it was the only time I ever wanted to knock her on her butt. There was a woman with three little kids, and Luz looks at me and says, 'Oh, there's another breeder.' I was devastated. I finally said, 'I take great offense at that word."

It is often difficult for a childless lesbian to understand the primal connection and protective instincts a mother feels for her children. "I think it was Luz's own stuff," Felice says. "Envy, sorrow at never having been a mother. Then she admitted to me, 'One of the things that attracted me to you was that you had these children, and you seemed to be so good at it.'"

As human beings, we continually struggle, torn by wanting to be who we really are and wanting to be who we feel we are supposed to be. We live with different degrees of repression. We often fake what we don't feel, say yes when we want to say no, pretend we don't care when we do. Every life is filled with these conflicts, but as the disparity grows between who we realize we are and the role we have played, the tension can become unbearable.

According to psychotherapist Hedda Begelman, director of the Gay and Lesbian Counselling Center of Long Island, "Should the woman be involved at the moment, not just with the thought that 'I love women,' but that 'I am in love with a particular woman,' the stress is multiplied even more. And leaving any marriage is not necessarily the easy way out. There are stresses involved with leaving: having children to deal with, going back and forth, having to keep a relationship with an ex-husband because there are children involved, and having to go through his anger. Having to go through all of the things you have to go through because you're a lesbian adds to the stress."[1]

Psychotherapist Gwenn A. Nusbaum, former clinical director of Identity House, a Manhattan-based peer counseling organization serving the lesbian, gay, bisexual, and transgender community, says, "Fear of expressing true sexuality keeps many people trapped, as does fear of being who they really are. Unfortunately, much of the fear is understandable. The American culture is basically a heterosexual one, dictating rules and values as to what types of attachments are right and which are wrong. A married woman tends to be perceived as correct and is often envied. A single woman or one involved in same-sexed attachments is often seen as strange or abnormal.

"Consider the Moral Majority and the repressive, dangerous factions around. When you talk about lesbians and gays, you are often talking about a hotbed of political activity fraught with hatred and fear. Individuals who are uninformed or may experience homosexual desires of their own, may use morality as a way to ward off fears connected with being more open to homosexual choices."[2]

Simone de Beauvoir points out in her book *The Second Sex* that among women artists and writers there are many lesbians. Their sexuality is not the source of their creative energy, but absorbed in their work, they do not want to waste time playing a feminine role or struggling with men.[3]

In previous centuries, women had been hospitalized for various mental illnesses known as "hysteria" or "madness." Their "symptoms" often were a strong independent streak or, according to Phyllis Chesler's *Women and Madness*, "sexual disinterest in their husbands." Today, the rates for depression are three times higher for women than for men. And again, in evaluating the mental health of women of any age group, it is important to consider societal factors and cultural expectations.[4]

Many of the MWLW I interviewed experienced some form of depression during their discovery period. For the first year or two of my discovery, I cried more than I ever had in my lifetime. The women I had confided in needed only ask, "How are you," and the floodgates would open. My therapist would look at me, and I'd grab a handful of tissues. I'd go to a consciousness-raising group, and regardless of the topic, tears would flow.

My tears were for many things; the void I felt at the loss of my best friend, the isolation my silence condemned me to, my own internalized homophobia. While I had always rationally been able to accept people who were different, now I was one of them. I felt like an outcast. My beliefs had proven to be false. After twenty-five years of marriage, I had betrayed my husband and children. I was living a lie.

Things I had always been able to talk about intellectually and with detachment now became emotionally charged. I felt like a giant balloon stretched to capacity with only a tiny hole from which to squeeze the pain that was threatening to make me explode. Until my worlds came together, I walked a line between the two. In one, my feelings were impenetrable, and I was able to function as I always had before, family and old friends none the wiser. In my new world, my pain could not be held in check.

At the most extreme level, some MWLW, like their counterparts during the nineteenth century, were committed by their families when their same-sex predilections were discovered.

Alice

Alice, the mother of three small children, needed a vacation and went away with her best friend. "I didn't know about myself, but when my friend found a waiter and didn't come back to the room that night, I was distraught. I wanted to be with her, and I wanted her to want to be with me. When we drove home, I got hysterical. I said, 'I wanted to spend the weekend with you.' She said, 'Do you know what that means? Are you a lesbian?' It had never crossed my mind. I had never thought about it. I said, 'I love you very much.' And she said, 'This could never be.'

"When you're Jewish, you're taught you go to school, listen to the teacher, get married, have children. Nowhere are you taught you might love a woman, but when I read *The Well of Loneliness,* I knew it was me. I became so distraught that tried to kill myself—twice."

Alice was committed to a mental institution. She decided she didn't want to die and from the facility called the lesbian hotline for help. "I was thirty-nine and had never seen a lesbian. Nadine walked in, and she was just a person. Eventually, we fell in love. When I left the hospital, she came to live with my family. I didn't tell my husband about us, but I told my parents. They were grateful that I was no longer suicidal and accepted her as my friend."

Leah

Leah was also committed to a mental hospital, but not because she tried to commit suicide. "My family found out I was having an affair with another woman when I was seventeen. They had me committed. I was given shock treatments. When I tried to escape, I was doped so badly that I was almost a vegetable. After seeing what they had done to me in the hospital, my same brother who had had me committed fought to have me released." Terrified of being locked away again, Leah sought safety in a heterosexual marriage and has remained there, silently and unhappily, ever since.

As women, we learn that our sexuality should be hidden, that it is dangerous or shameful. By announcing a same-gender attraction, a woman reveals not only her sexuality but also her rejection of the heterosexual model. While the media has made lesbianism "chic" of late, social mores have always shunned the openly sexual woman, consigning her the title of prostitute, whore, tease, or "bad girl," so just coming out can risk the consequence of social ostracism and rejection. For the MWLW already dealing with internalized homophobia, this anxiety may be overwhelming.

Rifka

Rifka believes that it was the humiliation of realizing her same-gender sexuality as well as a lifetime of bottled-up feelings that brought about her illness.

"I had left my marriage and my family for my best friend, Fran," Rifka says. "Still, I couldn't admit to being a lesbian. The shame and embarrassment at the thought of being one was totally overwhelming. I had always been a health food person, a physical educator, and a health educator, and after Fran and I had been together a year and a half, I came down with Crohn's disease. I was very sick, hospitalized for twenty-one days, and suddenly, like a spiritual transformation, I knew that only if I really changed my life would I come out of this. I began to come out, fully come out every day.

"I got rid of the feelings that I had bottled up for so many years ... childhood and everything else, and freeing myself to be a lesbian, I got rid of all that shit, too. Understanding what Crohn's was for me, self-subordination, it just clicked. I've never had another incident, and very few people are ever cured from it."

Joyce

Beth, who has been married for fifteen years, says, "I had a problem with sex in my marriage since my son was born. I nursed him for a long time, and any interest in sex with my husband went away. When my sexual feelings came back, they had nothing to do with men. I attended church, and I began to notice that if a woman stood near me, I had a sexual response. I think it was preverbal. There were no words for it.

"I went to a peer counseling center and started going to a coming-out group. It was very painful thinking about separating from my husband. I really care about him a lot. Although I don't have sexual feelings for him, he's one of my best friends.

"I stopped going to the counseling center and started focusing my energy on my marriage instead. I told my husband about my feelings, and initially he didn't think it was so threatening. He accepted what I told him, but he tried to understand it in terms of something that could be changed.

"We've been in therapy together for over a year and have done a fair amount of work, but my sexual feelings for him are still not there. I've been sick so much this year. The conflict of really trying to make things work with him and really wanting to be with a woman is making me sick, and I just suddenly got it. My insides and my outsides are not in alignment.

"Last year, there was guilt and suffering at the thought that maybe I was making the choice for my own pleasure, but now I understand that it's nonnegotiable and the way things have come to be. I don't feel much guilt now. I feel like my molecules changed, and I've become a different person."

It wasn't until the middle of the nineteenth century that psychologists, intent on establishing psychology as a science, chose to make homosexuality the object of a systematic study.

Methodical identification of people on the basis of same-sex relations had not been contemplated until sexologists first used the term *lesbian* in 1869. Prior to that, while same-sex eroticism and relationships have existed in every known culture, there was no concept of "the homosexual" as a particular kind of person. Homosexuality was a practice, not an identity.

In the creation of their new discipline of "sexology," psychologists chose to make homosexuality a categorical entity rather than a term that covers a widely diverse range of individuals. For this purpose, says Beverly Burch, author of *On Intimate Terms*, lesbians and gay men, noted primarily for their lack of heterosexuality, became "the Other." Their differences with respect to each other, and the internal differences within each group, were not considered.[5]

When the word *homosexual* was coined, *heterosexual* was also coined to be able to differentiate the "normal" from the "deviant."

In conjunction with the establishment of this new discipline of "sexology," the category of lesbian, also called a *sexual invert*, was formulated. Some described a sexual invert—taken from the word *inversion*—as one who is attracted to one's own sex rather than to the opposite sex. Some used it to mean having the steretypical characteristics of the other sex—effeminacy in the male and masculine strengths in the female. Neither group would include the majority of male homosexuals and lesbians, who do not show these traits. The terms *inversion* and *invert* have acquired a negative connotation and are not commonly used today.[6]

Lillian Faderman, in *Odd Girls and Twilight Lovers: A History of Lesbian Life in Twentieth-Century America*, says, "It was to a large extent the work of the sexologists, which was disseminated slowly to the layman, but finally became part of popular wisdom after World War I, that accounts for the altered views of women's intimacy with each other. It may be said that sexologists changed the course of same-sex relationships not only because they cast suspicion on romantic friendships, but also because they helped make possible the establishment of lesbian communities through their theories, which separated off the lesbian from the rest of womankind and presented new concepts to describe certain feelings and preferences that had before been within the spectrum of 'normal' female experiences."[7]

Since psychologists now depicted the lesbian as abnormal or sick, or men trapped in women's bodies, the taboo on a woman recognizing her love for another woman was increased tenfold. Fearful that her feelings were now unnatural, she might force herself to repress them, spend her life hiding "in the closet," or lead a double life.[8]

However, according to Faderman, "Experiences that are within the realm of the socially acceptable during one era may be considered sick or dangerous or antisocial during another—and in a brief space of time, attitudes may shift once again, and yet again.

"The period of World War II and the years immediately after illustrate such astonishingly rapid shifts. ... In the 1930s—an era when America needed fewer workers, the lesbian (a woman who needed to work and had no interest in making a man happy) was an antisocial being. During the war years that followed, when women had to learn to do without men ... and when female labor—in the factories, in the military, everywhere—was vital to the functioning of America, female independence and love between women were understood and undisturbed and even protected. After the war, when the surviving men returned to their jobs and the homes that women needed to make for them so that the country could return to 'normalcy,' love between women and female independence were suddenly nothing but manifestations of illness, and a woman who dared to proclaim herself a lesbian was considered a borderline psychotic. Nothing need have changed in the quality of the woman's desires for her to have metamorphosed socially from a monster to a hero to a sicko."[9]

Shirley

"Even though we're located geographically in one of the most les-bian-active and lesbian-friendly areas in the United States, I worry about how well my son will handle me being out in a small town," explains Shirley, who, with her husband, is redefining her marriage in the hopes that they can stay together. "I worry about the effect on our marriage: How much of my needs can I serve and our needs as well? How about my husband's needs? It's a continual balancing act, and the thing that most often tips my emotional balance is sorting out feelings that are indicators that I need to pay more attention to my family from the feelings that are unhealthy, unnecessary guilt.

"There's the irrational guilt: 'Why didn't I figure myself out before I got married and spare everyone this trauma? Why must I follow my needs instead of being a saint and subjugating them to the good of the family?' I can know all of the 'right' answers to these questions, and still spend time feeling like a shit.

"Then there is the anxiety. Will my needs eventually come into such conflict with my family's needs that there will be loss of love and mutual respect? Or a loss of the family? Will I never be able to have a complete, long-term relationship with a woman because she can't handle me being married?

"Despite the fear and guilt and anxiety, I've never been happier in my life. I am so elated that I have found me and that me feels wonderful to be. I feel charged—physically, mentally, emotionally, and spiritu-ally—which is good, because all these aspects of me have been working overtime in overdrive since I came out—and I need every bit of energy replenishment I can get."

Julia

Julia, who chose to remain in her marriage while she has maintained a long-term relationship with Tillie, says, "It drove me crazy. I had to lie a lot. I was lying so much I began not to know what the truth was. But I did it. I'm glad I did it. I don't regret it. I took care of my children, and then I went out for the evening. I definitely had feelings of anxiety. Wherever I went, I thought my husband would walk in. I worried if I was at a dance or in a bar or with a lot of lesbians. As the years rolled on, I became less concerned. I didn't want my children to know. I felt guilty and inappropriate, but as time went on I became more sure of myself, and I realized that what was going on for me was that I was thoroughly and very much in love."

Jean

Jean remembers the isolation both she and her lover felt when they first realized over thirty years ago that they were gay. "We didn't know there was anyone else around like us until we saw the movie *The Killing of Sister George*. We saw women relating to each other, socializing together, going places together. We planned a trip to England.

"Then, we saw a TV program on gay men and lesbians. They mentioned an organization called the Daughters of Bilitis, and we realized we didn't have to go to England to meet other women like us. We called and couldn't wait to go. I remember we had to go up a very long staircase, and it was hard for me because I'd just had surgery. My lover said, 'Are you sure you want to go?' and I said, 'Yes,' pulling myself up by the banister one step at a time. We actually saw other women like us. It was such a thrill, and I haven't lost that thrill. Every time I go someplace where there is a group of lesbians, I still get a shiver or a thrill."

Lena

"It was a dirty trick heaven played on me," says Lena. "If I had known about my true sexuality, I would not have suffered physically, emotionally, and spiritually as much as I did. But because I believe in my faith, I believe that there is a reason for all this, that the time for it to be revealed was that time, for particular people, for a certain reason. I left the Salvation Army because they have definite thoughts against homosexuality of any kind. I joined River City Metropolitan Community Church, which reaches out to lesbians and gays and all people. My husband and all of the family belong.

"This revelation has brought me more clarity and a lot of suffering. Pain is there because I want to be able to eat, sleep, and breathe and enjoy my life. Pain because I live in a society that won't let me do that. Pain because every two steps that I make in progress as an individual, I'm still black, I'm still poor, and I'm still stigmatized. That's where the pain is. The pain is saying I'm doing something strange or unusual with my life because I want to share all that I have with another woman. Pain because society says, 'No, you must choose.' My God didn't say I had to choose. And society says I have to."

Gwyn

"Most of my exposure to religion came from accompanying my good friends to their church and synagogue services and experiencing their different religious practices with their families in their homes. I realized as a young child that my own religious views flew in the face of traditional religions as I was coming to understand them. While I considered myself an extremely spiritual individual, I found myself objecting to the exclusionism and judgmental attitudes I heard expressed in places of worship. I searched for many years as a young adult for a church or religion where I could feel comfortable, where my views would be affirmed or at least tolerated.

"About five years ago, I discovered a Unitarian Universalist fellowship that is now my home. Homosexuality is acknowledged and accepted as a matter of official policy, but of course many individual members are still close-minded or inadequately enlightened.

"I believe if it were not for the critical, judgmental influence of traditional, conservative, organized religion, I would have achieved a healthy understanding of myself and realized true happiness much earlier in life.

"The morality stuff came from sources external to me; even before I understood my own gayness, I opposed mainstream society's judgmental attitudes toward gays and other oppressed groups. I didn't buy the package of close-mindedness and bigotry that was presented to me, but I still found myself victimized by it. Once I finally felt strong and healthy enough to reject these dangerous external voices, I experienced intense elation at the freedom and beauty of finally knowing and accepting and loving my lesbian self."

Sonia

For Sonia, it wasn't her religious upbringing but a sudden awareness of what lay in store for her that helped her to come to terms with who she was.

"I was in this incredible hell. I felt disassociated, losing weight, all these horrible things. I was upstate with my kids, and we were playing on the bed, and I remember in the past thinking, 'This is absolutely it. This is as good as it gets. I will never love anybody in my life as much as I love my children. I know I don't love my husband and haven't loved him in a really long time. This is what it's all about.'

"Something about that made me sad and disturbed me. What I was afraid of was similar to what happened to me when I was growing up. My parents didn't have the best marriage, and what happens is parents put so many expectations on their children. I was so afraid of doing that. My kids are the great love in my life, and fifteen years from now they'll be grown up and be their own people, and what will I be left with? I'm going to be sitting in a rocking chair with my husband, and we're going to have absolutely nothing, and that scared me, absolutely scared me.

"What am I going to want my kids to give back to me? What will I demand of them? What rightfully should they give to me? I can't expect them to fill this emptiness in me.

"Then, after Janie and I got together, I was playing with my kids, and I came to the realization that I really did love her. Before that I was in complete, total denial. I wanted to see her. I was obsessed, but I was in total denial about my sexuality, about loving her, about what this really meant. I couldn't deal with this at all. When I realized that, it was like a weight lifted off. All of a sudden I was in touch with my emotions, and I could see much clearer than I could before. It was a turning point for me."

When a woman discovers her true sexual identity, all of her senses are shaken up. Unquestioned teachings of her church and family—deeply instilled issues of morality and her sense of right and wrong—become suspect. She questions her previously held belief system. While she might try to deny the existence of her new identity, the passion, pain, and utter confusion she experiences during her journey serve as catalysts that bring other feelings to the surface. Some women likened their evolution to having gained a third dimension.

Unfortunately, many people go through their entire lives never having experienced passion of any kind, or the turbulent emotions that accompany it, and so it is almost impossible for them to comprehend what the MWLW is going through. When *The Bridges of Madison County* came out, an enormous part of the public embraced the book, and then the movie that followed, for just this reason. They were able to identify with, and live vicariously through, two individuals very much like themselves. And, at last, they were able to taste and to feel the passion they had never personally experienced.

Sarah

When Sarah was in her late thirties, she met Dotty, the woman who became her lifelong lover. Sarah and her husband had stopped living together intimately, as man and wife, some time before that. She had anticipated divorcing her husband, but his diminishing eyesight made her change her plans. Instead, Dotty moved in with Sarah's family. They told outsiders that Dotty was just staying with the family while she attended college—she remained for about thirty years.

Now seventy, Sarah explains, "It almost sounds like a ménage à trois, but it wasn't although there were times when she and I would gang up on Bill and times when they would gang up on me. My daughter [in high school at the time] and a lot of friends knew our situation, but not the local friends."

Dotty became ill and spent the last eighteen months of her life in and out of the hospital. "When she checked in, I was referred to as her friend," Sarah says. "I finally got sick of that and told the social worker on the unit, the director of nurses, and the doctor. Our relationship was not talked about, but it was pretty much an open secret. The hospital staff were very supportive. They never made us feel we were out of the ordinary and did as much for us as they did for anyone else.

"Dotty was standing after having been on a respirator for about seven weeks. A nurse was bustling around, and all of a sudden she turned around and put her hands on her hips and said, 'So how long have you been together?' Now, Dotty was an intensely private person. She didn't discuss her personal affairs with anyone and was always circumspect about everything. I said, 'Twenty-nine years.' It felt good to be able to say that.

"Even when Dotty died, people didn't know. We were very fortunate. When she was in the hospital, we met a young woman, Molly, who was in training to become a minister. It turned out she was a lesbian, so Dotty asked her to say a few words at her funeral."

Sarah says, "Dotty was a very traditional person, so I don't know how she ever got mixed up with me. I was her first, last, and only experience. She was a churchgoer and played the organ, and the church had been supportive during her illness, although they didn't know about her. She felt we had to do the traditional thing at the funeral, but she did ask the young woman we had met to say a few words, and Molly was very discreet. She spoke words that only those of us who were in the know were able to understand."

Still, Sarah says, "If I came out with my secret, my church would treat me with a cold shoulder. I haven't been there since Dotty died because of my anger. There would be snickering and laughing in my community, and I have a grandson in high school and another one starting next year. I wouldn't want to do that to them. It makes me angry that it has to be like this."

After Dotty died, loneliness brought Sarah out of her retirement, and she returned to her field of social work.

Sarah says, "One of our social workers said that one teenage boy had come out to him, and he wanted to know if we knew of any gay or lesbian social workers to whom we might refer the boy. I sat there silently. And so did the other social worker I knew was gay. I felt like I was really letting down people who needed my help. I felt this shit had to stop. So I went to my boss and told him, 'I feel like shit, and I'm getting angrier and angrier.' That's what I told my boss. It's bad enough when young people have to keep secrets, but when you've had to keep secrets for as long as I have, thirty years, you just get angrier and angrier. I said, 'You can do anything with it [this information] you want to.' He was accepting.

"I'm trying more and more to come out and to be as honest as I can.

"It's a hard life. People don't deliberately go out and stick their heads in a meat grinder because that's a pleasure to them. They go out and face this life because that's who they are."

The MWLW who had reached the point of being comfortable with themselves said the process of working through their identity issues had given them new insight, strength, awareness, and confidence. While these women had always been dutiful daughters and responsible wives and mothers, few had felt like real people in their own right. Now they began to take control of their lives, accepting responsibility for their own emotional, physical, and in some cases, financial well-being. The compulsion to fit some norm, or to expect their families to do so, disappeared. The metamorphosis freed and opened them to a kind of love that is unrestricted by society's demands or controls. They spoke with pride of the women they were becoming.

Several years ago, my husband and I attended a fiftieth birthday party for Jeff, one of our oldest friends. Before we were married, we had often group dated with Jeff and his wife Sherry and five other couples. Sherry had lovingly created a collage of memories spanning Jeff's high school years and on through the present, and his oldest friends had been asked to prepare small anecdotes about Jeff.

I watched as Sherry and Jeff stood arm in arm, listening to the stories. She looking up to him lovingly, and suddenly my eyes filled with tears, and I had to leave the room. This simple scene had stirred painful reminders of the times my husband and I had experienced similar closeness at joyous occasions years ago.

It took me some time before I learned that while we have changed and might never again share the picture-perfect relationship we once thought we had, we can appreciate ourselves for the new and honest understanding we have of each other.

Dealing with weddings, anniversaries, funerals—any rite of passage— can be awkward for everyone involved. Families can be at a loss regarding how to conduct themselves. Should they pretend they had forgotten the anniversary and avoid any mention of it? This was the issue my husband and I faced as our thirtieth anniversary, the first after my announcement, neared. My children, and my sister and brother-in-law who live nearby, were at a loss concerning how to conduct themselves. Should they avoid any mention of our anniversary, pretend they had forgotten it? My husband was all in favor of that. I myself was at a loss to know how to treat it. At first, I also thought forgetting it would be best. Then, the reality came to me. Through good and bad, my husband and I had weathered these years together. We went through job losses, moves, family illnesses, and deaths, and we raised two wonderful kids. In the process, we just happened to grow separately rather than as a couple.

While this anniversary was not the typical expression shared between two people "in love," for me it represented hurdles we had come through together, the caring we had for each other, and the new friendship we had established, regardless of the other issues. It was a landmark occasion and deserved not to be ignored.

I asked the family to join us for dinner at our favorite restaurant. Around the table, I could feel everyone's apprehension, my husband's included, until I verbalized what everyone had been afraid to say. I lifted my glass and acknowledged how difficult the last year had been for all of us. I made a toast recognizing my husband, then our children and other family members. I acknowledged their love for me and for my husband and appreciated their support through our difficulties without having taken sides or chosen abandonment, the easy way out. There was an audible sigh of relief. The discomfort and the tension left, and we had a very special evening.

Appendix

Where to Turn for Help and Information

For women in their earliest phases of discovery, making a long-distance phone call to a bookstore or a resource center used to be difficult. There was the fear of having to answer questions if a spouse saw an unusual number on the phone bill. Some women told me about calling long-distance operators to see how much a specific phone call would be and then, armed with the necessary amount of coins, making their calls anonymously from pay phones. If payment had to be sent for books, money orders (available at banks and post offices) were purchased to avoid a record of the purchases in checkbooks or on credit cards.

For those afraid of having literature sent to their homes, post office boxes, available for minimal rates, afforded privacy. Women paid cash in advance, and some used pseudonyms.

Married women who love women (MWLW) still use a multitude of plans to afford them the protection they feel they need when they visit a therapist, attend a support group or rap session, or meet and talk with other women like themselves. Pretexts range from registering for classes with hours that coincide with actual meetings, to keeping car trunks filled with packages so that a woman can produce a bag or two and say she has been shopping. One support group for MWLW has created a vague, nondisclosing cover flier so that women have something to show their husbands if they should be asked where they've been.

Women's bookstores, generally community minded, were once good places to find information on, and to become familiar with, local women's

233

activities. *The Feminist Bookstore News* used to have a list of almost 200 feminist and general interest bookstores across the country. Now, the Feminist Bookstore Network (www.litwomen.org/WIP/stores.html) has a locator on Google that will bring up stores by location. Unfortunately, there are only about fifty such stores remaining in the United States, and eleven in Canada.

Another national publication that lists resources, publications, organizations, religious associations, health services, and support groups and has a separate section for women is the *Gayellow Pages*. It is carried in most bookstores dealing with lesbian and gay issues. Their Web site will give specific locations. There is a fee for ordering a hard copy (mailed in a plain wrapper using the return address of Renaissance House), but it is also available for free download, updated every month at http://www.gayellowpages.com/online.htm. Their mailing address is Renaissance House, P.O. Box 533, Village Station, New York, NY 10014-0533.

Now, thanks to the computer, women can find help, guidance, advice, assistance, and information by searching for a multitude of phrases, such as married women who love women, lesbian counseling services, lesbian support groups, lesbian chat rooms, gay and lesbian centers. The word *lesbian* can also be replaced with *bisexual* for searches. (Most public libraries have computers for public use for women who are unable to access the Internet at home.)

The Lesbian, Gay, Bisexual, and Transgender Community Center (www.gaycenter.org), formerly called the Lesbian and Gay Community Services Center in New York City (212-620-7310) was established in 1983 and has grown to become the largest LGBT (lesbian, gay, bisexual, transgender) multiservice organization on the East Coast and second largest LGBT community center in the world. Every week, six thousand people visit the center, and more than three hundred groups meet there. They provide social service, public policy, educational, and cultural/recreational programs and have a national directory with which to assist long-distance callers in finding their nearest sources of help.

New York's Identity House (www.identityhouse.org) offers a walk-in center for one-on-one peer counseling or short-term referral for therapy for the lesbian, gay, and bisexual community. Identity House also offers workshops, including discussion groups for women in transition, and talk and listen rap groups.

The Lesbian Herstory Archives (www.lesbianherstoryarchives.org; 1-718-768-3953), located in Brooklyn, New York, houses the world's largest collection of materials by and about lesbians, including books, unpublished papers, newsletters, photographs, slides, periodicals, tapes, videos, films, subject and organization files, reference tools, artwork, calendars, manuscripts, music, and clothing. Volunteer staffers are available to assist long-distance guests and researchers alike.

Parents and Friends of Lesbians and Gays, also known as PFLAG (www.pflag.org), is a self-help group for parents and friends who are trying to understand their children's homosexuality or who have accepted it and are trying to help other parents do the same. Their national headquarters is PFLAG National Office, 1726 M Street, NW, Suite 400, Washington, D.C. 20036. More than five hundred local chapters can be found through the Internet as well.

For older women coming out, SAGE, www.sageusa.org 1-212-741-2247, is the world's oldest and largest non-profit agency addressing the needs of lesbian, gay, bisexual, and transgender elders. Incorporated as "Senior Action in a Gay Environment" in 1978, it is now "Services & Advocacy for GLBT Elders."

Not every city or small community phone book lists the kinds of lesbian services offered in New York, but resources can still be located. Professional groups such as the Family Services League, the National Association for Social Workers, the Society for Clinical Social Work, and the Organization of Gay and Lesbian Health Care Workers may have access to the information or can help a woman to locate individuals or groups who deal with gender-related issues.

In addition, listings that begin with "Women," such as Women's Counseling or Women's Health Care Services, are good sources as are psychological or psychotherapy services. Local YWCAs are another source for gathering information on woman-related issues and NOW, the National Organization for Women (www.now.org), has a lesbian rights director who can direct women to nearby support services. Local chapters of NOW can also assist.

Another option for finding help is a local AIDS hotline. AIDS hotlines have become information centers for the lesbian as well as gay community. Generally, they are staffed by volunteers who are sensitive to lesbian needs and will direct women to available services and support groups.

Colleges and universities are other places with access to information, through either their women's studies or gender studies programs. Most also have women's centers, where literature on topics of interest to women is disseminated, and their bookstores offer additional reading material. An Internet search for "universities with gender studies programs" will locate many.

The Metropolitan Community Church and the Unitarian Church have a history of social activism and are known to be gay friendly. Other places to search for literature for women in transition are alternative or new age learning centers. These are places that open-minded people frequent. Information on these centers can generally be found in health food stores.

Women used to place ads in newspapers to find others like themselves. Some still do this. For their own protection, rather than give out personal information such as phone numbers or addresses, they use post office box numbers. More and more women are now turning to the computer to find friends or lovers. While many individuals have met through newspaper ads or online, it is advisable to arrange first meetings at well-populated diners or restaurants.

When cities or towns do not have a center or services, women have established their own support groups. As frightened as a woman may feel about exposing herself, she is not alone. Many women are looking for someone to talk to.

Notes

New Introduction

1. Los Angeles *Hollywood Reporter*, June 6, 2006.
2. Jane Gross, "When the Beard Is Too Painful to Remove," *New York Times*, August 3, 2006.
3. Diane Anderson-Minshall, "Interview with Laura Innes, Dr. Kerry Weaver on ER," *Curve Magazine*, May 2002, 25.

Original Introduction

1. Shere Hite, *The Hite Report* (New York: Macmillan, 1976).
2. Amity Pierce Buxton, *The Other Side of the Closet* (Santa Monica, Calif.: IBS Press, 1991), xiv.
3. *Statistics of the United States* (Washington, D.C.: U.S. Department of Commerce, Bureau of Census, 1996), 105.
4. Carol Botwin, *Tempted Women,* (New York: William Morrow, 1994).
5. Dalma Heyn, *The Erotic Silence of the American Wife* (New York: Random House, 1992).
6. Sonya Friedman, *Secret Loves* (New York: Crown, 1994).

Chapter 1 Awakening

1. Arlene DiMarco, telephone interview, December 12, 1993.

Chapter 2 What Am I?

1. Eli Coleman, "The Married Lesbian," *Marriage and Family Review*, 14, no. 3/4 (1989): 121.
2. Buxton, *The Other Side*, xiv.

3. Lillian Faderman, *Surpassing the Love of Men* (New York: William Morrow, 1981), 16.
4. Ibid., 190.
5. Ibid., 16.
6. Ibid., 17.
7. Lillian Faderman, *Odd Girls and Twilight Lovers: A History of Lesbian Life in Twentieth-Century America* (New York: Penguin Books, 1991), 12–14.
8. New Hampshire Supreme Court Opinion, *David G. Blanchflower and Sian E. Blanchflower* 2003-050.
9. Associated Press, "News & Politics," *PlanetOut.com* November 7, 2003.
10. Benedict Cary, "Straight, Gay or Lying? Bisexuality Revisited," *New York Times*, July 5, 2005, sec. F, p. 1. http://www.nytimes.com/2005/07/05/health/05sex.html?_r=1&oref=slogin.
11. Tikva Frymer-Kensky, "Sex and Sexuality," in *The Anchor Bible Dictionary*, ed. David Noel Freedman (New York, Doubleday, 1992), 5:1144–1146. Typographical error in the source. The passage referenced is actually *Leviticus* 20:13.
12. Faderman, *Odd Girls*, 34.
13. Shari L. Thurer, *The Myths of Motherhood* (New York: Houghton Mifflin, 1994).
14. Hite, *Hite Report*, 151.
15. Margaret Mitchell, *Gone With the Wind* (New York: Macmillan, 1936).
16. Margaret Mitchell, *Lost Laysen* (New York: Scribner, 1996.)
17. Nancy Marvel, "The Case for Feminist Celibacy," *The Feminist,* (pamphlet) (New York, 1971).
18. Chandler Burr, "Homosexuality and Biology," *The Atlantic*, March 1993, 48.
19. Buxton, *The Other Side*, xv.
20. Dean Hamer and Peter Copeland, *The Science of Desire: The Search for the Gay Gene and the Biology of Behavior* (New York: Simon and Schuster, 1994), 20.
21. Del Martin and Phyllis Lyon, *Lesbian Woman* (New York: Bantam Books, 1972), 74.
22. Burr, "Homosexuality," 60.
23. Hamer and Copeland, *The Science of Desire*, 147.
24. Ibid., 146.
25. Burr, "Homosexuality, 168.
26. Ibid., 169.
27. Ibid.
28. Ibid., 171.
29. Gwenn A. Nusbaum, telephone interview, November 15, 1993.
30. Arnie Schwartz, "Surpassing the Odds," *10 Percent, Stonewall 25* June 1994, 66–70.
31. Martin S. Weinberg, Colin J. Williams, and Douglas W. Pryor, *Dual Attraction: Understanding Bisexuality* (New York: Oxford University Press, 1994), preface.
32. Anastasia Toufexis, "Bisexuality: What Is It?" *Time*, August 17, 1992, 49.
33. William H. Masters and Virginia Johnson, *Mirabella*, February 1994, 147–149.
34. Weinberg, Williams, and Pryor, *Dual Attraction*, 49.

Chapter 3 What Now?

1. Eileen Starzecpyzel, "The Persephone Complex," in *Lesbian Psychologies* (Champaign: University of Illinois Press, 1987), 264.
2. Ibid.
3. Beverly Burch, *On Intimate Terms*, (Champaign: University of Illinois Press, 1993), 27.
4. Ibid., 26.
5. Sue Vargo, "The Effects of Women's Socialization on Lesbian Couples," in *Lesbian Psychologies*, (Champaign: University of Illinois Press, 1987), 163.
6. Colette Dowling, *The Cinderella Complex* (New York: Pocket Books, 1981), 50.
7. Naomi Wolf, *Fire with Fire*, (New York: Random House, 1993), 70–71.
8. DiMarco, telephone interview.
9. Starzecpyzel, "The Persephone Complex," 263.
10. Ibid., 265.
11. Ibid.
12. Ibid., 265–281.
13. Hedda Begelman, interview, September 22, 1993.
14. Coleman, "The Married Lesbian," 119–135.
15. Begelman, interview.
16. Melody Beattie, *Codependent No More* (San Francisco: Harper and Row, 1987), 89.

Chapter 4 Do I Tell My Husband or Not?

1. Burr, "Homosexuality," 48.
2. Margaret Nichols, "Lesbian Sexuality: Issues and Developing Theory," in *Lesbian Psychologies* (Champaign: University of Illinois Press, 1987), 106.

Chapter 5 The Husbands

1. Robert T. Michael, John H. Gagnon, Edward O. Laumann, and Gina Kolata, *Sex in America, A Definitive Survey* (Boston: Little, Brown, 1994), 113.
2. Ibid., 214.
3. William H. Masters, Virginia E. Johnson, and Robert C. Kolodny, *Masters and Johnson on Sex and Human Loving* (Boston: Little, Brown, 1988), 392.
4. Ibid.
5. Tom Biracree and Nancy Biracree, *Almanac of the American People* (New York: Facts on File, 1988), 167.

Chapter 6 What Do the Kids Think?

1. Lois Wadas, telephone interview, January 19, 1997.
2. June M. Reinisch and Ruth Beasley, *The Kinsey Institute New Report on Sex* (New York: St. Martin's Press, 1990), 141.
3. Laura Benkov, *Reinventing the Family* (New York: Crown, 1994), 62.

4. William A. Henry III, "Gay Parents: Under Fire and on the Rise," *Time*, September 20, 1993, 66.
5. Benkov, *Reinventing the Family*, 207.
6. Ibid., 198–199.
7. Linda Garnets and Douglas C Kimmel, eds., *Psychological Perspectives on Lesbian and Gay Male Experience* (New York: Columbia University Press, 1993), 258.
8. Ibid.
9. Benkov, *Reinventing the Family*, 202.
10. Lee Salk, *Familyhood* (New York: Simon and Schuster, 1992), 94.
11. Paul Bohannan, *All the Happy Families* (New York: McGraw-Hill, 1985), 128.

Chapter 7 Coming Out to Friends and Family

1. Sherry Zitter, "Coming Out to Mom," in *Lesbian Psychologies* (Champaign: University of Illinois Press, 1987), 193.
2. Ibid.
3. Vargo, "The Effects of Women's Socialization," 165.
4. Zitter, "Coming Out to Mom," 183.

Chapter 8 The Reality of Marriage

1. Barbara Seaman, *Free and Female* (New York: Fawcett Crest, 1972), 205.
2. Radical Therapist Collective, ed., "Brainwashing and Women," in *The Radical Therapist* (New York: Ballantine Books, 1971), 123.
3. Seaman, *Free and Female*, 210–211.
4. Blanche Wiesen Cook, *Eleanor Roosevelt* (New York: Viking Penguin, 1992), 14.
5. Nigel Nicolson, *Portrait of a Marriage* (New York: Atheneum, 1980), 105–106.
6. Heyn, *The Erotic Silence*, 261.
7. Biracre and Biracre, *Almanac*, 203.
8. Ibid.
9. Catherine Whitney, *Uncommon Lives: Gay Men and Straight Women* (New York: New American Library, 1990), 11–12.
10. Friedman, *Secret Loves*, 205.

Chapter 9 Redefined Marriages

1. Helen Fisher, *Why We Love* (New York: Owl/Henry Holt, 2004), 217.
2. Karen S. Peterson, "Study: Divorce, Living Together, New Norms," *USA Today*, July 28, 2002. http://www.usatoday.com/news/health/2002-07-28-pro-divorce_x.htm.

Chapter 11 Labeling: Lesbian or Bisexual

1. Burch, *On Intimate Terms*, 37.
2. Loraine Hutchins and Lani Kaahumanu, *Bi Any Other Name: Bisexual People Speak Out* (Los Angeles: Alyson, 1991), 546.

3. John Leland, "Bisexuality," *Newsweek*, July 17, 1995, 44.
4. Toufexis, "Bisexuality," *Time*, August 17, 1992, 49–51.
5. Reinisch and Beasley, *Kinsey Institute New Report*, 143.
6. Burch, *On Intimate Terms*, 18–19.

Chapter 12 Sexual Intimacy

1. Hite, *The Hite Report*, xi.
2. Heyn, *The Erotic Silence*, 70.
3. Betty Dodson, *Sex for One: The Joy of Selfloving* (New York: Crown Trade Paperbacks, 1987), 108.
4. Nancy Friday, *Women on Top* (New York: Pocket Star Books, 1991), 236.
5. Begelman interview.
6. University of Chicago's National Opinion Research Center, "Sex in America," *U.S. News and World Report*, October 17, 1994, 74–81.
7. Dr. Joyce Brothers, *Daily News*, January 26, 2001, 48.
8. Frans de Waal, *Bonobo: The Forgotten Ape* (Berkeley: University of California Press, 1997).
9. Bruce Bagemihl, *Biological Exuberance: Animal Homosexuality and Natural Diversity* (New York: St. Martin's Press, 1999).
10. David Reuben, *Everything You Always Wanted to Know About Sex But Were Afraid to Ask* (New York: David McKay, 1969) as quoted in Martin and Lyon, *Lesbian Woman* (New York: Bantam, 1972), 57.
11. Martin and Lyon, *Lesbian Woman*, 57.
12. Hite, *The Hite Report*, 297.
13. Ann Landers, "Bed and Bored: Giving Up Sex," *Daily News*, June 25, 1990.
14. Joan Avna and Diana Waltz, *Celibate Wives* (Los Angeles: Lowell House, 1992), 4–5.
15. Fanny Flagg, *Fried Green Tomatoes* (New York: McGraw-Hill, 1988).
16. Hite, *The Hite Report*, 217.
17. Nigel Nicolson, *Portrait*.

Chapter 13 New Beginnings

1. Begelman interview.
2. Nusbaum interview.
3. Simone de Beauvoir, *The Second Sex* (New York: Vintage Books, 1989), 411.
4. Phyllis Chesler, *Women and Madness* (New York: Doubleday, 1972), 5.
5. Burch, *On Intimate Terms*, 18, 19.
6. Wayne R. Dynes, ed., *Encyclopedia of Homosexuality* (Garden City: Garland, 1990), 1:610.
7. Faderman, *Odd Girls*, 35.
8. Ibid., 3.
9. Ibid., 119.

Glossary

Lesbian, Gay, Bisexual, and Transgender Terminology

This glossary is taken from the 2006 National Lesbian and Gay Journalists Association *Stylebook Supplement on LGBT Terminology*, available at www.nlgja.org.

bisexual: As a noun, an individual who may be attracted to both sexes. As an adjective, of or relating to sexual and affectional attraction to both sexes. Does not presume nonmonogamy.

civil union: The state of Vermont began this formal recognition of lesbian and gay relationships in July 2000. A civil union provides same-sex couples some rights available to married couples in areas such as state taxes, medical decisions, and estate planning.

closeted, in the closet: Refers to a person who wishes to keep secret his or her sexual orientation or gender identity.

coming out: Short for "coming out of the closet." Accepting and letting others know of one's previously hidden sexual orientation or gender identity. *See* **closeted** and **outing**.

commitment ceremony: A formal, marriage-like gathering that recognizes the declaration of members of the same sex to each other. Same-sex marriages are not legally recognized by the U.S. government.

cross-dresser: Preferred term for person who wears clothing most often associated with members of the opposite sex. Not necessarily connected to sexual partners.

domestic partner: Unmarried partners who live together. Domestic partners may be of opposite sexes or the same sex. They may register in some counties, municipalities, and states and receive some of the same benefits accorded married couples. The term is typically used in connection with legal and insurance matters. *See* **gay/lesbian relationships**.

dyke: Originally a pejorative term for a lesbian, it is now being reclaimed by some lesbians. Caution: still extremely offensive when used as an epithet.

ex-gay: Describes the movement, mostly rooted in conservative religions, that aims to change the sexual attraction of individuals from same sex to opposite sex.

gay: An adjective that has largely replaced "homosexual" in referring to men who are sexually and affectionally attracted to other men. For women, "lesbian" is preferred. In headlines where space is an issue, "gays" is acceptable to describe both.

gay/lesbian relationships: Gay, lesbian, and bisexual people use various terms to describe their commitments. "Partner" is generally acceptable.

gender identity: An individual's emotional and psychological sense of being male or female. Not necessarily the same as an individual's biological identity.

heterosexism: Presumption that heterosexuality is universal or superior to homosexuality. Also: prejudice, bias, or discrimination based on such presumptions.

homophobia: Fear, hatred, or dislike of homosexuality, gay men, and lesbians.

homosexual: As a noun, a person who is attracted to members of the same sex. As an adjective, of or relating to sexual and affectional attraction to a member of the same sex.

intersex: People born with sex chromosomes, external genitalia, or an internal reproductive system that is not considered standard for either male or female. Parents and physicians usually will determine the sex of the child, resulting in surgery or hormone treatment. Many intersex adults seek an end to this practice.

lesbian: Preferred term, both as a noun and as an adjective, for women who are sexually and affectionally attracted to other women. Some women prefer to be called "gay" rather than "lesbian."

LGBT: Acronym for lesbian, gay, bisexual, and transgender.

lifestyle: An inaccurate term sometimes used to describe the lives of gay, lesbian, bisexual, and transgender people. Sexual orientation may be part of a broader lifestyle but is not one in itself, just as there is no "straight" lifestyle.

lover: A gay, lesbian, bisexual, or heterosexual person's sexual partner. "Partner" is generally acceptable. *See* **gay/lesbian relationships**.

openly gay/lesbian: As a modifier, "openly" is usually not relevant; its use should be restricted to instances in which the public awareness of an individual's sexual orientation is germane. Examples: Harvey Milk was the first openly gay San Francisco supervisor. *Ellen* was the first sitcom to feature an openly lesbian lead character.

outing (from "out of the closet"): Publicly revealing the sexual orientation or gender identity of an individual who has chosen to keep that information private. Also a verb: The magazine outed the senator in a front-page story. *See* **coming out** and **closeted**.

pink triangle: Now a gay pride symbol, it was the symbol gay men were required to wear in Nazi concentration camps during World War II. Lesbians sometimes also use a black triangle.

practicing: Avoid this term to describe someone's sexual orientation or gender identity. Use "sexually active" as a modifier in circumstances when public awareness of an individual's behavior is germane.

Pride (Day and/or march): Short for gay/lesbian pride, this term is commonly used to indicate the celebrations commemorating the Stonewall Inn riots of June 28, 1969. Pride events typically take place in June. *See* **Stonewall**.

queer: Originally a pejorative term for gay, now being reclaimed by some gay, lesbian, bisexual, and transgender people as a self-affirming umbrella term. Still extremely offensive when used as an epithet.

rainbow flag: A flag of six equal horizontal stripes (red, orange, yellow, green, blue, and violet) signifying the diversity of the lesbian, gay, bisexual, and transgender communities.

safe sex, safer sex: Sexual practices that minimize the possible transmission of HIV and other infectious agents.

sexual orientation: Innate sexual attraction.

special rights: Politically charged term used by opponents of civil rights for gay people.

Stonewall: The Stonewall Inn tavern in New York City's Greenwich Village was the site of several nights of raucous protests after a police raid on June 28, 1969. Although not the nation's first gay civil rights demonstration, Stonewall is now regarded as the birth of the modern gay civil rights movement.

straight: Heterosexual; describes a person whose sexual and affectional attraction is to someone of the opposite sex.

transgender: An umbrella term that refers to people whose biological and gender identity or expression may not be the same. This can include preoperative, postoperative, or nonoperative transsexuals, female and male cross-dressers, drag queens or kings, female or male impersonators, and intersex individuals.

transition: The process by which one alters one's sex. This may include surgery, hormone therapy, and changes of legal identity.

transsexual: An individual who identifies himself or herself as a member of the biological opposite sex and who acquires the physical characteristics of the opposite sex. Individual can be of any sexual orientation.

transvestite: *See* cross-dresser.

Two-Spirit: An American Indian believed to possess a mixture of masculine and feminine spirits. Some identify as gay, lesbian, bisexual, or transgender.

Selected Bibliography

Abbott, Deborah, and Ellen Farmer. *From Wedded Wife to Lesbian Life*. Freedom, CA: Crossing Press, 1995.

Alther, Lisa. *Other Women*. New York: Signet, 1984.

Anderson-Minshall, Diane. "Interview with Laura Innes, Dr. Kerry Weaver on ER," *Curve Magazine*, May 2002, 25.

Aona, Joan, and Diana Waltz. *Celibate Wives*. Chicago: Contemporary Books, 1992.

Bagemihl, Bruce. *Biological Exuberance: Animal Homosexuality and Natural Diversity*. New York: St. Martin's Press, 1999.

Barrett, Martha Barron. *Invisible Lives*. New York: William Morrow, 1989.

Beattie, Melody. *Codependent No More*. San Francisco: Harper and Row, 1987.

Benkov, Laura. *Reinventing the Family*. New York: Crown, 1994.

Biracree, Tom, and Nancy Biracree. *Almanac of the American People*. New York: Facts on File, 1988.

Bohannan, Paul. *All the Happy Families*. New York: McGraw-Hill, 1985.

Boston Lesbian Psychologies Collective, ed. *Lesbian Psychologies*. Champaign: University of Illinois Press, 1987.

Botwin, Carol. *Tempted Woman*. New York: William Morrow, 1994.

Braverman, Lois. "Chasing Rainbows," *Networker*, July/August 1995.

Brothers, Joyce. *Daily News*, January 26, 2001.

Brown, Rita Mae. *Rubyfruit Jungle*. New York: Bantam, 1977.

Brown, Rita Mae. *Venus Envy*. New York: Bantam, 1993.

Burch, Beverly. *On Intimate Terms*. Champaign: University of Illinois Press, 1993.

Burr, Chandler. "Homosexuality and Biology," *The Atlantic* 14, no. 3, 47–65 (1993).

Burr, Chandler. *A Separate Creation: The Search for the Biological Origins of Sexual Orientation*. New York: Hyperion, 1963.

Buxton, Amity Pierce. *The Other Side of the Closet*. Santa Monica: IBS Press, 1991.

Cary, Benedict. "Straight, Gay or Lying? Bisexuality Revisited," *New York Times*, July 5, 2005, sec, F, 1, http://www.nytimes.com/2005/07/05sex.html?_r=1&oref=slogin.

Chesler, Phyllis. *Women and Madness*. Garden City: Doubleday, 1972.

Chodorow, Nancy. *The Reproduction of Mothering: Psychoanalysis and the Sociology of Gender*. Berkeley: University of California Press, 1978.

Clarke, Donald. *Loving Someone Gay*. Berkley: Celestial Arts, 1987.

Coleman, Eli. "The Married Lesbian." *Marriage and Family Review* 14, no. 3/4, 21 (1989).

Cook, Blanche Wiesen. *Eleanor Roosevelt*. New York: Viking Penguin, 1992.

Coontz, Stephanie. "A Historian Upends Conventional Wisdom." *Newsweek*, June 5, 2006.

Corley, Rip. *The Final Closet, the Gay Parents Guide for Coming Out to Their Children*. Miami: Editech Press, 1990.

Cunningham, Amy. "The Good, the Bad, and the Phony: Why Women Smile." *Lears*, March 1993.

Cunningham, Amy. "Married Sex." *McCalls*, May 1993.

Curb, Rosemary, and Nancy Manahan, eds. *Lesbian Nuns Breaking Silence*. Tallahassee: Naiad Press, 1985.

de Beauvoir, Simone. *The Second Sex*. New York: Vintage Books, 1989.

de Waal, Fran. *Bonobo: The Forgotten Ape*. Berkeley: University of California Press, 1997.

Dodson, Betty. *Sex for One: The Joy of Selfloving*. New York: Crown, 1987.

Doup, Liz. "When Love and Marriage Don't Go Together." *Washington Post*, February 8, 1993.

Dowling, Colette. *The Cinderella Complex*. New York: Pocket Books, 1981.

Dymes, Wayne R., ed. *Encyclopedia of Homosexuality*. New York: Garland Press, 1990.

Elmer-Dewitt, Philip. "Sex in America," *Time*, October 17, 1994.

Erhart, Margaret. *Unusual Company*. New York: New American Library, 1987.

Faderman, Lillian. *Odd Girls and Twilight Lovers: A History of Lesbian Life in Twentieth Century America*. New York: Penguin Books, 1991.

Faderman, Lillian. *Surpassing the Love of Men*. New York: William Morrow, 1981.

Fairchild, Betty, and Nancy Hayward. *Now That You Know*. Orlando: Harvest/ HBJ, 1989.

Fisher, Helen. *Why We Love*. New York: Owl/Henry Holt, 2004.

Flagg, Fanny. *Fried Green Tomatoes*. New York: McGraw-Hill, 1988.

Friedman, Sonya. *Secret Loves*. New York: Crown, 1994.

Friday, Nancy. *My Mother My Self*. New York: Dell, 1977.

Friday, Nancy. *My Secret Garden*. New York: Pocket Books, 1973.

Frymer-Kensky, Tikva. "Sex and Sexuality." In *The Anchor Bible Dictionary*, Vol. 5, edited by David Noel Freedman. New York: Doubleday, 1992.

Garber, Marjorie. *Vice Versa: Bisexuality and the Eroticism of Everyday Life*. New York: Simon and Schuster, 1995.

Garnets, Linda D., and Douglas C. Kimmel, eds. *Psychological Perspectives on Lesbian and Gay Male Experiences*. New York: Columbia University Press, 1993.

Gross, Jane. "When the Beard Is Too Painful to Remove." *New York Times*, August 3, 2006.

Hamer, Dean, and Peter Copeland. *The Science of Desire: The Search for the Gay Gene and the Biology of Behavior*. New York: Simon and Schuster, 1994.

Heyn, Dalma. *The Erotic Silence of the American Wife*. New York: Random House, 1992.

Hite, Shere. *The Hite Report*. New York: Macmillan, 1976.

Hite, Shere. *Women and Love*. New York: St. Martin's Press, 1987.

Hite, Shere. *Women as Revolutionary Agents of Change*. Madison: University of Wisconsin Press, 1993.

Hollis, Judi. *Fat Is a Family Affair*. San Francisco: Harper/Hagelden, 1986.

Hutchins, Loraine, and Lani Kaahumanu. *Bi Any Other Name: Bisexual People Speak Out.* Los Angeles: Alyson, 1991.

Johnson, Sonia. *Wild Fire Igniting.* Albuquerque: Wild Fire Press, 1991.

Johnson, Sonia. *Ship That Sailed into the Living Room.* Albuquerque: Wild Fire Press, 1991.

Jong, Erica. *Fear of Flying.* New York: Penguin Books, 1973.

Kelly, Janis. "Sister Love: An Exploration of the Need for Homosexual Experiences." *Family Coordinator,* 21, no. 4, 473–475 (October 1972).

Kinsey, Alfred C. *Sexual Behavior in the Human Female.* New York: Pocket Books, 1965.

Leland, John. "Bisexuality," *Newsweek,* July 17, 1995.

Loulan, Jo Ann. *Lesbian Passion: Loving Ourselves and Each Other.* San Francisco: Spinsters, 1987.

Martin, Del, and Phyllis Lyon. *Lesbian Woman.* New York: Bantam, 1972.

Marvel, Nancy. "The Case for Feminist Celibacy," *The Feminists,* Pamphlet, New York, 1971.

Masters, William H., and Virginia Johnson. *Human Sexual Inadequacy.* New York: Little, Brown, 1970.

Masters, William H., Virginia E. Johnson, and Robert C. Kolodny. *Masters and Johnson on Sex and Human Loving.* Boston: Little, Brown, 1988.

Michael, Robert T., John H. Gagnon, Edward O. Laumann, and Gina Kolata. *Sex in America: A Definitive Survey.* Boston: Little, Brown, 1994.

Muller, Ann. *Parents Matter: Parents' Relationships with Lesbian Daughters and Gay Sons.* Tallahassee: Naiad Press, 1987.

National Lesbian and Gay Journalists. *Stylebook Supplement on LGBT* [Lesbian, Gay, Bisexual, and Transgender] *Terminology,* www.nlgja.org/resources/stylebook_english.html.

Nicolson, Nigel. *Portrait of a Marriage.* New York: Atheneum, 1980.

Penelope, Julia. *Call Me Lesbian.* Freedom, CA: Crossing Press, 1992.

Peterson, Karen S. "Study: Divorce, Living Together, New Norms." *USA Today,* July 28, 2002, online edition. http://www.usatoday.com/news/health/2002-07-28-pro-divorce_x.htm.

Pomeroy, Sarah. *Goddesses, Whores, Wives and Slaves.* New York: Schocken Books, 1975.

Price, Deb, and Joyce Murdoch. *And Say Hi to Joyce.* New York: Doubleday, 1995.

Rafkin, Louis. *Different Mothers: Sons and Daughters of Lesbians Talk About Their Lives.* Pittsburgh: Cleis Press, 1990.

Reinisch, June M., and Ruth Beasley. *The Kinsey Institute New Report on Sex.* New York: St. Martin's Press, 1990.

Reuben, David. *Everything You Always Wanted to Know About Sex But Were Afraid to Ask.* New York: David McKay, 1969.

Rosen, Judith. "Women's Bookstores: 20 Years and Thriving." *Publishers Weekly,* 239, no. 22 (May 11, 1992).

Russianoff, Penelope. *When Am I Going To Be Happy?* New York: Bantam, 1988.

Salk, Lee. *Familyhood.* New York: Simon and Schuster, 1992.

Saunders, Anne. "Planet Out News and Politics." *Associated Press,* November 7, 2003.

Scarf, Maggie. *Unfinished Business.* New York: Ballantine, 1980.

Schrof, Joannie M., and Betsy Wagner. "Sex in America." *U.S. News and World Report,* October 17, 1994.

Schwartz, Arnie. "Surpassing the Odds." *10 Percent, Stonewall 25,* June 1994.

Seaman, Barbara. *Free and Female*. New York: Fawcett Crest, 1972.

Sutphen, Dick. *Reinventing Yourself: A Metaphysical Self-Renewal System*. Malibu, CA: Valley of the Sun, 1993.

Tannahill, Reay. *Sex in History*. Lanham, MD: Scarborough House, 1992.

Toufexis, Anastasia. "Bisexuality: What Is It?" *Time*, August 17, 1992.

Walters, Marianne, Betty Carter, Peggy Papp, and Olga Silverstein. *The Invisible Web: Gender Patters in Family Relationships*. New York: Guildford Press, 1988.

Weil, Bonnie Eaker. *Adultery: The Forgivable Sin*. New York: Carol Publishing Group, 1993.

Weinberg, Martin S., Colin J. Williams, and Douglas W. Pryor. *Dual Attraction: Understanding Bisexuality*. New York: Oxford University Press, 1994.

Welsh, Patrick. "Gays in School." *Washington Post*, March 4, 1990.

Whitney, Catherine. *Uncommon Lives: Gay Men and Straight Women*. New York: New American Library, 1990.

Winterson, Jeanette. *Written on the Body*. New York: Knopf, 1993.

Woodman, Sue. "For the City's Lesbians, the Political and Social Climate Has Never Been So Conducive to Coming Out. Why, Then, Is the Decision Still So Wrenching?" *New York Woman*, February 1990.

Additional Reading

Atkins, Dawn. *Bisexual Women in the Twenty-First Century.* Haworth Press, 2003.
Baker, Jean. *How Homophobia Hurts Children: Nurturing Diversity at Home and at School.* Harrington Park Press, 2002.
Blakeslee, Sandra. *What About the Kids? Raising Your Children Before, During, and After Divorce.* Hyperion, 2004.
Clark, D. *Loving Someone Gay.* Celestial Arts, 1997.
Corvino, John. *Same Sex: Debating the Ethics, Science, and Culture of Homosexuality.* Rowman and Littlefield, 1997.
Degeneres, Betty. *Love, Ellen: A Mother/Daughter Journey.* Quill, 2000.
Esterberg, Kristin G. *Lesbian and Bisexual Identities.* Temple University Press, 1997.
Feinberg, Leslie. *Stone Butch Blues: A Novel.* Firebrand Books, 1993. Reprint, Alyson, 2004.
Fleisher, Joanne. *Living Two Lives.* Alyson, 2005.
Griffin, Carolyn Welch, Marian J. Wirth, Arthur G. Wirth, and Brian McNaught. *Beyond Acceptance: Parents of Lesbians and Gays Talk About Their Experiences.* St. Martins Press, 1997.
Hall, Radclyffe. *Well of Loneliness.* Anchor, 1990.
Jensen, Karol. *Lesbian Epiphanies: Women Coming Out in Later Life.* Harrington Park Press, 1999.
Kay, Karla, ed. *Lesbians/Bisexual Women.* Basic Books, 1996.
Klein, Fritz, and Timothy J. Wolf. *Two Lives to Lead: Bisexuality in Men and Women.* Harrington Park Press, 1985.
Lapovsky Kennedy, Elizabeth. *Boots of Leather, Slippers of Gold: The History of the Lesbian Community.* Penguin, 1994.
Larkin, Joan, ed. *A Woman Like That: Lesbian and Bisexual Writers Tell Their Coming Out Stories.* Perennial, 2000.
McGarry, Molly. *Becoming Visible: An Illustrated History of Lesbian and Gay Life in Twentieth-Century America.* Studio, 1998.
O'Neil, Sally M., and Barbee J. Cassingham. *And Then I Met this Woman.* Soaring Eagle, 1999.

Orndorff, Kata. *Bi Lives: Bisexual Women Tell Their Stories.* See Sharp Press, 1999.

Rodriguez Rust, Paula C. *Bisexuality in the United States.* Columbia University Press, 1999.

Sacks, Rhonda. *The Art of Meeting Women: A Guide for Gay Women.* Slope Books.

Weinstock, Jacqueline, and Esther D. Rothblum, eds. *Lesbian Friendships: For Ourselves and Each Other.* New York University Press, 1996.